THE ULTIMATE COLLECTION
of Grain- and Gluten-Free Recipes
to Meet Your Every N...

1,001 PALEO RECIPES

Arsy Vartanian, Rachel Ball, Jenny Castaneda, Hannah Healy, Katja Heino,
Nazanin Kovács, Rachel McClelland, Vivica Menegaz, Caroline Potter,
Kelly Winters and Amanda Torres

PAGE STREET
PUBLISHING CO.

PAGE STREET
PUBLISHING CO.

First published in 2021 by
Page Street Publishing Co.
27 Congress Street, Suite 105
Salem, MA 01970
www.pagestreetpublishing.com

Distributed by Macmillan, sales in Canada by The Canadian Manda Group.

24   23   22   21   20   1   2   3   4   5

ISBN-13: 978-1-64567-237-1
ISBN-10: 1-64567-237-9

Library of Congress Control Number: 2020943068

Cover and book design by Meg Baskis for Page Street Publishing Co.

Photography by Arsy Vartanian, Rachel Ball, Jenny Castaneda, Hannah Healy, Katja Heino, Nazanin Kovács, Rachel McClelland, Vivica Menegaz, Caroline Potter and Kelly Winters

Printed and bound in the United States

CONTENTS

INTRODUCTION

I've teamed up with ten of my favorite recipe developers in the Paleo community, to bring you the ultimate Paleo resource, *1,001 Paleo Recipes*. In this collection, we wanted to offer you any recipe you could possibly need to successfully transition to a Paleo lifestyle.

We understand that implementing Paleo principles can be time consuming and expensive. In offering so many recipes in one book, almost an encyclopedia of sorts, we hope that you can open up your fridge, take a look at what you have to work with, then find the perfect recipe in our book to guide you, saving you money, time and trips to the grocery store.

This book includes a wide range of recipes. You can use these recipes to host the perfect dinner party with mouth-watering appetizers to tantalizing desserts. Or turn to our "Easy, Fast, Few-Ingredient" section (page 172) and whip up a nourishing and satisfying weeknight dinner, after a long day of work.

Each chef brings a unique background and diversity to this book. You will find recipes from the author's ethnic backgrounds that have been reworked to maintain their authenticity, while providing a healthy Paleo alternative. You will also find recipes from chefs that have mastered the art of grain-free baking, ranging from breads, crackers to dessert. You will find recipes for Paleo lunches, weeknight dishes and using your slow cooker to keep you healthy, while keeping your work week manageable.

For the busy parents (which are all of them!), we have included kid-friendly recipes, budget-conscious main dishes, as well as those appropriate for large groups, such as for parties and potlucks.

Our ultimate goal is to provide you with a one-stop shop for your Paleo needs, to help you be successful on your Paleo journey! We hope this book will be your go-to resource to keep you healthy and on track, while keeping your meals interesting and satisfying!

—Arsy

WHAT IS THE PALEO DIET AND HOW DO YOU FOLLOW IT?

Some of you have been avid followers of the Paleo diet for years and just picked up this book to have a handy resource in your kitchen. However, as the Paleo diet has grown in popularity, there are many others that have heard about it through a friend or a colleague and want to try it for a number of reasons—ranging from weight loss to improved energy to managing symptoms of an autoimmune condition.

People that have a basic understanding of the Paleo diet and have some tips and tricks in their back pocket tend to be most successful. This section will explain everything you need to know to get started, as well as provide you with our top tips.

The Paleo diet is more of a lifestyle than a diet. It aspires to achieve optimal health by following a diet based on what and how our Paleolithic ancestors ate. The current Paleo movement uses our ancestors as a starting point, but leverages modern science to expand from there. Essentially, it is a diet focused on consuming whole, natural foods, such as meats, eggs, vegetables, fruits, nuts and healthy fats.

HOW TO GET STARTED

Eat plenty of meats, seafood, vegetables, eggs, healthy fats and some fruit and nuts. Avoid eating gluten, processed oils and refined sugar.

Always purchase the highest-quality ingredients that you can afford
Foods that are organic and grass-fed are not only void of toxins, such as pesticides and antibiotics, but are also highly nutritious. However, if you can't afford those at the moment, don't fret. Just focus on doing the best you can!

Avoid grains and legumes
It's especially important to avoid wheat and other gluten-containing grains, such as rye and barley. But also avoid soy, corn, beans and peanuts (they are actually a legume, not a nut).

Avoid added sugars
This includes artificial sweeteners and all refined sugars. Only occasionally consume natural sweeteners, such as honey, maple syrup and coconut sugar.

Avoid vegetable oils and industrial seed oils
This includes canola, corn, soybean, cottonseed, safflower and sunflower oil, among others.

Don't be afraid to include healthy fats in your diet
This includes animal fats, avocado, olive oil, coconut oil, palm oil, ghee, grass-fed butter (if you tolerate it well), lard (from pasture-raised pigs), tallow, etc. One of the biggest mistakes people make when adapting a Paleo diet is not consuming enough fats. Fats will keep you satiated and provide you with energy. If you feel hungry between meals, try increasing your fat intake.

Eat foods with minimal ingredients

If you don't recognize something in the ingredients list or if it is something your grandma didn't eat, chances are neither should you.

Typically a Paleo diet does not include dairy; only consume dairy if you digest it well

It is recommended to avoid dairy for the first 30 days of a Paleo diet. Then you can reintroduce it and observe how well you tolerate it. If you tolerate it well, then occasional dairy can be a healthy part of your diet. Whenever possible, it is best to use high-quality dairy, preferably raw and from grass-fed sources. Grass-fed dairy is richer in nutrients and has a better fat composition, plus it tastes amazing!

Is the Paleo diet a low-carb diet?

No, it is carb agnostic. It really depends on your lifestyle and your goals. There are people who choose to take a low-carb approach, particularly if weight loss is the goal. Depending on your needs, you can adjust accordingly. Athletes may choose to include more starchy options such as sweet potatoes, potatoes, tubers, plantains and bananas.

What are some of the benefits of the Paleo diet?

Paleo diet followers commonly report shedding unwanted weight, shrinking waistlines, better energy and focus, improved athletic performance, reduced chronic inflammation and joint pain, improvement in symptoms related to autoimmune conditions and reduction in the risk of modern day diseases.

TOP TIPS FOR FOLLOWING A PALEO DIET

Clean out your fridge and pantry

Before you get started, throw out all the foods in your fridge and pantry that you will not be consuming on the Paleo diet. If you only have healthy options to choose from when you get hungry, then chances are that you will make a healthy choice and stay on track.

Eat enough food and eat until you are full

This may seem counter-intuitive because we have been told so often to eat smaller portions. However, when we are eating the foods our bodies were designed to eat, our bodies also know when they have had enough. Trust your body. The Paleo diet typically has a much lighter caloric load than grain-based diets, so you may need to eat more in volume to stay full. If you eat larger meals, you will also need fewer snacks. Snack foods, even on a Paleo diet, are the ones that are easy to overeat, such as nuts and fruits. If you feel hungry between meals, try eating larger meals.

Be very strict the first 2 weeks

Many popular approaches like the Whole30 Program, which is my recommended starting point for the Paleo diet, include a 30-day protocol for best results. We completely agree that you will experience the most benefits if you complete the full 30 days.

However, I have found from my own experience and from talking to blog readers and clients, that the first two weeks are the most difficult. You may not feel great at this time because your body is adjusting to the changes in your diet. You may still be craving the foods you used to eat. Tell yourself that you will check in with yourself at the halfway point of your 30-day challenge and you will only move forward if it feels right. Stick to that first two weeks without any slip-ups and chances are high that you will decide to finish the 30 days at your half point check in. It will become much easier after the first two weeks. I promise! Once you are past the first couple of weeks, you will be feeling your best and you will be motivated to continue with the Paleo diet.

Be prepared

Preparation is key, especially when you are first starting out. Plan what you are going to eat in advance and prepare whatever you can ahead of time. I tend to focus on preparing meat in advance, as I find this to be the most time consuming; you can find some easy protein recipes in our slow cooker section. I make a large roast every Sunday and this lasts us for a few meals. This way, at dinner time we can throw together a well-balanced meal quickly.

As the typical American diet is heavily made up of grains, at first glance it seems overwhelming to exclude these foods. As we look at what we can eat, we see that the options are endless on the Paleo diet. You can have meats, seafood, fruits, vegetables, nuts/seeds, herbs/spices and healthy sources of fat. Any combination of these foods makes for a fantastic meal!

HOW TO STOCK YOUR PALEO KITCHEN

We don't need many fancy tools in the kitchen to make healthy and delicious Paleo meals, but having some good quality basics can be very helpful!

- Chef's knife
- Paring knife
- Knife sharpening steel
- Wood cutting boards (these are gentler on our knives than bamboo)
- Cast iron skillet
- Heavy-bottomed pot like a Dutch or French oven
- Stock pot
- Measuring cups
- Measuring spoons
- Microplane or zester
- Food processor
- Slow cooker
- Spiral vegetable slicer (to make veggie noodles)
- Glass containers for storage

HOW TO STOCK YOUR PALEO PANTRY

If you are new to Paleo cooking, you might notice some items in this book that you are unfamiliar with. Here are some common items that you might find in a Paleo pantry. You will notice many alternative flours. You can make many different Paleo treats for an occasional indulgence using flours made from nuts and roots.

- Nut butters (ranging from almond, to macadamia to cashew)
- Almond flour
- Coconut flour
- Arrowroot starch or flour
- Tapioca starch or flour
- Cacao powder
- Coconut milk
- Coconut oil
- Apple cider vinegar
- Coconut aminos (a great soy sauce alternative)
- Local, raw honey
- Ghee or clarified butter
- Herbs and spices
- Olive oil
- Sea salt
- Jarred tomato products (sauce, whole tomatoes, etc.)
- Sea salt
- Canned tuna, salmon and sardines
- Vanilla extract (gluten-free version)
- Baking soda

LET'S TALK ABOUT FATS

Mainstream headlines have had us believing that fat is detrimental to our health for decades. Observation of traditional cultures, as well as scientific studies, tell a different story. Contrary to conventional wisdom, healthy fats are actually essential to our health and a big part of the Paleo diet.

Additionally, this fabulous nutrient plays a key role in the brain, nervous system, skin and every cell in the body. Fat is mandatory for the absorption of the fat-soluble vitamins A, D, E and K and for hormone production.

Most of the recipes in this book call for some sort of fat. If you don't have what the recipe calls for on hand or if it calls for ghee or butter and you don't tolerate those well, refer to this list for an alternative fat.

FATS AND OILS SAFE FOR FRYING, SAUTÉING AND BROWNING

Saturated fats are the best options for cooking. Since they are chemically stable, they are resistant to damage from heat. Opt for grass-fed, organic and unrefined options.

FATS AND OILS SAFE FOR FRYING, SAUTÉING AND BROWNING	
Butter, ghee or clarified butter	Lard (pork fat)
Duck fat	Tallow (beef fat)
Schmaltz (chicken or goose fat)	Lamb fat
Goat fat	Coconut oil
Palm oil	

FATS AND OILS SAFE FOR COLD USE IN SALADS, SAUCES OR CONDIMENTS

These oils should be unrefined, expeller-pressed or cold-pressed to avoid high heat and chemical processing that will damage the oils.

FATS AND OILS SAFE FOR COLD USE IN SALADS, SAUCES OR CONDIMENTS	
Olive oil	Avocado oil
Nut oils (e.g., macadamia, walnut)	Seed oils (e.g., sesame*, flax, hemp, pumpkin)

In the book, Know Your Fats, Mary G. Enig explains, "Sesame oil has very good oxidative stability, which is thought to be related to sesamin or another antioxidant in the native oil" (p. 122). Meaning it can be heated without damaging the oil, so although it is a seed oil, it is actually safe for heat cooking.

UNHEALTHY FATS AND OILS TO AVOID

These fats are either man-made or highly processed with chemicals. These oils oxidize easily and become rancid, causing inflammation in the body. Avoid anything that is hydrogenated or partially hydrogenated.

FATS AND OILS TO AVOID	
Margarine or other butter substitutes	Sunflower oil
Vegetable oil	Rice bran oil
Canola oil	Grapeseed oil
Corn oil	Soybean oil
Cottonseed oil	Vegetable shortening
Safflower oil	

CHAPTER 1

MAIN DISHES

There is nothing more joyful than sitting down at the table with the people you love and sharing a delicious and healthful homemade meal, yet with our overly busy modern lives it can be tempting to go to the drive-thru on our way home from work or to microwave some pre-packaged frozen meals. With a little bit of planning and some time set aside in your week, it can be easy to prepare healthful, nutritious and tasty dishes to enjoy with your loved ones.

This is where Paleo comes in. When you remove things like fast-food, pre-packaged frozen meals, boxes of pasta and bags of bread, you are left with a whole new and exciting world of ingredients to cook with and the main dishes in this chapter will show you how to do just that.

The recipes featured in this chapter highlight some great sources of properly raised proteins, incredibly fresh and seasonal fruits and vegetables, aromatic spices and fresh herbs and great quality fats and oils, all of which are at the heart of a nutrient-dense Paleo diet.

So take a moment to read through this chapter and see for yourself just how many wonderful and tasty dishes you can prepare without the need for pre-packaged and boxed nutrient-poor foods. Some of my favorites in this section include the Perfectly Crispy Oven-Baked Asian Sesame Chicken Wings (page 78), Pistachio-Crusted Chicken Tenders with Currant Dipping Sauce (page 30) and the simple Pan-Seared Turmeric Salmon (page 100).

CAST IRON SKIRT STEAK WITH POMEGRANATE AND ORANGE MARINADE

Sometimes all it takes is a handful of simple ingredients and a couple of handy kitchen tools to create something magical. This easy and quick-to-make skirt steak topped with syrupy pomegranate molasses and citrusy orange zest and juice is sure to be a hit with anyone who tries it. —NK

SERVES 2

1 pound (454 g) skirt steak

1 tsp (6 g) sea salt, divided

½ tsp black pepper, divided

2 tbsp (30 ml) pomegranate molasses

Zest and juice of ½ an orange

¼ tsp garlic powder

2 tbsp (30 g) ghee

Use paper towels to completely pat dry the steak on all sides. Sprinkle ½ teaspoon of sea salt on each side of the steak and ¼ teaspoon of black pepper on each side. Allow to sit uncovered at room temperature for 1 hour.

Add pomegranate molasses, orange zest and juice and garlic powder to a small bowl and mix. Set aside.

Heat the ghee in a 12-inch (30.5-cm) cast iron skillet. Allow the skillet to heat up for 4 minutes, then carefully add the steak to the skillet using some kitchen tongs and allow it to cook for 5 minutes without moving it. After 5 minutes, using the kitchen tongs, carefully flip the steak over and allow to cook for another 4 to 5 minutes. While the steak is cooking on the second side, place a piece of aluminum foil onto a clean cutting board. When the steak has finished cooking, carefully remove it onto the aluminum foil and use a pastry brush to brush half of the pomegranate and orange mixture on either side of the steak. Wrap the steak in the foil and allow to rest for 10 minutes. Once rested, use a sharp knife to slice the steak against the grain. To serve, spoon the remaining pomegranate and orange mixture over the steak. Serve immediately over a bed of greens or with your preferred side dish.

CHEF'S TIP:
Pomegranate molasses can be found in Middle Eastern grocery stores or purchased online.

MAPLE APPLE SAUSAGE ACORN SQUASH

It doesn't take a lot of ingredients to make a deliciously flavorful meal and this recipe proves just that. It's full of fall flavor and is sure to please picky palates. —KW

SERVES 4

2 acorn squash, cut in half and seeded

2 tbsp (30 g) butter, ghee or coconut oil, melted

Pinches of ground cinnamon and ground nutmeg

2 apples—firm varieties like Fuji work best—cut into chunks

1 pound (454 g) rope sausage or kielbasa, cut into bite-size chunks, about 1–2 inches (2.5–5 cm)

1 medium onion, cut into chunks

2 tbsp (30 ml) pure maple syrup

Sea salt and pepper, to taste

4 skewers (if using wood skewers, make sure to soak in water for at least 15 minutes)

Preheat oven to 400°F (200°C, or gas mark 6). Place the halved acorn squash on a baking pan and brush each inside half with ½ tablespoon (7.5 ml) butter. Sprinkle the flesh of each acorn squash with a pinch of cinnamon and nutmeg. Bake for 1 hour.

While the acorn squash are baking, thread the apples, sausage and onion onto 4 skewers and place on a baking pan. Brush maple syrup all over the kabobs. Salt and pepper, to taste. Put the kabobs in the oven when there are 25 minutes left on the timer from the acorn squash (leave the acorn squash in the oven). The kabobs take 20 to 25 minutes to cook.

To serve you can either remove the sausage, apples and onion from the skewers and place in the acorn squash, or you can serve the kabobs alongside the acorn squash.

ROSEMARY LAMB BURGERS WITH PESTO

Nothing pairs better with lamb than fresh rosemary. Add a bit of fresh pesto, and you have a stellar meal. —KH

SERVES 4

1 pound (454 g) ground lamb

1 tbsp (4 g) fresh rosemary, minced

1 tsp (3 g) sea salt

1 tbsp (15 ml) coconut oil or ghee for cooking

FOR THE PESTO

1 bunch fresh basil, leaves only

¼ cup (60 ml) olive oil

1 tsp (5 ml) fresh lemon juice

1 clove garlic, minced

¼ tsp unrefined sea salt

¼ cup (32 g) hemp seeds or raw pumpkin seeds

FOR THE GARNISH

Salad greens of choice, arugula is good

Olive oil

White wine vinegar

Salt and pepper

Mix the ground lamb, rosemary and salt until thoroughly combined and form into 1-inch (2.5-cm)-thick patties. Melt fat of choice in skillet over medium-high heat. Cook patties, flipping once, until browned and cooked to desired doneness. I cook mine about 4 to 5 minutes on each side.

Meanwhile, place basil, olive oil, lemon juice, garlic and salt into a food processor. Process until you achieve a smooth texture. You will need to scrape the sides a few times. Then add the hemp seeds or pumpkin seeds and pulse until desired pesto consistency. Adjust taste with salt and lemon.

Toss the salad greens in a bit of olive oil, white wine vinegar and salt and pepper. Place the lamb burger on top. Add a dollop of pesto. Enjoy!

ROCK SALT ROASTED CHICKEN

My friend Alisa taught me this method of roasting a chicken on a bed of salt. The results are incredibly tender meat and the best, most perfectly crispy skin. —KW

SERVES 4

4 pounds (1.8 kg) rock salt

1 whole chicken, neck and insides removed

Salt and pepper

1 lemon

3 cloves garlic, peeled and sliced

3 sprigs fresh herbs—parsley, basil, oregano, rosemary, thyme, etc.

Preheat oven to 400°F (200°C, or gas mark 6). Pour the rock salt in a 9 × 13-inch (23 × 33-cm) baking dish. Season the inside and outside of the chicken with salt and pepper. Poke holes in the lemon with a fork or knife and insert it into the cavity of the chicken along with the garlic cloves and fresh herbs. Secure the cavity shut with toothpicks. Place chicken breast-side-up on the bed of salt. Roast for 40 minutes. Flip the chicken over and cook for 45 more minutes or until chicken is cooked through. Let rest for a few minutes before cutting.

CHEF'S TIP:

Rock salt is usually found in the baking aisle at the grocery store, on the bottom shelf around the other salt. It is also called ice cream salt.

SPAGHETTI SQUASH YOGA BOWL

This recipe combines fresh produce with a thick cashew lime sauce for the perfect veggie-heavy lunch, high in fiber and full of flavor. —RB

SERVES 4

2 pounds (908 g) spaghetti squash

1 tbsp (15 ml) coconut oil

2 bunches broccolini

4 kale stalks

FOR THE SAUCE

1 (1-inch [2.5-cm]) piece fresh ginger

2 cloves garlic

Juice of 1 lime

2 tbsp (30 g) cashew butter

1 tbsp (15 ml) apple cider vinegar

1 tbsp (12 g) coconut sugar

2 tbsp (30 ml) coconut aminos

1 tsp (5 ml) sesame oil

½ tsp salt

⅓ cup (80 ml) coconut oil

TO GARNISH

Chili flakes

Cashews

Sesame seeds

Pierce the spaghetti squash several times on each side with a sharp knife, and place on a plate. Microwave on high for 8 minutes and then rotate top side down and microwave for another 8 minutes. Slice open the spaghetti squash, being careful of the hot escaping steam, and set aside to cool. Using a fork, lift out the seeds and discard. Scrape out the insides into a medium mixing bowl.

In a large skillet, melt 1 tablespoon (15 ml) of coconut oil over medium heat. Trim the ends of the broccolini, then roughly chop and add it to the skillet. Trim the ends of the kale stalks, roughly chop and add to the broccolini. Cook until bright green and beginning to wilt, about 10 minutes, and then stir into the spaghetti squash. Divide the vegetable mixture into bowls.

To make the sauce, peel and roughly chop the fresh ginger. Add the ginger, garlic cloves, lime juice, cashew butter, apple cider vinegar, coconut sugar, coconut aminos, sesame oil, salt and coconut oil to a blender. Purée the ingredients for the sauce until smooth, then toss with the vegetables to thoroughly coat. Finish with chili flakes, cashews and sesame seeds.

PAD THAI

This authentic-tasting Thai dish is bursting with flavor and loaded with nutritious eggs and chicken. Spaghetti squash noodles make a great alternative to traditional pastas. —KH

SERVES 4

½ medium spaghetti squash

Coconut oil, butter or ghee for cooking

FOR THE SAUCE

½ cup (120 ml) coconut milk, homemade or canned

½ cup (120 ml) homemade broth

½ cup (125 g) almond butter

Juice of 1 large lime

1 tbsp (15 ml) apple cider vinegar

2 tbsp (30 ml) coconut aminos

2 tbsp (30 ml) toasted sesame oil

1 tbsp (8 g) fresh ginger, grated fine

¼ tsp sea salt

⅛ tsp cayenne pepper, powdered

Coconut oil, butter or ghee for cooking

1 pound (454 g) chicken, cut into 1-inch (2.5-cm) pieces

2 cloves of garlic, minced

2 eggs, beaten

3 cups (360 g) chopped veggies (I used carrots, zucchini and broccoli)

TO GARNISH

¼ cup (15 g) cilantro, chopped

3 green onions, thinly sliced

1 lime, cut into wedges

Cook the spaghetti squash until tender. I like to cut the squash in half and cook in a slow cooker on high for 2 to 2½ hours with about an inch (2.5 cm) of water in the bottom. It comes out perfect. Or pierce the outside of the squash several times with a fork and then roast whole squash in shallow baking dish for 1 hour in a preheated 375°F (190°F C, or gas mark 5) oven.

When cool enough to handle, cut the squash lengthwise (if you haven't already) and scoop the seeds and fibrous strings from the center. Gently scrape the tines of a kitchen fork around the edge of the spaghetti squash to shred the pulp into strands. These are the noodles. Set aside.

Combine all sauce ingredients (except cooking fat) in a medium pot over low heat. Stir until well combined. Set aside. Heat 1 tablespoon (15 ml) fat of your choice in a skillet over medium heat. Add the chicken pieces and cook until lightly browned, about 4 minutes. Add minced garlic and sauté for a minute or two. Remove from skillet and set aside.

Add a teaspoon of oil to the skillet and pour in beaten eggs and cook until the eggs are thoroughly heated, about 2 minutes. Remove from the skillet and set aside.

Add another teaspoon of oil to the skillet and the chopped sauté veggies until beginning to soften, about 4 to 5 minutes. Add the chicken, eggs and sauce to the skillet and mix thoroughly. Add the spaghetti squash noodles and mix again. Garnish with fresh cilantro, green onions and lime wedges. Serve immediately.

PROSCIUTTO-WRAPPED PESTO CHICKEN WITH ROASTED TOMATOES

I like to call this dinner a one-pot wonder because it just requires one pot. The light, garden fresh pesto and cherry tomatoes are a welcome contrast to the rich and salty prosciutto. Bonus—clean up is a breeze! Line your pan with parchment paper for even easier cleaning. —KW

SERVES 4

2 pints (600 g) cherry tomatoes

1 red onion, cut into half-moon slices

Sea salt and pepper, to taste

2 tbsp (30 g) fat of choice

4 boneless, skinless chicken breasts

¼ cup (60 g) Spinach Basil Pesto (page 510)

4 pieces prosciutto

Preheat oven to 450°F (230°C, or gas mark 8). Put the cherry tomatoes and onion on a rimmed baking pan. Salt and pepper the veggies. Pour the olive oil or other fat over the vegetables and toss to coat. Salt and pepper both sides of the chicken. Spread about 1 tablespoon (15 g) of pesto over each chicken breast. Wrap with one slice of prosciutto. Place the chicken breasts in the pan with the tomatoes and onions, and bake for 25 minutes or until tomatoes burst and chicken is cooked through.

BACON-WRAPPED CHICKEN THIGHS

I've yet to get a bad review of this recipe. It's easy, tasty and both kids and adults of all ages really enjoy it. Serve it with the Cool Ranch Avocado Dip (page 516) and you'll have a winning combo. —KW

SERVES 6

8 skinless chicken thighs

2 tbsp (16 g) Ranch Seasoning (page 512)

8 slices bacon

Cool Ranch Avocado Dip (page 516), for serving

Preheat oven to 375°F (190°C, or gas mark 5). Rub all sides of the chicken thighs with the Ranch Seasoning. Wrap each thigh with one slice of bacon. Place the thighs on a baking sheet and bake for 35 to 40 minutes or until bacon is crispy and chicken is cooked throughout. Serve with Cool Ranch Avocado Dip.

CHEF'S TIP:
For easy cleanup, line the baking pan with foil.

TUSCAN CHICKEN MINI ROULADE

These mini roulades are intensely flavorful, thanks to sundried tomatoes, prosciutto and juicy baked chicken. —RB

SERVES 6

3 pounds (1.4 kg) boneless, skinless chicken breasts

½ cup (60 g) sundried tomatoes

¼ pound (112 g) prosciutto, thinly sliced

Handful Tuscan kale, torn into bite-sized pieces

Salt and pepper to taste

Preheat the oven to 400°F (200°C, or gas mark 6). Set a roasting rack on top of a roasting pan, set aside.

Lay each chicken breast flat, and carefully cut them to make two pieces the same height and width yet half as thick. Lay 2 or 3 sundried tomatoes on each chicken breast, sprinkle with salt and pepper then layer a slice of prosciutto over them. Finish with a few pieces of Tuscan kale.

Roll each piece of chicken up around its filling, and secure by wrapping a piece of butcher's twine around it and tying at the top. Repeat with the remaining chicken.

Set each mini roulade on the roasting rack, and cook in the preheated oven for 40 minutes until the chicken is fully cooked. Untie each piece, and serve warm.

CHICKEN SCALLOPINI

This chicken scallopini variation uses the rich flavors of bacon, capers, parsley and sundried tomatoes to make a delicious combo with chicken and "zoodles." —RB

SERVES 4

4 zucchini

2 slices bacon

1½ pounds (680 g) boneless, skinless chicken thighs

1 tbsp (8 g) capers

¾ cup (225 g) packed artichoke hearts

¼ tsp salt

¼ cup (30 g) packed sundried tomatoes in oil, chopped

Handful flat-leaf parsley

Lemon

Using a spiralizer or vegetable peeler, process the zucchini into fine shreds. Heat a large skillet over medium heat and cook the bacon, turning once, until brown and crispy, approximately 5 minutes per side. Remove and let drain on a paper towel-lined plate. Don't drain the bacon fat from the skillet.

Fry the chicken in the bacon fat until crisped on the outside and cooked through, 15 to 25 minutes depending on size. Remove and let drain on a paper towel–lined plate.

Pour off the grease and cook the zucchini strands, tossing occasionally with tongs or a fork, 5 minutes to al dente or until softened to your preference. Drain the excess water rendered during cooking from the skillet and toss the zucchini noodles with the capers, artichoke hearts, salt and sundried tomatoes.

Crumble the strips of bacon over the vegetables and return the chicken thighs to the pan until reheated. Serve warm, garnished with parsley and a squeeze of lemon juice.

CHEF'S TIP:
The capers, bacon and sundried tomatoes are already salty, so be careful of over-salting.

ROASTED HERBED CHICKEN

It doesn't take much to create juicy, roasted chicken with extra crispy skin. The secret is to use bone-in chicken so it doesn't dry out as it cooks. Adding ghee under the skin and cooking it on convection setting guarantees that it will be crisp on the outside and juicy on the inside. —JC

SERVES 2

4 tsp (20 ml) ghee, melted

1 tsp (3 g) onion powder

½ tsp garlic powder

½ tsp dried chives

¼ tsp sea salt

¼ tsp black pepper

2 split chicken breasts, skin on

Preheat oven to 350°F (180°C, or gas mark 4) on convection setting.

In a small bowl, combine ghee, onion powder, garlic powder, chives, sea salt and black pepper. Rub the seasoning all over the chicken breasts and under the skin so it cooks extra crispy. Place chicken in an ovenproof dish and bake in the oven for 25 to 30 minutes until the thickest part has an internal temperature of 165°F (74°C). Let it rest for 5 to 8 minutes before serving.

CHEF'S TIP:

If your oven doesn't have a convection setting, preheat it to 425°F (220°C, or gas mark 7).

BROWNED BUTTER SAGE ROASTED CHICKEN

Walking into a kitchen that smells good always makes me hungry, so this is a great dish to serve for guests or a basic weeknight dinner. This recipe is simple with basics such as salt, butter, garlic and herbs but the combination of flavors is fantastic! —CP

SERVES 6–8

3 pounds (1.4 kg) bone-in, skin-on chicken breasts and legs

2 tbsp (30 ml) olive oil

1½ tsp (4.5 g) sea salt

½ tsp fresh cracked black pepper

5 cloves garlic, crushed

1 tbsp (4 g) fresh chopped sage, heaping full

1 red onion, sliced

2 tbsp (30 g) butter, sliced

FOR THE CRISPY SAGE BROWNED BUTTER SAUCE

8 tbsp (115 g) butter

¼ cup (16 g) fresh chopped sage

½ tsp sea salt

Cauliflower rice, optional

Parmesan cheese, optional

Preheat oven to 400°F (200°C, or gas mark 6).

Pat chicken dry with a paper towel and place in a large baking dish. Drizzle the olive oil onto the chicken, using your hands to coat all sides.

Season the chicken with salt and pepper, then rub in crushed garlic. Sprinkle chopped sage on top. Arrange the onion slices throughout the pan. Place slices of butter on top of the chicken, and throughout the pan.

Roast chicken for 32 to 37 minutes, depending on the size of your chicken pieces. Make the browned butter sauce about 5 minutes before you are ready to serve.

(continued)

Heat a small skillet to medium heat. Add butter and allow it to brown and sizzle for about 2 minutes, then turn down the heat. Once the butter is brown and gives off a nutty aroma, remove from heat and add in the chopped sage and salt. The sage will turn crispy as it hits the hot butter.

Serve the chicken over a scoop of cauliflower rice and generously drizzled with crispy sage browned butter. Garnish with Parmesan shavings if desired. Serve and enjoy!

CRISPY CHICKEN WITH BUTTERNUT SQUASH AND SAGE

The unique combination of crispy chicken, butternut squash and sage leaves makes this a delicious meal that everyone will love. —NK

SERVES 2–4

4 chicken thighs

Sea salt and black pepper, to taste

½ tsp red pepper flakes

1 tbsp (15 ml) coconut oil, melted

1 medium butternut squash, peeled and cubed

2 tbsp (30 g) butter, divided

6 fresh sage leaves

Preheat oven to 400°F (200°C, or gas mark 6). Line a large baking tray with parchment paper. Season chicken thighs with sea salt and pepper on both sides. Place onto the lined baking tray. Sprinkle the red pepper flakes evenly on top of each thigh. Pour melted coconut oil evenly onto the chicken thighs. Bake in the oven for 40 to 45 minutes.

While the chicken is baking, bring a pot of water to a boil. Place the cubed butternut squash in a steamer basket and carefully insert it into the pot. Cover and steam the squash until soft and tender, about 7 to 10 minutes . Once ready remove the squash from the steamer basket and mash with 1 tablespoon (15 g) butter.

Add 1 tablespoon (15 g) butter to a small skillet. Once the butter is frothy and turning a caramel brown color, add the sage leaves into the skillet and fry for a few minutes until the sage leaves crisp up. Place crispy sage leaves onto a paper towel–lined plate.

To serve, place some butternut squash mash on a plate and top with one or two pieces of chicken thigh. Top with some crispy sage leaves.

ROAST CHICKEN LEGS WITH YAMS

This one-pan meal is comforting and satisfying. It's a great go-to for busy weeknights. —AV

SERVES 4

1½ pounds (680 g) yams, peeled and cubed

4 tbsp (60 g) ghee, melted and divided

Sea salt and fresh pepper

4 chicken legs, thigh and drumstick, about 3 pounds (1.4 kg)

Bunch of thyme

Preheat oven to 450°F (230°C, or gas mark 8). Toss yams with 2 tablespoons (30 g) of ghee; season with salt and pepper.

Place chicken on a rimmed baking sheet and rub with remaining 2 tablespoons (30 g) of ghee, season with salt and pepper. Arrange the cubed yams around chicken. Tuck thyme leaves around the chicken and yams.

Roast until yams are fork-tender, chicken is cooked through, and skin is crisp, 35 to 45 minutes. Discard thyme leaves. Serve chicken with the yams.

BROCCOLI CHICKEN

Chinese takeout is usually filled with gluten, MSG and other unhealthy additives. Make this simplified broccoli chicken right at home and you can even eat it with rice without feeling guilty! —JC

SERVES 4

2 tbsp (30 g) tallow or coconut oil

1 (1-inch [2.5-cm]) piece of ginger, peeled and grated

4 cloves garlic, minced

1 pound (454 g) boneless, skinless chicken thighs, cut into bite-size pieces

½ tsp sea salt

¼ cup (60 ml) coconut aminos

¼ tsp black pepper

8 ounces (227 g) button mushrooms

12 ounces (336 g) broccoli, cut into bite-size pieces

1 tbsp (8 g) arrowroot dissolved in ¼ cup (60 ml) warm water

Add tallow to a wok over medium-high heat. Add ginger and garlic. Sauté for 1 minute until fragrant. Season chicken with sea salt and add to the wok. Sauté and cover to cook for 5 minutes until chicken is no longer pink. Season with coconut aminos and black pepper then stir to combine.

Add the mushrooms and broccoli. Stir-fry for 5 to 7 minutes until broccoli is cooked. Add dissolved arrowroot and stir for 1 minute until it thickens and coats the chicken and vegetables. Serve hot.

PESTO CHICKEN WITH ZUCCHINI NOODLES

A simple and fun dinner idea the whole family will love. You will never miss pasta again. —KH

SERVES 3–4

5 cups (600 g) zucchini noodles

Pinch of sea salt

FOR THE PESTO

1 large bunch fresh basil, leaves only

½ clove of garlic

¼ cup (60 ml) olive oil

¼ tsp sea salt

1 tsp (5 ml) fresh lemon juice

¼ cup (32 g) hemp seeds, pumpkin seeds or pine nuts

½ tsp sea salt

2 pounds (908 g) boneless chicken, cut into bite-sized pieces

2 tbsp (30 ml) coconut oil or ghee, divided

2 cloves of fresh garlic, minced

1 cup (150 g) cherry tomatoes, cut in half

3 tbsp (24 g) pine nuts, for garnish

Place zucchini noodles in a large strainer in the sink and sprinkle with a pinch of salt. Set aside. This will remove some of the moisture from the noodles.

To make the pesto, place the basil leaves and garlic into a food processor and process until completely broken up. Add olive oil, salt and lemon juice and continue to process until smooth. Add hemp seeds—or pumpkin seeds or pine nuts—and pulse until desired consistency.

Sprinkle ½ teaspoon salt over the chicken. In a large skillet, melt 1 tablespoon (15 ml) of fat of choice and sauté chicken pieces and minced garlic until cooked all the way through and starting to brown, about 8 to 10 minutes.

(continued)

Meanwhile, dump the noodles onto a clean dish towel and gently pat dry. Then, in another skillet, melt 1 tablespoon (15 ml) of fat of choice and sauté zucchini noodles for 2 to 3 minutes until just beginning to soften. Turn off heat and add the cooked chicken and pesto. Give a little stir. Top with cherry tomatoes and pine nuts. Serve immediately.

CHEF'S TIP:

I use 2 large skillets to make this dish because it is just easier. You can make this a one-skillet meal by removing the chicken after it is done and using the same pan to warm the noodles.

ROASTED CHICKEN WITH CILANTRO

This chicken offers the flavors of Mexico with green chili and cilantro. Pair this with a good salad and you're set! —VM

SERVES 4

2 cloves of garlic, chopped

1 green chili, seeded and chopped

1 cup (60 g) fresh cilantro, chopped

2 tbsp (30 ml) lemon juice

4 tbsp (60 ml) olive oil

1 tsp (6 g) sea salt

1 whole chicken

Fresh Mixed Salsa (page 249), optional, for serving

Add all of the ingredients, except for the chicken and salsa, to the food processor and blend well. Rub the chicken thoroughly with the marinade and refrigerate for at least 12 hours.

Preheat the oven to 350°F (180°F, or gas mark 4) once you have finished marinating the chicken.

Roast the chicken for 1½ hours in a roasting pan to preserve the juices.

Serve with salsa or a nice green salad.

LIME CILANTRO CHICKEN DRUMSTICKS

The lime cilantro marinade is really what makes this recipe excellent. The drumsticks take on that bright flavor and stay juicy after grilling. —HH

SERVES 2

4 drumsticks

¼ cup (60 ml) olive oil

1 tsp (5 ml) coconut aminos

Juice of half a lime

2 tbsp (8 g) chopped cilantro, plus more for garnish

½ tsp salt, pepper

½ tsp turmeric

½ tsp garlic powder

Place drumsticks in a large plastic container or large plastic resealable bag. Put all the remaining ingredients in the container, seal it and shake it around to completely coat the drumsticks. Leave in the fridge to marinate for 2 to 4 hours.

If using a cast iron grill pan, preheat the oven to 350°F (180°C, or gas mark 4). Heat the grill pan on the stove on medium heat until hot, then add the drumsticks to the pan and grill for 5 to 10 minutes on each side. You should have some grill marks on the drum sticks. Transfer the pan to the oven and cook for about 15 to 20 minutes or until the internal temperature reaches 165°F (74°C).

If using a BBQ grill, heat the barbecue until it's hot. Place the drumsticks on the grill for 5 minutes on each side. Then, cover the barbeque and allow the drumsticks to cook for another 10 to 20 minutes or until the internal temperature reaches 165°F (74°C).

Place the leftover marinade juices in a small saucepan and heat to a boil for a few minutes, then drizzle the drumsticks with the remaining marinade. Add some additional chopped cilantro to the drumsticks and enjoy!

LEMON BASIL CHICKEN DRUMSTICKS

Lemon Basil Chicken is our go-to chicken dish. The flavors are fresh and bright, and the dish is versatile enough to serve with almost any vegetables you have on hand. —KH

SERVES 4–6

FOR THE MARINADE

3 tbsp (45 ml) butter, ghee or coconut oil, melted

4 cloves of fresh garlic

¼ cup (60 ml) fresh lemon juice

½ cup (30 g) fresh basil, roughly chopped

1 tsp (3 g) sea salt

12 chicken drumsticks

Combine all the marinade ingredients in a blender and process until smooth, like salad dressing.

Pat the chicken drumsticks dry with paper towel and place into shallow baking dish. Pour the marinade on top, toss to evenly coat, cover and place in fridge to marinate for at least 2 hours. Overnight is even better.

Preheat the barbeque. Clean the grill well before cooking drumsticks and oil if necessary. Arrange marinated drumsticks on barbeque, turn heat down to medium and close the cover. Flip drumsticks every 8 to 10 minutes until thoroughly cooked. Mine usually take around 30 to 35 minutes, depending on how hot my grill is. Always be sure that the chicken reaches at least 165°F (74°C). Serve and enjoy.

HONEY ORANGE CHICKEN

Gone are the days of ordering orange chicken takeout where there is more breading than meat! Eliminate the extra step of coating and pan-frying by simmering chicken pieces directly in a sweet honey orange sauce. The result yields a lighter version with the same delicious taste. —JC

SERVES 6

1 tbsp (15 g) tallow or bacon fat

1 pound (454 g) boneless, skinless chicken thighs, cut into bite-size pieces

2 tbsp (16 g) ginger, grated

4 cloves of garlic, minced

2 tbsp (30 ml) coconut aminos

2 tbsp (30 ml) raw honey

1 tbsp (15 ml) chili sauce

½ cup (120 ml) fresh orange juice

Fish sauce

¼ cup (25 g) green onions, chopped

Add tallow to a wok or deep skillet over high heat. Add chicken pieces and stir-fry until they start to brown, about 2 to 3 minutes. Add ginger and garlic. Sauté for 1 minute until fragrant. Lower heat and add coconut aminos, honey, chili sauce and orange juice. Stir to incorporate everything together. Season with fish sauce to taste. Cover and simmer for 8 to 10 minutes until sauce thickens and chicken is cooked. Top with green onions before serving.

CHEF'S TIP:

Cara Cara oranges are sweeter and less acidic than other types of oranges but any variety will do. Adjust the amount of honey if the orange used is very tart.

BALSAMIC CHICKEN KABOBS WITH STRAWBERRY BASIL SALSA

A summertime favorite in our house, these juicy grilled chicken kabobs are drizzled in rich balsamic glaze and topped with sweet strawberries and fresh basil. —CP

SERVES 4–6

2 pounds (908 g) chicken breast

2 tbsp (30 ml) olive oil

1½ tsp (4.5 g) fresh rosemary, chopped

½ tsp sea salt

¼ tsp garlic granules

¼ tsp black pepper

1 pound (454 g) strawberries

½ cup (30 g) fresh basil, sliced

3 green onions, chopped

2 tbsp (30 ml) balsamic glaze

Fresh spring lettuce to garnish, optional

Slice chicken into 2-inch (5-cm) cubes. Place in a bowl and toss together with oil, rosemary, salt, garlic and pepper. Marinate in refrigerator for 30 minutes to 2 hours. When ready to grill, place chicken on kabob skewers.

Prepare the salsa by chopping strawberries, basil and onions and tossing together in a bowl.

When time to cook, preheat your grill to medium high heat, about 500°F (250°C, or gas mark 10). Grill chicken kabobs for 6 to 8 minutes, depending on the thickness of chicken, rotating halfway through.

Plate and drizzle generously with balsamic glaze. Serve with a garnish of spring lettuce leaves and strawberry basil salsa.

CHEF'S TIPS:
Chicken grilling time really depends on how you cut your chicken, due to size and thickness.

I keep a few fabulous herb-flavored poultry salt seasonings on hand and sometimes use that instead of the fresh rosemary rub to save time.

SAFFRON CHICKEN WITH ORANGE REDUCTION

Jazz up your chicken with the flavors of saffron and orange. Your taste buds will thank you for it. —NK

SERVES 4

1 cup (235 ml) Slow Cooker Chicken Broth (page 170)

Juice of 2 large oranges

2 tbsp (30 g) ghee, divided

1 yellow onion, sliced into half moons

1 pound (454 g) bone-in, skin-on chicken thighs

½ tsp ground saffron, dissolved in ¼ cup (60 ml) boiled water to make "saffron tea"

¼ cup (60 ml) water

Sea salt and black pepper, to taste

Fresh parsley, to garnish

Cauliflower rice or salad greens, optional, for serving

Add chicken broth and orange juice to a medium saucepan over medium–high heat. Reduce the liquid, stirring frequently, until it reduces down to about ⅓ cup (80 ml). Remove from the heat and set aside. Heat a large skillet with a lid, big enough to hold the chicken thighs over medium heat. Add in 1 tablespoon (15 g) ghee. Add in the onion and sauté for 10 minutes, then remove the onions to a clean plate.

Season both sides of each chicken thigh with salt and pepper. Add another 1 tablespoon (15 g) ghee to the skillet, add in the chicken thighs and cook for 6 to 7 minutes per side. Add the onions back into the skillet and add in the saffron tea. Rinse any leftover saffron with ¼ cup (60 ml) of water and pour that into the skillet. Pour the orange reduction in and stir to mix. Cover the skillet with a lid and reduce the heat down to a simmer. Cook for 15 to 20 minutes or until the chicken is cooked through. Serve with some fresh parsley on top.

To make this a complete meal serve over cauliflower rice or over a bed of salad greens.

ROASTED CHICKEN WITH APPLES

Another great, if a bit unusual, pairing I love is the combination of meat with the sweet flavor of fruit, especially chicken, which can often be bland and a bit dry. Combining it with apples enhances tenderness and sweet flavor, making it a hit with the whole family. —VM

SERVES 4

2 tbsp (30 g) lard, divided

½ tsp cayenne pepper

Sea salt and black pepper to taste

1 whole chicken

2 pounds (908 g) apples

1 tsp (3 g) ground cinnamon

¼ cup (60 ml) Slow Cooker Chicken Broth (page 170)

1 tbsp (8 g) coconut flour

2 cups (470 ml) apple cider

Preheat the oven to 350°F (180°C, or gas mark 4). In a bowl, mix together 1 tablespoon (15 g) of lard with cayenne and a pinch of sea salt and black pepper to create a paste. Give the chicken a nice massage with the rub. Put the chicken in a roasting pan and roast for 1½ hours. While the chicken is roasting, peel and core the apples. Cut them into quarters and quarter them again.

Add the remaining lard to a large pan and melt over high flame. Season the apples with cinnamon and sea salt, sautéing them until they are golden and soft, about 5 minutes. Once the apples are done, set them aside and keep warm.

When the chicken has roasted, cut the chicken into nice portions, set aside and keep warm.

Pour the pan drippings from the chicken into a small saucepan with the chicken broth, and bring it to a boil. Reduce the broth mixture over high heat for about 10 minutes and then remove from the heat. Add the coconut flour slowly to the broth while mixing thoroughly to form a delicious gravy.

Serve the chicken dressed in gravy, topping it with the apple mixture and enjoy!

CHICKEN TENDERS

These chicken tenders are the real deal! I've tried many alternative flours, and I have never found a combination that resembles the chicken tenders of my childhood so closely. My guests never realize that these are gluten-free. —AV

SERVES 4

1 cup (225 g) ground pork rinds

1 cup (120 g) tapioca flour

½ tsp cayenne

½ tsp dried oregano

1 tsp (3 g) garlic powder

1 tsp (3 g) onion powder

½ tsp sea salt

½ tsp ground black pepper

2 eggs

1 pound (454 g) boneless, skinless chicken thighs, cut into 1-inch (2.5-cm) chunks

Palm shortening or coconut oil, for frying

Honey Mustard Dipping Sauce (page 517), for serving

Blend pork rinds in the food processor until it has the consistency of flour. In a shallow bowl or a plate, combine the ground pork rinds, tapioca flour, cayenne, oregano, garlic powder, onion powder, salt and pepper. In a shallow bowl beat the eggs together. Dredge the chicken tenders one piece at a time in the flour mixture. Shake off the excess flour, then dip the chicken tenders in the egg and again in the flour. Make sure they are very well coated with the flour mixture. Set them aside on a clean dish.

Heat the palm shortening in a heavy-bottomed pan like cast iron over medium-high heat. Start with ¼ cup (58 g) palm shortening and add more if needed. You want enough oil in the pan to submerge the chicken tenders halfway in the oil. Add as many chicken tenders as you can fit without crowding the pan. Fry the chicken tenders on each side until the chicken is cooked through and no longer pink inside, about 4 to 5 minutes per side. The chicken will have to be cooked in batches. Place cooked tenders on a plate lined with paper towels to drain. Serve with Honey Mustard Dipping Sauce!

(continued)

PISTACHIO–CRUSTED CHICKEN TENDERS WITH CURRANT DIPPING SAUCE

Here, chicken strips are crusted in a grain-free pistachio mix, baked until golden and then served with a sweet black currant sauce for dipping. These are not your average chicken tenders! —RM

SERVES 6

FOR THE CHICKEN

Coconut oil or ghee, for greasing

1 cup (150 g) pistachios

½ cup (75 g) ground flaxseed

2 tbsp (8 g) fresh parsley

1 tsp (3 g) garlic powder

Salt, to taste

2 dashes cayenne pepper

1 egg

2 pounds (908 g) boneless, skinless chicken breast, cut in 1-inch (2.5-cm)-wide strips

FOR THE DIPPING SAUCE

3 tbsp (45 g) black currant jam (or a tart jam of choice)

3 tbsp (45 g) whole-grain mustard

1 tbsp (15 ml) raw honey

Preheat the oven to 500°F (250°C, or gas mark 10). Grease two baking sheets with coconut oil or ghee and set aside. Blend the pistachios using a food processor until you have a crumb consistency. Add the flaxseed, parsley, garlic powder, salt and cayenne pepper. Pulse until incorporated. Dump the breading onto a flat plate.

In a small shallow bowl, beat the egg well. Dip strips of chicken first in the egg and then coat with the pistachio breading. Line the baking sheets with the breaded chicken. Place trays in the oven, bringing the temp back down to 375°F (190°C, or gas mark 5). Bake for about 15 to 20 minutes until fully cooked.

In a small bowl, mix together the dipping sauce ingredients. Serve on the side of the hot chicken tenders.

BAKED CHICKEN WITH PISTACHIO TAPENADE

I prefer to make my own tapenade because it tastes fresher than the store-bought variety. I can also control what goes in it so I'm sure there are no unnecessary additives. This tapenade has a wonderful nuttiness from pistachios and dresses up plain ol' baked chicken! —JC

SERVES 4

¼ cup (25 g) pitted black olives

¼ cup (25 g) pitted green olives

3 cloves of roasted garlic

2 tbsp (20 g) roasted red peppers

½ cup (120 ml) extra-virgin olive oil

2 tbsp (16 g) raw pistachios, chopped

4 boneless, skinless chicken thighs

1 tbsp (15 ml) ghee or coconut oil, melted

Sea salt

Black pepper

Preheat oven to 375°F (190°C, or gas mark 5).

Prepare the tapenade by adding black olives, green olives, garlic, red peppers and olive oil to a food processor. Pulse until it is a rice-like consistency. Pulse it a little bit more if you like a smoother tapenade. Mix in the pistachios and set aside in a bowl.

Coat chicken with ghee and generously season with sea salt and black pepper. Place chicken on a baking dish and bake for 10 minutes. Flip the chicken and bake for another 10 minutes. Remove from oven and let it cool for 5 minutes. Top with pistachio tapenade before serving.

CHICKEN SCALOPPINI WITH ANCHOVY SAUCE

Chicken and anchovies might not be the most usual combination, but they really do complement each other well. The anchovies are full of flavor and their salty deliciousness really goes well with the milder chicken. If you want to try something a little different, I really recommend this dish. —VM

SERVES 2

10 ounces (280 g) chicken breast, sliced into thin filets

2 ounces (56 g) butter, divided

3 anchovy fillets

Juice of ½ a lemon

1 tbsp (4 g) fresh parsley, finely chopped, plus more for garnish

Begin by laying the chicken filets out between two sheets of parchment paper and beating them thin with a meat mallet. Be careful not to beat the living daylights out of the chicken, as you still need some for the dish!

In a large skillet over medium heat, melt half of the butter until it begins to brown. Add the chicken filets to the skillet and cook for 1 minute on each side until they slightly brown. Lower the heat and cook the chicken for another 5 minutes, turning often. Make sure to pay attention to the butter so that it does not burn; lower the heat if needed.

Once the chicken is done, set it aside on a plate. Smash the anchovies in a bowl with a fork or a pestle, until they form a paste. Add the anchovy paste to the skillet over low heat along with the lemon juice, the rest of the butter and parsley. Mix the ingredients well and cook for about 1 minute.

Spread the anchovy paste generously over the chicken filets, garnish with a sprinkle of chopped parsley and serve immediately.

SPICY GRILLED CHICKEN

Chicken can get a little redundant sometimes. When that happens to me, I spice it up and give it a nice kick with this 6-spice marinade. I love the blend of fragrant flavors and spices and I think you will too! —VM

SERVES 4

FOR THE MARINADE

2 tsp (6 g) ground cumin

2 tsp (6 g) ground coriander

1 tsp (3 g) ground cardamom

1 yellow onion, chopped

1 tbsp (8 g) fresh ginger, grated

½ tsp ground cayenne

½ tsp ground cloves

½ cup (120 ml) walnut oil

¼ cup (60 ml) apple cider vinegar

1 tsp (6 g) sea salt

FOR THE CHICKEN STRIPS

1 pound (454 g) chicken breast, sliced into 1-inch (2.5-cm) strips

Preheat the oven to 350°F (180°C, or gas mark 4). In a small skillet, start by toasting the cumin, coriander and cardamom for about a minute, being careful not to burn them. Let the spice mixture cool and then mix well with the remaining ingredients of the marinade.

In a large resealable bag, coat the chicken strips with the marinade, then refrigerate overnight.

Once the chicken is done marinating, heat the broiler to high, place the chicken strips on a grill pan and cook for about 4 minutes per side until well done.

CHICKEN FAJITA STUFFED PEPPERS

I drew inspiration for this recipe from two of our family's favorite recipes—chicken fajitas and stuffed peppers. These Chicken Fajita Stuffed Peppers are hands down a winner at our house and if you like chicken fajitas as much as we do, I think you'll really enjoy this recipe, too. —KW

SERVES 4

1 pound (454 g) boneless, skinless chicken breasts, cut into thin strips

1 red onion, sliced

1 zucchini, sliced

1 tbsp (15 ml) apple cider vinegar

1 tbsp (15 ml) coconut aminos

1 tbsp (15 ml) avocado oil or fat of choice

2 cloves of garlic, minced

1 tbsp (8 g) chili powder

1 tsp (3 g) onion powder

½ tsp ground cumin

Pinch of cayenne pepper

Sea salt and pepper, to taste

4 bell peppers, tops cut off and seeds removed

1 lime, halved

Chopped cilantro and Super Easy Guacamole (page 190), for garnish

Preheat oven to 350°F (180°C, or gas mark 4). Place the chicken strips, onion and zucchini on a baking pan. Set aside. In a small bowl, mix together the apple cider vinegar, coconut aminos, avocado oil, minced garlic, chili powder, onion powder, cumin, cayenne pepper and salt and pepper. Pour the liquid mixture on top of the pan and toss to coat. Bake for 20 minutes or until chicken is cooked through.

Divide the chicken mixture into 4 bell peppers. Place the stuffed peppers in a baking pan. Bake for 35 to 40 minutes or until peppers are softened to your liking. Squeeze lime juice over the top of each pepper. Serve with chopped cilantro and Super Easy Guacamole.

SPICY SHREDDED CHICKEN STUFFED SQUASH

This simple stuffed squash entrée is eye-catching yet easy to make. When they are in season, little patty-pan squash are a cute substitute for the more common oblong variety of summer squash. —RB

SERVES 3

3 summer squash

1 tsp (5 ml) coconut oil

2 cups (280 g) cooked, shredded chicken

¼ tsp salt

½ tsp sesame seeds

½ tsp black pepper

1 tsp (3 g) chili flakes

Preheat the oven to 350°F (180°C, or gas mark 4). Trim the ends and halve the squash lengthwise. Coat the squash in the coconut oil, and then place on a rimmed baking sheet.

Bake in the preheated oven for 15 minutes until softened. Remove the squash from the oven and allow to cool enough to handle. Scoop out a few tablespoons (24 g) of the seeds from each squash half and stir them into the shredded chicken.

Mix the salt, sesame seeds, black pepper and chili flakes into the squash/chicken mixture. Top each squash half with a small handful of this filling. Bake for an additional 15 minutes, or until the squash is fully soft and the chicken is hot.

CHEF'S TIP:

Experiment with diced chicken instead of the shredded chicken, or some other kind of meat entirely, whether diced, ground or shredded.

CHICKEN AND BISCUITS

In this version of the delicious Southern dish, vegetables are cooked in broth until soft, then mixed with chicken and topped with coconut-flour biscuits. —RB

SERVES 2

2 tbsp (30 ml) coconut oil

½ onion, thinly sliced

1 large carrot, sliced

2 ribs celery, chopped

1 cup (140 g) cooked shredded chicken

1½ cups (355 ml) chicken stock, divided

⅓ cup (40 g) arrowroot flour

½ cup (75 g) peas

¼ tsp salt

Crumbly Butter Biscuits (page 522)

Heat the coconut oil in a large skillet over medium heat. Add the sliced onion, chopped carrot and celery. Sauté until beginning to soften, approximately 5 to 10 minutes.

Add the shredded chicken, then pour in 1 cup (235 ml) of stock and simmer until reduced, approximately 10 minutes. Add the last ½ cup (120 ml) of stock plus the arrowroot flour, peas and salt.

Mix well until the peas are warmed and the consistency of the combination is soft with a touch of thickness from the arrowroot. Top with warm biscuits and serve.

BLT CHICKEN

One of my favorite things to eat pre-Paleo was the classic BLT sandwich, but this chicken dish is even better! It's bursting with fresh flavor that you're sure to love. —KW

SERVES 4–6

FOR THE MARINADE

¼ cup (60 ml) olive oil

¼ cup (60 ml) balsamic vinegar

4 cloves garlic, minced

2 tbsp (8 g) fresh basil, chopped

1 tsp (5 g) Dijon mustard or dry mustard

Salt and pepper, to taste

4-6 boneless, skinless chicken breasts

Salt and pepper, to taste

6 cups (420 g) fresh lettuce

3 tomatoes

2 slices cooked bacon per chicken breast

2 tbsp (8 g) fresh basil, chopped

(continued)

Mix all the marinade ingredients together in a small bowl. Reserve 2 tablespoons (30 ml) of the marinade for serving. Pour the remaining marinade all over the chicken and marinate in the fridge for at least 1 hour up to 24 hours.

Once the chicken is finished marinating, preheat the oven to 375°F (190°C, or gas mark 5). Salt and pepper the chicken and cook the chicken in a baking dish for 35 minutes or until cooked through.

While the chicken is cooking, place the lettuce on a large serving plate. Cut two of the tomatoes in thick slices. Place the tomato slices on top of the lettuce and add a pinch of salt and pepper to the tomato slices.

When the chicken is finished cooking, place the chicken on top of the sliced tomatoes. Lay two slices of cooked bacon over each chicken breast. Dice the remaining tomato, and put the diced tomatoes on top of the chicken. Pour the reserved 2 tablespoons (30 ml) of marinade all over the top of the diced tomatoes. Top with the 2 tablespoons (8 g) of fresh basil.

CHEF'S TIP:
You can cook the bacon before you cook the chicken. Put the bacon slices on a baking pan and put the pan in a cold oven. Turn the oven to 375°F (190°C, or gas mark 5) and bake for 20 minutes or until bacon is cooked to your liking.

CHICKEN MUSHROOM LETTUCE WRAPS

This recipe saved me when I first went grain-free. I love building the lettuce wraps, one by one, with the warm chicken stir-fry and the cool crunch of the lettuce. Then use the leftovers inside breakfast omelets to power start your day. —RM

SERVES 4

FOR THE SAUCE

¼ cup (60 ml) coconut aminos

2 tbsp (30 ml) rice vinegar

1 tbsp (8 g) freshly grated ginger

1 tbsp (15 ml) chili garlic sauce

1 tsp (5 ml) raw honey

Dash of sesame oil

3 cloves of garlic, minced

FOR THE STIR-FRY

1 tbsp (15 ml) extra-virgin olive oil

1 white onion, diced

3 ounces (84 g) shitake mushrooms, sliced

1 pound (454 g) ground chicken

1 (8-ounce [227-g]) can water chestnuts, drained

2 green onions, thinly sliced

Sea salt and pepper, to taste

1 head butter lettuce, separated into "wraps"

Mix all of the sauce ingredients together in a small bowl. Set aside.

Heat olive oil in a large wok over medium-high heat. Add the onion, mushrooms and chicken and then cook until lightly browned, stirring constantly, about 6 minutes. Add the sauce ingredients along with the water chestnuts. Continue sautéing until the flavors have been incorporated and excess liquid has been cooked off. Add in the sliced green onions and remove from heat. Thoroughly wash the head of lettuce and peel apart the leaves. Pat dry. Serve the hot chicken stir-fry in a bowl with a spoon and chilled lettuce wraps on the side. Spoon ¼ cup (60 g) of mixture onto each wrap as you eat it.

CHICKEN LIVERS WITH BACON & SHIITAKE MUSHROOMS

Bacon truly makes anything better. Add in the shiitake mushrooms and it's one of the best liver dishes you will ever have. Organ meats are very good for you, so I want to make sure you will love this recipe and make it one of the staples. Try it for dinner tonight! —VM

SERVES 2

6 slices of bacon

4 ounces (112 g) fresh shiitake mushrooms, thinly sliced

2 tbsp (30 ml) butter

2 cloves garlic, thinly sliced

½ pound (227 g) chicken livers

¼ tsp parsley flakes

¼ tsp red chili pepper flakes

Cut the bacon into 2-inch (5-cm) strips and cook in a large skillet over medium heat, until they begin to brown, about 3 to 4 minutes. Add the sliced mushrooms to the skillet and sauté for about 10 minutes, or until they are nicely cooked through.

Remove the bacon and mushrooms from the pan and set aside. Now add the butter and garlic to the pan, raising the heat to high, sautéing until the butter begins to brown, about 1 to 2 minutes. Add the chicken livers, parsley and red chili pepper flakes to the pan and sauté for about 5 minutes, turning once or twice until the liver has browned on all sides.

Add the mushrooms and bacon back to the skillet with the chicken livers, stirring well.

Cook this for another 2 minutes, making sure not to over-cook the liver or it will become hard. Serve immediately.

FEGATO CON LE CIPOLLE (LIVER WITH ONIONS)

While this dish might be quick and easy, it still has great nutritional proprieties. Marinating in apple cider vinegar removes the blood smell from the meat as well as any toxins that might have remained. The liver will be tender and full of flavor. —VM

SERVES 2

2 slices of beef liver, about ½-inch (1.3-cm) thick

2 tbsp (30 ml) apple cider vinegar

Sea salt

1 sweet onion, thinly sliced

Fresh thyme, de-stemmed and finely chopped

Fresh sage, finely chopped

3 tbsp (45 g) lard, butter or ghee

Marinate the beef liver overnight in apple cider vinegar.

Remove the liver from the refrigerator about 2 hours before cooking to bring it to room temperature.

Slice and chop the sweet onion and herbs. Add some fat to a large pan and sauté over low heat for about 5 to 7 minutes. Remove the onion and herbs from the pan and set to the side.

Raise the heat to high while adding more fat to the pan. Add the beef liver to the pan and sauté for about 2 to 3 minutes. Flip the liver over, add the onions and herbs back to the pan and cook for an additional 2 minutes.

Cook the liver until it reaches a light pink inside allowing for a nice juicy steak.

PALEO–TALIAN CARPACCIO

Carpaccio is a very popular dish in Italy. It consists of either raw beef or raw fish, very fresh, sliced paper thin and served with a variety of condiments. This one is the original classic carpaccio recipe! You can add ¼ cup (25 g) shaved Parmesan cheese to this finished recipe. Not strictly Paleo but extremely tasty! —VM

SERVES 2

1 steak of your choice, such as filet mignon or top sirloin

1 bunch fresh arugula

Extra-virgin olive oil

Sea salt and pepper to taste

¼ cup (25 g) shaved Parmesan cheese, optional

Take the meat and slice it very thinly directly onto the plate. In order to do that you might have to partially freeze it so it can be easily sliced. Use a meat slicer or a very sharp knife.

Cover the meat with the arugula and drizzle with olive oil, finishing off with salt and pepper to taste. Add the Parmesan, if desired. Enjoy!

CHEF'S TIP:

Please use only fresh organic meat for this recipe as the meat is consumed raw.

THE BEST CARNITAS EVER

These carnitas are flavorful and fork tender, with the perfect amount of crispiness. —AV

SERVES 6

2 tsp (6 g) ground cumin

1 tsp (3 g) dried oregano

1 tsp (3 g) paprika

1 tsp (3 g) salt

1 tsp (3 g) pepper

2½ pounds (1.1 kg) pork shoulder, cut into 2-inch (5-cm) cubes

4 cloves of garlic, minced

½ cup (120 ml) fresh orange juice

¼ cup (60 ml) fresh lime juice

4 cups (940 ml) chicken broth

Cilantro, cabbage and avocado for garnish

Combine cumin, oregano, paprika, salt and pepper. Place the pork in a Dutch oven and toss with spices until well coated. Add garlic, orange juice and lime juice. Add enough chicken broth to cover the pork. It was about 4 cups (940 ml) for me. Bring pot to right before boiling, then reduce to a simmer. Simmer uncovered until all of the liquid is gone. It takes between 1½ hours to 2 hours. If the liquid isn't evaporating quickly enough, increase the heat to medium. Once the liquid has evaporated, you will be left with the rendered pork fat. Cook pork until it is browned and crispy on the edges, about 8 to 10 minutes. Serve with toppings of your choice. Enjoy!

CARNE ASADA

There are dozens of variations of carne asada and each family has their own beloved recipe. Some would add either a light or dark beer to tenderize the meat while it marinates overnight. Swapping the beer for hard cider does the same job and adds an amazing flavor! Fire up the grill and give this one a try at your next backyard barbecue party. —JC

SERVES 8

FOR THE MARINADE

¼ cup (60 ml) hard cider

½ cup (120 ml) lemon juice

1 small red onion, thinly sliced

1 bell pepper, thinly sliced

2 tsp (6 g) garlic powder

2 pounds (908 g) flank steak, ½-inch (1.3-cm) thick

2 tsp (10 ml) coconut oil

Sea salt

Black pepper

Combine all the marinade ingredients in a gallon-sized zip top plastic bag. Place the flank steak in the bag. Press out excess air and seal. Lightly massage the bag to make sure the marinade coats every inch of the flank steak. Place it in the fridge to marinate overnight.

Preheat grill on high for 8 minutes, then reduce heat to medium. Lightly brush grates with coconut oil.

Remove flank steak from the marinade and generously season both sides with sea salt and black pepper. Grill flank steak for 5 minutes. Flip and grill the other side for 4 minutes for medium. Remove from grill and cover with foil to let it rest. Slice thinly and serve.

PAN-SEARED STEAK

Steak cooked on a cast iron pan comes out perfectly medium rare and juicy in under 10 minutes! A dry rub of simple everyday spices gives this steak great flavor without a lot of fuss. Top it off with the garlic rosemary butter sauce mixed with the pan drippings and you won't even need that fructose laden steak sauce! —JC

SERVES 2

2 (10-ounce [280-g]) rib eye steaks, about 1-inch (2.5-cm) thick

1 tsp (3 g) sea salt

1 tsp (3 g) black pepper

½ tsp paprika

¼ tsp onion powder

¼ tsp garlic powder

1 tsp (5 g) ghee or tallow

Cloves from 1 head of garlic, peeled

2 sprigs fresh rosemary

2 tbsp (30 g) butter

Bring the steaks to room temperature at least 30 minutes before cooking so they will cook evenly.

Make the dry rub by combining sea salt, black pepper, paprika, onion powder and garlic powder in a small bowl. Set aside.

Heat a cast iron pan over high heat. Rub the steaks with ghee and sprinkle dry rub on both sides. Gently press it in so the rub sticks to the steaks.

Once the pan starts smoking, add the steaks and cook for 3 minutes on the first side. Flip it and cook the other side for 3 more minutes for medium rare. Place cooked steaks on a plate and cover with foil to let them rest for a few minutes.

Prepare the sauce using the same cast iron pan. Reduce the heat to medium-low. Add the garlic cloves, rosemary and butter to the pan drippings. Cook until rosemary is fragrant and garlic is soft, about 5 minutes. Spoon the sauce on top of the cooked steaks and serve immediately.

CILANTRO LIME STEAK STRIPS

Cooking a steak properly can be tricky. I use this simple cheat method to prepare perfectly cooked steak every time. —KH

SERVES 2

1 pound (454 g) steak, cut into strips

1 tbsp (15 g) ghee (for cooking)

FOR THE MARINADE

¼ cup (60 ml) fresh lime juice

1 cup (60 g) loosely packed fresh cilantro

1 tbsp (15 ml) ghee, melted

2 cloves of fresh garlic

½ tsp sea salt

1 tsp (3 g) ground cumin

¼ tsp smoked paprika or chili powder

1 tbsp (15 ml) raw honey

2 tbsp (30 ml) water

Pinch of cayenne, optional

Place steak strips into a shallow bowl or pan. Process all marinade ingredients in a blender or small food processor until well blended like salad dressing. Pour marinade over steak strips and toss to evenly coat. Cover and allow to marinate for at least an hour in the fridge.

Melt the ghee over medium-high heat. Add steak strips and stir to coat. Cook about 2 minutes on each side for strips that are browned on the outside but still pink on the inside. Allow space between the strips as they will not cook properly if overcrowded. You may have to use two pans or do two batches. Cook times will vary depending on your type of steak and thickness of strips.

SIMPLE BEEF STIR-FRY

This Asian-inspired stir-fry combines quick-cooked colorful vegetables with a savory sprinkle of ground beef. —RB

SERVES 2

FOR THE MEAT

2 tsp (10 ml) coconut aminos

1 tsp (5 ml) fish sauce

2 tbsp (30 g) tomato paste

1 cup (225 g) ground beef

FOR THE VEGETABLES

2 tsp (10 ml) sesame oil

½ red cabbage

½ onion

½ red bell pepper

½ yellow bell pepper

1 head broccoli

2 large handfuls snow peas

Salt to taste

FOR THE GARNISH

Red pepper flakes

Sesame seeds

To make the meat, combine the coconut aminos, fish sauce and tomato paste in a small skillet over medium heat. Add the ground beef, mix thoroughly and cook for 10 minutes, breaking up large chunks as it browns, then remove from heat.

Make the vegetables by adding the sesame oil to a large skillet over medium heat. Thinly slice the red cabbage, onion and bell pepper, then sauté in the large skillet. Separate the head of broccoli into small florets and add to the skillet. Add the snow peas, and stir the vegetable mixture.

Cook the vegetables until softened to your liking, and then sprinkle the cooked ground beef over them and stir thoroughly. Add salt to taste. Serve warm, topped with red pepper flakes and sesame seeds.

BEEF AND EGGPLANT

Roasting eggplant over an open flame gives its skin a nice char and softens the inside while adding the right amount of smokiness. It can be made with just eggs but seasoned ground beef makes this more filling and satisfying. —JC

SERVES 2

4 Chinese eggplants

5 tbsp (75 ml) tallow or coconut oil

2 cloves of garlic, minced

½ pound (227 g) ground beef

¼ cup (30 g) carrot, chopped

¼ cup (30 g) potato, chopped

Sea salt

Black pepper

Fish sauce

¼ cup (25 g) green onions, chopped

2 large eggs

Ketchup

Work in batches and cook two eggplants at a time. The eggplant will be cooked directly on the stove to mimic an outdoor grill so keeping an eye on it is important. Arrange eggplant on a gas or electric stove over medium-high heat. Cook for 6 minutes until the purple skin turns black. Rotate each eggplant every 2 minutes so that all sides are evenly charred. Once cooked, the eggplant will be soft. Carefully remove it from heat and set aside on a paper towel-lined plate to cool. Once the eggplant is cool enough to handle, gently peel off the charred skin. Set one eggplant on a plate and flatten using the back of a fork until it is about ½-inch (1.3-cm) thick. Repeat for the remaining eggplant.

Add 1 teaspoon (5 ml) of tallow to a cast iron pan over medium-high heat. Add garlic and ground beef and sauté for 2 minutes. Reduce heat to medium and add carrot and potato. Season with sea salt, black pepper and fish sauce to taste. Sauté for 5 minutes until the vegetables are slightly softened. Mix in green onions. Remove from pan and set aside in a bowl. Add the remaining tallow to the pan.

Crack and whisk the eggs in a large bowl. Dip an eggplant in the egg until fully coated. Place the eggplant on the pan and spread ¼ cup (60 g) of the cooked beef mixture on top. Drizzle with 1 tablespoon (15 ml) of the egg mixture. Cover and cook for 3 minutes. Flip to the other side and cook for another 3 minutes until eggs are set and golden brown. Repeat for the remaining eggplant. Serve hot and enjoy with a generous serving of ketchup.

CHEF'S TIP:

Chinese eggplant is a thinner variety compared to the ones commonly found at grocery stores. They are similar in size to zucchini and can be found at most Asian markets.

VEGETABLE & BEEF STUFFED ACORN SQUASH

This stuffed squash recipe is a great way to add a variety of veggies to your diet. This is a perfect squash to stuff with meat too, as it isn't as sweet as many of its counterparts. —AV

SERVES 6

3 acorn squash

2 pounds (908 g) ground beef

2 tbsp (30 g) tomato paste

1 tsp (3 g) salt

1 tsp (3 g) black pepper

1 tbsp (8 g) ground cumin

2 tsp (6 g) oregano

1 tbsp (15 g) ghee

1 onion, diced

1 carrot, diced

1 rib celery, diced

½ red bell pepper, diced

4 cloves of garlic, crushed

1 zucchini, diced

(continued)

Preheat oven to 375°F (190°C, or gas mark 5). Place the whole squash in an oven-safe casserole dish. It can be cut in half first, but that is really difficult, so cooking it first makes it a bit easier to cut through. Add 1 cup (235 ml) of water to the dish and cook it for 30 minutes. Let it cool, then cut it in half lengthwise (from stem to end) and remove the seeds.

While the squash is baking and cooling, make the filling. Mix the ground beef with the tomato paste, salt, pepper, cumin and oregano. Set aside. Heat ghee in a heavy bottomed pan over medium. Add the onions and sauté until translucent, about 5 minutes. Then add the rest of the veggies to the pan and sauté for an additional 5 minutes or so. Then add the meat and sauté until browned and mixed with the veggies an additional 5 minutes. Fill the cavities of the squash with the meat mixture. Place the stuffed acorn squash back into the oven. Bake for another 30 minutes or until tender.

PERSIAN-SPICED BEEF AND ROASTED BUTTERNUT SQUASH

This dish uses a wonderful blend of spices, including cinnamon, nutmeg and rose petals that is reminiscent of the Persian cuisine I grew up eating. —NK

SERVES 4

2 pounds (908 g) butternut squash, peeled, seeded and cut into even-sized chunks

Sea salt and black pepper to taste

2 tbsp (30 ml) melted ghee, divided

1 medium red onion, sliced into half moons

1 pound (454 g) ground beef

2 tsp (6 g) Persian spice blend

¼ cup (38 g) organic raisins

¼ cup (38 g) crushed raw, unsalted pistachios

Handful fresh parsley, finely chopped

Preheat oven to 425°F (220°C, or gas mark 7). Place diced butternut squash into a large mixing bowl and season with sea salt and pepper. Add 1 tablespoon (15 ml) ghee and toss to coat. Place into a large baking tray lined with parchment paper and bake for 45 to 50 minutes or until the squash is roasted and tender.

While the squash is baking, heat a skillet over medium heat, add in 1 tablespoon (15 ml) of ghee. Add in the red onion and fry for about 10 to 15 minutes or until softened. Add in the beef and break up the meat as it cooks, around 8 to 10 minutes, or until no pink remains in the middle. When the beef is nearly browned season with sea salt, black pepper and the Persian spice blend. Mix to combine. Add in the raisins and stir to mix. Let cook for about 5 minutes then add in the pistachios and stir. When the meat is done cooking stir in the freshly chopped parsley. Add the butternut squash into the beef mixture and stir to combine.

CHEF'S TIP:
You can purchase the Persian spice blend called advieh online or at Persian grocery stores.

BEEF WITH PLANTAINS AND CURRANTS

Ever had beef with bananas before? Sounds unusual but you'll like this one! It takes on a bit of sweetness from the plantains and currants which in turn are complemented well by the savory seasoned beef. It contains a good balance of protein, carbs and fat that will keep you going for the rest of the day. —JC

SERVES 4

¼ cup (60 g) tallow or coconut oil

2 yellow plantains, sliced

1 beefsteak tomato, chopped

1 medium onion, chopped

3 cloves of garlic, minced

1 pound (454 g) ground beef

¼ cup (38 g) dried currants

¼ cup (32 g) green peas

Sea salt

Black pepper

¼ cup (25 g) green onions, chopped

Add tallow to a wok over medium-high heat. Add plantains and fry for 4 to 5 minutes until golden brown. Remove and set aside.

Drain excess oil from the wok, leaving about 1 tablespoon (15 ml) for sautéing. Add tomato, onion and garlic. Sauté for 3 minutes until tomatoes start to soften. Add beef and sauté until browned, about 5 minutes. Drain excess fat.

Return fried plantains to the wok and add currants and green peas. Season with sea salt and black pepper to taste. Sauté and let everything cook together for 1 to 2 minutes. Top with green onions before serving.

TANGY BEEF STEAK

Marinating beef in a garlicky sauce infuses it with so many flavors in just an hour. Sirloin is a tender cut of beef that can be cooked in a short amount of time without ending up being tough and hard to chew. If you can tolerate it, this is best served with white rice but substituting it with cauliflower rice is just as satisfying. —JC

SERVES 4

1 pound (454 g) sirloin, sliced into strips

8 cloves of garlic, minced

¼ cup (60 ml) + 2 tbsp (30 ml) coconut aminos

Juice of 2 lemons

½ tsp black pepper

2 tbsp (30 ml) tallow or coconut oil

1 large red onion, sliced

¼ tsp fish sauce

In a large bowl, add the sirloin strips, garlic, ¼ cup (60 ml) of coconut aminos, lemon juice and black pepper. Mix to combine. Cover and marinate in the fridge for 1 hour.

Add tallow to a wok over medium-high heat. Remove sirloin from the marinade and set aside the excess marinade for later. Add the sirloin to the wok. Pan-fry for 5 to 6 minutes until browned. Remove sirloin and set aside.

Add the red onion to the wok and sauté for 3 to 5 minutes until softened. Add the excess marinade, the remaining 2 tablespoons (30 ml) of coconut aminos, fish sauce and the cooked sirloin. Sauté and let it simmer for 2 to 3 minutes. Remove from heat and serve.

OSSOBUCO DELLA ROSY

My mom's famous Ossobuco is a delicious way to cook the meat on the bone. It also contains the marrow, full of tasty nutrients. Try it with just the lightest sprinkle of sea salt and enjoy! —VM

SERVES 2

Handful of dried porcini mushrooms

4 cups (940 ml) beef bone broth

Lard, tallow or ghee

2 beef shanks, about 2-inch (5-cm) thick

½ cup (80 g) onion, chopped

1 cup (130 g) carrots, chopped

1 cup (120 g) celery, chopped

¼ cup (60 ml) red wine

1 bay leaf

Sea salt and pepper to taste

Soak the porcini mushrooms in a bowl with 2 cups (470 ml) of hot broth until soft, about an hour.

Melt the fat over high heat in a large skillet and sear the shanks on both sides until nice and brown, about 3 minutes on each side. While you are browning the shanks, sweat the onion, carrots and celery with 2 tablespoons (30 g) of fat on low heat in a cast iron or heavy pot. When the vegetables are nice and soft, about 4 to 5 minutes, add the shanks, and raise the heat to high while adding the red wine.

Reduce the red wine for about 3 to 4 minutes and add the soaked porcini mushrooms, broth, bay leaf and salt and pepper to season. You will now want to lower the heat and cook for 2 hours, or until the meat is nice and tender.

Serve immediately with plenty of broth and vegetables.

BEEF HEART STEAK

Heart is not one of the most common cuts of beef! If you haven't tried beef heart at all, I highly recommend to at least try it once, because of the amazing nutritional properties. This is a great, easy recipe to start with. The flavor might surprise you too! —VM

SERVES 4

4 slices of beef heart, 1-inch (2.5-cm) thick

3 tbsp (45 ml) apple cider vinegar

Sea salt and black pepper to taste

1 tbsp (15 g) ghee

2 tbsp (30 ml) rosemary infused olive oil (or plain olive oil)

Marinate the beef heart overnight with the apple cider vinegar. When the beef heart is done marinating, prepare the meat by seasoning with salt and pepper.

In a cast iron skillet, melt the ghee over high heat and then add the beef hearts. Cook the beef hearts for about 5 minutes on each side until they have nicely browned.

Make sure you don't overcook the steaks as you will want the center of the meat to remain a light pink. When the steaks are done cooking, drizzle them with the rosemary infused olive oil and serve with a favorite salad.

CHEF'S TIP:
You can easily make the rosemary infused oil. Strip the leaves from a sprig of fresh rosemary and place them in a small jar with about 1 cup (235 ml) of olive oil. Make sure the oil covers the rosemary completely. Infuse for a week before using.

SKIRT STEAK WITH RADISH & CUCUMBER SALSA

This Skirt Steak with Radish & Cucumber Salsa is one of our favorite summer combos. The radish and cucumber salsa is so refreshing and a great alternative for those who are allergic to tomatoes. —AV

SERVES 4

FOR THE MARINADE

¼ cup (60 ml) olive oil

¼ cup (60 ml) lime juice

1 tsp (3 g) ground cumin

½ tsp chili powder

3 cloves garlic, minced

Salt and pepper

2 pounds (908 g) skirt steak

FOR THE RADISH & CUCUMBER SALSA

1 cup (120 g) radishes, chopped

1 cup (120 g) cucumber, chopped

¼ cup (16 g) fresh cilantro, chopped

2 cloves of garlic, minced

1 small jalapeño pepper, diced, optional

2 tbsp (30 ml) fresh lime juice

1 tbsp (15 ml) olive oil

Salt and pepper to taste

In a small bowl, mix olive oil, lime juice, cumin, chili powder and garlic. Generously add some salt and pepper. Place skirt steak in a glass bowl with a lid—I don't like to use plastic with acidic ingredients—and pour in marinade. Allow steak to marinate from 1 hour to overnight.

For the salsa, toss together radishes, cucumber, cilantro, garlic and jalapeño. Add lime juice and olive oil. Adjust salt and pepper to taste. Turn the grill to medium-hot and cook the steak about 3 to 4 minutes per aside. Let rest for 5 minutes. Cut steak across the grain, top with radish salsa and serve.

CHEF'S TIP:
If using Persian cucumber, I don't peel because the skin is soft, but peel if using a thicker skinned cucumber.

LAMB GALETTE WITH BURST TOMATOES AND FIGS

This rich, heavily spiced savory galette is a riff on a traditional Mediterranean tagine flavor combination. The burst tomatoes add a bright pop of flavor that's a perfect pairing with the meat and spices. —RB

SERVES 6

FOR THE FILLING

½ pound (226 g) cherry tomatoes

2 tsp (10 ml) coconut oil, divided

½ tsp salt, divided

½ pound (226 g) ground lamb

1 onion

½ cup (80 g) figs, packed

2 tsp (10 g) ground coriander

2 tsp (10 g) ground cumin

1 tsp (5 g) ground ginger

1 tsp (5 g) cinnamon

FOR THE CRUST

1 cup (96 g) almond flour

½ cup (48 g) arrowroot flour

2 tbsp (30 g) coconut flour

¼ tsp salt

2 tbsp (30 ml) coconut milk

1 tbsp (15 g) coconut oil, melted

1 egg, whisked

FOR THE GARNISH

Parsley

Oregano

Red chili flakes

(continued)

Preheat the oven to 350°F (180°C, or gas mark 4). Toss the cherry tomatoes in 1 teaspoon (5 ml) of coconut oil and ¼ teaspoon of salt. Roast in the preheated oven for 20 minutes, stirring halfway through, until soft and bursting.

While the tomatoes cook, melt 1 teaspoon (5 ml) of coconut oil in a large skillet. Cook the lamb over medium-high heat for 5–10 minutes, stirring occasionally and breaking up any large chunks, until browned. Use a slotted spoon to transfer the lamb to a plate.

Roughly chop the onion and figs, then whirl in a food processor until shredded (or dice manually).

Transfer the onion and figs to the skillet and reduce the heat to medium low. Stir in the coriander, cumin, ginger, cinnamon and ¼ teaspoon of salt. Cook until completely soft, then crumble the lamb back into the mixture and remove from the heat.

In a medium-size mixing bowl, combine the almond flour, arrowroot flour, coconut flour and salt. Add the coconut milk, coconut oil and egg to the dry ingredients, mix thoroughly and shape into a ball.

Roll the dough out to approximately ¼-inch (6.3-mm) thick on a sheet of wax paper with a sheet of wax paper laid over to prevent sticking.

Layer the onion and fig mixture with the burst tomatoes in the center of the dough. Using the edges of the wax paper, fold the edges of the crust up and over the perimeter of the filling. Grip the edges of the wax paper and transfer the galette to a baking sheet.

Bake in the preheated oven for 20 minutes, rotating the sheet halfway through, or until the edges of the crust are browned but not burnt. Top with a sprinkling of parsley, oregano and red chili flakes.

CABBAGE WITH LAMB, SUMAC & PINE NUTS

Sumac and allspice give this lamb and cabbage dish an exotic, Middle Eastern flavor. —RB

SERVES 2

½ large purple cabbage

½ onion

1 tbsp (15 ml) coconut oil

1 tsp (3 g) ground sumac

1 tsp (3 g) salt

1 tsp (3 g) ground allspice

1 pound (454 g) ground lamb

¼ cup (38 g) pine nuts

FOR THE GARNISH

Purple cabbage

Pine nuts

Flat-leaf parsley

Roughly chop the cabbage and onion. Transfer to a food processor and shred.

Melt the coconut oil over medium heat in a large skillet. Cook the shredded cabbage and onion in the skillet until beginning to soften, approximately 10 minutes. Add the sumac, salt and allspice to the vegetables and stir in the raw ground lamb.

Cook, breaking up the chunks with a spoon and stirring thoroughly, until the lamb is browned, approximately 10 minutes. Stir in the pine nuts, then serve warm on a bed of whole purple cabbage leaves with extra pine nuts and parsley as garnish.

BROILED LAMB AND BUTTERED FENNEL

Lamb and fennel are beautiful ingredients to start with. Pair them together and they make a wonderful dish. —VM

SERVES 1

¼ pound (112 g) lamb stew meat, cut in 1-inch (2.5-cm) cubes

Sea salt and black pepper to taste

1 ounce (28 g) onion, cut in rounds, about ¼-inch (6-mm) thick

3 tbsp (45 g) butter

3.5 ounces (98 g) fennel bulb, sliced into ¼-inch (6-mm)-thick slices

¼ cup (60 ml) water

Start by seasoning the lamb with salt and pepper, placing the meat and onion on a baking sheet. Place the meat in the broiler on high for 5 to 6 minutes, or until the lamb cubes have browned on the outside.

Melt the butter in a skillet over medium heat, sautéing the sliced fennel for a few minutes. Add a pinch of salt with the water to the skillet and cover for 10 minutes. Serve the fennel with the lamb and enjoy!

SPICED LAMB DENVER RIBLETS

This is an easy and delicious recipe that you can whip up at the last minute when you have some unexpected guests pop by. It's a very rich and satisfying dish which pairs well with a light green salad. —VM

SERVES 4

DRY RUB

6 tsp (16 g) ground cumin

½ tsp cayenne pepper

1 tsp (6 g) sea salt

2 pounds (908 g) lamb riblets

Combine all of the dry rub ingredients in a bowl and mix well. Generously rub the lamb riblets on all sides. Cover with a towel and let them sit at room temperature for about an hour.

Preheat the oven to 350°F (180°C, or gas mark 4). Place the riblets on a rack and roast for about an hour or until they have nicely browned.

Remove the riblets from the oven and let them cool for about 5 minutes before slicing them. Serve with a nice salad and side dish.

PERSIAN SPICED LAMB

Lamb cutlets are one of my favorite cuts of meat. Sprinkle them with some Persian spice and grill them in a hot pan to make a simple and tasty protein to add to your plate. —NK

SERVES 3

6 lamb cutlets, trimmed

Sea salt and black pepper, to taste

2 tbsp (16 g) Persian spice mix (advieh)

2 tbsp (30 ml) ghee, melted

Salad, for serving, optional

Heat a medium square grill pan over medium-high heat. While the pan is heating up place lamb cutlets onto a clean surface and season both sides with sea salt and black pepper. Sprinkle the Persian spice mix over the lamb and use your hands to rub the mixture into the lamb. Brush both sides of each cutlet with the melted ghee. Cook in batches for 3 to 5 minutes per side on the hot grill pan. Serve warm alongside some salad of your choice.

CHEF'S TIP:

You can find Persian spice mix, called advieh, online or at Persian grocery stores.

LAMB CHOP HERBES DE PROVENCE

This is my grandmother's favorite way to cook lamb chops. It's a simple yet tasty recipe using a dried herb mixture typical of the south of France called Herbes de Provence. The herb blend includes rosemary, thyme, lavender and marjoram. I use it in many grilled meat dishes as well as in my Bacon & Beet Breakfast Root Hash (page 432). —RM

SERVES 4–5

2½ pounds (1.1 kg) lamb chops (about 1½ inches [3.8 cm] thick)

1 sprig rosemary

1 clove garlic, smashed

1 tbsp (15 ml) olive oil, plus more for cooking

1 tbsp (4 g) Herbes de Provence

Sea salt and pepper, to taste

Place the lamb chops, rosemary and garlic in a large freezer bag. Add the olive oil and Herbes de Provence until fully coating the lamb chops. Marinate in the fridge for at least 5 hours. Take the bag out 30 minutes prior to cooking so it can warm to room temperature.

Heat a large skillet over medium-high heat. Salt and pepper both sides of the lamb chops. Drizzle the skillet with olive oil and cook both sides of the lamb chops for about 3 minutes, until a nice brown crust forms. Serve immediately.

PAN-GRILLED LAMB CHOPS WITH SUNCHOKE PURÉE

Sunchokes are a very underrated root. They make a delightful purée with a great nutty flavor. Here, pairing the creamy sunchoke purée with the savory lamb chops makes for a great dish. —VM

SERVES 2

1½ pounds (680 g) sunchokes, washed, peeled and cut into 2-inch (5-cm) pieces

3 tbsp (45 g) butter

1 tbsp (18 g) sea salt, plus extra for seasoning

4 lamb chops

2 tbsp (30 ml) olive oil

Black pepper

2 tbsp (8 g) fresh rosemary, finely chopped

¼ tsp red pepper flakes

Add the sunchokes, butter and salt to a saucepan over low heat and submerge them with enough water to cover everything. Cook the sunchokes until they are tender to the touch of a fork, about 30 minutes, adding water if necessary.

Drain the sunchokes and then add them to the food processor and purée. Set the sunchoke purée aside and keep warm.

Remove the lamb chops from the fridge about 1 hour before cooking so they come to room temperature. This ensures even cooking. Once they have warmed up, drizzle them with olive oil and season with salt, pepper, rosemary and red pepper flakes.

Warm a cast iron skillet over medium heat and cook the lamb chops, turning once, until they reach 130°F (54°C). This can take 5 to 7 minutes, depending on the thickness. When the lamb is finished, serve with the sunchoke purée.

SMOTHERED PORK CHOPS

Pork chops and apples usually go hand in hand like peanut butter and jelly. In this dish, a thick and luscious sauce made with caramelized onions and homemade Slow Cooker Apple Butter (page 168) creates a comforting gravy that will make your pork chops good to the last bite. —JC

SERVES 2

2 bone-in pork chops, 1-inch (2.5-cm) thick

Sea salt

Black pepper

¼ cup (58 g) tallow or ghee

2 tbsp (30 g) butter

1 small onion, thinly sliced

1 tbsp (15 g) whole grain mustard

1 cup (235 ml) vegetable broth

1 tbsp (15 ml) apple cider vinegar

½ cup (120 g) Slow Cooker Apple Butter (page 168)

Bring the pork chops to room temperature at least 30 minutes before cooking so they won't be cold in the middle and overcooked on the outside. Generously season the pork chops with sea salt and black pepper on both sides.

Add tallow to a cast iron pan on high heat. Add the pork chops and reduce heat to medium. Fry the first side for 6 to 8 minutes. Flip to the other side and cook for another 6 minutes or until the internal temperature is about 145°F (63°C). Remove from pan and set aside.

Drain excess oil from the pan and reduce heat to medium-low. Add butter and onion. Fry until onion is browned and caramelized, about 25 to 30 minutes. Add mustard, vegetable broth, apple cider vinegar and apple butter. Simmer for 10 minutes. Adjust sea salt and black pepper if necessary. Stir and pour it on top of the pork chops. Serve immediately.

CIDER-BRAISED PORK CHOPS

Using hard cider as a braising liquid does a good job of tenderizing pork chops as they cook in the oven. Choose green apples over any other red variety since they are both slightly tart and sweet at the same time. They also caramelize nicely when fried in ghee. —JC

SERVES 4

4 (8-ounce [227-g]) bone-in pork chops

Sea salt

Black pepper

Onion powder

1 tbsp (15 g) ghee or coconut oil

2 green apples, quartered

4 large shallots, peeled

12 ounces (355 ml) hard cider

Bring pork chops to room temperature about 30 minutes before cooking. Generously season both sides with sea salt, black pepper and onion powder.

Preheat oven to 375°F (190°C, or gas mark 5).

Add ghee to a Dutch oven over medium-high heat. Add pork chops and sear for 3 minutes. Flip to the other side and sear for another 3 minutes. Remove and set aside. Add apples and shallots to the pan and fry for 5 minutes. Remove and set aside.

Add hard cider and deglaze the bottom of the pan. Reduce heat. Adjust sea salt and black pepper to taste. Once it starts to simmer, return pork chops to the pan. Cover and place it in the oven for 30 minutes. Evenly distribute apples and shallots among the pork chops. Cover and return the pan to the oven for an additional 15 minutes. Let it cool for 5 to 8 minutes before serving.

SKILLET PORK CHOP SAUTÉ WITH PEACHES

Savory pork chops paired with sweet peaches and aromatic thyme. —AV

SERVES 4

1 tbsp (15 g) ghee

4 (4-ounce [112-g]) center-cut boneless pork loin chops, trimmed

½ tsp salt

½ tsp freshly ground black pepper

¼ cup (40 g) sliced shallots

2 tsp (2 g) chopped fresh thyme

2 peaches, each cut into 8 wedges

2 tbsp (30 ml) balsamic vinegar

1 tbsp (15 g) butter

Heat a large skillet over medium-high heat. Add the ghee to the pan and swirl to coat.

Sprinkle the chops evenly with salt and pepper. Add the chops to the pan; cook for 3 minutes on each side or until done.

Remove chops from pan, and keep warm. Add shallots, thyme and peaches to pan; cook for 5 minutes until peaches and onions are soft. Stir in vinegar, scraping pan to loosen browned bits. Remove from heat and stir in the butter. Spoon the sauce over the chops and serve.

OVEN-ROASTED PORK CHOPS WITH GREEN BEANS AND SPINACH PESTO

Using spinach to make pesto has a lighter flavor compared to basil but it definitely goes well with the green beans. Don't forget to slather a good amount of pesto onto each bite of pork chop. —JC

SERVES 4

4 center cut boneless pork chops, ½-inch (1.3-cm) thick

1 tbsp (15 ml) ghee or coconut oil, melted

Sea salt

Black pepper

1 pound (454 g) green beans, trimmed

FOR THE SPINACH PESTO

1 bunch spinach

¼ cup (38 g) raw almonds, sliced

¼ cup (60 ml) extra-virgin olive oil

1 clove of garlic

¼ tsp red pepper flakes

¼ tsp sea salt

¼ tsp black pepper

Preheat the oven to 375°F (190°C, or gas mark 5). Line a baking sheet with foil or parchment paper.

Coat the pork chops with ghee. Season both sides generously with sea salt and black pepper. Place them a few inches apart on the baking sheet. Bake for 30 to 35 minutes on the first side. Flip the pork chops and bake for another 10 minutes on the second side. Remove from the oven and set aside.

Prepare the pesto by combining the spinach, almonds, olive oil, garlic, red pepper flakes, sea salt and black pepper in a food processor. Pulse until smooth.

Place a steamer basket in a large pot. Add the water and bring to a boil. Arrange the green beans evenly on the steamer basket. Cover the pot and reduce heat until the water is just simmering. Let it cook for 5 to 8 minutes until the green beans have softened but still have a nice crunch to them. Turn off heat and immediately transfer to a colander to cool for 5 minutes.

Toss the steamed green beans with half of the pesto sauce. Serve with the baked pork chops and the remaining pesto sauce on the side.

PORK CHOPS WITH CRANBERRY SAUCE

This recipe is a simple way to make pork chops by searing, then baking. The cranberry sauce adds a wonderful sourness to the rich and savory pork chops. —HH

SERVES 2

2 pork chops

½ tsp salt

½ tsp pepper

½ tsp garlic powder

½ tsp thyme

½ tsp oregano

½ tsp rosemary

2 tbsp (30 g) ghee, lard or avocado oil

Cranberry Sauce (page 520)

Preheat the oven to 350°F (180°C, or gas mark 4). Rub both sides of the pork chops with salt, pepper, garlic powder, thyme, oregano and rosemary. Heat the ghee or oil in an oven-safe skillet (cast iron or enamel) over medium-high heat. Once the oil is hot, place the pork chops in the pan and sear for 4 to 5 minutes on each side to brown the chops.

Place the oven-safe pan with the pork chops in the oven and cook for about 15 to 20 minutes or until a meat thermometer inserted reads 140°F (60°C). Drizzle with Cranberry Sauce.

PORK–STUFFED ACORN SQUASH

Stuffed acorn squash is one of my fall favorites. The oregano, thyme, rosemary and sage in the pork stuffing bring a warm, satisfying flavor to this dish. —HH

SERVES 4

2 acorn squash

1 medium onion

6 cloves garlic

1 tbsp (15 g) ghee, lard or oil

½ tsp each of oregano, thyme, rosemary, turmeric, salt, pepper

1 pound (454 g) ground pork

¼ tsp sage

¼ tsp ground cumin

Preheat the oven to 375°F (190°C, or gas mark 5). Cut the acorn squashes in half widthwise. Chop off the stem and remove the inner seeds and membrane. Place the acorn squash on a baking sheet or glass baking dish in the oven and cook for about 25 to 30 minutes until fork tender. Remove from the oven and let cool.

Finely chop the onion and garlic. Heat the ghee in a skillet on medium-high heat and cook the onions for about a minute. Then, add the garlic, oregano, thyme, rosemary and sage. Mix and cook until the onions are translucent, about 3 to 5 minutes. Add in the ground pork and use a spatula to break up the pork into small bits. Add the turmeric, cumin, salt and pepper to the pork and mix well. Sauté until the pork is fully cooked and browned, about 5 to 7 minutes. Turn off the heat and set aside. If necessary, scoop out part of the acorn squash meat to allow enough room for the pork stuffing. Evenly stuff the acorn squash halves until they are full. Reheat in the oven at 375°F (190°C, or gas mark 5) for about 10 to 15 minutes. Serve and enjoy.

STUFFED PORK TENDERLOIN

This stuffed tenderloin is packed with a sweet and savory filling that takes plain ol' pork to an entirely different dimension. Ground Italian sausage flavors the meat well as it roasts in the oven and the sweet potato and dried fruit adds the right amount of sweetness. Slicing into the tenderloin reveals the wonderful colors of the ingredients, making it a feast for the senses. —JC

SERVES 4

2 (1-pound [454-g]) pork tenderloins

1 tbsp (8 g) garlic powder

1 tbsp (8 g) onion powder

1 tsp (3 g) sea salt

1 tsp (3 g) black pepper

2 raw Italian sausages, casing removed

1 small sweet potato, chopped

1 small onion, chopped

2 tbsp (16 g) dried cranberries

2 tbsp (16 g) dried apricots, chopped

1 tbsp (15 ml) coconut oil

Preheat oven to 375°F (190°C, or gas mark 5). Line a baking sheet with parchment paper.

Butterfly each pork tenderloin by making a lengthwise incision, cutting from one end to the other. Stop at about ¾ inch (2 cm) from the edge so the sides will remain attached. Cover with parchment paper or plastic wrap and pound it flat with a meat mallet until it is about ½-inch (1.3-cm) thick. Season both sides of each pork tenderloin with garlic powder, onion powder, sea salt and black pepper.

Lay a piece of tenderloin flat on a cutting board. Spread half of the ground sausage evenly on top. Add half of the sweet potato, onion, cranberries and apricots. Carefully roll the tenderloin until the stuffing is wrapped up tightly. Secure the seams with toothpicks and tie it completely with kitchen string. Repeat the same process for the other pork tenderloin.

Rub the stuffed pork tenderloins with coconut oil. Place them on the baking sheet and bake in the oven for 35 to 40 minutes or until the thickest part reaches an internal temperature of 145°F (63°C). Let it rest for 10 to 15 minutes before slicing and serving.

SIZZLING PORK BELLY SISIG

Sisig is traditionally made out of pig's ears, face and snout, which gives it that crunchy texture and unique taste. Those ingredients are not always easily accessible unless you have an Asian market close by so using pork belly from a reputable source is a good alternative. A dish that is near and dear to almost every Filipino's heart, its tantalizing aroma will make your mouth water and crave that porky goodness! —JC

SERVES 4

5 cups (1175 ml) water

¼ cup (60 ml) apple cider vinegar

1 pound (454 g) boneless pork belly with skin, about ¼-inch (6-mm) thick

1 tbsp (15 g) sea salt

¼ cup (40 g) chicken liver, chopped

½ cup (80 g) red onion, chopped

1 jalapeño pepper, seeded and chopped

3 cloves of garlic, minced

3 tbsp (45 ml) coconut aminos

1 tsp (5 ml) fish sauce

1 tsp (3 g) onion powder

2 tsp (6 g) black pepper

3 tbsp (45 ml) coconut cream

Juice of 1 lime

1 large egg

In a large pot, add water, apple cider vinegar, pork belly and sea salt. Turn on heat and bring to a boil. Reduce heat to low and cook for an additional 5 to 8 minutes. Turn off heat. Drain water and let it cool for at least 20 minutes until cool enough to handle. Chop the pork belly into ½-inch (1.3-cm) pieces.

In a dry cast iron pan over medium heat, add chicken liver. Cook for 5 minutes until no longer pink. Mash it into smaller pieces using the back of a wooden spoon. Add pork belly and cover. Let it cook for 15 to 20 minutes stirring occasionally to prevent the bottom from burning. Take the pan off the heat before removing the lid to stir the pork belly. This will prevent unexpected splatters! Remove cover and add onion, jalapeño, garlic, coconut aminos, fish sauce, onion powder and black pepper. Sauté for 2 to 3 minutes.

Turn off heat and mix in the coconut cream and lime juice. Crack an egg on top and mix well before serving.

CHEF'S TIP:
Mayonnaise can be substituted for the coconut cream.

COCONUT GINGER CAULIFLOWER PORK

This simple one-skillet dish combines cauliflower and pork with ginger, coconut milk, scallions and black sesame seeds for an easy Asian-inspired dinner. —RB

SERVES 2

1 tbsp (15 ml) coconut oil

1 pound (454 g) ground pork

1 (2-inch [5-cm]) piece of ginger root, peeled

2 cloves of garlic

2 tsp (10 ml) fish sauce

½ tsp salt

1 small cauliflower

½ cup (120 ml) coconut milk

5 large scallions

Black sesame seeds

Melt the coconut oil in a large skillet over medium heat. Add the ground pork, and cook a few minutes until beginning to brown.

Grate the ginger and mince the garlic, add to the pork. Stir in the fish sauce and salt, then cook, stirring frequently, until the meat is no longer pink.

Roughly chop the cauliflower, coarsely shred in a food processor (or dice by hand) then add to the meat mixture. Stir in the coconut milk and cook, stirring occasionally, until cauliflower is softened, approximately 10 minutes.

Finely chop the scallions, add to the skillet and cook for 2 minutes, stirring. Transfer to a serving bowl, top with black sesame seeds and serve warm.

SWEET AND SAVORY GARLIC SAUSAGE

Garlicky, savory and slightly sweet, longanisa (sausage) can be found as a breakfast staple in most Filipino households. Every commercial brand contains fillers and preservatives, so making it at home is always your best bet. Enjoy with a big helping of cauliflower rice and fried eggs. —JC

SERVES 4

1 pound (454 g) ground pork

2 tbsp (16 g) garlic, minced

1 tbsp (15 ml) apple cider vinegar

2 tbsp (30 ml) coconut aminos

3 tbsp (36 g) coconut sugar

¾ tsp sea salt

1½ tsp (4.5 g) black pepper

¼ tsp paprika

2 tbsp (29 g) tallow or coconut oil

Ketchup for dipping

Cauliflower rice, for serving

4 fried eggs, for serving

In a medium bowl, add ground pork, garlic, apple cider vinegar, coconut aminos, coconut sugar, sea salt, black pepper and paprika. Mix well by hand. Cover and marinate overnight in the fridge.

Scoop 1 ounce (28 g) of sausage mixture and shape into a 2-inch (5-cm)-long log using your hands. Repeat until all the meat is formed into logs.

Add tallow to a cast iron pan over medium-high heat. Add sausages and fry for 8 to 10 minutes. Roll occasionally to evenly cook all sides. They are ready once they turn golden brown and are cooked through. Serve with ketchup on the side, some cauliflower rice and fried eggs.

ITALIAN SAUSAGE RAGU

A savory Italian sausage ragu sauce served over zucchini noodles or spaghetti squash or even eaten by the spoonful. A comforting blend of herbs and marinara makes this Paleo pasta dish come to life. —CP

SERVES 4

1½ pounds (680 g) assortment of sweet and spicy Italian sausage links, casings removed

1 medium red onion, thinly sliced

6 crimini mushrooms, thinly sliced

3 cloves garlic, crushed

1 tsp (3 g) sea salt

1 tsp (3 g) dried oregano

½ tsp dried Italian herbs

½ cup (120 g) tomato paste

2 cups (480 ml) marinara sauce

Zucchini noodles, for serving

Fresh basil, for serving

Parmesan cheese, for serving

Heat a large skillet to medium heat.

Brown and crumble sausage, cooking thoroughly, about 10 minutes. Using a slotted spoon, remove sausage from pan and set aside.

Heat the pan back to medium heat. Sauté onions, mushrooms, garlic and herbs in the leftover grease for 5 minutes, or until fragrant. Stir in the tomato paste and briefly sauté again. Add the sausage crumbles and marinara.

Simmer on low for 30 minutes, stirring occasionally.

Serve over a bed of zucchini noodles, spaghetti squash or sautéed spinach. Garnish with fresh basil and a pinch of Parmesan, if desired.

CHEF'S TIP:
I use a combination of sweet and spicy sausages, but if you prefer a milder dish, use all sweet Italian sausages.

VENISON RAGOUT

A ragout is any combination of meat, vegetables and spices slow cooked over a low heat. I wanted to take this dish to the next level using wild caught venison meat and sun-dried tomatoes. The result is just delicious, and I know you will think so too. —VM

SERVES 4

2 cups (260 g) whole, dried sun-dried tomatoes

2 tbsp (29 g) lard or ghee

1 sweet onion, chopped

2 carrots

1 pound (454 g) ground venison

½ cup (120 ml) red wine

Sea salt and black pepper, to taste

1 tsp (1.5 g) fresh thyme, finely chopped

1 tsp (1.5 g) fresh rosemary, finely chopped

1 tsp (1.5 g) fresh sage, finely chopped

Soak the sun-dried tomatoes in a bowl of hot water for 10 minutes and set aside.

Heat the Dutch oven over low heat and melt the lard/ghee. Add the onions to the pot to sweat. Add the carrots to the pot as well.

In a separate skillet, brown the meat over high heat until it is evenly cooked through, about 10 minutes. Add the meat and wine to the onion/carrot mixture and raise the heat to high. Cook for about a minute to evaporate the alcohol. Add the sun-dried tomatoes with their soaking liquid to the pot along with the salt, pepper and herbs.

Bring the heat to low and cook for an hour and a half.

BACON-WRAPPED HOTDOGS AND STIR-FRY VEGETABLES

Amidst the hustle and bustle of wholesale stores in downtown Los Angeles, there is an abundance of small carts or trucks that are built with a makeshift kitchen comprised of portable butane stoves with foil-lined trays. The aroma coming from these tiny carts will draw you to them and their bacon wrapped hotdogs with onions, peppers and jalapeños. This homemade version is definitely up to par and the best part is, there's no mystery meat lurking in the ingredients list! —JC

SERVES 4

2 tsp (10 g) tallow or bacon fat

2 green bell peppers, sliced

1 large onion, sliced

2 jalapeño peppers, sliced

8 strips of bacon

8 beef hotdogs

Preheat oven to 375°F (190°C, or gas mark 5) on convection setting. Line a baking sheet with parchment paper.

In a skillet or cast iron pan, melt tallow or bacon fat over medium-high heat. Add bell peppers, onion and jalapeños. Sauté until soft and slightly caramelized, about 5 to 8 minutes. Remove from heat and set aside.

Wrap a strip of bacon around each piece of hotdog and set it down on the baking sheet. Tuck the bacon end at the bottom of the hotdog to prevent it from unraveling and curling while baking. Bake for 25 to 30 minutes until golden brown. Keep a close eye on it during the last 5 minutes to make sure the bacon doesn't burn. Drain excess oil before serving with the sautéed vegetables.

CHEF'S TIP:

If your oven doesn't have a convection setting, preheat it to 425°F (220°C, or gas mark 7).

CAJUN PORK BURGERS

Andouille sausage and Cajun seasoning add a smoky kick to these pork burgers. —AV

SERVES 4

½ pound (227 g) Andouille sausage, uncooked, removed from casing

3 cloves of garlic, minced

½ a small white onion, cut into chunks

¼ cup (16 g) fresh cilantro

1 pound (454 g) ground pork

2 tsp (6 g) Cajun seasoning

½ tsp sea salt

½ tsp pepper

1 tbsp (15 g) ghee

Lettuce for serving

Cut sausage into large chunks and place in a food processor with the garlic, onions and cilantro. Blend it until the sausage is in crumbles. In a large bowl combine the sausage mixture, pork, Cajun seasoning and salt and pepper. Form the mixture into 4 large patties. Heat a cast iron skillet or heavy bottomed pan over medium-high heat and add the ghee. Cook the burgers for about 5 minutes per aside or until cooked to your liking. Serve in lettuce wraps with toppings of your choice.

CHIPOTLE BACON SLIDERS

All you have to say is BACON and I'm in. These slightly spicy burgers topped with bacon and caramelized onions are my kind of meal. Mini burgers are a nice alternative to regular burgers and make a fun and creative party food. —KH

MAKES 9

2 tbsp (30 g) butter, ghee or coconut oil

1 large yellow onion, sliced into thin rounds

1 avocado

Lime juice

Sea salt

A few dashes of your favorite hot sauce, optional

1 pound (454 g) ground meat

4 strips of precooked bacon

1 tsp (3 g) sea salt

½ tsp chipotle chili powder

½ tsp chili powder

1 tsp (3 g) ground cumin

1 tbsp (15 g) butter, ghee or coconut oil

Lettuce, for garnish

To make the caramelized onions, melt the ghee, butter or coconut oil on medium heat. Add onion rounds and sauté slowly until golden brown. Stir occasionally to make sure they cook evenly. You can add a tablespoon (15 ml) of water if they begin to stick to the pan. Usually takes 20 to 25 minutes.

Mash together avocado, lime and salt in a small bowl. Add optional hot sauce for some heat. Set aside. Combine ground meat, chopped bacon, salt and spices in a medium bowl. Mix to combine.

Form into 9 small patties. Heat 1 tablespoon (15 g) of fat of choice in skillet on medium to medium-high heat. Cook patties 4 to 5 minutes on each side, or until cooked the way you like them. Serve over a bed of fresh lettuce. Top with caramelized onions and avocado.

BUILD YOUR OWN BURGER

I use this recipe as the base of all of my creative Sunday Night Burgers. It's a juicy knock-off of the old Fuddruckers Burger, and then I add toppings like roasted jalapeños, grilled onions and even guacamole. —RM

SERVES 4

FOR THE SEASONING

1½ tsp (4 g) maple sugar

2 tsp (6 g) paprika

1½ tsp (4 g) black pepper

1¼ tsp (4 g) salt

¼ tsp garlic powder

¼ tsp onion powder

¼ tsp cayenne pepper

FOR THE BURGER

1 pound (454 g) ground beef

Lettuce wraps

FOR THE TOPPINGS

Bacon, optional

Sweet Onion Marmalade (page 501), optional

Super Easy Guacamole (page 190), optional

Roasted jalapeño peppers, optional

Mix the maple sugar and seasoning together in a bowl and then put into an empty spice shaker. Form beef into patties. Season both sides of the patties with mix from the shaker and then with your thumbs make a small indentation in the middle of the patty. This will help alleviate the common "bloating center" problem.

Heat your grill as hot at it can get, then place your patties on the hottest part of the grill. Cook until you see juices starting to get pushed through to the top of the patty. This is going to vary by grill but should be about 5 minutes. Flip, and cook on the other side for about 2 minutes less than the first side. Sandwich the burgers between two lettuce wraps and add nitrate-free bacon, Sweet Onion Marmalade, Super Easy Guacamole and roasted jalapeños.

CHEF'S TIP:
It's best to pack your beef patties loosely. Tightly packed patties make for dried out, non-juicy burgers.

TRIPLE PEPPER BURGERS

Grilled burgers with a kick of heat—spicy and sweet peppers take burger night to a new level! —CP

SERVES 4

FOR THE ROASTED SWEET POTATO "BUNS"

1 medium sweet potato

1 tbsp (15 ml) olive oil

½ tsp sea salt

¼ tsp fresh cracked black pepper

Avocado slices or guacamole

½ red bell pepper

1 jalapeño pepper

1 small red chili pepper

2 cloves garlic

1½ pounds (680 g) ground beef

½ tsp sea salt

Warm the grill to medium-high heat. Preheat oven to 400°F (200°C, or gas mark 6). Line a baking sheet with parchment paper.

Thinly slice sweet potatoes into ¼-inch (6-mm) rounds. Place on the baking sheet and lightly drizzle both sides with olive oil. Sprinkle with salt and pepper.

Roast sweet potatoes for 20 minutes, flip and continue roasting for an additional 15 to 20 minutes or until edges are slightly crispy.

While the sweet potatoes are roasting, finely chop all peppers and garlic. Mix peppers and garlic with ground beef and shape into hamburger patties. Sprinkle burgers with salt.

Grill burgers for 4 minutes, flip to the other side and continue cooking for an additional 4 minutes. Place one sweet potato slice on the plate and top with the burger. Layer with sliced avocado or a spoonful of guacamole and top with another slice of roasted sweet potato "bun."

SMOKY SAGE BISON BURGERS WITH BUTTER MUSHROOMS

Lettuce wrapped hamburgers are my go-to favorite comfort food, and I love creating different flavors using fresh herbs and spices. Bison is a leaner cut of meat made flavorful with the addition of smoked salt and fresh herbs. Serve with Root Vegetable Hash (page 213) for a satisfying dinner. —CP

SERVES 6

2 pounds (908 g) ground bison

2 tbsp (30 g) Dijon mustard

1 tbsp (15 ml) balsamic vinegar

1 tbsp (4 g) fresh sage, finely chopped

1 tsp (3 g) sea salt

½ tsp smoked salt flakes + a few pinches for garnishing

½ tsp fresh cracked black pepper

2 tbsp (30 g) butter

1 clove garlic, crushed

8 cremini mushrooms, sliced

2 cups (140 g) fresh baby arugula

Dijon mustard, optional, for garnish

Preheat your grill or barbecue to medium-high and warm a small skillet on low for sautéing the mushrooms.

In a bowl combine the bison, mustard, balsamic vinegar, sage, salt and pepper, working together with your hands to combine. Shape the burgers into 6 meat patties, about 1-inch (2.5-cm) thick.

Grill the burgers for 4 minutes, carefully flip and grill for an additional 4 minutes for medium.

While the burgers are cooking, melt butter in the skillet and sauté garlic and mushrooms for a few minutes or until soft.

Serve burgers on a bed of arugula, topped with sautéed mushrooms and a pinch of smoked salt. They taste great with a spoonful of Dijon mustard on the side as well.

CHEF'S TIP:

Bison is a leaner cut of meat so searing the burgers at high heat helps them keep their moisture; however, you do not want to overcook. These burgers are delicious topped with a slice of raw Gruyere cheese if you can tolerate dairy.

DOUBLE CILANTRO SLIDERS

These are tender and delicious green sliders packed with cilantro and warmed with garlic and Indian spices. —RB

SERVES 6

1 onion

½ pound (227 g) mushrooms

4 tbsp (60 ml) coconut oil, divided

1 tsp (3 g) salt

½ pound (227 g) frozen spinach, chopped

¼ cup (60 ml) coconut milk

½ cup (60 g) diced celery

2 cloves garlic

½ cup (30 g) chopped cilantro

1 pound (454 g) ground beef

¼ cup (30 g) coconut flour

2 eggs

1 tsp (3 g) coriander

1 tsp (3 g) ground cumin

½ tsp cayenne pepper

1 tsp (3 g) black pepper

Finely dice the onion and mushrooms. Heat 2 tablespoons (30 ml) of coconut oil in a skillet over medium heat, then add the diced mushrooms, onions and salt. Cook until soft and most of the liquid has steamed off, approximately 10 minutes.

While the onion and mushrooms cook, heat the spinach until defrosted (either in the microwave for approximately 4 minutes or on the stove-top). Transfer to a large sieve or colander and squeeze the water out with your hands until the spinach is stiff and only slightly damp. Transfer to a large mixing bowl.

Place the coconut milk, celery, garlic and cilantro in a blender and pulse until smooth. Pour the sauce over the spinach. Add the mushroom and onion to the spinach mixture. Mix in the ground beef, coconut flour, eggs, coriander, cumin, cayenne and black pepper. Shape into small patties approximately 3 inches (7.5 cm) in diameter.

Heat 2 tablespoons (30 ml) of coconut oil in a skillet over medium heat and transfer the first batch of patties once the oil is hot (being careful not to crowd the pan). Brown the patties for 4 to 5 minutes on each side, being careful to brown but not burn. Serve warm.

PESTO MEATBALLS

Bursting with the flavors of summer, these pesto meatballs have become a family favorite. I always make a double batch to freeze for later. —KH

MAKES 48

1 bunch fresh basil, leaves only

1 clove fresh garlic, minced

1 tsp (5 ml) fresh lemon juice

1 tsp (3 g) sea salt

⅛ tsp black pepper

3 tbsp (45 ml) coconut oil or ghee, melted

2 pounds (908 g) ground meat—beef, bison or pork

2 eggs, beaten

Preheat the oven to 400°F (200°F C, or gas mark 6) and line baking sheets with parchment paper.

To make the pesto, process basil leaves in a food processor until they're completely broken up. Add garlic, lemon juice, salt, pepper and fat of choice and continue to process until well incorporated and smooth.

Mix ground beef and eggs together in a large bowl. Add basil pesto and mix again. Form into small balls and place onto lined baking sheets. Bake for 22 to 24 minutes, or until cooked all the way through and starting to brown. Enjoy!

CHEF'S TIP:
To freeze for later, freeze in single layers then place into airtight container.

GARDEN VEGGIE AND HERB MEATBALLS

Meatballs are my favorite way to get nutrient-dense goodness into my family. Enjoy them as a main meal or keep them on hand for easy snacking. —KH

MAKES 20–24

1 pound (454 g) ground beef

1½ cups (200 g) packed shredded vegetables (I use zucchini, yellow summer squash and carrots)

¼ small onion, finely chopped

1 clove garlic, minced

2 tbsp (8 g) fresh herbs, finely chopped (I use basil, cilantro or parsley)

1¼ tsp (4 g) sea salt

1 egg, beaten

2 pinches sea salt

Preheat the oven to 400°F (200°F C, or gas mark 6) and line a baking sheet with parchment paper.

Place shredded vegetables into a colander in the sink. Sprinkle with two pinches of sea salt and mix well. Allow to sit for 10 minutes. Then place veggies into a clean hand towel and squeeze out all of the moisture in them. Set aside.

Meanwhile, purée onion and garlic together in a small food processor. Combine ground beef, squeezed out veggies, onion/garlic mixture, chopped herbs, sea salt and egg in a large bowl. Mix with your hands until well combined. Roll into desired sized meatballs and place onto baking sheet. Bake for 25 to 30 minutes until brown and cooked all the way through. Serve immediately or allow to cool and freeze for later.

OLIVE ROSEMARY MEATBALLS

Spaghetti and meatballs are the ultimate comfort food! These meatballs are simple to make for a weeknight dinner or even a great option to serve when having guests over. I love to serve them with spaghetti squash and a sprinkle of Parmesan cheese, if you can tolerate dairy! —CP

SERVES 3

1 egg

2 tsp (6 g) fresh rosemary

½ cup (50 g) Kalamata olives

½ cup (60 g) almond flour

1 clove garlic, crushed

1¼ tsp (4 g) salt

1 tsp (3 g) dried oregano

½ tsp dried basil

1 pound (454 g) ground beef

2 cups (480 ml) marinara sauce

Warm a large skillet to medium high.

In a small bowl, whisk the egg. Finely chop the rosemary and olives. Combine all ingredients except marinara, working together with your hands. Shape the meat mixture into medium-sized meatballs.

In the hot non-stick skillet, brown meatballs for 8 minutes, rotating to cook on all sides. Reduce heat to low and cover meatballs with marinara. Place lid on skillet and simmer on low for 25 to 30 minutes.

Serve over a plate of spaghetti squash or zucchini noodles with a spoonful of sauce on top!

CHEF'S TIP:

I always keep a rosemary plant on my patio as it lasts forever and cooking with fresh herbs adds irreplaceable flavor to your meals.

SPAGHETTI SQUASH WITH THYME MEATBALLS

Missing that bowl of pasta and meatballs? Why not try some spaghetti squash instead! This tasty squash filled with spaghetti-like strands makes a perfect replacement for that old packaged pasta and of course we can't forget those delicious meatballs. —NK

SERVES 4

1 spaghetti squash, around 2 pounds (908 g)

½ cup (120 ml) water

1 pound (454 g) ground beef, left to chill in the fridge

½ tbsp (4 g) dried thyme

¼ tsp garlic powder

¼ tsp black pepper

½ tsp sea salt

2 tbsp (30 g) ghee

Sea salt and black pepper, to taste

Preheat oven to 425°F (220°C, or gas mark 7). Line a large baking tray with parchment paper. Cut spaghetti squash in half length-wise and remove the seeds. Season the inside of the squash with some sea salt and black pepper. Place cut side down in the baking tray and pour in ½ cup (120 ml) of water. Place in the oven to bake for 30 to 45 minutes or until the squash is tender. Remove from the oven and place onto a clean plate to cool.

Remove ground beef from the fridge, add in the thyme, garlic powder, black pepper and sea salt. Mix well. Form into small-medium meatballs and set on a clean plate as they are formed. Turn the oven temperature down to 350°F (180°C, or gas mark 4). Put the meatballs on a parchment paper-lined baking tray and cook for 20 to 25 minutes. Remove from the oven and set aside.

Heat 2 tablespoons (30 g) ghee in a large skillet over medium heat. Using a fork, remove the spaghetti squash strands from the cooked squash. Add the strands to the skillet and fry for around 5 minutes. Add in the meatballs and mix through.

ITALIAN MEATBALLS

These Italian Meatballs are best served with a homemade pasta sauce with sautéed spiralized zucchini or a baked spaghetti squash. You can even freeze these meatballs so you have a quick meal option in a hurry. —KW

SERVES 6

1 pound (454 g) ground beef

1 pound (454 g) ground pork

1 cup (160 g) onion, finely diced, about 1 medium onion

1 cup (70 g) mushrooms, finely diced (or any vegetables)

2 tsp (6 g) garlic powder

2 tsp (6 g) onion powder

Pinch or two of red pepper flakes

Sea salt and pepper to taste

2 heaping tbsp (8 g) fresh basil, finely chopped

2 heaping tbsp (8 g) fresh oregano, finely chopped

Preheat oven to 350°F (180°C, or gas mark 4). Mix all ingredients together in a large bowl until well mixed.

Shape into desired size meatballs. Bake on a rimmed baking sheet for 25 minutes or until thoroughly cooked.

CHEF'S TIP:

If you eat dairy, ¼ cup (25 g) of Romano or Parmesan cheese is an excellent addition.

SPICED LAMB MEATBALLS

The addition of exotic spices like cinnamon and turmeric bring a new flavor to these lamb meatballs. Serve with zucchini noodles or spaghetti squash. —HH

SERVES 4–5

1 pound (454 g) ground lamb

3 tbsp (24 g) arrowroot powder

½ tsp baking soda

1 tsp (3 g) salt

1 tsp (3 g) oregano

1 tsp (3 g) thyme

½ tsp sage

½ tsp garlic powder

¼ tsp ground cinnamon

½ tsp turmeric

1 small onion, finely diced

6 cloves garlic, finely diced

1–2 tbsp (15–30 g) ghee, lard or oil

In a large bowl mix the ground lamb, arrowroot, baking soda, all spices and chopped onion and garlic until all of the ingredients are well incorporated.

Place the oil in a large pan on medium-high heat and allow to heat up for a minute or two.

Form the meat into meatballs. Once the oil is hot, fill the pan with meatballs. Let cook on one side for 3 to 5 minutes, then flip and allow to cook for another 4 to 6 minutes. Break one meatball open to make sure it is cooked through to determine proper cooking time for all the meatballs.

Place the finished meatballs on a plate and continue forming balls from the raw meat and cooking in the oil until all the meat is gone.

LIVER BACON MEATBALLS

You won't believe it's liver! "I can't believe it's not . . . or I mean I can't believe it is!! Oh it's delicious! What did you do to make it taste so good . . ." These are some of the many comments I got from non-liver-lovers on this recipe! Try it to believe it! —VM

SERVES 4

½ pound (227 g) beef liver

2 tbsp (30 ml) apple cider vinegar

8 ounces (227 g) uncured bacon, diced small

1 egg

¼ cup (60 ml) full-fat coconut cream

Sea salt and black pepper to taste

1½ pounds (680 g) ground beef

1 shallot, finely chopped

1 pinch of cayenne pepper

Ghee or cooking fat, optional

Place the liver in a bowl with apple cider vinegar and refrigerate overnight.

Heat a large pan over low heat and sauté the chopped bacon until it's cooked, but not too crispy, for about 5 minutes. Remove the bacon and any excess grease from the pan and place the bacon on a paper towel to drain fat.

In a bowl, whisk the egg with coconut cream, sea salt and black pepper. Set aside. In a food processor reduce the cooled bacon to rough crumbles. Then add the liver to the bacon and process until it turns to a coarse liquid.

Add the ground beef, shallots, egg mixture, cayenne and a little more sea salt and pepper. Process the mixture just enough to blend all of the ingredients. Once mixed, form the meat mixture into balls about the size of a golf ball.

Brown the meatballs on all sides in a large pan over medium heat, approximately 2 to 3 minutes per side. You can add some ghee, or other cooking fat if needed. Or you can save the bacon fat and just use that. Cover the pan and allow the meatballs to cook for approximately 10 minutes over low heat.

TURKEY MEATBALLS

Semi-homemade meatballs is a great time saver especially if you can find a good brand of store bought marinara sauce that has clean ingredients and no added sugar in it. Simmering the meatballs in marinara sauce after baking makes them juicy and flavorful! —JC

SERVES 8

½ tsp coconut oil

1 large onion, chopped

1 cup (60 g) fresh parsley, loosely packed

4 cloves garlic, minced

2 pounds (908 g) ground turkey

3 large eggs

½ cup (60 g) almond flour

1 tsp (3 g) sea salt

1 tsp (3 g) black pepper

2 (15.5-ounce [434-ml]) jars of Paleo-friendly marinara sauce

Preheat oven to 375°F (190°C, or gas mark 5). Lightly grease a baking sheet with coconut oil.

In a food processor, add onion, parsley and garlic. Pulse until finely chopped, about 5 to 10 seconds. Transfer to a large bowl. Add ground turkey, eggs, almond flour, sea salt and black pepper. Gently mix everything until just combined but do not overmix. Form into 1½- to 2-inch (3.8- to 5-cm)-sized meatballs and arrange them on the baking sheet. Bake in the oven for 15 to 20 minutes until cooked through with an internal temperature of 160° to 165°F (71° to 74°C).

In a big pot, add the marinara sauce and bring to a simmer over medium-low heat. Add the cooked meatballs. Cover and simmer for 10 to 15 minutes until the sauce has slightly thickened.

Let it cool for a couple of minutes before serving.

CHIPOTLE MEATBALLS

Ground beef is a staple in the Paleo diet. I never get tired of finding new ways to transform ground beef into different flavorful dishes. I think you'll really enjoy the bold flavors in these chipotle meatballs. —KW

SERVES 3–4

1 pound (454 g) ground beef

½ cup (80 g) onion, finely chopped, about ½ a medium onion

½ cup (35 g) mushrooms, finely chopped

¼ cup (15 g) fresh cilantro, chopped

1 chipotle chile in adobo, seeds removed, finely chopped—or ½–1 tsp (1.5–3 g) chipotle chili powder

1 tsp (3 g) garlic powder

1 tsp (3 g) onion powder

1 tsp (3 g) ground cumin

Sea salt and pepper, to taste

Preheat oven to 350°F (180°C, or gas mark 4).

Combine all the ingredients in a large bowl and mix until incorporated. Shape into desired size meatball and place on a rimmed baking pan.

Bake for 25 to 30 minutes or until cooked through.

CHEF'S TIP:

For extra spice do not remove the chipotle chile seeds.

JERK MEATBALLS

If you like bold flavors, be sure to give these jerk meatballs a try. I especially enjoy pairing these meatballs with some sliced fresh pineapple and guacamole for a taste of the tropics. —KW

SERVES 6–8

1 pound (454 g) ground beef

1 pound (454 g) ground pork

1 lime, juiced

1 bell pepper, finely minced

1 medium red onion, finely diced

1 tbsp (8 g) ground allspice

2 tbsp (24 g) coconut sugar

¼ tsp ground cinnamon

1 tsp (3 g) red pepper flakes

¼ tsp ground cloves

¼ tsp ground cumin

2 tsp (6 g) sea salt

1 tsp (3 g) black pepper

2 tbsp (8 g) fresh cilantro, finely chopped

FOR OPTIONAL TOPPINGS

Super Easy Guacamole (page 190)

Pineapple Coleslaw (page 190)

Mango Habanero Hot Sauce (page 517)

Preheat oven to 375°F (190°C, or gas mark 5). Combine all ingredients together. Roll into 2-inch (5-cm) balls. Bake on a baking pan for 20 minutes or until thoroughly cooked. Top with your desired toppings.

ASIAN-STYLE MEATBALLS WITH CILANTRO AND GREEN ONION

Coconut aminos are a great Paleo substitute for soy sauce. They really make the salty-sweet flavor of these Asian-style meatballs. —KH

MAKES 24

1 tbsp (15 ml) coconut aminos

1 tbsp (15 ml) honey

1 tbsp (15 ml) toasted sesame oil

1 tsp (3 g) grated fresh ginger

1 clove garlic, minced

½ tsp sea salt

1 pound (454 g) ground beef

1 egg, beaten

1 tbsp (8 g) coconut flour

¼ cup (15 g) fresh cilantro, finely chopped

2 tbsp (12 g) green onions, chopped

Preheat the oven to 400°F (200°F C, or gas mark 6) and line a baking sheet with parchment paper.

In a small bowl, mix coconut aminos, honey, sesame oil, ginger, garlic and salt. Set aside.

Place ground beef, egg and coconut flour into large bowl. Mix well. Add prepared amino and honey mixture. Mix again to combine. Fold in cilantro and green onions. Roll into desired size meatballs and place onto baking sheet. Bake for 25 minutes until brown and cooked all the way through. Serve immediately or allow to cool and freeze for later.

TERIYAKI COCKTAIL MEATBALLS

Whether you are looking for a fun dinner recipe or a crowd-pleasing appetizer, these flavorful meatballs, packed with ginger and cilantro, are sure to be a hit. —KH

MAKES 40

1 pound (454 g) ground beef

1 pound (454 g) ground pork

2 eggs, beaten

1 tbsp (8 g) coconut flour

1 tsp (3 g) unrefined sea salt

¼ cup (15 g) fresh cilantro, finely chopped

1 tbsp (8 g) fresh ginger, grated

A few grinds of fresh pepper

FOR THE SAUCE

¼ cup (60 ml) water

1 tbsp (8 g) arrowroot powder

½ cup (120 ml) coconut aminos

½ cup (120 ml) good quality homemade broth

1 tbsp (8 g) fresh ginger, grated

2–3 cloves garlic, crushed

½ tsp sea salt

2 tbsp (30 ml) toasted sesame oil

2 tbsp (30 ml) apple cider vinegar

4 tbsp (60 ml) raw honey

FOR THE GARNISH

Sesame seeds

Cilantro

Preheat the oven to 350°F (180°F C, or gas mark 4). Liberally oil a baking rack with coconut oil or ghee and place the rack on top of a large baking sheet. Set aside. In a large bowl, combine ground meat, eggs, coconut flour, salt, cilantro, grated ginger and pepper. Mix until well combined—I use my hands here. Using moistened hands, form the meat mixture into 40 small meatballs and place onto the prepared baking rack. Bake for 20 minutes.

Make the sauce by combining the water with arrowroot powder. Set aside. Add coconut aminos, broth, ginger, garlic and salt to a sauté pan. Bring to a simmer and simmer for about 4 minutes to reduce. Add arrowroot mixture and cook for a minute or two, stirring constantly, until the sauce thickens and becomes glossy. Turn off heat and stir in the sesame oil, vinegar and honey.

Add the baked meatballs to the sauce and stir to coat evenly. You will have to do this in batches. Use a slotted spoon to transfer to serving platter. Pour remaining sauce over meatballs on platter, if you like. Garnish with sesame seeds and cilantro. Serve warm.

GYRO MEATBALLS

Meatballs are a personal favorite of mine and I love creating all different variations of the classic meatball. These Gyro Meatballs have the bold flavors of Greek cuisine. Serve them with the Avocado Tzatziki Sauce (page 511) for the perfect combination. —KW

MAKES 25–30

1 pound (454 g) ground lamb (or ground beef)

½ medium red onion, finely diced (about ½ cup [80 g])

2 cloves garlic, minced

Zest of ½ lemon

1 tbsp (4 g) fresh oregano, chopped or 1 tsp (3 g) dried oregano

1 tbsp (8 g) ground coriander

½ tsp ground cumin

Sea salt and pepper, to taste

Avocado Tzatziki Sauce (page 511), for serving

Preheat oven to 350°F (180°C, or gas mark 4). Combine all the meatball ingredients together and form into approximately 1½- to 2-inch (3.8- to 5-cm) balls. Place on a raised-edge baking pan and bake for 25 minutes.

Serve with Avocado Tzatziki Sauce.

CHEF'S TIPS:

If you eat dairy, adding ¼ cup (30 g) feta cheese to the meatballs is delicious.

BOBOTIE (SOUTH AFRICAN CURRIED MEATLOAF)

A grain-free spin on a traditional South African dish, this savory and sweet meatloaf is a version you've probably never tasted before. —RB

SERVES 6

1 cup (235 ml) strong black tea

½ cup (75 g) raisins

½ cup (75 g) chopped dried apricots

1 large onion

2 cloves garlic

2 tbsp (30 ml) olive oil

2 tsp (4.5 g) ground turmeric

2 tsp (4.5 g) ground coriander

1 tsp (3 g) cayenne pepper

½ tsp ground cumin

½ tsp ground black pepper

½ tsp fennel seeds

1 tsp (3 g) salt

2 tbsp (30 ml) apple cider vinegar

½ pound (227 g) ground beef

½ pound (227 g) ground lamb

1 egg

¾ cup (90 g) almond flour

¼ cup (38 g) sliced almonds

(continued)

Preheat the oven to 375°F (190°C, or gas mark 5). Line a loaf pan with foil, set aside.

Combine the tea, raisins and apricots in a bowl, let soak for 30 minutes. Drain, and reserve ⅓ cup (80 ml) soaking liquid. Set both aside.

Roughly chop the onion and finely shred with the garlic in a food processor. Heat olive oil in a heavy-bottomed skillet over medium heat. Cook garlic and onion until lightly caramelized, stirring frequently, about 15 minutes.

Add the turmeric, coriander, cayenne, cumin, pepper, fennel and salt. Cook while stirring until fragrant, about 1 minute. Add soaked fruit and soaking liquid plus the vinegar. Cook until almost all liquid evaporates, about half an hour. Remove from heat and transfer to a large bowl and then add the beef, lamb, egg and almond flour. Mix until evenly combined.

Transfer meat mixture to the foil-lined loaf pan. Scatter almonds in a single layer over the top of the meat loaf, pressing gently to adhere the slivers to the meat mixture. Bake for approximately 40 minutes. Cool enough to handle, then gently remove from the pan and slice.

BACON AND TURKEY MEATLOAF

This is inspired by my favorite 50/50 beef and bacon burger at a neighborhood joint. Any dish with bacon never fails in my book! This is the perfect comfort food that tastes like a cheat but it's 100% Paleo, grain-free and dairy-free as well. Make a complete meal by serving it with Cauliflower Mash (page 237) and Caramelized Onion Gravy (page 246). —JC

SERVES 4

1½ pounds (680 g) ground turkey

8 ounces (227 g) bacon, chopped

1½ cups (180 g) carrots, shredded

2 ribs celery, shredded

1 small onion, finely chopped

¼ cup (30 g) almond flour

3 large eggs

2 tbsp (16 g) black pepper

Preheat oven to 375°F (190°C, or gas mark 5).

Combine all ingredients in a large bowl. Place meatloaf mixture in a loaf pan and bake for 60 to 65 minutes. Remove from the oven and let it rest for 8 to 10 minutes before slicing and serving.

CHEF'S TIP:
Freeze bacon so that it's easy to chop into really small pieces.

FRENCH PÂTÉ MEATLOAF

If French pâté and American meatloaf got married and had a baby, this would be it! Of course any modern baby would follow Paleo guidelines. No grains or dairy here! —VM

SERVES 6

¼ cup (35 g) sun-dried tomatoes

3 tbsp (43 g) ghee

1 cup (160 g) onion, chopped

3 cloves garlic, minced

½ pound (227 g) chicken liver, cleaned and separated

2 tsp (6 g) herbes de Provence

¼ cup (60 ml) cognac

1 pound (454 g) ground beef

10 slices bacon, divided

1 tsp (6 g) sea salt

½ tsp ground black pepper

1 tsp (3 g) ground allspice

2 large eggs

½ cup (120 ml) coconut cream

½ cup (60 g) cassava flour

French-style cornichons, for garnish

Preheat the oven to 350°F (180°F, or gas mark 4). Soak the sun-dried tomatoes in hot water to rehydrate for about 10 minutes. Melt the ghee in a skillet over medium heat. Add the chopped onion and minced garlic, sautéing them until they turn soft and translucent, about 3 to 4 minutes.

Add the chicken livers to the skillet, seasoning with the herbes de Provence over high heat. Quickly sear the chicken liver on all sides, leaving the insides pink, about 3 to 5 minutes. When you are done searing the chicken liver, add the cognac and sauté until the alcohol has evaporated, about 1 minute. Remove the chicken liver mixture to a plate and let cool. Once the chicken liver mixture has cooled, chop the mixture into small pieces and place into a large bowl.

Sear the ground beef in a skillet on high heat until browned but not too dry, about 10 minutes. Remove the ground beef, and add it to chicken liver mixture.

Chop four slices of the bacon into small pieces. Add the chopped bacon to the mixture and season with sea salt, ground black pepper and allspice.

Beat the eggs and coconut cream and until frothy. Add the egg mixture to the chicken liver-ground beef mixture, along with the cassava flour, and mix well.

Line a glass baking dish or loaf pan with the six remaining bacon slices, laying them across the width of the dish or pan. Pour the meat mixture into the pan, pressing it down into the dish or pan. Fold the bacon slices over the top of the meat mixture if you can, then cover the dish with foil.

Place the dish inside a bigger metal baking pan, filling the baking pan with water until halfway full. Now place the whole dish into the oven carefully, and bake until a meat thermometer reads 155°F (68°C), which usually takes about 2½ hours.

When the dish is done baking, take it out of the oven and let it cool. Once it has finished cooling, take a serving plate and lay it face down on the top of the dish. Flip the entire dish over, so the meatloaf will come to rest on the plate. Serve lukewarm with French style cornichons.

SUN-DRIED TOMATO AND MUSHROOM MEATLOAF

This meatloaf is flavorful, but not overwhelming. This recipe calls for ground beef, but the flavors of this dish would work well with ground turkey, or even ground pork! Meatloaf is a perfect dish to make over the weekend, and divvy up into separate containers to grab-and-go for the work week. It works for breakfast well too! —AV

SERVES 6

¼ cup (20 g) dried mushrooms, or substitute fresh mushrooms

½ cup (80 g) sun-dried tomatoes, chopped

2 pounds (908 g) ground beef

2 pieces bacon, chopped

4 cloves garlic, minced

½ onion, diced

1 tsp (3 g) chili powder

2 tsp (6 g) sea salt

½ tsp black pepper

½ cup (30 g) fresh parsley, chopped

¼ cup (15 g) fresh basil, chopped

1 jalapeño pepper, minced

1 egg

FOR THE GLAZE

¼ cup (40 g) sun-dried tomatoes

¼ cup (20 g) dried mushrooms, or substitute fresh mushrooms

1 clove garlic

1 tsp (5 ml) olive oil

2 tbsp (30 ml) water from the sun-dried tomatoes

2 tbsp (30 ml) water from the mushrooms (if using fresh mushrooms just use filtered water)

(continued)

Rehydrate the sun-dried tomatoes by placing them in a bowl and covering them with warm water. Let them soak at room temperature for at least 45 minutes or until they feel flexible. If they feel stiff, soak them longer. Reserve the water. Rehydrate dried mushrooms by placing them in a bowl and covering with warm water for 30 to 45 minutes. Reserve water.

Preheat the oven to 375°F (190°C, or gas mark 5). Combine the beef, bacon, garlic, onion, sun-dried tomatoes, mushrooms, chili powder, salt, pepper, parsley, basil and jalapeño. Then add the egg and mix gently; do not overdo it or you will risk making the loaf dry. Pat the mixture into a loaf pan and smooth the top. Bake for 1 hour.

To make the glaze, purée all of the glaze ingredients in a food processor until smooth. After the meatloaf has cooked for 1 hour, remove it from the oven and drain some of the fat out of the loaf pan. Brush the top of the meatloaf with the glaze, then place back in the oven for about 20 minutes or until the top looks browned and caramelized. Drain some more fat out, if needed. Allow to rest for 10 minutes and serve!

SHEPHERD'S PIE

I have to say this is one of my absolute favorite recipes! I think the rich and creamy sweet potato topping (in place of the traditional white potato topping) makes the recipe even better than the original. —HH

SERVES 4–5

2½ cups (300 g) sweet potato

1 small onion

2 tbsp (30 g) ghee or avocado oil

6 cloves garlic

½ tsp oregano

½ tsp thyme

½ tsp marjoram

½ tsp sage

1 cup (70 g) mushrooms, chopped

1 pound (454 g) ground beef

1 tsp (3 g) salt, divided

½ tsp pepper

½ tsp ground cumin

2 medium carrots, chopped

1 cup (150 g) frozen peas

¼ cup (60 ml) + 2 tbsp (30 ml) chicken bone broth

Preheat the oven to 400°F (200°C, or gas mark 6). Place all of the sweet potatoes on a baking sheet in the oven and cook for about 45 minutes or until the sweet potatoes are soft and fork tender. Set aside.

Dice the onion and sauté in the ghee or avocado oil for about 1 minute. Add the garlic, oregano, thyme, marjoram and sage and sauté until onions are almost translucent. Add the mushrooms and sauté for 1 to 2 minutes. Add the ground beef in small amounts then sprinkle with ½ teaspoon salt, pepper and cumin. Stir and break up the beef with a wooden spoon or a spatula. Sauté until the beef is browned, then add carrots and peas and continue cooking.

There should be a layer of liquid for the peas and carrots to cook in. If there is minimal or no liquid add about ¼ cup (60 ml) of chicken bone broth. Cook until the carrots have softened.

Once the roasted sweet potatoes have cooled, remove the skin and place the potato into a separate bowl and add 2 tablespoons (30 ml) of chicken bone broth and ½ teaspoon of salt. Use a potato masher, immersion blender or regular blender to purée the mixture. If it is too thick or difficult to purée, add more chicken bone broth, 1 tablespoon (15 ml) at a time until you reach the desired consistency.

Place the beef and vegetable sauté mixture in a pie plate or a 9 × 9-inch (23 × 23-cm) baking dish. Place the sweet potato purée on top of the beef and vegetable mixture and smooth evenly over the beef and vegetables. Cook at 425°F (220°C, or gas mark 7) for 20 minutes. Let cool and serve.

TRICOLOR SHEPHERD'S PIE (HACHIS PARMENTIER TRICOLORE)

This French take on traditional English comfort food is grain-free and dairy-free while still maintaining its rich, savory flavor. —RB

SERVES 4

FOR THE TOPPING

2 pounds (908 g) potatoes

1 pound (454 g) yams

⅓ cup (80 ml) coconut milk

½ tsp salt, divided

¼ cup (15 g) parsley leaves

FOR THE FILLING

2 tbsp (30 ml) coconut oil

2 leeks, white part only

1 carrot

2 cloves garlic

1 pound (454 g) ground beef

3 sprigs thyme

1 bay leaf

2 tbsp (30 g) tomato paste

½ tsp salt

¼ tsp pepper

Peel the potatoes and yams, then roughly chop. Transfer to a medium pot, cover with water and bring to a boil. Simmer at medium low, covered, until the root vegetables are soft, approximately 20 minutes.

To prepare the filling, heat the coconut oil over medium heat in a large skillet. Thinly slice the white parts of the leeks, and add them to the skillet. Peel the carrot, smash and peel the garlic cloves, and then pulse them together in a food processor until finely shredded.

Add the carrot mixture to the leeks in the skillet, along with the ground beef. Cook until the beef is no longer pink, about 10 minutes. Add the thyme, bay leaf, tomato paste, salt and pepper. Stir. Remove from the heat and allow to cool, then pack evenly into an 11-inch (28-cm) oval baking dish.

To finish the topping, remove the potatoes and yams from the pot and when cool enough to handle, mash the potatoes until very smooth using a food processor with the coconut milk and ¼ teaspoon salt. Set aside.

Divide the mashed potatoes in half and purée one half with the parsley leaves until uniformly green. Purée the yams with ¼ teaspoon salt in a food processor. Set aside.

Preheat the oven to 400°F (200°C, or gas mark 6).

Put together a pastry bag, coupler and large round frosting tip. Fold the top half of the bag over to form a cuff and spoon in the white mashed potatoes. Slowly squeeze the potatoes down into the tip and out in a ribbon across one-third of the surface of the filling. Clean the pastry bag, then fill with mashed yams. Cover one-third of the filling, leaving room for the green potatoes. Clean the pastry bag, then fill with green potatoes and pipe out to fill the last remaining third of the dish's surface.

Bake in the preheated oven for 25 minutes until lightly browned and bubbly around the edges. Serve warm.

COTTAGE PIE

Cottage pie and shepherd's pie can easily be confused with each other. Technically, the preparation and ingredients are the same except for the type of meat used. Cottage pie uses beef while shepherd's pie uses lamb! Using Cauliflower Mash (page 237) yields the same consistency and texture as regular white potatoes so no one will ever notice that this is a Paleo recipe. —JC

SERVES 4

2 pounds (908 g) ground beef

1½ cups (180 g) carrots, shredded

1 medium onion, chopped

1 cup (235 ml) Slow Cooker Beef Broth (page 171)

2 tbsp (16 g) dried thyme, crushed

2 tbsp (16 g) dried rosemary, crushed

2 tbsp (16 g) coconut flour

Sea salt

Black pepper

3 cups (750 g) Cauliflower Mash (page 237)

Preheat oven to 400°F (200°C, or gas mark 6).

In a cast iron pan over medium-high heat, add ground beef, carrots and onion. Sauté until browned, 5 to 8 minutes. Reduce heat. Add beef broth, thyme, rosemary and coconut flour to the meat. Stir and simmer until the mixture has thickened, about 1 to 2 minutes. Season with sea salt and black pepper to taste.

Divide the meat equally among eight ramekins. Spread the cauliflower mash evenly on top of each one. Place the ramekins on a baking sheet and bake for 25 minutes. Turn on the broiler and broil for an additional 5 to 8 minutes to give it a nice golden brown crust. Serve hot.

CHEF'S TIP:

A regular baking dish can also be used instead of the individual ramekins. The cooking time remains the same.

BEEF KEBABS

The orange juice (my dad's secret ingredient) helps tenderize the meat, while the tomato paste adds a punch of flavor to these otherwise traditional beef kebabs. —AV

SERVES 4–6

FOR THE MARINADE

1 small onion, chopped

5 cloves garlic

1 tsp (3 g) orange zest

1 tbsp (4 g) fresh rosemary, chopped

¼ cup (60 ml) fresh squeezed orange juice

¼ cup (60 ml) olive oil

2 tbsp (30 g) tomato paste

1 tsp (3 g) sea salt

½ tsp black pepper

2 pounds (908 g) sirloin, cut into 2-inch (5-cm) pieces

1 zucchini, cut into 1-inch (2.5-cm) rounds

1 yellow summer squash, cut into 1-inch (2.5-cm) rounds, halve the large pieces

1 red onion, cut into chunks

½ green bell pepper, cut into 1½-inch (3.8-cm) chunks

½ red bell pepper, cut into 1½-inch (3.8-cm) chunks

To make the marinade, place all ingredients in a food processor and blend until smooth, about 1 minute. Reserve ¼ cup (60 ml) marinade for the vegetables. Place beef in a bowl and cover with the marinade. Toss to make sure it is well coated. Refrigerate for 4 hours to overnight. Remove the beef from the refrigerator 30 minutes before cooking, to allow it to come to room temperature.

Thirty minutes before grilling, toss the vegetables with the ¼ cup (60 ml) reserved marinade. Remove the beef from the marinade and thread onto skewers. Do the same with the vegetables. Heat your grill to medium. Cook the kebabs on the grill, turning the skewers every 3 to 4 minutes, to allow all sides to cook evenly, for about 10 to 12 minutes. Timing can really vary from grill to grill, so either check by feeling the meat or taking off a piece and slicing it open and checking for doneness. If it still pink inside cook it a little longer. Do the same with the vegetables. Cook until tender and just slightly charred.

PERSIAN LAMB KEBABS

These kebabs can be made ahead of time and enjoyed as a simple weeknight meal. Pair with some greens or your side dish of choice for a complete meal. —NK

SERVES 4

2 pounds (908 g) ground lamb

1 medium onion, grated and excess water removed

2 tsp (12 g) sea salt

¼ tsp black pepper

2 tbsp (30 ml) ghee, melted

Sumac to taste

Place the lamb into a food processor and process the meat 2 to 3 times until it clumps together. Place lamb into a large mixing bowl and add the onion. Add sea salt and black pepper and mix well. Cover and set aside at room temperature for an hour. When ready to cook take a golf ball-sized piece of mixture and roll into a ball with your hands. Place onto a clean surface and roll into a long cigar shape. Use the palm of your hand to flatten out the mixture and form into a kebab shape. Place each kebab onto a plate until the mixture is all used. Heat a medium square grill pan over medium-high heat. Add the ghee. Once hot, cook the kebabs in batches for 5 to 6 minutes per side. Serve with some sumac sprinkled on top.

CHEF'S TIP:

The kebab mixture can be refrigerated up to 12 hours before cooking.

EASY PERSIAN OVEN KEBABS

Kebabs are something I grew up eating all the time. Usually it was my dad making them outside on the BBQ but sometimes when the weather wouldn't permit, my mum would make them in a skillet. I have found this oven version to be the easiest way to make them. These are great enjoyed with some salad on the side or even with some cauliflower rice. Don't forget the sumac either, it's a must when enjoying Persian kebabs. —NK

SERVES 4–6

2 pounds (908 g) ground beef or lamb

1 medium yellow onion, grated and extra juice discarded

¼ tsp ground turmeric

½ tsp crushed saffron, dissolved in 2 tbsp (30 ml) water

Sea salt and black pepper to taste

Sumac, to serve

Preheat oven to 350°F (180°C, or gas mark 4). Line a small baking tray around 12 × 9 inches (30.5 × 23 cm) with parchment paper. Place beef, onion, turmeric and saffron into a large mixing bowl. Season with sea salt and black pepper to taste. Add the mixture to the baking tray and use your hands to spread the mixture evenly into the baking dish, making sure to cover the entire surface. Place in the oven and bake for 20 to 25 minutes. Remove from the oven and carefully drain the excess liquid from the baking tray. Cut the meat into kebab strips and serve with some sumac sprinkled over the top.

CHEF'S TIP:

You can find sumac online or at Persian grocery stores.

LEBANESE KAFTA

Traditional kafta is usually cooked on a grill but using the oven on convection setting works just as well. Pair this with a refreshing side dish such as the Cucumber and Tomato Salad (page 330) for a Mediterranean inspired meal. —JC

SERVES 4

1 pound (454 g) ground beef

1 pound (454 g) ground lamb

1 medium onion, finely chopped

¼ cup (30 g) sun-dried tomatoes, chopped

¼ cup (15 g) dried parsley

3 tbsp (12 g) fresh mint, finely chopped

1 tsp (3 g) red pepper flakes

1½ tsp (7.5 g) sea salt

1 tsp (3 g) garlic powder

2 tsp (6 g) ground cumin

2 tsp (6 g) black pepper

2 tsp (6 g) oregano

1 tsp (3 g) paprika

¼ tsp cayenne pepper

1 tbsp (8 g) ground coriander

Preheat oven to 350°F (180°C, or gas mark 4).

Line a baking sheet with foil and place a baking rack on top.

Add all the ingredients to a large bowl. Use your hands to combine everything together making sure not to overwork the meat. Form the meat around each metal skewer. Press it flat so the meat does not fall off. Arrange kafta on the baking rack and cook for 10 to 15 minutes until the meat is cooked through but not tough. Let it cool and remove the kafta from the skewers before serving.

CHEF'S TIP:

Pan-fry a little bit of the meat mixture to check if it is seasoned according to your preference. Add more spices if necessary before forming the meat on the skewers.

RAS EL HANOUT PIZZA

A cauliflower crust makes a grain-free pizza possible. Lamb, vegetables and spices make it delicious. —RB

MAKES 1

FOR THE CRUST

3 cups (300 g) diced cauliflower

¾ cup (90 g) almond flour

3 tbsp (24 g) coconut flour

1 tbsp (8 g) ras el hanout

½ tsp salt

3 eggs

FOR THE TOPPING

1 tsp (5 ml) olive oil

¼ pound (112 g) ground lamb

½ red bell pepper

½ yellow bell pepper

½ Chinese eggplant

1 zucchini

6 ounces (168 g) tomato paste

½ tsp salt

1 tsp (3 g) ras el hanout

1 tsp (3 g) red pepper flakes

2 ounces (56 g) fresh feta cheese, optional

Preheat the oven to 400°F (200°C, or gas mark 6). Line a baking tray with wax paper and set aside.

Add the diced cauliflower to a mixing bowl. Add the dry ingredients for the crust and mix thoroughly. Stir in the eggs, then transfer the mixture to the baking tray and form into a pizza base by flattening the dough with your hands. Pre-bake for 25 minutes or until golden.

While the crust is baking, warm the olive oil over medium heat in a medium skillet. Brown the ground lamb briefly until no longer pink, approximately 10 minutes.

Dice the bell peppers and thinly slice the eggplant and zucchini. Mix the tomato paste with 2 tablespoons (30 ml) of water to thin it, then mix in the salt ras el hanout and red pepper flakes.

Once the crust is pre-baked, remove from the oven and spread the tomato mixture over it with the back of a spoon. Lay the sliced zucchini and eggplant rounds over it and sprinkle with the bell pepper. Top with the browned lamb and feta cheese, if using.

Return the pizza to the oven, and bake for 10 additional minutes until the veggies are softened.

BEEF MASSAMAN CURRY

This rich, thick curry gets its flavor from exotic spices, hearty beef and sweet squash. —RB

SERVES 4

1 pound (454 g) cubed chuck beef or stewing beef

3 tbsp (45 g) red curry paste

3 tbsp (45 ml) olive oil, divided

1 butternut squash, approximately 1½ pounds (680 g)

½ onion

10 green cardamom pods

2 cinnamon sticks

3 star anise

2 (13.5-ounce [378-g]) cans coconut milk

2 tbsp (30 ml) fish sauce

⅓ cup (80 g) cashew butter

4 kaffir lime leaves

Handful fresh Thai basil leaves, torn

Handful dry-roasted cashews

In a medium mixing bowl, combine the raw beef with the red curry paste and 2 tablespoons (30 ml) of olive oil. Toss lightly and let marinate while you prepare the squash.

Peel the squash, cut it lengthwise, remove the seeds and chop into 1-inch (2.5-cm) cubes. Peel the onion, and roughly chop. Heat 1 tablespoon (15 ml) of olive oil in a large pot over medium heat and brown the marinated meat briefly, then add the onion and squash. Tie the cardamom pods, cinnamon sticks and star anise and in cheesecloth or a cooking-safe spice bag (the goal is to prevent the spices from being loose in the pot). Add to the meat mixture in the pot, and cover with the coconut milk.

Add the fish sauce and cashew butter, and stir well to combine. Bring to a boil, then turn heat to low and let simmer, covered, for 1 hour. After an hour, add the kaffir lime leaves and basil. Simmer for an additional ½ hour uncovered (to thicken), then remove and discard the lime leaves and spice bag. Garnish with cashews and serve.

CHEF'S TIP:

Kaffir lime leaves are available in gourmet grocery stores and in ethnic markets.

SRI-LANKAN GRILLED CHICKEN

This is a fun twist on a classic grilled chicken. The lemongrass adds a bright and vibrant flavor. —AV

SERVES 4

1 stalk of lemongrass

¾ cup (48 g) fresh cilantro sprigs

4 cloves garlic

1 tsp (3 g) turmeric

1 tsp (3 g) ground coriander

1 tsp (3 g) ground cumin

¼ tsp cayenne

1 tsp (3 g) fresh ginger, grated

1 tbsp (15 ml) sesame oil

¼ cup (60 ml) chicken broth

Juice of 1 lime

½ tsp sea salt

¼ tsp pepper

8 skinless, bone-in chicken thighs

Cucumber Salad (page 330), for serving

Prepare the lemongrass by removing the leaves in the tough outer layers, until you get to the softer, fleshier part. You want to use the pale yellow stalk that is easier to slice. Remove the bulb and slice the lemongrass. Stop slicing when it is no longer fleshy, about two thirds of the way down.

Combine the lemongrass, cilantro, garlic, turmeric, coriander, cumin, cayenne, ginger, sesame oil, chicken broth, lime juice, salt and pepper in a food processor. Blend into a smooth paste.

Cover chicken with the sauce and marinate for 1 to 4 hours or overnight. Grill the chicken over medium heat for 20 to 25 minutes, flipping once, until cooked through. Serve with Cucumber Salad.

LAMB CURRY

The fragrant spices in this dry curry enhance the mild flavor of ground lamb. It is best paired with cooling Cucumber and Tomato Salad (page 330) and cauliflower rice for a quick weeknight dinner with an exotic flair. —JC

SERVES 4

2 tbsp (30 g) ghee or tallow

2½ tsp (7.5 g) ground cumin

2½ tsp (7.5 g) curry powder

4 cloves garlic, minced

1 tbsp (8 g) ginger, grated

2 leeks, white parts only, thinly sliced

1 pound (454 g) ground lamb

2 medium carrots, sliced

½ bunch cilantro, roughly chopped

Cucumber and Tomato Salad (page 330), for serving

Cauliflower rice, for serving

Melt ghee in a wok over medium heat. Add cumin, curry powder, garlic and ginger. Fry for 1 minute until fragrant. Add leeks and sauté for 1 minute until they begin to soften. Add ground lamb and sauté for 3 minutes. Add carrots, sauté and cook for 5 minutes.

Turn off heat and mix in chopped cilantro. Serve with Cucumber and Tomato Salad and cauliflower rice on the side.

VINDALOO

This vindaloo with chicken and sweet potatoes is thick, spicy, tangy and delicious. —RB

SERVES 6

½ serrano pepper

1 (3-inch [7.5-cm]) piece ginger

1 tbsp (8 g) whole black peppercorns

1 tbsp (8 g) black mustard seeds

1 tbsp (8 g) cumin seeds

1 tbsp (8 g) coriander seeds

1 tbsp (8 g) ground turmeric

1 tsp (3 g) fenugreek seeds

1 tsp (3 g) ground cinnamon

5 whole cloves

¼ cup (30 g) paprika

½ cup (120 ml) apple cider vinegar

2 tbsp (30 ml) honey

½ head garlic, peeled and smashed

½ cup (120 ml) water

3 pounds (1.4 kg) boneless, skinless chicken thighs, cut into bite-size pieces

2 tbsp (30 ml) coconut oil

2 large yellow onions

2 pounds (908 g) Japanese sweet potato

4 cups (940 ml) chicken broth

Core and roughly chop half of the serrano pepper—wear gloves or wash your hands thoroughly after handling, being careful not to touch your face. Peel and roughly chop the ginger. Combine the peppercorns, mustard seeds, cumin seeds, coriander seeds, turmeric, fenugreek seeds, cinnamon, cloves, paprika, apple cider vinegar, honey, garlic, ginger, serrano and water in a blender. Purée until smooth.

Combine the chopped chicken thighs with the spice paste in a glass storage container. Allow to marinate in the refrigerator for 24 hours.

Heat the coconut oil in a large, heavy-bottomed pot. Finely chop the onions and cook in the oil until translucent, approximately 10 minutes. Add the marinated chicken and any leftover paste to the onions, then peel and chop the sweet potatoes and add to the pot. Cover the contents with the broth and bring to a boil. Lower the heat to medium, then boil covered for a half hour. Uncover the pot and boil until thickened to your preference, approximately 30 minutes.

CHEF'S TIP:
If you prefer a milder vindaloo, substitute jalapeño pepper for the serrano pepper or omit entirely.

GREEN CURRY CHICKEN LETTUCE WRAPS

These Asian-inspired lettuce wraps are healthy, light and satisfying. —AV

SERVES 4

3 tbsp (45 ml) fresh lime juice

2 tbsp (30 g) green curry paste

2 tbsp (30 ml) fish sauce

1 tbsp (6 g) fresh ginger, grated

2 cloves of garlic, minced

½ tsp sea salt

½ tsp freshly ground black pepper

1 tbsp (15 ml) coconut oil

2 pounds (908 g) boneless, skinless chicken thighs, cut into 1-inch (2.5-cm) chunks

FOR GARNISHES

1 head butter lettuce leaves, separated

½ cup (50 g) green onions, chopped

¼ cup (40 g) cashews, chopped

1 large carrot, peeled and julienned

1 cup (120 g) radish, julienned

1 cup (64 g) fresh mint, chopped

1 cup (64 g) Thai (or regular) basil, chopped

(continued)

In a small bowl mix together the lime juice, curry paste, fish sauce, ginger, garlic, salt and pepper. Set aside. Heat the coconut oil in a large sauté pan, add the chicken and sauté until browned, stirring occasionally, about 5 to 7 minutes. Add the curry sauce to the pan and cook until chicken is cooked through, an additional 10 to 12 minutes.

Serve chicken in lettuce cups, topped with green onions, cashews and the rest of the garnishes.

CHICKEN CURRY PEPPERS

These stuffed bell peppers are the fastest version of curry you can make, yet still taste great and look fun! Dress them up with cilantro, chili flakes or chopped egg as toppings if you're in the mood. —RB

SERVES 4

3 tbsp (24 g) curry powder

3 cups (420 g) cooked chicken, either shredded or cubed

1 cup (235 ml) coconut milk

1 tsp (3 g) salt

4 bell peppers

In a medium mixing bowl, mix the curry powder, chicken, coconut milk and salt together. Halve the peppers lengthwise, scoop out the pith and seeds. Load the chicken curry into the bell pepper halves and serve, either warm or cold.

CHEF'S TIP:

The shredded chicken can be subbed for cooked diced or ground chicken.

EASY RED CURRY

There's no need to sacrifice taste when throwing quick meals together. This easy recipe can be made on a weeknight using leftover meats from the fridge and frozen organic veggie mixes. It will taste like you spent hours slaving over a hot stove. —RM

SERVES 4–6

1 pound (454 g) spicy sausage

2 (13.5-ounce [378-g]) cans full-fat coconut milk

2½ tbsp (37 g) red curry paste

½ cup (120 ml) chicken stock

1 tbsp (4 g) red pepper flakes

1 kaffir lime leaf (or 1 tsp [5 ml] of lime juice)

1 tbsp (15 ml) fish sauce

4 cloves garlic, minced

1 pound (454 g) frozen veggie mix

2 cups (240 g) sliced frozen pepper and onion mix

2 cups (240 g) cooked chicken, chopped

Cauliflower rice, optional, for serving

Remove the skin and cook the sausage in a large deep skillet over medium heat for 10 to 15 minutes, or until browned. Remove the cooked sausage from the skillet, reserving on the side. Add the coconut milk to the skillet along with the curry paste, chicken stock, red pepper flakes, lime leaf, fish sauce and garlic. Cook for 5 minutes, stirring occasionally.

Then add the frozen veggies and peppers to the skillet, stir and cover while cooking for 5 minutes. Remove the lid and stir in the chicken and sausage. Uncover and cook for the last 5 minutes or until the coconut milk reduces slightly. Remove the lime leaf before serving in a bowl over cauliflower rice or by itself.

CHICKEN ADOBO

I've always made Filipino Chicken Adobo without measuring the ingredients because I can just eyeball the right ratio of coconut aminos to apple cider vinegar and make adjustments as it simmers. This is a good one-pot meal that can be enjoyed with cauliflower rice or regular white rice. It usually lasts up to a week in the fridge due to the amount of vinegar used in cooking it. —JC

SERVES 4

1½ pounds (680 g) skin-on boneless chicken thighs, cut into bite-sized pieces

¾ cup (180 ml) apple cider vinegar

½ cup (120 ml) coconut aminos

1 tsp (5 ml) fish sauce

3 cloves garlic, minced

2 dried bay leaves

½ tsp black pepper

Sea salt

2 tbsp (30 g) tallow or coconut oil

Cauliflower rice, for serving

Add chicken, apple cider vinegar, coconut aminos, fish sauce, garlic, bay leaves and black pepper to a Dutch oven. Place it on the stove and turn on heat to medium. Let it simmer for 3 to 5 minutes. Reduce heat to low, cover and cook for 20 to 25 minutes.

Increase heat back to medium and remove cover. Season with sea salt according to taste. Stir and simmer for 5 minutes. Remove chicken and place it in a bowl. Pour the sauce in a separate bowl and set aside.

Add tallow to the same pan over medium heat. Add the cooked chicken and fry for 2 to 3 minutes until golden brown. Pour the sauce back into the pan. Stir and simmer until the sauce reduces slightly, about 2 minutes. Serve with cauliflower rice.

STEAMED CHICKEN WITH SCALLION SAUCE

This recipe reminds me of a traditional Asian dish that I grew up eating called Hainanese Chicken. It is typically a whole chicken submerged and cooked in boiling water then served with rice, clear broth and a ginger sauce. For quicker cooking time, chicken thighs are much more ideal and steaming instead of boiling locks in their juices. The scallion sauce adds a wow factor so make sure you don't skimp on that! —JC

SERVES 2

FOR THE SCALLION SAUCE

2 cups (200 g) scallions, green and white parts, chopped

⅓ cup (40 g) ginger, grated

1 tsp (3 g) coarse salt, I like Himalayan

¼ cup (58 g) tallow or coconut oil

2 tbsp (30 ml) extra-virgin olive oil

¼ tsp chili pepper flakes (optional)

1 pound (454 g) skin on, boneless chicken thighs

1 tbsp (15 g) tallow or coconut oil

Sea salt

1 inch (2.5 cm) fresh ginger, thinly sliced

4 cups (940 ml) water

Prepare the scallion sauce by combining the scallions, ginger and coarse salt in a glass bowl.

Place the tallow in a small saucepot over high heat. It is ready once it starts to smoke, about 2 to 3 minutes. Remove from heat and carefully pour the hot tallow on the ginger scallion mixture. It will immediately sizzle so be careful. Add the olive oil and chili pepper flakes. Stir and set aside.

Pat chicken with paper towels to remove excess moisture. Rub each piece with tallow and generously season with sea salt. Cut 2 to 3 slits on top (about ¼-inch [6-mm] deep) and insert a slice of ginger in each one. This will give the chicken added flavor while steaming.

(continued)

Place a steamer basket in a large pot. Add the water and bring to a boil. Arrange the chicken evenly on the steamer basket. Cover the pot and reduce heat until the water is just simmering. Cook for 30 to 35 minutes or until juices run clear.

Once the chicken is cooked, slice it and top with the scallion sauce. Serve immediately.

CHEF'S TIPS:

Tallow is the best choice for the Scallion Sauce because it has a neutral taste that doesn't affect the flavor of the sauce. Coconut oil is a good alternative if you are okay with the added coconut taste.

Freeze ginger overnight to make it easier to grate.

CHICKEN STIR-FRY WITH ALMOND SATAY SAUCE

Since it takes some work to chop everything up for this recipe, I like to make a huge batch, so that we can enjoy it for a few days. This stir-fry is so flavorful, delicious and satisfying! —AV

SERVES 6

2 tbsp (30 ml) unrefined, cold-pressed sesame oil, divided

1½ pounds (680 g) boneless, skinless chicken thighs, cut into 1½-inch (3.8-cm) chunks

Salt and pepper

2 carrots, chopped

1 onion, sliced

4 cups (280 g) broccoli, florets and stems diced up

2 zucchinis, chopped

1 red bell pepper, sliced

1 jalapeño pepper, sliced

4 cloves garlic, minced

2 cups (140 g) cremini mushrooms, sliced

1-inch (2.5-cm) piece fresh ginger, peeled and grated

1 cup (235 ml) Almond Satay Sauce (page 515)

Heat 1 tablespoon (15 ml) of sesame oil in a wok over medium-high heat. Add the chicken to the wok and generously salt and pepper it. Consistently stir the meat with a wooden spoon until it is cooked through and no longer pink inside, about 10 to 15 minutes. Remove the cooked chicken and set aside. If a lot of liquid has accumulated in the wok, drain it and wipe the wok out.

Add the additional tablespoon (15 ml) of sesame oil to the wok, then add the vegetables that require longer cooking times first: Add the carrots, onions and broccoli stems (if you are using them), cook until vegetables are softened, stirring constantly, about 5 to 7 minutes. Then add the broccoli florets, zucchinis, bell pepper, jalapeño, garlic, mushrooms and ginger. Generously salt and pepper the vegetables and cook until crunchy tender. Add the chicken back in and add the satay sauce. Stir until the chicken is mixed in with the vegetables and all the vegetables are well coated with sauce. Adjust salt and pepper to taste. Serve and enjoy!

CHEF'S TIP:

I recommend making the entire serving of Almond Satay Sauce and using the leftovers for other meals throughout the week, like lettuce wraps. Alternatively, you can halve the recipe and it will make the right amount for this stir-fry.

INDIAN-STYLE BAKED CHICKEN

Learning to cook with spices is a great way to add variety to a Paleo diet. This perfectly spiced recipe using whole-food ingredients adds an exotic touch to regular baked chicken. —KH

SERVES 8–10

FOR THE CURRY SAUCE

2 tbsp (30 ml) coconut oil, ghee or butter

½ onion, chopped

1 tsp (3 g) cumin seeds

1 tsp (3 g) ground cumin

1 tsp (3 g) ground coriander

1 tsp (3 g) ground turmeric

½ tsp garam masala

¼ tsp ground cinnamon

⅛ tsp ground cardamom

1 medium tomato, quartered

¼ cup (60 ml) full-fat coconut milk

4 cloves garlic

2-inch (5-cm) piece fresh ginger

1 tsp (3 g) sea salt

¼ cup (15 g) fresh cilantro

¼ cup (60 ml) Slow Cooker Chicken Broth (page 170), or water

¼ tsp cayenne, optional for a bit of heat

6 chicken drumsticks

6 bone-in chicken thighs

Melt fat of choice in a skillet and sauté onions for 5 minutes. Add cumin seeds and continue to cook until onions are translucent and beginning to brown, about 4 to 5 minutes. Add cumin powder, coriander, turmeric, garam masala, cinnamon and cardamom to onions and sauté for 2 to 3 minutes to bring out the flavor of the spices. If spices begin to stick, turn down heat and add a bit of fat. Remove from heat.

Place tomato, coconut milk, garlic, ginger, salt and cilantro into a blender. Pour broth, or water, into skillet with onions and carefully scrape all of the onions and spices into the blender as well. Purée until smooth to make curry sauce.

In a Dutch oven or covered casserole, pour curry sauce over chicken pieces and mix to thoroughly coat. Allow to marinate in fridge for at least 2 hours, longer is even better.

Preheat the oven to 350°F (180°F C, or gas mark 4). Bake marinated chicken, covered, for 40 minutes, stirring the chicken halfway through to evenly coat with curry sauce. Remove cover and bake another 20 to 25 minutes until chicken is cooked all the way through.

TERIYAKI CHICKEN THIGHS

The secret to tender, falling-off-the-bone chicken is patience. I like to cook my chicken at a lower temperature for a longer period of time. This recipe combines ginger, garlic and coconut aminos for a simple, yet impressive, dinner dish. —KH

SERVES 4–6

3 tbsp (45 ml) coconut aminos

1 tbsp (15 ml) apple cider vinegar

1 tbsp (15 ml) honey

2 cloves garlic, minced

½ tbsp (4 g) fresh grated ginger

¼ tsp sea salt

6 bone-in chicken thighs with skin on

Combine all marinade ingredients in a small bowl and mix well. Pour over chicken thighs and allow to marinate for at least 2 hours—overnight is even better.

Preheat the oven to 300°F (150°C, or gas mark 2). Arrange chicken thighs in the bottom of a heavy baking pan, making sure they are not overlapping. Bake, covered, for 50 minutes. Remove cover and broil for 2 to 3 minutes, until chicken thighs are beginning to brown.

PERFECTLY CRISPY OVEN–BAKED ASIAN SESAME CHICKEN WINGS

If you like Asian flavors, I think you'll love the Asian Sesame Sauce that coats these crispy wings. A few years ago, I discovered that baking powder is the secret ingredient for wings. It helps give the wings super crispy skin, but keeps the meat tender and moist. If you've never tried this method before, I think you'll be pleasantly surprised with the results. —KW

SERVES 4

FOR THE WINGS

2 tbsp (16 g) baking powder

½ teaspoon sea salt

3 pounds (1.4 kg) chicken wings, about 18, cut at joints and wing tips discarded

FOR THE ASIAN SESAME SAUCE

⅓ cup (80 ml) coconut aminos

1 tbsp (15 ml) balsamic vinegar

1 tsp (3 g) ground ginger

3 cloves garlic, minced

2 green onions, chopped

½ tsp red pepper flakes

Sesame seeds and extra green onion, for serving

Preheat oven to 250°F (120°C, or gas mark ½). Combine baking powder and salt in a bowl or resealable plastic bag. Pat wings dry with a paper towel. Toss wings in the baking powder/salt until evenly coated. Place the wings in a single layer on a wire rack that's on a baking sheet. Bake for 30 minutes on the lower-middle oven rack. After 30 minutes, move the wings to the upper middle rack, turn the oven heat to 425°F (220°C, or gas mark 7) and bake for 45 minutes.

While the wings are cooking, prepare the Asian Sesame Sauce by combining the coconut aminos, balsamic vinegar, ginger, garlic, green onions and red pepper flakes in a small bowl and stir until combined.

When the wings are done, remove them from the oven and toss with sauce. Let sit a few minutes to soak in the sauce. Toss again. Top with extra green onions and sesame seeds.

THAI BEEF SATAY WITH SPICY SUNFLOWER SEED SAUCE

This is my take on one of the most popular Thai food dishes. It is quite easy to make and it will be even better than the one you get at restaurants, without the unwanted ingredients! You can cook these on a BBQ or in the oven under the broiler! —VM

SERVES 6

Bamboo skewers

2 pounds (908 g) steak of choice, cut into 2-inch (5-cm)-long strips

FOR THE MARINADE

2 cups (470 ml) coconut milk

1 tbsp (15 ml) fish sauce (I use Red Boat)

1 tsp (3 g) curry powder

1 tbsp (8 g) ground turmeric

1 tbsp (8 g) fresh ginger, zested

FOR THE SAUCE

¼ cup (60 g) Thai red curry paste

2 tbsp (30 ml) chili oil

1 tbsp (8 g) cayenne pepper

1 tsp (3 g) ground cinnamon

½ tsp ground cumin

3 tbsp (45 ml) fish sauce (I use Red Boat)

4 cups (940 ml) coconut cream

3 tbsp (45 g) sunflower seed butter

Start by soaking the bamboo skewers in a bowl of water.

In a mixing bowl add the steak and all of the ingredients for the marinade. Mix well. Submerge the steak strips in the marinade and refrigerate for 4 hours. When the steak is done marinating, bring the BBQ to a medium-high heat.

Thread the steak with the skewers and grill them to the desired tenderness. Keep in mind that grass-fed meat cooks faster, so you want to make sure you don't overcook the meat. If cooking under the broiler, turn broiler on high, let the oven warm up for about 10 minutes, then place the skewers on a broiling pan and cook for about 10 to 15 minutes turning often; check often for doneness so to not overcook.

For the sauce, add the curry paste, chili oil, cayenne pepper, cinnamon, cumin, fish sauce and 1 cup (235 ml) of coconut cream to a sauce pan over medium heat and bring to a boil. Cook the sauce for 5 minutes, making sure the ingredients are well blended. Add the remaining coconut cream and continue to cook over low heat until the sauce has reduced. The sauce will take about 20 minutes to reduce. Right before you finish reducing the sauce, add the sunflower butter to the sauce and mix well.

Serve the beef satay hot off the grill, drizzled with sauce.

THAI CURRY CHICKEN

One thing that I love about Thai food is that most of the ingredients used are already Paleo-friendly. The coconut milk adds a rich creaminess that blends well with the curry spices and coats the chicken, broccoli and sweet potatoes. —HH

SERVES 4–6

1 large onion

8 cloves garlic

2 small to medium sweet potatoes

5 carrots

1 cup (70 g) thick-cut broccoli

2 boneless skinless chicken breasts

2 tbsp (30 g) ghee, lard or oil

½ tsp dried parsley

1¼ cups (290 ml) chicken broth

½ tsp ground cumin

¼ tsp paprika

½ tsp salt

½ tsp pepper

1½ tsp (4.5 g) curry powder

1¼ cups (290 ml) full-fat canned coconut milk

Dice the onions and garlic. Cut sweet potatoes, broccoli and chicken breasts into thick uniform pieces. The chicken breasts should be chopped into about 1- to 2-inch (2.5–5-cm) bite-sized cubes.

Heat the ghee in a large pan or pot. Add the onions and cook for a minute, then add the garlic and parsley and cook until the onions are almost translucent, about 3 to 5 minutes. Add the chopped sweet potatoes, carrots, broccoli and chicken breasts and cook for about a minute to brown a bit. Add the chicken broth, cumin, paprika, salt, pepper and 1 teaspoon (3 g) of curry powder and allow to simmer, covered, for about 10 minutes. Uncover and stir, then let cook uncovered until the potatoes and carrots are soft and the chicken is cooked through, about 5 to 10 minutes. Add the coconut milk and the remaining ½ teaspoon of curry powder and stir. Let cool and serve.

SPICY CURRIED BUTTERNUT SQUASH GALETTE

In addition to being the best way to repurpose leftover roasted squash, this galette is a rustic crowd-pleaser, due to the combination of crispy crust, sweet golden raisins and softened onion. —RB

SERVES 8

FOR THE FILLING

1 tbsp (15 ml) coconut oil

1 onion

1 tsp (3 g) fresh ginger

2 heaping cups (450 g) roasted butternut squash, cubed

1 tsp (3 g) curry powder

1 pinch of chili flakes

¾ tsp salt

2 tbsp (28 g) golden raisins

FOR THE CRUST

2¼ cups (270 g) almond flour

1¼ cups (150 g) arrowroot flour

1 tsp (3 g) ground coriander

1 tsp (3 g) ground cumin

¼ tsp cayenne pepper

¼ tsp salt

¼ cup (60 ml) coconut oil

4 eggs

Preheat oven to 350°F (180°C, or gas mark 4). To make the filling, heat the coconut oil in a medium skillet, and thinly slice the onion into rounds. Grate the fresh ginger over the onions. Sauté the mixture in the oil over medium heat until translucent, approximately 15 minutes. Remove from heat and stir in the roasted squash, curry powder, chili flakes, salt and golden raisins. Mix well.

To make the crust, combine the almond flour, arrowroot flour, coriander, cumin, cayenne and salt in a large bowl. Gradually stir in the coconut oil and eggs, and then form the dough into a ball.

Lay down parchment paper, and roll the dough out into a large disc approximately ¼-inch (6-mm) thick. Heap the squash mixture in the center, then use the edges of the parchment paper to fold the perimeter of the dough over to hold the filling in. Cook in the preheated oven for 30 minutes, or until the edges of the crust begin to brown. Serve warm.

CHEF'S TIP:

To roast the squash, peel and cut it into ½-inch (1.3-cm) cubes, mix with a few tablespoons (30 to 45 ml) of coconut oil and cook it spread on a cookie sheet at 350°F (180°C, or gas mark 4) for 30 minutes.

ASIAN CHICKEN HEARTS

No one will ever know you snuck organ meat into their diet with this recipe! It's absolutely rich and full of flavor. Serving chicken hearts sliced has the added benefit of masking the original shape of the heart, which can make some family members queasy. Kids will love this meal. —RM

SERVES 3–4

1½ pounds (680 g) chicken hearts

2 tbsp (30 ml) tamari (or coconut aminos)

1 tbsp (15 ml) rice wine vinegar

1 tsp (5 ml) sesame oil

1 tsp (5 ml) ginger juice (I use Ginger People)

1 tsp (3 g) red pepper flakes

4 cloves garlic, minced

2 slices thick-cut bacon

½ cup (60 g) leeks, sliced

½ cup (46 g) red and orange bell pepper, sliced

Wash the chicken hearts and slice them in thirds lengthwise. Add tamari, vinegar, sesame oil, ginger juice, red pepper flakes and minced garlic to a large bowl and mix well. Add the chicken hearts and marinate in the refrigerator, covered, for 1 to 2 hours.

Chop the bacon into small pieces and fry over medium heat in a fry pan until crispy, about 5 minutes. Scoop the bacon pieces out when finished and add the sliced leeks and chopped bell pepper. Cook down for about 5 minutes and then turn the heat up to medium-high and add the chicken hearts along with the marinade. Cook for 4 minutes or so until just cooked through, then add the bacon. Plate and serve.

CHICKEN MOFONGO

Mofongo is a Puerto Rican dish that's made by mashing fried green plantains and chicharrones, or pork cracklings, in a pilon—a mortar and pestle. The mashed plantains are then formed into a dome and surrounded by a red sauce or broth. In this recipe, I used bacon instead of chicharrones because it is easier and just as tasty. —RM

SERVES 4

4 green plantains

Water

1 tsp (3 g) salt

5 slices bacon

1 tbsp (8 g) minced garlic

½–1 cup (120–235 ml) chicken stock

Black pepper, to taste

Salt, to taste

FOR THE CHICKEN SAUCE

1 tbsp (15 ml) coconut oil

½ white onion, finely chopped

¼ green bell pepper, finely chopped

2 cloves garlic, chopped

2 tbsp (8 g) chopped cilantro, plus extra for garnish

1 (15-ounce [420-ml]) can tomato sauce

1 cup (235 ml) chicken stock

3 tbsp (45 ml) red wine vinegar

2 tsp (6 g) salt

1½ tsp (4 g) onion powder

1½ tsp (4 g) ground cumin

1½ tsp (4 g) garlic powder

1 tsp (3 g) oregano

1 tsp (3 g) coriander

½ tsp black pepper

½ tsp achiote seed powder

2 boneless chicken breasts, cubed

Peel the plantains by slicing a sharp knife down each ridge. Slide your fingers under and along the edge of each strip, slowly peeling the strip off. Cut the plantains into 1-inch (2.5-cm) chunks and soak covered in water with 1 teaspoon (3 g) salt for 15 minutes. Transfer plantains to a pot, covered with water, and boil for 15 to 20 minutes until tender. Drain.

Fry the bacon in a deep skillet and then reserve the slices on a paper towel. Use the rendered fat to fry the plantain chunks until golden.

Add the plantains, garlic, and salt and pepper to a pilon (mortar and pestle) and mash until fully incorporated. Slowly drizzle the chicken stock to keep it moist. If you are using a food processor instead of hand-mashing it, then you want it to be thick with a mashed potato texture; not too wet and not too dry. If it's too dry, add more chicken stock.

Meanwhile make the chicken sauce. In a deep skillet over medium heat, heat the coconut oil and sauté the white onion, green pepper, garlic and cilantro for about 4 minutes. Add the tomato sauce, chicken stock, red wine vinegar and seasonings. Cook for another 3 to 4 minutes. Add the cubed chicken and cook, covered, for 8 to 10 minutes.

Ladle the chicken sauce onto a plate. Form the warm plantain mixture into balls or use the pilon or small bowl to form the shape of a dome. Flip it over and place it in the center of the plate, dome side up, garnishing with extra cilantro.

SAMBAR (INDIAN ONION STEW)

This simple Indian onion stew is an exotic winner of a dish, with savory Indian spices, the tang of tamarind and the sweetness of onions and sweet potatoes. —RB

SERVES 6

2 tbsp (30 ml) coconut oil

1 tsp (3 g) black mustard seeds

1 tbsp (8 g) ground turmeric

2 tsp (4.5 g) ground coriander

2 tsp (4.5 g) ground cumin

2 tsp (4.5 g) salt

2 tsp (4.5 g) black pepper

3 pounds (1.4 kg) sweet potatoes, peeled and cut into 1-inch (2½-cm) cubes

2 quarts (1880 ml) chicken broth

2 (12-ounce [340-g]) bags pearl onions

3 tsp (15 g) tamarind paste

FOR THE GARNISH

Red pepper flakes

Mustard seeds

Cilantro

Heat the coconut oil in a large pot over medium heat. Add the mustard seeds and then partially cover the pot when they pop. Once the mustard seeds have popped, add the turmeric, coriander, cumin, salt and black pepper.

Stir the spices in the oil and then add the sweet potatoes, broth, onions and tamarind. Stir thoroughly, bring to a boil and then lower the heat and simmer for 30 minutes.

Remove the lid and let the stew reduce for a further 30 minutes, or until thickened to your preference. Serve hot.

BASIL BEET BURGERS WITH LEMON GARLIC AIOLI

Beets and basil are perfect for each other. Topped with a bit of zesty lemon garlic aioli, these light little patties make a unique and flavorful meal. —KH

MAKES 16–18

FOR THE LEMON GARLIC AIOLI

½ cup (125 g) Homemade Mayonnaise (page 496)

2 tbsp (30 ml) fresh lemon juice

¼ tsp sea salt

1 clove garlic, crushed

1 tbsp (4 g) fresh basil, cilantro or parsley, finely chopped

Coconut oil, ghee or butter for cooking

½ medium onion

½ cup (30 g) fresh basil leaves

3 cups (360 g) shredded raw beets, washed and trimmed

3 eggs, beaten

1 tsp (3 g) sea salt

½ cup (60 g) almond flour or 2 tbsp (16 g) coconut flour

To make lemon garlic aioli, mix all ingredients together until smooth and creamy. Place in fridge until ready to serve.

To make beet burgers, finely chop onion and basil leaves and add to shredded beets. Add salt and eggs. Mix well. Add either almond flour or coconut flour. Mix to combine.

Heat skillet over medium-high heat and cover bottom of pan liberally with fat of choice. Form small patties about ½-inch (1.3-cm) thick and drop into pan. Cook patties 3 to 4 minutes on one side, until crispy. Flip, and cook other side. Press them down a bit to make sure they are not too thick. The center will not cook well if too thick. Serve immediately with lemon garlic aioli.

ROASTED CELERIAC WITH SMOKED PANCETTA, MUSHROOMS AND LEEK

Seasonal fall vegetables and salty pancetta come together to make this an absolutely delicious meal. —NK

SERVES 4–6

2 (1-pound [454-g]) celeriac, thick outer layer removed and cut into ⅓-inch (2-cm) chunks

½ tbsp (3 g) dried thyme

½ tsp sea salt

½ tsp black pepper, divided

1 tbsp (15 ml) ghee, melted

7 ounces (196 g) smoked pancetta, diced

1 medium leek (white and light green parts only), sliced into thin rounds

9 ounces (252 g) mushrooms, sliced

Preheat oven to 425°F (220°C, or gas mark 7). Line a large baking sheet with parchment paper. Place diced celeriac onto the baking sheet and add the dried thyme, sea salt and ¼ teaspoon black pepper. Mix well. Pour over the melted ghee. Place in the preheated oven for 40 to 45 minutes, making sure to turn the diced celeriac halfway through.

While the celeriac is baking place a large skillet on medium heat. Once hot, add the diced pancetta and cook until it starts to crisp up and the fat starts to render, about 5 minutes. Once crispy, remove the pancetta onto a paper-lined plate, reserving the leftover fat in the skillet. Add the sliced leek and cook for 5 minutes until just softened. Add the sliced mushrooms and cook for another 5 to 8 minutes. Season with ¼ teaspoon black pepper. Add the pancetta back in and lower the heat. Add the roasted celeriac to the skillet and mix everything together. Serve warm.

CAULIFLOWER AND GHEE SOUFFLÉ

An easy Cauliflower Ghee Soufflé that makes a great impression. With this recipe, you get all the buttery flavor without the dairy. —VM

SERVES 6

1 whole cauliflower

Ghee

6 eggs

1 cup (235 ml) coconut cream

Sea salt and black pepper to taste

3 egg whites

Preheat the oven to 400°F (200°C, or gas mark 6). Cut the cauliflower into florets, rinsing them off, and then spread them onto a baking sheet. Place a dab of ghee onto each floret, and then season with sea salt. Place the cauliflower in the oven and roast the florets for about 20 minutes, or until they get a nice golden brown.

While the cauliflower is roasting, take the 6 eggs as well as the coconut cream, and add them to a blender. Season the egg mixture with sea salt and black pepper, and then blend until nice and frothy. In a bowl, beat the egg whites until they create nice, foamy peaks. Gently fold the egg whites into the egg mixture until they are nicely combined.

Once the cauliflower florets have cooled from roasting in the oven, slowly and gently mix them into the egg mixture so as to not to deflate the egg mixture. Generously grease the soufflé dish with the ghee. Pour in the cauliflower egg mixture, leaving an inch (2.5 cm) of room at the top to allow for rising while cooking. Bake the soufflé for about 30 minutes, or until nicely browned on top. Serve immediately.

SHREDDED RED CABBAGE AND APPLE HASH

The flavor of sweet apples is mixed with the savory notes of ground beef and red cabbage to make this a delicious and easy to prepare meal that is full of flavor. —NK

SERVES 4

2 pounds (908 g) red cabbage, shredded

2 apples, cored and diced into chunks

2 tbsp (30 ml) raw apple cider vinegar

1 tsp (6 g) sea salt, divided

½ tsp black pepper, divided

2 tbsp (30 g) ghee, divided (can substitute coconut oil)

1 medium red onion, sliced into half moons

1 pound (454 g) ground beef

1 tsp (3 g) ground cinnamon

Preheat oven to 400°F (200°C, or gas mark 6). Line a large baking dish with parchment paper. In a large mixing bowl add the shredded red cabbage and apple. Pour over the raw apple cider vinegar and mix. Season with ½ teaspoon sea salt and ¼ teaspoon black pepper. Stir to mix. Pour mixture into the prepared baking dish and drizzle with 1 tablespoon (15 g) ghee or coconut oil. Place in the oven and bake for 35 to 40 minutes or until the cabbage and apples are softened and the top layer is roasted.

While the cabbage and apples are baking in the oven, heat a large skillet on medium heat and add 1 tablespoon (15 g) ghee or coconut oil. Add the sliced onion and cook for 10 minutes. Add the ground beef and break up the meat as it cooks. Once the meat is almost browned through, about 8 to 10 minutes, add in ½ teaspoon sea salt, ¼ teaspoon black pepper and the ground cinnamon. Stir to mix. Cook until the meat is done then remove from the heat. Remove the baking dish from the oven and mix in the meat. Taste and add more salt and pepper before serving.

CHEF'S TIP:
If you have any leftovers you can enjoy them the next day with a fried egg on top for breakfast.

SWEET POTATO, APPLE AND FENNEL HASH

This is a delicious fall-inspired dish. Try it out during apple season for a different way to add apples to your meals. —NK

SERVES 2–4

2 tbsp (30 g) ghee, divided

1 medium sweet potato, peeled and diced

Sea salt to taste

1 small red onion, diced

1 pound (454 g) ground beef

3 small fennel bulbs, cored and diced

3 small apples, cored and diced

1 tbsp (8 g) ground cinnamon

½ tsp ground allspice

¼ tsp ground cloves

¼ tsp ground nutmeg

¼ tsp ground ginger

Heat 1 tablespoon (15 g) ghee in a large skillet over medium heat. Once the ghee is melted, add the sweet potato and stir to cook for 5 minutes. Sprinkle in some sea salt and continue to cook for another 10 to 15 minutes. Once the sweet potato is softened but still holding its shape remove onto a clean plate and set aside, covered to keep warm.

In the same skillet heat another 1 tablespoon (15 g) ghee over medium-low heat. Add the onion and sauté for 5 minutes until softened. Add the ground beef and break up the meat as it cooks. When the meat is nearly cooked through, around 8 to 10 minutes, season with some sea salt. Add the diced fennel and stir through. Cook for another 5 minutes then add the apple and cook for another 5 minutes. Add the sweet potato back to the skillet. Add the cinnamon, allspice, cloves, nutmeg and ginger. Stir well. Turn the heat down to low and cook for a few more minutes. Serve warm.

GRAIN-FREE DELICATA SQUASH CROSTATA

Try this grain-free take on a traditional crostata. Made with minimal ingredients and filled with the flavors of sweet delicata squash and earthy sage, this is sure to be a winner at your table. —NK

SERVES 6–8

2 pounds (908 g) yuca root

¼ cup (60 ml) avocado oil

1 pound (454 g) delicata squash

3 tbsp (24 g) coconut flour, optional

8 large fresh sage leaves

Sea salt and black pepper, to taste

Preheat oven to 425°F (220°C, or gas mark 7). Line a large baking sheet with parchment paper.

Place a large pot of water with a lid to boil on the stove. While the water is getting ready slice the tops and ends off the yuca. Slice off the thick outer layer on the yuca, making sure to remove any brown or blemished spots. Then cut into medium-sized chunks. Carefully place the yuca into the pot of boiling water and cover with the lid. Boil yuca for 20 to 25 minutes or until easily pierced with a fork.

Strain the yuca and allow to cool for 5 minutes. Place in a high-powered blender or food processor with the avocado oil. Blend the yuca until it reaches a "dough-like" consistency. Remove dough onto a clean surface lined with parchment paper and leave it to cool.

Slice the ends off the delicata. Slice the squash lengthwise and remove the seeds with a spoon. Place it flesh-side down on a cutting board and cut crosswise into thin slices. Set aside.

Remove any of the tough fibrous pieces left behind in the yuca dough after cooling. Allow it to cool for 10–15 minutes, then check the dough for stickiness. If the yuca is still a little sticky, sprinkle 1 tablespoon (8 g) coconut flour at a time and press into the dough to help absorb any stickiness.

Use your hands to shape the yuca dough into a circular or oval shape, about ½-inch (1.3-cm) thick. Spread the delicata squash in the center of the dough, avoiding the outside edges. Stack the fresh sage leaves on top of each other then roll into a cigar shape, use a sharp knife or kitchen shears to slice the sage into thin strips. Add the sage strips evenly on top of the delicata squash. Using your hands, start folding the outside edges of the yuca dough to create a raised edge all around the dough. Season the squash all over with sea salt and freshly cracked black pepper. Carefully place onto the parchment-lined baking sheet. Place in the oven and bake for 30 to 40 minutes or until the edges of the dough become crispy and the delicata squash is softened. Remove from the oven and allow to cool before slicing and serving.

CHEF'S TIP:

I learned about making yuca dough from my friend Jennifer over at Predominantly Paleo. This dough is perfect for those who have nut or egg allergies and for those who are following the Autoimmune Paleo Protocol.

ROASTED STUFFED DELICATA SQUASH

I love to pair sweet and savory flavors together and one of the best ways to do this is to add dried fruits to a savory dish as I did with this recipe. —NK

SERVES 4

4 small delicata squash cut in half, seeds removed

1 tsp (6 g) sea salt, divided

2 tbsp (30 g) ghee, divided

¼ cup (60 ml) water

1 small red onion, diced

2 small cloves garlic, minced

1 pound (454 g) ground beef

¼ tsp black pepper

¼ tsp ground nutmeg

3 ounces (84 g) ground cherries

2 ounces (56 g) pecans, roughly chopped

(continued)

Preheat oven to 400°F (200°C, or gas mark 6). Line a large baking tray with parchment paper. Place delicata squash halves cut-side up onto the baking tray. Season with ½ teaspoon sea salt. Pour 1 tablespoon (15 g) ghee over the delicata squash halves. Pour the water into the baking tray. Bake for 30 to 40 minutes or until the delicata squash are easily pierced with a fork.

Heat a medium skillet on medium-low heat. Add 1 tablespoon (15 g) ghee and the onion and cook until softened, about 10 minutes. Add the garlic and cook for another minute. Add the beef and break it up as it cooks. Add the nutmeg, ½ teaspoon sea salt and black pepper and mix. Add the ground cherries and pecans. Once the meat is cooked through, about 8 to 10 minutes, remove from the heat. Spoon the mixture into the baked delicata squash and serve warm.

CHEF'S TIP:
Save any leftover meat mixture to enjoy the next day.

ROASTED ROOT VEGETABLE FRITTATA

One thing I can never get enough of are roasted root vegetables. From carrots, to parsnips, to beets and more, roasting brings out a deliciously sweet flavor from these vegetables. Throw in some eggs and you have a tasty frittata on your hands that everyone will be sure to love. —NK

SERVES 6–8

5 ounces (140 g) diced parsnips

9 ounces (252 g) diced carrots

6 ounces (168 g) diced beets

1 tsp (6 g) sea salt

¼ tsp black pepper

2 tbsp (30 g) ghee, divided

3 sprigs fresh rosemary

1 medium red onion, diced

1 pound (454 g) ground beef

1 tbsp (8 g) finely chopped fresh rosemary

8 eggs

Sea salt and black pepper, to taste

Preheat oven to 375°F (190°C, or gas mark 5). Line a large baking tray with parchment paper. Place chopped parsnips, carrots and beets into a medium-sized mixing bowl, add 1 teaspoon (6 g) sea salt and ¼ teaspoon black pepper. Mix and pour in a single layer into the baking tray. Drizzle with 1 tablespoon (15 ml) melted ghee. Add the rosemary sprigs on top. Bake for 30 to 40 minutes.

While the vegetables are cooking, heat 1 tablespoon (15 g) ghee in a 12-inch (30.5-cm) cast iron skillet or 12-inch (30.5-cm) oven-proof skillet over medium-low heat. Once heated, add the diced onion and cook for 10 minutes until softened and turning golden. Add the ground beef and break up the meat as it cooks. Season with the chopped fresh rosemary, sea salt and black pepper to taste. Continue to cook until the meat has browned, around 8 to 10 minutes. Remove from the heat and set aside until the vegetables are done.

Once vegetables have finished baking, stir them into the meat mixture. Turn the oven temperature down to 350°F (180°C, or gas mark 4). In a medium-sized mixing bowl whisk the eggs until well mixed. Pour the eggs over the meat and vegetable mixture in the skillet. Carefully place in the oven and bake for 18 to 20 minutes or until the eggs are set. Remove from the oven and allow to cool before slicing and serving.

BUTTERNUT BAKE

Seasoned with the warm spices of fall, this gratin is reminiscent of Thanksgiving brunch but you are welcome to serve it at any time of the year. Feel free to use other types of winter squash or even sweet potatoes for variety. —JC

SERVES 4

1½ pounds (680 g) butternut squash, chopped into ¾-inch (2-cm) cubes

¾ tsp dried sage

¼ tsp sea salt

¼ tsp black pepper

1 tbsp (15 g) ghee or bacon fat

2 large shallots, sliced

1 pound (454 g) raw sausage, casing removed and crumbled

1 bunch spinach

¾ cup (180 ml) Homemade Coconut Milk (page 503)

2 tbsp (16 g) toasted pecans, chopped

Preheat oven to 350°F (180°C, or gas mark 4).

In a large bowl, add butternut squash and season with sage, sea salt and black pepper. Toss to combine and set aside.

Add ghee to a cast iron pan over medium-high heat. Add shallots and sauté for 1 minute. Add the sausage and sauté for 5 minutes until it starts to brown. Use the back of a spatula to break large chunks into smaller pieces while sautéing so that the sausage meat cooks evenly. Add butternut squash and cook for 3 minutes. Add spinach and mix for a minute until the spinach wilts. Turn off heat. Pour in coconut milk and mix everything to combine.

Cover the pan with foil. Bake it in the oven for 30 minutes. Top with toasted pecans and let it cool for 5 to 10 minutes before serving.

GRAIN-FREE "SPAGHETTI" BOATS

A Paleo version of a family favorite. The squash, zucchini, greens and meat make this meal so hearty you won't miss the real pasta. —KH

SERVES 4

2 medium-sized spaghetti squash

1 pound (454 g) ground meat

1 medium zucchini, chopped into ¼-inch (6-mm) pieces

1 cup (70 g) kale, spinach or chard, finely chopped

3 cups (750 g) homemade or store-bought marinara or tomato sauce

Cook spaghetti squash until tender. Cut the squash in half lengthwise and cook in slow cooker on high for 2 to 2½ hours with about an inch (2.5 cm) of water in the bottom. Or you can bake the squash halves skin-side up in a shallow baking dish for 40 minutes in a preheated 375°F (190°C, or gas mark 5) oven or until pierced easily with a fork.

When cool enough to handle, scoop the seeds from the center of the cooked spaghetti squash and discard. Set the squash aside.

Brown the ground meat in a medium pan. Add the zucchini and greens. Add the tomato sauce. Simmer on medium heat for 15 minutes, stirring occasionally.

With a fork, gently scrape the strands of the squash into the tomato/veggie mixture and mix thoroughly. Fill all 4 spaghetti squash shells with the mixture. Bake for 25 minutes on 375°F (190°C, or gas mark 5).

SPAGHETTI SQUASH PIZZA ROLL

Spaghetti squash can be drained and mixed with eggs and coconut oil to make a flexible, plant-based crust. Stuff the roll with your favorite sauce, meat and vegetable toppings and enjoy the taste of pizza! —RB

SERVES 4

2 spaghetti squash (approximately 3 pounds [1.4 kg] each)

½ pound (227 g) sausage meat

2 eggs

¼ tsp salt

⅓ cup (40 g) coconut flour

⅓ cup (80 g) sugar-free pizza sauce

1 (2.25-ounce [63-g]) can sliced black olives

Handful spinach

Preheat the oven to 350°F (180°C, or gas mark 4). Line a cookie sheet with parchment paper and set aside.

Pierce the spaghetti squash several times on each side with a sharp knife, and place on a plate. Microwave on high for 8 minutes, then rotate top-side down and microwave for another 8 minutes (it may be necessary to cook the spaghetti squash one at a time). Slice open the two spaghetti squashes, being careful of the hot escaping steam, and set aside to cool.

While they cool, cook the sausage meat in a dry skillet over medium heat until no longer pink. Drain off any fat, and set aside.

Once the squash are cool enough to handle, remove the seeds, scrape the flesh from the skin, and squeeze the excess water out of the spaghetti squash strands using your hands or by rolling tightly in paper towels.

The spaghetti squash is drained enough when the strands have been reduced to 1½ cups (383 g) total. Pulse the drained squash, eggs, salt and coconut flour in a food processor for 1 minute until thoroughly mixed and the spaghetti squash threads are chopped very fine.

Transfer to the parchment paper-lined cookie sheet, and roll out into a rectangle approximately 12-inches (30.5-cm) long and 6-inches (15-cm) wide.

Smooth the pizza sauce over the spaghetti squash crust, then top with the cooked sausage meat, the sliced olives, and the handful of spinach. Using the edge of the parchment paper, begin to roll the edge of the crust up over the toppings.

Continue rolling until you have a tight cylinder. Bake in the preheated oven for 45 minutes, until the crust is cooked through. Slice and serve warm.

CHEF'S TIP:

These ingredients are just suggestions to get you started, as far as toppings are concerned. Other suggestions include Brussels sprouts, smoked pancetta, bacon, pineapple, roasted red peppers or sun-dried tomatoes, broccoli rabe, mushrooms, chili flakes and roasted jalapeños.

SPAGHETTI SQUASH BACON BOWL

This is a simple entrée that still delivers on presentation and taste. The rich flavors of sun-dried tomatoes, bacon and pine nuts round out the subtler taste of the spaghetti squash and spinach (the latter adds a pop of green and a nutritious boost to a hearty meal). Pile back into one of the hollowed out squash halves for a fun serving style! —RB

SERVES 2

5 ounces (140 g) chopped spinach

1 small spaghetti squash, approximately 1½ pounds (680 g)

5 slices bacon, cooked and crumbled

½ cup (60 g) oil-packed sun-dried tomatoes, drained and chopped

1 tsp (3 g) chili flakes

¼ tsp salt

2 tbsp (16 g) pine nuts

To wilt the spinach, stir in a dry skillet over medium heat until soft, very dark green and any liquid has cooked off, approximately 10 minutes.

Place the spaghetti squash on a plate, then prick 4 to 5 times on various sides with the tip of a sharp knife. Microwave on high for 4 minutes, then rotate top-side down and microwave for 4 minutes more. Remove and let cool enough to handle.

Once the squash is cool, cut in half lengthwise. Scoop out the seeds and discard. Scrape out the cooked strands and transfer to a large mixing bowl. Stir in the crumbled bacon, wilted spinach, sun-dried tomatoes, chili flakes and salt.

Pile back into one of the squash halves or into a serving platter, and top with the pine nuts.

SPAGHETTI SQUASH WITH SPICY CAVEMAN SAUCE

Another Paleo-talian creation! A little bit of Bolognese and a little bit of Amatriciana, with just a touch of creaminess and a spicy kick. Enjoy! —VM

SERVES 4

1 large spaghetti squash

1 pound (454 g) ground beef, at room temperature

2–3 slices bacon, chopped in small pieces

2 carrots, small, chopped

1 pint (300 g) Italian tomato purée

Sea salt and pepper to taste

2 small chilies, like pepperoncini or chile de arbol

¼ cup (60 ml) coconut cream

Ghee or butter

Preheat the oven to 350°F (180°C, or gas mark 4). Cut the squash in half and scrape out the seeds with a spoon. Rub the face of the squash with some coconut oil and lay the squash face down on a foil-lined baking sheet. Roast the squash for about 40 minutes or until soft and shreddable with a fork.

Crumble the ground beef into a hot pan, letting it sit and brown on the bottom. Once the meat has browned on the bottom, start stirring the ground beef, breaking it up and browning on all sides as you go. When the meat is completely browned, remove the meat from the pan and set aside.

Now lower the heat to medium and sauté the bacon pieces for about 5 minutes. While the bacon is sautéing, chop up the carrots and add them to the pan. Sauté the bacon and carrots for another 5 minutes, or until the bacon is well done.

Add the ground beef back into the pan with the bacon and carrots and the tomato purée. Salt and pepper the meat mixture and stir well. Add the chilies, either whole or crushed, depending on the level of spiciness you desire. If you add the chili whole it will be less spicy and it can also be removed before eating.

Reduce the heat to low and let the mixture simmer for about an hour. If it begins to get dry, add some water and continue simmering. Before removing from the flame, add the coconut cream and stir well.

Shred the roasted squash into noodle-like strands using a fork while scraping it out of its shell. You can toss the shredded squash with some ghee or butter, lightly seasoning it with some salt and pepper. Once you are done seasoning the squash, place a generous serving in a bowl, topping with the tasty sauce, and serve immediately.

SPAGHETTI SQUASH WITH CILANTRO–MACADAMIA PESTO

Although uncooked fennel has a licorice flavor, once it is cooked, the flavor becomes much more mild and the texture becomes much softer, adding a very pleasant and refreshing flavor to this Paleo spaghetti. I also recommend making the pesto in advance to allow the flavors to meld and intensify. —AV

SERVES 4

FOR THE CILANTRO-MACADAMIA PESTO

2 cups (120 g) cilantro, firmly packed

1 cup (60 g) fresh basil

3 cloves garlic, chopped

¼ cup (25 g) green onion, chopped (use mostly green parts)

½ tsp paprika

½ cup (75 g) macadamia nuts

½ cup (120 ml) olive oil

Zest from 1 lemon

Juice from 1 lemon

Salt and pepper to taste

1 large spaghetti squash

1 tbsp (15 g) ghee

1 fennel bulb, diced

2 pounds (908 g) boneless, skinless chicken, cooked and chopped

Cherry tomatoes and fresh basil for garnish

In a food processor, blend all of the pesto ingredients to desired consistency. Adjust salt and pepper to taste. Preheat the oven to 375°F (190°C, or gas mark 5). Place the spaghetti squash in a baking dish and cook for 30 minutes or until you can easily pierce it with a knife. Remove from oven and cut lengthwise. Place back into baking the dish, rind-side up. Add ½ inch (1.3 cm) of water to baking dish. Cook in the oven for 20 minutes, or until you can easily lift the strands. Let cool for 20 minutes.

Discard seeds and use a fork to pull apart the stands of spaghetti squash. They should come off very easily. Place the strands of spaghetti squash in a separate bowl. Heat ghee over medium heat in a heavy-bottomed pan. Add fennel and sauté until soft, about 5 minutes, then add cooked chicken and sauté until chicken is warm. Add spaghetti squash and some pesto to the pan. Use enough pesto to nicely coat all the squash and chicken. Serve the rest of the pesto on the side, or save it to top over lettuce wraps and eggs throughout the week. Garnish with tomatoes and fresh basil.

CHEF'S TIP:
You can use whichever chicken parts you prefer; leftover rotisserie chicken works well for this too!

PESTO BACON SPAGHETTI SQUASH

A fun combination of spaghetti squash, pesto and bacon. The spaghetti squash mimics the texture of traditional grain pasta, making it a great way to add variety to a Paleo diet. —KH

SERVES 4

2 spaghetti squash

1 tsp (5 ml) coconut oil or ghee

1 bunch fresh basil, leaves only

¼ cup (60 ml) olive oil

1 tsp (5 ml) fresh lemon juice

1 clove garlic, minced

¼ tsp sea salt

¼ cup (32 g) hemp seeds or raw pumpkin seeds

4 strips cooked bacon, chopped

Preheat the oven to 400°F (200°F C, or gas mark 6). Cut the squash in half lengthwise, scrape out the seeds and place skin-side up on a greased baking sheet. Lightly oil the outside skin as well. Bake for 35 to 45 minutes, or until fork-tender. Allow to cool slightly.

Place basil, olive oil, lemon, garlic and salt into a food processor. Process until smooth. You will need to scrape the sides a few times. Add the hemp seeds or pumpkin seeds and pulse until desired pesto consistency is reached. Adjust for salt and lemon.

Once squash are a bit cool, scrape out the tender noodles into a large bowl and toss with the pesto. Fill squash shells with pesto noodles, garnish with chopped bacon and serve.

SAVORY SWEET POTATO SLICE

Most of us know how good nutrient-dense foods like liver are, but for a lot of us adding these foods into our diet can be tricky. Here's a delicious and simple way to get liver into you and the best part is by the time this Savory Sweet Potato Slice is cooked, you won't even notice the liver is there. —NK

SERVES 6–8

1 pound (454 g) ground beef

4 ounces (112 g) beef or lamb liver, ground up in a food processor

2 tbsp (30 g) ghee

1 medium red onion, diced

1 clove garlic, minced

Sea salt and black pepper, to taste

10 eggs

¼ tsp baking soda

1 red bell pepper, diced

7 ounces (196 g) mushrooms, diced

1 pound (454 g) sweet potato, grated

½ tbsp (4 g) dried oregano

½ tsp red pepper flakes

Preheat oven to 375°F (190°C, or gas mark 5). Line a 10½ × 7-inch (26.7 × 17.8-cm) baking dish with parchment paper. In a medium-sized mixing bowl add the ground beef and ground liver. Mix to combine. Heat a large skillet over medium heat, add the ghee. Once heated, add the onion and stir to cook until softened, about 5 to 8 minutes. Add the garlic and stir for another minute. Add the meat mixture and use a spoon to break up the meat as it cooks. When almost browned, season the meat with sea salt and black pepper to taste. When the meat is just cooked through, turn off the heat and set the skillet aside to cool.

In a large mixing bowl add the eggs and baking soda. Whisk the eggs until well mixed and season the eggs with sea salt and black pepper. Add the meat mixture along with the diced bell pepper, mushrooms and grated sweet potato to the eggs. Mix well then season with dried oregano and red pepper flakes. Pour mixture into the prepared baking dish. Bake for 45 to 50 minutes. Remove from the oven and allow to cool before serving.

SWEET POTATO PATTIES

Enjoy these tasty Sweet Potato Patties made with beef and warming spices like cinnamon and cumin. Eat with a green salad on the side or serve up in some lettuce for some bun-less burgers. —NK

SERVES 4

1 large sweet potato

1 pound (454 g) ground beef

1 tsp (3 g) ground cinnamon

½ tsp ground cumin

½ tsp sea salt

¼ tsp ground cloves

¼ tsp black pepper

Ghee or coconut oil, for frying

Preheat oven to 400°F (200°C, or gas mark 6). Using a fork poke holes all over the sweet potato. Wrap sweet potato in aluminum foil. Place sweet potato onto the middle rack of the oven. Bake for 40 to 50 minutes or until easily pierced with a fork. Remove from the oven and allow to cool before removing the skin and mashing. Place mashed sweet potato in the fridge for an hour to cool completely.

Remove from the fridge and place in a mixing bowl with the rest of the ingredients. Mix well. Heat a 10- to 12-inch (25- to 30.5-cm) skillet on medium-high heat. Add some ghee or coconut oil. While the skillet is heating, use your hands to form the sweet potato mixture into balls, about golf-ball sized, then flatten them out to form patties. Cook in batches for around 6 to 7 minutes per side.

SOUTHWESTERN–STYLE STUFFED SWEET POTATOES

The combination of sweet potatoes and spiced meats in this easy dinner dish really works. The rich flavors of the cumin and chili powder make the meal. The best part is adding all of the fun toppings. —KH

SERVES 4

4 large sweet potatoes

1 tbsp (15 g) butter, ghee or coconut oil

¼ onion, chopped fine

½ pound (227 g) ground beef, bison or turkey

½ tsp sea salt

1 tsp (3 g) ground cumin

1 tsp (3 g) chili powder

2 tbsp (30 ml) filtered water

2 cups (140 g) baby spinach, chopped

FOR THE SPICY AVOCADO SAUCE

1 ripe avocado, mashed

1 tbsp (15 ml) olive oil

Juice from 1 lime or lemon

Pinch of sea salt

A few dashes of your favorite hot sauce

FOR THE GARNISH

Green onions

Cilantro

1 tomato, chopped

Preheat the oven to 400°F (200°C, or gas mark 6). Pierce each sweet potato several times with the tines of a fork. Place the sweet potatoes on a rimmed baking sheet, and bake until tender and completely soft, about 45 to 60 minutes.

Prepare avocado sauce by combining all avocado sauce ingredients and mixing until creamy and smooth. Set aside.

About 30 minutes into baking the sweet potatoes, melt fat of choice in skillet and sauté onions for 7 to 9 minutes until they're beginning to brown. Add ground meat and continue to cook until meat is completely browned, about 8 to 10 minutes. Add salt, cumin, chili powder and water to skillet. Mix to combine and cook another 5 minutes on low-medium, until water is all cooked off, stirring occasionally. Add chopped spinach and cook another couple of minutes until spinach is wilted. Cover and remove from heat.

When sweet potatoes are done, make a slit in the top of each sweet potato and squeeze the ends to create a little well inside. Gently loosen up some of the inside of each sweet potato with a fork. Then top with a big mound of spiced ground meat. Drizzle with spicy avocado sauce, and garnish with green onions, cilantro and tomato. Serve with fresh green salad or steamed greens.

BUFFALO RANCH STUFFED PEPPERS

This is one of the most popular dinner recipes on my blog! It's also a personal and family favorite. I recommend serving these stuffed peppers with Super Easy Guacamole (page 190). —KW

SERVES 4

½ tsp each: dried parsley, dried dill, dried chives, garlic powder, onion powder

4 chicken breasts

1 medium onion, sliced

Sea salt and pepper, to taste

Extra butter, ghee or other fat of choice for greasing and baking

¼ cup (58 g) butter or ghee

½ cup (120 ml) hot sauce

4 peppers, tops cut off and seeds cleaned out

Super Easy Guacamole (page 190), optional, for serving

Preheat oven to 350°F (180°C, or gas mark 4). Mix the dried spices together. Place the chicken breast and sliced onions in a single layer on a greased or parchment paper-lined baking pan. Sprinkle the entire pan with dried spices. Salt and pepper, to taste. Place a small pat of butter or other fat of choice over each chicken breast. Bake for 25 to 30 minutes or until chicken is cooked through.

While chicken is cooking, melt ¼ cup (58 g) butter in a pot over medium-low heat. Once melted add in hot sauce and stir. Set aside.

Once chicken is cooked, run a knife through the chicken and onions until chicken is in small bite-size pieces. Combine chicken with the hot sauce mixture. Spoon chicken mixture evenly in all 4 peppers. Place stuffed peppers in a baking pan. Bake for 35 to 40 minutes or until peppers are softened to your liking. Serve with Super Easy Guacamole.

CARROTS ALLA CARBONARA

Pasta carbonara is an Italian dish characterized by a mixture of bacon, cheese, egg and black pepper added to the pasta to make it thick, savory and hearty. This is the grain-free and dairy-free version, but it doesn't skimp on flavor. —RB

SERVES 2

4 slices bacon

8 carrots

1 onion

2 cloves garlic

4 tbsp (60 ml) coconut milk

2 eggs

½ cup (75 g) peas

1 tsp (3 g) salt

1 tsp (3 g) black pepper

¼ cup (15 g) chopped parsley

(continued)

Heat a large skillet over medium heat. Cook the bacon until crispy, then set aside to drain and cool. Pour off all but 1 tablespoon (15 ml) of the bacon fat, reserved in the skillet.

Using a spiralizer or peeler, cut the carrots into thin strands, set aside. Dice the onion and garlic then sauté the onions, garlic and carrots in the bacon fat (stirring frequently to avoid burning and sticking) until very soft and caramelized, about 15 to 20 minutes. Remove from the heat.

Whisk the coconut milk and eggs together, then add to the carrot mixture with the peas, salt and pepper. Mix thoroughly, and then crumble the bacon on top. Top with the parsley, and serve warm.

PARSNIP FRA DIAVOLO

This is a twist on the classic Italian dish Fra Diavolo using parsnips in place of spaghetti and fresh herbs to intensify the flavor of the warming, spicy tomato sauce. Sub lobster, crab or chicken for the shrimp if preferred. —RB

SERVES 2

2 pounds (908 g) parsnips

4 tbsp (60 ml) coconut oil, divided

½ pound (227 g) shrimp

4 cloves garlic

1 tsp (3 g) chili flakes

½ tsp salt

2 cups (500 g) tomato purée

¼ cup (15 g) basil

¼ cup (15 g) parsley

¼ cup (15 g) mint

Wash and peel the parsnips. Using a spiralizer or a vegetable peeler, process the parsnips into thin strips. Melt 2 tablespoons (30 ml) of coconut oil in a large skillet over medium high heat. Add the parsnips and cook, stirring frequently, until softened and reduced to approximately half size (approximately 20 minutes). Transfer the parsnips to a plate, then melt 1 tablespoon (15 ml) of coconut oil in the skillet.

Peel and devein the shrimp, then fry in the skillet for 5 minutes over medium heat until pink. Transfer out of the skillet, then melt the last tablespoon (15 ml) of coconut oil over medium-high heat.

Dice the garlic cloves, fry for 1 minute until golden and fragrant. Add the chili flakes and salt and cook for one minute more. Add the tomato purée, and cook, stirring frequently to minimize spatters, for 10 minutes.

Dice the herbs, add them to the spicy tomato mixture along with the cooked shrimp and parsnips. Stir to thoroughly combine the sauce with the other ingredients, then serve warm.

PARSNIP "PASTA" PUTTANESCA

This parsnip "pasta" puttanesca is a grain-free re-creation of an Italian classic. —RB

SERVES 4

4 medium parsnips, washed and peeled

1 tbsp (15 ml) coconut oil

1 onion

3 cloves garlic

1 tbsp (8 g) capers

4 anchovy fillets

1 cup (250 g) diced tomatoes

¼ tsp salt, plus more to taste

1 tsp (3 g) red chili flakes

Handful flat-leaf parsley

Black pepper

Using a spiralizer or vegetable peeler, process the parsnips into fine shreds.

Melt the coconut oil over medium heat in a large skillet, then cook the shredded parsnips for 15 to 20 minutes, or until soft but still al dente. Transfer to a paper towel-lined plate, set aside.

Dice or finely shred the onion and garlic, add to the skillet and cook until soft and translucent, stirring occasionally to prevent scorching, about 10 to 15 minutes.

Dice the capers and anchovies, stir into the onions and garlic. Add the diced tomatoes, salt and chili flakes and stir. Stir in the cooked parsnips, adjust with additional salt to taste.

Top with fresh parsley, sprinkle with black pepper, and serve hot.

ITALIAN CABBAGE ROLLS (INVOLTINI CON LA VERZA)

This is a typical northern Italian dish from the region where I grew up. I was missing this dish, which is originally made with bread stuffing, so I decided to re-create it in a way that would preserve the flavor but remove the unwanted gluten. I was very happy with the results! —VM

SERVES 4

1 quart (1 l) water

1 tsp (6 g) sea salt + a good pinch

1 savoy cabbage, cut off the bottom and separate the leaves

1 pound (454 g) ground beef

2 eggs

½ cup (60 g) cassava flour

½ cup (120 ml) coconut cream, optional

1 tsp (3 g) herbes de Provence

¼ tbsp (2 g) red chili flakes

Black pepper to taste

Cooking fat of choice (lard, ghee, butter, coconut oil)

Preheat the oven to 350°F (180°C, or gas mark 4). Place a large, shallow pot over high heat and boil the water with a pinch of sea salt. Add the cabbage leaves to the pot and let cook for about 5 minutes until the leaves begin to soften. Drain the water from the pot and set the leaves aside to cool.

In a large bowl, mix together the ground beef, eggs, cassava flour, coconut cream, herbs, chili flakes and black pepper, mixing well to create the stuffing.

Lay out the cabbage leaves on a cutting board and then fill with a couple of full tablespoons of stuffing. Wrap the leaves tightly around the stuffing, then place them face down in a greased oven dish. Repeat this process until you have used all of the stuffing.

Bake the rolls for 45 minutes and then serve immediately.

ROASTED CABBAGE CARBONARA

A wonderful pasta substitute dish! Perfect for those cold winter days when we need some comfort food and cabbage is in season. Can be made with other sauce options too. —VM

SERVES 4

1 small green cabbage

4 cloves garlic, peeled

¼ cup (60 ml) extra-virgin olive oil

1 tsp (6 g) sea salt

FOR THE SAUCE

8 slices uncured bacon (or guanciale if you can find it)

2 egg yolks

4 tbsp (60 ml) butter, melted

½ cup (120 ml) coconut cream, melted

Sea salt to taste

½ tsp freshly ground black pepper

(continued)

Preheat the oven to 350°F (180°C, or gas mark 4). Remove the cabbage outer leaves and trim off the hard part at the bottom. Slice the cabbage in ½-inch (1.3-cm)-thick slices and lay it on a pre-oiled cookie sheet. You might need to use several cookie sheets to accommodate the whole cabbage.

In a small food processor, mix the garlic cloves with the olive oil and the salt, until they form a smooth, runny paste. With a pastry brush, brush the paste onto the cabbage slices evenly. Put the cabbage in the oven and bake for about 30 minutes, turning the slices once and brushing the other side with more oil.

While the cabbage cooks, prepare the carbonara sauce. Cut the bacon into small pieces, about 1-inch (2.5-cm) wide, then put in a frying pan and cook on a moderate flame until crispy, then drain from fat and set aside. In a large bowl whisk together the eggs, melted butter, coconut cream, salt and pepper to form a smooth cream. The cream should be quite peppery—that is why the name is carbonara, which means full of coals. You can add more fresh pepper if you like it spicy.

As soon as the cabbage is ready—it should be well cooked and caramelized with slightly burnt edges—toss it in the bowl with the carbonara sauce and the bacon pieces. Serve immediately while still very hot!

ITALIAN PEPPERS WITH ANCHOVY AND GARLIC SAUCE

Also known as Peperoni Alla Bagna Cauda, salty bagna cauda is fragrant with garlic and buttery flavors and is the perfect complement for roasted sweet bell peppers. A great traditional dish from the Italian region of Piemonte. —VM

SERVES 4

5–6 bell peppers, in all colors

8 tbsp (115 g) butter

1 head of garlic

¾ cup (112 g) walnuts, plus a little extra for garnish

10 anchovies (Italian are the best quality)

Char the bell peppers by placing them on a baking sheet and under the broiler. Slowly roast them, turning every few minutes until they are evenly burnt on all sides.

Remove the peppers and let them cool inside a paper bag.

Thinly slice the garlic and cook with the butter in a saucepan over extremely low flame for about 10 minutes, until the garlic starts to dissolve.

While the garlic is cooking, reduce the walnuts to a rough powder in a food processor. Add them to the garlic butter when done, then add the anchovies and cook for about 5 minutes. Remove from the heat. Whisk all the ingredients together until well blended.

Once the peppers have cooled, peel off the charred skin. Remove the tops, cut the peppers in half and remove all of the seeds. Do not rinse the peppers as that will ruin the flavor. You can clean them gently with a paper towel if desired. Lay the peppers out on plates, spooning the Bagna Cauda onto them, and finishing them off with a walnut garnish.

LAZY LAYERED EGGPLANT

This Mediterranean-inspired dish is a rework of lasagna or moussaka. It's easy enough for a weeknight but tastes like you spent hours at the stove. —RB

SERVES 2

2 eggplants

1 large onion

1 clove garlic

1 tbsp (15 ml) olive oil

½ pound (227 g) ground lamb

1 can diced tomatoes

1 tsp (3 g) salt

1 tsp (3 g) black pepper

½ tsp Aleppo pepper, plus more for garnish, optional

1½ tsp (4.5 g) ground cumin

1 tsp (3 g) ground coriander

½ tsp cayenne pepper

2 tbsp (8 g) flat-leaf parsley, chopped

½ lemon

Preheat oven to 350°F (180°C, or gas mark 4). Slice the eggplant into rounds approximately ½-inch (1.3-cm) thick. Place on a cookie sheet and bake in preheated oven for 30 minutes, until al dente.

While the eggplant is cooking, prepare the sauce: dice the onion and garlic, or pulse together in a food processor until finely shredded. Heat the olive oil in a medium skillet over medium heat and add the onion and garlic. Cook until translucent, stirring frequently, about 10 minutes.

Add the ground lamb and cook until no longer pink. Pour in the tomatoes and add salt, black pepper, Aleppo pepper, cumin, coriander and cayenne. Stir, and spoon the mixture out of the skillet.

Layer half of the cooked eggplant in concentric circles in the skillet. Spread half of the lamb mixture over the eggplant layer. Follow with the other half of the eggplant, layered in the same way.

Mix the parsley into the remaining half of the lamb mixture, then spoon over the second eggplant layer. Cook over medium heat for 5 to 10 minutes. Finish with a dusting of Aleppo pepper and a squeeze of lemon. Serve warm.

EGGPLANT LASAGNA

Ever thought of using thinly sliced eggplant in lieu of pasta sheets? This gluten-free and grain-free lasagna is very low in carbs but filled with a nutrient rich meaty Bolognese. Since it is not too heavy, anyone can easily finish this in one sitting. —JC

SERVES 4

2 tbsp (30 g) ghee or bacon fat, divided

2 whole eggplants, thinly sliced lengthwise

3 cups (750 ml) Paleo-friendly Bolognese sauce

¼ cup (15 g) fresh basil, torn into pieces

Preheat oven to 350°F (180°C, or gas mark 4).

Add 1 teaspoon (5 g) of ghee to a pan over medium-high heat. Add eggplant strips three at a time and lightly fry for 30 seconds each side. Remove from pan and set aside. Do this in batches and add 1 teaspoon (5 g) of ghee for each one until all the eggplant is fried.

Spread ½ cup (125 g) of Bolognese sauce evenly at the bottom of a loaf pan and sprinkle with some basil. Add 1 layer of eggplant with the edges overlapping. Repeat this step for the rest of the Bolognese sauce, eggplant and basil. Make sure the Bolognese sauce is the top most layer.

Cover the loaf pan with foil. Bake it in the oven for 30 to 35 minutes until the sauce is bubbly around the edges. Let it cool for 5 to 8 minutes before cutting and serving.

CHEF'S TIP:

Use a mandolin to evenly slice the eggplant into strips.

ZUCCHINI LASAGNA

This lasagna is not quite what you would think of as a regular dish of lasagna. These are individual stacks of veggies and cashew cheese. Think of it like individual lasagna appetizers. Great for a dinner party! —HH

SERVES 2

2 zucchinis

2 medium-large tomatoes

1 tbsp (15 g) ghee or oil

About 1 cup (120 g) Cashew Cream Cheese (page 507)

1 tsp (3 g) Italian seasoning (blend of oregano, thyme, basil, marjoram, rosemary)

½ tsp salt

½ tsp pepper

Slice the zucchini lengthwise into slices about ¼- to ½-inch (6–13-mm) thick. Slice the tomato similarly, but a little bit thicker so it will hold up in the skillet. Sprinkle salt on the zucchini slices and let sit on a paper towel for a few minutes to draw out the water, then blot the zucchini slices with a paper towel to dry.

Heat ghee in a skillet on high heat. Once the oil is hot place the zucchini in the pan. You only want to slightly brown the zucchini on each side for a minute or two. It won't take long, so be watchful. If it cooks too long it will become too flimsy. Set the zucchini aside. Then repeat with the tomatoes.

Cut the zucchini slices in half and place a few on the plate in a square shape. Spread a layer of Cashew Cream Cheese over the zucchini slices, then top that with tomato slices—you can cut the tomato slices in half to accommodate. Repeat this until the ingredients are used up. You should have about three layers. Top with a sprinkle of Italian seasoning, salt and pepper. These do not need to be baked. They can be eaten right after forming the layers. However, if you want to heat it so the cashew cheese is warm, place in the oven at 325°F (170°C, or gas mark 3) for about 10 minutes until warm.

ZUCCHINI SPAGHETTI WITH CREAMY ALFREDO SAUCE

The base of the alfredo sauce is coconut milk. However, the herbs and spices dominate the flavor so it tastes like a creamy savory sauce. The nutritional yeast in this recipe provides a "cheesy" flavor to give this non-dairy sauce a more dairy-like flavor. —HH

SERVES 2

FOR THE CREAMY ALFREDO SAUCE

1 cup (235 ml) full-fat coconut milk, canned

¼ tsp oregano

¼ tsp salt

¼ tsp garlic powder

½ tsp nutritional yeast

1 tsp (3 g) arrowroot

FOR THE ZUCCHINI SPAGHETTI

3 whole zucchinis

1 tbsp (15 g) butter or ghee

To make the creamy alfredo sauce, place all the ingredients except arrowroot into a pot. Heat the pot on medium-high heat while stirring. Cook for about 5 minutes to allow the sauce to thicken a little bit with evaporation. To thicken further, place 1 teaspoon (3 g) of arrowroot in a separate small bowl and add 1 tablespoon (15 ml) at a time of the coconut milk mixture to the small bowl until you have the arrowroot fully incorporated as a liquid (this helps prevent clumps of arrowroot in the sauce). Then, add the arrowroot mixture into the pot and stir continuously as the sauce thickens. Turn off the heat and set aside.

To make the zucchini spaghetti you'll need a spiralizer tool. Wash the zucchini and chop the ends off. Place each zucchini on the spiralizer and twist to make noodles.

In a large pan, heat the oil on medium-high heat and place the zucchini noodles in the pan. Cook the zucchini while stirring occasionally until the zucchini is cooked and softened, about 7 to 10 minutes. Reheat the alfredo sauce if necessary. Place the zucchini noodles in a dish and top with the alfredo sauce.

ZUCCHINI PASTA WITH AGRETTI AND LEMON

An easy modification on the original recipe for grain- and gluten-free pasta! Agretti is a springtime Mediterranean succulent which resembles the thin leaves of fennel. Agretti is not easily found, as it is only harvested for a few weeks at the end of spring. You will most likely be able to find it at farmers markets and if you can find it, it's totally worth it! —VM

SERVES 2

1 bunch agretti

3 tbsp (45 ml) olive oil

3 cloves garlic, sliced thin

Juice of 1 lemon

2 large zucchini, for pasta

Lemon zest, for garnish

Rinse the agretti, then remove the hard bottom of the stems. Dry what remains with a towel, then chop into 1-inch (2.5-cm) pieces. In a large skillet, heat the olive oil over medium heat. When the oil is nicely heated, add the sliced garlic and sauté until lightly browned. Once the garlic is browned, add the agretti and cook for about 5 minutes, stirring occasionally.

Turn off the heat and stir the lemon juice into the agretti mixture. Spiralize the zucchini into noodles. You can lightly sauté the noodles, or serve them raw. I like them raw myself. Once you are done preparing the noodles the way you like them, divide them between two plates, top with the agretti and zest a little lemon on top. Dinner is served!

CHEF'S TIP:

If you cannot find agretti, you could use fresh purslane or dandelion greens as a substitute, although agretti has a sour/salty taste that is very difficult to replicate.

ZUCCHINI PASTA WITH SORREL, BASIL AND HEMP SEED PESTO

Spaghetti al pesto! Who does not love this famous Italian dish? So what do you do when you have left behind grains and cheese? You can still enjoy it, just in an entirely new way! In this recipe I used zucchini noodles because they taste so good. The great thing about zucchini noodles is that you can steam them or lightly sauté or just eat them raw. —VM

SERVES 2

2 cloves garlic, peeled

4–5 sorrel leaves

Bunch of fresh basil

½ cup (75 g) raw hemp seeds

½ cup (120 ml) extra-virgin olive oil, plus extra to sauté with

3 medium zucchini

Make the pesto by blending the garlic, sorrel, basil, hemp seeds and olive oil in a food processor until a smooth paste has formed. If the paste is too dry, add a little olive oil until it reaches a smooth consistency.

Grate the zucchini, or use a spiralizer to create spaghetti-like noodles. You can have this dish several ways. Some like the zucchini fresh, and some like to steam or sauté them. Either way, plate the zucchini with a generous serving of the Basil and Hemp Seed Pesto and enjoy!

SMOKY SALMON

Here's an easy, healthy dinner that you can have on the table in 15 minutes. The smoky spices transform ordinary salmon into a flavorful, vibrant dish. The fresh Avocado Salsa (page 249) pairs nicely with this recipe. —KW

SERVES 4–6

2 pounds (908 g) salmon fillet

1 tsp (3 g) ground cumin

1 tsp (3 g) smoked paprika

1 tsp (3 g) onion powder

Sea salt and pepper, to taste

1–2 tbsp (15–30 ml) butter or ghee, melted

Avocado Salsa (page 249)

Preheat oven to 400°F (200°C, or gas mark 6). Place the salmon skin-side down on a lightly greased baking pan. Combine the spices in a small bowl. Rub the spice mixture over the top of the salmon. Pour the melted butter over the salmon. Bake for 12 to 15 minutes or until salmon flakes easily with a fork. Serve with Avocado Salsa.

SALMON FILLETS WITH OLIVE SAUCE

You might be surprised how well salmon and olives complement each other's flavors. If you want to try a unique dish, then give this one a shot. I think you will be pleasantly surprised. —VM

SERVES 4

6 ounces (168 g) kalamata olives, pitted

3 shallots, sliced

4 tbsp (60 ml) coconut oil, divided

½ cup (120 ml) coconut cream

Sea salt and black pepper to taste

4 (8-ounce [227-g]) salmon fillets

4 tbsp (60 ml) coconut aminos

To prepare the olive sauce, purée the olives in the food processor.

In a saucepan over low heat, sweat the shallots with 2 tablespoons (30 ml) coconut oil for about 10 minutes. Add the olive purée and coconut cream to the sauce-pan and cook for another minute. Season with salt and pepper to taste. Keep warm over very low heat.

For the fish, melt 2 tablespoons (30 ml) of coconut oil in a large pan over high heat. Add the salmon to the pan skin-side down, cooking for about 10 minutes. Flip and cook for another minute.

Take the fillets off the heat. You can check for doneness by breaking off a small piece. The salmon should easily flake.

Dress the salmon with the olive sauce and enjoy!

PAN-SEARED TURMERIC SALMON

I love making this simple seared salmon dish for dinner. Not only does the fish provide beneficial anti-inflammatory omega-3 fats and easily digested protein, but dressed in garlic, turmeric and coconut oil it tastes great too! —HH

SERVES 2

2 salmon fillets

½ tsp turmeric

½ tsp garlic powder

½ tsp salt

½ tsp pepper

1 tbsp (15 ml) coconut oil, tallow or lard

Sprinkle the exposed flesh part of the salmon fillets with the turmeric, garlic powder, salt and pepper. Place the oil in a large pan and start heating it up on medium heat. Once the pan is hot, place the salmon fillets in the pan and cook, flesh side down, for about 3 to 5 minutes. Then flip them over and cook for about 5 minutes or until cooked through. If your salmon fillet has skin on it, you can eat it or peel the skin off after cooking.

HONEY-GLAZED SALMON WITH MACADAMIA CRUST

Delicate and flaky salmon coated with crunchy ground macadamia nuts, spiced with cinnamon and sweetened with a touch of honey makes this a tasty dish. —NK

SERVES 4

1⅓ cups (160 g) ground macadamia nuts

1 tsp (3 g) ground cinnamon

Sea salt, to taste

4 medium salmon fillets

1 tbsp (15 ml) raw honey, melted

2 tbsp (30 ml) coconut oil

Preheat oven to 400°F (200°C, or gas mark 6). Line a large baking tray with parchment paper. Place ground macadamia nuts onto a plate and add the ground cinnamon and pinch of sea salt. Stir to combine. Pat dry both sides of each piece of salmon with a paper towel. Using a pastry brush, brush both sides of each piece of salmon with raw honey. One at a time place each piece of salmon into the macadamia mixture and press the mixture into the salmon. Place each piece of fish onto a clean plate as you go.

Heat a medium-large skillet over medium heat and add the coconut oil. Fry each piece of salmon on either side for 1 to 2 minutes to form a golden crust. Remove each piece to the baking tray as you go. Place all salmon into the preheated oven to bake for 15 to 18 minutes or until the salmon is cooked through.

MANGO-GLAZED SALMON

Slather a sweet mango purée with a hint of ginger and chili on top of fresh salmon. It caramelizes and takes on a nice golden brown color when broiled in the oven. Serve it with the Roasted Portobello Tray (page 234) or any of your favorite vegetables on the side. —JC

SERVES 4

1 ripe mango, peeled, pitted and chopped

2 tbsp (30 ml) raw honey

1 tsp (5 ml) apple cider vinegar

½ tsp chili powder

1 tsp (3 g) ginger, grated

Pinch of red pepper flakes

4 (4-ounce [112-g]) skin-on salmon fillets

Sea salt

Preheat oven to 375°F (190°C, or gas mark 5). Line a baking sheet with parchment paper.

Prepare glaze by combining mango, honey, apple cider vinegar, chili powder, ginger and red pepper flakes in a food processor or blender. Pulse until smooth. Set aside ½ cup (120 ml) of glaze as drizzling sauce.

Generously season salmon fillets with sea salt. Arrange salmon fillets skin-side down next to each other on the baking sheet. Top each one with 2 tablespoons (30 ml) of mango glaze. Bake in the oven for 20 to 25 minutes. Turn on the broiler and broil on low for 5 minutes to caramelize the glaze. Remove from the oven and let the salmon fillets cool for 5 minutes before drizzling with the remaining mango glaze.

CAJUN GRILLED SALMON

Smoky, spicy and sweet—the Cajun rub will have everyone loving this grilled salmon. Top with a colorful, Mango Basil Salsa (page 250) for a beautiful dinner dish to serve on a warm summer evening. —CP

SERVES 4

1 tbsp (15 ml) olive oil

1 tbsp (15 ml) butter, melted

2 cloves of garlic, crushed

1 tsp (3 g) sea salt

1 tsp (3 g) paprika

½ tsp fresh cracked black pepper

¼ tsp smoked paprika

¼ tsp ground cumin

¼ tsp cayenne pepper

¼ tsp dried thyme

¼ tsp chili powder

1½–2 pounds (680–908 g) fresh salmon

Mango Basil Salsa (page 250), to serve

In a bowl, melt together oil, butter and garlic. In a separate bowl, mix the dry rub.

Slice salmon into 3 to 4 fillet pieces. Brush each side of the fish with the butter-garlic sauce and generously rub with Cajun dry rub.

Heat grill to medium-high, keeping the heat about 500°F (250°C, or gas mark 10). Grill salmon, skin side down first, for 3 to 5 minutes, carefully flip to other side and continue to grill 3 to 5 more minutes—total time depends on the thickness of the fish.

Serve topped with Mango Basil Salsa.

SESAME–CRUSTED SALMON

This recipe is a spin-off of a fantastic salmon dish I ate at a Japanese restaurant. Serve it with the Asian Cucumber Salad (page 323) for a complete meal. —KW

SERVES 4

FOR THE ASIAN-INSPIRED MARINADE

1 clove of garlic, minced

1 tsp (3 g) fresh ginger, grated

1 tbsp (15 ml) olive oil

1 tbsp (15 ml) toasted sesame oil

1 tbsp (15 ml) coconut aminos, tamari or soy sauce

1 tbsp (15 ml) apple cider vinegar

1 tsp (5 ml) honey, optional

1 pound (454 g) salmon fillet

¼–⅓ cup (38–50 g) toasted sesame seeds

Optional toppings: sliced green onion, sliced avocado, fresh greens

Preheat oven to 400°F (200°C, or gas mark 6). Mix the marinade ingredients together in a small bowl. Pour over the salmon and marinate in the fridge for 30 minutes. After it's done marinating, take the salmon out of the marinade and press the sesame seeds on the top and bottom on the salmon. If you are using skin-on salmon, just press the sesame seeds on the top side. Bake on a lightly greased raised-edge pan for 12 or 15 minutes or until salmon is done to your liking. Top the salmon with sliced green onions and avocado and serve with fresh greens.

SALMON WITH SUN-DRIED TOMATO BUTTER

Sun-dried tomatoes add a nice flavor to creamy butter and give salmon an extra layer of oomph. Look for oil-infused sun-dried tomatoes so they will easily blend with the butter. If you can't find any, make your own by soaking sun-dried tomato pieces in extra-virgin olive oil the day before you need it. —JC

SERVES 4

4 (8-ounce [227-g]) salmon fillets

1 tsp (5 ml) coconut oil

¼ tsp sea salt

¼ tsp black pepper

1 tbsp (8 g) dried oregano, crushed

3 tbsp (43 g) salted butter, softened

¼ cup (60 ml) extra-virgin olive oil

4 pieces olive oil–infused sun-dried tomato halves

2 tbsp (8 g) fresh parsley

Preheat oven to 375°F (190°C, or gas mark 5). Line a baking sheet with parchment paper.

Season salmon with coconut oil, sea salt, black pepper and dried oregano. Place the salmon fillets on the baking sheet a couple of inches apart. Bake in the oven for 15 to 20 minutes until they flake easily with a fork.

Prepare the sun-dried tomato butter by combining butter, olive oil, sun-dried tomatoes and parsley in a food processor. Pulse until everything is well incorporated.

Once the salmon is cooked, add a generous dollop of sun-dried tomato butter on top of each piece before serving.

SALMON CROQUETTES WITH CREAMY AVOCADO SAUCE

This recipe turns that boring canned salmon into something delicious! The turmeric adds a smoky earthiness while the herbs bring freshness to this canned fish. Enjoy it with creamy avocado-lime sauce as a dip. —HH

MAKES 5–6

FOR THE SALMON CROQUETTES

1 (6-ounce [168-g]) can salmon

¼ tsp turmeric

½ tsp garlic

½ tsp thyme

½ tsp oregano

½ tsp pepper

½ tsp salt

½ medium onion, diced

1 green onion stalk

2 eggs

¼ cup (30 g) arrowroot

2 tbsp (30 g) ghee, lard or avocado oil

FOR THE CREAMY AVOCADO SAUCE

1 avocado

Juice of half lime

⅓ cup (80 ml) coconut milk

1 tbsp (4 g) chopped fresh cilantro

½ tsp garlic powder

¼ tsp salt

¼ tsp pepper

¼ tsp coconut aminos

For the salmon croquettes, combine all ingredients except the ghee or oil in a bowl and mix to combine. Heat the oil in a skillet on medium-high heat for about a minute. Form palm-sized patties and place in the pan. Cook for about 4 to 6 minutes on each side. Repeat until all of the mixture is used up.

(continued)

For the creamy avocado sauce, place all of the ingredients in a blender and blend on high for a minute or two until all ingredients are puréed and you have a creamy sauce texture.

CHEF'S TIP:

The amount of arrowroot needed may differ depending on the moisture level of the canned salmon that you are using. Be sure to drain any excess liquid from the can if your salmon is packed in water or oil. The batter should be wet, but you should be able to form a patty from it. If the batter seems too wet or you try frying one patty and the texture isn't right, try adding more arrowroot, 1 tablespoon (7 g) at a time, until you achieve the right texture.

SALMON BALLS

I stock cans of salmon in my pantry just for this recipe and because I always have canned salmon in my pantry, this is my go-to meal when I've had a busy day and need to get a healthy meal on the dinner table quickly. —KW

MAKES ABOUT 20 BALLS

12 ounces (340 g) canned salmon, drained

1 shallot or ¼ cup (40 g) red onion, finely diced

1 egg

½ lemon, zested and juiced

1 tbsp (8 g) green onion, chopped

1 tbsp (4 g) fresh dill or basil, chopped

Sea salt and pepper to taste

1 tbsp (15 ml) fat of choice for greasing—olive oil, avocado oil, coconut oil, etc.

Preheat oven to 350°F (180°C, or gas mark 4). Mix all of the ingredients, except your fat of choice, together in a bowl until well incorporated. Form into 1- to 2-inch (2.5 to 5-cm) balls. Add your fat of choice to a baking pan and then place the salmon balls on the pan. Lightly roll the salmon balls in the oil so they get coated. Bake for 20 minutes or until light golden brown on top.

CHEF'S TIP:

We love to eat these with an easy homemade dipping sauce. Add 1 tablespoon (4 g) of fresh herbs—I usually use dill and/ or basil—to ⅓ cup (80 g) Homemade Mayonnaise (page 496).

FISH STICKS

Goodbye gluten-loaded fish sticks. The next time you get a craving for classic fish sticks, give these a try. They are kid-friendly and pair well with the Lemon Dill Dipping Sauce (page 517). —KW

SERVES 4

1 pound (454 g) white fish

⅓ cup (40 g) coconut flour

Sea salt and pepper, to taste

1 tsp (3 g) garlic powder

¼ tsp cayenne pepper

2 eggs

1½ cups (120 g) unsweetened shredded coconut

Coconut oil, or other fat of choice, for frying

Lemon Dill Dipping Sauce (page 517)

Lemon wedges

Cut the fish in strips. Combine the coconut flour, sea salt and pepper, garlic powder and cayenne pepper in a bowl. Whisk the eggs in another bowl. Place the shredded coconut in another bowl. Coat each fish stick in the coconut flour. Then coat the fish stick in the eggs.

Next, press the fish stick in the shredded coconut. Repeat with all the fish sticks.

Place about 1 to 2 tablespoons (15 to 30 ml) of the coconut oil, or other fat, in a large skillet. Fry the fish sticks in batches for about 2 to 3 minutes each side over medium-low heat or until browned. Add more fat to the skillet as needed and push any burnt/brown coconut crumbs off to the side of the skillet. Serve the fish sticks with Lemon Dill Dipping Sauce and fresh lemon wedges.

SPICY FISH STICKS

Breaded fish fingers were something I ate growing up. I remember my mum coating the fish in eggs, flour and breadcrumbs and serving it alongside some salad and sometimes some fries. Of course these days I forgo the flour and breadcrumbs but that doesn't mean I can't still enjoy crispy fish and the same goes for you. Try these delicious, spicy fish sticks paired with some Green Herb Mayonnaise (page 496) and some homemade fries or greens on the side. If you're making these for the little ones feel free to leave out the red pepper flakes and change up the seasoning as you like. —NK

SERVES 4

1 pound (454 g) cod fillet, or other firm white fish

2 eggs

½ cup (60 g) tapioca flour

1 cup (120 g) almond flour

½ tbsp (4 g) red pepper flakes

1 tsp (3 g) dried thyme

Sea salt and black pepper, to taste

2 cups (470 g) shortening

Green Herb Mayonnaise (page 496), optional, for dipping

Rinse and dry the cod fillet with paper towels. Then cut it into strips, about ¼- to ½-inch (6-mm to 1.3-cm) wide. Add eggs to a medium-sized mixing bowl and whisk. In a shallow plate, add the tapioca flour, and in another shallow plate add the almond flour, red pepper flakes and dried thyme; stir to mix. Season the fish sticks well with sea salt and black pepper on both sides. Place another clean plate nearby.

One at a time dip each fish stick first into the tapioca flour, then into the eggs and then into the almond flour mixture, making sure to coat the fish all over. Place each one onto the clean plate as you go. Once you have placed batter on all the fish set aside.

Heat a large skillet over medium-high heat. Add the shortening to heat. To check if the cooking fat is ready to fry the fish, stick the end of a wooden spoon into the oil—when bubbles form around the spoon the oil is hot enough. In batches fry the fish sticks for around 3 minutes per side. Remove to a paper towel-lined plate. Serve warm with Green Herb Mayonnaise on the side.

MAHI MAHI TACOS

Do you love tacos? I do! And fish tacos remind me of summer, vacation and fun beach times. Not to mention they are quick and easy to prepare and a definite crowd pleaser. This is my easy but super tasty and satisfying version of fish tacos. —VM

SERVES 2

6 ounces (168 g) mahi mahi fillets

½ cup (60 g) coconut flour

1 tbsp (8 g) ground cumin

1 tsp (3 g) cayenne

½ tsp sea salt

½ cup (120 ml) avocado oil for frying

4 large leaves of romaine lettuce

1 cup (240 g) Super Easy Guacamole (page 190)

1 cup (240 g) Fresh Mixed Salsa (page 249)

Dry the mahi mahi fillets and cut them into 1-inch (2.5-cm)-wide strips.

In a bowl, mix together the coconut flour, cumin, cayenne and sea salt. Dredge the fish in the coconut flour mixture, making sure you coat them well.

In a large skillet, heat the avocado oil over high heat, add the mahi mahi and fry them for about 3 to 4 minutes per side, until they turn a nice golden brown. Place the fish on a paper towel to soak up any excess oil.

Serve on the romaine lettuce leaves used as taco shells. Top the fish tacos with the Super Easy Guacamole and Fresh Mixed Salsa. Enjoy!

BAJA MAHI TACO LETTUCE WRAPS

Make it a party with these gourmet Baja fish tacos. Golden fried mahi fillets on lettuce wraps with slaw, guacamole and lime. Serve with Paleo margaritas! —RM

SERVES 6

FOR THE BREADING

¼ cup (20 g) finely shredded coconut flakes, unsweetened

¼ cup (30 g) ground flax seed

½ tsp ground cumin

½ tsp Cajun seasoning

½ tsp sea salt

¼ tsp cayenne pepper

¼ cup (60 ml) virgin coconut oil

2 egg yolks

1 tbsp (15 ml) unsweetened almond milk

1 pound (454 g) fresh mahi mahi, or cod

FOR THE RED CABBAGE SLAW

2 tbsp (30 ml) apple cider vinegar

1 tbsp (15 ml) olive oil

1 tbsp (15 ml) honey

Pinch of red pepper flakes

¼ head red cabbage, finely sliced

1 medium head butter lettuce, cut in half

Super Easy Guacamole (page 190)

¼ cup (15 g) chopped cilantro

Lime wedges

Hot sauce

Sift together the dry breading ingredients onto a plate. Heat a medium-sized skillet over medium heat on the stove. Add the coconut oil and heat until 350°F (180°C, or gas mark 4). Whisk the egg yolks and almond milk in a shallow bowl.

Cut the fish into six equal pieces and dry with a paper towel. In steps, coat a piece of fish with the egg wash and then coat it thoroughly on all sides with the breading. Immediately drop it gently into the oiled skillet, cooking on all sides for about 4 minutes total, depending on the thickness. I like to swirl the skillet around it so that the fish is covered deep in the hot oil instead of frying in a shallow layer; two fillets at a time work best. Check the insides to make sure the fish is fully cooked, and then transfer to a paper towel-lined plate.

For the Red Cabbage Slaw, mix the apple cider vinegar, olive oil, honey and red pepper flakes until fully combined. Toss the sliced cabbage in the dressing until every bit is coated.

Use one or two lettuce wraps to hold each fish fillet and top with Red Cabbage Slaw, guacamole and cilantro. Garnish with a lime wedge and hot sauce!

SEARED SESAME-CRUSTED AHI

Seared ahi is one of my favorite dishes to order when eating out. Whenever I see sushi grade ahi on sale, I jump on the opportunity to make it at home for a fraction of the cost. Serve this with coconut aminos for dipping and you have a gourmet meal without breaking the bank. —JC

SERVES 2

¼ tsp sea salt

3 tbsp (24 g) sesame seeds

1 pound (454 g) sushi grade ahi tuna

1 tbsp (15 g) tallow or coconut oil, divided

2 tsp (10 ml) toasted sesame oil

¼ cup (60 ml) coconut aminos

1 tsp (3 g) fresh ginger, grated

1 tbsp (8 g) fresh radish, grated

¼ tsp red pepper flakes

Sea salt

Combine sea salt and sesame seeds in a small bowl. Coat the ahi tuna with 1 teaspoon (5 g) of tallow to help the sesame seeds stick while cooking. Gently press the sesame seed mixture on the ahi tuna until the entire surface is covered.

Heat a cast iron pan over medium-high heat. Add the remaining 2 teaspoons (10 g) of tallow to the pan. Once the pan starts to smoke, add the ahi tuna and sear each side for 2 to 3 minutes. The outside will be opaque and cooked while the inside is still red and raw. Remove from heat and set aside to rest before slicing.

Prepare the dipping sauce by combining sesame oil, coconut aminos, ginger, radish and red pepper flakes in a small bowl. Season with sea salt to taste. Serve with the seared ahi tuna.

AHI POKE

Poke is a wonderful summertime meal. It is so light and refreshing. It's tough to find Paleo poke out at restaurants, as they often use soy sauce. As many of you know, soy sauce isn't gluten-free. The first ingredient is usually wheat, unless you are using pure tamari. Luckily, Paleo-friendly, soy-free poke is super easy to whip up at home! —AV

SERVES 4 FOR AN APPETIZER OR 2 FOR A MEAL

1 pound (454 g) sashimi grade ahi tuna, cut into 1-inch (2.5-cm) cubes

¼ cup (30 g) green onions, chopped

1 serrano pepper, seeded and chopped

1 (½-inch [1.3-cm]) piece fresh ginger, grated

¼ cup (30 g) English cucumber, peeled and chopped

½ tsp sea salt

¼ cup (60 ml) coconut aminos

1 tsp (5 ml) fish sauce

1 tbsp (15 ml) macadamia nut oil

1 large clove garlic, minced

1 tbsp (8 g) sesame seeds

2 tbsp (15 g) macadamia nuts, chopped

Juice of ½ a lime for garnish

Place the ahi in a medium size bowl, preferably glass. Add the green onions, serrano pepper, fresh ginger, English cucumber and salt to the ahi. In a small bowl, whisk together coconut aminos, fish sauce, macadamia nut oil and garlic. Add the coconut aminos mixture to the ahi. Fold in the sesame seeds and macadamia nuts. Cover and refrigerate for at least 2 hours. Adjust salt to taste. Add fresh lime juice right before serving.

PANFRIED HALIBUT WITH AVOCADO SALSA

Incredibly quick to make, this is one of my favorite meals to enjoy after a day at the beach. The avocado salsa is so refreshing. —AV

SERVES 4

FOR THE AVOCADO SALSA

2 scallions, chopped

1 small jalapeño pepper, minced

¼ cup (40 g) cherry tomatoes, halved

¼ cup (16 g) cilantro, chopped

3 cloves garlic, minced

¼ tsp sea salt

¼ tsp pepper

⅛ tsp ground cumin

3 tbsp (45 ml) fresh lemon juice

2 avocados, peeled and chopped

2 tbsp (30 g) butter or ghee

Sea salt and pepper

4 (4-ounce [115-g]) halibut fillets

In a medium bowl, combine scallions, jalapeño, cherry tomatoes, cilantro, garlic, salt, pepper, cumin and lemon juice. Fold in avocados, taking care not to smash.

Heat a large frying pan over medium-low heat. Add butter. Generously salt and pepper the halibut. Once the butter is warm, cook the halibut until lightly browned, about 5 minutes. Flip and cook until the fish is cooked through, opaque and flakes easily, about 3 minutes. Top with the avocado salsa and serve.

SEA BASS WITH CHILI LIME BUTTER

Sea bass has a firm and meaty texture that holds together well when baked in the oven. A zesty butter sauce adds a touch of creaminess and a little bit of a kick thanks to the jalapeño. —JC

SERVES 2

1 pound (454 g) sea bass fillets

1 tbsp (15 ml) coconut oil

Sea salt

Black pepper

4 tbsp (60 g) salted butter or ghee

2 shallots, finely chopped

1 jalapeño pepper, finely chopped

Juice and zest of 1 lime

Preheat oven to 375°F (190°C, or gas mark 5). Line a baking sheet with parchment paper.

Rinse fish fillets and pat dry with paper towels. Lightly coat each piece with coconut oil and generously season with sea salt and black pepper. Place them on the baking sheet, 2 inches (5 cm) apart. Bake for 10 to 15 minutes until fish is opaque and flaky.

Prepare the sauce by combining butter, shallots, jalapeño, lime juice and zest in a small saucepan over medium heat. Simmer for 2 to 3 minutes until shallots are softened. Once the fish is cooked, pour the chili lime butter sauce on top and serve immediately.

CHEF'S TIP:

Any mild white fish such as mahi mahi or tilapia is a good substitute for sea bass.

SPICY MUSSELS AND SHRIMP MARINARA

This classic seafood marinara dish has some heat behind it. Mussels and shrimp are cooked in a spicy broth with a touch of wine and garlic. Serve as an appetizer or as a main dish with a salad. —RM

SERVES 2

1 tbsp (15 ml) extra-virgin olive oil

2 cloves garlic, minced

1 cup (250 g) marinara sauce

½ cup (120 ml) white wine

Cayenne pepper, to taste

½ pound (227 g) mussels, scrubbed

½ pound (227 g) shrimp, peeled & deveined

Salt and pepper, to taste

Heat the olive oil in a large skillet over medium heat. Add the garlic and sauté for about 1 minute. Add the marinara sauce and wine and reduce by about one third. Spice it up with cayenne pepper, to taste. Then add the mussels and shrimp. Sprinkle with salt and pepper. Cover and cook for about 5 minutes. Stir and flip shrimp, and then cook covered for another 4 minutes. The shrimp should be pale and the mussels open. Serve with a spoon and extra bowl for the shells.

SEARED TUNA STEAKS

These simple tuna steaks make a quick and easy weeknight dinner. Serve with mashed sweet potatoes or cauliflower rice. —HH

SERVES 2

2 (5-7 ounce [140-196 g]) tuna steaks

½ tsp turmeric

½ tsp oregano

½ tsp cracked black pepper

½ tsp salt

½ tsp garlic powder

2 tbsp (30 g) ghee, butter or palm oil

Cauliflower rice or mashed sweet potatoes, optional, for serving

Sprinkle tuna steaks on both sides with the turmeric, oregano, pepper, salt and garlic powder. Heat the ghee or butter in a skillet on medium-high. Once the oil is hot, place the tuna steaks in the skillet to sear for about 3 to 4 minutes on each side. They should be opaque in the center. If you prefer your tuna more well-done, cook for another 1 to 2 minutes. Serve over cauliflower rice or mashed sweet potatoes.

SPICY TUNA PIE

This unusual fish entrée with a rich spaghetti squash crust is inexpensive to make with easily accessible ingredients. Substitute canned salmon if you prefer, or experiment with swapping different shredded vegetables for the onion, jalapeño and bell pepper. —RB

SERVES 8

FOR THE CRUST

2 spaghetti squash (approximately 3 pounds [1.4 kg] each)

1 tsp (5 ml) coconut oil

2 eggs

¼ tsp salt

FOR THE FILLING

1 jalapeño pepper, cored and seeded

1 onion

1 bell pepper

1 tsp (5 ml) coconut oil

15 ounces (420 g) canned tuna

3 eggs

¼ cup (15 g) chopped cilantro

½ tsp salt

½ tsp black pepper

Preheat the oven to 350°F (180°C, or gas mark 4). Pierce the spaghetti squash several times on each side with a sharp knife, and place on a plate. Microwave on high for 8 minutes, then rotate top-side down and microwave for another 8 minutes (it may be necessary to cook the spaghetti squash one at a time).

Slice open the two spaghetti squashes, being careful of the hot escaping steam, and set aside to cool. Once they have cooled, rake the strands of the squash out of the skin and combine with the rest of the ingredients for the crust in a medium mixing bowl, and then press into a 9-inch (23-cm) pie plate with sides at least 2 inches (5 cm) high. Press the crust mixture evenly into the bottom of the pie plates and evenly up the sides. Bake in the preheated oven for 15 minutes.

While the crust bakes, dice the jalapeño, onion and bell pepper by hand (or finely shred in a food processor). Melt the coconut oil in a medium skillet over medium high heat. Cook the jalapeño, onion and bell pepper for 5 to 10 minutes or until softened, and then remove from the heat and allow to cool enough to touch.

Transfer to a large mixing bowl, and stir in the tuna, eggs, cilantro, salt and black pepper. Combine thoroughly, and then spoon the filling into the pre-baked crust. Return to the oven and cook for 30 minutes, or until the filling is set and the crust is browned but not burnt.

Serve warm, garnished with more diced jalapeño if desired.

GARLIC BUTTER SHRIMP

Incorporate more seafood into your diet by making this classic dish. The garlicky morsels of shrimp served with the Sweet Carrot and Butternut Purée (page 243) will tantalize your taste buds! —JC

SERVES 4

1 pound (454 g) jumbo shrimp, shell on, deveined

2 tbsp (30 g) salted butter, cubed

3 cloves garlic, minced

1 tbsp (4 g) fresh parsley, chopped

¼ tsp red pepper flakes

Sweet Carrot and Butternut Purée (page 243)

Preheat oven to 375°F (190°C, or gas mark 5).

Rinse shrimp and pat dry. In a small bowl, mix together butter, garlic, parsley and red pepper flakes. Place shrimp on a baking dish and top with the butter mixture. Bake uncovered until shrimp turns pink, about 8 to 10 minutes. Serve with Sweet Carrot and Butternut Purée on the side.

CAULIFLOWER FRIED RICE WITH SHRIMP AND BACON

One of the first recipes I made after switching over to eating Paleo was cauliflower-based fried rice. I added my favorite ingredients and kept it really simple to minimize chopping and clean up. Bacon and shrimp complement each other and create a comforting but light dish, made even lighter by substituting cauliflower for white rice. —JC

SERVES 4

3 strips bacon, chopped

1 large carrot, chopped

1 small onion, chopped

3 cloves garlic, minced

1 pound (454 g) raw medium shrimp, peeled

6 cups (1500 g) cauliflower rice

¼ cup (25 g) green onions, chopped

Add bacon to a wok over medium-high heat. Fry until crispy and set aside in a bowl. Add carrot and onion to the rendered bacon fat in the wok. Stir-fry until onion is translucent, about 3 minutes. Remove and set aside in the same bowl as the bacon.

Add garlic and shrimp to the same wok. Stir-fry for 3 to 5 minutes until the shrimp turns pink and opaque throughout. Return the bacon, carrots and onions to the wok and combine with the shrimp. Add the cauliflower rice and stir-fry for 2 to 3 minutes to cook everything together. Turn off heat and mix in the green onions. Serve immediately.

PINEAPPLE SHRIMP FRIED RICE

Homemade fried rice tastes so much better compared to its greasy take out counterpart plus it doesn't contain any unhealthy hidden ingredients. Using cauliflower rice is a time saver and you'll have a piping hot bowl chock full of zesty shrimp and pineapple ready in no time. —JC

SERVES 4

2 tsp (10 g) tallow or coconut oil

1 medium onion, chopped

1½ cups (225 g) fresh pineapple, cut into chunks

2 medium carrots, chopped

1 pound (454 g) medium shrimp, peeled and deveined

1 jalapeño pepper, stem and seeds removed, chopped

¼ cup (60 ml) vegetable broth

¼ cup (60 ml) coconut aminos

Sea salt

Black pepper

4 cups (100 g) cauliflower rice

Add tallow to a deep skillet or wok over medium-high heat. Add onion, pineapple and carrots. Stir-fry for 8 minutes until lightly browned. Add shrimp and cook for 3 to 5 minutes until it turns pink. Add jalapeño, broth and coconut aminos. Season with sea salt and black pepper to taste. Stir-fry for 1 minute. Add cauliflower rice and mix well to combine. Let it cook for 2 to 3 minutes, mixing occasionally until the cauliflower rice has softened. Spoon into bowls and serve.

PINEAPPLE SHRIMP STIR-FRY

Serving this quick and delicious stir-fry in hollowed out pineapple halves is a fun finishing touch. —RB

SERVES 4

1 tbsp (15 ml) coconut oil

1 onion

1 cauliflower

1 pound (454 g) shrimp

½ tsp salt

½ tsp pepper

1 pineapple

Scallions, chopped

Black sesame seeds

Heat the coconut oil over medium heat in a large skillet. Thinly slice the onion and finely chop the cauliflower. Sauté the vegetables in the coconut oil until very soft, about 15 to 20 minutes.

Add the shrimp, salt and pepper, and cook, stirring occasionally, until shrimp is cooked through, approximately 5 minutes.

Slice the pineapple lengthwise, then cut out and discard the woody core. Hollow out both side of the pineapple, chop the fruit and then add it to the skillet. Toss with the shrimp and vegetables until warm and the juice has cooked off.

Mound the filling into the halves of the pineapple and top with chopped scallions and black sesame seeds. Serve warm.

COCONUT SHRIMP CURRY

This coconut shrimp curry is a quick, easy and colorful weeknight dinner option. —RB

SERVES 4

½ onion

1 red bell pepper

1 tbsp (15 ml) coconut oil

1 tsp (3 g) salt

2 tbsp (16 g) curry powder

½ pound (227 g) shrimp

1 cup (80 g) shredded unsweetened coconut

1½ cups (355 ml) coconut milk

Handful snow peas

Roughly chop the onion and bell pepper, then shred coarsely in a food processor. Melt the coconut oil over medium heat in a large skillet and add the onion, bell pepper, salt and curry powder and sauté until soft, approximately 10 minutes.

Add the shrimp and cook until pink, approximately 5 minutes. Stir in the shredded coconut, coconut milk and snow peas. Cook for 15 minutes, until the shredded coconut has softened. Serve warm.

SHRIMP PAD THAI

This recipe gives traditional pad Thai a grain-free spin while keeping the flavors authentic. —RB

SERVES 2

FOR THE SAUCE

1 tbsp (15 ml) fish sauce

1 tbsp (15 g) tamarind paste

1 tbsp (12 g) coconut sugar

FOR THE PAD THAI

½ cup (60 g) dried shrimp

2 (7-ounce [196-g]) packages shirataki noodles in water

2 shallots

4 pickled mustard stem

1 bunch chives

4 tbsp (60 ml) coconut oil, divided

12 large fresh shrimp

2 eggs

2 heaping cups (100 g) mung bean sprouts

½ cup (75 g) chopped cashews

FOR THE GARNISH

Chives

Red pepper flakes

Coconut sugar

Cashews

Mung bean sprouts

Fresh limes

Combine the ingredients for the sauce in a small dish. Set aside.

Soak the dried shrimp in warm water until they begin to soften, and then finely dice.

Drain the noodles, set aside. Thinly slice the shallots, dice the pickled mustard stem, and cut several 1-inch (2.5-cm) lengths from the bundle of chives. Save the rest of the chives to serve with the finished dish.

In a large skillet, heat 2 tablespoons (30 ml) of coconut oil and add the sliced shallots. Cook the shallots over high heat, keeping them moving, until they begin to lose their color but don't burn—this should only take a minute or so if the skillet is hot enough. Add the chopped mustard stem and diced dried shrimp. Stir for 1 minute, letting the flavors mix, then add the drained noodles and fresh shrimp.

Stir to mix the contents of the skillet and push to one side to make room for the eggs. Crack the eggs on one side of the skillet, and scramble briefly before working into the rest of the skillet's ingredients.

Turn off the heat under the skillet, and add the bean sprouts, chopped cashews and chopped chives. Mix thoroughly, letting the remaining heat wilt the vegetables. Serve hot, with the reserved chives and topped with red pepper flakes, more coconut sugar, cashews, bean sprouts and a squeeze of lime.

CHERMOULA WITH PARSNIP "NOODLES" AND SHRIMP

Chermoula is a spicy herb sauce often used in North African cuisine. It's used here to complement the subtle natural spiciness of parsnip "noodles." The dish is rounded out by quick-cooking shrimp for an easy, light meal. —RB

SERVES 2

1 tsp (3 g) ground cumin

⅓ cup (20 g) coarsely chopped flat-leaf parsley

⅓ cup (20 g) coarsely chopped cilantro leaves and tender stems

3 cloves garlic, peeled and smashed

1 tsp (3 g) paprika

2 tsp (10 ml) lemon juice

⅓ cup (80 ml), plus 1 tbsp (15 ml) coconut oil

½ tsp salt

½ tsp chili flakes, plus more for garnish

4 parsnips (approximately 2 pounds [908 g]), peeled

¾ pound (340 g) shrimp, peeled and deveined

To make the chermoula, combine the cumin, parsley, cilantro, garlic, paprika, lemon juice, ⅓ cup (80 ml) coconut oil, salt and chili flakes in a blender. Purée for 3 to 5 minutes until smooth.

Using a spiralizer or vegetable peeler, process the parsnips into fine shreds. Melt the remaining 1 tablespoon (15 ml) coconut oil over medium heat in a large skillet, then cook the shredded parsnips for 15 to 20 minutes, or until soft but still al dente. Transfer to a paper towel-lined plate, set aside.

Cook the shrimp in the same skillet as you cooked the parsnips over medium heat for 5 minutes until pink and cooked through. Combine the cooked shrimp and cooked parsnips in a large mixing bowl, then pour the chermoula over and mix well. Serve warm.

SHIRATAKI SHRIMP STIR-FRY

Rely on this stir-fry as a fast, easy and tasty way to get a balanced meal. A shrimp stir-fry is particularly quick to cook. —RB

SERVES 2

½ tsp coconut oil

1 tbsp (15 ml) coconut aminos (optional)

1 bell pepper, sliced

¼ pound (112 g) shrimp

¼ tsp salt

1 (7-ounce [196-g]) package shirataki noodles

1 soft-boiled egg, chopped

2 scallions, chopped

½ tsp red chili flakes

¼ tsp black sesame seeds, for garnish

Heat the coconut oil and coconut aminos, if using, over high heat in a large skillet, then add the sliced bell pepper, shrimp, salt and shirataki noodles. Toss them in the hot oil and aminos until shrimp are pink and the peppers are softened, approximately 5 minutes.

Transfer to bowls, and top with chopped egg, chopped scallions, chili flakes and black sesame seeds. Serve hot.

SLOW ROASTED GOAT LEG

Goat can be prepared so many different ways. Slow roasting has to be one of my favorites, as it yields a tasty but tender result. Pairing with the apples and peaches highlights the great flavor of the goat meat. You definitely will not be disappointed with this dish! —VM

SERVES 6–8

1 goat leg

1 pound (454 g) peach slices, frozen

1 Meyer lemon, zested

Sea salt

Pink peppercorn, freshly ground

2 apples, coarsely chopped

2½ cups (588 ml) white wine, divided

Water

Defrost the goat leg, if frozen, and peaches two days before you want to serve the dish.

Lay the defrosted goat leg on some long pieces of aluminum foil on a cookie sheet. Zest the lemon, and then season the goat leg with it, along with the salt and pepper. Pack the peaches and chopped apples all over the leg and wrap tightly in the foil. Once the leg is wrapped up, place the leg in the refrigerator overnight to soak in all the flavors.

When the leg is done marinating, take it out of the refrigerator about 2 hours before cooking, to come to room temperature.

Preheat the oven to 250°F (120°C, or gas mark ½) and unwrap the goat leg. Lay the leg on a deep cookie sheet or roasting pan if you have one large enough. Pour any leftover marinade over the leg and then add the white wine to the pan. Cover the leg in a foil tent and then place in the oven.

Reduce the temperature to 200°F (100°C) and roast the leg for 5 to 6 hours, checking the fluid levels periodically. If the liquid is low or completely absorbed, you can refill it with a second cup of wine. Temp the leg. and when it reaches 120°F (49°C), turn the broiler on high and remove the foil tent. Let the leg brown nicely on top for about 5 minutes. When the inside temperature of the meat reaches 125°F (52°C) remove the leg from the oven.

Cover the leg with foil to keep it warm while it rests for about 15 minutes. Once the leg has finished resting, slice the meat against the grain at an angle.

If the pan drippings have not burnt, you can reduce them in a saucepan with ½ cup (120 ml) of white wine for a nice sauce. Serve with your favorite side dishes and enjoy!

ROASTED GOAT SHOULDER SWEETLY SPICED

A roasted goat shoulder can be just as tender and juicy as any lamb cut. Spices and dried fruits enhance the flavors of the meat, and create a nice counterpoint to the savory notes. —VM

SERVES 6

1 goat or lamb shoulder

FOR THE MARINADE

2 tbsp (24 g) coconut sugar

2 tbsp (16 g) ground cumin

1 tbsp (8 g) ground cayenne

1 sweet onion, peeled and quartered

3 cloves garlic, peeled

1 cup (130 g) dried apricots, plus more for serving

1 cup (175 g) Medjool dates, plus more for serving

1 cup (235 ml) water

½ cup (120 ml) white wine, optional

Marinate the meat the day before you plan on serving it.

Blend all of the marinade ingredients in a food processor until they create a smooth paste. Massage the paste into the meat and place into a resealable bag and refrigerate overnight.

Preheat the oven to 425°F (220°C, or gas mark 7). Lay the shoulder in a glass baking dish and bake for 20 minutes to sear and seal the juices. Lower the heat to 300°F (150°C, or gas mark 2) and cover the shoulder loosely with foil. Bake for an additional 2 hours, and then add the dates and apricots to the dish. If the fluid is running low, feel free to add a little more water if needed. Bake the shoulder for one more hour and then take it out of the oven.

Let the meat rest for about 10 minutes before slicing. Plate the shoulder with a nice serving of dates and apricots along with any favorite side dishes and enjoy.

PALEO KOOFTEH (PERSIAN MEATBALLS)

Like most Middle Eastern dishes, koofteh takes a while to make because the meatballs are simmered in broth, low and slow. This dish is perfect for a leisurely weekend dinner. Traditionally this recipe calls for white rice, but I've substituted cauliflower rice, which works surprisingly well! No one in my family has ever even noticed the missing rice. —AV

SERVES 4 (MAKES 10 MEATBALLS)

2 strands of saffron

2 tsp (10 ml) of filtered water

FOR THE FILLING

1 tbsp (15 g) ghee

½ onion, diced

½ cup (60 g) walnuts, chopped

½ cup (85 g) prunes, chopped

FOR THE SAUCE

1 tbsp (15 g) ghee

½ onion, diced

2 cloves garlic, crushed

½ tsp turmeric

6 tomatoes, peeled, chopped and seeds removed

2 cups (475 ml) filtered water

½ tsp sea salt

FOR THE MEATBALLS

1 cup (100 g) cauliflower

½ tsp sea salt

¼ tsp pepper

1 pound (455 g) ground beef

½ onion, grated

1 egg

½ cup (20 g) fresh parsley, chopped

¼ cup (10 g) mint, chopped

½ tsp turmeric

Tomato broth

Place the strands of saffron in a small bowl and cover with the water and set aside. Prepare the filling. Heat a large sauté pan over medium heat, preferably one with a large, flat base and shallow sides. Add the ghee and sauté the diced onion in ghee until translucent. Add the walnuts and prunes and sauté for a few minutes until well combined. Set the filling aside.

Prepare the sauce. Add the ghee to the same pan and sauté the onion until soft and translucent, about 10 minutes. Add garlic and turmeric. Stir well and sauté for 2 more minutes. Add chopped tomatoes, water and salt. Cover and simmer on low heat while you form the meatballs.

To form the meatballs, remove the stem of the cauliflower and put through a food processor until it resembles rice. In a large bowl, combine cauliflower, salt, pepper, meat, onions, egg, parsley, mint, turmeric and soaked saffron and mix well. Round mixture into balls, poke a hole in the middle, fill with filling and close. You should be able to make about 10 meatballs.

Slowly place the meatballs in the simmering sauce. Cook on low heat for an hour or until meatballs are cooked through. Carefully turn the meatballs halfway through cooking so both sides have a chance to be immersed in the liquid. Serve meatballs in bowls along with tomato broth.

PALEO PERSIAN KOTLET (CUTLET)

This was one of my favorite meals my mom made for us growing up. She often served the kotlets with homemade French fries. I have made a few minor Paleo adjustments to her original recipe: I have omitted white flour and swapped out the white potato for sweet potato. Although you can make kotlets with white potato, I think the sweet potato adds a note of complexity to this Middle Eastern comfort food.

Traditionally, these are served hot or cold. They are great to pack for a Paleo picnic. —AV

SERVES 4

1 sweet potato, peeled and chopped (about 3 cups [710 ml])

½ large onion, chopped

3 cloves garlic

3 tbsp (8 g) fresh parsley

1 pound (455 g) ground beef

¼ tsp turmeric

½ tsp sea salt

¼ tsp pepper

1 egg

3 tbsp (45 g) ghee, lard or duck fat for frying

Tomatoes, pickles, olives (garnish)

Place sweet potato, onion, garlic and parsley in a food processor. Pulse until well combined. If the mixture gives off any liquid, drain the liquid before combining it with the meat. Combine the mixture with the meat, turmeric, salt, pepper and egg. Mix until well combined.

Heat a heavy-bottomed skillet such as cast iron over medium heat. Add ghee or fat. Take a handful of the meat mixture and shape into a ball. Continue to flatten into an oval shape.

Place flattened kotlets into the skillet. This will have to be done in batches. Take care not to overcrowd the pan. Fry until both sides are well browned and cooked through, about 5 minutes per side. Add more fat as needed. Drain the kotlets on a paper-towel-lined plate. Serve with sliced tomatoes, pickles and olives.

BEEF CHEEK BRAISED WITH TOMATOES

Beef cheeks, called *joues de boeuf* in French, are an inexpensive and often overlooked cut of meat. As a result of the extensive chewing cows do, they are one of the toughest cuts of meat on the cow. When cooked properly, the connective tissue softens and the meat melts in your mouth. The result is a tender and heavenly piece of meat. —AV

SERVES 6

2 beef cheeks

1 tsp (5 g) sea salt

½ tsp pepper

½ tsp chili powder

2 tbsp (30 g) ghee

1 white onion, diced

6 cloves garlic, minced

2 tbsp (30 ml) tomato paste (preferably from a jar)

6 tomatoes, chopped, peeled and cored

2 cups (472 ml) Slow Cooker Beef Broth (page 171)

Rub beef cheeks with salt, pepper and chili powder on both sides. Heat a heavy-bottomed skillet over medium heat. Add ghee to hot pan. Once ghee is hot, add the beef cheeks and brown on both sides, about 3 minutes per side. Set aside. Add the onion to the pan and sauté until soft, about 5 minutes, then add garlic and sauté until fragrant, about 1 minute. Add tomato paste and tomatoes and scrape the pan with a wooden spoon to get up any brown bits. Place browned beef cheeks in the slow cooker. Pour the tomato-onion mixture and beef broth over it. Cook on low heat for 8 hours.

SLOW-COOKER HORSERADISH AND PARSNIP POT ROAST

The slow-cooking process tames the heat of the horseradish in this dish, but it still offers enough savory flavor to complement the sweetness of the parsnips. —AV

SERVES 8

2 tbsp (30 g) ghee

Sea salt and pepper

3–4 pounds (1.4–1.8 kg) beef chuck roast

1 onion, sliced

2 tbsp (10 ml) tomato paste (preferably from a jar)

3 tbsp (30 g) Paleo horseradish

6 cloves garlic, minced

¼ tsp paprika

½ cup (120 ml) Slow Cooker Beef Broth (page 171)

2 bay leaves

3 sprigs fresh thyme

2 carrots, peeled and chopped

4 large parsnips, cubed and chopped

Heat a heavy-bottomed pan or cast iron skillet on medium-high heat. Add the ghee. Generously salt and pepper the roast. When the ghee is warm, add the roast to the pan and brown on all sides, about 1 to 2 minutes per side. Set aside.

Add the onions to the pan and sauté until translucent, about 5 minutes. Add the tomato paste and cook until the color of the paste changes from a bright red to a brick color, about 1 minute. Transfer the onion mixture to the slow cooker.

In a small bowl combine the horseradish, garlic and paprika. Generously rub the mixture all over the roast. Place the roast in the slow cooker. Add broth, bay leaves, thyme, carrots and parsnips to the slow cooker. Turn to low and cook for 8 hours. Discard the sprigs of thyme and bay leaves. Serve roast with parsnips and carrots.

CHEF'S TIP
To avoid soggy vegetables, add the carrots and parsnips halfway through cooking time.

SAUTÉED BEEF OVER WATERCRESS

Inspired by a delicious meal at a Vietnamese restaurant in New York City, this dish skips the oyster sauce but stays true to the notion of beef sautéed with lots of onions, garlic and scallions, and is served over watercress. The sweetness of the well-cooked onions with the peppery watercress and the flavorful beef offer a tantalizing treat to the taste buds. —AV

SERVES 6

FOR THE MARINADE

¼ cup (60 ml) coconut aminos

2 tbsp (30 ml) fresh lime juice

2 tbsp (30 ml) sesame oil (unrefined, expeller- or cold-pressed)

3 cloves garlic, minced

1 tbsp (20 g) raw honey

1 tbsp (15 g) fresh ginger, minced

2 tbsp (5 g) green onions, chopped

1 tbsp (15 g) fish sauce

1½ pounds (680 g) flank steak

FOR THE DRESSING

1 tbsp (15 ml) fresh orange juice

1 tbsp (15 ml) fresh lime juice

1 tbsp (15 ml) coconut aminos

1 tsp (7 g) raw honey

1 tbsp (15 ml) sesame oil (unrefined, expeller- or cold-pressed)

¼ tsp red chili flakes

3 tbsp (45 ml) expeller-pressed coconut oil

2 cups (260 g) white onion, sliced

¾ cup (40 g) scallions, chopped

4 large cloves garlic or 6 medium, minced

2 bunches watercress leaves

Make the marinade by mixing together the coconut aminos, lime juice, sesame oil, garlic, honey, ginger, green onions and fish sauce. Pour over the flank steak. Make sure it is well coated. Cover and marinate for at least 4 hours, up to overnight. Flank steak can be tough, so the longer it marinates the more tender it will become.

Make the dressing by whisking together orange juice, lime juice, coconut aminos, honey, sesame oil and chili flakes. Set aside.

Heat a wok or a large, heavy-bottomed skillet to medium-high heat. Add the coconut oil. Once the oil is warm, add the beef and sauté until cooked through, about 6 to 8 minutes. Set beef aside. Add onions and sauté until translucent, about 7 minutes. Add scallions and garlic and sauté until scallions are soft, about 3 minutes. Add beef back in and sauté until beef is warm, about 2 minutes. Place a large handful of watercress on a plate, drizzle with 2 teaspoons (10 ml) of dressing and top with warm beef and onion sauté.

CHEF'S TIP

I prefer using expeller-pressed coconut oil for this dish, as it does not have a strong coconut flavor.

PANFRIED FILET WITH SHALLOT SAUCE

Most of us reserve indulging in an elegant filet mignon for a celebratory restaurant meal. That restaurant filet can easily be made at home, with higher quality ingredients and at a fraction of the price. Even fancy restaurants are likely going to use vegetable oil for searing their steaks. At home you can use grass-fed butter or another fat of your choice. Once you top your steak with this luscious shallot pan sauce, it will triumph over most of the steaks you have had at a restaurant. —AV

SERVES 4

4–6 ounces (115–170 g) beef filets

2 tbsp (30 ml) unsalted butter, melted

FOR THE SAUCE

2 tbsp (30 ml) unsalted butter, melted

1 cup (240 g) shallots, thinly sliced

Sea salt and pepper

1 tbsp (15 ml) red wine vinegar

½ cup (120 ml) Slow Cooker Beef Broth (page 171)

1 tbsp (2 g) fresh rosemary, finely chopped

Let the steaks come to room temperature, about 30 minutes. Preheat oven to 400°F (204°C). Place an oven-safe, glass baking dish in the oven to warm up. Heat a large cast iron skillet over medium-high. Brush melted butter onto one side of the steak. When the skillet is ready, add the steaks. While the first side is browning, brush the other side with butter. Once a nice brown crust forms, about 2 to 3 minutes, use tongs to flip the steaks and sear the other side. Using tongs transfer steaks to the warm dish in the oven and roast for 6 to 8 minutes for medium-rare.

While the steaks are roasting, make your sauce. Add 1 tablespoon (15 ml) of butter to the same cast iron skillet used to brown the steaks. Add the shallots and season generously with salt and pepper. Continue to cook until the shallots are softened, about 10 minutes. Add the vinegar and cook until it evaporates. Add the broth and bring to a boil. Allow the sauce to cook until it has reduced by half. Pull the pan from the heat, stir in the remaining tablespoon of butter and rosemary. Remove steaks, salt and pepper and let rest for 5 minutes. Serve topped with shallot sauce.

SUN-DRIED-TOMATO-AND-FENNEL-BRAISED SHORT RIBS

Beef short ribs are packed with flavor and become unbelievably tender when slowly cooked. The sun-dried tomatoes and fennel give these braised short ribs a Mediterranean twist. —AV

SERVES 4

2½ pounds (1.1 kg) beef short ribs

2 tsp (10 g) coriander

2 tsp (10 g) cumin

Sea salt and pepper

2 tbsp (30 g) ghee

1 onion, sliced

1 medium fennel bulb, sliced

¼ cup (40 g) green garlic, chopped

¼ cup (40 g) sun-dried tomatoes, chopped

1 cup (235 ml) dry red wine

3 cups (710 ml) Slow Cooker Beef Broth (page 171)

2 bay leaves

Preheat oven to 350°F (177°C). Toss ribs with coriander and cumin, and generously salt and pepper. Heat a Dutch oven or heavy-bottomed, ovenproof pan on medium-high heat. Add the ghee to the pan. Once the ghee is hot, add the ribs and brown on all sides, about 3 minutes per side. Transfer to a plate and set aside.

Add the onion to the pan and sauté until translucent, about 5 minutes. Add the fennel, green garlic and sun-dried tomatoes and sauté until fragrant, about 2 to 3 minutes. Add the wine and scrape up any brown bits from the bottom of the pan. Add the broth and bay leaves and the ribs to the pan. Cover and transfer the pan to the oven. Cook for 1½ hours, basting and turning 1 or 2 times. Uncover and cook for an additional 45 minutes. Discard bay leaves before serving.

CHEF'S TIP

If you can't find green garlic, then substitute 4 cloves garlic, minced.

GRAPE LEAF AND CABBAGE DOLMAS

Many Armenian dishes require long prep times and then cook "low and slow." I remember spending half a day making these with my mom and grandma! So we always made dolmas in bulk for a few meals. You can halve the recipe or freeze the leftovers for another night. Dolma is traditionally paired with plain, thick yogurt. —AV

SERVES 10

1 bunch fresh cilantro

2 bunches fresh parsley

1 bunch scallions

1 bunch fresh dill

1 head cabbage, halved

1 jar grape leaves

2 pounds (900 g) grass-fed ground beef

1 tbsp (15 g) sea salt

1 tsp (5 g) pepper

½ tsp cayenne

½ tsp turmeric

2 tbsp (30 g) butter, softened (not needed if using conventional beef)

½ lemon

2 tbsp (30 ml) tomato paste (preferably from a jar)

4 cups (950 ml) of water, divided

Wash and thoroughly dry the herbs. If they are wet, you will risk making the meat mixture soggy. Pulse the cilantro, parsley, scallions and dill in the food processor until well minced but not too smashed. Set aside.

Bring a pot of water to a boil and add the cabbage. Cook for 15 minutes, until soft. Strain in a colander.

Drain the grape leaves and separate them. Mix the meat, herb mixture, salt, pepper, cayenne and turmeric. Mix in butter only if using grass-fed beef; conventional beef has enough fat and won't need additional butter. Squeeze the half-lemon's juice into the mix. Use your hands to make sure the mixture is well combined.

Lay the grape leaves, vein-side up, stem toward you. Place 1 tablespoon of filling at the base of the leaf and roll up, tucking in the excess leaf at the sides to make a bundle. Remove the core from the cabbage and separate the leaves. Place 1 heaping tablespoon of filling at the base and roll up, tucking in the sides to make a bundle.

Using a heavy-bottomed pot with a lid, line the bottom of the pan with excess cabbage leaves. Place your dolmas on top of the excess cabbage leaves, placing grape leaf dolmas on the bottom and cabbage dolmas on top, with the bottom of your bundles facing down. Dissolve the tomato paste in 1 cup (240 ml) of water. Pour the dissolved tomato paste into the pot. Add 3 more cups (700 ml) of water. Place an oven-safe, heavy plate over the dolmas to weigh them down. (This is to keep them from unraveling.)

Cover the pot and bring to a light boil. Tilt the lid so the pot is only partially covered. Simmer for 2½ hours. Remove the lid and the plates. Simmer for an additional 30 minutes uncovered.

Preheat oven to 400°F (204°C). Heat a large Dutch oven or a heavy-bottomed, oven-safe pan over medium heat. Generously salt and pepper the chicken. Add the ghee to the pan.

Add the chicken to the pan, skin side down. When the skin releases easily, after about 5 minutes, flip and brown the other side for about 3 minutes. Transfer chicken to a plate. Add the onions and sauté until soft, about 5 minutes. Add garlic and sauté until fragrant, about 1 minute. Add the balsamic vinegar and scrape the bottom of the pan with a wooden spoon to get up any brown bits. Turn the heat off the pan. Add the yams and toss with the onion mixture. Generously salt and pepper the mixture. Lay the sprigs of rosemary on top of the yams. Place your browned chicken on top of the rosemary.

Cover the pan with a lid and bake for 45 minutes. Turn your oven from bake to broil. Remove the lid and broil for 10 minutes or until your chicken skin is nice and crispy but not burned. Discard rosemary sprigs.

BALSAMIC ROSEMARY ROASTED CHICKEN AND YAMS

The balsamic vinegar balances out this one-pot meal by adding the perfect hint of sweetness and acidity. I recommend using a high-quality balsamic vinegar for the best results.—AV

SERVES 4

1 whole chicken, cut into 8 pieces

Sea salt and pepper

2 tbsp (30 g) ghee

1 red onion, sliced

3 cloves garlic, minced

2 tbsp (30 ml) balsamic vinegar, preferably an aged, syrupy variety

3 yams, peeled and chopped

2 sprigs rosemary

FRUIT–STUFFED CHICKEN

This is an impressive dish to make for a holiday gathering in the fall, when apples are in season. The sweet and tart flavor of the apples combined with the zesty orange will fill your house with the comforting scents of autumn.—AV

SERVES 4

1 roasting chicken (approximately 3½ pounds [1.6 kg])

1 large orange

Sea salt and pepper

4 tbsp (60 g) butter, divided

1 cup (150 g) red onion, diced

3 cloves garlic, minced

2 apples, unpeeled, cored and diced

1 tbsp (1 g) fresh rosemary, minced, plus a few sprigs

(continued)

Preheat the oven to 350°F (77°C). Remove any organs from the chicken's cavity and reserve for another use. Rinse the bird with cold water and pat dry. Grate the zest from the orange and reserve. Cut the orange in half and rub all over the chicken. Liberally salt and pepper the entire bird.

Melt 2 tablespoons (15 g) butter in a skillet. Add red onion and cook over low heat until tender. Add garlic and apples and sauté until apples are soft but not cooked through, about 10 minutes. Salt and pepper generously. Turn off the heat and combine orange zest and rosemary with the apple and onion mixture.

Stuff the chicken with the mixture. Stuff rosemary sprigs under the skin. Tie the legs together with kitchen twine. Place the chicken breast-side up in a roasting pan. Dot each breast with a tablespoon of butter. Roast for 1½ hours. Let chicken rest, and carve.

SLOW-COOKER CHOCOLATE CHICKEN MOLE

I have been perfecting the recipe for a slow-cooker chicken mole for several years. I think I finally got it right! The dark chocolate adds richness and complexity, while the peppers add a smoky flavor and the tomatoes brighten up the dish.—AV

SERVES 6

2 pounds (900 g) chicken pieces (breasts and legs work well), bone in, skins removed

Salt and pepper

2 tbsp (30 g) ghee

1 medium onion, chopped

4 cloves garlic, crushed or minced

6–7 whole tomatoes, peeled, seeded and chopped

5 dried New Mexico chili peppers, rehydrated and chopped

¼ cup (60 g) almond butter

2½ ounces (70 g) dark chocolate (70% or above)

1 tsp (5 g) sea salt

1 tsp (3 g) cumin

½ tsp ground cinnamon

½ tsp guajillo chili powder

Avocado, cilantro and jalapeño, all chopped (garnish)

Generously salt and pepper the chicken. Place a pan over medium heat and add ghee. Once the ghee has warmed, add the chicken and brown on all sides. This may need to be done in batches. Move chicken to the slow cooker.

Add onion to the same pan and sauté until translucent. Add garlic and sauté for 1 to 2 minutes, until fragrant. Transfer onion and garlic to slow cooker. Add the tomatoes, chili peppers, almond butter, dark chocolate, salt and spices (cumin, cinnamon, chili powder) to the slow cooker. Cook on low for 4 to 6 hours or until chicken is tender and pulls apart easily. If you are home when making this dish, lift the lid once and give a stir to make sure all the ingredients are well combined. Remove chicken bones. Top mole with avocado, cilantro and jalapeño and serve!

GRILLED CHICKEN CHERMOULA

Chermoula is a marinade often used for fish or seafood in Algerian, Moroccan and Tunisian cuisines. The bright flavors of the fresh herbs lend themselves to chicken dishes, too. This dish is best if you allow the chicken to marinate overnight. —AV

SERVES 4

6 tbsp (90 ml) extra-virgin olive oil

2 tsp (5 g) cumin

½ tsp sea salt

½ tsp coriander

½ tsp sweet paprika

1 medium red chili pepper, seeded and chopped

Finely grated zest and juice of 1 lemon

2 cloves garlic, crushed

1½ cups (40 g) fresh cilantro leaves

½ cup (13 g) fresh parsley leaves

1 whole chicken, cut into 8 pieces

Combine all ingredients except chicken in a food processor. Blend for 1 minute or until well mixed. Reserve ¼ cup (60 ml) of the marinade to serve with the chicken. Pour the rest of the marinade over the cut chicken pieces, making sure they are well coated. Tuck as much marinade as you can under the chicken skin. Cover and set in the fridge for at least 4 hours, up to overnight.

Heat the grill to medium-high. Grill chicken, turning once halfway through. Grill for 30–40 minutes or until internal temperature reads 165°F (74°C). Serve drizzled with extra sauce.

TANDOORI CHICKEN

Tandoori chicken is an Indian dish, traditionally prepared in a clay oven called a tandoor. You can now find recipes for grilled and roasted variations. This dish is typically prepared with yogurt and spices. I have made this recipe with yogurt and all my taste testers preferred the coconut milk version!

The mild heat from the cayenne in this dish is balanced out by the coconut milk and zesty lemon juice.—AV

SERVES 4

1 tsp (5 g) fenugreek, whole

1 tsp (5 g) peppercorn, whole

1 tsp (5 g) coriander

1 tsp (3 g) cumin

1 tsp (3 g) garam masala

½ tsp cayenne

¼ tsp turmeric

1 tsp (5 g) sea salt

1 (1-inch [2-cm]) piece fresh ginger, minced

1 jalapeño, minced

2 tbsp (30 ml) fresh lemon juice

½ cup (118 ml) coconut milk

2 pounds (907 g) chicken legs and thigh, bone in, skin removed

Preheat the oven to 375°F (190°C). Place fenugreek and peppercorn through a spice grinder. In a small bowl mix the fenugreek, peppercorn, coriander, cumin, garam masala, cayenne, turmeric and salt. Next, mix in the ginger, jalapeño, lemon juice and coconut milk. Stir until well mixed.

Make a few deep slashes in each piece of chicken. This will help the chicken absorb more of the flavor. Pour the spice mixture over the chicken. Make sure the chicken is well coated. Place in fridge for at least 4 hours, up to overnight.

Preheat oven to 375°F (190°C). Place chicken on a wire rack on top of a baking sheet so the baking sheet catches the drippings. Cook for 50-60 minutes or until a meat thermometer reads 165°F (74°C).

MACADAMIA-CRUSTED DUCK BREAST WITH SPICY "SOY" GINGER SAUCE

Coconut aminos are a great Paleo substitute for soy sauce. They have a similar salty flavor, with a slight hint of sweetness. I use real soy sauce made from fermented soybeans as a condiment. Soybeans have a high level of phytates, which tend to block the body's absorption of minerals. However, fermentation substantially reduces levels of phytic acid, so fermented soy is preferable.

In recipes such as this one, I prefer the subtler flavor of coconut aminos to soy sauce. The bold flavors of this spicy sauce complement the creaminess and rich flavor of the duck.—AV

SERVES 4

1 cup (120 g) macadamia nuts

4 duck breast halves, boneless, skin on

Sea salt and pepper

1 tbsp (15 g) duck fat or ghee

2 tsp (15 g) raw honey

FOR THE SAUCE

1 cup (240 g) shallots, diced

2 cloves garlic, minced

1 jalapeño, minced

1 tbsp (8 g) fresh ginger, grated

¼ cup (60 ml) coconut aminos

2 tbsp (30 ml) fresh lime juice

1 tsp (7 g) raw honey

Preheat oven to 350°F (177°C). Place macadamia nuts in a food processor and blend until crushed. Heat a skillet, preferably cast iron, over medium-high heat. Generously season both sides of the duck breasts with salt and pepper. Add the duck fat or ghee to the pan, then add the duck skin-side down. Brown until the skin has a nice golden crust, about 5 minutes. Flip over and brown the other side for 1 to 2 minutes.

Transfer the duck breasts to a glass baking dish, skin-side up. Allow to cool for a few minutes. Spoon ½ teaspoon of honey on the skin side of each duck breast. Spoon enough of the crushed macadamia nuts over the honey so the entire top of the duck breast is covered. Make sure the breast is well coated. Do this to the remaining duck breasts. Place in the oven and roast for 20 minutes until medium well.

While the duck breasts are roasting, make the sauce. Using the same pan that the duck was seared in, drain all but about 1 tablespoon (15 ml) of fat. Add the shallots. Cook until soft, about 5 minutes. Add the garlic, jalapeño and ginger. Sauté until fragrant, about 1 minute. Stir in the coconut aminos, lime juice and honey. Simmer until slightly reduced. Adjust salt to taste. Remove duck breast from the oven, let rest for 5 minutes and serve drizzled with sauce.

WINE-BRAISED DUCK LEGS

I recommend buying whole ducks for this dish. Buying a whole duck is more cost-effective and almost all of the parts can be used. Use the skin to render for duck fat and the carcass to make stock. —AV

SERVES 4

½ bunch fresh parsley

½ bunch fresh thyme

1 tsp (5 g) sea salt

½ tsp pepper

¼ tsp red chili flakes

4 duck legs

2 tbsp (30 g) duck fat or ghee

1 large onion, diced

1 carrot, peeled and diced

2 cloves garlic, minced

1 cup (235 ml) dry red wine

1 cup (160 g) tomatoes, peeled, seeded and diced

1 bay leaf

2 cups (475 ml) Slow Cooker Chicken Broth (page 170)

2 tbsp (30 g) butter

Kitchen twine

Preheat oven to 375°F (190°C). Tie the parsley and thyme together with some kitchen twine. Combine the salt, pepper and red chili flakes in a small bowl. Rub each duck leg on the meat side with the mixture. Heat the duck fat or ghee in a Dutch oven or a large, ovenproof, heavy-bottomed pan. Add the duck legs, skin-side down, and sear until lightly browned, about 3 minutes. Turn the duck legs over and sear the other side, about 2 minutes. Transfer to a platter and set aside.

If there is too much fat in the pan, drain all but 2 tablespoons (30 ml). Add the onion and carrots and sauté for 5 minutes. Add the garlic and sauté for an additional minute. Add the wine and tomatoes and bring to a light boil, scraping up any brown bits from the bottom of the pan. Add the thyme, parsley, bay leaf and chicken broth.

Place the duck legs skin side down in the pan. Cover and place in the oven to cook for 1½ hours. Halfway through, flip the duck legs so the skin side is up. Change your oven setting to broil and cook uncovered for the last 10 minutes. Remove duck legs and strain the sauce through a sieve and into a sauté pan. Bring the liquid to a boil, then turn down to a simmer and reduce it by half or to desired consistency. Turn off the heat, stir in the butter and adjust salt to taste. Put the duck on individual plates, spoon the sauce over and serve.

JAMAICAN JERK PORK CHOPS

When I started the Paleo diet, one of my closest friends brought me some jerk seasoning from Jamaica. I read the ingredients and noticed a few questionable items, so I decided to make my own. This is what I came up with! —AV

SERVES 4

2 scallions, chopped

2 cloves garlic, minced

1 tbsp (8 g) fresh ginger, peeled and grated

1 serrano chili pepper, seeded and minced

1 tbsp (20 g) raw honey

1 tbsp (6 g) allspice

1 tbsp (2 g) dried thyme

1 tsp (8 g) ground cinnamon

1 tsp (3 g) ground nutmeg

¼ tsp cayenne pepper

1 tsp (5 g) sea salt

1 tsp (5 g) pepper

Juice of 1 lime

Juice of 1 orange

2 tbsp (30 ml) coconut vinegar

2 tbsp (15 g) coconut aminos

¼ cup (60 ml) extra-virgin olive oil

4 pork chops, bone in

2 tbsp (30 ml) coconut oil

Combine all of the ingredients in a bowl except the coconut oil and pork. Make sure it is all mixed well. Place pork chops in a shallow bowl and pour marinade over the chops. Cover and marinate for at least 1 hour, up to overnight.

Heat the coconut oil in a large skillet over medium heat. When it has melted, remove the pork chops from the marinade and place in the skillet, making sure they are not crowding each other. If your skillet is not large enough, you may need to do this in batches. Cook 3–4 minutes per side; the length will depend on the thickness of your chops. Flip over as soon as one side is well browned.

PORK CHOPS WITH POMEGRANATE–GINGER SAUCE

Pomegranates are one of the most recognizable symbols of Armenia; they represent fertility, abundance and marriage. Pomegranate season was a special time for us growing up. My younger brother and I always looked forward to sitting at the dining table and enjoying the seeds that our mom had carefully removed.

Now I enjoy leveraging their unique and tantalizing flavor to elevate simple meals like these pan-fried pork chops. —AV

SERVES 4

FOR THE SAUCE

½ cup (120 ml) unsweetened pomegranate juice

½ cup (120 ml) Slow Cooker Chicken Broth (page 170)

½ cup (120 g) shallots, diced

1 clove garlic, minced

1 tsp (5 g) fresh ginger, minced

1 tbsp (20 g) raw honey

3 sprigs thyme

Dash of sea salt

1 tsp (2 g) arrowroot starch

1 tsp (3 g) coriander

½ tsp onion powder

½ tsp garlic powder

4 pork chops, center cut

Sea salt and pepper

2 tbsp (30 ml) coconut oil

In a medium-sized saucepan, combine all of the ingredients for the pomegranate-ginger sauce, except the arrowroot starch. Cook until reduced by half, about 10 minutes. Remove sauce from the heat and set aside. Once the sauce is cool, strain it through a fine mesh strainer to remove the solids.

In a small bowl, mix coriander, onion powder and garlic powder. Rub the seasonings mix on both sides of the pork chops. Generously salt and pepper.

Heat a large skillet to medium-high heat. Once the pan is hot add the coconut oil. Place the chops in the pan and make sure that they are not crowding each other too much. Cook chops on each side for about 4 minutes or until well browned and cooked through. Remove the chops from the pan and set aside to rest.

As your chops are resting, add the strained pomegranate-ginger sauce to the same pan and bring to a simmer. Stir for a couple of minutes and scrape up any browned bits. Place your arrowroot starch in a small bowl and add enough filtered water to make a thin paste. Add this paste to the sauce and whisk until the sauce is slightly thickened. Spoon the warm sauce over the pork chops and serve.

CHINESE FIVE-SPICE PLUM PORK RIBS

While no one knows its exact origins, some believe that the Chinese created five-spice powder to encompass all of the five flavors: sour, bitter, sweet, pungent and salty. These five elements combined create a powerful flavor. The five-spice powder brings a unique flavor to this dish. Remember when using it, a little goes a long way! —AV

SERVES 4

2 tbsp (40 g) raw honey

⅓ cup (80 ml) fresh orange juice

1 tsp (2 g) Chinese five-spice powder

1 tsp (5 g) fresh ginger, minced

1 serrano pepper, minced

3 cloves garlic, minced

1 tsp (5 g) sea salt

2 pounds (900 g) pork spare ribs, cut into 4 slabs

1 pound (455 g) plums, pitted and halved or, if very large, quartered

Preheat the oven to 300°F (150°C). In a small bowl, mix all the ingredients except ribs and plums until well combined. Place ribs meat-side down in an oven-safe pan with a lid, such as a Dutch oven. Pour sauce over the ribs and make sure they are well coated. Arrange the cut plums around the ribs. Cover and bake for 2 hours. Halfway through remove the lid and baste the pork.

Increase the oven to 375°F (190°C). Remove the cover and flip the pork so the meat is facing up. Bake for an additional 15 to 20 minutes or until ribs are browned. Place ribs on a plate with some plums and drizzle with sauce.

BRAISED GOAT SHOULDER

Goat is the most widely consumed red meat in the world, a staple among many cultures but rarely eaten in the United States. I am not sure why, because it is truly delicious! Pasture-raised goat meat tastes more like beef than lamb. Because goat is very lean, the shoulder can be quite tough, but becomes tender and tasty when braised with moist heat. Next time you see some goat at your farmers market, pick some up and give this recipe a try —AV

SERVES 8

2 tbsp (30 g) ghee

Sea salt and pepper

3 pounds (1.4 kg) boneless goat shoulder

1 onion, thinly sliced

2 tbsp (30 ml) tomato paste (preferably from a jar)

4 cloves garlic, minced

1 leek, thinly sliced

1 rib celery, diced

1 carrot, peeled and diced

1 tbsp (15 ml) red wine vinegar

4 cups (945 ml) Slow Cooker Beef Broth (page 171)

6 ripe tomatoes, quartered

4 sprigs thyme

2 bay leaves

Preheat oven to 375°F (190°C). Heat a large Dutch oven to medium-high heat and add ghee. Generously salt and pepper the goat shoulder. When the ghee is warm, add the meat and brown on all sides, about 5 minutes on the first side. Set the meat aside.

Add the onion to the Dutch oven and cook until soft, about 5 minutes. Add the tomato paste, garlic, leek, celery and carrot. Cook for a few minutes until fragrant. Add the red wine vinegar and scrape up any brown bits from the pan. Add the meat, broth, tomatoes, thyme and bay leaves. Cover and place in the oven. Cook for 2 hours or until goat shoulder is tender. Discard thyme sprigs and bay leaves before serving.

SLOW-COOKER LAMB VINDALOO

My grandma taught me that food always tastes best when it is made from scratch. Although I have curry pastes in my pantry for when I am short on time, I always jump at an opportunity to make my own. This exquisite spicy curry dish is surprisingly simple to make. —AV

SERVES 6

FOR THE PASTE

6 dried chili peppers

½ yellow onion, diced

4 cloves garlic, crushed

2 tsp (10 g) fresh ginger, grated

1 tsp (3 g) ground cinnamon

½ tsp ground cloves

¼ tsp ground turmeric

1 tbsp (8 g) coriander

1 tbsp (8 g) cumin

1 tsp (5 g) fenugreek

1 tsp (5 g) sea salt

2 tbsp (30 ml) distilled white vinegar

2 pounds (900 g) lamb (shoulder or stew meat)

2 tbsp (30 g) ghee

½ cup (120 ml) Slow Cooker Beef Broth (page 171)

Soak chili peppers in warm water for 30 minutes. In a food processor, combine chili peppers and all other paste ingredients. Spread the paste over the lamb and marinate for at least several hours, up to overnight. Save any remaining paste to add to your broth later. Brown the lamb in the ghee. This may have to be done in batches. Place lamb with remaining paste in the slow cooker and add broth. Cook on low for 6–8 hours.

LAMB SHANKS WITH APRICOTS

It is difficult to describe the distinct flavor of saffron. For me, it has a nostalgic flavor, reminding me of the many dishes that I enjoyed growing up. If you have never cooked with saffron, one thing to note is that a little goes a long way. This is a good thing, as it is the most expensive spice in the world!

Juicy and sweet apricots are the perfect accompaniment to the pungent saffron in this dish. —AV

SERVES 6

FOR THE RUB

½ tsp ground ginger

½ tsp allspice

1 tsp (3 g) cumin

¼ tsp turmeric

¼ tsp cayenne

½ tsp lemon zest

3 pounds (1.4 kg) lamb shanks

Sea salt and pepper

3 tbsp (45 ml) ghee

1 red onion, sliced

5 cloves garlic, minced

3–4 cups (710–945 ml) Slow Cooker Beef Broth (page 171)

2 strands saffron

2 cups (360 g) fresh apricots, pitted and halved (or ½ cup [75 g] dried, chopped)

Preheat oven to 400°F (204°C). Combine all the ingredients for the rub and rub all over the lamb. Generously season with salt and pepper. Heat a Dutch oven to medium-high heat. Add the ghee. Once it is hot, brown lamb on all sides. Remove the lamb and set aside.

Sauté the onion in the same Dutch oven until soft, about 5 minutes, and then add the garlic. Cook for a minute or two. Add the broth, bring to a boil and scrape the bottom of the pan to get up any brown bits. Add the saffron and apricots. Return the meat and cover the pot and place into preheated oven. Cook for 1½ to 2 hours or until shanks have become tender. Turn the shanks over halfway through cooking. Remove the lid for the last 20 minutes to allow the shanks to get a nice brown crust. Serve the lamb shanks with the cooked apricots and drizzled with juice from the pan.

SUN-DRIED TOMATO AND MUSHROOM LAMB BURGERS

When it comes to burgers, most people think of beef. Lamb offers cooks a more complex and sophisticated flavor to work with. The sweet and savory sun-dried tomatoes and earthy mushrooms harmonize perfectly with the rich lamb. My favorite way to enjoy burgers is on top of grilled portobello mushrooms. —AV

SERVES 6

½ cup (80 g) sun-dried tomatoes, chopped

½ cup (40 g) dried porcini mushrooms, chopped

2 pounds (900 g) ground lamb

2 pieces bacon, chopped

4 cloves garlic, minced

½ onion, grated

1 tsp (3 g) chili powder

2 tsp (10 g) sea salt

½ tsp pepper

½ cup (20 g) fresh parsley

¼ cup (5 g) fresh basil

1 jalapeño, minced

1 egg, lightly beaten

FOR THE PORTOBELLO MUSHROOMS:

6 portobello mushrooms, stemmed

Sea salt and pepper

2 tbsp (30 g) butter, melted

Rehydrate sun-dried tomatoes by placing them in a bowl and covering them with warm water. Let them soak at room temperature for at least 45 minutes or until they feel flexible. Rehydrate dried mushrooms by placing them in a bowl and covering them with warm water for 30 to 45 minutes.

Preheat a grill over medium-high heat. Combine the sun-dried tomatoes, mushrooms, lamb, bacon, garlic, onion, chili powder, salt, pepper, parsley, basil, jalapeño and egg. Mix gently. Form into six patties. Remove the stems from the portobello mushrooms. Generously salt and pepper them and liberally brush with melted butter. Grill burgers for about 4 minutes a side for medium burgers. Cook portobello mushrooms for 5 minutes per side or until heated through and tender. Top each portobello mushroom with a burger and serve.

CHEF'S TIP

For an added flavor boost, top this burger with sautéed onions and sliced avocado.

GRILLED LAMB CHOPS WITH MINT PESTO

Armenian and Persian cooking liberally use fresh herbs, fruits and nuts. Even when I am not making a Middle Eastern dish, the influence on my cooking is very noticeable. I am drawn to developing recipes centered around herbs, such as pestos, chimichurri and herb sauces. —AV

SERVES 6

2 pounds (907 g) lamb

1 tbsp (15 ml) extra-virgin olive oil

2 tbsp (30 ml) fresh orange juice

2 tbsp (3 g) mint leaves, minced

½ tsp fresh thyme

½ tsp pepper

½ tsp sea salt

3 cloves garlic, minced

½ tsp finely grated orange zest

2 pounds (900 g) lamb loin chops, about 8 to 10 chops

FOR THE MINT PESTO

½ cup (15 g) mint leaves

¼ cup (5 g) fresh basil

¼ cup (30 g) macadamia nuts

1 tbsp (10 g) garlic, minced

¼ cup (60 ml) extra-virgin olive oil

2 tbsp (30 ml) fresh lemon juice

1 tbsp (15 ml) fresh orange juice

¼ tsp sea salt

¼ tsp pepper

Preheat grill to medium-high. In a small bowl, combine olive oil, orange juice, mint, thyme, pepper, salt, garlic and orange zest. Rub the mixture all over the lamb and let it rest at room temperature for 30 minutes.

In the meantime, prepare the mint pesto by placing all of the ingredients in a food processor and pulsing a few times until well combined. Adjust salt and pepper to taste.

Grill the lamb chops 3 to 4 minutes per side for medium. Serve the lamb chops drizzled with mint pesto.

MEDITERRANEAN STUFFED PEPPERS

Vibrant peppers are packed with bright and fragrant flavors. A light salad is the perfect accompaniment to this flavorful dish. —AV

SERVES 4

1 tbsp (15 g) ghee

½ yellow onion, chopped

¼ cup (40 g) sun-dried tomatoes, chopped

2 cloves garlic, crushed

1 tbsp (15 ml) tomato paste (preferably from a jar)

1 pound (455 g) ground lamb

½ tsp sea salt

¼ tsp pepper

¼ cup (10 g) fresh parsley, chopped

1 tbsp (2 g) mint, chopped

3 red bell peppers, halved and cores removed

Rehydrate sun-dried tomatoes by placing them in a bowl and covering them with warm water. Let them soak at room temperature for at least 45 minutes or until they feel flexible.

Preheat oven to 350°F (177°C). Heat a heavy-bottomed skillet to medium-high heat and add ghee. Add onions and sauté until soft, about 5 minutes. Add sun-dried tomatoes, garlic and tomato paste. Sauté for 1 minute. Add lamb, salt and pepper and cook until browned, using a wooden spoon to break up the clumps. Turn off the heat and fold in the parsley and mint. Use a slotted spoon to pick up the mixture from the pan, leaving the extra fat behind.

Stuff the peppers, place in an oven-safe baking dish and cook for 20 minutes or until meat is browned and peppers are soft.

GINGER LIME BUTTER-SAUTÉED SHRIMP

Aromatic and spicy ginger paired with tart lime give the shrimp a unique and zesty flavor.—AV

SERVES 4

Salt and pepper

1 pound (455 g) uncooked shrimp, peeled and deveined

2 tbsp (30 g) butter

¼ cup (60 g) shallots, minced

2 cloves garlic, minced

1 tbsp (15 g) fresh ginger, minced

½ tsp crushed red pepper flakes

3 tbsp (45 ml) fresh lime juice

1 tsp (5 g) lime zest

¼ cup (60 ml) coconut aminos

2 tbsp (5 g) scallions, chopped (garnish)

Generously salt and pepper the shrimp and set aside. In a large skillet, heat the butter over medium heat. When the butter is melted, add the shallots and sauté until soft, about 5 minutes. Add the garlic and ginger and cook until fragrant, about 1 minute. Add the crushed red pepper and cook for 30 seconds. Add the lime juice, lime zest and coconut aminos and stir to combine.

Add the shrimp and cook, stirring occasionally, until white throughout, about 4 minutes. Make sure the shrimp is well coated with the sauce. Spoon the shrimp and sauce into shallow bowls and serve topped with scallions.

PAN-ROASTED HALIBUT WITH MUSHROOMS AND LEEKS

The smooth, buttery texture of halibut is complemented by the delicate flavor of the leeks and the earthy flavor of the mushrooms. This dish is relatively quick to make, ideal for a weeknight dinner and fancy enough to serve to guests. —AV

SERVES 4

2 tbsp (30 g) unsalted butter

4 cups (300 g) crimini mushrooms, sliced

2 large leeks, white and light green parts only, thinly sliced

Sea salt and pepper

4 skinless halibut fillets (about 4 ounces [120 g] each)

5 sprigs fresh thyme

1 tbsp (2 g) fresh flat-leaf parsley

Heat a large skillet with a lid over medium heat. Melt the butter and add the mushrooms and leeks. Season with salt and pepper. Cook carefully until leeks and mushrooms are softened but not browned. Generously season the halibut with salt and pepper and nestle the fish among the vegetables in the skillet. Add the thyme. Cover tightly. Cook gently until the fish is just cooked through, about 7 minutes. Discard thyme sprigs. Serve the fish with mushrooms and leeks, topped with fresh parsley.

CHEF'S TIP

Freeze the green parts of the leeks to add to stocks and broths (pages 170–171).

SLOW-COOKED MACADAMIA ROSEMARY SALMON

I can't recall where I picked up this method of cooking salmon, but it's become my favorite technique. This method does take a bit longer, but the end result is a tender, juicy and silky fish.—AV

SERVES 6–8

1 (3-pound [1.4-kg]) salmon fillet

2 tbsp (30 ml) macadamia nut oil

½ tsp sea salt

¼ tsp pepper

3 sprigs fresh rosemary

4 cloves garlic, minced

1 whole lemon, sliced

Preheat oven to 200°F (93°C). Place a pan of warm water on the lowest rack to keep the heat moist. Place the salmon in a baking dish. Lightly brush the salmon with macadamia nut oil. Season with salt and pepper, top with rosemary sprigs, garlic and slices of lemon. Cook for 1 hour. Do not open the oven often, since it is set at such a low heat. Serve.

STEAMED SALMON WITH CURRIED PEAR AND MANGO CHUTNEY

The curry powder and the lemon juice combine to give this chutney a bold flavor, a perfect complement to a simply steamed salmon fillet.—AV

SERVES 4

1 tbsp (15 g) ghee

¼ cup (40 g) red onion, diced

1 small pear, peeled, cored and finely diced

1 ripe mango, peeled and finely diced

1 serrano pepper, minced

1 large or 2 small cloves garlic, minced

2 tbsp (10 g) dried cherries, rehydrated and finely diced

2 tsp (15 g) raw honey

2 tsp (10 g) fresh ginger, grated

1 tsp (3 g) spicy curry powder, divided

¼ cup (60 ml) fresh lemon juice

¼ cup (60 ml) fresh lime juice

4 (6-ounce [170-g]) salmon fillets

Sea salt and pepper

Warm a heavy-bottomed frying pan over medium heat. Add the ghee. Add the onion and cook until translucent, 3 to 4 minutes. Toss in the pear, mango, pepper, garlic, dried cherries, honey, ginger and ½ teaspoon curry powder. Cook for 1 to 2 minutes. Add the lemon and lime juices and bring to a simmer. Cook until the chutney is reduced by half. Remove from the heat and set aside. This can be made in advance and reheated before serving, or it can be served at room temperature.

Generously season the salmon with salt and pepper, and with the remaining curry powder. Place a steamer basket in a large pot. Bring a small amount of water to a boil. The water should not come into the basket. Place the salmon fillets on the steamer tray, skin-side down. Cover and steam until the fish is opaque, about 10 minutes. Serve the salmon topped with chutney.

PANFRIED COD WITH HERB SAUCE

Mild-flavored cod is the perfect pairing for this herb sauce. The fish takes a back seat and allows the sauce to be the star of the show. Cod is often dredged in flour, but I prefer fresh cod to be lightly seasoned with salt and pepper and panfried with some butter. —AV

SERVES 4

FOR THE SAUCE

4 tbsp (10 g) fresh parsley, coarsely chopped

1 tbsp (3 g) mint leaves

1 tbsp (3 g) fresh basil leaves

1 tbsp (3 g) scallions, chopped

1 tbsp (8 g) tarragon

1 medium red chili, chopped

3 tbsp (45 ml) extra-virgin olive oil

1 clove garlic

2 tbsp (30 ml) lemon juice

Sea salt and pepper

2 tbsp (30 g) butter

Sea salt and pepper

4 (6-ounce [170-g]) cod fillets, without skin

Make the herb sauce. Pulse all of the ingredients in a food processor. Adjust salt and pepper to taste. Set aside.

Heat a large skillet to medium-high and add butter. Generously salt and pepper the cod. Cook until crisp and golden, about 4 minutes per side. Top with herb sauce and serve.

THAI COCONUT CURRIED MUSSELS

Wild mussels have a mild, delicate flavor and are slightly chewy. They are easily influenced by the flavors in which they are cooked. The Thai coconut curry broth provides a bright and bold flavor.—AV

SERVES 2

1 pound (455 g) mussels

1 stalk lemongrass

2 tbsp (30 ml) coconut oil

⅓ cup (80 g) shallots, sliced

1 tbsp (10 g) garlic, minced

2 tsp (10 g) fresh ginger, peeled and minced

1 tbsp (15 ml) red curry paste

2 cups (475 ml) coconut milk (for homemade page 503)

½ cup (120 ml) chicken stock

½ tsp lime zest

1 tbsp (15 ml) fresh lime juice

2 Thai red peppers, chopped

2 tsp (10 ml) fish sauce

2 kaffir lime leaves

¼ cup (7 g) cilantro, minced

Discard any damaged or open mussels. Soak the mussels in fresh water for 20 minutes. Remove the tougher outer leaves of the lemongrass until you get to the soft, yellow stalk. Trim off the bulb and slice up the yellow, fleshy parts of the lemongrass. Place the lemongrass in a food processor and process well on high. Individually remove each mussel from the water, trim the beard and set in another bowl of clean, cold water.

(continued)

Heat the coconut oil in a sauté pan over medium heat. Add the shallots and sauté until soft, about 5 minutes. Add the lemongrass, garlic, ginger and red curry paste and sauté for 1 to 2 minutes. Add the coconut milk, chicken stock, lime zest, lime juice, Thai peppers, fish sauce and lime leaves. Cook for 8 to 10 minutes. Add the mussels. Cover and cook over medium heat until the mussels open, 3 to 5 minutes. Discard lime leaves. Uncover and spoon the opened mussels into serving bowls along with the broth. Garnish with cilantro.

PANFRIED MACKEREL WITH GREEN OLIVE RELISH

Mackerel is one of the most underrated fish, and perhaps for this reason is quite inexpensive. Mackerel is a nutrition powerhouse. In addition to being high in omega-3 fats, it is loaded with minerals such as calcium, phosphorous, potassium, selenium and magnesium, and vitamins such as A, D, K, niacin, B12, Vitamin C, choline and folate.—AV

SERVES 4

FOR THE RELISH

¼ cup (60 g) shallots, diced

Filtered water

½ cup (90 g) green olives, pitted

½ tsp lemon zest

1 tbsp (3 g) fresh parsley

1 tbsp (3 g) chives

½ cup (75 g) watercress

2 tbsp (30 ml) fresh lemon juice

2 tbsp (30 ml) extra-virgin olive oil

¼ tsp sea salt

¼ tsp pepper

2 tbsp (30 g) butter

6 (4-ounce [115-g]) mackerel fillets

Cover shallots with filtered water and let sit for 10 minutes. Strain liquid. This will help take the bite out, so the shallots don't overwhelm the rest of the relish. Combine all of the ingredients for the relish in a food processor. Pulse a few times to combine, but do not overblend. Set aside.

Heat the butter in a large frying pan and fry the mackerel for 2 to 3 minutes per side. Serve topped with the green olive relish.

THAI GREEN CURRY CHICKEN

Thai food is my absolute favorite. I dream of one day eating my way through Thailand, and keeping it Paleo of course! We used to love getting takeout from Thai restaurants, but like most foods, now I prefer to make it at home myself. This green curry chicken bursts with flavor. —AV

SERVES 6

1 tbsp (15 ml) coconut oil

2 green onions, chopped

3 cloves garlic, minced

1 tsp (3 g) fresh ginger, grated

1 tbsp (15 ml) coconut aminos

1 tbsp (15 ml) fish sauce

3 tbsp (45 g) green curry paste

3 cups (700 ml) coconut milk (for homemade, see page 503)

2 kaffir lime leaves

1 small jalapeño, chopped, optional

¼ tsp sea salt

2 pounds (900 g), boneless and skinless chicken thighs

½ of a fresh lime

Cilantro for garnish

Heat coconut oil in a large sauté pan with a tight-fitting lid over medium heat. Sauté the green onion until soft, about 3 minutes. Then add the garlic, ginger, coconut aminos, fish sauce and curry paste and cook for an additional minute, until fragrant. Pour in the coconut milk, kaffir lime leaves, jalapeños and salt. Lay the chicken pieces in the mixture to poach. Bring the mixture to a simmer. Reduce to low heat and cook with the lid on for 50 minutes, or until chicken pulls apart with a fork easily. Pull the chicken apart, use a slotted spoon to remove it from the coconut milk. Squeeze in the lime juice and shower with chopped cilantro.

CHEF'S TIP

Use the remaining broth to cook vegetables for a side dish. Cook vegetables over medium heat until soft. Yams, carrots and zucchini all work well!

ADOBO MOJADO MARINATED PORK ROAST

The flavor that this seasoning blend, called adobo, imparts into the pork roast is absolutely incredible. This is my mother-in-law's famous pork roast recipe that family always requests when visiting her. It is especially popular during the holiday season and can make a great alternative to cured ham if you're looking for something new and exciting. Scale the recipe up to accommodate a whole shoulder roast or fresh ham and start a new tradition! —AT

SERVES 4-6

2 tbsp (20 g) minced garlic (about 1 whole head)

1½ tsp (9 g) fine Himalayan salt

1½ tsp (3 g) dried oregano

1 tsp (2 g) freshly ground black pepper

½ tsp ground turmeric

1 tsp (2 g) ground coriander seeds

1½ tbsp (25 ml) extra-virgin olive oil

1½ tbsp (25 ml) freshly squeezed lime juice

1 (4-5-pound [1.8-2.3-kg]) bone-in pork shoulder roast

In a small bowl, combine all the ingredients, except the pork, to form a paste.

Cut slits in the skin on the top of the roast and pierce all sides of the roast with a knife to help the seasoning blend penetrate the meat. Coat the roast with the paste and place in a large resealable plastic bag or wrap it in a few layers of plastic wrap. Allow to marinate overnight, up to 24 hours.

Before roasting, remove the pork from the refrigerator and allow to stand at room temperature for 30 minutes. Preheat the oven to 400°F (200°C).

Remove the wrappings from the pork. Roast the pork for 1 hour, uncovered and skin-side up, in a pan with sides a few inches tall to accommodate all the fat that will render out during roasting. Then, without opening the oven, lower the temperature to 300°F (150°C) and continue to roast until a meat thermometer inserted into the thickest part of the roast (not touching the bone) reads 185°F (85°C), or for 2 to 3 hours longer (40 to 45 minutes per pound [455 g] of roast). You may wish to check the roast after 1½ hours' roasting at 300°F (150°C).

The roast is done when the meat shreds easily with a fork and the fat on top is nicely crisped.

GARLIC–LIME FRIED SHREDDED BEEF

Vaca frita literally means "fried cow" and is, hands-down, my favorite Cuban dish. Some real culinary magic happens when you take slow-cooked beef, season it intensely with garlic and lime and then fry it until it achieves this tantalizing crispy-on-the-outside yet delightfully tender-on-the-inside texture. —AT

SERVES 4–6

FOR THE STEAK

2 pounds (905 g) flank steak

1 onion, quartered

1 bell pepper, stemmed, seeded and quartered

2 cloves garlic, crushed

1 bay leaf

6 black peppercorns

FOR SEASONING

1 tbsp (10 g) minced garlic

2 tsp (12 g) fine Himalayan salt

Juice of 1–2 limes

FOR FRYING

About ¼ cup (56 g) lard, avocado oil or extra-virgin olive oil, divided

1 large white onion, sliced thickly, divided

2 limes, cut into wedges

Chopped fresh cilantro, for garnish (optional)

To prepare the steak, cut it crosswise into 2 or 3 pieces and place in a large pot. Add the quartered onion, bell pepper, garlic, bay leaf and peppercorns and cover everything with water. Bring to a boil over high heat, then cover and lower the heat to a moderate simmer. Cook until the steak is falling-apart tender, 2½ to 3 hours.

Remove the steak from the pot and shred with two forks. Strain the broth and reserve for another use, discarding the cooked onion, bell pepper, bay leaf and peppercorns.

To season the steak, combine the shredded steak with the seasoning ingredients in a bowl. Tip: You can leave the cooked shredded meat in the seasoning, refrigerated, for several hours or overnight. It will make the meat more flavorful, but is not necessary. If you do batch cooking, you can actually leave it in the marinade for up to 3 days, frying it up fresh each time you eat a portion.

To fry the steak, work in batches to fry the meat. In a large skillet, heat about 2 tablespoons (28 g) of your fat of choice over medium heat for 3 to 4 minutes. Add the meat shreds to the pan without crowding them to ensure that the meat fries and does not steam. Spread out the meat with spacing throughout. Allow it to fry for 5 to 8 minutes, stirring a few times. Add about one-third of the sliced onion and continue to fry until the onion has softened, 3 to 5 minutes. Transfer the mixture to a serving plate and keep warm. Continue until all the meat and onion is cooked.

Serve with lime wedges and garnish with cilantro, if desired.

CHEF'S TIP

For a less hands-on cooking method, place all the ingredients for the steak in a slow cooker and cook on low for about 8 hours, shred the meat, then finish cooking as directed.

Although flank steak is the traditional cut used, thanks to the pronounced look of the shreds once cooked, you may also substitute a chuck roast, which usually weighs about 4 pounds (1.8 kg). Double the remaining ingredients and increase the cooking time to 3 to 4 hours for tender, fork-shreddable chuck. Or, put it all in the slow cooker as described above.

STEAK AND FRENCH FRY STIR-FRY

Lomo saltado is a fusion of Chinese and Peruvian cuisine, which arose as a result of indentured Chinese workers coming to Peru in the mid-1800s and introducing stir-frying and soy sauce to the region. The flavors and textures in this dish, with the quick-seared steak, spicy peppers and crispy fried potatoes, are sure to delight your senses and quickly turn this into a new household favorite. For a strictly Paleo version, use coconut aminos to replace the soy sauce, but note that using gluten-free tamari will result in a bolder flavor. —AT

SERVES 2

FOR THE POTATOES

1 pound (455 g) russet potatoes (about 4 medium potatoes)

About ½ cup (112 g) fat for frying (lard or duck fat recommended), or if oven-roasting, 2 tbsp (30 ml) melted fat to coat the fries

Fine Himalayan salt, to taste

FOR THE MEAT

1 pound (455 g) trimmed sirloin steak, cut into slices ½-inch (1.3-cm) thick and about 2 inches (5 cm) long

1 tbsp (15 ml) coconut aminos (or gluten-free tamari if you tolerate soy)

2 large cloves garlic, minced

½ tsp fine Himalayan salt

½ tsp freshly ground black pepper

4 tbsp (60 ml) avocado oil for frying (avocado is the only Paleo oil suitable for frying at such high temperatures)

FOR THE VEGETABLES

2-3 cloves garlic, peeled and minced

1 red onion, thickly sliced

1-2 ajíes amarillos (sold frozen or dried at some Latin American markets), or jalapeño or serrano peppers, stemmed and seeded and sliced thinly (if you prefer a nonspicy dish, substitute 1 yellow bell pepper)

3 plum tomatoes, cut into wedges

4 tbsp (60 ml) coconut aminos (or gluten-free tamari if you tolerate soy)

1 tbsp (15 ml) coconut vinegar or white wine vinegar

¼ cup (4 g) chopped fresh cilantro

To prepare the potatoes, peel and cut them lengthwise into sticks ½-inch (1.3-cm) thick, then place the sticks in a large bowl. Cover with water and let sit for at least 20 minutes. Drain and pat dry. Soaking the potatoes like this before frying is the secret to French fries that are tender on the inside and crispy on the outside. If frying the potatoes, melt the fat in a large skillet over medium heat for 4 to 5 minutes. Working in batches if necessary, carefully drop the potato sticks into the fat and cook, turning once or twice during frying, until golden brown and crispy, 20 to 25 minutes. Drain on a paper towel-lined plate and season to taste with salt.

If oven-roasting, preheat the oven to 450°F (230°C). Soak and drain as directed for frying, then coat with the melted fat and salt. Arrange the fries in a single layer on a rimmed baking sheet and bake for 25 to 35 minutes, flipping once halfway through for even cooking.

To prepare the meat, combine the strips of steak and all the meat ingredients, except the avocado oil, in a bowl and toss well. In a large skillet or wok, heat the avocado oil over high heat for 2 to 3 minutes. Cook the meat in batches as necessary; do not overcrowd the meat in the pan. Rapidly stir-fry the meat for 3 to 5 minutes, until both sides are seared. Remove with a slotted spoon and set aside.

To prepare the vegetables, using the same skillet, lower the heat to medium and add the garlic, stirring quickly for 10 to 20 seconds, then add the red onion, quickly stir-frying for 2 to 3 minutes. Add the ajíes amarillos and cook for 1 to 2 more minutes. Remove everything with a slotted spoon and set aside. Add the tomato wedges and cook, stirring frequently, for 2 to 3 minutes.

Increase the heat back to high and return the reserved vegetables and meat to the pan. Stir in the coconut aminos and vinegar. Cook, stirring frequently, for 2 to 3 minutes. Turn off the heat and stir in the cilantro. Just before serving, add the potatoes, stirring to combine with the meat and juices. Serve immediately. Traditionally paired with white rice, which you can replace with the White or Yellow Malanga "Rice" (page 286).

RIPE PLANTAIN LASAGNA OR MEAT PIE

Piñon and pastelón are two variations of a similar casserole made with ripe plantains and ground beef. Depending on where in Puerto Rico or the Dominican Republic you are, the names can be used interchangeably or even reversed. It can be confusing. One features ripe plantains cut into strips, fried and layered like lasagna. The other features mashed ripe plantains turned into a pie crust. Either way, they are both delicious and perfect for feeding a crowd. The lasagna version is not AIP-friendly but the crust version is! —AT

SERVES 8

FOR PLANTAIN LASAGNA

6 ripe plantains

¼ cup (56 g) lard, coconut oil or avocado oil for frying, plus more as needed

1½ pounds (680 g) ground beef

4 tbsp (55 g) sofrito

1 onion, diced

1 red bell pepper, diced

1½ tsp (3 g) dried oregano

2¼ tsp (11 g) fine Himalayan salt, divided

2 tbsp (13 g) sliced green olives

2 tsp (6 g) drained capers

Juice of 1 lime

6 large eggs, beaten

ADJUSTMENTS FOR THE PLANTAIN CRUST VERSION

¼ cup (30 g) sifted cassava flour

¼ cup (60 g) lard or coconut oil

1 tsp (6 g) fine Himalayan salt

Prepare the lasagna: Preheat the oven to 350°F (180°C).

To peel ripe plantains, first slice off both tips with a knife, then cut a slit in the skin down the length of the plantain. Lift off the peel with your fingers. Cut each plantain lengthwise into strips about ½-inch (1.3-cm) thick. Aim for getting five slices per plantain.

In a large skillet, heat your fat of choice over medium heat until shimmering, 3 to 5 minutes. Carefully arrange the plantain slices in a single layer in the skillet and cook until lightly browned on both sides, 3 to 5 minutes per side. Drain on a paper towel–lined plate, cooking the remaining plantains in batches until all the strips are cooked. Try to keep them whole, but it's okay if some of them break apart during cooking.

Meanwhile, in a second large skillet, you can cook the meat filling while the plantains are frying. Place the ground beef and sofrito in the pan and cook over medium heat until the meat is about three-quarters of the way browned, about 10 minutes. Add the onion and bell pepper and cook until the meat is fully browned, about 5 more minutes. Stir in the oregano, 1½ teaspoons (9 g) of the salt and the olives, capers and lime juice. Lower the heat to low and cook until the plantain slices in the other pan are all cooked.

To assemble the lasagna, grease a large baking dish (9 × 13 inches [23 × 33 cm], at least 2 inches [5 cm] deep). Beat the eggs and the remaining ¾ teaspoon of salt with a whisk and pour half of this mixture into the bottom of the prepared pan. Arrange the fried plantain slices in a single layer across the bottom of the dish, using whole strips if possible. Save any broken strips for the middle layer. You should need 9 to 10 strips per layer. Next, add half of the ground meat mixture and spread evenly. Add another layer of plantains (using up any broken strips), then the remaining meat mixture, and finish it off with the top layer of plantain, using whole slices if possible for presentation. Pour the remaining beaten egg mixture evenly on top of the casserole.

Bake for 30 minutes, or until the egg is set and top of the casserole is golden brown. Allow to rest about 5 minutes before serving. Divide into 8 square servings and enjoy!

For the crust version, after peeling the plantains, place them in a pot and cover with water. Boil until fork-tender, 15 to 20 minutes. Drain and mash with the cassava flour, fat of choice and the salt. Grease a 9 × 13-inch (23 × 33–cm) baking dish and spread about half of the plantain mash across the bottom and up the sides. Fill with the meat mixture, then cover with the remaining plantain mash (you can roll the remaining mash into small balls and flatten between your hands, arranging these pieces side by side, then smoothing the seams together with your fingers).

Bake for 30 minutes at 350°F (180°C) and allow to rest for about 5 minutes before serving.

MARINATED ROASTED CHICKEN

Pollo a la brasa is a flavorful marinated roasted chicken recipe that is traditionally cooked in a rotisserie, but that you can roast in your oven with excellent results. Thanks to the rich marinade, the skin is very well seasoned and turns out extra crispy. Be aware that restaurants may use beer and/or soy sauce (which contains gluten) so be sure to ask about the marinade if you ever dine at a Peruvian restaurant. —AT

SERVES 2–4

2 tbsp (30 ml) coconut aminos (or gluten-free tamari if you tolerate soy)

1 tbsp (10 g) minced garlic

1 tbsp (14 g) huacatay paste (also known as black mint)

½ tsp fine Himalayan salt

¼ tsp freshly ground black pepper

½ tsp dried oregano

1 tbsp (15 g) ají panca paste

1 tbsp (15 ml) extra-virgin olive oil

Juice of 1 lime

1 (3–4-pound [1.4–1.8-kg]) whole chicken

In a small bowl, combine all the ingredients except the chicken to create a marinade. Remove the giblets from the cavity of the chicken and gently separate the skin from the breast and from the thighs. Rub some of the marinade underneath the skin and use the rest to generously cover the skin of the chicken. Place the chicken in a large resealable plastic bag and remove all the air to allow the marinade to be in close contact with the skin. Place in the refrigerator for a minimum of 2 hours, but ideally overnight for the most flavor.

Preheat the oven to 375°F (190°C). Place the chicken, breast side up, in a roasting pan fitted with a rack. Bake, uncovered, for about 1½ hours, or until a meat thermometer inserted into the thickest portion of the thigh (not touching bone) reads 165°F (74°C) and the skin is browned and crispy. Serve with some salsa verde.

CHEF'S TIP

Both huacatay paste and ají panca paste are readily available to order online and highly recommended. However, to replace huacatay paste, use a mixture of 2 parts regular fresh mint, 2 parts fresh cilantro and 1 part fresh basil. Blend them together with a little olive oil to create a paste, and freeze extra in portions in an ice cube tray. You can use pasilla peppers or ancho chiles to replace the ají panca.

MOFONGO STUFFED WITH SHRIMP

Mofongo is one of my all-time favorite Puerto Rican dishes. It is incredible to me just how flavorful the combination of fried plantains, garlic and chicharrónes (cracklings) is! It can be served as a side dish, but it transforms into a hearty main dish when stuffed with shrimp cooked in a rich tomato sauce. —AT

SERVES 4

1 batch Mofongo (page 81)

FOR THE CAMARONES

2 tbsp (30 ml) extra-virgin olive oil

4 tbsp (55 g) sofrito

2 large cloves garlic, minced

1 (15-ounce [425-g]) can plain tomato sauce

1 orange or yellow bell pepper, minced

1 small onion, minced

¼ tsp fine Himalayan salt

¼ tsp freshly ground black pepper

1 pound (455 g) medium peeled and deveined shrimp

2 tbsp (2 g) minced fresh cilantro, for garnish

(continued)

Cook the mofongo and the camarones simultaneously so they are both ready at the same time.

To prepare the camarones, in a large sauté pan, heat the olive oil over medium heat for 1 to 2 minutes, add the sofrito and stir for 2 to 4 minutes (longer if cooking with frozen sofrito), until sizzling and fragrant. Add the garlic and cook for an additional 60 seconds.

Pour in the tomato sauce, add the bell pepper, onion, salt and black pepper and bring to a simmer. Cook for 3 to 4 minutes to soften the bell pepper and onion. Add the shrimp and simmer until they are cooked through, 6 to 8 minutes.

Divide the mofongo into four portions. Shape each portion into a mound and then create an indentation in the center, forming a bowl shape (just like making mashed potato volcanoes when you were a kid!). Generously fill with the shrimp and sauce, allowing it to overflow out from the center. Garnish with the cilantro and serve immediately.

SHREDDED BEEF IN TOMATO SAUCE

Ropa vieja literally translates as "old clothes," and the legend attached to this dish says that there was once a peasant who had no meat to feed his family, so he put his old clothes into the stew pot and they were magically transformed by his love and good intentions into this delicious dish. Others say the dish got its name because the shredded meat resembles tattered cloth. Regardless, it is a hearty, classic dish and is excellent for batch cooking. —AT

SERVES 4–6

3 tbsp (45 ml) olive oil

2 pounds (905 g) flank steak, cut crosswise into 3 or 4 pieces

6–8 cloves garlic, minced

1 large onion, diced

1 large bell pepper (any color), seeded and diced

½ tsp fine Himalayan salt

¼ tsp freshly ground black pepper

1 (8-ounce [235-g]) can plain tomato sauce

2 bay leaves

1½ tsp (3 g) dried oregano

1½ tsp (4 g) ground cumin

3–4 cups (710–946 ml) water or Slow Cooker Chicken Broth (page 170)

1 (1-ounce [28-g]) jar capers, drained

½ cup (50 g) sliced green Manzanilla olives

2 tbsp (2 g) minced fresh cilantro

In a large Dutch oven or heavy-bottomed pot, heat the olive oil over medium-high heat for 3 to 4 minutes. Brown the meat on both sides, 5 to 8 minutes. Transfer to a plate and set aside.

Lower the heat to medium and add the garlic, cooking briefly until fragrant, 15 to 20 seconds. Then, add the onion and bell pepper and cook, stirring frequently, for about 5 minutes. Add the salt, black pepper, tomato sauce, bay leaves, oregano, cumin and water or broth and bring to a boil over high heat. Return the browned meat to the pan and cover, lowering the heat to a simmer. Cook until the meat is tender and shreds easily with two forks, 2½ to 3 hours, stirring the pot every 30 to 45 minutes; if the sauce thickens too much, you can add extra water in ½-cup (120-ml) increments. During the last 30 minutes or so of cooking, add the capers and olives.

Once the meat is tender enough to shred, remove it from the pot and carefully shred it with two forks. Add the shreds back to the pot and stir in the cilantro.

Serve immediately with White or Yellow Malanga "Rice" (page 286) and/or Fried Ripe Plantains (page 283).

CHEF'S TIP

For a less hands-on cooking method, place all the ingredients, except the capers, olives and cilantro, in a slow cooker and cook on low for about 8 hours. Shred the meat, stir it together with the sauce and add the capers, olives and cilantro.

While flank steak is the traditional cut used because of the pronounced look of the cooked shreds, you may also substitute a more economical chuck roast, which usually weighs about 4 pounds (1.8 kg). Double the other ingredients and increase the cooking time to 3 to 4 hours for tender, fork-shreddable chuck. Or put it all in the slow cooker as described above.

MOJO MARINATED PORK ROAST

The term lechón asado typically refers to the Cuban method for roasting a whole suckling pig, but can also mean a flavorful pork roast done right in your oven. Allowing a pork roast to marinate overnight in mojo criollo, which is a blend of sour orange juice and garlic, results in a moist and tender roast of which you'll certainly be asking for seconds. —AT

SERVES 4–6

1½ cups (355 ml) Mojo Criollo (page 520)

½ cup (80 g) finely diced onion

2 large onions, sliced into rings

1 (4-5-pound [1.8-2.3-kg]) bone-in pork shoulder roast

Cut slits in the skin on the top of the pork roast and pierce all sides of the roast with a knife, to help the mojo criollo marinade penetrate the meat. Coat the roast with the marinade and the diced onion and place in a large resealable plastic bag. Allow to marinate overnight, up to 24 hours.

Before roasting, remove the pork from the refrigerator and allow to stand at room temperature for 30 minutes. Preheat the oven to 400°F (200°C). Arrange the onion rings across the bottom of a pan that has sides a few inches (cm) tall (this is to accommodate all of the fat that renders out during roasting). Remove the pork from the bag. Place the roast, skin side up, on top of the bed of onions and roast, uncovered, for 1 hour. Then, without opening the oven, lower the temperature to 300°F (150°C) and continue to roast until a meat thermometer inserted into the thickest part of the roast (not touching the bone) reads 185°F (85°C), or 2 to 3 hours longer (40 to 45 minutes per pound [455 g] of roast). You may wish to check the roast after 1½ hours' roasting at 300°F (150°C).

The roast is done when the meat shreds easily with a fork and the fat on top is nicely crisped.

MOJO MARINATED AND FRIED PORK CUBES

At most Cuban restaurants you will see masas de puerco as a main dish option. Well, these are masitas, or "little pieces," because this version is pan-fried rather than deep-fried, and cutting the pork into small chunks makes it faster and easier to cook this dish. Marinating in mojo criollo gives these fried chunks of delicious pork their signature flavor. You will love the contrasting textures in this dish: crispy and caramelized on the outside, yet tender on the inside. —AT

SERVES 6–8

1 (2-2¼-pound [905–1021-g]) pork loin roast, trimmed of fat

1 cup (235 ml) Mojo Criollo (page 520), made using only 2 tbsp (30 ml) extra-virgin olive oil

6-8 tbsp (84-112 g) lard or avocado oil for frying (using extra as needed)

1 large white onion, peeled and cut into rings, divided

Cut the trimmed loin roast into chunks no larger than 1 inch (2.5 cm) in any dimension. Place the pork chunks in an airtight container, pour in the mojo criolo to coat evenly and allow to marinate in the refrigerator a minimum of 4 hours, ideally overnight.

Remove the chunks from the marinade and pat them dry on paper towels. Reserve the marinade for the end of the recipe.

Preheat the oven to 275°F (140°C) to keep the pork warm as you fry it in batches.

(continued)

In a medium or large skillet or Dutch oven, heat your fat of choice over medium heat until shimmering, about 5 minutes. You will need at least ½ inch (1.3 cm) of fat in the pan. (The larger the pan, the more fat you will use, but the faster you can cook the batches. It is up to you whether you prefer to use less fat or cook faster.) Add pork chunks to the hot oil without crowding the pieces and fry, turning often, until all sides are browned and crispy, 8 to 12 minutes total. Transfer with a slotted spoon to an ovenproof dish and place in the warm oven. Repeat until all the chunks are cooked.

After the last pieces of pork have been cooked, drain all but about 2 tablespoons (30 ml) of fat from the pan. Add about half of the sliced onion rings to the pan and cook briefly, about 1 minute, before adding the reserved marinade. Toss to combine and cook, stirring often, for about 5 minutes, scraping the bottom of the pan with a wooden spoon to scrape up any burnt bits. Add the remaining onion rings and continue to cook for about 5 minutes more.

Combine the cooked onions with the fried pork chunks in a serving dish and serve immediately. Pairs wonderfully with Twice-Fried Green Plantains (page 284) or Fried Ripe Plantains (page 283).

CHAYOTE SQUASH STUFFED WITH MEAT

Chayotes are delicious tropical squashes that are perfect to stuff with meat and bake like stuffed peppers. They do take quite a while to cook, though, but the hands-on time in this recipe is minimal. Make a big batch to feed a crowd. Leftovers reheat very well, too, making this recipe great for batch cooking. —AT

SERVES 6–8

6 large chayotes, cut in half lengthwise

1 tbsp plus 1 tsp (24 g) fine Himalayan salt

2 tbsp (30 ml) extra-virgin olive oil

2 tbsp (30 g) sofrito

4 medium cloves garlic, minced

1 small onion, diced finely

1 pound (455 g) ground beef

4 tbsp (64 g) tomato paste

Juice of 2 limes

2 tsp (6 g) drained capers

1 tsp (2 g) dried oregano

12 pieces dairy-free white cheese, optional

Place the halved chayotes in a large pot and cover with water; add 1 tablespoon (18 g) of the salt. Bring to a boil over high heat, then lower the heat to a low boil, cover and cook until the chayotes are fork-tender, about 45 minutes to 1 hour.

Meanwhile, in a large skillet, heat the olive oil over medium heat for 1 to 2 minutes. Add the sofrito and remaining teaspoon (6 g) of salt and cook for 2 to 3 minutes, until fragrant (longer if using frozen sofrito). Add the garlic and onion and cook for 3 to 4 minutes. Add the remaining ingredients except the "cheese" and break up the ground beef, cooking, stirring occasionally, until the meat is no longer pink, about 15 minutes. Reduce the heat to low to keep warm until the chayotes are ready.

Preheat the oven to 400°F (200°C).

Drain the chayotes and carefully scoop out and discard the tough, fibrous core from the center, leaving as much flesh as possible. Then, be very careful to scoop out the flesh while leaving the shell intact. Add the flesh to the meat mixture, increase the heat to medium and allow to simmer for 5 to 10 minutes to allow the flavors to meld.

Arrange the chayote shells on cookie sheets or in glass baking dishes and fill with the meat mixture. Bake for 10 minutes. If desired, you may top them with slices of dairy-free white cheese during the last 5 to 7 minutes of baking. Serve with your favorite side dishes.

TROPICAL STARCH STEW

Sancocho is a type of hearty stew popular in many countries. It is traditionally prepared on Sundays, using up leftover ingredients from the week. It is an easy one-pot meal to put together and share with loved ones. My mother-in-law likes to use a wide variety of starchy fruits and tubers in her sancocho and would traditionally put corn on the cob in hers as well, which I have omitted here to keep it grain-free and Paleo. Yuca and plantains are typically the easiest to find, and you can use another squash for the calabaza and white potatoes in place of the malanga and taro. —AT

SERVES 6–8

2–4 tbsp (30–60 ml) extra-virgin olive oil (use more if cooking raw meat)

4 tbsp (55 g) sofrito

1½ pounds (680 g) cubed fresh meat (such as stew beef or pork or chicken breast)

1 large onion, diced

2–3 quarts (1.9–2.8 L) Slow Cooker Chicken Broth (page 170), divided

1 pound (455 g) peeled and cored yuca (frozen recommended)

1 green plantain, peeled and sliced into 1-inch (2.5-cm) rounds

1 ripe plantain, peeled and sliced into 1-inch (2.5-cm) rounds

1 small piece (½–1 pound [225–455 g]) calabaza squash, peeled and cut in 1-inch (2.5-cm) pieces (can substitute butternut squash or regular pumpkin)

1–2 malangas, peeled and cut into 1-inch (2.5-cm) pieces

1 small taro root, peeled and cut into 1-inch (2.5-cm) pieces

1 tsp (6 g) fine Himalayan salt

½ tsp freshly ground black pepper

1 tsp ground turmeric

In a large stockpot, heat the olive oil over medium heat for 1 to 2 minutes, then add the sofrito. Cook, stirring constantly, until sizzling and fragrant, about 2 to 4 minutes (longer if using frozen).

If using raw meat, add it now and stir frequently to sear all sides, about 5 minutes. Add the onion and continue to sauté until it is translucent, 3 to 5 minutes more. If you are using leftover shredded meat, add it together with the onion, cooking for 3 to 5 minutes.

Use a wooden spoon to scrape up any browned bits from the bottom of the pan, if necessary, and add a few cups (235 to 475 ml) of broth to deglaze the pan. Next, add all the remaining ingredients, topping off with enough broth to cover. Note that traditionally this is not a watery soup. Bring to a boil over high heat, then cover the pot and lower the heat to a simmer. Cook for at least 30 minutes, or until all the starches are tender. Overcooking will cause the ripe plantains and calabaza to fall apart.

SHREDDED BEEF, RIPE PLANTAINS, "BEANS" AND "RICE"

Pabellón criollo is considered to be the national dish of Venezuela and consists of four parts: tender shredded meat (called carne mechada), fried sweet plantains (called plátanos maduros), black beans (called caraotas negras) and white rice. To create a strictly Paleo version, I have devised not one but two options to replace both the white rice and the black beans. This dish is served as a hearty meal, but you can also take a small portion of each of the four components and stuff them inside an arepa or even inside an empanada. —AT

SERVES 4–6

FOR THE *CARNE MECHADA*

2 pounds (905 g) flank steak

2 onions (1 quartered, 1 diced), divided

1 bay leaf

1 fresh mint leaf, or ½ tsp dried

3 tbsp (45 ml) extra-virgin olive oil

1 red bell pepper, diced

3 large cloves garlic, minced

2 tbsp (30 ml) coconut aminos

1 tsp (5 ml) cider vinegar or lime juice

1½ tsp (9 g) fine Himalayan salt

Freshly ground black pepper

2 tbsp (2 g) chopped fresh cilantro

½ tsp ground cumin

TO SERVE

Cauliflower rice or White or Yellow Malanga "Rice" (page 286)

Vegetable Black "Beans" (page 290) or Yuca Black "Beans" (page 291)

2 or 3 yellow plantains, cooked according to the directions for Fried Ripe Plantains on page 283

To prepare the carne mechada, cut the flank steak crosswise into two or three pieces and place in a large pot. Add the quartered onion, bay leaf and mint and cover everything with water. Bring to a boil over high heat, then cover and lower the heat to a moderate simmer. Cook until the steak is falling-apart tender, 2½ to 3 hours. During the last half hour or so of cooking, you can work on preparing the rice, beanless caraotas and plantains.

When the meat is cooked, remove the steak and shred with two forks. Strain the broth and reserve for another use, discarding the cooked onion and leaves.

In a large skillet, heat the olive oil over medium heat for 2 to 3 minutes. Add the diced onion and red pepper and cook for 6 to 8 minutes. Add all the remaining carne mechada ingredients and mix well, then stir in the shredded beef. Let it all simmer together for about 5 minutes to let the flavors meld.

When plating the pabellón criollo, you can divide the plate into equal quarters and fill one with carne mechada, one with rice, one with the beanless caraotas and one with fried plantain slices. Alternatively, you can arrange the four components in parallel lines across the plate.

PUPUSAS CON CHICHARRÓN O "QUESO"

Pupusas are a beloved dish in El Salvador. The dough is traditionally made from *masa harina* (nixtamalized corn, which tortillas are also made from), which was tough to replace but I think this blend of flours works very well. This type of seasoned pork filling is called *chicharrón*, but it is not to be confused with fried pork belly—yes, different countries use the same word to mean different things! You can also fill them with a blend of a little meat and a little "cheese." Have fun with it! —AT

MAKES 8 *PUPUSAS*

FOR THE *CHICHARRÓN* FILLING

1 pound (455 g) ground pork

¾ tsp (5 g) fine Himalayan salt

½ tsp (1 g) freshly ground black pepper

½ medium tomato, diced

½ medium onion, diced

2 tsp (4 g) dried oregano

FOR THE DOUGH

1 cup (112 g) sifted coconut flour

1 cup (128 g) tapioca starch

½ tsp fine Himalayan salt

1½ cups (355 ml) filtered water

Olive oil, for forming the dough

8 slices dairy-free white cheese, optional

2 tbsp (28 g) fat of choice for frying (lard, ghee, coconut oil or avocado oil), plus extra as needed

Fermented Curtido (page 253), for garnish

First, prepare the filling. Heat a large skillet over medium heat for 1 to 2 minutes. Add the ground pork and cook, stirring occasionally, for about 5 minutes. Add the remaining filling ingredients to the pan and cook for an additional 5 to 10 minutes, or until the pork is cooked through. Remove from the heat and allow to cool while you prepare the dough.

To prepare the dough, it is important to measure coconut flour precisely. I prefer measuring for baked goods by weight rather than volume since it is more accurate. I use a fine-mesh strainer to sift my flours, then scoop with my measuring cups and level with a knife.

In a large mixing bowl, combine the flours and salt and stir well. Add the water and use a spoon to stir and form a dough. Continue to work the dough using your hands, then allow the dough to rest for several minutes to soak up the water.

Rub a little olive oil into your hands to make it easier to work with the dough. Divide the dough into eight portions. Roll a portion into a ball between your palms, then press your thumb in the middle a few times to form a pocket. Add about 2 tablespoons (30 g) of the filling, a slice of dairy-free white cheese or a mixture of both, and press the opening closed. Gently flatten the ball into a disk shape. Repeat with the remaining dough.

In a medium skillet, heat your fat of choice over medium heat for 2 to 3 minutes. Cook the *pupusas* in batches so you don't overcrowd the pan. Cook them for 3 to 4 minutes on each side, or until browned and crispy. Drain on a paper towel–lined plate.

Serve with generous amounts of *curtido*. This recipe works well to make a double or triple batch of *pupusas* and freeze for later. To reheat from frozen, cook in a skillet for 5 to 10 minutes, or until warmed through.

CHEF'S TIP
The pupusas will hold their shape more easily if the meat filling is chilled. You can place the meat in the freezer to chill it quickly, or simply make the meat filling in advance and refrigerate it.

CHAPTER 2

SLOW COOKER

For busy people following a Paleo diet, the slow cooker will become your best friend. For some of us, this is the only way we are able to stay committed to this lifestyle. Preparing healthful meals from fresh ingredients can be really time consuming.

The slow cooker allows us to spend less time in the kitchen but still enjoy a nourishing and tasty meal. You can toss some of these recipes in your slow cooker before you head to the office, and you can come home to a warm dinner waiting for you.

The slow cooker is also a great way to save money. It gives us a chance to use tough, inexpensive cuts of meat that become juicy, tender and delicious when they are cooked low and slow.

Some of my personal go-tos from this chapter include Easy Slow Cooker Chicken Verde (page 153), Slow Cooker Stuffing (page 169) and Butternut Squash N'Oatmeal (page 167).

BLACKBERRY, BALSAMIC SHORT RIBS

Sweet and tart blackberries give these slow-cooked short ribs a unique, rich flavor. These can be made with fresh or frozen berries, depending on the season. These short ribs will fall apart with a fork for a scrumptious dinner everyone will love! Serve over a bed of Root Vegetable Hash (page 213) or cauliflower rice. —CP

SERVES 4–6

3 pounds (1.4 kg) boneless beef short ribs

1½ tsp (4.5 g) sea salt

¾ tsp black pepper

1 tsp (3 g) smoked paprika

½ tsp dried thyme

1 pound (454 g) fresh blackberries

1½ cups (360 g) tomato purée

⅓ cup (80 ml) balsamic vinegar

1 tbsp (15 ml) butter or ghee

Root Vegetable Hash (page 213) or cauliflower rice, to serve

Remove the short ribs from the refrigerator. Mix together salt, pepper, paprika and thyme, creating a rub mixture. Pat short ribs dry with a paper towel to remove any excess moisture. Sprinkle both sides of short ribs with the spices, using your fingers to rub into the meat. Set aside for 30 minutes and bring meat to room temperature.

Preheat oven to 225°F (105°C). Warm a Dutch oven to medium heat on the stove.

Place blackberries, tomato purée and vinegar in a blender. Blend on high for at least 30 seconds. Scrape down the sides of the blender and briefly blend again.

Melt the butter in the hot pan. Working in batches sear the short ribs for 1 minute, flip and sear on the other side for an additional minute. Pour the blackberry sauce over the short ribs and place in the oven.

Bake for 5 hours or until meat easily shreds apart. You may want to skim the top layer of blackberry foam off the top of the ribs about halfway through the cooking process.

Serve warm with Root Vegetable Hash or cauliflower rice.

CHEF'S TIP:

If you use a high-speed blender the blackberry seeds will be broken down and become unnoticeable; if you do not have a high-speed blender you will want to strain out the seeds.

WEEKNIGHT SHREDDED PORK TACOS

Growing up in southern California, tacos were always my favorite food and I have grown to love wrapping my favorite meats and salsas in butter leaf lettuce for a Paleo alternative. Cook the pork all day and chop up the Spicy Pear Salsa (page 251) just as you are about to serve. Dinner can be on the table in minutes with minimal clean up and stress! —CP

SERVES 6–8

2 tsp (6 g) salt

1½ tsp (4.5 g) chili pepper

½ tsp fresh cracked black pepper

¼ tsp ground cinnamon

3½ pounds (1590 g) boneless pork shoulder roast

2 tbsp (30 ml) bacon grease

⅓ cup fresh orange juice

2 tbsp (30 ml) fresh lime juice

Butter lettuce leaves, guacamole and Spicy Pear Salsa (page 251) for serving

(continued)

Preheat oven to 225°F (105°C) and warm a Dutch oven on the stove to medium heat.

Mix together salt, chili, pepper and cinnamon, to make a spice rub. Slice pork roast into four chunks and rub spices into both sides of meat.

Melt bacon grease in the pan on the stove. Brown meat chunks for 1 minute, then turn and continue browning on the other side. Pour juices on top and place the lid on the Dutch oven. Bake for 5½ hours, turning the meat halfway through to incorporate the juices. Meat will shred apart very easily when fully cooked.

Serve shredded pork taco meat in a butter lettuce leaf cup garnished with guacamole and Spicy Pear Salsa.

LOADED MEXICAN NACHOS

Easy slow-cooked and flavorful chicken tops this fun spin on traditional nachos. I am a huge fan of Southwest flavors and these loaded Mexican nachos hit the spot. I think you'll enjoy using peppers instead of tortilla chips. Pile high the toppings and dig in! —KW

SERVES 2–3 AS A MEAL OR 4–6 AS AN APPETIZER

CROCKPOT CHICKEN INGREDIENTS

2–3 chicken breasts, fresh or frozen

2 tsp (6 g) chili powder

1 tsp (3 g) ground cumin

½ tsp smoked paprika

½ tsp garlic powder

½ tsp dried oregano

Salt and pepper, to taste

1 cup (237 ml) chicken stock

1 tbsp (4 g) fresh cilantro

Peppers of choice (bell peppers, poblanos, jalapeños, banana peppers, etc.)

OPTIONAL TOPPINGS

1–2 tomatoes, diced

4 green onions, chopped

1–2 avocados, diced

1–2 cups (70–140 g) romaine lettuce, shredded

¼ cup (15 g) fresh cilantro

Black olives, sliced

Place the chicken in the slow cooker. Mix all the spices together in a small bowl and pour over the chicken. Next add the chicken stock. Give it a good stir and then add in the cilantro. Cover and cook on high for 3 to 4 hours or low for 6 to 8 hours. After the chicken is done cooking, take it out of the cooker and shred it with two forks. You can add about ¼ cup (60 ml) of the remaining liquid to the chicken if you like the chicken juicier.

Once the chicken is finished slow cooking, preheat oven to 350°F (180°C, or gas mark 4). Cut the peppers into the size of tortilla chips and remove any seeds. If they are small peppers like jalapeño or banana, they just need to be cut in half. If they are larger peppers like bell peppers, they will need to be cut a few times.

Place the peppers on a baking tray. Add the chicken on top of the peppers. Add any toppings you wish. Bake for 10 to 15 minutes.

SLOW COOKER INDIAN CHICKEN CURRY

This curry takes a little extra effort, but it's worth it. It is hearty, filling and bursts with flavor. —AV

SERVES 8

1 large onion, chopped

1 small cauliflower, chopped (about 4 cups [428 g])

1 large carrot, chopped

1 large sweet potato, peeled and chopped

4 cloves garlic, minced

2 tsp (6 g) ground cumin

2 tsp (6 g) ground coriander

½ tsp turmeric

½ tsp cayenne

½ tsp garam masala

½ tsp ground ginger

1½ pounds (680 g) boneless, skinless, chicken thighs, cut into 1½-inch (3.8-cm) chunks

1 tbsp (15 g) tomato paste

1 cup (235 ml) chicken broth

3 cups (705 ml) coconut milk

4 ounces (112 g) baby spinach

Optional garnishes: cilantro and chili pepper flakes

Place onions, cauliflower, carrot, sweet potato and garlic in the slow cooker. In a small bowl, combine the cumin, coriander, turmeric, cayenne, garam masala and ginger. Toss the chicken with the tomato paste and the spice mixture. When it is well coated, place the chicken in the slow cooker. Add the broth and the coconut milk. Cook on low for 4 to 6 hours, or until chicken is cooked through. Add the spinach the last 10 minutes of cooking. Top with cilantro and chili pepper and serve.

CHEF'S TIPS:

You can add the cauliflower and sweet potato halfway through cooking to avoid overcooking.

LAZY SUNDAY POT ROAST

Prep this comforting and nourishing meal in minutes, toss it in the slow cooker and have a healthy meal ready for dinner. —AV

SERVES 8

3-4 pounds (1362-1816 g) chuck roast

1 tsp (3 g) dried oregano

½ tsp paprika

2 tsp (6 g) ground cumin

Salt and pepper

2 tbsp (30 g) ghee, divided

1 onion, sliced

3 cloves garlic

3 carrots, chopped

2 ribs celery, chopped

1 cup (235 ml) beef stock

Coat the chuck roast with oregano, paprika and cumin. Salt and pepper generously. Heat 1 tablespoon (15 g) of ghee in a heavy-bottomed pan. Sauté onions until translucent, about 5 minutes. Add garlic, carrots and celery and sauté for a few minutes until fragrant, about 3 to 4 minutes. Move all vegetables into the slow cooker.

Heat the remaining tablespoon (15 g) of ghee in the same pan. Brown roast for a few minutes on each side, about 2 to 3 minutes per side. Move to slow cooker. Add beef stock and cook on low for 6 to 8 hours. Salt and pepper before serving.

BBQ PULLED PORK

This BBQ Pulled Pork is an easy recipe for a weeknight. It packs plenty of heat and robust flavor and pairs very well with a side of Creamy Bacon Brussels Sprouts (page 224). Leftovers are great on a grain-free sandwich roll, like Grain-Free Fluffy White Dinner Rolls (page 522). —RM

SERVES 6

1 small white onion, chopped

1 tbsp (8 g) chili powder

1 tbsp (8 g) unsweetened cocoa powder

1 tbsp (12 g) coconut sugar or maple syrup

2 tsp (6 g) garlic salt

1 tsp (3 g) onion powder

1 tsp (3 g) ground cumin

1 tsp (3 g) paprika

¾ tsp cayenne pepper

½ tsp black pepper

½ tsp ground cinnamon

3 pounds (1.4 kg) pork butt (or shoulder)

1 cup (250 g) Paleo-approved BBQ sauce

Place onions at the bottom of the slow cooker. In a bowl, mix all of the dry seasonings together. Rub on all sides of the pork butt. Place it in the slow cooker then pour the BBQ sauce on top. Cover and cook on low heat for 6 to 8 hours. Remove the pork from the slow cooker and set it on a large plate. Use two forks to lightly shred the meat while removing any fatty pieces. Drizzle the leftover BBQ juice on top of the pulled pork and serve immediately.

SMOKY BBQ BEEF

This BBQ beef with barbeque sauce made from scratch only takes about 15 minutes to assemble! If you are going to make this first thing in the morning before you head to work, you can slice the onion the night before and mix the BBQ sauce. In the morning, it will only take you a few minutes to make this delicious meal. —AV

SERVES 6

1 onion, sliced

3–4 pounds (1362–1816 g) beef brisket

Salt and pepper

FOR THE BBQ SAUCE

8 ounces (227 g) tomato paste

3 tbsp (45 ml) apple cider vinegar

2 tbsp (30 ml) honey

½ tsp cayenne

½ tsp crushed red pepper

2 tsp (6 g) sea salt

1 tsp (3 g) dry mustard

1 tsp (3 g) paprika

1 tsp (3 g) onion powder

3 cloves garlic, crushed

2 tbsp (30 ml) coconut aminos

1 tap liquid smoke

Place the onions in the bottom of the slow cooker. Generously salt and pepper the brisket and place on top of the onions. In a separate bowl, mix the tomato paste, apple cider vinegar, honey, cayenne, crushed red pepper, sea salt, dry mustard, paprika, onion powder, garlic, coconut aminos and liquid smoke. Pour the BBQ sauce over the beef. Cook on low for 8 to 10 hours, or until meat is fork tender and shreds easily. Adjust salt and pepper to taste. Serve and enjoy!

SLOW COOKER SLOPPY JOES

For a more sophisticated take on sloppy joes, I recommend serving these over some roasted sweet potatoes. The slight sweetness from the beef combines with the sweet potato wonderfully to make a delicious and filling meal. When choosing chili powders, take care to purchase one that is made of spices only. Read the ingredient label carefully. Chili powder ingredients often include additives and anti-caking agents. —AV

SERVES 6

2 pounds (908 g) ground beef

1 green bell pepper, chopped

1 leek, diced, white and light green parts only

4 cloves garlic, minced

2 tbsp (30 ml) honey

2 cups (480 g) strained tomatoes (find this near the marinara sauces)

6 tbsp (90 g) tomato paste

2 tbsp (30 ml) coconut aminos

1 tsp (3 g) chili powder

½ tsp chili pepper flakes

Salt and pepper to taste

Place the ground beef, bell pepper and the leeks in the slow cooker. In a medium sized bowl, combine the garlic, honey, strained tomatoes, tomato paste, coconut aminos, chili powder and chili pepper flakes. Pour the tomato mixture over the meat and vegetables in the slow cooker. Use a wooden spoon to break up the ground beef. Cook on low for 4 to 6 hours, or until the meat is cooked through. Adjust salt and pepper to taste. Serve and enjoy!

SLOW COOKER BARBACOA

Barbacoa is a Mexican dish that is often served with corn tortillas and guacamole. We often enjoy this over salad or with Tortillas (page 529). —AV

SERVES 8

5 dried chipotle peppers, rehydrated

1 cup (240 g) strained tomatoes

¼ cup (60 ml) apple cider vinegar

½ cup (80 g) onion, chopped

4 cloves garlic

2 tbsp (30 ml) honey

1 tbsp (15 g) sea salt

1 tsp (3 g) ground cumin

½ tsp ground cinnamon

¼ tsp ground allspice

⅛ tsp ground cloves

1 tsp (3 g) oregano

2 tsp (6 g) fish sauce

½ cup (120 ml) Slow Cooker Beef Broth (page 171)

¼ cup (60 ml) liquid from rehydrating peppers

3-4 pounds (1362–1816 g) chuck roast, cut into 3-4 large chunks

2 bay leaves

Tortillas (page 529), for serving

Rehydrate the peppers by covering them with hot water for 30 minutes. Reserve the water. In a food processor, combine all of the ingredients, except for the bay leaves and the chuck roast. Blend until all the ingredients are well combined. Place the chuck roast in the slow cooker. Add the bay leaves. Pour the sauce over the roast. Cook on low for 8 hours or until the meat pulls apart easily. Use a slotted spoon to remove the meat from the slow cooker. Adjust salt and pepper to taste. Serve on Tortillas and enjoy!

EASY SLOW COOKER TACO MEAT

Taco meat is a Paleo go-to food. Top a salad with guacamole, salsa, green onions and this taco meat for a quick, easy and tasty dinner. —AV

SERVES 6

1 tbsp (8 g) chili powder

1 tsp (3 g) ground cumin

1 tsp (3 g) sea salt

1 tsp (3 g) black pepper

½ tsp ground coriander

½ tsp dried oregano

½ tsp garlic powder

½ tsp onion powder

¼ tsp paprika

¼ tsp crushed red pepper

2 pounds (908 g) ground beef

3 tbsp (45 g) tomato paste

In a small bowl combine all of the spices. Add the beef, tomato paste and spices to the slow cooker. Use a spoon to mix up the ingredients and break up the meat. Cook on low for 4 hours.

Break up the meat some more. Use a slotted spoon to remove the meat from the slow cooker and serve!

CHEF'S TIP:

You can reserve 2 teaspoons (10 g) of the taco seasoning and add it in the last 30 minutes of cooking. This extra step isn't necessary, but it will heighten the flavor of the meat!

SLOW COOKER CARNITAS

A fatty cut of pork, a slow cooker and some basic spices are all that's needed to create a dish that melts in your mouth and requires very little effort. Just combine everything together, check it every once in a while and let your slow cooker do the heavy lifting for you. This carnitas tastes even better as leftovers the next day. —JC

SERVES 8

3½ pounds (1590 g) pork shoulder

4 cloves garlic, crushed

1 medium onion, sliced

1½ cups (355 ml) Slow Cooker Chicken Broth (page 170), plus extra if needed

1 tbsp (8 g) ground cumin

1 tbsp (8 g) paprika

1 tbsp (8 g) dried oregano

1 tsp (3 g) ground coriander

2 tbsp (16 g) black peppercorns

1 tsp (3 g) salt

3 bay leaves

Place all ingredients in a slow cooker. Cover and cook on low for 8 hours. Check every couple of hours to make sure there is enough liquid left. If it starts to dry out, add a little bit more broth.

Once cooked, skim off excess fat that rises to the top. Let it rest uncovered until it is cool enough to handle, about 20 minutes. Shred the meat using two forks. Discard the bay leaves and whole peppercorns before serving.

EASY SLOW COOKER ROAST CHICKEN

Slow cooker chicken is a go-to on the Paleo diet. It's flavorful, but not bold, so you can serve it with a variety of vegetables throughout the week. —AV

SERVES 6–8

1 (3–4-pound [1362–1816-g]) roasting chicken

Salt and pepper

1 tbsp (15 ml) ghee, melted

¼ tsp allspice

1 small orange, zested and quartered

2 cloves garlic, minced

1 small apple, chopped

Remove the giblets from the chicken, if there are any. Rinse the chicken and pat it dry. Liberally salt and pepper the inside of the chicken. Rub the chicken with the ghee and sprinkle with salt and pepper. Rub with allspice, orange zest and garlic. Stuff the cavity with the chopped apple and quartered orange. Tie the legs together with kitchen string and tuck the wing tips under the body of the chicken. Place the chicken in the slow cooker, breast side down. You don't need any cooking liquid, it will make its own. Cook on low for 6 hours.

EASY SLOW COOKER CHICKEN VERDE

We always keep some organic chicken thighs in our freezer and bottled salsa verde in our pantry. On the busiest of days, all I have to do is remember to pull the chicken out of the freezer the night before. Some blog readers have told me that when they forget to take the chicken out of the freezer, they just add it to the slow cooker still frozen and it still works. I haven't tried that myself yet! —AV

SERVES 6

2 pounds (908 g) boneless, skinless chicken thighs

16 ounces (454 g) salsa verde

Add chicken to the slow cooker. Cover with salsa verde and cook on low for 5 hours. If you are home, you can open the lid at the 4-hour mark and shred the chicken with two forks; if not, no worries, it will still turn out fine! Use a slotted spoon to remove the chicken from the cooker, leaving the liquid behind. Salt and pepper to taste and serve. Prepared salsa is already quite salty, so it doesn't require additional salt.

CHEF'S TIP:
The recipe is great as is, but these are some optional things you can do to enhance the flavor:

- *Brown the chicken in some ghee or cooking fat of your choice before placing it in the slow cooker.*

- *When choosing packaged salsa, read the ingredients carefully and make sure that there is nothing listed that you don't recognize as food.*

SLOW COOKER TERIYAKI CHICKEN

Easy and flavorful, slow cooker recipes like this one are invaluable when following a Paleo diet. Coconut aminos are key in making a Paleo teriyaki sauce. Naturally slightly sweet, it doesn't require as much sweetener to get that teriyaki flavor. —AV

SERVES 4–6

2 pounds (908 g) skinless chicken thighs (bone-in or boneless)

½ cup (120 ml) coconut aminos

1 tbsp (15 ml) honey

1 tbsp (6 g) fresh ginger, grated

2 cloves garlic, minced

Salt and pepper

Place chicken in the slow cooker. In a small bowl, mix coconut aminos, honey, fresh ginger and garlic. Pour the sauce over the chicken and cook on low for 4 to 5 hours. Use a slotted spoon to remove the chicken from the slow cooker. Adjust salt and pepper to taste. Serve and enjoy!

EASY SLOW COOKER CHICKEN CURRY

Easy and flavorful slow cooker dishes like this help us stay on track with the Paleo diet. You can add your favorite vegetables to make this a one-pot meal! —AV

SERVES 6

2–3 pounds (908–1362 g) boneless, skinless chicken thighs

1 (14.5-ounce [406-g]) can coconut milk or 2 cups (470 ml) Homemade Coconut Milk (page 503)

3 tbsp (45 g) green curry paste

Add chicken, coconut milk and curry paste to the slow cooker. Use a fork to mix in the curry paste. Cook on low for 4 to 5 hours. Use two forks to pull apart the chicken. Use a slotted spoon to remove the chicken from the liquid. Serve and enjoy!

SLOW COOKER CHICKEN WITH SUN-DRIED TOMATOES & ARTICHOKES

This dish bursts with flavor. No one would ever guess that it only took you 5 minutes to prepare! Read the ingredients that are in the jar of sun-dried tomatoes and artichokes carefully to make sure that there are no unhealthy oils or other additives. —AV

SERVES 6–8

2–3 pounds (908–1362 g) skinless chicken, boneless or bone-in, any parts you like

1 (8-ounce [227-g]) jar sun-dried tomatoes packed in olive oil

1 tbsp (15 g) tomato paste

1 (16-ounce [454-g]) jar artichokes, drained

Salt and pepper

Place chicken in the slow cooker, then add sun-dried tomatoes, tomato paste and artichokes. Cover and cook on low for 4 to 5 hours. Salt and pepper to taste. Serve and enjoy!

CHEF'S TIP:
If you are home when this dish is cooking, you can add the artichokes later and allow them to cook during the last 2 hours. This will result in a tender, but not mushy vegetable.

SLOW COOKER HONEY MUSTARD CHICKEN

This chicken is moist and has a mild sweet flavor. It pairs well with lettuce wraps and my Almond Satay Sauce (page 515). —AV

SERVES 6

2 pounds (908 g) skinless chicken thighs, bone-in or boneless

2 tbsp (30 ml) coconut oil, melted

3 tbsp (45 ml) honey

1 tbsp (15 g) stoneground prepared mustard

1 tsp (3 g) madras curry powder

Salt and pepper

Lettuce wraps, optional, for serving

Julienned carrots, optional, for serving

Almond Satay Sauce (page 515), optional, for serving

Place chicken in the slow cooker. In a small bowl, mix coconut oil, honey, prepared mustard and curry powder. Pour the sauce over the chicken and cook on low for 4 to 5 hours. Salt and pepper to taste. Enjoy in lettuce wraps, with julienned carrots and my Almond Satay Sauce.

EASY SLOW COOKER CHICKEN MARENGO

Serve this easy-to-make chicken marengo with zucchini noodles and olives for a delicious and satisfying meal. —AV

SERVES 6–8

2-3 pounds (908-1362 g) skinless chicken, any parts that you prefer

Salt and pepper

1 onion, sliced

½ cup (120 ml) dry white wine

1 (16-ounce [474-ml]) jar marinara sauce

¼ pound (112 g) fresh mushrooms, sliced

Zucchini noodles and olives, optional, for serving

Place the chicken at the bottom of the slow cooker. Generously season with salt and pepper. Add the onions around the chicken. Add the white wine and the marinara sauce. Cover and cook on low for 4 hours. Add mushrooms, and then cook for an additional hour. Adjust salt and pepper to taste. Serve and enjoy!

SLOW COOKER LEMON GARLIC ROAST CHICKEN

This dish makes an appearance on our menu regularly. It's flavorful, but not bold, so you can serve it with a variety of vegetables throughout the week. —AV

SERVES 6

2 tbsp (30 ml) fresh squeezed lemon juice

1 tbsp (15 ml) avocado oil (you can substitute olive oil)

1 tbsp (8 g) dried parsley

1 tsp (3 g) garlic powder

1 tsp (3 g) dried basil

½ tsp oregano

½ tsp sea salt

½ tsp black pepper

1 whole roasting chicken, 3-5 pounds (1362-2270 g)

1 lemon, quartered

1 onion, quartered

In a small bowl, combine lemon juice, avocado oil, parsley, garlic powder, dried basil, oregano, sea salt and black pepper. Rub the herb mixture all over the chicken. If you have some left, you can also rub it in the cavity. Stuff the cavity with the lemon and onion. Place chicken in the slow cooker. Cook on low for 7 hours. I have found that in my Hamilton Beach slow cooker, 7 hours is the perfect timing to keep the chicken intact, but cooked and moist. At 8 hours, it starts falling off the bone. This can vary depending on the brand of slow cooker.

CHEF'S TIPS:

Save the bones and use for making broth. If you want chicken with a crispy skin, transfer the chicken from the slow cooker to an oven-safe dish and bake at 350°F (180°C, or gas mark 4) for 5 to 10 minutes.

EASY SLOW COOKER POACHED CHICKEN

This chicken makes a great filling for a traditional chicken salad, chicken soup, casserole or a Mexican style meal. —AV

SERVES 8

1 whole chicken

Vegetable scraps, optional, to add more flavor to the broth

2 tbsp (30 ml) apple cider vinegar

Filtered water

If the bird came with a bundle of giblets stuffed in the cavity, remove the bundle before cooking. You can toss the giblets (minus the liver) into the stock to give it a richer flavor. The liver can give the stock a bitter flavor, so set that aside for another use. Place the chicken in the slow cooker. Leave the skin on, as this will help you make a more gelatinous broth. Fill up the slow cooker with enough water so the chicken is mostly submerged. Depending on the size of the chicken, you may not be able to completely cover it, but cover it as best you can. If adding any vegetable scraps, you can also toss those in now. Add the apple cider vinegar.

Cook on low for 8 hours. Remove the chicken from the broth and allow it to sit until it is cool enough to handle. It is easiest to pull apart the chicken with the fingers. The meat will essentially just fall off the bones. Separate the meat from the skin and tendons. Strain the broth and set it aside for another use.

LEMON, TARRAGON AND GARLIC CHICKEN

Slow cooking a whole chicken is a great way to enjoy a simple tasty meal. Using fresh herbs and adding creamy butter to the chicken turns this into a flavorful meal that saves you time in the kitchen. —NK

SERVES 6–8

1 whole chicken

Sea salt and black pepper, to taste

3 tbsp (45 g) softened Almond Butter (page 506), divided

4 sprigs fresh tarragon

3 cloves garlic, peeled

1 lemon, sliced into thin rounds

Season chicken all over, including the cavity, with sea salt and black pepper. Carefully separate the skin on the breast with your fingers making sure not to tear. Add 2 tablespoons (30 g) of the Almond Butter in between the skin and flesh of the chicken breast and use your hands to spread out the mixture. Take another 1 tablespoon (15 g) of the Almond Butter and spread it over the rest of the chicken. Add the fresh tarragon, garlic and most of the lemon slices, reserving a few, to the cavity of the chicken. Place chicken in a slow cooker and place the rest of the lemon slices on top of the chicken. Cook on low for 5 to 7 hours. Remove from the slow cooker and allow to rest for about 10 minutes before shredding.

CHEF'S TIP:
Save the leftover bones from the chicken to make broth.

SLOW COOKER SPICY CHICKEN WITH GRILLED PEACHES

Pairing fruit with meat is a great way to brighten up a meal. Try this delicious dish for a sweet take on a chicken dinner. —NK

SERVES 6

1 whole chicken

Sea salt and black pepper, to taste

3 tbsp (45 g) ghee, divided

1 tbsp (8 g) red pepper flakes

½ cup (120 ml) balsamic vinegar

3 medium peaches

Season the chicken all over with some sea salt and black pepper including the cavity. In a small bowl mix 2 tablespoons (30 g) ghee and the red pepper flakes. Using your hands massage the ghee mixture all over the chicken. Use your fingers to carefully get under the skin of the chicken breast and spread the mixture under there too. Place the chicken in a slow cooker and cook on low for 5 to 7 hours. Once cooked remove the chicken and allow to rest.

While the chicken is resting add balsamic vinegar to a small pot and bring to a boil over medium heat. Turn the heat to a simmer and continue to cook, making sure to stir often until the balsamic is reduced by half and has thickened. Remove from the heat and set aside. Shred the chicken and set aside.

Heat a medium square grill pan over medium-high heat. While the pan is heating slice peaches in half and remove the stones. Brush the flesh side of each peach with another 1 tablespoon (15 g) ghee. In batches place the peaches cut-side-down in the hot grill pan and let cook for 4 to 5 minutes on one side before flipping over to cook the other side for another 2 to 3 minutes. Remove from the heat and cut peaches into quarters. Serve peaches alongside some chicken.

SLOW COOKER MAPLE-GLAZED TURKEY BREAST WITH CRANBERRIES

These maple-glazed turkey breasts pair really nicely with some simple roasted Brussels sprouts. When purchasing maple syrup, read the ingredients closely to make sure that it is pure maple syrup with no added ingredients, such as high fructose corn syrup. —AV

SERVES 4

4 filets of turkey breast, or you can substitute thighs

4 tbsp (60 ml) maple syrup

1 tbsp (15 g) sea salt

¼ tsp ground cinnamon

1 (16-ounce [454-g]) bag cranberries, fresh or frozen

1 onion, sliced

Salt and pepper to taste

Place the turkey in the slow cooker. Then rub the top of each breast with 1 tablespoon (15 ml) of maple syrup. Sprinkle the turkey with sea salt and cinnamon. Then add the cranberries and onions and cook on low for 4 hours. Adjust salt and pepper to taste. Serve and enjoy!

CLASSIC ITALIAN MEATBALLS

I love using jarred marinara sauce to add more flavor to slow cooker meals. You can often find organic marinara sauce with no questionable ingredients at your local health food store. Read the ingredients carefully to make sure that you purchase one that only has vegetables, spices and olive oil. —AV

SERVES 6

1 tbsp (15 g) ghee

½ cup (80 g) chopped onions

2 pounds (908 g) ground beef

4 cloves garlic, minced

1 tbsp (15 ml) balsamic vinegar, preferably a thick syrupy variety

1 tbsp (15 g) tomato paste

¼ tsp crushed red pepper

1 tbsp (6 g) Italian seasoning

2 tsp (6 g) sea salt

1 tsp (3 g) black pepper

1 egg, lightly beaten

1 (16-ounce [454-ml]) jar tomato and basil marinara sauce

Heat a heavy-bottomed pan over medium heat; add the ghee and sauté the onions until translucent, about 2 to 3 minutes.

In a large bowl, combine the ground beef, sautéed onions, garlic, balsamic vinegar, tomato paste, crushed red pepper, Italian seasoning, sea salt, black pepper and egg. Using your hands, mix all the ingredients until they are well incorporated. Shape the mixture into about 2-inch (5-cm) meatballs. This mixture should make between fifteen and seventeen meatballs.

Line the bottom of the slow cooker with the meatballs. Pour the marinara sauce into the slow cooker. Cook on low for 4 to 6 hours, or until the meat is cooked through.

SLOW COOKER MARINARA SAUCE

This is a great recipe to make when tomato season is at its peak and you don't know what to do with them all. You can freeze it and enjoy it over zucchini noodles or spaghetti squash all year long. —AV

MAKES 4 (16-OUNCE [474-ML]) JARS

2 tbsp (30 g) ghee

2 small onions, diced

6 cloves garlic, chopped

7 ounces (196 g) tomato paste

4 pounds (1816 g) tomatoes, peeled, seeded and chopped

3 anchovy fillets, minced

½ cup (120 ml) dry white wine

1½ tsp (4.5 g) salt

1 tsp (3 g) black pepper

1 tbsp (9 g) dried basil

2 tsp (6 g) dried oregano

1 tbsp (15 ml) balsamic vinegar

Heat ghee in a medium sized skillet over medium heat. Add onions and sauté until translucent, about 7 minutes. Add garlic and tomato paste and sauté until tomato paste turns from a bright red to a brick color, about 1 to 2 minutes. Transfer onion and garlic mixture to slow cooker. Add tomatoes, anchovies, wine, salt, pepper, basil, oregano and vinegar. Cook on low for 8 hours. Allow to cool and store in wide-mouth mason jars.

BACON CABBAGE CHUCK ROAST STEW

With a rich bacon flavor, this stew will become one of your favorite Paleo comfort foods! Since it's gently slow cooked to retain all the wonderful nutrients, it's healthy to boot. —VM

SERVES 4

½ pound (227 g) uncured bacon

2–3 pounds (908–1362 g) chuck roast

2 large red onions, cut in slices

1 clove garlic, peeled and smashed

1 small green or savoy cabbage, roughly chopped

Celtic sea salt

Black pepper to taste

1 sprig fresh thyme

1 cup (235 ml) Slow Cooker Beef Broth (page 171)

Line the bottom of the slow cooker with the bacon slices. Add the remaining ingredients and cook on low for 7 hours. Easy and delicious!

SLOW COOKER POT-AU-FEU

Pot-au-feu is a classic French dish of boiled meat and vegetables. It literally means "pot on the fire." It is made using tough, but flavorful, parts of the beef, such as shank or brisket, making it a perfect candidate for the slow cooker. It calls for a great variety of vegetables—carrots, celery, onions, leeks, etc. You can choose your vegetables based on what's in season or priced well. But my favorite part of this dish is the array of condiments it is served with! —AV

SERVES 8

FOR THE BOUQUET GARNI

3 sprigs fresh thyme

2 bay leaves

Leafy greens from 2 celery ribs

6 sprigs fresh parsley

1 pound (454 g) marrow bone, cut into 2-inch (5-cm) pieces

1 small cinnamon stick

1 tsp (3 g) black peppercorns

1 bouquet garni, see above

1 pound (454 g) beef shanks

1½ pounds (680 g) rump roast, tied with string so it keeps its shape

3 leeks, peeled and cut in half

8 carrots, peeled and halved

8 ribs celery, peeled and halved

4 turnips, peeled and quartered

1 small head cabbage, cored and cut into 6 wedges

1 large onion, quartered

6 whole cloves garlic, peeled

1–2 tsp (3–6 g) sea salt

FOR THE GARNISHES

Stone-ground mustard

Cornichons or small pickles

Prepared horseradish

Coarse sea salt

Arrange the herbs in a stack and tie them together into a tight bundle with a string.

Wrap the marrow-bones in cheesecloth and secure the cloth tightly with kitchen string. Wrap the cinnamon stick, peppercorn and bouquet garni in cheesecloth and secure with a string. Combine all ingredients in the slow cooker. Pour enough water to cover all ingredients. Cook on low for 8 to 10 hours. Discard bundle of herbs. Place the meat on a platter and surround with the vegetables. Scoop the soft marrow from bones and also serve separately. Strain the broth through a fine-mesh sieve into a clean saucepan.

Bring the broth to a boil for 10 to 15 minutes, until it has reduced. Season it with additional salt if needed. Serve the broth alongside the platter of meat and vegetables. Include garnishes for the meat and vegetables, such as whole grain mustard, pickled vegetables, grated horseradish and sea salt.

CHEF'S TIP:
If you can, add the vegetables halfway through the cooking time to avoid overcooking the vegetables. Substitute the rump roast with oxtail for an extra gelatinous broth!

SLOW COOKER BALSAMIC BRAISED SHORT RIBS

These beef short ribs are braised to luscious tenderness, while slow cooking in a flavorful balsamic sauce. —AV

SERVES 6–8

4-5 pounds (1816–2270 g) bone-in beef short ribs, each about 3 inches (7.5 cm) long

2 tsp (6 g) sea salt

1 tsp (3 g) black pepper

⅔ cup (160 ml) balsamic vinegar

1 cup (235 ml) dry red wine

2 tbsp (30 g) tomato paste

½ cup (80 g) red onions, diced

4 cloves garlic, minced

1 carrot chopped, optional

1 rib celery chopped, optional

Sprinkle the short ribs with the salt and pepper. Then place them in the bottom of the slow cooker. In a separate bowl mix the balsamic vinegar, red wine, tomato paste, red onions and garlic. Pour over the ribs. If using carrots and celery, add those to the slow cooker. Cook on low for 6 to 8 hours or until beef is fork tender. Adjust salt and pepper to taste. Serve and enjoy!

CHEF'S TIP:

If you have time, heat up 1 tablespoon (15 g) of ghee or coconut oil in a heavy-bottomed pan and sear the short ribs on each side for 2 to 3 minutes before placing them in the slow cooker. This will produce nicely browned ribs. Defat and reduce the leftover sauce and serve it drizzled over the short ribs. This will add an additional flavor boost to your dish.

SLOW COOKER BALSAMIC ROAST BEEF

This is my go-to beef roast recipe. The balsamic vinegar is the secret ingredient and transforms an ordinary roast into a flavorful masterpiece. I hope you have some leftovers, too—they are fabulous! —KW

SERVES 6–8

1 (3-4-pound [1362–1818-g]) beef roast

1 medium onion, diced

6 cloves garlic, minced

1 cup (235 ml) chicken or beef stock or broth

½ cup (120 ml) balsamic vinegar

2 tbsp (30 ml) coconut aminos

Pinch or two of red pepper flakes

Sea salt and pepper, to taste

Place the whole roast in a slow cooker fat side down. Add remaining ingredients over the top of the roast. Add additional salt and pepper to the top of the roast. Cover and cook on low for 8 hours. You know it is done when the top is browned and the meat shreds very easily with a fork.

Remove the roast from cooker. Blend remaining juices and onion/garlic in the cooker with an immersion blender for the gravy until you reach desired consistency. Serve this gravy with the roast beef.

SLOW COOKER CITRUS BRAISED CARNITAS

These carnitas are another staple at our house. It's easy to make a large batch in the slow cooker and enjoy it all week as part of a variety of meals. Have it for breakfast with some eggs, enjoy it for lunch on top of a hefty salad, or enjoy it for dinner with roasted vegetables. —AV

SERVES 6–8

1 tbsp (8 g) ground cumin

2 tsp (6 g) ground coriander

1 tsp (3 g) paprika

1 tsp (3 g) sea salt

1 tsp (3 g) onion powder

½ tsp garlic powder

½ tsp cayenne pepper

½ tsp oregano

3 pounds (1.4 kg) boneless pork shoulder, cut into 4 large chunks

½ cup (120 ml) fresh squeezed orange juice

¼ cup (60 ml) fresh squeezed lime juice

In a small bowl, combine cumin, coriander, paprika, sea salt, onion powder, garlic powder, cayenne and oregano. Rub the spice mixture all over the pork. Place the pork in the slow cooker. Add the fresh-squeezed orange juice and the fresh squeezed lime juice. Cook on low for 6 to 8 hours or until the meat is fork tender.

CHEF'S TIP:

To get the carnitas crispy, use a slotted spoon and place the carnitas in an oven safe dish. Broil for about 5 minutes.

SLOW COOKER BEEF & BUTTERNUT SQUASH STEW

This hearty beef stew, is filling and comforting. The butternut squash adds a hint of sweetness without overwhelming the savory flavors in the dish. —AV

SERVES 6

3 tbsp (45 g) ghee, divided

2 leeks, light parts only, diced

4 cloves garlic, minced

2 pounds (908 g) beef stew meat, cut into 2-inch (5-cm) cubes

Salt and pepper

2 tbsp (30 g) tomato paste

¼ cup (30 g) sun-dried tomatoes, finely chopped

4 cups (940 ml) Slow Cooker Beef Broth (page 171)

4 cups (600 g) butternut squash, peeled, seeded and chopped

1 tbsp (6 g) fresh rosemary, minced

Chopped fresh parsley for garnish

Heat 2 tablespoons (30 g) of ghee in a medium-sized skillet over medium heat. Add the leeks and sauté until soft, about 5 minutes. Add garlic and sauté for another minute or two. Transfer the mixture into the slow cooker. Add the additional tablespoon (15 g) of ghee to the same pan. Generously salt and pepper the beef. Add the beef to the pan and cook until it is browned on all sides, about 5 minutes. Add the tomato paste and cook until it turns from a bright red to a brick color.

Transfer the beef to the slow cooker. Add the sun-dried tomatoes and beef broth. You can either add the butternut squash now, or you can add it half way through cooking time. They will turn out much softer if you add them at the beginning, but they will still be delicious! Cook on low for 6 to 8 hours. Add rosemary in the last hour of cooking. Salt and pepper to taste. Garnish with fresh parsley and serve!

EASY SLOW COOKER BEEF CURRY

With only 5 minutes of prep, you can come home to a flavorful and delicious meal. Serve this over cauliflower rice and some steamed vegetables for a complete meal. —AV

SERVES 6

2–3 pounds (908–1362 g) beef stew meat or chuck roast, cut into several big chunks

1 (14.5-ounce [406-g]) can coconut milk or 2 cups (470 ml) Homemade Coconut Milk (page 503)

3 tbsp (45 g) red curry paste

Add beef, coconut milk and curry paste to the slow cooker. Use a fork to mix in the curry paste.

Cook on low for 6 to 8 hours. Use two forks to pull apart the beef into smaller chunks. Use a slotted spoon to remove the beef from the liquid. Serve and enjoy!

SLOW COOKER TAGINE OF MUTTON WITH LEMON AND OLIVES

This dish is a Moroccan classic, revisited. I love the warm spices and tanginess of Moroccan foods. It will keep the taste buds and the stomach happy. —VM

SERVES 4

1 pinch saffron

¼ tsp ground turmeric

1 tsp (3 g) ground ginger

¼ tsp ground cayenne

½ tsp ground black pepper

¼ tsp ground cumin

1 large yellow onion

1 small bunch fresh cilantro

1 small bunch fresh parsley

2 pounds (908 g) mutton shoulder, cut in large cubes

2 lemons, quartered, or 2 preserved lemons, discard the pulp

1 cup (100 g) green olives, drained and pitted.

Juice of 1 lemon

Sea salt and pepper, to taste

In a large mixing bowl add all of the spices with a few pinches of sea salt and mix well. Add the spice mixture to a food processor along with the onion, cilantro and parsley and blend well. Be careful to not over blend as you want the mixture to maintain a chunky consistency. Add the mixture to the slow cooker along with the mutton, mixing meat well with the spice blend.

Add the lemons, and cook for 4 hours on low. In the last half hour, add the olives and lemon juice and finish cooking. Taste for seasoning and add salt and pepper if needed.

CHEF'S TIP:

The best olives to use for this dish are the ripe, green Moroccan-style olives. However any green olives could be used just as easily. Most Moroccan dishes also tend to use preserved lemons, but I thought I would try this one with fresh lemons. To my delight it came out just as good with the fresh lemons. If you have the opportunity to use traditional Moroccan ingredients, then definitely use those, otherwise you have some easy alternatives to make a very tasty dish.

MEXICAN BIRRIA (LAMB STEW)

Birria is a Mexican stew made of lamb or goat using a base of toasted dried chilies and stock. Traditionally it is served with corn tortillas, but I love it over cauliflower rice or with a side of baked yuca fries. —RM

SERVES 4

4 guajillo chilies

3 ancho chilies

4 arbol chilies

3 cups (705 ml) chicken stock

1 (14-ounce [397-g]) can diced tomatoes

3-4 pounds (1362–1880 g) lamb shoulder and neck bones (for stew)

1 white onion, sliced

6 cloves garlic, minced

2 tsp (6 g) oregano

1 tsp (3 g) black pepper

1 tsp (3 g) salt

1 tsp (3 g) thyme

½ tsp ground cinnamon

½ tsp ground cumin

2 tbsp (30 ml) vinegar

8 ounces (227 g) white mushrooms, quartered

Chopped cilantro, for garnish

Cauliflower rice or baked yuca, optional, for serving

Bring about 3 cups (705 ml) of water to a boil in a medium saucepan. At the same time, heat a skillet over medium heat. Cut the stems off the chilies and remove the seeds and veins. Toast the chilies in the skillet for 5 minutes. Submerge the chilies in the boiling water and immediately turn off the stove. Soak them for 20 minutes. Purée the chilies, 2 cups of chicken stock and tomatoes in a blender.

Layer the bottom of your slow cooker with the lamb meat and bones. Cover with sliced onions, the chili purée, garlic and spices. Add the remaining 1 cup (236 ml) of chicken stock and vinegar. Cook on low for 8 to 10 hours. When there are 3 hours remaining, add the chopped mushrooms and stir the stew. Serve in a bowl over cauliflower rice or accompanied by yuca fries. Garnish with fresh cilantro.

SLOW COOKER CHIPOTLE PORK

This pulled pork is slightly spicy and slightly smoky. If you want to try a fantastic combination of sweet and spicy, serve this pork with the Pineapple Coleslaw (page 190). —KW

SERVES 4–6

1 tbsp (8 g) black pepper

1 tsp (3 g) chipotle chili powder, more if you like it spicy

4 pounds (1818 g) pork roast

¼ cup (60 ml) balsamic vinegar

1 tsp (5 ml) all natural liquid smoke

OPTIONAL TOPPINGS

Avocado slices

Freshly torn cilantro

BBQ sauce

Combine the salt, pepper and chipotle chili powder in a small bowl. Rub the entire pork with the spices. Place the spiced pork in the slow cooker. Add in the stock, balsamic and liquid smoke. Give it a stir, cover the slow cooker and cook on low for 8 hours.

When it's finished cooking, take the pork out of the slow cooker and shred it. Feel free to add in ¼ to ½ cup (60 to 120 ml) of some of the slow cooker juice if you like a juicier shredded pork. Serve with any optional toppings.

EASY SLOW COOKER MAPLE ORANGE PORK SHOULDER

This recipe bursts with fall flavors and it only takes 5 minutes to prep! Win-win in my book! —AV

SERVES 6

2½–3 pounds (1.1–1.3 kg) pork shoulder, cut into several big chunks

1 tsp (3 g) sea salt

½ tsp black pepper

½ tsp dried sage

1 apple, peeled and chopped

½ cup (120 ml) fresh-squeezed orange juice

1 tbsp (15 ml) pure maple syrup

Rub the pork with the salt, pepper and sage. Place it in the slow cooker. Add the apples, orange juice and maple syrup. Cook on low for 6 hours. Once it is cooked, use two forks to pull the pork apart. Enjoy!

CHEF'S TIP:

Although the recipe is delicious as is, if you have a few extra minutes, you can brown the pork before adding it to the slow cooker for a little extra oomph!

ASIAN SLOW-COOKED PORK

This is by far one of my favorite ways to eat slow-cooked pork. The flavor combination of tamari, ginger and rice vinegar makes the meat so succulent. Then the mustard greens and mushrooms elevate it to a whole other level. —RM

SERVES 8

½ cup (120 ml) chicken stock

½ cup (120 ml) tamari, or ⅓ cup (80 ml) coconut aminos

½ cup (120 ml) rice wine vinegar, plus 1 tbsp (15 ml)

2 tbsp (30 ml) fresh-squeezed orange juice

1 tsp (5 ml) sesame oil

½ tsp Chinese five spice

1 tsp (3 g) red pepper flakes

4–5 cloves minced garlic, plus 1 clove

1 thumb-sized ginger knob, grated

Salt and pepper, to taste

2–3 pounds (908–1362 g) Boston butt pork

8 ounces (227 g) mushrooms, sliced

1 pound (454 g) mustard greens or kale, stemmed and julienned

Pour all of the liquid ingredients, Chinese five spice, red pepper flakes, garlic and ginger into the slow cooker. Salt and pepper the Boston butt pork on both sides, and then add it to the cooker mixture. Cook on low for 7 hours and then remove the pork.

Add the sliced mushrooms to the cooker and shred the pork on a plate. Mix the pork back in the pot and cook for 1 more hour.

Before serving, boil the mustard greens in a pot of water for 10 minutes. Then sauté them in a sauce pan with 1 tablespoon (15 ml) rice vinegar and 1 clove of minced garlic. Add the greens to the cooker and serve.

SLOW COOKER ASIAN-STYLE SHORT RIBS

Slow cooker meals are a great way to save time in the kitchen. This Asian-inspired recipe is wonderful served over cauliflower rice or on simple lettuce cups. —KH

SERVES 6

4 pounds (1816 g) beef short ribs

FOR THE SAUCE

½ cup (120 ml) coconut aminos

½ cup (120 ml) good quality broth

2 tbsp (30 ml) apple cider vinegar

4 tbsp (60 ml) raw honey

1 tbsp (8 g) grated ginger

5 cloves fresh garlic, minced

FOR THE GARNISH

1 tbsp (15 ml) toasted sesame oil

Green onions

Sesame seeds

Cauliflower rice or lettuce cups, for serving

Place short ribs at the bottom of the slow cooker. Combine all sauce ingredients and pour over top of ribs. Toss to evenly coat. Cook on low for at least 6 hours. turning the ribs once for more even cooking. Remove ribs from slow cooker and set aside to cool.

Skim fat from top of liquid in the slow cooker. Pour it into a large measuring cup and place it in the fridge for a bit so the fat rises to the surface. Pour the liquid from the slow cooker into a small pot on the stove top. Bring to a boil, then lower heat and simmer for 8 to 10 minutes to reduce liquid. Remove from heat and stir in 1 tablespoon (15 ml) toasted sesame oil.

Using your fingers, pull the meat off of the bones and shred into small chunks. Pour desired amount of sauce over top and stir to evenly coat. Garnish with green onions and sesame seeds. Serve over cauliflower rice or lettuce cups.

SLOW COOKER APPLE GINGER PORK WITH BEET APPLE FENNEL SLAW

The best way to cook a pork roast is in the slow cooker. It comes out juicy and tender every time. —KH

SERVES 4–6

½ cup (120 ml) good quality broth

4 apples, peeled, cored and sliced

1 large onion

2 tbsp (16 g) fresh ginger, minced

3 cloves fresh garlic, minced

½ tsp sea salt

1 tbsp (15 ml) honey

1 tsp (3 g) ground cinnamon

2 pinches ground cloves

¼ tsp ground cumin

1 tsp (3 g) sea salt to rub on pork

1 (2–2½-pound [908–1590-g]) pork roast (butt or shoulder)

FOR THE SLAW

3 tbsp (45 ml) extra-virgin olive oil

1½ tbsp (23 ml) fresh lemon juice

½ tsp grated fresh ginger

2 pinches sea salt

2 grinds fresh pepper

1 small red beet, sliced into matchsticks

1 medium apple, sliced into matchsticks

½ fennel bulb, cored and thinly sliced lengthwise

1 small golden beet, sliced into matchsticks

2 tbsp (8 g) chopped fresh basil, cilantro or parsley

(continued)

Pour broth into the slow cooker and add apples, onion, ginger, garlic, salt, honey and spices. Give a little stir to combine. Rub the salt all over the pork roast. Then nestle the roast into the apple onion mixture. Cover and cook for 8 to 10 hours on low.

Before eating, carefully shred the roast with two forks and mix into juicy goodness in the slow cooker.

Make slaw just before serving: Whisk together olive oil, lemon juice, ginger, salt and pepper. Separate red beets and toss with 1 tablespoon (15 ml) of dressing. Combine apple, fennel and golden beets in another bowl and toss with remaining dressing. Gently combine red beets into rest of slaw to prevent red from staining entire slaw. Sprinkle with fresh herbs. Dig in and enjoy!

CROCKPOT PORK AND PUMPKIN CHILI

I have to give my husband the credit for this recipe. He has a knack for putting different spices together and this recipe contains his special chili spice blend. This recipe serves a crowd and the slow cooker does the work for you. —KW

SERVES 10–12

3 pounds (1.4 kg) pork roast

Salt and pepper, to taste

2 onions, diced

2 (14.5-ounce [406-g]) cans fire-roasted diced tomatoes

2 chipotle peppers in adobo sauce, chopped

2 tbsp (30 ml) adobo sauce

1 (7-ounce [196-g]) can diced green chilies

4 cloves garlic, minced

¼ cup (32 g) chili powder

2 tbsp (16 g) ground cumin

1 tbsp (8 g) smoked paprika

2 tsp (6 g) ground cinnamon

2 tsp (6 g) cocoa powder

2 cups (470 ml) chicken stock or bone broth

¼ cup (15 g) cilantro, plus more for garnish

2 cups (500 g) roasted pumpkin or squash; or 1 (14-ounce [392-g]) can pumpkin purée

1 bunch kale or mustard greens, roughly chopped

Avocado, for serving

Super Easy Guacamole (page 190), for serving

Place the pork in the slow cooker and season with salt and pepper. Add the onions, fire roasted tomatoes, chipotle peppers, adobo sauce, green chilies, garlic and spices. Add the chicken stock and then toss in the cilantro. Cover and cook on low for 8 to 10 hours or high for 4 to 5 hours.

An hour before it's done, take out the pork and shred it with two forks. Put the pork back into the cooker. Pour the roasted pumpkin/squash in the cooker and give it a good stir. Add the kale or mustard greens and give it a final stir. Cook for an hour. Serve with avocado, extra cilantro or Super Easy Guacamole.

CHEF'S TIP:
The spiciness of this recipe is perfect to me—it's not too spicy, but it does give a smoky and slightly spicy heat. If you like a spicier chili, add in another chipotle pepper or add in some additional chipotle chili powder.

BUTTERNUT SQUASH N'OATMEAL

This N'Oatmeal is a nice change from the usual eggs. Since this recipe is made in a slow cooker, you can always make this overnight and have delicious, warm, Paleo N'Oatmeal ready for you in the morning. —AV

SERVES 8

½ cup (75 g) raw almonds

½ cup (75 g) raw walnuts

Dash of sea salt

1 medium butternut squash, peeled and cubed

2 apples, peeled and cubed

1 tsp (3 g) ground cinnamon

½ tsp ground nutmeg

1 tbsp (12 g) coconut sugar

1 cup (235 ml) Homemade Coconut Milk (page 503)

TOPPINGS

Coconut milk

Currants

Desiccated coconut

Maple syrup

Cover the almonds and walnuts with filtered water. Add a dash of sea salt. Soak for 12 hours. Rinse the nuts with some more filtered water. Place in a food processor and blend until you have a meal or flour consistency.

Place the butternut squash, apples, cinnamon, nutmeg, ground nuts, coconut sugar and coconut milk into the slow cooker. Cook on low for 8 hours. Use a potato masher to mash the N'Oatmeal into your preferred consistency. Top with your favorite toppings and serve.

SLOW COOKER CINNAMON VANILLA APPLESAUCE

We have an apple tree in our yard and one of my favorite things to make with our apples is this easy cinnamon vanilla applesauce. Your house will smell divine while it is slow cooking. —KW

MAKES 4+ QUARTS (3.6+ L)

10 apples, peeled, cored and sliced

1 tbsp (15 ml) vanilla extract

2 tsp (6 g) ground cinnamon

Pinch of sea salt

Place all ingredients in a slow cooker. Cover and cook on high for 4 hours, stirring halfway through. After 4 hours is up, give it a final stir, breaking up any large chunks. Cool and refrigerate.

CHEF'S TIP:

If you like a super smooth applesauce, use an immersion blender to process until you reach the desired consistency.

SLOW COOKER APPLESAUCE

Applesauce is a healthy Paleo dessert option. The pears in this recipe add a little lightness to the flavor. —AV

SERVES 10

10 apples, peeled, cored and sliced

Juice of half a tangelo (you can also use an orange)

1 tbsp (8 g) ground cinnamon

¼ cup (60 ml) honey

Place all ingredients in a slow cooker and cook on low for 6 to 8 hours. Mash apples with a fork.

Remove from the slow cooker and place in a medium size bowl and refrigerate overnight. You can eat this right away, but the flavors are much better if you let it sit overnight.

SLOW COOKER APPLE CRUMBLE

Slow cooker desserts are wonderful for dinner parties. Get this started before you start prepping dinner and pop it in the oven right after dinner. Your guests will be beyond impressed with this fresh-made, warm dessert. This recipe is delicious served with coconut milk ice cream or Coconut Whipped Cream (page 504). —AV

SERVES 6

FOR THE FILLING

1 tbsp (15 ml) coconut oil

12 cooking apples, such as Granny Smith, peeled, cored and sliced

1 tbsp (15 ml) lemon juice

1 tsp (3 g) ground cinnamon

½ tsp ground nutmeg

⅛ tsp ground allspice

⅛ tsp ground cardamom

2 tbsp (30 ml) maple syrup

FOR THE TOPPING

2 tbsp (30 ml) coconut oil

¾ cup (90 g) almond flour

½ cup (70 g) pecans

Dash of sea salt

⅛ tsp ground cardamom

½ tsp ground nutmeg

½ tsp ground cinnamon

2 tbsp (30 ml) maple syrup

Coconut Whipped Cream (page 504) or coconut milk ice cream, to serve

In the slow cooker, mix the coconut oil, apples, lemon juice, cinnamon, nutmeg, allspice, cardamom and maple syrup. Cook on high for 2 hours.

Preheat the oven to 375°F (190°C, or gas mark 5). Mix all the topping ingredients and stir to incorporate. The mixture should resemble crumbles. Transfer the filling to an oven-safe pie dish. Spread the crumbles over the top of the filling and place the pie dish into the oven for 15 to 20 minutes, until top is crisp. Let it rest for 5 minutes. Serve topped with Coconut Whipped Cream or coconut milk ice cream.

SLOW COOKER APPLE BUTTER

Using a slow cooker will turn Pink Lady or Fuji apples into spreadable butter that you can eat as a snack or with Smothered Pork Chops (page 47). Apple butter can also be a wonderful homemade gift to friends and family during the holidays. It's definitely healthier than store bought brands since there are no added sugars or preservatives in the ingredient list. —JC

SERVES 8

3 pounds (1.4 kg) apples, chopped (I like Pink Lady or Fuji)

2 tbsp (16 g) ground cinnamon

1 tsp (3 g) pumpkin spice

¼ tsp sea salt

Place all ingredients in a slow cooker. Cook on low for 5 hours. Check every hour and give the apples a quick stir. This will prevent the apples at the bottom from burning. Let it cool for at least 30 minutes.

Place cooked apples in a blender and purée until smooth. Store in glass jars and refrigerate for up to a week.

SLOW COOKER APPLE AND FIG STEW

This Apple and Fig Stew makes a delicious, warming and hearty meal. Tender meat, mixed with juicy tart apples and sweet dried figs make this stew a real treat. —NK

SERVES 4–6

2 tbsp (30 ml) ghee

1 medium red onion, sliced into half moons

2 cloves garlic, minced

2 pounds (908 g) beef stew meat, diced into even pieces

¼ tsp ground nutmeg

1 tsp (3 g) ground cinnamon

½ tsp sea salt

15 ounces (420 ml) organic tomato sauce

2 Granny Smith apples, cored and diced

7 ounces (196 g) dried figs, quartered

½ cup (120 ml) Slow Cooker Chicken Broth (page 170)

Heat the ghee in a large skillet over medium heat. Once heated, add the onions and cook for 10 minutes until softened. Add the minced garlic cloves and stir to cook for a minute. Add the beef, nutmeg, cinnamon and sea salt. Stir to mix and cook until the meat has browned on the outside. Stir in the tomato sauce and cook for another 2 to 3 minutes. Remove from the heat. Stir in the apples and figs. Add everything to a slow cooker and add the chicken broth. Cook on low for 6 hours. Serve warm.

SLOW COOKER STUFFING

This Slow Cooker Stuffing will free up your oven for the many other things you will need it for on Thanksgiving. Plus, it will be a guaranteed hit with your non-Paleo guests, at least it always is for us! —AV

SERVES 8

3 Italian sausages, removed from casing (I recommend 2 hot Italian and 1 mild)

2 cups (140 g) mushrooms, sliced

½ yellow onion, diced

2 ribs celery, diced (about ¾ cup [90 g])

3 cloves garlic, crushed

1 Granny Smith apple, peeled and diced

2 yams, peeled and chopped

6 fresh sage leaves, minced

½ cup (70 g) pecans, chopped

¼ cup (38 g) dried cranberries

2 tbsp (30 ml) butter or ghee, melted

Salt and pepper

¼ cup (60 ml) Slow Cooker Beef Broth (page 171)

3 sage leaves, chopped for garnish

Brown the sausage in a heavy-bottomed pan over medium heat for about 5 to 7 minutes and transfer to the slow cooker.

Add the mushrooms, onion, celery, garlic, apple, yams, sage, pecans and cranberries to the slow cooker. Pour the melted butter or ghee over it and mix with a wooden spoon. Generously salt and pepper. Add the broth and cook on low for 4 to 5 hours or until meat is cooked through and the yams are tender. Salt and pepper to taste, then serve with sage for garnish.

CHEF'S TIP:

If you are in a hurry, you can skip browning the meat and this dish will still turn out great. Browning the meat just gives this recipe a little extra oomph!

SLOW COOKER CHICKEN BROTH

Although the heads and feet are listed as optional, I highly recommend that you include them when making broth, as these are the most gelatinous parts of the animal. Chicken skin is rich in collagen, and also a great addition to broth.

If you don't have all the vegetables on hand, just skip them. Each adds more depth and flavor to the broth, but no one vegetable is necessary. The only three ingredients that are necessary are the bones, water and vinegar! —AV

MAKES 10–12 CUPS (2.3–2.8 L)

3 pounds (1.4 kg) chicken carcass pieces, including necks and backs

2 chicken heads, optional

4 chicken feet, optional

1 leek, cut into several pieces, optional

1 large onion, quartered, optional

2 carrots, peeled and cut in half, optional

2 ribs celery, cut in half, optional

2 bay leaves, optional

10 sprigs parsley, optional

Filtered water

1 tbsp (15 ml) apple cider vinegar

Place the bones, chicken heads and feet, if using, in the slow cooker. Add the vegetables, bay leaves, parsley (if using) and enough water so the bones are completely covered, usually between 8 to 12 cups (1.9 to 2.8 l) for me. Add apple cider vinegar. Cook on low for 10 to 12 hours. Remove all vegetables and bones and put broth through a strainer. Refrigerate overnight. The fat will have solidified at the top by the next day. Remove fat and discard or reserve for another use. Refrigerate broth and use within a few days or freeze.

CHEF'S TIP:

For the stovetop, follow the same steps above, but place all of your ingredients in a large stockpot. Bring them to a light simmer, not a boil, and then reduce the heat to very low and cook for 2 to 3 hours or longer, if you are available to keep an eye on the stove.

SLOW–COOKED CHICKEN GIZZARD

This is one of my favorite recipes of all. It comes from a very famous bar in Salvador Bahia, Brazil. After many attempts I finally replicated their very secret recipe. You will never taste a more delicious gizzard in your life, I promise! —VM

SERVES 2

1 bunch of cilantro, stems removed, plus additional (chopped) for serving

3 cloves garlic, peeled and sliced

1 onion, sliced

1 pound (454 g) chicken gizzards, opened and cleaned from the contents

¼ cup (30 g) Italian tomato purée

½ cup (120 ml) white wine

¼ cup (60 ml) water

Sea salt to taste

Cauliflower rice, for serving

Place all of the ingredients in the slow cooker, adding the liquids last and a good pinch of sea salt.

Cook on high for about 6 hours.

Serve in shallow bowls with plenty of broth, and a sprinkle of chopped cilantro on top of cauliflower rice. In Brazil toasted cassava flour is used instead of rice to absorb the broth, it's delicious!

SLOW COOKER
BEEF BROTH

Adding roasted bones and vegetables to broth makes it more aromatic and flavorful. If you are in a hurry, throw the bones in to the slow cooker with filtered water and apple cider vinegar. You will still make a nutritious broth that will be much more flavorful than any store-bought variety. When you do have the time, I recommend taking the extra steps. —AV

MAKES 10–12 CUPS (2.3–2.8 L)

3–4 pounds (1362–1816 g) beef bones

Onions, carrots, celery; coarsely chopped, optional

A few sprigs thyme, optional

Bay leaf, optional

Filtered water

1 tbsp (15 ml) apple cider vinegar

Preheat oven to 450°F (230°C, or gas mark 8). Place the bones in a roasting pan and roast uncovered for 30 minutes.

Transfer the bones to the slow cooker. Add the vegetables, thyme and bay leaf. Add enough water to cover the bones. Add apple cider vinegar. Cook on low for 8 to 24 hours. Remove all vegetables and bones, and put broth through a strainer. Refrigerate overnight. The fat will have solidified by the next day; remove it and discard or reserve for another use. Discard thyme and bay leaf. Refrigerate broth and use within a few days or freeze.

CHEF'S TIP:

For the stovetop, follow the same steps above, but place all of the ingredients in a large stockpot. Bring them to a light simmer, not a boil, and then reduce the heat to very low and cook for 2 to 3 hours or longer, if you are available to keep an eye on the stove.

SLOW COOKER
AFRICAN CASHEW STEW

This slow cooker cashew stew combines the thick sweetness of cashew butter with soft slow-cooked vegetables and rich, dark chicken meat. —RB

SERVES 6

1 onion

1 carrot

1–3 bell peppers

4 cloves garlic

3 pounds (1.4 kg) boneless, skinless chicken thighs

1 (6-ounce [170-g]) can tomato paste

½ cup (90 g) cashew butter

2 tsp (10 g) salt

1 tsp black pepper

1 cup (240 ml) broth

½ habanero, optional

Fresh cilantro, optional

Whole cashews, chopped, optional

Roughly chop the onion, carrot and bell peppers. Smash and peel the garlic cloves and then load them with the chopped vegetables into a food processor. Pulse until finely shredded.

Layer half of the shredded vegetables in a slow cooker, and add the chicken thighs. Top with the remaining half of the vegetables. Add the tomato paste, cashew butter, salt and pepper. Pour the broth in, and cook on low for 8 hours.

Stir the contents together, shredding the chicken into the rest of the ingredients with a fork. Mince the ½ habanero, stir it into the stew and top with fresh cilantro and chopped cashews if desired.

CHAPTER 3

EASY, FAST, FEW-INGREDIENT

A common misconception about the Paleo diet is that it's time consuming, but that doesn't have to be the case thanks to the easy, fast and few-ingredient recipes like the ones you'll find in this chapter.

If you have some go-to and easy-to-make delicious meals, desserts and snacks up your sleeve, you will be able to stick to your Paleo diet without sacrificing too much of your time. After all, when you combine fresh, whole ingredients like meat, vegetables, spices and herbs, it really doesn't take much to make a fabulous meal.

In this chapter you'll find everything from main dishes to desserts, snacks and smoothies. Each recipe is delicious yet simple, and each will save you time and money in the kitchen. Some of my go-tos are the Prosciutto-Wrapped Pesto Chicken Pasta (page 176), Roasted Delicata Squash with Brown Butter Sage Sauce (page 183) and Smoky, Salty Coconut Crisps (page 191).

BAKED APPLE SAGE CHICKEN MEATBALLS

These simple-to-make meatballs make a great appetizer or pair them with some zucchini noodles for a complete meal. —NK

SERVES 4

2 pounds (908 g) ground chicken thigh

½ tsp sea salt

¼ tsp black pepper

4 fresh sage leaves, finely chopped

¼ cup (28 g) grated apple

½ cup (60 g) apple flour (can substitute almond flour)

Zucchini noodles, optional, for serving

Preheat oven to 400°F (200°C, or gas mark 6). Line a large baking sheet with parchment paper. Remove ground chicken from the fridge and add the sea salt, black pepper and sage. Add the grated apple and sift in the apple flour or almond flour. Work quickly to mix everything together using your hands. Use an ice-cream scoop or your hands to form the meatballs into even-sized balls. Place prepared meatballs on the baking sheet as you go, making sure to space them out. Place in the oven and cook for 15 to 20 minutes or until cooked through.

CHEF'S TIP:

Make sure the ground chicken thigh, grated apple and mixing bowl are all chilled before forming the meatballs. This will keep the fat in the ground chicken thigh from melting and keeping the apple and mixing bowl chilled will help maintain the temperature of the chicken thigh.

ROASTED BRUSSELS SPROUTS WITH GARLIC TAHINI SAUCE

If you have ever had a fear of Brussels sprouts like I used to, try roasting them, you won't be disappointed! This rich, garlic tahini sauce is creamy and full of quality proteins, fats and minerals. —CP

SERVES 4

2 pounds (908 g) Brussels sprouts

¼ cup (60 ml) olive oil, divided

1 tsp (3 g) sea salt, divided

¼ tsp fresh cracked black pepper

¼ cup (60 g) tahini

1 tbsp (15 g) Dijon mustard

1 tsp (5 ml) lemon juice

2 large cloves garlic, crushed

⅛ tsp cayenne pepper

Preheat oven to 400°F (200°C, or gas mark 6).

Slice Brussels sprouts into quarters. Place in a baking dish and toss together with half the olive oil, salt and black pepper.

Roast for 25 to 30 minutes or until crispy, stirring halfway through.

Make the sauce by whisking together remaining olive oil and salt, tahini, mustard, lemon, garlic and cayenne pepper.

Drizzle garlic tahini sauce over roasted Brussels sprouts and serve warm.

BACON-WRAPPED SCALLOPS

These bacon-wrapped scallops make such a rich and decadent appetizer that's actually quite easy to make! —HH

SERVES 4

8 scallops

8 slices bacon

Preheat the oven to 425°F (220°C, or gas mark 7). Use stainless steel barbeque skewers or soak wooden barbeque skewers in cool water for about 10 minutes. This will help avoid burning the wood in the oven. Wrap a slice of bacon around each scallop, trimming the bacon to fit evenly around the scallop if necessary. Secure the bacon around the scallop by piercing a trimmed skewer through the middle. Place all the scallops on a baking sheet lined with aluminum foil and place in the oven. Cook for about 25 minutes, turning over halfway through, until the bacon has browned and crisped.

CURRY PLANTAIN CHIPS

These plantain chips are crisp and salty, like potato chips! It is very important for this recipe that you get green plantains and not ripened yellow plantains. Getting them green ensures that they will be salty, not sweet, and a better texture for chips. I like to use avocado oil for this recipe because it's a liquid oil that makes it easier to coat the plantains and it doesn't dominate the flavor, like olive oil would. —HH

SERVES 3–4

2 green plantains

1½ tbsp (23 ml) avocado oil

½ tsp salt

1 tsp (3 g) curry powder

Preheat the oven to 350°F (180°C, or gas mark 4). Use a paring knife to cut the peel off of the plantains. Slice the plantains into very thin slices. Place the slices in a bowl and pour the avocado oil over them and mix so that all the slices are covered in oil. Arrange the slices on a baking sheet lined with parchment paper so that none of them are overlapping. Sprinkle the slices with salt and curry powder. Bake for 25 to 30 minutes or until crispy. Be careful not to burn.

ZUCCHINI BLENDER BREAD

This zucchini bread takes five minutes to prepare and both kids and adults really enjoy it. The best part is that there is no added sugar in this recipe. The dates naturally sweeten this delicious bread. —KW

MAKES 1 LOAF

1 medium zucchini, seeded and cut into chunks

4 eggs

¼ cup (60 ml) melted butter, ghee or coconut oil

1 tsp (5 ml) pure vanilla extract

½ cup (60 g) coconut flour

1 tbsp (8 g) ground cinnamon

1 tsp (3 g) baking soda

1 tbsp (15 ml) apple cider vinegar

¼ tsp sea salt

⅓ cup (60 g) chocolate chips, walnuts or any other nuts or seeds, optional

Preheat oven to 350°F (180°C, or gas mark 4). Add zucchini chunks, dates, eggs, butter, and vanilla to a blender and blend until smooth. Add the coconut flour, cinnamon, baking soda, apple cider vinegar and sea salt and blend once again until thoroughly mixed. Add optional items now and briefly stir. Pour into a regular-sized well-greased or parchment-lined loaf pan and bake for 60 minutes.

TRUFFLE AND HERB BUTTER ROASTED CHICKEN

Sometimes it's the most classic and simple of dishes that satisfy our tastes. Butter roasted chicken—slightly crispy skin, flavorful herbs and savory truffle oil. I like to serve this roasted chicken over a bed of zucchini noodles for a complete comfort food meal. —CP

SERVES 3–4

FOR THE TRUFFLE BUTTER

2 tbsp (30 g) butter

2 tbsp (30 ml) truffle oil, divided

3 large cloves of garlic, crushed

1 tsp (3 g) fresh rosemary, chopped

½ tsp sea salt

¼ tsp cracked black pepper

2 pounds (906 g) bone-in, skin-on chicken pieces

FOR THE ZUCCHINI NOODLES

2 medium zucchini, noodled

1 cup (70 g) fresh spinach leaves

1 tbsp (15 ml) butter

¼ cup (40 g) pine nuts, lightly toasted

¼ cup (16 g) fresh basil, thinly sliced

Preheat oven to 400°F (200°C, or gas mark 6).

In a small saucepan, melt the butter, half of truffle oil, garlic and spices, setting aside the remaining truffle oil for garnishing.

Place chicken in a baking dish and generously brush butter over chicken. Drizzle any remaining butter on top. Roast chicken for 25 to 30 minutes, depending on the size and thickness of the pieces.

As the chicken is roasting, make the zucchini noodles and briefly sauté noodles and spinach in butter just until they soften.

Serve roasted chicken on a bed of zucchini noodles, garnishing with toasted pine nuts and basil.

AUTUMN APPLE, SAGE GRILLED CHICKEN KABOBS

Juicy, grilled chicken kabobs with fresh herbs and tart green apples have a unique fall flavor. Serve over a bed of Herbed Cauliflower Rice (page 206) for a complete dinner. Balsamic reduction can be found at most stores; however double check the ingredients as some brands contain added sugars or preservatives. —CP

SERVES 4–6

2 pounds (908 g) chicken breasts

2 small Granny Smith apples

1 red onion

2 tbsp (30 ml) olive oil

1 tbsp (4 g) fresh sage, chopped

3 cloves garlic, crushed

1½ tsp (4 g) salt

½ tsp fresh cracked black pepper

Herbed Cauliflower Rice (page 206), to serve

2 tbsp (30 ml) balsamic glaze, to garnish

Preheat grill to medium-high heat.

Cube chicken, apples and onions into small squares. Toss together with oil, sage, garlic, salt and pepper. Place the seasoned chicken, apples and onions on wooden skewers.

Grill for 6 to 8 minutes, rotating halfway through. Adjust grilling time based off thickness of chicken.

Serve with a scoop of Cauliflower Rice and a drizzle of balsamic reduction.

CHEF'S TIP:

I often add leftovers to fresh leafy greens and toss with Grainy Mustard Champagne Vinaigrette (page 513) for a simple lunch.

PROSCIUTTO-WRAPPED PESTO CHICKEN PASTA

Pan searing chicken holds in the flavor and tenderness of the chicken as it simmers in the creamy dairy-free pesto sauce. This meal is full of flavors, nutrients and is just such a happy, simple dish to prepare! I usually keep a batch of homemade pesto on hand to use throughout the week and this pesto pasta is nightshade-free for those with sensitivities. —CP

SERVES 2–3

4 tbsp (60 g) butter, divided

1 crown broccoli, chopped

1 pound (454 g) boneless and skinless chicken breast

8 slices prosciutto

½ cup (120 g) Fresh Basil Pesto (page 509)

¼ cup (60 ml) coconut milk

2 zucchini, noodled

Warm a large skillet to medium heat. Melt half the butter in the skillet and sauté the broccoli for 5 minutes. Remove and set aside.

Slice chicken breast in half and then in half again, creating 8 strips of chicken. Tightly wrap each piece in prosciutto.

Melt the remaining butter in the skillet and sear chicken for 1 minute, flip to the other side and sear for an additional minute.

Reduce the heat to low. Stir in the pesto, coconut milk and broccoli, covering the chicken in the pesto sauce. Place a lid on the skillet and simmer for 15 to 20 minutes or until chicken is thoroughly cooked.

Serve over a bed of warm zucchini noodles or spaghetti squash.

CHEF'S TIPS:

I love having a batch of pesto to keep on hand for a quick yet gourmet weeknight dinner. If you can tolerate dairy, I love topping this dish with a sprinkle of Parmesan cheese.

THAI BASIL CHICKEN

Thai basil chicken is always my favorite meal at our local Thai restaurant. I wanted to re-create this using Paleo-friendly ingredients, so I use coconut aminos for a soy-free alternative to soy sauce. Serve with zucchini noodles or even Garlic Sesame Roasted Broccoli (page 182) for a simple weeknight meal. —CP

SERVES 6

FOR THE MARINADE

2 tbsp (30 ml) sesame oil

4 tbsp (60 ml) coconut aminos

2 tsp (10 ml) fish sauce

½ tsp chili flakes

½ tsp ground ginger

Fresh cracked black pepper

4 cloves garlic, crushed

2 pounds (908 g) chicken breast, thinly sliced

2 tbsp (30 ml) coconut oil

1 red bell pepper, thinly sliced

¾ cup (45 g) fresh Thai basil, thinly sliced

Zucchini noodles or Garlic Sesame Roasted Broccoli (page 182), to serve

Green onions, to garnish

In a medium mixing bowl, whisk together the marinade ingredients and add chicken. Marinate chicken in sauce for 6 hours.

In a large skillet or wok, heat coconut oil over medium-high heat.

Add chicken with sauce, browning all sides before lowering heat. Stir in red pepper and basil, continuing to sauté until chicken is completely cooked.

Serve with zucchini noodles or Garlic Sesame Roasted Broccoli and top with a sprinkle of green onions.

5-MINUTE CHICKEN LIVER PATE

The easiest and most delicious way to use sautéed liver leftovers! —VM

SERVES 1

3½ ounces (98 g) sautéed chicken livers, preferably leftover, cooled

3 tbsp (45 g) butter, softened

1 tsp (1.5 g) fresh mixed herbs, thyme, oregano, sage, chopped

Sea salt and black pepper, to taste

Sliced radishes or crackers, for serving

Take all of the ingredients and place them in the blender. Blend everything until a smooth paste has formed, then serve with sliced radishes or crackers.

SAUTÉED CHICKEN LIVER WITH A BABY KALE SALAD

This is a quick and simple but very nutritious dish. Sautéing in butter always brings the best out of any food, and here it makes the chicken liver especially delicious! —VM

SERVES 2

FOR THE CHICKEN LIVER

4 ounces (112 g) chicken liver, veins and ligaments removed

2 tbsp (30 g) butter or ghee

1 small onion, sliced

Sea salt and black pepper

FOR THE KALE SALAD

4 ounces (112 g) baby kale, or any kind of kale

2 tbsp (30 ml) apple cider vinegar

Sea salt to taste

Bring liver to room temperature. In a medium skillet, melt the butter or ghee over low heat. Add the sliced onion and sauté until soft. about 3 to 5 minutes.

Pat the liver dry. Increase the heat to high, add the liver to the skillet and sauté for about 5 minutes. Turn them over and sauté for another 2 to 3 minutes until they are nicely browned. Season with salt and pepper.

While the liver is cooking. wash the kale and chop it into small pieces. Add the kale to a bowl and toss with the apple cider vinegar and salt.

Serve the chicken liver over the kale salad.

BBQ CHICKEN LIVERS AND HEARTS

If you have had chicken livers and hearts, then you know how tasty they are. They're even better when you BBQ them! They will get that wonderful smoky flavor and that nice browned outside we love of BBQ meat! —VM

SERVES 6

1 pound (454 g) chicken hearts

1 pound (454 g) chicken livers

Bamboo skewers, pre-soaked in water for 1 hour

Sea salt and black pepper to taste

Tahini, for serving

Make sure the grill is ready at a medium-high heat. Start by cleaning the hearts and liver of veins and fat with a good knife.

Thread about 5 to 7 separately on each skewer, and season them with sea salt and black pepper. Place the skewers into a nicely oiled grill basket and grill to desired tenderness.

Fresh tahini sauce is a great topping for both meats.

CHEF'S TIP:

Tahini sauce can be purchased pre-made or made from scratch using sesame seed butter, garlic, lemon juice and water.

CHICKEN LIVERS WITH GINGER SAUCE

A different flavor for a classic superfood. You can love chicken livers because of the tender and delicious taste or because they are a powerhouse of nutrition. My main concern is to make them taste amazing! —VM

SERVES 4

4 tbsp (60 g) ghee, divided

3 sweet onions, thinly sliced

1 pound (454 g) chicken livers

2 inches (5 cm) of fresh ginger root, peeled and grated

¼ cup (15 g) fresh cilantro, finely chopped

Sea salt and black pepper to taste

Melt half of the ghee in a frying pan over low heat. Add the onions, sweating them slowly. Remove the onions from the pan, and then add the remaining ghee.

Raise the heat to high and add the chicken livers, sautéing for about 2 minutes on each side until they are nicely browned. Make sure you do not overcook the livers as you want them to remain a little pink on the inside. Add the ginger and cilantro to the pan along with salt and pepper to taste.

Cook for an additional minute and serve warm.

LIVER WITH FIG SAUCE

I just love when figs come into season. Figs have always been my favorite fruit and I try to use them in any recipe I can. Combining the figs with the liver and the balsamic adds a tangy sweetness to the dish that transforms that livery taste that not everyone enjoys! —VM

SERVES 2

1 pound (454 g) beef liver, cleaned and sliced into ½-inch (1.3-cm) steaks

¼ cup (60 ml) balsamic vinegar

3 ripe figs

Ghee or butter

¼ cup (60 ml) white wine

Salt to taste

Marinate the liver overnight with the balsamic vinegar. Wash the figs and remove stems, then blend them in a food processor until smooth.

Once the liver is done marinating, add the fat to a large skillet over medium heat. Place the liver in the skillet and let it brown for about 5 minutes. Turn the liver over and add the white wine to the pan, cooking off the alcohol for about 1 minute.

Add the puréed figs and stir well. Cover the liver for about 2 minutes to let the sauce warm up. Once the liver and sauce are ready, season with salt and serve immediately.

SPINACH CILANTRO TURKEY BURGERS

Every time I make these burgers, they are always a crowd pleaser. I just love the fresh and bright flavors of cilantro and the rich and earthy flavors of cumin. Serve on a big bed of lettuce and lots of toppings for an easy and satisfying meal. —KH

SERVES 5

1 pound (454 g) ground dark meat turkey

½ small onion, finely chopped

2 handfuls baby spinach, washed and chopped

1 tsp (3 g) sea salt

¼ cup (15 g) fresh cilantro, finely chopped

1 tbsp (15 g) ghee or butter for cooking

Lettuce, for serving

Caramelized onions, for serving

Avocado, for serving

In large bowl, combine all burger ingredients except for the ghee or butter and mix well. Form into five patties. Melt ghee or butter in a skillet on medium heat. Cook patties until nice and brown, about 4 minutes on each side, flipping a couple of times. This usually takes about 10 minutes. Serve over a bed of lettuce and top with caramelized onions and avocado (and whatever else you like on your burgers).

SPINACH CILANTRO MEATBALLS

I keep pre-made meatballs in the freezer for quick and easy weeknight meals. You can whip these meatballs up with any ground meat that you have on hand. —KH

MAKES ABOUT 40

2 pounds (908 g) ground meat

½ medium onion, finely chopped

1½ tsp (4.5 g) sea salt

1 tsp (3 g) ground cumin

2 cups (140 g) packed baby spinach, chopped

½ cup (30 g) fresh cilantro, finely chopped

2 eggs, whipped

Preheat the oven to 400°F (200°C, or gas mark 6). Line a baking sheet with parchment paper.

Combine all ingredients in a large bowl and mix well until fully combined. Roll into small balls and place onto prepared baking sheet. Bake for 25 minutes, until meatballs are beginning to brown and are cooked all the way through. Freeze meatballs in a single layer then place frozen meatballs in an airtight container.

APPLE TARRAGON MEATBALLS

These bite-sized pork meatballs are infused with the sweetness of apples and the aromatic note of tarragon. Serve alongside some zucchini noodles for a complete meal. —NK

SERVES 2–4

1 pound (454 g) ground pork

1 apple (a sweet variety works best), peeled, cored and grated

2 tsp (6 g) dried tarragon

Sea salt and black pepper to taste

Preheat oven to 350°F (180°C, or gas mark 4). Line a large baking tray with parchment paper. Place ground pork, apple and tarragon into a mixing bowl. Season with sea salt and black pepper and mix well. Form into medium-sized meatballs and place onto the lined baking tray as you go. Place in the oven and bake for 25 to 30 minutes or until the meatballs are cooked through.

CHEF'S TIP:

Make sure the pork is chilled before making these meatballs so that you keep the fat from melting and breaking down before the meatballs are cooked.

PEACH HONEY MUSTARD SAUCE

This easy sauce is a summertime staple for us. It pairs well with all types of meat and fish. We even enjoy it as a salad dressing in the summer months when peaches are the most flavorful and in season. —KW

MAKES ¾ CUP (180 G)

1 peach, peeled and chopped

¼ cup (60 ml) honey

¼ cup (60 g) Dijon mustard

In a food processor, process the ingredients until smooth and creamy.

CHEF'S TIP:

Use half the recipe for a meat marinade and save the other half to pour over the finished meat.

KALE AND SAUSAGE

My favorite 15-minute meal. No time for cooking? Keep this easy recipe on hand for busy times. —KH

SERVES 3–4

1 bunch kale, chopped into thin ribbons

1 tbsp (15 ml) coconut aminos

1 pound (454 g) sausage

1 tsp (5 g) butter or ghee

Steam kale for 8 to 10 minutes. Remove from heat and toss with coconut aminos. Meanwhile chop sausage into bite-sized pieces and sauté in butter or ghee until thoroughly browned and thoroughly cooked. Remove sausages from heat and add cooked kale. Mix to combine and serve.

GRILLED LAMB SKEWERS

In Italy this dish is sometimes called Arrosticini. In Sanremo, where I grew up, it is Rostelle! It's my favorite dish in the whole world!—In Italy they are eaten as a main course, served with a green salad. —VM

SERVES 6

2 pounds (908 g) lamb shoulder

Salt and pepper to taste

Bamboo skewers, soaked in water for 1 hour

Start by cutting the meat into 1-inch (2.5-cm) cubes.

Season the lamb with salt and pepper to taste. Once the skewers are done soaking, go ahead and skewer enough lamb to fill up two-thirds of the skewer. Throw the skewers on the grill over medium high heat, turning about every minute until the meat reaches the desired level of doneness.

Serve immediately with a green salad with a balsamic vinaigrette.

QUICK AND EASY PALEO BULGOGI

Bulgogi, a type of Korean marinated beef, is one of the most popular Korean dishes. But if you're sensitive to gluten like me, then it's usually not an option for us. You can't have Bulgogi without the soy sauce, otherwise it's not Bulgogi. Lucky for us we have coconut aminos to help pull this dish together quite nicely. So enjoy all the flavors of the garlic, ginger, apples and pear tonight! —VM

SERVES 4

FOR THE MARINADE

½ cup (120 ml) coconut aminos

4 cloves garlic

½ apple, sliced and peeled

½ pear, sliced and peeled

1 tbsp (8 g) ginger, finely chopped

1 tbsp (12 g) coconut sugar

2 tbsp (30 ml) toasted sesame oil

1 white onion, roughly chopped

1 pound (454 g) steak sirloin, thinly sliced

FOR THE DIPPING SAUCE

¼ cup (32 g) Korean hot pepper flakes, or red chili pepper flakes

3 cloves garlic, minced

½ cup (80 g) white onion, chopped

½ pear, peeled and seeded

½ cup (80 g) pineapple chunks

2 tbsp (30 ml) honey

2 tbsp (30 ml) toasted sesame oil

Leaf lettuce, for wrapping

Purée all of marinade ingredients in the food processor until nice and smooth. Add the marinade and meat to a bowl, mixing everything until it's nice and coated. Cover and refrigerate overnight.

For the dipping sauce, blend all of the sauce ingredients in the food processor until nice and smooth.

The best way to cook Bulgogi is over a charcoal grill, but a cast iron skillet will do just fine as well. Heat the skillet over high heat and sear the meat on all sides until nicely browned. Set aside when done.

Fill the lettuce leaves with meat and dress them with sauce.

AROMATIC DOVER SOLE FILLETS

Delicate flavors of lemon zest and cardamom, combined with the best olive oil, just a touch of aromatic cilantro and a melt-in-your mouth texture—sounds like a perfect dish to me! —VM

SERVES 2

¼ cup (60 ml) olive oil, divided

Zest of 1 Meyer lemon

3 whole cardamom pods, crushed, or a sprinkle of cardamom powder

1 cup (60 g) cilantro, chopped, divided

4–6 Dover sole filets

Sea salt

Turn the broiler to high. Coat a baking dish with half of the olive oil. Then add the lemon zest, crushed cardamom and half of the chopped cilantro.

Lay the fillets over the oil mixture and top with the remaining ingredients.

Season with sea salt and place under the broiler for 7 to 8 minutes. Cook thoroughly until the fish breaks easily with a fork, and serve immediately.

CHILI LIME SALMON

In about fifteen minutes, you can have a healthy meal on the table. While the salmon is cooking, I like to whip up some Super Easy Guacamole (page 190) and a big salad. —KW

SERVES 4

1 pound (454 g) salmon fillet

1 tbsp (15 g) fat of choice, for greasing

2 limes

2 tsp (6 g) chili powder

½ tsp ground cumin

Sea salt and pepper, to taste

Mango Habanero Hot Sauce (page 517), optional, for garnish

Preheat oven to 400°F (200°C, or gas mark 6). Place the salmon skin-side down in a greased baking dish. Squeeze the juice from one of the limes all over the salmon. Combine the chili powder, cumin, sea salt and pepper together. Sprinkle the seasoning all over the salmon. Bake for 12 to 15 minutes or until fish flakes easily with a fork. Use the other lime and Mango Habanero Hot Sauce for serving.

GARLIC SESAME ROASTED BROCCOLI

Roasted broccoli with plenty of garlic is my favorite way to eat this green vegetable. Roasting brings out a certain sweetness and the aroma of toasted sesame oil will fill your kitchen. Serve with salmon or chicken for a simple, healthy meal. —CP

SERVES 4–6

2 large crowns broccoli

3 tbsp (45 ml) toasted sesame oil, divided

4 large cloves garlic, crushed

½ tsp sea salt

¼ tsp black pepper

2 tbsp (30 g) butter

2 tbsp (16 g) sesame seeds

Preheat oven to 400°F (200°C, or gas mark 6).

Cut broccoli into small florets. Place in a baking dish and toss together with 2 tablespoons (30 ml) sesame oil, garlic, salt and pepper. Slice butter into small cubes and arrange throughout the pan.

Roast for 20 minutes, stir and continue roasting for 15 to 20 additional minutes or until broccoli is tender.

Garnish with remaining tablespoon (15 ml) of sesame oil and sesame seeds.

BRUSSELS SPROUT AND BACON HASH

Pan-seared Brussels sprouts made crispy as they fry up in bacon grease. Top with a fried or poached egg for a nutritious, hearty breakfast. —CP

SERVES 2

10 Brussels sprouts

1 shallot

4 slices bacon, preferably thick cut

2 tbsp (30 ml) bacon grease

2–4 eggs, poached or fried

¼ tsp sea salt

¼ tsp fresh cracked black pepper

Warm a skillet to medium heat for several minutes so that the skillet is evenly heated.

Use a mandolin to shred Brussels sprouts, or simply use a knife to slice into thin shreds. Slice the shallot into thin slices and cut the bacon into small cubes.

Add the bacon grease to the pan and sauté the sprouts and shallot for several minutes or until they start to turn crispy. Stir in the bacon and sauté for an additional minute.

Plate topped with a poached or fried egg and salt and pepper to taste.

ROASTED DELICATA SQUASH WITH BROWN BUTTER SAGE SAUCE

This is a delicious side dish that pairs the sweetness of delicata squash with the classic combination of butter and sage. —NK

SERVES 4

2 delicata squash (1 pound [454 g] each), peeled, seeded and diced into even-sized chunks

½ tsp sea salt

¼ tsp black pepper

1 tbsp (15 ml) melted ghee or coconut oil

3 tbsp (45 g) butter

10 fresh sage leaves

Preheat oven to 400°F (200°C, or gas mark 6). Line a large baking sheet with parchment paper. Mix diced delicata squash with sea salt and black pepper in a mixing bowl. Mix in the melted ghee or coconut oil. Spread onto the baking sheet and place in the oven and bake for 20 to 25 minutes or until fork tender.

Once ready remove from the oven and set aside, covered to keep warm. Heat a medium stainless steel skillet on medium-high heat and add the butter. Heat the butter until it starts to foam. Once the foam has reduced and the butter has changed color to a caramel brown add the sage leaves and carefully swirl the skillet around so the butter covers the sage leaves and they start to crisp up, about 3 minutes or so. Quickly add the delicata squash into the pan and toss to coat in the brown butter and sage. Serve warm.

GRILLED RAINBOW CARROTS WITH GARLIC HERB BUTTER

Grilled rainbow carrots are not only beautiful but also tasty and sweet! They have quickly become one of my favorite summer side dishes and can be tossed on the grill with your meat or main entrée. —CP

SERVES 6–8

2 bunches rainbow carrots

Whipped Garlic Herb Butter (page 497), to serve

½ cup (75 g) pine nuts, toasted

Handful of micro greens

Pinch of coarse sea salt

Preheat the grill to medium heat.

Lightly scrub the carrots and cut top greens off if desired.

Grill carrots on warmed grill for 10 to 20 minutes, rotating frequently. Grill time will depend on the thickness of your carrots.

Plate and top with whipped garlic herb butter, toasted pine nuts, microgreens and a sprinkle of coarse sea salt.

BAKED CARROT FRIES

Carrot fries are one of my favorite snacks! They're nutritious, tasty and fun too. These carrots are baked instead of fried, which allows you to use less oil and creates a tender texture and rich roasted flavor. —HH

SERVES 2

1 pound (454 g) carrots

1½ tbsp (23 ml) olive oil

1 tsp (3 g) sea salt

½ tsp pepper

½ tsp garlic powder

½ tsp thyme

Preheat the oven to 400°F (200°C, or gas mark 6). Line a cookie sheet with parchment paper. You can wash and peel the carrots if you want to. I use organic carrots and don't peel them and they turn out fine. Cut the carrots into even sticks that are roughly 4 inches (10 cm) long and about ½-inch (1.3-cm) thick. Put the cut carrots into a bowl and drizzle with olive oil. Then sprinkle the salt, pepper, garlic powder and thyme on top. Stir the carrots to evenly coat with the oil and spices. Place the carrots on the cookie sheet. Make sure the carrots are evenly spread and not stacked on top of each other.

Bake for about 25 to 35 minutes, checking halfway through to move the carrots around or flip them on the sheet to get even cooking. Once you can pierce the carrots easily with a fork and there is a slight browning or crisping on the edges, they are done. Remove them from the oven and allow to cool for a few minutes.

GRILLED ZUCCHINI WITH LEMON ROSEMARY BUTTER

Grilled zucchini is my favorite way to eat this summer vegetable as you can toss it on the grill with the rest of your meal. Butter, rosemary and lemon create a savory butter sauce that will have everyone eating their vegetables! —CP

SERVES 6–8

2 tbsp (30 ml) butter, melted

1 lemon, juiced

2 cloves garlic, crushed

1 tsp (3 g) fresh rosemary, chopped

½ tsp sea salt

Pepper, to taste

4 zucchini

Warm grill to medium-high heat.

While the grill is warming, prepare the butter sauce by whisking together all ingredients, except the zucchini.

Slice the zucchini, long-ways, into 3 to 4 slices depending on the thickness.

Brush half of the lemon rosemary butter on both sides of squash slices. Set aside remaining butter.

Grill the zucchini for 3 minutes, flip and continue to grill on the other side for 3 additional minutes.

Plate on a serving tray and drizzle remaining butter on top of grilled zucchini.

CHEF'S TIP:
Use this savory butter with other grilled vegetables you may find at the market or have in your kitchen.

LEMON TARRAGON HERB BUTTER

Compound butters are a great way to add flavor to a dish. For this one I used fresh tarragon and lemon to make a vibrant butter. —NK

MAKES ½ CUP (100 G)

8 ounces (227 g) or 1 stick salted butter, softened at room temperature

2 tbsp (8 g) fresh tarragon, chopped

Zest of 1 small lemon

¼ tsp sea salt (if using unsalted butter)

Place softened butter into a medium-sized mixing bowl. Add in the chopped tarragon and lemon zest. Mix well then place mixture onto a piece of parchment paper. Fold the parchment paper over the butter mixture and using your hands roll the mixture into a log. Twist both ends of the parchment paper to seal. Store in the freezer and use as needed.

CHEF'S TIP:
There are so many different ways to flavor compound butter so have fun with it. Add to vegetables when roasting or frying or add to a piece of steak or fish.

PIMIENTOS DE PADRÓN

Pimientos de Padrón, or Padron peppers in English, are small, green, mild peppers that originate from the Padrón region of Galicia in northwestern Spain. These can make a fun, conversation-stimulating appetizer since some of these peppers are medium spice and some random ones are really hot. You never know which one you're going to get! —HH

SERVES 2

½ pound (227 g) Padron peppers

2 tbsp (30 ml) olive or avocado oil

Coarse sea salt to taste

Wash and dry the peppers. In a small cast iron skillet heat the oil on medium heat, wait a minute for it to get hot. Put the peppers in the skillet and let them brown on one side for a minute or two, then turn them over to brown on the other side. Once they're sufficiently browned, remove them from the pan and place on a plate. Sprinkle with coarse sea salt and enjoy!

CAULIFLOWER PURÉE

This cauliflower purée recipe is one of my absolute favorite side dishes! It's creamy and delicious just like mashed potatoes. When you season it just right, the flavor is incredible. —HH

SERVES 4

2 medium heads cauliflower

1–1½ cups (235–355 ml) Slow Cooker Chicken Broth (page 170)

5 cloves garlic

½ tsp salt

½ tsp pepper

½ tsp sage

½ tsp thyme

½ tsp onion powder

1 tbsp (15 g) butter, ghee or olive oil

Wash the cauliflower heads and chop into small pieces. Place the chopped cauliflower into a large pot and pour in 1 cup (235 ml) of the broth. The broth should come up just short of the top of the cauliflower; it shouldn't be covering the cauliflower. Add more if necessary.

Turn on the heat to high. Add the whole peeled garlic cloves—they do not need to be chopped since they will be puréed later. Then add the salt, pepper and spices and stir. Cover the pot with a lid and bring it to a boil. Once the cauliflower is boiling, stir it and turn the heat to medium-high. It should continue to boil gently. Simmer for about 30 minutes or until the cauliflower is very soft and tender. You should be able to easily mash it with a fork.

Turn the heat off. Remove from heat, add butter or oil and purée with an immersion blender. If you are using a blender, add the butter or ghee and wait for it to cool. Once it's cooled blend it until it becomes a smooth purée. Add more salt or pepper to taste if necessary and enjoy!

COCONUT CREAMED SPINACH

A knock-off recipe from a famous local Haitian restaurant on Miami Beach. This is a light and creamy staple side dish in my house. —RM

SERVES 2–3

1 (13½-ounce [378-g]) can coconut milk

½ roasted red pepper, diced

2 plum tomatoes, cored and diced

½ tsp salt

3 cloves garlic, minced

2 tbsp (30 g) butter, optional if dairy-free

8 ounces (227 g) cooked frozen spinach, drained

Sauté coconut milk, red pepper, tomatoes, salt and garlic over medium-low heat for 10 minutes. Slowly add butter while stirring, then add the spinach and allow to simmer for 5 minutes. If you have fresh spinach on hand, simply add it to the sauce at the end until it wilts to your satisfaction and serve.

CHILLED LEMON ASPARAGUS

This is a crisp and refreshing twist on your average asparagus side dish. It is a true palate cleanser that pairs well with heavy meats, fish or creamy entrées. —RM

SERVES 5–6

1 pound (454 g) asparagus, trimmed

Olive oil

Half of a fresh lemon

Salt and pepper, to taste

Bring a medium pot of water to a boil. Cook the asparagus al dente, about 4 minutes. Drain the asparagus using a colander and then immediately submerge them into icy water, to stop the cooking process. Once chilled, remove from water and pat dry on a serving platter. Drizzle with olive oil and squeeze the lemon half—without the seeds—over it. Season with salt and fresh pepper, then serve immediately.

BOK CHOY STIR-FRY

Stir-fried bok choy with salty coconut aminos and healthy medicinal turmeric. This is a simple side dish to serve with slow-cooked pork or meat kebabs. —RM

SERVES 2–4

1 tbsp (15 ml) extra-virgin olive oil

1 bunch bok choy, trimmed and sliced

1 tbsp (15 ml) coconut aminos

2 tsp (10 ml) chili garlic sauce

½–1-inch (1.3–2.5 cm) piece fresh ginger, grated

¼ tsp turmeric

Heat olive oil in a large skillet over medium-low heat. Fry the chopped bok choy until semi-soft, about 4 minutes. Add the coconut aminos and garlic sauce and fry for another 30 seconds, then add the ginger and turmeric. Continue stirring and cooking for about another 2 minutes, until the bok choy has absorbed the flavor and the liquid has reduced. Serve immediately.

BOK CHOY SALAD WITH GARLIC TAHINI DRESSING

This salad uses sliced raw bok choy for a refreshing crunch, and is then tossed in a homemade garlic tahini dressing for a spicy peppery tang. —RM

SERVES 2–3

1 medium bunch bok choy, trimmed and thinly sliced

¼ cup (30 g) matchstick carrots

FOR THE GARLIC TAHINI DRESSING

3 tbsp (45 ml) extra-virgin olive oil

2 tbsp (30 ml) apple cider vinegar

1 clove garlic

1 tbsp (15 g) sesame tahini

½ tsp black pepper

1 tsp (5 ml) lemon juice

Pinch of salt

Place the chopped bok choy and carrots in a large mixing bowl. In a food processor, blend together all of the dressing ingredients until smooth, stopping to scrape the sides of the processor, about 4 minutes. Drizzle the dressing over the raw bok choy salad and toss. Serve immediately.

EASY GREENS

Greens are some of the healthiest and most nutrient-dense vegetables and should be eaten liberally on a Paleo diet. This is a quick and easy way to prepare greens that the whole family will love. —KH

SERVES 3–4

1 bunch greens—kale, chard or collard

2 tsp (10 g) ghee

2 tsp (10 ml) coconut oil

Sea salt, to taste

Place greens into large bowl in kitchen sink, fill the bowl with water and gently swish them around in the water to remove any gritty dirt. Empty the water out and repeat a couple of times. Drain greens. Stack leaves on top of each other, roll into a tube-shape and slice into thin strips.

Place shredded greens into a steamer basket and steam for 5 to 10 minutes—depending on the type of green and your personal preference. More for collards and kale, less for chard.

Remove from heat, place into glass bowl, add 2 teaspoons (10 g) of ghee and 2 teaspoons (10 ml) of coconut oil and mix to combine. Salt to taste and serve.

SIMPLE CARROT NOODLE SALAD

Having simple side dishes to throw together makes eating healthy easier. This simple carrot salad takes just minutes to prepare and pairs well with just about any Paleo meal. I sometimes add a few raisins for a sweeter salad. —KH

SERVES 2

2 large carrots, peeled

2 tbsp (30 ml) apple cider vinegar

⅛ tsp sea salt

1 tbsp (4 g) cilantro, finely chopped

2 tbsp (18 g) raisins, optional

Spiralize, grate or use a vegetable peeler to make thin noodle-like strips from the carrots. Add apple cider vinegar, sea salt, chopped cilantro and optional raisins. Mix to combine. Enjoy.

SUMMER TOMATO BALSAMIC SALAD

A delightful summer salad full of flavor and color is a great addition to any backyard barbecue or gathering. Savory prosciutto gives this simple tomato salad a rich flavor tossed together with a balsamic vinaigrette. —CP

SERVES 6

10 slices prosciutto

1½ tbsp (23 ml) olive oil

1 tbsp (15 ml) balsamic vinegar

1 large clove of garlic, crushed

½ tsp sea salt

¼ tsp fresh cracked black pepper

1 pint (300 g) fresh cherry tomatoes

1 shallot

1 avocado

½ cup (30 g) fresh basil, thinly sliced

Use your hands to twirl prosciutto slices into ribbon-like spirals. Place around the edges of a serving platter.

Whisk together the olive oil, balsamic vinegar, garlic, salt and pepper.

Chop the tomatoes, shallot and avocado.

Toss together the salad with the dressing.

Plate salad in the middle of the prosciutto slices and garnish with fresh basil.

CHEF'S TIP:

If you are entertaining you can make this salad up ahead of time, cover and chill in the refrigerator. Just top with avocado slices when ready to serve so they don't turn brown.

PARSNIP CHIPS

Parsnips are a root vegetable with a sharp flavor that is perfect for making chips. Enjoy these as a snack or appetizer. —HH

SERVES 4

4 medium parsnips

Salt, to taste

Preheat the oven to 325°F (170°C, or gas mark 3). Wash and peel the parsnips. Using a mandolin slicer, thinly slice the parsnips. Arrange the sliced parsnips on a baking sheet lined with parchment paper. Do not layer the slices on top of other slices. The slices can be extremely close to fit more on the sheet because they will shrink while baking. Sprinkle the slices with salt. Place in the oven for 25 to 30 minutes or until the parsnip slices have lightly browned and are crispy.

FRIED PLANTAINS

Plantains are in the banana family and make for a wonderful Paleo side dish. They pair well with savory meats. This recipe works best with very ripe plantains. —KH

SERVES 3

4 tbsp (60 ml) coconut oil

3 very ripe plantains, sliced diagonally

In a heavy skillet, melt coconut oil on medium-high heat, liberally coating the entire bottom. When a drop of water sizzles in the oil, add the plantain slices and cook until the bottom is golden brown. Carefully flip slices over and brown on other side until just beginning to caramelize. Remove from pan and drain off excess oil by placing onto paper towel. Serve warm.

BAKED PLANTAIN STRIPS

Plantain strips are an easy snack to keep on hand for a day at the office or hiking on trails. I think the best kinds of snacks are ones that conveniently don't have to be refrigerated. They also pair well with a soup and salad for lunch. —RM

SERVES 2–3

1 green plantain

1 tbsp (15 g) bacon fat (or oil of choice)

Salt, to taste

Pepper, to taste

Garlic powder, to taste

1 lime

Super Easy Guacamole (page 190), optional, for serving

Preheat the oven to 375°F (190°C, or gas mark 5). Cut off both ends of the plantain with a sharp knife. Slice the knife down the full length of the plantain peel along each ridge. You can peel each strip off by first gliding your fingers along and under the peel strip, and slowly wedging your fingers against the plantain. Using a mandolin with a finger guard, slice the plantain in thin strips down the length so that the pieces are long, instead of small circles. Try a few test slices to make sure they are a nice thickness. Deposit the slices in a mixing bowl and add the bacon fat. Gently toss and coat each slice evenly.

Layer two baking sheets with parchment paper. Lay out each plantain slice in a single layer, and then sprinkle with salt, pepper and garlic powder to taste. Finish with a squeeze of lime. Bake for about 20 minutes, flipping over halfway through. The last 5 minutes you're going to want to keep an eye on them because the ends might brown. Serve with guacamole or store them in an airtight container for a later snack.

CHEF'S TIP:

Use a mandolin slicer for best results. A consistent thickness throughout the slices will ensure an even baking time.

TURMERIC APPLE CHIPS

Turmeric adds an earthy element to these apple chips, along with beautiful color—and health benefits! Turmeric has been known for its role in regulating cell function, as well as being an anti-inflammatory for arthritis. It also boasts high concentrations of geranylgeranoic acid, which is a cancer-fighting chemical. —RM

SERVES 3–4

1 red delicious apple

1 tsp (5 ml) fresh lemon juice

Ground turmeric, to taste

Ground cinnamon, to taste

Powdered ginger, to taste

For best results use a mandolin to get uniform thickness of slices. Preheat the oven to 225°F (107°C) and line two to three baking sheets with parchment paper. Wash the apple and then pat it dry. Cut off the end of the apple, and then start slicing thin rings with the seeds in the center of each ring. The seeds will fall out during baking, don't worry.

You may need to adjust the setting after a few test slices in order to get the right thickness. I prefer mine pretty thin. In a bowl, coat the slices in lemon juice to preserve them before baking. This also adds a nice tartness. Lay out the apple rings in a single, non-overlapping layer on the baking sheet. I was able to cover three baking sheets. Lightly dash each apple with the ground turmeric, cinnamon and ginger on one side only. Bake for about an hour and a half, turning over once halfway through.

CHEF'S TIP:

The apples may still feel slightly flimsy when you take them out of the oven, but they will crisp up once they cool. Enjoy the same day or store in an airtight container for up to a week.

SUPER EASY GUACAMOLE

Just like an easy salsa, an easy guacamole recipe is a kitchen must have. The great thing about this recipe is that it is so simple and takes no time at all. Pair this with the Chorizo Omelet (page 441) or the Mahi Mahi Tacos (page 105) and enjoy! —VM

SERVES 2

2 avocados

Juice of 1 lime

¼ cup (15 g) fresh cilantro, finely chopped

1 clove garlic

½ red onion, or 2 shallots for a milder flavor

¼ tsp sea salt

Add all of the ingredients to the food processor, blend to the desired consistency and enjoy. It doesn't get any easier than this!

CHEF'S TIP:

To prevent the guacamole form turning dark, place an avocado seed in the finished guacamole and refrigerate.

PINEAPPLE COLESLAW

Pineapple adds a fresh flair to typical coleslaw. For a fabulous contrasting flavor, serve this with the Slow Cooker Chipotle Pork (page 163). —KW

SERVES 4–6

½ head green cabbage, shredded

½ head red cabbage, shredded

2 carrots, shredded

½ cup (120 g) Homemade Mayonnaise (page 496)

1½ tbsp (23 ml) apple cider vinegar

2 cups (330 g) fresh pineapple

Sea salt and pepper, to taste

Combine all ingredients in a bowl and stir. Keep any leftovers in the refrigerator for up to one week.

SMOKY, SALTY COCONUT CRISPS

Watching movies just isn't the same without popcorn, but this is my favorite grain-free alternative for something salty and crunchy! You also can make simple dessert parfaits with layers of whipped coconut cream, pomegranate seeds or your favorite fruit and these smoky coconut crisps. —CP

SERVES 2–4

2 cups (160 g) thick shredded coconut flakes

1 tsp (3 g) smoked sea salt flakes, divided

½ tsp ground cinnamon

¼ tsp ground nutmeg

¼ tsp sea salt

Warm a non-stick skillet over medium low heat.

In a bowl, toss together coconut flakes, half the salt and spices. Add to the skillet and sauté for 2 to 4 minutes or until fragrant and golden brown.

Remove from the pan and toss in remaining smoked sea salt flakes. Cool completely. Enjoy!

CARDAMOM SPICE NUTTY SNACK BARS

These spiced nut bars are a simple snack without all the processed ingredients that make up most packaged snack bars. The smoky cardamom flavor provides a nice contrast to the sweetness of the golden raisins. I also like to crumble a few pieces atop yogurt for a simple breakfast option. —CP

MAKES 8–12

1 cup (150 g) raw almonds

1 cup (85 g) finely shredded coconut flakes, unsweetened

½ cup (120 g) raw cashew butter

½ cup (75 g) golden raisins

2 tbsp (16 g) ground flaxseed

2 tbsp (30 ml) coconut oil

2 tsp (10 ml) vanilla extract

¾ tsp ground cardamom

½ tsp ground cinnamon

¼ tsp ground nutmeg

¼ tsp sea salt

Place all ingredients in the food processor. Pulse for about 30 seconds, then scrape down the sides of the bowl and pulse again for about 30 seconds or until the mixture begins to smooth and become crumbly. Do not blend to a complete nut butter.

Line a square or small rectangular baking dish with parchment paper. Scoop nut mixture into the baking dish and firmly pat down using your fingers or a flat spatula.

Chill in the refrigerator for 2 hours before slicing. Wrap each snack bar in parchment paper and store in the refrigerator to eat and enjoy when desired.

CHEF'S TIP:
Coconut oil turns solid when chilled and helps keep these snack bars firm and intact. They will soften and become slightly crumbly when at room temperature.

CASHEW BUTTER STUFFED DATES

These make a great Paleo appetizer. The salty quality of the cashew butter mixed with the sweetness of the date creates a delightfully flavorful snack! —HH

MAKES 24

1 cup (150 g) raw cashews

Dash salt

24 dates

Zest of ½ lemon

Cover the cashews with warm water and let soak for 2 to 3 hours. After the cashews have soaked, drain the water. Place the cashews into a food processor or blender, add a dash of salt and blend until it's creamy like cashew butter. Cut a slit lengthwise down the dates and remove the pits, leaving a basin in which to put the cashew cheese. Using a knife or small spoon, fill the dates with cashew cheese. Using a fine grater, grate the lemon rind over the cashew stuffed dates.

CINNAMON-TOASTED COCONUT CHIPS

This coconut chip recipe is a great healthy snack idea—especially for kids! The best part is that they are super simple to make and only take about 5 minutes! —HH

SERVES 4

1½ cups (120 g) thick, unsweetened coconut flakes

About 1 tsp (3 g) ground cinnamon

1 tsp (4 g) coconut sugar, optional, for added sweetness

Preheat the oven to 325°F (170°C, or gas mark 3). Spread out the coconut flakes on a cookie sheet. Sprinkle the cinnamon on top of the flakes evenly. If you want them to be sweet sprinkle a little coconut sugar over them. Place in the oven for about 5 minutes, mixing the coconut halfway through so they toast evenly. Make sure you keep an eye on them because they can burn quickly. Remove them from the oven when they are lightly toasted and golden brown. Let cool before eating.

CHEF'S TIP:

You'll need thick coconut flakes for this recipe to turn out—not the thinly shredded coconut that is commonly used for baking.

conut Almonds, page 272

Weeknight Shredded Pork Tacos, page 147

g-Free Chocolate Pie, page 366

Sweet Carrot and Butternut Purée, page 243

Carrot Ginger Muffins, page 467

Southwest Chicken Salad, page 305

Matcha Pomegranate Panna Cotta, page 389

Slow Cooker Indian Chicken Curry, page 149

Blueberry Cobbler Pancakes, page 455

Crispy Ham Eggs Benedict, page 437

Butternut Squash Soup, page 309

Stuffed Pork Tenderloin, page 50

Easy Roasted Vegetable Soup, page 316

Sweet Potato Latkes, page 433

Ahi Poke, page 107

Warm Bacon Dressing, page 514

rskish Delight Panna Cotta, page 390

Whipped Jalapeño Honey Butter, page 500

ow Cooker Chicken Broth, page 170

Raw Cheesecake, page 360

Autumn Apple, Sage Grilled Chicken Kabobs, page 175

Tostones with Galic-Infused Ghee, page 224

Spaghetti Squash Bacon Bowl, page 88

Thai Coconut Soup with Shrimp or Chicken, page 319

Rosemary Lamb Burgers with Pesto, page 18

Roasted Stuffed Delicata Squash, page 85

Bacon & Beet Breakfast Root Hash, page 432

Zucchini and Sweet Potato Fritters, page 222

Chicken Dippers, page 207

Prosciutto-Wrapped Pesto Chicken Pasta, page 176

Italian Cabbage Rolls, page 95

Fruity Breakfast Pizza with Granola Crust, page 426

ol Ranch Avocado Dip, page 516

Chocolate Chip Cookies, page 416

live, Pomegranate and Walnut Salad, page 326

Chicken Mushroom Lettuce Wraps, page 34

Herbed Bacon Loaded Potatoes, page 227

Maple Glaze Donuts, page 408

Eggy Onion Breakfast Bread, page 449

Sliced Baked Sweet Potato, page 221

Curried Carrot Waffle Stack, page 448

Zucchini Blender Bread, page 174

Pork Chops with Cranberry Sauce, page 49

Honey Sweetened Lemon Curd, page 383

Chocolate Protein Smoothie, page 484

Gingerbread Men Cookies, page 344

Steamed Chicken with Scallion Sauce, page 75

Pumpkin French Toast, page 460

Coffee Jelly and Almond Milk Tea, page 491

Butternut Squash N'Oatmeal, page 167

Quick and Easy Pickled Red Onions, page 511

Creamy Chocolate Ice Cream, page 377

CHOCOLATE-COVERED COCONUT CHIPS WITH HONEY DRIZZLE

Here's a simple snack made especially for coconut and chocolate lovers. These coconut chips are an irresistible treat that both kids and adults love. —KW

SERVES 6

2 cups (160 g) unsweetened coconut chips or large flakes

2 tbsp (30 ml) coconut oil, melted

1 tsp (3 g) cacao powder

Few pinches of sea salt

2 tsp (10 ml) honey

Preheat oven to 300°F (150°C, or gas mark 2). In a shallow baking pan, add the coconut flakes and coconut oil and stir until well mixed. Sprinkle the cacao powder and sea salt all over the coconut. Stir briefly. Bake for 8 to 10 minutes, stirring every 3 minutes. Watch carefully towards the end of the cooking time, as it can burn. Once it is done cooking and right before serving, drizzle a teaspoon or two (5 to 10 ml) of honey all over the chips.

COCONUT DATE ROLLS

Have you ever seen or bought coconut date rolls at the grocery store? I've bought them a few times because I love that they only have 3 ingredients, but they can be so expensive. Making your own makes it easier on your budget! —HH

SERVES 4

4 tbsp (60 ml) boiling water

24 dates, pitted

¼–½ cup (20-40 g) shredded coconut

Add boiling water to a shallow dish with pitted dates inside. The dates shouldn't be totally submerged in water, just enough to soak up some water. Let dates soak for about 10 to 15 minutes then drain the water. Empty dates into a food processor and run until dates are chopped. Form chopped dates into a ball and roll them in shredded coconut. Place in the fridge and let harden for about an hour.

RAISIN "CEREAL"

Do you ever miss breakfast cereal as a Paleo or real-foodie? I love this Paleo "Raisin Bran!" It only has 3 ingredients and doesn't contain any added sugar, grains or GMOs like those unhealthy store-bought cereals. —HH

SERVES 4

2 cups (160 g) thick, unsweetened coconut flakes

1 tsp (3 g) ground cinnamon

⅓ cup (50 g) raisins

Preheat the oven to 325°F (170°C, or gas mark 3). Spread out the coconut flakes on a cookie sheet. Sprinkle the cinnamon evenly on top of the flakes. Place in the oven for about 5 minutes, mixing the coconut halfway through so they toast evenly. Make sure you keep an eye on them because they can burn quickly. Remove them from the oven when they are lightly toasted to a golden brown color. Let cool. Then transfer the coconut to a sealed jar, container or bag. Add the raisins and the "Raisin Bran" is finished! Enjoy this Paleo "Raisin Bran" in a bowl with some additive-free coconut milk poured over it for part of your breakfast or a snack.

CHEF'S TIP:
You'll need thick coconut flakes for this recipe to turn out— not the thinly shredded coconut that is commonly used for baking.

FLUFFY BANANA PANCAKES

Saturday mornings in our house usually revolve around making banana pancakes together and sipping on hot cups of coffee. These are my husband's favorite and weekend pancakes are a special tradition we both look forward to! These banana pancakes are made from coconut flour, but the whipped egg whites give them a soufflé like texture. We like to make a simple, warm maple syrup as a topping, but most often I eat them with melted butter. —CP

SERVES 3–4

FOR THE SIMPLE MAPLE SYRUP

½ cup (120 ml) maple syrup

2 tbsp (30 g) butter

2 tbsp (30 ml) water

1 cup (225 g) mashed bananas, firm and not fully ripe

4 eggs, whites and yolks separated

¼ cup (32 g) + 1 tbsp (8 g) coconut flour, sifted

1½ tsp (7.5 ml) vanilla extract

½ tsp ground cinnamon

2 tbsp (30 g) butter for melting on griddle

First, warm a griddle to medium-low heat.

Next, in a small saucepan, melt together all ingredients for the simple maple syrup and slowly warm.

While the syrup is warming, start making the pancakes by mashing the bananas on a plate. Measure out 1 cup (225 g) and set aside.

Separate the eggs, placing the yolks in one bowl and the whites in another. Use a hand mixer to whip the egg whites until soft, foamy peaks begin to form. Add remaining ingredients to the bowl with the yolks and blend together, scraping down the sides of the bowl to incorporate all the ingredients.

Fold the whites into the banana pancake batter, stirring until they are completely mixed.

Working in batches, melt a pat of butter on the griddle. Drop a large spoonful of batter onto hot griddle. Cook for 2½ minutes, carefully flip and cook for an additional 2½ minutes or until pancakes are cooked through. Repeat process with remaining batter.

Serve warm with a drizzle of simple maple syrup.

CHEF'S TIP:
I have found that when working with coconut flour, a firm banana works best as it will not result in a soggy or eggy taste. So, if you are impatient to let your bananas ripen like me, this recipe is for you!

ROSE WATER MIXED BERRY CHIA JAM

Want to enjoy some homemade jam? Try this delicious rose water-scented jam that comes together in no time. —NK

MAKES 3 CUPS (750 G)

20 ounces (560 g) mixed frozen berries

6 tbsp (90 ml) filtered cold water

¼ cup (60 ml) raw honey

2 tbsp (30 ml) rose water

5 tbsp (40 g) chia seeds

Add frozen berries and the filtered cold water to a medium saucepan. Place over medium heat and stir until the berries start to break down, around 10 to 15 minutes. Add the raw honey and rose water and stir to mix. Pour mixture into a blender and add in the chia seeds. Blend until well mixed. Pour into a glass jar or jars and allow to cool before storing in the fridge for up to 2 weeks.

WHIPPED COCONUT BERRY PARFAIT

This rich and creamy coconut berry parfait is a healthy yet decadent dessert. The texture of the fluffy rich coconut cream brings out the juicy sweetness of the fruit. Serve at a dinner party or for an intimate meal. —HH

SERVES 2

1 cup (235 ml) coconut cream

2 tbsp (24 g) coconut sugar

1 tsp (5 ml) vanilla

½-¾ cup (75-112 g) strawberries, chopped

¼-½ cup (38-75 g) walnuts

¼-½ cup (38-75 g) blueberries

Using a manual hand whisk, whip the coconut cream in a bowl with coconut sugar and vanilla until it's fluffy.

In a glass—I use a wine glass—put a layer of coconut cream, then add chopped strawberries around the edge, top with some blueberries and walnuts. Repeat this layering until all ingredients are gone!

5-INGREDIENT SMOKY AND SPICY SCOTCH EGGS

I make a big batch of scotch eggs so I can keep a few in my refrigerator for busy days. They are my go-to food when I need to run out of the door in a hurry. They are packed with healthy fats and protein and can keep me full for hours. —KW

SERVES 6

6 eggs

1½ pounds (680 g) ground pork sausage

1 tsp (3 g) chili powder

½ tsp smoked paprika

2 tbsp (8 g) fresh chives, chopped

Sea salt and pepper, to taste

Preheat oven to 375°F (190°C, or gas mark 5). Put eggs in a pot and cover with water. Bring to a boil. Once the water is boiling, remove the pot from heat and cover. Let sit for 10 to 12 minutes or until yolks are done to your liking. Remove the eggs from the water and let cool until they are cool enough to handle. Peel the shell off the eggs.

While the eggs are cooling, mix sausage, chili powder, smoked paprika and chives and salt and pepper in a bowl until well combined. Divide sausage mixture into six portions. Flatten each sausage portion and mold it around the cooked egg and then place the sausage-wrapped egg on a baking pan. Repeat with remaining sausage portions and eggs. Bake for 30 minutes or until sausage is cooked throughout and slightly browned on top. Eat just as they are or serve with Dijon mustard or Sriracha sauce.

MARINATED GRILLED CHICKEN KEBABS

Pinchos are traditional street food in Puerto Rico and can be made from pork or chicken that has been marinated in a tangy sauce and then grilled to perfection. You can serve these as an appetizer or a light meal. Leftovers are great to put on top of a salad, too! —AT

SERVES 3–4

1 tbsp (10 g) minced garlic

½ tsp fine Himalayan salt

½ tsp freshly ground black pepper

2 tsp (2 g) minced fresh oregano, or 1 tsp (2 g) dried

1 tbsp (15 ml) extra-virgin olive oil

1 tbsp (15 ml) freshly squeezed lime juice (from about ½ lime)

1½ pounds (680 g) boneless, skinless chicken breast

Have ready seven to nine skewers. If using wooden or bamboo skewers, soak them in water for at least 30 minutes before grilling.

In a bowl, combine the garlic, salt, pepper, oregano, oil and lime juice and stir to form a paste.

Cut chicken breasts into 1-inch (2.5-cm) chunks and place in a glass container with a lid. Pour the marinade over the chicken and stir to combine. Cover the chicken and refrigerate for a minimum of 2 hours, up to overnight.

Prepare a grill for direct cooking over medium heat (325 to 375°F [170 to 190°C]). Depending on the type of grill this may take 15 to 20 minutes.

Remove the chicken from the refrigerator and thread it onto the skewers, spreading each piece as flat as possible and leaving a very small space between each piece.

Once the grill is hot, brush the cooking grates clean, if necessary (to prevent sticking). Grill the kebabs over direct medium heat, keeping the lid closed as much as possible, until the chicken is firm to the touch and no longer pink in the center, 8 to 10 minutes total, turning once or twice during cooking. Take care not overcook.

Remove from the grill and serve immediately. Pairs wonderfully with Tostones with Garlic-Infused Ghee (page 224), and you can make mini sandwiches by placing one chunk of chicken between two tostones.

CHICKEN AVOCADO SALAD

Reina pepiada is a dish that was meant to be fit for a queen—a beauty queen, that is. The 1955 winner of the Miss World Pageant was the first woman from Venezuela (or anywhere in South America, for that matter) to ever win the title, and a restaurant owner in Caracas created this dish to serve the winner. It is now arguably the most popular filling for arepas, for good reason! —AT

SERVES 4

1 ripe Hass avocado, peeled and sliced

Juice of 1 lime

4 tbsp (4 g) chopped fresh cilantro

1 small yellow onion, minced

½ tsp fine Himalayan salt

Freshly ground black pepper, to taste

4 tbsp (56 g) mayonnaise plus 1 clove garlic, minced

2 cups (280 g) shredded chicken

Place the avocado in a medium bowl and squeeze the lime juice on top. Use a fork or a potato masher to mash the avocado until creamy. Add all the remaining ingredients and mix well.

Cover and place in refrigerator for at least 1 hour before serving.

Serve it on top of Tostones with Garlic-Infused Ghee (page 224) or serve it alone as a delicious and flavorful chicken salad.

CHICKEN IN SOFRITO

When I was living in Miami and strictly following the Paleo Autoimmune Protocol (AIP), I used to make this chicken all the time. While it is not technically a traditional Puerto Rican dish per se, it still tastes authentically Puerto Rican, thanks to the sofrito, and is a dish I'm sure you'll love to add to your rotation, too. You can also deviate a bit from tradition and bulk it up with additional AIP-compliant vegetables of choice, such as carrots or zucchini. —AT

SERVES 4–6

3 tbsp (45 ml) extra-virgin olive oil

4 tbsp (55 g) sofrito

1 medium onion, diced

2 cups (260 g) diced carrot, zucchini or other AIP-approved vegetable, optional

4–6 cloves garlic, minced

1 tsp (6 g) fine Himalayan salt

1 tsp (2 g) dried oregano

Juice of 1 lime

2 tbsp (30 g) pure pumpkin purée, to thicken the sauce, optional

2 cups (280 g) shredded chicken, or 2 pounds (905 g) boneless, skinless chicken breast, cut into 1–1½-inch (2.5–4-cm) pieces

Chopped fresh cilantro, for garnish

In a large skillet over medium heat, heat the olive oil. Add the sofrito and cook until the sofrito is fragrant, 2 to 4 minutes (longer if cooking with frozen sofrito). If using shredded chicken, first add the onion and cook for 3 to 4 minutes, stirring occasionally. If using additional veggies, add them with the onion. Add the garlic and cook for 2 minutes more. Add all the remaining ingredients, except the cilantro, and cook for an additional 10 minutes, or until the onion and additional veggies, if using, are tender and the chicken is warmed throughout.

If using raw chicken, add it to the pan with the sofrito and allow to cook, stirring occasionally, until all the chicken pieces are white on the outside, 5 to 7 minutes. Add all the remaining ingredients, including the veggies (if using) and cook for an additional 6 to 8 minutes, or until the chicken is cooked through and the vegetables are tender.

Garnish with chopped cilantro and serve as a main dish.

MEAT–STUFFED RIPE PLANTAINS

Canoas means "canoes" in Spanish, and as you will see, this is due to the look of the finished dish: The sweet plantains are turned into little canoes filled with delicious meat! This dish has such a fun presentation and can be made without a lot of fuss. It is one that my husband remembers fondly from his childhood and loves for me to make today. —AT

SERVES 4–6

6 ripe to very ripe plantains, peeled (yellow with some black)

About ¼ cup (56 g) fat for frying (lard, coconut oil or avocado oil), plus more for baking dish

½ batch Ground Beef Hash (page 200)

Dairy-free white cheese, to top, optional

Chopped fresh cilantro, for garnish

(continued)

Slice the tips off the plantains and cut a slit down the length of the peel and lift to remove.

In a medium skillet, heat your fat of choice over medium heat until shimmering, 3 to 5 minutes. Working in batches if necessary, carefully add the plantains to the heated fat (they should sizzle when dropped in), cooking on each side for 3 to 5 minutes, or until they have turned a nice golden brown and have partially caramelized. Be careful not to burn. Drain on a paper towel–lined plate.

Preheat the oven to 350°F (177°C).

Lightly grease the bottom of a 9 × 13-inch (23 × 33-cm) glass baking dish with coconut oil or lard. When the plantains have cooled enough to handle, place them so that the curved ends are pointing up and cut a slit down the length of each plantain along the center, being careful not to cut all the way through. Arrange them in the bottom of the dish and stuff generously with the meat filling. Bake for 15 to 20 minutes. If desired, top with pieces of the dairy-free white cheese for the last 5 to 7 minutes. Sprinkle chopped cilantro on top and serve immediately.

CITRUS MARINATED PORK CHOPS

Mojo Criollo (page 520) and pork are such a match made in heaven! Although this dish does require an overnight marinade, the actual hands-on time is minimal and this dish is quick to cook. Be sure to make these at your next cookout to wow your guests with the intense flavor! —AT

SERVES 6

1 cup (235 ml) Mojo Criollo (page 520), divided

6 bone-in pork chops, ¾–1-inch (3–2.5-cm) thick (about 3 pounds [1.4 kg])

1 medium onion, thinly sliced

1 tbsp (15 ml) extra-virgin olive oil

2 limes, cut into wedges

Reserve about ¼ cup (60 ml) of the mojo criollo in a covered container in the refrigerator.

Place the pork chops in a glass baking dish in a single layer and pour the remaining ¾ cup (175 ml) of marinade on top, covering both sides of each chop. Cover and refrigerate for a minimum of 2 hours or up to overnight for the most flavor.

Remove the pork chops from the refrigerator 30 minutes before grilling. Gently pat the pork chops dry and discard their marinade.

Prepare the grill for direct cooking over medium-high heat (375 to 400°F [190 to 200°C]), or heat a large grill pan over medium-high heat on the stovetop. Place the pork chops on the hot grill grates. Grill the pork chops 3 to 4 minutes per side, until browned and the center of the pork is no longer pink. The pork chops are done when the pork's internal temperature (using a meat thermometer) reaches 160°F (71°C).

While the pork is grilling, sauté the onion in the olive oil until it is translucent. Set aside.

Transfer the pork chops to a serving platter. Top with the sautéed onion and drizzle with the reserved mojo criollo. Serve with the lime wedges.

CHICKEN WITH "RICE"

Arroz con pollo—chicken with rice—is true comfort food in many Latin American countries. This is a quick option, thanks to the shredded chicken, and adheres to strict Paleo by using cauliflower to replace the rice. —AT

SERVES 4

1 head cauliflower

¼ cup (60 ml) extra-virgin olive oil

4 tbsp (55 g) sofrito

2 tsp (4 g) ground turmeric

1 tsp (6 g) fine Himalayan salt

1 red bell pepper, diced

1 small onion, diced

2–3 cups (280–420 g) shredded chicken

¼ cup (44 g) sliced green olives

Remove the stem and outer leaves from the cauliflower and cut it into several smaller chunks. In a food processor fitted with the blade attachment, pulse the cauliflower for about 10 seconds. Scrape down the sides and continue to pulse until all the cauliflower is riced, working in batches if necessary.

In a large skillet, heat the olive oil over medium heat. Add the sofrito and cook until it is fragrant, 2 to 4 minutes (longer if cooking with frozen sofrito).

Add the turmeric, salt, bell pepper, onion and shredded chicken and cook, stirring frequently, for about 3 minutes. Add the cauliflower and cook for 5 to 7 minutes more, until the cauliflower is cooked throughout and the pepper and onion are tender. Stir in the olives just before removing the pan from the heat.

CHEF TIP:

If you do not have a food processor, you can grate the cauliflower with a box grater instead. The pieces won't be as uniform, but it will still work!

GARLIC-LIME FRIED SHREDDED CHICKEN

Translating the name of this dish is a bit nonsensical since it would be "fried cow of chicken," but it is simply a version of the classic vaca frita—"fried cow"—made with chicken instead of beef. I like to keep plain shredded cooked chicken on hand in my freezer so I can use it to quickly make meals like this. —AT

SERVES 4

2 cups (280 g) shredded chicken

¼ cup (60 ml) freshly squeezed lime juice

1 tbsp (10 g) minced garlic

1 tsp (6 g) fine Himalayan salt

4–6 tbsp (56–84 g) fat of choice for frying (lard, avocado oil or extra-virgin olive oil)

1 white onion, cut into thin rings

Lime wedges, for garnish

In a mixing bowl, combine the shredded chicken, lime juice, garlic and salt and stir well. You can let it marinate for 30 to 60 minutes in the refrigerator or cook it right away if you're in a hurry.

In a large skillet, heat your fat of choice over medium heat until shimmering, 3 to 5 minutes. Add the chicken and spread into a thin even layer in the pan. Let it fry undisturbed for 10 to 15 minutes, or until it is browned and crispy on the bottom. This may seem like a long time, but it is correct.

Add additional cooking fat as needed. Stir the chicken and let it fry undisturbed for another 5 minutes. Add the onion rings and stir to mix in with the chicken, frying for an additional 5 to 10 minutes while stirring occasionally. The end result should be crispy and browned and the onion softened but not mushy. Garnish with lime wedges and serve.

GROUND BEEF HASH

Carne molida translates as "ground meat," but don't let the simple name fool you into thinking it is a boring dish! It is easy to throw together on a busy weeknight and is full of flavor, thanks to the sofrito cooking base. This is how my mother-in-law learned to make this dish in Puerto Rico. This dish also freezes well if you make a double batch. —AT

SERVES 6–8

2 tbsp (30 ml) extra-virgin olive oil

4 tbsp (55 g) sofrito

2 large cloves garlic, minced

½ tsp fine Himalayan salt

½ tsp freshly ground black pepper

1 small onion, diced

2 pounds (905 g) ground beef

2 tbsp (32 g) tomato paste

1 medium yellow potato, cut into ½-inch (1.3-cm) dice

½ cup (65 g) diced carrot

12–15 green Manzanilla olives, sliced

In a large sauté pan with a lid, heat the olive oil over medium heat for 1 to 2 minutes. Add the sofrito, garlic, salt and pepper and cook, stirring, 2 to 4 minutes, until sizzling and fragrant (longer if using frozen sofrito).

Add all the remaining ingredients, except the olives. Cook for about 10 minutes, until the meat is browned, stirring occasionally to break up the meat.

Lower the heat to low or medium-low to bring the mixture to a simmer, cover and cook for 20 to 30 minutes more, until the potatoes and carrot are tender when pierced with a fork.

SWEET AND SAVORY GROUND BEEF

Picadillo has such an interesting contrast of flavors and is well spiced without being hot. You don't often think to pair raisins or "sweet" spices like allspice with ground beef, but it works incredibly well in this dish to balance the umami from the tomatoes, olives and capers. —AT

SERVES 4–6

2 tbsp (30 ml) extra-virgin olive oil

1 cup (150 g) diced red bell pepper

1 cup (160 g) diced onion

2 tbsp (20 g) minced garlic (about 1 whole head)

2 pounds (905 g) ground beef

1½ tsp (4 g) ground cumin

1½ tsp (3 g) dried oregano

1 tsp (2 g) ground allspice

1½ tsp (9 g) fine Himalayan salt

3 tbsp (48 g) tomato paste

2 tbsp (17 g) drained capers

⅓ cup (33 g) sliced green Manzanilla olives

⅓ cup (50 g) raisins

¼ cup (4 g) chopped fresh cilantro or flat-leaf parsley

In a large sauté pan with a lid, heat the olive oil over medium heat for 1 to 2 minutes. Add the bell pepper and onion and cook until the onion is translucent, 4 to 5 minutes. Add the garlic and cook for about 2 minutes more. Add the ground beef and cook until browned, about 15 minutes, stirring occasionally and breaking up all the chunks.

Next, add all the remaining ingredients, except the cilantro, and stir well to combine. Lower the heat, cover and cook for about 15 more minutes, or until the sauce has thickened.

Turn off the heat and stir in the cilantro. Serve with your favorite side dishes.

THIN-CUT STEAK AND ONIONS

Palomilla steaks are very common in Cuban restaurants. They are cut ultrathin from sirloin steaks or top round, marinated and then cooked ultrafast. The key is to have the meat no more than ¼-inch (6-mm) thick so that you can cook them in under 5 minutes flat over high heat. If you live near a Cuban butcher, they will likely sell these sliced steaks, but ask them if they will slice your preferred cut for you. Otherwise, cut them at home yourself (see Chef's Tip). —AT

SERVES 4

4 large cloves garlic, minced

Juice of 2 limes

½ tsp fine Himalayan salt

4 sirloin or top round steaks, cut to ¼-inch (6-mm) thick and weighing about 8 ounces (225 g) each

2 tbsp (30 ml) avocado oil (do not substitute another oil)

1 onion, thinly sliced

¼ cup (15 g) chopped fresh parsley, for garnish

In a small bowl, combine the garlic, lime juice and salt. Place the steaks in a single layer in a glass dish with a lid and cover with the lime marinade. Cover the dish and refrigerate for 15 to 60 minutes. Do not marinate for longer than 1 hour. Due to the thinness of the steak, a longer marinade can tenderize the meat too much and result in an unpleasant texture. While your steak is marinating, prepare your side dishes of choice.

In a large skillet, heat the avocado oil over high heat for 2 to 3 minutes. You want the pan to be very hot and to hear those steaks sizzle loudly as soon as they hit the pan. Cook the steaks in two batches if necessary; do not overcrowd the pan. Rapidly cook the meat for 1 to 2 minutes per side, until both sides are seared. Remove with a slotted spoon and set aside.

Lower the heat to medium and add the onion, cooking until it is softened but still crunchy, 3 to 5 minutes. Turn off the heat and stir in the parsley. Serve the steaks immediately with a generous portion of the onion mixture.

CHEF'S TIP:
Cut the steaks into thin slices if you were not able to buy them already sliced. One trick to make cutting meat easier is to partially freeze it for 30 to 60 minutes before cutting. It does take some skill, a steady hand and a good knife to cut the steak to only ¼-inch (6-mm) thick. Work carefully and if your steaks slices turn out thicker, simply place between two pieces of plastic wrap and pound with the flat side of a meat mallet until they are ¼-inch (6-mm) thick.

SEASONED SHREDDED CHICKEN

This shredded chicken tastes just like the chicken at my favorite Colombian restaurant here in Memphis. I love how incredibly fast and easy it is to throw this dish together on a busy day and it is amazing just how versatile it is. —AT

SERVES 4–6

3 tbsp (45 ml) extra-virgin olive oil

2 large yellow or orange bell peppers, diced

1 small onion, diced

4-6 cloves garlic, minced

2 tbsp (32 g) tomato paste

2 plum tomatoes, diced

1 tsp (6 g) fine Himalayan salt

½ tsp freshly ground black pepper

½ tsp ground cumin

½ tsp paprika

2 cups (280 g) shredded chicken

Chopped fresh cilantro, for garnish

(continued)

In a large skillet, heat the olive oil over medium heat for 2 to 3 minutes. Add the bell peppers and onion and cook for 3 to 4 minutes, stirring occasionally. Add the garlic and cook for 2 minutes more. Add all the remaining ingredients, except the cilantro, stir to combine and cook for an additional 10 minutes, or until the vegetables are tender and the chicken is warmed throughout.

Garnish with the cilantro and serve as a main dish.

MARINATED GRILLED CHICKEN BREAST

"Chicken on the grill" may sound plain, but this dish is so perfectly seasoned you'll never think grilled chicken is boring again. The color of the cooked chicken is also exquisite and makes for a beautiful, delicious meal you can cook on any busy weeknight. Make a double batch to have leftovers for salads! —AT

SERVES 2

2 boneless, skinless chicken breasts

½ tsp ground paprika

¼ tsp granulated garlic

¼ tsp granulated onion

¼–½ tsp ground cumin

¼ tsp fine Himalayan salt

Zest and juice of 1 lime

1½ tsp (8 ml) extra-virgin olive oil

Prepare a grill for direct cooking over medium heat (325 to 375°F [170 to 190°C]). Depending on type of grill, this may take 15 to 20 minutes.

While the grill is heating, wrap the breasts in a layer of plastic wrap and use a flat meat mallet or the bottom of a sturdy glass or jar to pound the breasts to a uniform thickness of about ½ inch (1.3 cm).

Combine the remaining ingredients in a bowl and stir to form a paste. Coat the pounded breasts with the mixture.

Once the grill is hot, brush the cooking grates clean, if necessary (to prevent sticking). Grill the chicken breasts over direct medium heat, with the lid closed as much as possible, until the meat is firm to the touch and no longer pink in the center, 8 to 12 minutes total, turning once or twice.

Remove from the grill and let rest for 3 to 5 minutes before serving.

MARINATED BEEF HEART KEBABS

Beef heart is an excellent choice if you are new to eating offal, because it tastes like a fine steak. If you are lucky, your butcher will be able to sell you cleaned and cut heart rather than an entire heart. This traditional Peruvian dish marinates the heart in a delicious sauce that you can actually use to marinate any cut of meat. If you are too squeamish to cook heart, you can use any steak or even cubed chicken breast instead. But I highly recommend that you give beef heart a chance! —AT

SERVES 2–4

½ cup (120 ml) freshly squeezed lime juice

3–4 tbsp (48–64 g) ají panca paste (see note for substitutes)

6 cloves garlic, peeled and minced

1½ tsp (9 g) fine Himalayan salt

1 tsp (2 g) freshly ground black pepper

1 tsp (3 g) ground cumin powder

4 tbsp (60 ml) extra-virgin olive oil, divided

1 pound (455 g) beef heart, trimmed

Combine the lime juice, ají panca paste, garlic, salt, black pepper, cumin and 2 tablespoons (30 ml) of the olive oil in a glass container with a lid.

If not already cleaned, trim the heart of fat, connective tissue and blood vessels. Cut the meat into equal-size chunks, 1 to 2 inches (2.5 to 5 cm) across and ½-inch (1.3-cm) thick.

Place the heart chunks in the marinade and toss to combine. Cover and refrigerate for a minimum of 1 hour, up to overnight.

Before grilling, have ready 6 to 8 skewers. If using wooden or bamboo skewers, soak them in water for at least 30 minutes.

Meanwhile, prepare the grill for direct cooking over medium heat (325 to 375°F [170 to 190°C]). Depending on type of grill, this may take 15 to 20 minutes.

Thread the heart pieces onto the skewers. Make sure each piece is spread as flat as possible and leave a very small space between each piece.

Once the grill is hot, brush the cooking grates clean, if necessary (to prevent sticking). Grill the skewers over direct medium heat for 2 to 3 minutes per side for medium rare or 4 to 5 minutes for medium well done. Brush the kebabs with the remaining olive oil at least once during cooking. Do not overcook or else the beef heart will become tough and rubbery.

Serve immediately as an appetizer or with your favorite sides for a meal. This pairs very well with Tostones with Garlic-Infused Ghee (page 224).

NOTE:

Ají panca paste can be ordered online if you can't find it locally, or you can substitute 1 to 2 tablespoons (7.5 to 15 g) of pasillo or ancho chile powder. Taste the marinade before adding the meat and adjust to your preferred level of spiciness.

GRILLED SKIRT STEAK

When I lived in Miami Beach, my neighborhood was called "Little Argentina." I had the privilege of living down the street from an incredible Argentinean steakhouse where I was first introduced to churrasco steak, which refers to grilled skirt steak. I also befriended several neighbors in my condo building who hailed from Argentina and enjoyed many churrasco grilling sessions with them on our back patio. Churrasco is extremely simple—all you need is skirt steak and salt. Pair it with chimichurri sauce for an incredible meal perfect to share with friends. —AT

SERVES 4

2 pounds (905 g) skirt steak (each steak is usually 1 pound [455 g])

1 tsp (6 g) fine Himalayan salt

Cilantro Chimichurri (page 510) to serve

Prepare a grill for direct cooking over medium heat (325 to 375°F [170 to 190°C]). Depending on type of grill, this may take 15 to 20 minutes.

Immediately before grilling, rub both sides of the steak with salt. Cook the steak for 3 to 5 minutes per side for medium rare.

Transfer to a plate and let stand for 5 minutes. Slice into 1- to 2-inch (2.5- to 5-cm) strips across the grain at an angle and serve generously topped with chimichurri.

CHAPTER 4

APPETIZERS, SNACKS & SIDES

A gathering isn't complete without important elements such as appetizers, sides and snacks. Not only are the recipes in this section easy to make, but they're also extremely versatile. There's something here for everybody. Tantalizing morsels such as Tostones with Garlic-Infused Ghee (page 224) pack just the right amount of flavor to fire up your senses and awaken your tastebuds. You may want to ask yourself, how can something so simple be mind-blowingly amazing?!

Sometimes eating multiple appetizers as sides to a main dish is the next best thing. I mean, how can you go wrong with pairing Herbed Bacon Loaded Potatoes (page 227) and Honey Mustard Brussels Sprouts (page 225) with just about any type of protein? If you don't feel like wolfing down such a big serving or aren't feeling hungry enough to feed your inner beast, enjoy them as a light snack. They're pretty much interchangeable and can even fly solo.

As you dive into this chapter, have your grocery list in front of you, because I guarantee you will want to cook a few!

BUTTERNUT SQUASH MINI-PIZZA

Try a variety of toppings on this fun appetizer. Some of our other favorites are chicken, artichoke, sundried tomato or sausage, olives and capers! —AV

SERVES 10

1 medium butternut squash

2 tbsp (30 ml) ghee, melted

Salt and pepper

1 cup (240 g) Macadamia Nut Pesto (page 510)

¼ cup (60 g) red onion, thinly sliced

6 ounces (168 g) kielbasa sausage, chopped

Preheat the oven to 400°F (200°C, or gas mark 6). To get the right shape for this recipe, we'll only be able to use the neck of the squash, not the section where the seeds live. Slice that section off and save it for another use, such as cubed and roasted butternut squash. Peel the remaining part of the squash, then slice it into ½ inch (1.3 cm) slices, keeping the circular shape.

Grease a baking sheet with some softened ghee. Place the squash on the baking sheet. Brush with the remaining ghee and sprinkle with salt and pepper. Cook for 25 to 30 minutes, until almost done and soft, not quite browned. Sprinkle each piece with some pesto, red onion and sausage. Bake for another 5 minutes to brown. Serve hot.

FRESH HERB CAULIFLOWER RICE WITH PARSLEY, CORIANDER AND DILL

This dish was inspired by a Persian dish called Sabzi Polow, which translates to Herb Rice. Here I use cauliflower rice and fresh herbs to make this a delicious Paleo and low-carb friendly version for those who can't eat rice. Pair it with my Fresh Grilled Sardines with Persian Salad (page 324) recipe for a complete meal. —NK

SERVES 6

1 medium head cauliflower, washed, cored and cut into small florets

2 tbsp (30 g) ghee

Sea salt and black pepper, to taste

½ cup (30 g) packed fresh flat leaf parsley, finely chopped

½ cup (30 g) packed fresh coriander, finely chopped

½ cup (30 g) packed fresh dill, finely chopped

½ cup (50 g) packed green onions, green part only finely chopped

Zest of 1 small lemon

Place cauliflower into a food processor and process until the cauliflower reaches a rice-like shape. Heat a large heavy-bottomed pot with a lid over medium heat. Add the ghee. Once heated add in the cauliflower and cook, stirring frequently, for 10 minutes. Season with sea salt and black pepper. Add the flat leaf parsley, coriander, dill and green onions, stir to mix through. Place the lid on the pot and turn the heat down to low. Cook for another 10 to 15 minutes. Remove the lid and add the lemon zest. Stir to mix through. Taste to check for seasoning.

HERBED CAULIFLOWER RICE WITH SAGE, THYME, ROSEMARY & GARLIC

A classic side dish made healthy using cauliflower but full of delicious flavor. Serve with Browned Butter Sage Roasted Chicken (page 23). —CP

SERVES 6

6 tbsp (90 g) butter

¾ cup (75 g) green onions, chopped

1 tsp (3 g) fresh sage, chopped

1 tsp (3 g) fresh thyme, chopped

1½ tsp (4.5 g) fresh rosemary, chopped

3 large cloves garlic, crushed

1 tsp (3 g) salt

½ tsp fresh cracked black pepper

1 large head cauliflower

Heat a large skillet to medium heat. Melt butter in skillet and sauté onions, herbs, garlic, salt and pepper for about 5 minutes or until fragrant.

Next make the cauliflower rice. Slice cauliflower into small florets, removing and discarding most of the stems.

Using the grating attachment of a food processor to rice or shred the cauliflower florets. Working in batches, pulse cauliflower florets several times, repeating the process until all the cauliflower is used.

Add grated cauliflower to skillet and sauté for 20 minutes or until cauliflower softens.

Serve cauliflower rice with any of your favorite grilled or roasted meats such as Browned Butter Sage Roasted Chicken (page 23).

Keep remaining cauliflower rice in the refrigerator and use a scoop as desired.

LEMON PEPPER CHICKEN WINGS

Chicken wings and buffalo sauce always go hand in hand, but I wanted something different and not slathered in sauce for a change. This homemade lemon pepper seasoning gives a fresh burst of flavor and a peppery kick to oven-baked chicken wings. This definitely tastes better than store bought seasoning and does not have any added preservatives. —JC

SERVES 2

2 pounds (908 g) chicken wings

1 tbsp (15 ml) lemon juice

¼ cup (60 ml) butter or ghee, melted

2 tbsp (16 g) lemon zest

1 tbsp (8 g) freshly cracked black pepper

1 tsp (3 g) sea salt

Preheat the oven to 375°F (190°C, or gas mark 5) on convection setting. Cover a baking sheet with foil and place a baking rack on top.

Pat the chicken wings dry and remove as much moisture as you can using paper towels. Place them on the rack 1 inch (2.5 cm) apart from each other. Roast the first side in the oven for 6 to 8 minutes. Flip to the other side and cook for another 6 to 8 minutes. Check them periodically to ensure that they do not get overcooked.

While the chicken wings are cooking, combine the lemon juice and melted butter in a large bowl. Combine the lemon zest, black pepper and sea salt in a smaller bowl.

Remove the chicken wings from the oven. Add them to the bowl with the lemon-butter mixture and toss until each piece is coated. Sprinkle the lemon pepper seasoning on the chicken wings and toss until the seasoning is well distributed. Serve immediately.

CHEF'S TIP:
If your oven doesn't have a convection setting, preheat it to 425°F (220°C, or gas mark 7).

CHILI LIME CHICKEN WINGS

I make this chili lime version to serve with the Lemon Pepper Chicken Wings (page 206) while watching football on Sundays. It's a different spin on classic buffalo wings with the addition of zesty lime for some added freshness. —JC

SERVES 2

1½ pounds (680 g) chicken wings
¼ cup (60 ml) cayenne hot sauce
1 tsp (3 g) onion powder
1 tsp (3 g) garlic powder
¼ tsp sea salt
Juice and zest of 1 lime

Preheat oven to 375°F (190°C, or gas mark 5) on convection setting. Cover a baking sheet with foil and place a baking rack on top.

Pat the chicken wings dry and remove as much moisture as you can using paper towels. Place them on the rack 1-inch (2.5-cm) apart from each other. Roast the first side in the oven for 6 to 8 minutes. Flip to the other side and cook for another 6 to 8 minutes. Check periodically to ensure that they do not get overcooked.

While the chicken wings are cooking, combine the cayenne hot sauce, onion powder, garlic powder, sea salt, lime juice and zest in a large bowl.

Remove the chicken wings from the oven. Add them to the bowl with the hot sauce mixture and toss until each piece is coated. Serve immediately.

CHEF'S TIP:
If your oven doesn't have a convection setting, preheat it to 425°F (220°C, or gas mark 7).

CHICKEN DIPPERS

There's something about chicken fingers that appeals to everyone. This recipe is no exception. These chicken dippers are best served with a homemade dipping sauce. My favorite and the one I recommend is the Buffalo Ranch Dipping Sauce (page 516). —KW

SERVES 4

2 eggs
2 tbsp (30 ml) melted butter or fat of choice
¾ cup (90 g) ground flaxseed
¼ cup (30 g) almond flour
1 tsp (3 g) chili powder
½ tsp garlic powder
½ tsp onion powder
¼ tsp salt
¼ tsp pepper
4 chicken breasts, cut into 2-inch (5-cm) pieces
Buffalo Ranch Dipping Sauce (page 516), for serving

Preheat oven to 400°F (200°C, or gas mark 6). In a shallow bowl, mix together the egg and melted butter.

In another shallow bowl, mix together the flax, almond flour, chili powder, garlic powder, onion powder, salt and pepper. Coat each piece of chicken in the egg mixture and then roll in flax mixture. Place chicken dippers on a parchment-lined cookie sheet. Bake for 10 minutes. Flip. Bake for an additional 10 minutes or until cooked through. Serve with Buffalo Ranch Dipping Sauce.

GINGER PORK MEATBALLS

Ginger adds a nice warm flavor and aroma to ground pork and I find myself using this combination as a base in some of my Asian dishes. These simple meatballs are great as finger food appetizers at a party or even just as a quick breakfast or snack. Make a batch and keep it in the fridge for easy access anytime. —JC

SERVES 4

1 pound (454 g) ground pork

1 large egg

1 medium carrot, finely chopped

¼ cup (30 g) almond flour

¼ cup (32 g) fresh ginger, grated

1 tsp (3 g) sea salt

1 cup (235 g) tallow or coconut oil for frying

In a large bowl, combine all the ingredients except the tallow. Mix lightly until everything is combined and form mixture into 1-inch (2.5-cm) bite-sized meatballs.

Heat the tallow in a cast iron or frying pan over medium heat. Cook meatballs in two to three batches and make sure they do not touch each other so they cook evenly. Fry each side for 2 to 3 minutes until golden brown and cooked through. Drain excess oil and serve hot.

SAUSAGE PACKETS

These sausage packets are so easy to make so double them up to make enough leftovers for the next day. Use Andouille if you want something with a kick, or for a more classic flavor, you can never go wrong with Italian. A combination of the two tastes great as well! —JC

SERVES 6

6 fully cooked sausages, sliced into 1-inch (2.5-cm) pieces

1 large onion, chopped into 1-inch (2.5-cm) pieces

¼ pound (112 g) grape tomatoes, whole

½ pound (227 g) baby potatoes, quartered

½ tsp paprika

½ tsp black pepper

2 tbsp (30 g) salted butter, cubed

Preheat oven to 350°F (180°C, or gas mark 4).

In a large bowl, add sausages, onion, tomatoes and potatoes. Season with paprika and black pepper. Mix well to combine.

Prepare packets by cutting six 12 × 12-inch (30.5 × 30.5–cm) pieces of heavy-duty foil. Evenly distribute the sausage and vegetables among the six pieces of foil. Add butter cubes on top. Fold each packet until the filling is secured inside. Poke three to four holes on the outside to release steam as it cooks. Place the sausage packets on a baking sheet. Bake packets in the oven for 40 to 45 minutes.

Remove from the oven and let cool for 10 minutes before opening the foil packets.

LASAGNA ROLLS

These would be a wonderful healthy appetizer to serve at a dinner party or to bring to a potluck. The strips of savory zucchini and eggplant wrapped around the rich, creamy cashew cheese make for a delightful snack. —HH

MAKES 8–12

FOR THE CASHEW CHEESE

1 cup (150 g) raw cashews

Enough water to cover the cashews

Sprinkle of sea salt

½ tsp garlic powder

½ tsp salt

FOR THE ROLLS

1 eggplant

1 zucchini

Salt and pepper to taste

1 tsp (5 ml) ghee, coconut oil or sustainable palm oil

8 ounces (227 g) cashew cheese

½ cup (125 g) organic tomato sauce

1 tsp (3 g) Italian seasoning or a blend of dried oregano and thyme

Soak the cashews in water and sea salt for 8 to 24 hours. Drain the water and process in a food processor or blender along with garlic powder and salt. Blend until creamy. If you want it to be a little thinner you can add a little more water. This will make about 8 to 12 ounces (227 to 340 g). Store in a jar in the fridge.

Thinly slice the eggplant and zucchini lengthwise. Sprinkle salt over the slices and place salt-side down on a paper towel. Sprinkle salt on the other side of the slices and let sit for about 10 minutes. This will draw the water out of the eggplant and zucchini. Get another paper towel and dab the moisture off of the eggplant and zucchini until it's dry. Heat oil in a skillet on high. Once the oil is hot, brown the eggplant and zucchini slices in the pan for about 1 to 2 minutes on each side. Set cooked slices aside until you've seared all of them.

Put about 1 tablespoon (10 g) of the cashew cheese in the middle of one slice of eggplant, then fold it over to cover the cheese and put on a plate. If you want, you can double wrap the cashew cheese with a slice of eggplant and a slice of zucchini or you can just do one slice for each, it's up to you. Once all of the slices have been used take about 1 teaspoon (5 ml) of organic tomato sauce and drizzle over each roll. Sprinkle salt, pepper and herbs to taste and serve!

CHILI HAND PIES

Spicy chili in savory, grain-free pockets of crust makes cute, portable finger-food. —RB

SERVES 12

FOR THE FILLING

1 small onion

½ bell pepper

2 cloves garlic

1 tbsp (15 ml) coconut oil

2 tbsp (16 g) chili powder

1 tbsp (8 g) ground cumin

¼ tsp ground cinnamon

¼ tsp cayenne

½ tsp sea salt

¼ tsp pepper

1 pound (454 g) ground beef

4 tbsp (60 g) tomato paste

2 tbsp (16 g) coconut flour

FOR THE CRUST

2¼ cups (270 g) almond flour

1 cup (120 g) arrowroot flour

¼ tsp salt

¼ cup (60 ml) coconut oil, softened

4 eggs

(continued)

Preheat the oven to 350°F (180°C, or gas mark 4). To make the chili, coarsely chop the onion and bell pepper and pulse in a food processor with the garlic cloves until finely shredded. Fry in a large skillet with the coconut oil over medium heat until soft, about 15 to 20 minutes.

Add the chili powder, cumin, cinnamon, cayenne, salt and pepper to the vegetables while they cook. Stir in the ground beef and tomato paste and cook for an additional 5 minutes. Remove from the heat and add the coconut flour. Mix until crumbly and the meat's grease has been absorbed, then set aside.

To make the crust, combine the almond flour, arrowroot flour and salt together in a large mixing bowl. Add the softened coconut oil. Using a fork or pastry cutter, break it into the flour. Keep working it in until evenly distributed and the flour is crumbly.

Create a well in the dry mixture and crack the eggs in. Whisk the eggs together, and then slowly incorporate the surrounding dry mix until a ball of dough forms. Knead briefly until smooth and place in the refrigerator to chill for approximately 5 minutes.

Cut the dough in half, working half now and placing the other half in the refrigerator. Lay the dough on top of plastic wrap or parchment paper. Roll out the dough to about ⅛-inch (3-mm) thickness. Using a 4-inch (10-cm) circle cookie cutter, biscuit cutter or ramekin, cut rounds of crust.

Place a scant handful of chili in the middle of the dough circles and fold the dough over. Using the tines of a fork, press the edges together, being careful not to rip the dough. Place the hand pies on a parchment-lined cookie sheet. Bake for 25 minutes or until browned. Serve warm.

CHEF'S TIP:
These are best served the day they are made, but will keep in an air-tight container for a day.

BUFFALO RANCH CHICKEN SALAD

When regular chicken salad gets too boring, try this Buffalo Ranch Chicken Salad. I like to eat it with celery sticks and Super Easy Guacamole (page 190). —KW

SERVES 2

1½ cups (210 g) cooked shredded or chopped chicken, about 2 breasts

1 green onion (both white and green parts), chopped

1 celery rib, chopped

½ tsp dried parsley

¼ tsp each: onion powder, garlic powder, dried dill, dried chives, sea salt and pepper

2 tbsp (30 g) Homemade Mayonnaise (page 496)

2 tbsp (30 ml) hot sauce

Celery sticks, for serving

Super Easy Guacamole (page 190), for serving

Combine all ingredients together in a bowl. Refrigerate and serve cold. Serve with celery sticks and Super Easy Guacamole.

CHEF'S TIP:
The flavor is best when left in the refrigerator for a few hours.

SUMMER GARDEN RATATOUILLE

Ratatouille is considered a summer garden dish. It is bright and perfectly acidic. Topped with a poached egg, it makes a perfect light summer lunch. —AV

SERVES 4

2 tbsp (30 g) ghee

1 onion, diced

1 medium eggplant, diced

2 tbsp (30 g) tomato paste

6 tomatoes, peeled, seeded and chopped

4 cloves garlic, minced

1 red bell pepper, diced

1 green bell pepper, diced

1 jalapeño pepper, diced

2 medium zucchini, diced

1 tbsp (6 g) fresh oregano

2 tbsp (12 g) fresh thyme

¼ cup (24 g) fresh parsley, chopped

½ cup (120 ml) Slow Cooker Chicken Broth (page 170)

Salt and pepper

Olive oil

Poached eggs

Heat the ghee in a large skillet with a lid over medium-high heat. Add the onion and sauté until translucent, about 5 minutes. Add the eggplant and sauté for about 10 minutes. Eggplants are very thirsty, so you might have to add a little more ghee.

Add the tomato paste and sauté until it turns from a bright red to a brick color, about 1 minute. Add chopped tomatoes and let the vegetables cook for about 5 to 7 minutes. Then add garlic, bell peppers, jalapeño pepper, zucchini and chopped herbs. Stir to combine. Add chicken broth and place the lid on the skillet. Turn the temperature down to very low and simmer the vegetable stew for 10 minutes. Remove the lid and simmer for an additional 10 minutes or until the broth has evaporated and the vegetables have become very tender. Salt and pepper to taste. Drizzle with olive oil and top with a poached egg.

SMOKED PAPRIKA ROASTED CARROTS

The smoky-spicy paprika balances with the naturally sweet carrots and coconut oil. —AV

SERVES 6

2 tbsp (30 ml) coconut oil, melted

2 tsp (6 g) smoked paprika

½ tsp sea salt

½ tsp black pepper

2½ pounds (1.1 kg) medium carrots, peeled and halved lengthwise

2 tbsp (8 g) finely chopped fresh cilantro

Preheat oven to 375°F (190°C, or gas mark 5). In a large bowl, combine the coconut oil, paprika, salt and pepper with the carrots. Toss well to ensure that carrots are well coated. Arrange carrot mixture in a single layer on a baking sheet. Bake for 30 minutes or until carrots are tender. Stir once halfway through. Sprinkle with cilantro and serve.

MAPLE–GLAZED CARROTS

This recipe is a great lower-carb substitute for a sweet potato side dish during the holidays. Cinnamon dazzles the senses while maple and butter bring out the rich sweetness of the carrots. —RM

SERVES 6

1 pound (454 g) carrots, cut on the bias into coins

½ cup (120 ml) water

2 tbsp (30 g) butter (I prefer Kerrygold)

1½ tbsp (23 ml) grade B maple syrup

Pinch of salt

Ground cinnamon, to taste

In a skillet, bring the carrots, water, butter and maple syrup to a boil. Add a pinch of salt and lots of cinnamon to taste. Reduce the heat to a simmer and cook for 6 minutes covered. Remove the lid and cook for another 4 to 5 minutes until the carrots are tender—but not mushy—and the maple butter has reduced. Serve warm.

SIMPLE ROASTED ROOT VEGGIES

This recipe calls for some of the more overlooked root vegetables, such as turnips and parsnips. These vegetables are loaded with nutrients, inexpensive and available in the winter when other vegetables are hard to find. When roasted, they become slightly sweet and caramelized. —AV

SERVES 4

1 large purple top turnip

3 parsnips

2 yams

1 tablespoon (4 g) fresh thyme

3 cloves garlic, minced

Salt and pepper

3 tbsp (45 ml) ghee, melted

Cut the turnip, parsnips and yams evenly and place in a bowl. Toss with thyme, garlic, salt, pepper and ghee. Ensure that the vegetables are coated evenly. Spread the vegetables in a single layer on a cookie sheet and bake at 400°F (200°C, or gas mark 6) for 30 to 40 minutes. Turn veggies over, once halfway through.

ROOT VEGETABLE HASH

Roasted root vegetables are my go-to side for weeknight meals as they are healthy and comforting all at the same time. This dish just requires a few minutes of tossing together, then place in the oven while you prepare the rest of your meal! I love this with a simple side salad and grilled steak or even leftovers with eggs for breakfast. —CP

SERVES 6

2 medium sweet potatoes or yams

2 parsnips

1 rutabaga

1 pound (454 g) pearl onions

4 tbsp (60 ml) olive oil

4 tbsp (60 g) butter

1½ tsp (4.5 g) sea salt

1 tsp (3 g) paprika

1 tsp (3 g) garlic granules

½ tsp smoked paprika

½ tsp fresh cracked black pepper

Preheat oven to 400°F (200°C, or gas mark 6).

Cube all root vegetables into 1-inch (2.5-5-cm) cubes. Peel the onions and slice in half.

Place into two large baking dishes and toss together with olive oil and spices. Slice butter into small cubes and arrange throughout the pan.

Roast for 30 minutes, stirring halfway through. Turn the heat up to 425°F (225°C, or gas mark 7) and roast for an additional 15 minutes or until roots are tender and golden brown. Serve warm.

MASALA SWEET POTATO BITES

These little sweet potato cakes are a warm and comforting Paleo side dish. The savory Indian spices, finished off with lemon and cilantro, create a fun and unique addition to any dinner menu. —KH

SERVES 3–4

2 cups (500 g) mashed sweet potatoes

2 eggs, whipped

1 tbsp (8 g) arrowroot powder

½ tsp ground cumin

½ tsp ground coriander

½ tsp ground turmeric

½ tsp ground ginger

½ tsp sea salt

Coconut oil or ghee for cooking

Fresh lemon juice and cilantro, for garnish

Combine all ingredients in a medium bowl—except for cooking oil and garnish—and mash until well combined. Let mixture sit in fridge for 15 minutes. Heat the fat in a large skillet. Spoon out tablespoon (15 g)-sized scoops of mixture into pan and allow to cook for 3 to 4 minutes before flipping. Continue to cook until golden brown on both sides. Serve with a squeeze of fresh lemon juice sprinkled on top and some fresh cilantro.

SWEET POTATO NOODLES WITH GINGER ALMOND BUTTER SAUCE

Noodles can be made out of just about anything. Sweet potato noodles are a sweet and satisfying alternative to traditional noodles. And combining them with this creamy, flavorful, gingery sauce creates a wonderful comforting side dish. You can use a spiralizer, vegetable peeler or sharp knife to julienne the sweet potato in this recipe. —KH

SERVES 2

FOR THE SAUCE

1 tbsp (15 g) almond butter

3 tbsp (45 ml) hot homemade broth or water

1 tbsp (15 ml) coconut aminos

1 tbsp (15 ml) fresh lime juice

½ tsp fresh grated ginger

Pinch of sea salt

Pinch of cayenne, optional

Fresh cilantro, for garnish

1 large sweet potato, peeled

Combine all sauce ingredients in a small bowl until well incorporated. Set aside.

Either julienne or spiralize sweet potato into small noodles or strips. Steam lightly for 2 to 3 minutes to soften. Pour sauce over "noodles," mix to combine and serve. Garnish with fresh cilantro.

SWEET POTATO WEDGES

Sweet potato wedges are a Paleo favorite. These are delicious paired with burgers wrapped in lettuce, for a go-to weeknight meal. —AV

SERVES 4

4 tbsp (56 g) ghee

1 tsp (3 g) ground cumin

½ tsp paprika

3 sweet potatoes, cut lengthwise into wedges

Salt and pepper

Preheat the oven to 400°F (200°C, or gas mark 6). In a large saucepan over medium heat, melt the ghee. Remove the pan from the heat and stir in the cumin and paprika. Add the potato wedges to the melted ghee and toss to combine. Season the potatoes with the salt and pepper.

Spread the potatoes in an even layer on a baking sheet. Roast the potatoes, stirring occasionally, until tender, about 20 to 25 minutes. Remove from the oven to a serving dish and serve.

GREEK SWEET POTATO FRIES

Sweet potato fries never get old in our house, but this Greek inspired version combines for a unique flavor for a healthy, yummy dish to pass and share around the table. —CP

SERVES 4–6

2 medium sweet potatoes or yams

2 tbsp (30 ml) olive oil

1 tsp (3 g) sea salt

¼ tsp garlic granules

¼ tsp paprika

4 ounces (112 g) feta cheese crumbles, optional

½ cup (50 g) kalamata olives, chopped

8–10 fresh basil leaves, thinly sliced

2 tbsp (30 ml) balsamic reduction or glaze

Preheat oven to 400°F (200°C, or gas mark 6). Line two baking sheets with parchment paper.

Thinly slice sweet potatoes into skinny fries. Toss with olive oil, salt and spices, coating but not drenching with oil.

Arrange sweet potatoes on baking sheets with room in-between each fry, as this helps them crisp in the oven.

Bake for 35 minutes, rotating halfway through, or until fries begin to crisp and turn golden brown.

While fries are baking, crumble feta cheese and slice olives and basil.

Remove fries from oven, topping with cheese, olives, basil and a generous drizzle of balsamic glaze. Serve and enjoy!

CHEF'S TIP:

Traditional Greek style feta cheese is made from sheep's milk or a combination of goat and sheep's milk, making this a great option for those sensitive to cow's milk; however, you can omit the cheese all together.

PARSNIP FRIES TWO WAYS

Parsnips are a great blank canvas for flavor. Next time you're after something different to eat or serve try these simple to make parsnip fries with two different flavorings. —NK

SERVES 4

4 medium parsnips, peeled and cut into fries

3 tsp (8 g) Pumpkin Pie Spice (page 505)

3 tsp (8 g) hot Hungarian paprika powder

Sea salt, to taste

2 tbsp (30 ml) coconut oil, melted

Preheat oven to 450°F (230°C, or gas mark 8). Line a large baking tray with parchment paper. Divide parsnip fries evenly into two medium-sized mixing bowls. Add the pumpkin pie spice to one bowl and the Hungarian paprika powder to the other. Add a pinch of sea salt to each bowl. Mix well. Arrange fries onto a large baking tray so that the pumpkin pie spiced and the Hungarian paprika spiced fries are separated from each other. Drizzle with coconut oil and bake for 10 to 15 minutes on one side before carefully removing from the oven, turning the fries over and baking for another 10 to 15 minutes on the other side. Sprinkle with a bit more sea salt before serving.

SPICED BUTTERNUT SQUASH FRIES

These butternut squash fries infused with the warming spices of cinnamon, nutmeg, cloves and ginger make a delicious side or snack to enjoy. —NK

SERVES 2

1 medium butternut squash, peeled, seeded and cut into fries

2 tsp (6 g) ground cinnamon

¼ tsp ground nutmeg

⅛ tsp ground cloves

⅛ tsp ground ginger

¼ tsp sea salt

1 tbsp (15 ml) coconut oil, melted

Hazelnut oil, for topping, optional

Preheat oven to 425°F (220°C, or gas mark 7). Line a large baking tray with parchment paper. Place butternut squash fries in a large mixing bowl and add the cinnamon, nutmeg, cloves, ginger and sea salt. Mix well. Place the fries onto the lined baking tray and drizzle with the melted coconut oil. Bake for 15 to 20 minutes then remove from the oven, flip the fries over and bake for another 15 to 20 minutes. Serve warm with a drizzle of hazelnut oil on top.

OVEN-ROASTED PARSNIP FRIES WITH RAS EL HANOUT

Ras el Hanout is a North African spice mix that can be found in certain grocery stores or you can purchase it online. It pairs perfectly with parsnips for delicious spiced homemade fries. —NK

SERVES 4

2 pounds (908 g) parsnips, peeled and cut into fries

2 tbsp (16 g) Ras el Hanout

½ tsp sea salt

2 tbsp (30 ml) ghee, melted

Preheat oven to 400°F (200°C, or gas mark 6). Line a large baking tray with parchment paper. Place parsnip fries into a large mixing bowl and add the Ras el Hanout and sea salt. Using your hands, mix everything together, making sure to coat all of the parsnip fries in the spice mixture. Place parsnip fries on the lined baking tray in a single layer as best as possible. Drizzle with the melted ghee. Bake for 20 minutes on one side then carefully remove from the oven, flip the fries over and bake for another 20 minutes. Remove from the oven and allow to cool before serving.

LOMO SALTADO
WITH YUCA FRIES

Lomo saltado is the national dish of Peru. Traditionally, the stir-fry is served over French fries and accompanied by white rice. This recipe replaces the potato-based fries with yuca and gets rid of the rice altogether. —RM

SERVES 4

1 pound (454 g) tri-tip steak

Salt and pepper to taste

2 tbsp (30 g) duck fat (or bacon fat), divided

½ teaspoon ground cumin

4 cloves garlic, chopped

1 aji amarillo pepper

1 red onion, sliced thin

¼ cup (60 ml) apple cider vinegar

1 tbsp (15 ml) tamari or coconut aminos

3 tomatoes seeded, peeled, and sliced, or 2 cups (500 g) chopped tomatoes, drained

Yuca Fries (page 218), for serving

2 tbsp (8 g) fresh parsley to garnish

Slice beef in to ¼-inch (6-mm)-wide strips. Salt and pepper. Heat 1 tablespoon (15 g) duck fat in a wok. Add the cumin and garlic and sauté for 1 minute. Add beef to wok and cook over medium heat until brown on all sides, 2 to 3 minutes. Remove beef and set aside.

Chop aji amarillo and then add to wok along with the sliced onion. Cook on medium heat until onions are soft, about 5 minutes. Add vinegar and tamari and cook 2 to 4 minutes. Add beef and tomatoes and cook for 2 more minutes.

Serve on top of Yuca Fries and garnish with parsley.

CHEF'S TIP:

If you don't have access to aji amarillo, then habanero, Hungarian wax peppers or serranos make good substitutes.

BAKED ZUCCHINI FRIES

These zucchini fries make the ideal healthy appetizer. If you eat dairy, substituting 3 tablespoons (15 g) Romano or Parmesan cheese instead of the almond flour is absolutely fantastic. Be sure to make the Blooming Onion Sauce (page 516) for dipping! —KW

SERVES 4–6

2 medium-sized zucchini

2 eggs

⅓ cup (40 g) coconut flour

⅓ cup (40 g) arrowroot flour/powder

3 tbsp (24 g) almond flour

1½ tsp (4 g) dried Italian seasoning

1 tsp (3 g) garlic powder

Sea salt and pepper, to taste

1–2 tbsp (15–30 ml) coconut oil or other oil/fat of choice, melted

Blooming Onion Sauce (page 516), for dipping

Preheat oven to 425°F (220°C, or gas mark 7). Cut the zucchini in thirds so that each chunk is about 3 to 4 inches (7.5 to 10 cm) long. Then cut each chunk into nine fries. Whisk the eggs in a bowl until well mixed.

In a separate bowl, combine the coconut flour, arrowroot flour, almond flour and spices.

Pour melted coconut oil onto a cookie sheet. Dip the zucchini into the egg and then into the flour mixture. Put the coated zucchini fries onto the cookie sheet. Bake for 15 minutes. Flip. Bake 15 to 20 more minutes or until golden brown. Serve with the Blooming Onion Sauce.

DUCK FAT PLANTAIN FRIES

Duck fat gives these plantain fries a characteristically rich flavor. I love dipping them in homemade Parsley Garlic Aioli (page 518) on burger night. —RM

SERVES 3

2 greenish yellow plantains

2 tbsp (30 g) duck fat

1½ tsp (4 g) garlic salt

Cayenne pepper, to taste

Parsley Garlic Aioli (page 518), for dipping

Preheat the oven to 400°F (205°C, or gas mark 6). Line a baking sheet with parchment paper for easy cleanup. Peel the plantains by cutting the tips off and slicing down each ridge with a knife. Slide your fingers underneath each ridge until the peel easily comes off. Cut each plantain in half, and then quarter each half. Cut into fry shapes. I like slicing my plantains just slightly thicker than shoestring fries. If they are too thick then they become too dry, but if they are too thin then they aren't soft enough in the middle.

Toss the plantains with the duck fat in a large mixing bowl. Add the seasoning. Layer the fries on the parchment paper in a single layer. Bake for 17 to 20 minutes, turning over about halfway through. Serve immediately with your favorite Paleo dipping sauce or Parsley Garlic Aioli.

YUCA FRIES

Yuca, or cassava, is a popular starchy tuber in Latin American cuisine. It is typically served as a boiled side dish or fried in thick strips. Yuca is the perfect complement to any slow cooker pork dish. —RM

SERVES 2

1 pound (454 g) frozen yuca root

1 tbsp (8 g) salt

1 tbsp (15 ml) lemon juice

4 tbsp (60 g) lard

Garlic sea salt to taste

Parsley Garlic Aioli (page 518), for serving

Boil yuca in 6 cups (1410 ml) of water with salt and lemon juice for 40 minutes. Remove and strain in a colander. Allow to cool. Cut any full chunks in half lengthwise and remove the fibrous strings that might be present in the center of the yuca. Slice into 1-inch (2.5-cm)-thick strips. Heat lard in a frying pan or skillet to medium heat and then add yuca strips. Cook for about 10 minutes, flipping over halfway through. Both sides should be lightly golden. Lay fried yuca on paper towels to sop up extra grease. Sprinkle with garlic sea salt and serve with Parsley Garlic Aioli.

CHEF'S TIP:

You can also use fresh yuca from a market, but for simplicity's sake I use the already peeled and cut frozen kind which can be found in most supermarkets.

BAKED ONION RINGS

These Paleo baked onion rings make a fun, healthy alternative snack for special occasions! —HH

SERVES 4

1 large yellow onion

1 egg

2 tbsp (30 ml) coconut milk, whole milk or almond milk

1 tbsp (15 ml) high-heat oil—avocado oil, sustainable palm oil, etc.

½ cup (60 g) almond flour

¼ tsp sea salt

¼ tsp garlic powder

Preheat the oven to 450°F (230°C, or gas mark 8). Cut the onion into thick rings. In one bowl, whisk the egg and mix in the other wet ingredients. Then, in a separate bowl, combine the almond flour, salt and garlic powder.

Set aside a cookie sheet lined with parchment paper. With a fork dip one onion ring slice into the wet ingredients, then place it in the dry ingredients so it gets coated with the flour mixture. Then place the coated ring on the cookie sheet. Repeat this process until all of the ingredients have been used up.

Place the rings in the oven for about 8 to 10 minutes. Keep an eye on the rings so they don't burn. They should be browned on the edges when they're done.

ROASTED SWEET POTATO CHIPS

These sweet potatoes aren't as crispy as fried chips but the edges are crunchy enough that you'll end up wanting more. Ghee with parsley, chives and garlic makes it so yummy you'll want to drizzle a good amount all over the sweet potatoes. Pair these chips as a side to sausages and brats or enjoy as a quick snack. —JC

SERVES 4

4 tbsp (60 ml) ghee, melted, divided

2 tbsp (16 g) parsley, chopped

1 tbsp (8 g) chives, chopped

1 clove garlic, minced

1 pound (454 g) sweet potatoes, thinly sliced

Sea salt

Preheat oven to 375°F (190°C, or gas mark 5). Line two baking sheets with parchment paper.

In a small bowl, combine 3 tablespoons (45 ml) of ghee with the parsley, chives and garlic. Let it sit for at least half an hour to infuse the flavors together.

In a large bowl, add sweet potatoes and the remaining 1 tablespoon (15 ml) of ghee. Mix well until the sweet potatoes are lightly coated with ghee. Distribute them evenly among the two baking sheets and arrange them in a single layer. Roast in the oven for 25 to 30 minutes. Flip the sweet potatoes at the 15 minute mark to cook evenly. Remove and set aside to cool for 5 minutes. Drizzle the herb infused ghee on top and season with sea salt to taste before serving.

CHEF'S TIP:
Use a mandolin to slice the sweet potatoes evenly.

STUFFED BAKED SWEET POTATOES

This is no ordinary baked potato. Packed with three complementing ingredients—mushrooms, bacon and egg—it is a great meal for either breakfast or dinner. In the absence of cheese and sour cream, the yolk of a perfectly cooked sunny side up egg coats everything in a creamy, rich sauce that turns this dish from savory to spectacular. —JC

SERVES 4

4 sweet potatoes

8 strips bacon

6 ounces (168 g) shiitake mushrooms, sliced

6 ounces (168 g) oyster mushrooms, sliced

1 medium onion, chopped

4 large eggs

Preheat oven to 375°F (190°C, or gas mark 5).

Wrap each sweet potato with foil. Place them on a baking sheet and bake for 25 to 30 minutes until they can easily be pierced with a fork.

Add bacon to a cast iron pan over medium heat. Pan-fry until crispy, flipping every couple of minutes for even cooking. Remove from heat and let it cool for a few minutes. Chop bacon into pieces and set aside.

Reserve 2 tablespoons (30 ml) of bacon grease in the pan. Add the mushrooms and onion, and sauté until soft, about 3 to 5 minutes. Combine mushrooms and onion with the cooked bacon. Set aside.

Cook the eggs sunny side up using the left over bacon grease for about 2 to 3 minutes. Remove them from the pan and set aside.

Once sweet potatoes are cooked, cut a slit on top of each one. Gently squeeze the opposite ends of each sweet potato to create a cavity. Spoon in the bacon mushroom mixture and top with the sunny side up egg. Serve immediately.

CHESTNUT AND SWEET POTATO PASTA

Roasting fresh chestnuts is one our favorite things to do at home during the cooler months. This recipe is a fun way to enjoy those roasted chestnuts. —NK

SERVES 4

9 ounces (252 g) chestnuts

1 medium sweet potato, peeled

2 tbsp (30 g) ghee, divided

1 tbsp (8 g) ground cinnamon, divided

¼ tsp sea salt

Raw honey to serve, optional

Preheat oven to 400°F (200°C, or gas mark 6). Line a large baking tray with parchment paper. Using a paring knife score an X into the flat side of each chestnut, making sure not to cut into the flesh of the chestnut. Place onto the prepared baking tray and bake for 20 to 30 minutes. Remove from the oven and allow to cool slightly before peeling. Set chestnuts aside.

Run the sweet potato through a spiralizer to create pasta-like strands. Heat a large skillet over medium heat and add 1 tablespoon (15 g) ghee. Once melted, add the sweet potato and ½ tablespoon (4 g) cinnamon. Mix well. Add the sea salt and cook until the sweet potato is softened, about 5 to 7 minutes. Remove from the heat and place onto a clean plate. Slice the prepared chestnuts in half. In the same skillet as you cooked the sweet potato, add 1 tablespoon (15 g) ghee over medium heat. Add another ½ tablespoon (4 g) cinnamon and the sliced chestnuts. Mix well and fry for 3 to 4 minutes. To serve, place sweet potato pasta onto a plate and add the chestnuts on top. Serve with a drizzle of raw honey if desired.

CHEF'S TIP:

Peel the chestnuts when they are still warm—the shells will come off easier.

ROASTED SWEET POTATOES WITH CAULIFLOWER CREAM SAUCE

When you're Paleo or sensitive to dairy, you sometimes miss the rich creamy decadence of dairy—and the milk, cream and cheese you can use to make lovely sauces to put over vegetables or pasta. Luckily, cauliflower can pretty easily take dairy's place in creamy sauces and taste delicious on its own! This dish would make a great side for any old weeknight dinner or even for a Thanksgiving dinner. —HH

SERVES 4

⅔ cup (80 g) Cauliflower Purée (page 186)

3 medium sweet potatoes

2 tbsp (30 ml) olive oil

1 tsp (3 g) sea salt

½ tsp pepper

½ tsp thyme

½ tsp oregano

First make the Cauliflower Purée and set it aside. Preheat the oven to 400°F (200°C, or gas mark 6). Wash the sweet potatoes, then slice them into thin slices about ½-inch (1.3-cm) thick. Place them in a bowl and drizzle with the olive oil and sprinkle with the salt, pepper and spices. Stir the sweet potatoes around in the bowl to coat each slice with olive oil and spices. Place them in rows, slightly overlapping the edges, so they stack across a 8 × 8-inch (20 × 20-cm) glass baking dish. Bake for about 45 to 55 minutes or until fork tender. Heat up the Cauliflower Purée and add a little water or broth to make it thinner if necessary. Drizzle it over the roasted sweet potatoes.

SLICED BAKED SWEET POTATO

This baked sweet potato is like a personal Thanksgiving Dinner side dish for one. You can even make it a day prior, as sweet potato is delicious reheated. —RM

SERVES 1

1 sweet potato, washed

1 tbsp (15 g) butter or ghee, divided

Ground cinnamon

1 tbsp (8 g) finely chopped pecans

¼ tbsp (18 g) coconut sugar

Preheat the oven to 400°F (200°C, or gas mark 6). Make slits three quarters of the way into the potato, down the entire length, as if you were trying to scallop the potato but still keeping the entire thing intact. Slather the whole potato with butter. Sprinkle with cinnamon and then place in the center of a baking sheet and bake for 45 minutes. Remove from the oven and use a spoon to wedge pecan crumbs, sugar and remaining butter in between the potato slices. Top with more cinnamon and bake for another 15 minutes. Serve hot.

ZUCCHINI AND SWEET POTATO FRITTERS

These sweet and savory cakes can be enjoyed on their own or topped with an egg for breakfast. —AV

MAKES 12 (3 PER PERSON)

2 small zucchini

2 tsp (6 g) sea salt

½ an onion

1 sweet potato, peeled

2 eggs, beaten

1 tbsp (8 g) coconut flour

Coconut oil for frying

Grate zucchini into a colander. Toss with 2 teaspoons (6 g) of sea salt and let it sit for 10 minutes. In the meantime, grate the onion. Be sure to grate the onion first. Then grate the sweet potato and place it in the same bowl as the onion; this will keep the sweet potato from browning. Squeeze the remaining liquid from the zucchini. Add the zucchini, eggs and coconut flour to the onion and sweet potato mixture. Mix to combine.

Heat 2 tablespoons (30 ml) of coconut oil in a heavy-bottomed skillet. Place spoonfuls of the sweet potato mixture into the pan; fit as many as you can without overcrowding. Flatten the fritters with a spatula. Cook 3 to 4 minutes per side, until they are browned. Move to a paper towel–lined plate to drain. Repeat until you don't have any of the mixture left. Add more coconut oil as needed. Serve immediately.

BEET CARROT FRITTERS

You may be used to zucchini fritters, but beets and carrots also make for a delightful fritter. This recipe creates a great crunchy outer layer and tender flavorful inner layer. Just make sure you squeeze all of the liquid out of the shredded beets first or your fritters may fall flat! —HH

MAKES 10–12

2 medium beets

3 carrots

½ of a medium onion

½ tsp thyme

½ tsp oregano

½ tsp salt

½ tsp pepper

½ tsp garlic powder

2 eggs

½ cup (60 g) arrowroot

2 tbsp (30 g) ghee, avocado oil or lard

Using a grater or the grater setting on a food processor, grate the beets and put into a bowl, then sprinkle them with salt. Set aside for about 5 minutes. Separately grate the carrots and set aside. Then, slice the onions into thin strips to resemble the grated beets and carrots.

Once the beets have rested for about 5 minutes, use a cheesecloth, nut milk bag or clean flour sack-style dish cloth to wring out their moisture. Squeeze as much liquid out of the beets as possible.

Place the beets, carrots and onions into a mixing bowl and add the thyme, oregano, salt, pepper, garlic powder and mix. Add the eggs and mix thoroughly, then add the arrowroot and mix to combine.

Heat the ghee or oil in a large pan on medium-high heat and allow to heat up for about a minute. Once the oil is hot, place a dollop of the beet mixture into the pan with a spoon and flatten into a pancake shape, allow to fry on each side for about 3 to 5 minutes and flip and cook until it's firm and toasted on each side. Repeat until all of the beet mixture has been used up.

SPAGHETTI SQUASH FRITTERS

These cinnamon and cumin spiced Spaghetti Squash Fritters are easy to make and make a delicious snack or side. —NK

SERVES 3

1 (2-pound [908-g]) spaghetti squash

½ cup (120 ml) water

1 tsp (3 g) ground cinnamon

¼ tsp ground cumin

¼ tsp sea salt

1 cup (235 ml) refined coconut oil or red palm shortening, for frying

Preheat oven to 425°F (220°C, or gas mark 7). Cut spaghetti squash in half and remove the seeds. Place the squash cut-side down in a baking dish. Pour in the water and bake for 60 to 90 minutes or until tender. Remove from the oven and allow to cool until cool enough to handle. Then use a fork to scoop out the strands like pasta and place on a clean kitchen towel or cheesecloth. Use the cloth to squeeze out any excess water and place the squash in a medium-sized mixing bowl. Add the cinnamon, cumin and sea salt, and mix.

Heat a 10- to 12-inch (25- to 30.5-cm) skillet over medium-high heat. Add the refined coconut oil or red palm shortening. Heat until when you stick the end of a wooden spoon into the oil, bubbles form around it, checking the oil every 2 to 3 minutes. Use your hands to take a roughly 1 tablespoon (15 ml) portion of the spaghetti squash mixture and roll into a ball, then flatten it out to about ¼-inch (6-mm) thick. Place into the cooking fat and cook in batches, frying for 3 to 4 minutes per side.

PERSIAN SAFFRON POTATO PATTIES (KOOKOO SIBZAMINI)

Persian Saffron Potato Patties are a delicious and simple to make side dish. They're traditionally spiced with turmeric, but I decided to use saffron instead in this recipe and added some parsley for a twist. —NK

SERVES 7

2 pounds (908 g) Russet potatoes

½ tsp saffron, ground

2 tbsp (30 ml) boiled water

1 tbsp (8 g) finely chopped flat leaf parsley

½ tsp sea salt

¼ tsp black pepper

¼ tsp garlic powder

Refined coconut oil or ghee, for frying

Add enough cold water to just cover the potatoes in a pot. Place on high heat and bring to a boil. Reduce heat slightly and place lid on the pot. Boil for 20 to 30 minutes or until the potatoes are tender. Drain and rinse with cold water. Set aside to cool for about 5 to 10 minutes until cool enough to handle. Remove the skin from the potatoes and set aside to cool completely.

Once cooled, run them through a potato ricer into a large mixing bowl or use a potato masher to mash. Mix the ground saffron with the boiled water and add to the potatoes. Add the parsley, sea salt, black pepper and garlic powder and use your hands to mix well.

Form mixture into even golf ball-sized balls, then flatten out into patties about ½-inch (1.3-cm) thick. Heat ½- to 1-inch (1.3- to 2.5-cm) refined coconut oil or ghee in a 10- to 12-inch (25- to 30.5-cm) skillet over medium-high heat. When the oil is hot, carefully add the potato patties in batches to the skillet and fry for 3 to 4 minutes per side. Move onto a paper towel-lined plate as they finish frying.

CHEF'S TIP:
It's important to let the potatoes cool completely in this recipe. The mixture will hold together much better this way and there's no need to add eggs or flour to the mixture to bind it together.

TOSTONES WITH GARLIC–INFUSED GHEE

Tostones are twice-fried plantains that are crunchy on the outside and slightly soft on the inside. They are seriously addicting, especially when dipped in garlicky ghee! Pre-soaking the plantains helps cook the tostones evenly and minimizes any burnt spots. When pressed for time, this step can be omitted without affecting the taste of the tostones once they are cooked. —JC

SERVES 4

3 cups (705 ml) cold water

½ tsp sea salt

2 green plantains, peeled and cut into ½-inch (1.3-cm) pieces

1 cup (235 g) tallow or coconut oil

3 tbsp (45 g) ghee

3 cloves garlic, minced

Mix together the cold water and ¼ teaspoon sea salt in a bowl until the sea salt is dissolved. Add the sliced plantains and soak for 30 minutes. Drain plantains and pat dry with paper towels.

Add tallow to a cast iron pan over medium heat. Add half of the plantains to the pan. Make sure they are not touching each other so each piece cooks evenly. Fry for 5 minutes on the first side. Flip to the other side and fry for another 5 minutes. Remove from the pan and drain on paper towels. Repeat the same process for the remaining plantains.

Grab one piece of fried plantain and using the flat bottom of a small bowl or drinking glass, gently press onto the plantain in a clockwise motion until it is flattened to about ¼-inch (6-mm) thick. Repeat this for the rest of the fried plantains.

In the same pan over medium heat, fry the flattened plantains for a second time in three to four batches. Fry for 2 minutes each side. Remove from heat and drain on paper towels. Place tostones on a serving plate and season with the remaining ¼ teaspoon of sea salt.

While the tostones are cooling, melt ghee in a small saucepan on low heat. Add garlic and cook for 2 to 3 minutes until golden brown. Stir it frequently so the garlic doesn't burn and stick to the bottom of the saucepan. Remove from heat and drizzle on top of the tostones or serve on the side as a dip.

CREAMY BACON BRUSSELS SPROUTS

This unique recipe is to die for! These will make a believer out of anyone who turns their noses up at Brussels sprouts. Kids and picky eaters are sure to love them. —RM

SERVES 4

1 pound (454 g) Brussels sprouts, trimmed and quartered

2 tbsp (30 ml) butter, melted

Sea salt and freshly ground pepper to taste

4 slices of bacon, chopped up

6 crimini mushrooms, chopped

1 shallot, chopped

1 clove garlic, minced

½ cup (120 ml) full-fat coconut milk

¼ cup (60 ml) cooking sherry

Preheat the oven to 475°F (240°C, or gas mark 9). Mix the Brussels sprouts, butter and salt and pepper in a bowl. Line a baking sheet with tin foil and then spread out the Brussels evenly on it. Bake for 15 minutes, tossing once halfway through.

Meanwhile, over medium-high heat, cook the bacon in a deep skillet until slightly browned, about 7 minutes. Reduce the heat to medium and then add the mushrooms and shallots. Salt and pepper to taste. Cook for 5 minutes until the shallots are translucent, stirring occasionally.

Add the garlic and stir, about 1 minute. Add the coconut milk and cooking sherry to the skillet, mixing thoroughly. Bring to a boil and simmer until reduced by half. Constantly stir. When the sauce is thick enough to coat the back of a spoon, about 5 to 7 minutes, stir in the Brussels sprouts to evenly coat them. Serve immediately.

BACON AND LEEK BRUSSELS SPROUTS

Leeks and bacon pair magnificently together to elevate these Brussels sprouts from boring to flavor explosion! —RM

SERVES 3–4

4 slices thick cut bacon, diced

1 pound (454 g) Brussels sprouts, trimmed and quartered

1 clove garlic, smashed

¼ cup (30 g) sliced leeks

Salt and pepper, to taste

First fry the bacon bits in a large deep skillet over medium heat. Once the bacon is crispy, about 5 minutes, remove it with a slotted spoon, keeping the remaining grease in the pan. Fry the Brussels sprouts in the bacon fat until lightly browned and tender, about 8 minutes. Add the garlic and leeks, sautéing for another 4 minutes until the leeks are cooked. Mix the crispy bacon into the Brussels sprouts and serve immediately.

HONEY MUSTARD BRUSSELS SPROUTS

The Brussels sprouts of yesteryear used to be bland, boring and so mushy nobody wanted to even attempt to eat them. Nowadays, Brussels sprouts are very popular among almost everyone who eats Paleo because they go really well with almost everything. This is a different spin that is flavored with sweet, tangy honey mustard and toasted pine nuts. —JC

SERVES 2

¼ cup (38 g) raw pine nuts

1 tbsp (15 g) bacon fat or coconut oil

1 pound (454 g) Brussels sprouts, cut in half

1 tbsp (15 g) Dijon mustard

2 tbsp (30 ml) raw honey

Add pine nuts to a skillet over medium-low heat. Toast for 3 to 5 minutes stirring constantly to prevent one side from burning. Remove from heat and set aside to cool.

Add bacon fat to the same skillet. Increase heat to medium and add Brussels sprouts cut-side down. Cover and cook for 5 minutes. Flip, cover and cook the other side for 5 to 7 minutes. Turn off heat and let sit covered for 2 to 3 minutes. Mix mustard and honey in a small bowl and pour it on top of the Brussels sprouts. Add the pine nuts and mix everything until well combined. Serve immediately.

MAPLE BACON BRUSSELS SPROUTS

The strong flavor of Brussels sprouts is smoothed and enhanced with the sweetness of apple, the saltiness of bacon and the complex finish of maple vinegar. —RB

SERVES 2

4 slices of bacon

1 pound (454 g) Brussels sprouts

1 apple

⅔ cup (100 g) slivered almonds

¼ tsp salt

2 tsp (10 ml) maple vinegar

Preheat oven to 350°F (180°C, or gas mark 4). Cook bacon over medium heat in a skillet until crispy. Remove to drain and cool on a paper towel-lined plate then dice or crumble into bits. Reserve 1 tablespoon (15 ml) of bacon fat.

Wash and trim the Brussels sprouts, cutting off the woody base of each bud and removing any shriveled or discolored leaves. Halve or quarter each sprout, then toss to coat in the reserved bacon fat and spread evenly in a roasting pan. Roast for 20 minutes or until soft and the outer leaves are crisped.

Core the apple, then dice or shred in a food processor. Combine with the bacon bits in a medium serving bowl, then mix in the slivered almonds.

Remove the Brussels from the oven and transfer to the serving bowl. Sprinkle with the salt and maple vinegar, or to taste. Toss thoroughly and serve warm.

CHEF'S TIP:

Maple vinegar is available online or in gourmet grocery stores. Substitute 1½ teaspoons (7.5 ml) maple syrup plus ½ teaspoon champagne vinegar, white vinegar or apple cider vinegar for the maple vinegar if desired.

LEMON GARLIC BRUSSELS SPROUTS WITH BALSAMIC GLAZE

I absolutely love these lemon garlic Brussels sprouts! I always find it funny when people talk about Brussels sprouts like they're the worst of the worst. Brussels sprouts can be incredibly delicious if prepared well, like these ones that contain rich balsamic glaze and a pop of lemon zest! —HH

SERVES 2–3

2 cups (470 ml) balsamic vinegar

About 2 cups (180 g) Brussels sprouts

5 cloves garlic

2 tbsp (30 g) ghee or oil

Salt and pepper to taste

1 tsp (3 g) lemon zest

To prepare the balsamic glaze, bring the balsamic vinegar to a boil in a saucepan, then turn down to a simmer. Stir occasionally. It will take around 10 to 15 minutes to thicken depending on the consistency you want. Turn off the heat when it reaches a syrupy consistency. It will thicken very slightly after turning off the heat. Set aside to let cool.

Wash the sprouts and chop off stem end of each one. Then cut each sprout in half lengthwise. Put the sprouts in a skillet and pour a small amount of water in, just enough to come halfway up the Brussels sprouts. You don't want to completely cover the Brussels sprouts in water. Turn the heat on medium-high and cover skillet. Let simmer until the Brussels sprouts are tender and can be pierced with a fork, but are not too soft or mushy, about 5 to 10 minutes. Turn the heat off and strain the water out using a colander.

Finely chop the garlic. Heat the ghee into the skillet on high heat. Once the ghee is hot, put the Brussels sprouts in the pan and sprinkle with garlic, salt and pepper. Let cook for a couple minutes on one side to brown then stir and mix the sprouts to evenly heat. Once the Brussels sprouts have browned for a few minutes, they are done. Put the Brussels sprouts on a plate, then drizzle with the balsamic glaze. Then, zest with some organic lemon. Add a little more salt and pepper if desired and enjoy!

HERBED BACON LOADED POTATOES

A small dollop of mayonnaise, a generous serving of bacon and savory seasoning turn plain potatoes into a scrumptious dish. Don't overcook the potatoes so they do not turn mushy but are tender with a nice bite. Enjoy this with any type of meat and make an extra batch since it refrigerates really well and tastes great even the next day. —JC

SERVES 4

1 tsp (3 g) garlic powder

1 tsp (3 g) onion powder

½ tsp black pepper

¼ tsp paprika

1 pound (454 g) baby red potatoes

3 cups (710 ml) cold water

2 cups (473 g) ice

2 tbsp (30 g) Homemade Mayonnaise (page 496)

2 stalks green onions, chopped

4 strips cooked bacon, chopped

Combine garlic powder, onion powder, black pepper and paprika in a small bowl. Set aside.

Add potatoes to a large pot. Add water until it covers the top of the potatoes by about an inch (2.5-cm). Turn on heat to high and bring water to a boil. Reduce heat and simmer uncovered for 25 minutes. Remove pot from heat and drain off the water. Add cold water and ice to cool the potatoes immediately. Let sit for 3 to 5 minutes. Transfer potatoes to a large colander to drain excess water and dry the potatoes.

Halve each potato and place them in a large bowl. Add mayonnaise, green onions and bacon, and sprinkle the seasoning on top. Stir gently until everything is combined. Serve immediately or chill in the fridge before serving.

GREEN BEANS WITH BACON

This classic combo is savory and comforting. It can be whipped up for a weeknight dinner or reserved for your Thanksgiving menu. —AV

SERVES 4

1 pound (454 g) green beans, trimmed and chopped into 2-inch (5-cm) pieces

2 slices bacon, chopped

½ small onion, chopped

1 tbsp (15 ml) red wine vinegar

Place the green beans in a medium-sized skillet with a tight fitting lid. Add about an inch (2.5-cm) of water and cook covered for about 7 minutes. Set aside green beans and drain the skillet Return the skillet to the stove and add the bacon to the pan, cooking over medium heat. When the fat begins to render, about 5 minutes, add the onions. Cook until bacon is getting crispy and onions are translucent, another 5 minutes. Return the cooked green beans to the pan, and coat in the bacon dripping and cook until bacon is crispy at the edges. Add the vinegar to the pan and stir to combine with the bacon drippings, about 1 minute. Allow the vinegar to evaporate, 1 to 2 minutes. Adjust salt and pepper to taste!

GREEN BEANS, POTATOES AND HAM SALAD

Make this dish if you are looking for something easy to bring to your next potluck event. Cooking the ingredients just right results in tender potatoes and crisp green beans. The mayonnaise acts as a binder and adds an overall creaminess to the salad so it tastes great when served either hot or cold. —JC

SERVES 4

1 pound (454 g) fingerling potatoes

½ tsp sea salt

4 cups (947 ml) water

1 pound (454 g) green beans, cut into 2-inch (5-cm) pieces

½ pound (227 g) cooked ham, chopped

¼ cup (60 g) Homemade Mayonnaise (page 496)

½ tsp black pepper

¼ tsp red pepper flakes

2 large hard-boiled eggs, finely chopped

2 tbsp (8 g) chives, chopped

Place potatoes and sea salt in a medium sized pot. Add enough water until it covers the potatoes by about an inch (2.5-cm). Turn on heat to high and bring to a boil. Reduce heat to low and let it simmer for 8 to 10 minutes. Potatoes are cooked when they can easily be pierced with a fork. Cook for a couple of minutes more if the potatoes are still firm. Remove and drain in a colander to cool.

Fill the same pot halfway and bring it to a boil. Add the green beans and blanch for 3 minutes, stirring occasionally. Remove and set aside to drain in the colander with the potatoes.

In a large bowl, add the potatoes, green beans, ham, mayonnaise, black pepper and red pepper flakes. Stir until everything is well combined. Top with chopped eggs and chives. Serve warm. If a cold salad is preferred, cover and let it chill in the fridge for 1 hour before serving.

ROASTED GREEN BEANS WITH TRUFFLE OIL AND CASHEWS

Roasting brings out a sweetness of the green beans and provides such a fabulous texture, especially when paired with crunchy cashew nuts. Toss with truffle oil when the beans come out of the oven for a rich, buttery flavor. This vegetable combination makes for a great entertaining or holiday side dish. —CP

SERVES 4–6

1 pound (454 g) French green beans

1 tbsp (15 ml) olive oil

2 cloves garlic, crushed

½ tsp sea salt

¼ tsp black pepper

½ cup unsalted cashews

1 tbsp (15 ml) truffle oil

Preheat oven to 400°F (200°C, or gas mark 6).

Toss green beans in olive oil, garlic, salt and pepper. Spread beans evenly in a large baking dish. Roast for 20 to 25 minutes, stirring halfway through. Stir in the cashews during the last 5 minutes of roasting.

When the beans come out of the oven, drizzle on truffle oil, stirring one last time. Best served warm.

CHEF'S TIP:

French style beans, known as haricots verts, are longer and skinnier than regular beans and I think they have better texture and taste. They cook up fabulously, making this a great dish for entertaining or the holidays.

HARICOTS VERTS WITH BROWNED BUTTER

Browned butter has a nutty taste that gives plain vegetables that extra pop. It can turn from golden brown to black in a blink of an eye so make sure you don't get distracted or else you'll end up throwing good butter in the trash! —JC

SERVES 4

3 tbsp (45 g) butter, cubed

1 pound (454 g) haricots verts or green beans, trimmed

¼ cup (38 g) sliced raw almonds

Add butter to a large pan over medium heat. Gently stir the butter until it melts completely. Once it simmers and forms a white foam on top, stir it constantly for about 3 to 5 minutes. Turn off heat when the white solids turn into brown bits and sink to the bottom of the pan. Stir for 1 more minute and set aside in a small bowl.

Add haricot verts to the same pan. Sauté until tender but still crispy, about 3 to 5 minutes. Drizzle in the browned butter and add the almonds. Sauté for 1 minute and remove from heat. Serve warm.

TOASTED ALMOND HARICOTS VERTS

Spruce up ordinary green beans with an earthy almond crunch. This is an easy recipe to whip up for family dinners or the holidays. The toasted almond adds an extra gourmet element to these green beans. —RM

SERVES 5

1 pound (454 g) haricots verts (French green beans)

⅓ cup (50 g) almond slivers

½ tsp coconut oil

Garlic salt, to taste

Dash cayenne pepper, to taste

½–1 tbsp (7.5–15 g) butter

½ tsp dried dill

Snap off the stem ends of the green beans and any ends that look browned. Bring a large pot of water to a boil on the stove.

Meanwhile, in a large skillet over medium-low heat, toast the almonds along with the coconut oil, garlic salt and cayenne for about 5 minutes. Stir constantly to avoid burning.

Add the green beans to the boiling water and cook for 7 minutes, al dente. A knife tip should be able to pierce them and they should still be a nice shade of green. Immediately strain the green beans and drench them in cold water to stop the cooking process.

Add the green beans and butter to the skillet of almonds, gently melting the butter, still over medium-low heat, until the butter is fully melted, a couple of minutes. Add the dill and more garlic salt, to taste. Serve immediately.

ZUCCHINI BLOSSOM APPETIZER

Battered and fried zucchini blossom is a traditional dish from the region of Liguria, where I was born. I substituted the wheat flour for almond flour, and it still came out as delicious as ever. I hope you like them as much as I do! —VM

SERVES 4

8–12 fresh zucchini blossoms

2 eggs

2 cups (240 g) almond flour

Lard for frying (you can use coconut oil if you prefer)

Sea salt and black pepper to taste

Clean the zucchini blossoms well, checking for any damage and removing the green part at the bottom.

In one bowl whisk the eggs lightly. In the other bowl add the almond flour for dredging. Gently roll the blossoms in the egg and then the almond flour.

In a skillet over high heat, fry the blossoms in the fat of choice until they turn a nice golden brown, turning them often, about 3 to 5 minutes.

Lay the fried blossoms on a paper towel to absorb any excess oils, sprinkle with salt and pepper and serve immediately.

CHEF'S TIP:

Zucchini blossoms can be found seasonally at farmers markets, or you can easily grow your own zucchini plants, so you will have plenty of flowers to cook!

SIMPLE SPICED SPAGHETTI SQUASH

Warmly-spiced, simple squash is what you want to accompany a weeknight dinner. —RB

SERVES 4

1 large spaghetti squash

1 tbsp (15 ml) coconut oil

½ tsp salt

1 tsp (3 g) coriander

1 tsp (3 g) ground cumin

½ tsp ground turmeric

¼ tsp cayenne

1 tbsp (4 g) parsley

Pierce the spaghetti squash several times on each side with a sharp knife, and place on a plate. Microwave on high for 8 minutes and then rotate top-side down and microwave for another 8 minutes.

Slice open the spaghetti squash, being careful of the hot escaping steam, and set aside to cool. Using a fork, lift out the seeds and discard. Scrape out the insides into a medium mixing bowl. Mash and shred until the strands are separated. Add the coconut oil, salt, spices and parsley. Combine thoroughly, serve warm.

CURRIED BUTTERNUT SQUASH AND GREENS

Add a little warmth to a cozy fall meal with hearty butternut squash and greens. This is almost a meal on its own. —KH

SERVES 4–6

1 tsp (3 g) ground turmeric

1 tsp (3 g) ground cumin

1 tsp (3 g) ground coriander

¼ tsp garam masala

¼ tsp ground ginger

¼ tsp ground cinnamon or ground cardamom

1 tsp (3 g) sea salt

1 medium butternut squash

4 tbsp (60 g) ghee, butter, or coconut oil, divided

2 tbsp (30 ml) honey

1 bunch of your favorite greens (kale, collard, chard)

2 tbsp (30 ml) water

Preheat the oven to 400°F (200°C, or gas mark 6). Grease a large baking sheet.

Combine spices and salt in a small bowl. Set aside.

Peel squash, cut in half lengthwise and scoop out the seeds. Chop into 1-inch (2.5-cm) cubes.

Melt 2 tablespoons (30 g) fat of choice in a large pot over medium heat. Add spices and temper them for 2 to 3 minutes until flavors release. Do not let it smoke. Turn off heat. Add honey to fat-spice mixture and stir to combine.

Pour chopped squash into the pot and mix until thoroughly coated. Spread evenly onto prepared baking sheet. No need to wash pot because you will use again. Bake for 15 minutes.

Flip the squash and bake another 15 to 20 minutes until squash is soft and beginning to brown.

Meanwhile, wash and chop the greens. Melt 2 tablespoons (30 g) of fat of choice in the same pot as above and sauté greens on medium heat. Sprinkle with a bit of salt to release the water in the greens for better cooking and add 2 tablespoon (30 ml) of water. If they start to stick, add a bit more water. Cook until greens are done to your liking, about 5 minutes for chard; kale and hardier greens a few minutes longer. Pour cooked squash into skillet with greens and lightly toss to combine. Serve and enjoy.

TWICE COOKED BUTTERNUT SQUASH ROUNDS

These butternut squash rounds are a tasty and fun side or snack to enjoy. The little ones will love them I'm sure. —NK

SERVES 4

1 butternut squash with a 6-inch (15-cm)-long neck

½ tsp sea salt, divided

1 tbsp (15 ml) ghee, melted

2 eggs

½ cup (60 g) arrowroot flour

1¼ cups (150 g) almond flour

2 tbsp (16 g) Pumpkin Pie Spice (page 505)

2 cups (470 g) sustainable shortening

(continued)

Preheat oven to 350°F (180°C, or gas mark 4). Line a large baking tray with parchment paper. Slice the neck off the squash, placing the rest of the squash aside to use in another recipe. Peel the neck of the neck and slice into ½-inch (1.3-cm) slices. Place butternut squash rounds on the baking tray. Sprinkle ¼ teaspoon sea salt over the squash rounds. Pour over the melted ghee. Place butternut squash in the oven and bake for 10 minutes. Remove from the oven carefully, flip the squash rounds over and sprinkle over another ¼ teaspoon sea salt over the squash. Place back in the oven and bake for another 10 minutes. Remove and allow to cool completely.

Once cooled, add eggs to a medium-sized mixing bowl and whisk. On a shallow plate place the arrowroot flour. In another shallow bowl add the almond flour and mix in the pumpkin pie spice. Place a 10- to 12-inch (25- to 30.5-cm) skillet to heat over medium heat. Add the shortening and allow it to heat up, about 3 to 5 minutes. Test the cooking fat by sticking the end of a wooden spoon in; when bubbles form around the end of the spoon the cooking fat is ready for frying. Take one butternut squash round at a time and dip into the arrowroot mixture, then into the eggs and then into the almond flour mixture. Set onto a clean plate as you go. Fry in batches for 2 to 3 minutes per side. Remove onto a paper towel-lined plate as you go. Serve warm.

HONEY SESAME YAMS

Perfectly roasted yams covered in sesame seeds and honey make for a delicious Paleo side dish. This is my go-to recipe for potluck dishes. —KH

SERVES 6–8

2 tbsp (30 ml) honey

2 tbsp (30 ml) butter or ghee, melted

2 tbsp (30 ml) coconut oil, melted

8 cups (960 g) yams, chopped into 1-inch (2.5-cm) cubes

2 tbsp (16 g) sesame seeds, raw

2 pinches of sea salt

Preheat the oven to 375°F (190°C), or gas mark 5. Combine honey, butter or ghee and coconut oil and pour over chopped yams and mix until well coated. Place yams onto a large baking sheet and bake for 10 minutes.

Remove baking sheet from oven and sprinkle sesame seeds over yams. Carefully combine seeds by using a flat spatula to flip yams. Return to oven and bake for another 40 minutes, or until yams are soft and starting to brown, turning at least once. Remove from oven and sprinkle with a pinch or two of sea salt.

CHEF'S TIP:

Maple syrup can be substituted for honey if you prefer. Also, if you prefer to not use butter or ghee, you can use 4 tablespoons (60 ml) of coconut oil instead.

BAKED DELICATA MOONS

This is my all-time favorite squash to eat. Delicata squash is smaller and easier to prepare than butternut squash, and has such a delectably sweet flavor, which I highlight here with maple syrup. —RM

SERVES 4

1 delicata squash

1 tbsp (15 ml) butter, melted

1 tsp (5 ml) grade B maple syrup, optional

Salt to taste

Ground cinnamon to taste

Preheat the oven to 400°F (200°C, or gas mark 6). Wash the skin of the squash, getting in the creases of each ridge, but don't peel. Cut off both ends and then cut longways down the length of the squash. Taking a spoon, scoop out the stringy seeds and reserve on the side. Then vertically cut ½-inch (1.3-cm) pieces, so the squash looks like crescent moons.

Line a baking sheet with parchment paper for easy cleanup. Lay out each moon, and cover with melted butter, maple syrup, salt and cinnamon. Add the washed squash seeds for a nice crunch! After making sure each side is evenly coated, pop the tray in the oven for 25 to 30 minutes, gently flipping occasionally. They should be soft in the center and lightly crisp and browned on the edges.

ARTICHOKES IN PINZIMONIO

I love when artichokes come into season. They are hands down one of my favorite vegetables! The dipping sauce is so flavorful while being so simple. I know you will love this dish as much as I do! —VM

SERVES 4

4 globe artichokes

Juice of ½ a lemon

1 cup (235 ml) olive oil

1 cup (235 ml) balsamic vinegar

1 tsp (6 g) sea salt

Prepare the artichokes by cutting off the stems and peeling off the outer layer of leaves. Submerge the artichokes in a bowl with water and lemon juice for about 10 minutes.

Once the artichokes are done soaking, place them into a large pot, submerged in water, over high heat. Bring the pot to a boil and cook for about 15 minutes. Make sure you do not overcook the artichokes. You want them to be tender, not mushy.

While the artichokes are cooking, whisk together the olive oil, balsamic vinegar and salt until everything has emulsified. Plate the artichokes with the dipping sauce in a little bowl on the side and enjoy!

SWEET TOMATO SURPRISE

Plump and juicy tomatoes filled with sausages and vegetables soften and caramelize as they bake in the oven. Eat one at any time of the day and top it with a sunny side up egg for an extra treat! —JC

SERVES 6

6 beefsteak tomatoes

2 cooked sausages, chopped

1 small green apple, chopped

1 rib celery, chopped

1 medium carrot, chopped

¼ cup (60 g) cold butter, cut into cubes

2 tbsp (16 g) raw pecans, chopped

2 tbsp (16 g) dried apricots, chopped

¼ tsp sea salt

¼ tsp black pepper

Preheat oven to 350°F (180°C, or gas mark 4).

Prepare tomatoes by slicing off the top, scooping out the seeds and the fleshy part inside each one to make it hollow. Pat inside dry with paper towels. Place the hollowed tomatoes with the bottom sides down on a 9 × 9-inch (23 × 23-cm) baking dish.

In a bowl, make the stuffing by mixing together the sausage, green apple, celery, carrot, butter, pecans and apricots. Season with sea salt and black pepper. Spoon the stuffing inside each tomato, filling it generously until it overflows.

Bake the stuffed tomatoes for 35 minutes until the tomatoes are soft and skins have blistered. Let cool for 5 minutes before serving.

ROASTED PORTOBELLO TRAY

Portobello mushrooms are very hearty and surprisingly filling. This is a good option for meatless Mondays because it's packed with colorful and nutrient dense vegetables. Enjoy it as a light meal or a side to any type of entrée. —JC

SERVES 4

4 portobello mushrooms, cut into 1-inch (2.5-cm) slices

1 pound (454 g) Brussels sprouts, cut in half

12 ounces (340 g) baby carrots

2 medium onions, quartered

Cloves from 1 head of garlic, smashed

3 tbsp (45 ml) ghee or tallow, melted

2 sprigs fresh rosemary, stems removed and leaves chopped

½ tsp onion powder

¼ tsp sea salt

Zest and juice of 2 lemons

Preheat oven to 375°F (190°C, or gas mark 5). Line a baking sheet with parchment paper.

Place the mushrooms, Brussels sprouts, carrots, onions and garlic in a single layer on the baking sheet. Drizzle with ghee and season with rosemary, onion powder and sea salt. Toss vegetables with your hands to combine. Arrange the vegetables in a single layer on the baking sheet.

Roast in the oven for 15 minutes. Flip and re-arrange the vegetables on the tray to cook the other side. Return to the oven for another 15 minutes. Turn on the broiler to low and broil for 5 to 8 minutes. Top with lemon zest and drizzle with lemon juice before serving.

END OF SUMMER RATATOUILLE

In this modified version of the original, tomatillos take the place of eggplant. This dish is meant to use the last of the summer veggies from the garden. You can add peppers, eggplants and onions too if you like. —VM

SERVES 4

2 tomatoes

2 zucchini (even the oversized ones)

2–3 tomatillos

Bell peppers, optional

Eggplants, optional

Onions, optional

Herbes de Provence

Olive oil

Sea salt

Prepare the vegetables by slicing them nice and thin. Preheat the oven to 350°F (180°C, or gas mark 4), and oil a baking dish. Layer the baking dish with the vegetables, mixing them throughout the dish.

Once you have finished lining the dish with all of the vegetables, drizzle them generously with olive oil and season with the spices. Bake the dish for about an hour and serve alongside the main dish.

PERSIAN JEWELED RICE

Inspired by the classic Persian dish Javaher Polow, which translates to Jeweled Rice, and which gets its name from its colorful ingredients that resemble jewels, this simpler version made with cauliflower rice is perfect for those following a Paleo or lower-carb template. —NK

SERVES 4

2 tbsp (30 g) ghee, divided

2 medium carrots, julienned

Zest of 1 orange

¼ cup (38 g) chopped pistachios

¼ cup (38 g) slivered almonds

1 head cauliflower processed into rice-like pieces

2 tsp (6 g) Persian spice (advieh)

Sea salt and black pepper, to taste

4 dried figs, chopped finely

Heat a small frying pan over medium heat. Add 1 tablespoon (15 g) ghee. Once heated add the carrots. Cook for 5 minutes before adding a pinch of sea salt and the orange zest. When the carrots are almost cooked through, add the pistachios and almonds, mix well. Once the carrots are done, around 5 to 7 minutes, remove from the heat and set aside.

In a large heavy-bottomed pot with a lid, heat 1 tablespoon (15 g) ghee over medium heat. Add in the cauliflower for 10 minutes. Add the advieh, sea salt and black pepper. Cook for another 5 minutes then add in the carrot mixture and chopped figs. Place a lid on the pot and lower the heat to a simmer. Cook for another 10 minutes. To serve, add a few more crushed pistachios and almonds on top.

CHEF'S TIP:
You can purchase advieh in Persian grocery stores or online.

CINNAMON AND PAPRIKA ROASTED CAULIFLOWER

Roasting vegetables is one of my favorite ways to cook them. Try this tasty roasted cauliflower with cinnamon and paprika and I'm sure you will agree. —NK

SERVES 2–4

1 head cauliflower (about 2 pounds [908 g]), cut into medium chunks

½ tsp sea salt

½ tsp ground cinnamon

½ tsp sweet Hungarian paprika

¼ tsp garlic powder

2 tbsp (30 ml) melted ghee or coconut oil

Preheat oven to 450°F (230°C, or gas mark 8). Place cauliflower chunks into a large mixing bowl and season with sea salt, cinnamon, paprika and garlic powder. Mix well. Place onto a large baking sheet lined with parchment paper. Drizzle with the melted ghee or coconut oil and bake for 20 to 25 minutes. Serve warm.

CRANBERRY ORANGE AND ALMOND CAULIFLOWER RICE

Who said cranberries can only be used to make sauces or sweets? This deliciously tangy and sweet Cranberry Orange and Cauliflower Almond Rice will have you thinking differently about those little red fruits. —NK

SERVES 6–8

2 tbsp (30 g) ghee, divided

6 ounces (168 g) fresh cranberries

Zest and juice of 1 small orange

2 tbsp (30 ml) raw honey

1 (2-pound [908-g]) cauliflower, washed, cored, diced into small florets and processed into rice-like pieces

Sea salt and black pepper, to taste

2 ounces (56 g) slivered almonds

Heat a small saucepan over medium heat. Add in 1 tablespoon (15 g) ghee. Once heated add in the fresh cranberries, orange zest and juice and raw honey. Stir to mix. Cook, stirring frequently, for 10 to 15 minutes. Remove from the heat and set aside.

Heat a large heavy-bottomed pot on medium heat. Add another 1 tablespoon (15 g) ghee. Add the cauliflower rice and mix. Cook for 10 minutes, stirring frequently. Season with sea salt and black pepper to taste. Add in the cranberry orange mixture and slivered almonds. Use a fork to fluff the cranberry mixture thoroughly. Lower the heat and cover the pot with a lid. Cook for another 5 minutes.

PERSIAN BARBERRY CAULIFLOWER RICE (ZERESHK POLOW)

Barberries are a small, tart, dried fruit used plentifully in Persian cuisine. One of the most popular dishes they are used in is called Zereshk Polow, which translates to Barberry Rice. Here I take the traditional recipe and turn it into a delicious alternative. This recipe pairs perfectly with some chicken or even fish. —NK

SERVES 4

½ cup (65 g) dried barberries, soaked in cold water for 30 minutes

3 tbsp (45 g) ghee, divided

½ tsp saffron, ground, mixed with 2 tbsp (30 ml) boiled water

1 tsp (5 ml) raw honey

1 medium head cauliflower, processed into rice-like pieces

½ tsp sea salt

¼ tsp black pepper

Drain the barberries. Place a small saucepan over medium heat. Add 1 tablespoon (15 g) ghee. Add the barberries, saffron-water mixture and raw honey. Mix and cook for a few minutes. Remove from the heat and set aside.

Place a large heavy-bottomed pot with a lid over medium heat. Add 2 tablespoons (30 g) of ghee; once heated, add the cauliflower and stir frequently for 10 minutes. Add the sea salt and black pepper. Stir to mix. Add the barberry mixture and mix again. Cover the pot with a lid and reduce the heat. Cook for another 10 minutes.

CHEF'S TIP:
You can find barberries online or at Persian grocery stores.

CURRIED CAULIFLOWER

This is one of my favorite side dishes. The roasted flavor of this spiced cauliflower pairs well with just about any meal. —KH

SERVES 4–6

1 tsp (3 g) ground turmeric

1 tsp (3 g) ground cumin

1 tsp (3 g) ground coriander

½ tsp ground ginger

¼ tsp ground cinnamon

4 tbsp (60 ml) coconut oil

1 head of cauliflower, cut into bite-sized florets

½ tsp unrefined sea salt

3–4 cloves fresh garlic, minced

Preheat the oven to 450°F (230°C, or gas mark 8).

Mix turmeric, cumin, coriander, ginger and cinnamon in a small bowl. Set aside.

Melt coconut oil on low heat in a large pot. Add spice mixture and allow spices to temper for 2 to 3 minutes on low to medium heat, stirring occasionally. Do not let it smoke. Turn off heat.

Add cauliflower, salt and fresh garlic. Mix well to thoroughly coat the cauliflower. Transfer to large baking pan and bake for 25 to 30 minutes, until golden brown, turning the cauliflower a time or two while baking.

CAULIFLOWER MASH

This cauliflower mash is a staple at our house because it's a quick and easy low carb alternative to potatoes. The coconut milk and ghee make it smooth and luxurious. This dish pairs really well with any type of grilled or roasted meat! —JC

SERVES 4

4 cups (940 ml) water

1 head of cauliflower, cut into florets

4 tbsp (60 g) ghee or bacon fat

½ cup (120 ml) Homemade Coconut Milk (page 503)

Sea salt

Place a steamer basket in a large pot. Add the water and bring to a boil. Arrange the cauliflower evenly on the steamer basket. Cover the pot and reduce heat until the water is just simmering. Let it cook for 10 to 15 minutes until the cauliflower is soft but not mushy. Remove cover and turn off heat. Let it cool for at least 10 minutes until it is no longer steaming.

Place the cooked cauliflower in a food processor or blender. Add ghee and coconut milk. Pulse until the cauliflower mash is smooth and creamy. Season with sea salt to taste. Transfer to a bowl and serve.

ROSEMARY CAULIFLOWER MASH

Cauliflower mash allows me to get in some extra veggies during my dinners while it masquerades as a starch. Very tricky! This recipe is also delicious as leftovers, unlike traditional mashed potatoes. —RM

SERVES 4

1 head cauliflower

4 large cloves garlic

1 tsp (3 g) salt

3 tbsp (45 g) butter

½ tbsp (2 g) fresh rosemary, minced

Black pepper, to taste

Cut the florets and stems of the cauliflower into medium-sized pieces, discarding the leaves and core. Place the cauliflower and whole bare garlic cloves in the steamer basket—the garlic stays whole because it will later be puréed together. Sprinkle an even layer of the salt over the cauliflower. Steam for 10 minutes or until soft. You can boil the florets until soft if you don't have a steamer, but make sure you squeeze the water out before puréeing or else the mash will be too watery.

Throw the steamed cauliflower and garlic into a food processor. Add the butter, rosemary and fresh black pepper. Mix on high until thoroughly puréed, about 5 minutes, stopping to scrape the sides down periodically. Do a taste test to see if you need more salt or pepper. Serve hot, or store covered in the fridge.

CHEF'S TIP:

For a special occasion, if you can handle dairy, try adding ½ cup (45 g) grated raw cheddar cheese. For a creamier texture, add almond milk to taste.

TRUFFLED CAULIFLOWER MASH

Mashed cauliflower is a great alternative to mashed potatoes and roasting the cauliflower adds such rich flavor to this dish. Delicious served with Pan-Seared Steak (page 37) for the ultimate comfort food meal! —CP

SERVES 6–8

1 large head of cauliflower

1 tbsp (15 ml) olive oil

4 tbsp (60 g) butter, divided

¾ tsp sea salt

¼ tsp pepper

1 cup (235 ml) Slow Cooker Chicken Broth (page 170)

2 cloves garlic, crushed

2 tbsp (30 ml) truffle oil

2 green onions, sliced

½ cup (35 g) micro greens

½ cup (50 g) Parmesan cheese shavings, optional

Preheat oven to 400°F (200°C, or gas mark 6). Cut cauliflower into small florets. Place in a baking dish and drizzle with olive oil, 2 tablespoons (30 g) butter, salt and pepper. Roast for 30 minutes, stirring halfway through.

Remove cauliflower from the oven and place in a blender along with any roasting juices. Add chicken broth and garlic. Blend until smooth.

In a small saucepan, melt remaining butter. Remove from heat and stir in truffle oil.

Scoop cauliflower mash onto plate and drizzle with truffle butter.

Garnish with green onions, micro greens and Parmesan shavings.

CAULIFLOWER WITH MUSTARD SAUCE

Cauliflower is quickly becoming everyone's new favorite side dish. With this dish the mustard sauce ends up being the highlight, well complemented by the smooth flavor of the cauliflower. —VM

SERVES 4

4 tsp (12 g) whole mustard seeds

1 tsp (3 g) ground turmeric

⅓ cup (80 ml) water

3 tbsp (45 ml) mustard oil, or avocado oil

2 cloves garlic, chopped

½ sweet onion, chopped

1 jalapeño pepper, seeded and finely chopped

5 cups (650 g) cauliflower florets

2 tbsp (12 g) whole cumin seeds

Preheat the oven to 350°F (180°C, or gas mark 4). In a coffee grinder, grind the mustard seeds to a fine powder. Mix the ground mustard with the turmeric and the water to make a smooth paste.

In a large skillet, heat the oil over high heat, adding the mustard paste, garlic, onion and jalapeño and sauté until it has turned a nice golden brown, about 3 to 5 minutes. Remove the mixture from the skillet and set aside. Add a little more oil to the skillet and sauté the cauliflower and onions until the florets have browned on all sides, about 5 to 10 minutes.

Place the cauliflower and onion mixture in a well-oiled baking dish and spread the mustard paste evenly over the florets. Sprinkle the florets with the cumin seeds and bake for 30 minutes. Make sure you check the cauliflower while it is baking so it does not burn. If it does begin to burn, add a little water to the dish.

Serve immediately while hot.

ROASTED CAULIFLOWER WITH CAPER BAGNA CAUDA

An easy and tasty side dish inspired by my childhood in Piemonte, where Bagna Cauda originates. Bagna Cauda is a very tasty combination of garlic, butter and anchovy that marries well with many meats and vegetables. —VM

SERVES 4

FOR THE CAULIFLOWER

1 head of cauliflower, chopped into florets

2 tbsp (30 ml) butter, melted

Sea salt to taste

FOR THE CAPER BAGNA CAUDA

2 tbsp (16 g) capers in salt, or capers in vinegar

3 tbsp (45 g) butter

2 cloves garlic, finely chopped

2 anchovy fillets

Preheat the oven to 400°F (200°C, or gas mark 6). Toss the cauliflower florets in the melted butter and place on a baking dish. Season with salt and roast for about 30 to 40 minutes.

While the cauliflower is roasting, soak the capers in warm water for 10 minutes. Rinse the capers and repeat one more time. If you are using capers in vinegar, just drain and add to the recipe.

Melt the butter in a small saucepan over low heat. Add the garlic and sauté slowly for about 10 minutes. Smash the anchovies and add them to the saucepan along with the capers and mix well. Cook the anchovy mixture for an additional 5 minutes and then set to the side.

When the cauliflower is finished roasting, plate the cauliflower and dress with the caper bagna cauda and enjoy!

ROASTED PARSNIP MASH WITH CARAMELIZED ONIONS

This buttery, root vegetable mash with caramelized onions and creamy goat cheese is a low-carb, healthy alternative to mashed potatoes. —CP

SERVES 6–8

2 pounds (908 g) parsnips, peeled and cubed

3 tbsp (45 ml) olive oil, divided

1 tsp (3 g) sea salt, divided

¼ tsp paprika

¼ tsp fresh cracked pepper

1 sweet white onion, finely chopped

2 cups (140 g) kale, deveined and chopped

1½ cups (355 ml) Slow Cooker Chicken Broth (page 170)

4 cloves garlic, crushed

6 tbsp (90 g) butter

2 tbsp (30 g) Dijon mustard

4 ounces (112 g) soft goat cheese, optional

Preheat oven to 350°F (180°C, or gas mark 4). Peel and cut the parsnips into small cubes. Arrange on a large baking sheet and toss together with 1½ tablespoons (23 g) olive oil and spices. Roast for 50 to 55 minutes, stirring halfway through.

While the parsnips are roasting, heat a skillet on low and caramelize the onions with the remaining olive oil and salt. Sauté for 20 minutes or until the onions are soft. Add in the kale and continue sautéing for 5 more minutes.

Once parsnips are cooked, add parsnips, chicken broth, garlic, butter, mustard and goat cheese (if using) to a blender or to a large bowl if using an immersion blender. Blend until a thick, yet creamy mixture has formed.

Add the parsnip mash to serving bowl and fold in caramelized onions and kale.

Best served hot with a side of grilled or roasted dinner sausage links.

SPICY PARSNIP HUMMUS

I wanted to make hummus similar to the kind that I enjoyed growing up. My mom's version uses a lot of garlic. I stayed mostly true to her recipe but slightly enhanced it by adding a little kick! I had her test it and she said the flavors were unbelievably close. I often serve hummus with sliced cucumber. —AV

SERVES 8

2 cups (320 g) parsnips

2 cups (480 g) tahini

3 tbsp (45 ml) lemon juice

4 cloves garlic

½ tsp sea salt

2 tbsp (30 ml) extra-virgin olive oil

1 tsp (3 g) crushed red pepper flakes

Paprika, for garnish

Bring a large pot of salted water to a boil. Add the parsnips and boil until soft, about 15 minutes. Drain the parsnips and place them into the food processor. Add the tahini, lemon juice, garlic, salt, olive oil and red pepper flakes. Purée until smooth. Taste and adjust salt accordingly. Sprinkle with a pinch of paprika for garnish.

ROASTED GARLIC PUMPKIN HUMMUS

Don't do beans? No problem! The tahini, olive oil, cumin and lemon juice give this Paleo version an authentic flavor. People will be begging for your recipe. —KH

MAKES ABOUT 2 CUPS (500 G)

1 cup (130 g) cauliflower florets

1 tsp (5 g) ghee or coconut oil

1 large head of garlic

1½ cups (375 g) cooked pumpkin purée

¼ cup (65 g) tahini

2 tbsp (30 ml) olive oil, plus more for garnish

2 tbsp (30 ml) fresh lemon juice

¼ tsp ground cumin

Sea salt, to taste

1-2 tsp (5-10 ml) honey, optional

Pinch paprika, for garnish

Preheat the oven to 400°F (200°C, or gas mark 6). Toss cauliflower florets in fat of choice and place on a baking sheet. Then cut the top half inch (1.3-cm) off of the garlic head, place into small baking dish, cut-side up, and cover. Place both into hot oven.

Bake cauliflower for 15 to 20 minutes, until soft and starting to brown a bit. Bake head of garlic for 20 to 25 minutes, until cloves are nice and soft.

Once everything is cooked, allow to cool. Gently squeeze the contents of 2 to 3 garlic cloves into food processor. Place rest of the ingredients into food processor and purée until creamy smooth. Adjust for salt and garlic, and optional honey if you like a bit of sweet. Serve with fresh veggies, your favorite crackers, or whatever else makes you happy!

ROASTED EGGPLANT & GARLIC BABA GANOUSH

Roasted eggplant replaces beans in the traditional hummus dip. Full of flavor, this dip is a great nutrient-dense snack, served with root vegetable chips or fresh vegetables. —CP

SERVES 6

1 large eggplant

8 cloves garlic, peeled

2 tbsp (30 ml) olive oil, divided

1 tbsp (15 g) butter

¼ cup (60 g) tahini

2 tsp (10 ml) lemon juice

½ tsp sea salt

¼ tsp cayenne pepper

¼ tsp paprika

Preheat oven to 400°F (200°C, or gas mark 6). Line a baking sheet with parchment paper.

Slice the eggplant in quarters, placing face down on the baking sheet with the garlic cloves. Drizzle olive oil on top and cube butter arranging throughout the baking sheet.

Roast for 30 to 35 minutes or until eggplant and garlic are soft and begin to caramelize.

Allow to cool for 15 minutes. Scoop eggplant meat out of the skins and place in a bowl with tahini, lemon and spices.

Use an immersion blender or food processor to purée until smooth. Chill in the refrigerator for 1 hour or until ready to serve.

Garnish with a drizzle of olive oil and dash of cayenne pepper and serve with root vegetable chips or fresh vegetable crudités.

CELERY ROOT PURÉE

This celery root purée is a wonderful change of pace from simple mashed potatoes. When cooked, celery root sweetens and has a delightful flavor. It is perfect paired with lamb, beef or chicken. —AV

SERVES 4

1 large celeriac root, about 2 pounds (908 g), peeled and cut into ½-inch (1.3-cm) pieces

2 cloves garlic, minced

½ cup (120 ml) Slow Cooker Chicken Broth (page 170)

¼ cup (60 g) ghee

Salt and pepper

Add the celeriac, garlic and chicken broth to a skillet with a tight-fitting lid. Turn the heat to medium. Steam the celeriac for about 20 minutes, until it is cooked through. Keep an eye on it, to make sure that the liquid doesn't run out. If it does, you can add some water. Once the celeriac is tender, add the ghee and mash the celeriac. Use an immersion blender for a more creamy consistency. Season with salt and pepper to taste.

RED PEPPER AND CARROT PURÉE

My husband thinks this is the best side dish that I have ever made and I think I agree! —AV

SERVES 4

2 red bell peppers, halved and seeded

1½ pounds (680 g) carrots, peeled and chopped

2 tbsp (30 ml) balsamic vinegar

½ tsp sea salt

¼ tsp pepper

¼ cup (60 g) butter

½ tsp sweet paprika

2 tbsp (8 g) cilantro

Preheat oven to 350°F (180°C, or gas mark 4). Place peppers on a baking sheet, cut-side down. Bake for 45 minutes or until peppers are blackened. Remove the skins. While the peppers are baking, place carrots in a large pot, cover with water and bring to a boil. Boil until carrots are soft, about 30–45 minutes. Drain carrots.

Using an immersion blender, purée the peppers, carrots, balsamic vinegar, salt, pepper, butter, paprika and cilantro. Serve warm.

SWEET CARROT AND BUTTERNUT PURÉE

This sweet carrot and butternut purée is a good alternative to regular mashed potatoes. Just add ghee and sea salt and you have a nutritious side dish packed with antioxidants such as beta-carotene and vitamin C! —JC

SERVES 4

4 cups (940 ml) water

½ pound (227 g) carrots, cut into 2-inch (5-cm) pieces

½ pound (227 g) butternut squash, cut into 2-inch (5-cm) pieces

2 tbsp (30 g) ghee or bacon fat

½ tsp sea salt

Place a steamer basket in a large pot. Add the water and bring to a boil. Arrange the carrots and butternut squash evenly on the steamer basket. Cover the pot and reduce heat until the water is just simmering. Let it cook for 15 to 20 minutes until the carrots and squash are soft and can easily be pierced with a fork. Remove cover and turn off heat. Let cool for at least 10 minutes until no longer steaming.

Place the cooked carrots and butternut squash in a food processor or blender. Add ghee and sea salt. Pulse until purée is smooth and creamy. Transfer to a bowl and serve.

RED PEPPER "HUMMUS"

This "hummus" is also a raw vegan dish, made with zucchini and cashews in place of traditional chickpeas. It's a healthy snack substitute when the afternoon munchies strike. —RM

SERVES 6

½ cup (75 g) raw cashews, unsalted

½ roasted red pepper

2½ cups (300 g) zucchini, peeled and cubed

2 tbsp (30 g) sesame tahini

1 tbsp (15 ml) olive oil

3 tsp (15 ml) lemon juice

1½ tsp (4 g) sea salt

1 large clove garlic

½ tsp cayenne pepper

Pine nuts, optional topping

Paprika, for garnish

First soak the cashews for at least an hour, and then pat dry. Place the roasted red pepper in a wad of paper towels and then squeeze any excess moisture out. Put all ingredients in a food processor and blend until fully smooth, stopping to scrape the sides down, for about 4 minutes. Garnish with pine nuts and a sprinkle of paprika. Serve with raw veggies and Paleo pita bread.

TURNIP PURÉE

If you are tired of the same old cauliflower purée and want something similar but with a sharp flavor kick, try this turnip purée. It goes great underneath a fillet of fish or roasted chicken. —HH

SERVES 4

6 large turnips

6 cloves garlic, chopped

½ tsp salt

½ tsp pepper

½ tsp oregano

2 tbsp (30 g) butter, ghee or coconut oil

Wash and peel the turnips, then chop into 1- to 2-inch (2.5- to 5-cm) pieces. Place the turnips, chopped garlic and salt in a pot and fill the pot with water until it reaches about half the height of the turnips. The water should not be covering the chopped turnips. Cover the pot and boil on medium-high heat until the turnips are soft and easily pierced with a fork, about 15 to 25 minutes, depending on the size of the turnips. Turn the heat off and remove the cover.

Add the remaining ingredients to the pot—pepper, oregano, butter. Then use an immersion blender to purée. You can also use a blender to purée the mixture, but wait about 30 minutes for the mixture to cool before blending to avoid damaging the blender.

MASHED TURNIPS WITH BACON AND CHIVES

I belong to a CSA (Community Supported Agriculture) and turnips frequently show up in my winter box. I've learned that the secret to making turnips less bitter and super tasty is a long simmer time. This recipe is a fun twist on loaded mashed potatoes. —KW

SERVES 4–6

8 cups (1200 g) chopped turnips

Bone broth or water for boiling

½ pound (227 g) bacon

2 tbsp (30 g) bacon fat

2 tbsp (30 ml) butter or ghee, melted

¼ tsp garlic powder

⅛ tsp onion powder

Sea salt and pepper, to taste

2 tbsp (8 g) fresh chives, snipped or chopped

Put diced turnips in a large pot and fill with water or bone broth. Bring to a boil and let simmer, uncovered, for at least 30 minutes or until tender. The longer you simmer, the better because the less bitter it will be. Sometimes I let them simmer for over an hour!

While the turnips are cooking, cook the bacon in a skillet over medium heat until crispy. Reserve 2 tablespoons (30 ml) of bacon grease and then crumble the bacon. Once turnips are done simmering, drain well.

Return turnips to pot and add all remaining ingredients, except the bacon and chives. Mash to desired consistency. Fold in bacon. Top with fresh chopped chives.

CAULIFLOWER HUMMUS

Who knew cauliflower can be made into hummus? This super versatile vegetable is the perfect substitute for chickpeas and a good source of Vitamins C and K and folate. Not to mention that the unsuspecting non-Paleo individual will never guess that they are eating something healthy. —JC

SERVES 4

4 cups (940 ml) water

1 head of cauliflower, cut into florets

¼ cup (60 g) tahini

3 cloves garlic

¼ cup (60 ml) extra-virgin olive oil, plus more for drizzling

Juice and zest of 1 lemon

¼ tsp red pepper flakes

¼ tsp sea salt

¼ tsp black pepper

Place a steamer basket in a large pot. Add the water and bring to a boil. Arrange the cauliflower evenly on the steamer basket. Cover the pot and reduce heat until the water is just simmering. Let it cook for 10 to 15 minutes until the cauliflower is soft but not mushy. Remove cover and turn off heat. Let it cool for at least 10 minutes until it is no longer steaming.

Place the cooked cauliflower and the remaining ingredients in a food processor or blender. Pulse for 20 to 25 seconds. Transfer to a serving bowl and drizzle olive oil on top before serving.

ROASTED CELERIAC MASH WITH PAPRIKA

Celeriac mash is a great alternative to traditional potato mash. Roasting the celeriac adds a great depth of flavor to this dish. —NK

SERVES 4

2 (1-pound [454-g]) celeriac root pieces, thick outer layer removed, diced into ¾-inch (2-cm) chunks

Sea salt and black pepper, to taste

1 tbsp (15 ml) ghee, melted

1 cup (235 ml) full-fat coconut milk

½ tbsp (4 g) sweet Hungarian paprika, plus more for sprinkling on top

1 tbsp (8 g) collagen hydrolysate, optional

Preheat oven to 425°F (220°C, or gas mark 7). Line a large baking sheet with parchment paper. Season diced celeriac with sea salt and black pepper in a mixing bowl. Add to the prepared baking sheet and drizzle with the melted ghee. Roast in the oven for 40 to 45 minutes or until fork tender, making sure to turn the celeriac halfway through.

Remove from the oven and allow to cool for 10 minutes. Add to a blender or food processor with the coconut milk. Blend until well combined and smooth. Add in the Hungarian paprika and collagen hydrolysate, if you're using it, and mix again until well incorporated. Taste to check for seasoning and adjust as needed. Sprinkle over a bit more Hungarian paprika before serving.

CARAMELIZED ONION GRAVY

I can literally eat this gravy by the spoonful without feeling guilty. Gone are the days of flour-laden gravy to create that thick texture that we all love. Caramelized onions are wonderful in providing that same texture. As an added bonus, it doesn't thin out when it gets cold! —JC

SERVES 4

2 large onions, thinly sliced

3 tbsp (45 g) ghee or bacon fat

½ cup (120 ml) Slow Cooker Chicken Broth (page 170)

¼ cup (60 ml) Homemade Coconut Milk (page 503)

Sea salt

Black pepper

In a saucepot over low heat, add the onions and ghee. Let the onions cook slowly for 35 to 45 minutes until they soften and are caramelized. Stir them every 5 minutes to prevent one side from burning and to achieve that golden brown color.

Add bone broth and simmer for 3 to 5 minutes. Remove from heat and let it cool for 10 minutes. Place onions in a blender and add coconut milk. Blend until smooth and thick. Season with sea salt and black pepper to taste. Transfer to a gravy boat before serving.

SWEET SQUASH DIP

Shake things up with this delicious sweet dip. Perfect for those holiday celebrations. —NK

SERVES 8

1 butternut squash, around 2 pounds (908 g)

½ tsp sea salt

2 tsp (6 g) ground cinnamon

2 tbsp (30 ml) coconut oil, melted

½ cup (120 ml) full-fat coconut milk

⅓ cup (80 ml) tahini

4 tbsp (60 ml) raw honey

2 tbsp (16 g) pomegranate seeds, optional

Preheat oven to 400°F (200°C, or gas mark 6). Peel, seed and dice the butternut squash into chunks. Line a large baking sheet with parchment paper. Add the diced butternut squash to a mixing bowl and add the sea salt, cinnamon and coconut oil. Stir to mix. Pour the butternut squash into the prepared baking tray and bake for 30 to 35 minutes or until the butternut squash is easily pierced with a fork.

Remove from the oven and allow to cool to room temperature. Once cooled, add the butternut squash, coconut milk, tahini and raw honey to a food processor or blender. Blend until the ingredients are well combined. Pour into a glass container with a lid and place in the fridge to cool for at least a couple of hours or overnight. When ready to serve, add the pomegranate seeds on top.

CHEF'S TIP:

Don't want to use pomegranate seeds? Try sprinkling some more ground cinnamon or Pumpkin Pie Spice (page 505) over the top of this dip instead.

SUN-DRIED TOMATO SPREAD

Sun-dried tomatoes are a staple in Italy. I remember my mom drying them in the sun on big racks when I was a kid. This spread is going to be the new favorite on Paleo bread and in Paleo Sandwiches. It is also great for a party appetizer with some Paleo crackers! —VM

MAKES 8 OUNCES (224 G)

8 ounces (227 g) sun-dried tomatoes

8 ounces (227 g) water

1 bay leaf

Extra-virgin olive oil

In a small saucepan, heat the sun-dried tomatoes in the water for about 10 minutes over low heat. Drain the tomatoes, add them to the food processor and blend them until they create a smooth paste. You can add a little water if needed as you blend.

Once the paste is smooth, even, and of a fine enough consistency, scoop the paste into a jar, placing the bay leaf on the top.

Smooth the top of the tomato paste and then add the olive oil on top, so it seals the paste from any air. Now seal the jar.

Can be stored at room temperature but make sure to refrigerate the spread once you have opened the jar.

ZESTY ITALIAN KALE CRISPS

Crunchy, savory and slightly spicy, these kale crisps are a great way to eat your vegetables in style! I like to dip these Italian flavored kale crisps in a warmed tomato sauce for a complete pizza-like flavor. —CP

SERVES 4–6

1 bunch kale

2 tsp (10 ml) olive oil

½ tsp sea salt

½ tsp dried basil

½ tsp dried oregano

⅛ tsp cayenne pepper

1 cup (240 g) marinara sauce, warmed

Preheat oven to 250°F (120°C, or gas mark ½). Line 2 baking sheets with parchment paper.

Rinse kale leaves and pat dry with a towel, making sure to remove all moisture.

Use a knife to devein the kale and then slice into 2-inch (5-cm) squares.

Drizzle in olive oil and sprinkle with spices. Use your hands to massage kale, thoroughly working in the oil and spices. Spread onto parchment-lined baking sheets, making sure none of the leaves are piled on top of each other.

Bake for 35 to 40 minutes or until leaves crisp up. Remove kale chips from the oven and set aside to cool for 3 to 5 minutes, as this will allow the chips to become more crunchy.

Serve dipped in warm marinara sauce.

SPICY SOUTHERN COLLARD GREENS

This dish is a cross between traditional collard greens and pork soup. The "lickings," or broth, is an elixir full of nutrients and healthy fat. Serve with Grain-Free Fluffy White Dinner Rolls (page 522) to make it the perfect comfort food meal. —RM

SERVES 8

2 pounds (908 g) pork for stew, cut into chunks

2 tbsp (16 g) Cajun seasoning

1 pound (454 g) collard greens, trimmed and chopped

3 tbsp (45 ml) Paleo-friendly hot sauce

2 tbsp (30 ml) apple cider vinegar

1 tsp (3 g) red pepper flakes

Grain-Free Fluffy White Dinner Rolls (page 522), for serving

Whipped Jalapeño Honey Butter (page 500), for serving

Heat a large stock pot over medium-high heat. Coat pork chunks with 1 tablespoon (8 g) Cajun seasoning. Quickly sear the pork in the stock pot until lightly browned on all sides, about 1 minute per side. Place collards on top of pork and then fill with water until the greens are submerged. Add hot sauce, apple cider vinegar, red pepper flakes and remaining Cajun seasoning. Cook for 3 hours until the pork is tender. Serve in bowls with a side of Grain-Free Fluffy White Dinner Rolls and Whipped Jalapeño Honey Butter.

CHEF'S TIP:

If you can't find Cajun seasoning at the grocery store, use a mix of garlic salt and cayenne pepper to taste.

BELL PEPPER "NACHOS"

Bell pepper nachos are not the same as the regular version, but they may be better! These bell peppers are heavily loaded with all of the delicious toppings and can be eaten by hand or sliced up and enjoyed with a knife and fork. —RB

SERVES 5

Coconut oil for cooking

1 pound (454 g) ground beef

1 tsp (3 g) paprika

1 tsp (3 g) black pepper

½ tsp salt

5 bell peppers

3 handfuls shredded cabbage

½ cup (60 g) pickled jalapeño peppers

½ cup (50 g) sliced black olives

1½ cups (350 g) pico de gallo

¼ cup (15 g) chopped cilantro

1 avocado

Heat the coconut oil in a medium skillet over medium heat. Add the ground beef, breaking apart with a spoon into chunks as it cooks. When the meat is no longer pink, about 10 minutes, remove from heat and stir in the paprika, pepper and salt. Set aside and allow to cool to room temperature.

Halve the bell peppers lengthwise and remove the seeds and white pith. Placing the pepper halves concave-side up, sprinkle the shredded cabbage evenly into them. Follow by sprinkling the cooled ground beef over the cabbage, then add the jalapeños, olives, pico and cilantro.

Halve the avocado and remove the pit. Slice widthwise and lengthwise, then scoop a spoon between the skin and flesh to separate the avocado into chunks. Finish by sprinkling over the loaded bell pepper halves.

ROASTED SALSA

This salsa has a delicious roasted flavor and is a great mild-medium level of spiciness that is suitable for most people. —HH

MAKES ABOUT 1 PINT (473 ML)

8 roma tomatoes

3 Anaheim peppers

1 small onion, cut into quarters

5 cloves garlic

Juice of ¼ lemon

1 tsp (5 ml) apple cider vinegar

2 tbsp (8 g) chopped cilantro

1 tsp (3 g) ground cumin

½ tsp salt

½ tsp pepper

Preheat the oven to 450°F (230°C, or gas mark 8). Cut the tomatoes in half and place them on a baking sheet along with the Anaheim peppers and the onion quarters. Roast for 20 to 30 minutes.

Remove tomatoes, peppers and onion from the oven and place in a bowl or pot with a cover. Leave covered for at least 10 minutes. This creates steam that makes it easier to peel the skin off of tomatoes and peppers.

Peel the skin off of the tomatoes and peppers. Remove inner seeds and membrane from the peppers. Put the garlic and onion in a food processor or blender and blend. Then add tomatoes, peppers and remaining ingredients and blend. Let cool, then store the salsa in a jar in the fridge.

FRESH MIXED SALSA

Who doesn't have a great salsa recipe? Sometimes simple is best and that's what I give you here. I hope you enjoy it as much as I do. —VM

SERVES 2

3 tomatillos

2 cloves garlic, peeled and chopped

1 heirloom tomato

1 jalapeño pepper, seeded and chopped

½ red onion

Juice of 1 lime

¼ tsp sea salt

Add all of the ingredients to a food processor and pulse until you reach the desired consistency and enjoy!

CHEF'S TIP:
Pair with the Chorizo Omelet (page 441) and the Mahi Mahi Tacos (page 105).

AVOCADO SALSA

Avocados make an appearance in this flavorful salsa making it a fun variation over traditional salsa. This avocado salsa is the perfect accompaniment to the Smoky Salmon recipe (page 100). Or if you prefer, use plantain chips for dipping. —KW

SERVES 4

2 avocados, peeled and diced

1 small red onion, finely diced

3 mild to hot peppers, seeded and finely diced

Juice of 3 limes

2 tbsp (30 ml) olive oil

2 tbsp (8 g) fresh cilantro, chopped

Sea salt and pepper, to taste

Combine all the salsa ingredients in a bowl. Place the salsa in the fridge until ready to use.

TOMATILLO AVOCADO SALSA

This salsa is bursting with amazing fresh flavors. It goes exceptionally well with all types of meat. I even use it for a salad dressing, too. —KW

MAKES ABOUT 4 CUPS (1000 G)

1 pound (454 g) tomatillos, husk removed, about 4–5 tomatillos

1 jalapeño pepper, seeds removed

½ bunch cilantro

1 medium onion

2 cloves garlic

1 avocado, seed and skin removed

1 lime, juiced

1 tsp (3 g) salt

Put everything in a high-powered blender and blend for a few minutes until puréed or to desired consistency. If you don't have a high-powered blender, make sure to at least quarter the tomatillos, onion, avocado, jalapeño, etc. before adding it to the blender. This will keep for 2 weeks in the refrigerator.

MANGO AVOCADO SALSA

This salsa is the perfect accompaniment to a lightly flavored fish, such as halibut. —AV

SERVES 4

1 mango, peeled and diced

¼ cup (40 g) red onion, chopped

1 habanero pepper, seeded and chopped

2 tbsp (8 g) cilantro, chopped

2 tbsp (30 ml) olive oil

1 tablespoon (15 ml) lime juice

1 clove garlic, crushed

Salt and pepper to taste

1 avocado, diced

Mix all ingredients in a bowl, except for the avocado. Gently toss together and then fold in avocado. This way the avocado will not get mashed. Adjust lime juice, olive oil, salt and pepper to taste. Refrigerate for 30 minutes to 1 hour prior to serving.

MANGO BASIL SALSA

Mangos are my absolute favorite tropical fruit and I love to eat this salsa by the spoonful in the summertime! This fruit salsa is a fabulous addition to your summer barbecue table and pairs well with Cajun Grilled Salmon (page 102). —CP

MAKES ABOUT 1 CUP (235 ML)

1 mango, peeled

½ cup (75 g) grape or cherry tomatoes

1 shallot

¼ cup (15 g) fresh basil, thinly sliced

1 lime, juiced

Finely chop all ingredients and add to a mixing bowl. Drizzle with lime juice and stir together.

Serve with Cajun Grilled Salmon or eat with sweet potato chips.

CHEF'S TIP:

Mangos can take a while to ripen depending on how fresh they are when you purchase them at the market. Keep a few on hand when they are in season, so you can make this salsa whenever you want!

SPICY PEAR SALSA

Sweet juicy pears meet spicy jalapeños for an explosion of flavor in this fruity salsa! The fresh fruit pairs nicely with Weeknight Shredded Pork Tacos (page 147). —CP

MAKES ABOUT 3 CUPS (709 ML)

3 green pears, slightly firm, I prefer Bartlett or Green Anjou variety

1 small red onion

¾ cup (45 g) cilantro

1 jalapeño pepper, seeds removed

3 limes, juiced

Chop all ingredients and add to a mixing bowl. Drizzle with lime juice and stir together.

Serve with Weeknight Shredded Pork Tacos or with root vegetable chips.

CHEF'S TIP:

I have found that a firmer pear works best so that your salsa is not too mushy. Make sure to wear gloves when seeding and chopping the jalapeño!

PEACH SALSA

If you want a sweet taste of summertime, be sure to try this easy Peach Salsa. Sweet juicy peaches paired with spicy jalapeños and garden fresh vegetables is a combination that you are sure to love. —KW

MAKES ABOUT 8 CUPS (1800 G)

4 peaches, peeled and diced

2 medium tomatoes, diced

2 cloves garlic, minced

1 medium red onion, finely diced

1 jalapeño pepper, finely chopped

1 lime, juiced

¼ cup (15 g) cilantro, chopped

Sea salt, to taste

Combine all ingredients in a large bowl. Keep any leftovers in the refrigerator for up to a week.

CHEF'S TIP:

To make the prep even easier, put all the whole ingredients in a food processor and pulse until desired consistency is achieved. You can leave the jalapeño seeds in or out depending on how spicy you like it.

KALE GUACAMOLE

Kale and guacamole? Yes! Trust me. You will thank me later. —KH

SERVES 4

5 leaves of kale

¼ small red onion

½ clove fresh garlic, minced, more if you like it garlicky

3 ripe avocados

2 tbsp (8 g) fresh cilantro

½ tsp sea salt

1 tbsp (15 ml) fresh lime juice

¼ tsp ground cumin

A small jalapeño pepper or a pinch of cayenne, optional, for some heat

Steam kale for about 7 to 9 minutes. Drain well and allow to cool. Once kale has cooled, process onions, kale and garlic in a food processor until smooth. Add the rest of the ingredients and process until desired consistency. Adjust with lime and salt. Enjoy!

BACON GUACAMOLE

Avocados are a good source of healthy fats, which are beneficial for heart health. This guacamole is extremely versatile and the addition of bacon will make you want to eat it by the spoonful! —JC

SERVES 6

3 large ripe avocados

3 strips cooked bacon, crumbled

1 jalapeño pepper, chopped

1 roma tomato, chopped

2 tbsp (16 g) onion, chopped

1 tsp (3 g) garlic powder

Juice of 2 limes

Pinch of sea salt

Scoop out the avocado flesh into a medium-sized bowl. Add the bacon, jalapeño, tomato, onion, garlic powder, lime juice and sea salt. Mash everything with a fork until combined. Adjust the sea salt if necessary. Serve immediately or cover and place in the fridge to chill.

PICKLED JALAPEÑOS

These pickled sliced jalapeños add a punch of flavor and spice to so many different dishes. I especially enjoy adding a few slices to salads. —KW

MAKES 4 QUARTS (3.6 L)

25 jalapeño peppers, sliced in ¼-inch (6-mm) slices

3 cloves garlic, minced

1 tsp (3 g) dried oregano

¼ tsp ground turmeric

3 tbsp (24 g) sea salt

¼ cup (60 ml) honey

2 cups (470 ml) distilled water

2 cups (470 ml) apple cider vinegar

Divide the sliced jalapeños among four 1-quart (1-l) canning jars. In a large bowl, stir together the garlic, oregano, turmeric, sea salt, honey, water and apple cider vinegar. Add the liquid mixture to each jar, completely covering the jalapeño slices. Refrigerate for at least 3 days and up to 6 months.

ISRAELI LACTO FERMENTED PICKLES

This recipe comes from my husband's grandfather, Grandpa Ruven. These are the easiest lacto fermented pickles you will ever make, and some of the best! The recipe works best when made in a ½-gallon (2-l) canning jar. —VM

SERVES 8

2 pounds (908 g) small pickling cucumbers

4–5 jalapeños peppers

6–8 cloves garlic, peeled

1 tbsp (18 g) sea salt

1 tsp (3 g) cayenne pepper

¼ cup (60 ml) apple cider vinegar

3–4 fresh grape leaves

Sterilize a jar in boiling water for about 5 minutes.

Wash the cucumbers and jalapeños. When the jar has cooled down, dry it and put the garlic cloves, salt and cayenne in the bottom. Add cucumbers and jalapeños up to 2 inches (5 cm) from the top, then add the apple cider vinegar. Fill the remaining space in jar with cold water. Close with the lid and shake a few times to mix the contents well.

Re-open the lid and stuff in grape leaves to cover the top so that the contents will not touch the lid or come in contact with air. Set your jar on the kitchen counter over a plate in case liquid overflows.

You can start checking the pickles after 5 or 6 days, they should be fully pickled, tangy, crunchy and a little spicy. Enjoy!

FERMENTED CURTIDO (SALVADORIAN SAUERKRAUT)

Curtido is like a spicy sauerkraut from El Salvador. It is usually fermented for 5 days; however, I choose to do a full ferment for maximum probiotic benefits. Curtido s typically served alongside pupusas, a ground corn patty stuffed with cheese, as a spicy palate cleanser. If you are looking for a unique gluten-free cheat meal with an added probiotic benefit, this is it! —RM

MAKES ABOUT 6 CUPS (1500 G)

2 heads of cabbage, cored

1 onion

2 carrots

2 jalapeño peppers

1 tbsp (4 g) dried red pepper flakes

1 tbsp (4 g) dried Mexican oregano

Salt according to the ratio of 3 tbsp (24 g) per 5 pounds (2.3 kg) of vegetables

Slice the cabbage into ⅛-inch (3-mm) ribbons using a mandolin, cabbage slicer or chef's knife—I strongly recommended a mandolin. Use the same setting to slice the onion. Grate the carrots with a peeler. Seed, core and chop the jalapeños. Put all the vegetables, along with the oregano and pepper flakes, into a huge bowl and mix well.

Weigh contents of the bowl on a kitchen scale. At this point, start adding the salt according to a 3 tablespoons (24 g) salt per 5 pounds (2.3 kg) of vegetable ratio. Mix the salt in slowly and evenly as you massage and pound the contents of the bowl. Continue to pound and squeeze the salted veggies for about 10 minutes to release all the water.

Transfer the contents of the bowl to a Fido type jar—a 2 l to 2.5 l jar would probably be right for this amount but it really depends on the size of your cabbage—making sure to smash the veggies down with your fist so that you have about 2 inches (5 cm) of brine covering them on the top. Seal the jar and store undisturbed in a dark place for at least 5 days if you are only worried about taste, 2 weeks if you want some probiotic benefit and 2 months if you want the ultimate probiotic benefit.

CHEF'S TIP:

Mixing the salt in evenly is just as important as getting the ratio correct. If the salt isn't evenly distributed you run the risk of having pockets of spoiled curtido. Be sure to put a rimmed plate underneath your Fido jar. Liquid is going to seep through the airlock ring as the carbon dioxide builds up, which is normal.

KIMCHI-KRAUT

A child of two worlds and two different lacto-fermentation cultures: Kimchi from Korea and Kraut from Germany! If you want a vegetarian version, skip the anchovy and fish sauce. —VM

MAKES 1 QUART (1 L)

1 head of heirloom cabbage, chopped into small pieces

¼ cup (72 g) sea salt

1 tbsp (8 g) fresh ginger, zested

3 cloves garlic, peeled

3 green onions, sliced

¼ cup (32 g) ko choo kah rhoo (Korean red pepper), or use red chili flakes

2 tbsp (30 ml) fish sauce (I use Red Boat)

2–3 anchovy fillets

½ apple (very ripe)

½ pear (very ripe)

1 sweet onion

Start by placing the chopped cabbage into a large bowl. Dissolve the salt in a cup of lukewarm water. Pour the salt water into the bowl with the cabbage and toss well. Weigh the cabbage down, submerging it in the brining liquid, and let it sit from 4 to 12 hours. Drain and rinse the cabbage from the brine and set to the side.

In a food processor add the ginger, garlic, green onions, pepper flakes, fish sauce and anchovies. Blend the mixture to a rough consistency. Add the apple, pear and onion to the food processor and purée all of the ingredients. The sugar from the fruit will feed the fermentation process naturally.

During the next part of the process make sure to wear rubber gloves as your hands might get irritated by the pepper flakes. Add the purée to the cabbage and mix well with your hands, rubbing the paste into the cabbage.

Fill a sterilized quart (1 L)-sized jar to about 2 inches (5 cm) from the top of the jar and close the lid.

Let the kimchi sit for at least 24 hours at room temperature before placing it in the fridge. You can start enjoying the kimchi after 4 to 5 days depending on the degree of fermentation you prefer. The longer you ferment it the more sour it will be. The kimchi should last a month in the refrigerator once you have opened the jar.

CRANBERRY SIDE SLAW

This is not your run-of-the-mill slaw that is drenched with goopy globs of sweet mayo. It's light, refreshing and has a hint of crunch and tanginess courtesy of the easiest vinaigrette you will ever make. Keep a jar handy in your fridge so you'll have fresh, homemade dressing whenever you need it! —JC

SERVES 2

FOR THE VINAIGRETTE
¼ cup (60 ml) extra-virgin olive oil
1 tbsp (15 g) Dijon mustard
1 tbsp (15 ml) apple cider vinegar
1 tsp (3 g) honey
¼ tsp black pepper
Pinch of sea salt

FOR THE SLAW
1 cup (90 g) green cabbage, shredded
1 cup (90 g) red cabbage, shredded
¼ cup (40 g) red onion, thinly sliced
1 rib celery, chopped
2 tbsp (16 g) sesame seeds
2 tbsp (16 g) dried cranberries

Combine vinaigrette ingredients in a jar. Cover it tightly and give it a good shake to combine and emulsify.

Prepare slaw by adding cabbages, onion, celery, sesame seeds and cranberries in a large bowl. Drizzle vinaigrette on top of the slaw. Toss lightly to combine. Serve immediately or give it a quick chill in the fridge for 20 to 30 minutes.

BEET AND CARROT CREAMY SLAW

The sweetness of the carrots and beets is accented here by a creamy and tangy dressing. A very easy and healthy recipe to make. —VM

SERVES 2

2 carrots, cut into small pieces
1 beet, cut into small pieces
½ cup (120 ml) coconut cream, or full-fat coconut milk
Juice of 1 lemon
¼ tsp cayenne pepper
¼ tsp ground cumin
Sea salt to taste

Add all of the ingredients to a food processor and blend until roughly chopped.

Season with salt to taste and enjoy!

COUNTRY SLAW

This simple slaw is an easy take on the classic Southern side dish, with a bright citrus note from the orange juice. —RB

SERVES 4

½ medium head of cabbage

½ onion

2 carrots

¼ cup (60 g) Homemade Mayonnaise (page 496)

1 tbsp (15 ml) orange juice

2 tbsp (30 ml) apple cider vinegar

1 tbsp (8 g) mustard powder

1 tsp (3 g) black pepper

½ tsp celery salt

In a food processor, shred the cabbage, onion and carrots. Work in batches if needed, then transfer to a large mixing bowl.

In a small mixing bowl, mix the mayonnaise, orange juice, apple cider vinegar, mustard powder, black pepper and celery salt. Add to the cabbage, onion and carrot mixture, combine thoroughly. Serve chilled.

AVOCADO EGG SALAD

This avocado egg salad is a perfect recipe for an on-the-go-breakfast, wrapped in lettuce for lunch, or as a quick snack. —AV

SERVES 4

10 eggs

2 ripe avocados, seeded and coarsely mashed

1 tbsp (15 g) stone ground mustard (I use Organicville)

3 tbsp (45 ml) fresh lemon juice

1 tbsp (4 g) dill, finely chopped

2 tbsp (8 g) fresh parsley, finely chopped

1 tsp (3 g) paprika

Salt and pepper to taste

Chopped tomatoes for garnish, optional

To boil the eggs, place them in a large saucepan and fill with enough cold water so the eggs are covered, at least by an inch or two (2.5 to 5 cm). Turn the burner on high and bring the eggs to a boil. As soon as the water boils, turn off the heat and let eggs sit for 8 to 10 minutes. Run the eggs under cold water immediately to stop the cooking process. Shell eggs and place in a large bowl. Add the avocado and mash with a fork, until eggs are minced and avocado is mixed in well. Add the remainder of the ingredients to the egg and avocado mixture. Mix until mixed through. Adjust salt and pepper to taste. Top with fresh chopped tomatoes if desired and serve.

DEVILED EGGS WITH PARSLEY, GREEN ONIONS & JALAPEÑO

Homemade mayo takes these classic deviled eggs to the next level. These are always the first to go at parties and potlucks. —AV

MAKES 12

12 hardboiled eggs

¾ cup (180 g) Homemade Mayonnaise (page 496)

2 tsp (10 g) stone-ground or Dijon mustard

2 tbsp (12 g) fresh parsley, minced, plus extra sprigs for garnish

2 tbsp (10 g) green onions, minced

1 small jalapeño pepper, minced

1 tsp (2 g) cilantro, fresh

Pinch cayenne pepper

¼ tsp salt

Pepper to taste

½–1 tsp (1.5–3 g) paprika, depending on how spicy you like

Slice each egg in half lengthwise. Scrape out yolks and place in a bowl. Add mayonnaise, mustard and blend together with a fork. Add the rest of the ingredients, except the paprika, and use a fork to blend until the mixture gets creamy. Spoon mixture into each egg half. Sprinkle with paprika and garnish with a sprig of parsley.

AVOCADO DEVILED EGGS

The creamy, tangy, slightly spicy filling for these avocado deviled eggs makes them perfect for every occasion, from a formal cocktail party to a quick snack. —VM

SERVES 1

2 eggs, hard-boiled

1 tsp (5 ml) chili-infused olive oil

Pinch of sea salt

Juice of ½ a lime

½ avocado

Fresh cilantro or thyme, for garnish

When the eggs are cooled, peel and cut them in half. Remove the yolks, setting them aside in a bowl. Mix the yolks with the chili-infused olive oil, salt, and lime juice until they're creamy and smooth.

Cut the avocado in half, discarding the pit. Cut the avocado into cubes inside the skin. Scoop the avocado out of the skin, and then gently mix it into the egg mixture. Once you have completely incorporated the avocado with the egg yolk mixture, fill the egg whites with generous servings of the avocado-egg mixture and sprinkle with a touch of fresh cilantro or thyme.

ALTERNATE VERSION

Once you have finished making the avocado-egg mixture, dice up the egg whites, incorporating them into the mixture making an Avocado Deviled Egg Salad. You can serve the egg salad in lettuce cups, or use as a stuffing for a hollowed out tomato.

CHEF'S TIP:
You can buy chili-infused olive oil in a specialty kitchen store, on the internet, or you can make it yourself by just soaking a cup of red chilies in a cup of olive oil for at least a week.

BACON AND BALSAMIC DEVILED EGGS

On my blog, I call these the best deviled eggs because that's what so many people have told me they are! Bacon and balsamic are the secret ingredients that transform ordinary deviled eggs into a flavorful masterpiece. —KW

MAKES 24

12 eggs, hard-boiled

5 bacon slices, cooked and crumbled

⅓ cup (80 g) Homemade Mayonnaise (page 496)

2½ tbsp (25 g) onion, finely chopped

1 tbsp (15 g) Dijon mustard

1 tsp (5 ml) balsamic vinegar

Salt and pepper to taste

Cut the eggs in half lengthwise and scoop out all the yolks. Put the yolks in a separate bowl and mash. Add the bacon, mayonnaise, onion, mustard, balsamic vinegar and salt and pepper. Stir until well combined. Spoon the mixture into the egg halves evenly.

PICKLED DUCK EGGS WITH HERBS

Pickled eggs make a wonderful anytime snack or an easy appetizer! Duck eggs are very much like chicken eggs, but richer and creamier. I like to boil my eggs only 8 minutes so the yolks are still soft. I do not use any sugar in this recipe, but the eggs will still taste great and will keep fine in the fridge! —VM

SERVES 6

2 cups (470 ml) water

1 cup (235 ml) apple cider vinegar

1 tsp (3 g) whole peppercorns

1–2 sweet onions, sliced

1 tbsp (16 g) sea salt

1 dozen duck eggs, hard-boiled

1 jar, quart (1 l) size

4–5 cloves garlic

1 bunch fresh mixed herbs (thyme, oregano, rosemary, basil)

In a small saucepan add the water along with the apple cider vinegar, peppercorns, sliced onions and salt, and bring everything to a rolling boil. When it has reached a rolling boil, take the saucepan off the heat and set to the side—this is the brining mixture.

Shell the hard-boiled eggs and place them into a large, sterile jar. Add the garlic, herbs and brining mixture to the jar, submerging the eggs entirely. Close the jar, making sure there are no air bubbles left in the jar, you can do this by gently shaking it or tapping the bottom against the kitchen counter.

Refrigerate the eggs for 2 weeks before enjoying. Once you have opened the jar of eggs they will last about 3 weeks in the refrigerator.

CHEF'S TIP:

Pickled eggs make great deviled eggs!! Use Avocado & Golden Flax Crackers (page 530) to serve.

CUCUMBER AND SALMON PINWHEELS

Impress your friends with this clean, crisp, elegant, yet simple to make appetizer. —AV

MAKES 12

1 large whole English cucumber

1 avocado, peeled and smashed

Salt and pepper

2 ounces (56 g) smoked salmon, cut into thin strips

Coconut aminos for dipping

Slice the cucumber in half lengthwise. Using a mandolin, slice the cucumber into long thin strips, lengthwise. Place the strips on a clean kitchen towel to absorb the liquid.

Smash the avocado in a small bowl, and season with salt and pepper to taste. Place one strip of cucumber on a cutting board. Place a strip of salmon on the cucumber and top it with a teaspoon (5 g) of the avocado mixture on the salmon towards the top of the cucumber. Roll up the cucumber strip and secure it with a toothpick. Chill until ready to serve.

SPICY SAUTÉED SHRIMP

This fiery little appetizer is big on spice and flavor. —AV

SERVES 4 (3 PER PERSON)

2 tbsp (30 g) ghee

12 large shrimp, peeled and deveined, tails left on

¼ tsp sea salt

⅛ tsp black pepper

¼ tsp crushed red pepper flakes

1 tsp (3 g) paprika

3 cloves garlic, minced

1 tbsp (15 ml) fresh lemon juice

2 tbsp (8 g) fresh cilantro, chopped

Heat the ghee in a large heavy-bottomed skillet, such as cast iron, over medium heat. Toss the shrimp in a bowl with the salt, pepper, red pepper flakes and paprika. Add the shrimp to the skillet. Cook, stirring frequently, until just slightly translucent inside, about 3 minutes.

Stir in the garlic and cook for an additional minute, stirring frequently, until the shrimp is opaque. Remove from the heat, stir in the lemon juice and garnish with cilantro and serve.

CHIPOTLE PINEAPPLE SHRIMP LETTUCE CUPS

This dish right here is summer in a bowl. The fresh flavors of pineapple combined with the smokiness of shrimp seasoned with chipotle peppers and adobo seasoning will create a flavor explosion in your mouth! —JC

SERVES 2

2 slices bacon, chopped

1 pound (454 g) raw shrimp, peeled, deveined and chopped into ½-inch (1.3-cm) pieces

1 red bell pepper, chopped

1 cup (160 g) fresh pineapple, chopped

1 tsp (3 g) ground chipotle peppers

1 tsp (3 g) ground adobo seasoning

1 egg, scrambled and chopped

¼ cup (25 g) green onions, chopped

1 head butter leaf lettuce

Add bacon to a skillet over medium heat. Pan-fry until crispy and golden brown. Set aside.

Keep the bacon fat in the skillet and add shrimp. Sauté until it just begins to turn pink, about 1 to 2 minutes. Add bell pepper and pineapple. Season with chipotle peppers and adobo seasoning. Sauté to cook for 2 to 3 minutes. Turn off heat and stir in the bacon, chopped egg and green onions. Let it cool for 5 to 8 minutes before serving on butter lettuce leaves.

STEAMED CHERRYSTONE CLAMS

Delicate clams simmered with aromatics such as garlic and onion are the perfect appetizer and don't take long to prepare. Soaking the clams in water with sea salt allows them to expel sand so you don't end up eating gritty clams and broth. A little bit of red pepper flakes before serving gives it just the right amount of heat. —JC

SERVES 2

2 pounds (908 g) cherry stone clams

Water

1 tbsp (15 g) sea salt

2 tbsp (30 g) ghee

6 cloves garlic, minced

1 small onion, chopped

½ cup (120 ml) vegetable broth

¼ cup (16 g) parsley, chopped

¼ tsp red pepper flakes

Place clams in a large bowl. Add water until it covers the top of the clams about an inch (2.5 cm) and sprinkle in the sea salt. Soak clams for 30 minutes to remove the sand inside each shell. Scrub the clams with a soft-bristled brush to clean the shells. Drain water and rinse the clams.

Melt ghee in a large deep pot over medium heat. Add garlic and onion and sauté for 1 minute until fragrant. Add vegetable broth and bring to a simmer. Add clams, sauté and cover to cook for 8 to 10 minutes until the shells open. Turn off heat and add parsley and red pepper flakes. Stir and spoon clams and sauce into bowls. Serve immediately.

SARDINE BOATS

These sardine boats, filled with flavors like fresh parsley, Dijon mustard and artichoke hearts, make a great appetizer or you can enjoy them as a light lunch. —NK

SERVES 2–4

1 small radicchio

2 (4¼-ounce [120-g]) cans sardines

¼ cup (15 g) fresh parsley, chopped

1 tsp (5 g) Dijon mustard

1 tsp (3 g) red pepper flakes

¼ tsp garlic powder

3 ounces (84 g) artichoke hearts, chopped

Sea salt and black pepper to taste

Juice of half a small lemon

Remove the outer leaves of the radicchio. Then remove four of the larger leaves and split those in half so you have eight smaller leaves or boats. Set aside. In a medium-sized mixing bowl, mash the sardines. Add the fresh parsley, Dijon mustard, red pepper flakes, garlic powder, artichoke hearts, sea salt and black pepper. Squeeze the lemon juice over and mix. Fill each radicchio boat with the sardine filling and enjoy fresh.

SHRIMP & COLD CUCUMBER MOUSSE

This is a quite new and unusual way to prepare cucumbers, but you will love it, especially in the summer when the body is craving refreshing foods. The shrimp adds just the right amount of flavor and healthy protein to make it a meal! —VM

SERVES 4

2 large cucumbers

2 shallots, thinly sliced

16 ounces (480 ml) Slow Cooker Chicken Broth (page 170), cold

12 ounces (355 ml) coconut milk, unsweetened

Sea salt and black pepper to taste

16 shrimp, pre-cooked and shelled

1 tsp (3 g) sweet paprika

1 bunch chives, finely chopped

Peel the cucumber and slice it length-wise. Remove the seeds and cut into bite-size pieces. Add the cucumber to a food processor along with the shallots, chicken broth, coconut milk and salt and pepper, and blend it all into a nice purée. Place the purée in the refrigerator for about an hour while you prepare the shrimp.

Shell and dry the shrimp, seasoning with the sweet paprika and a pinch of salt.

Take the purée from the refrigerator and blend one more time in the food processor.

Serve the purée in nice little bowls, garnishing with the chives and shrimp. Enjoy!

CRAB–STUFFED ZUCCHINI

Zucchini makes a great vessel for just about anything, including crab! This recipe makes a really good appetizer for a party or any other occasion. —VM

SERVES 4

3 large zucchini

3 small sweet onions, thinly sliced

2 tbsp (30 ml) olive oil

8 ounces (227 g) tomatoes, chopped and juice drained

4 ounces (112 g) crabmeat, canned or fresh

1 small bunch of parsley, finely chopped

Sea salt and black pepper to taste

Preheat the oven to 350°F (180°C, or gas mark 4). Blanch the zucchini in boiling water for about 4 to 5 minutes. Drain the zucchini from the water and let cool.

Sweat the sliced onions in a saucepan with the olive oil over low heat for about 5 minutes. Add the tomatoes and cook for another 5 minutes. Next add the crab, parsley, salt and pepper. Mix well and then turn off the heat.

Cut the zucchini in half. Form boats by carefully scooping out the meat. Add the meat from the zucchini to the crab and mix well. Place the zucchini boats on a greased cookie sheet, filling them with the crab mixture.

Bake the zucchini boats for 15 to 20 minutes and serve.

TUNA-STUFFED AVOCADOS

If you like fresh tuna and avocado, this is a marriage made in heaven. The best part about it is how easy it is to make when you are just too busy to do anything else. —VM

SERVES 4

1 (5-ounce [140-g]) can tuna

2 large ripe avocados

1 rib of celery, diced into small pieces

1 egg, hard-boiled

Juice of 1 lemon

1 shallot, finely chopped

2 tbsp (30 g) Homemade Mayonnaise (page 496)

4 Kalamata olives, finely chopped

Sea salt & black pepper to taste

Avocado & Golden Flax Crackers (page 530), optional, for serving

Open the can of tuna and drain the liquid, scooping it into a mixing bowl. Smash the tuna with a fork until you get the desired level of chunkiness. Cut the avocados in half, then separate the flesh from the skin with a spoon, being careful to keep the skin intact so it can be used as a small cup.

Cut the avocado flesh in very small cubes and add to the tuna. Add the remaining ingredients to the avocado and tuna, mixing thoroughly.

Once you have finished mixing the ingredients together, spoon the mixture into the avocado skins and refrigerate for an hour before serving.

I recommend pairing this with my Avocado & Golden Flax Crackers, making for a very tasty combination.

TUNA TARTARE WITH HOMEMADE MAYONNAISE

If you love fresh tuna, you will really enjoy this recipe. It makes for a great appetizer at any party or Sunday brunch. —VM

SERVES 4

5 cloves garlic

2 egg yolks

Sea salt and black pepper to taste

Juice of 3 lemons, divided

½ cup (120 ml) extra-virgin olive oil

1½ pounds (680 g) tuna fillet, sashimi grade

1 green bell pepper

4 shallots

1 small bunch of chives

12 cherry tomatoes

12 green olives, pitted

Start by making the garlic mayonnaise. Add the garlic, egg yolks, a pinch of salt and a teaspoon of lemon juice to the food processor. Begin to blend the mixture while slowly adding the olive oil at the same time. Keep blending until you have added all of the olive oil, and a mayonnaise is formed. Set aside.

For the Tuna Tartare, pat the tuna dry with a towel. Cut the fillet into small, ½-inch (1.3-cm) cubes and place in a bowl along with the remaining lemon juice, a pinch of salt and pepper. Mix well. Place the tuna in the refrigerator for about 10 minutes while you move on to the other ingredients.

Clean and dice the bell pepper, shallots and chives. Add the vegetables to the tuna and mix well.

Form the tartare into little towers on serving plates with the aid of a cup.

Decorate the tartare with cherry tomatoes and olives, and serve with a side of garlic mayonnaise.

BACON-WRAPPED SHRIMP DATES

Sweet and savory meets seafood. This simple finger food recipe makes for elegant hors d'oeuvres at any party. —RM

SERVES 6

Bamboo skewers

12 slices of thick cut bacon

6 Medjool dates, pitted and quartered

2 dozen medium uncooked shrimp, peeled and deveined

Cajun seasoning

Soak the bamboo skewers in water for an hour, ensuring the ends don't brown too much when broiling the shrimp.

Then lay the bacon strips on a baking sheet and broil them in the oven for about 5 minutes. You want the bacon to be cooked but still pliable (not crispy). Remove from oven and cut in half. Save the rendered bacon fat for later use.

Cut the dates in half, longways, and remove the pits. Then cut them in half again, quartering them so that it's a long skinny strip. Season the shrimp with Cajun spice, to taste. Pair a date strip with one shrimp. Wrap a bacon slice around it, then skewer it at the seal.

Once assembled, lay the skewers back on the baking sheet and broil for 4 minutes on each side, until the shrimp is cooked and the bacon is crispy.

BACON-WRAPPED JALAPEÑOS STUFFED WITH CASHEW "CHEESE"

These stuffed jalapeños are the first to go at any tailgating party. Spicy jalapeños are stuffed with a tangy nut cheese and then wrapped in bacon and baked to perfection. —RM

SERVES 4

Mini skewers or tooth picks

10 slices of sugarless bacon

10 jalapeño peppers

Jalapeño Cashew "Cheese" Spread (page 508)

Soak the wooden skewers in water so they become more flame-retardant. Preheat the oven at 375°F (190°C, or gas mark 5). Line a baking sheet with parchment paper.

Layer the bacon on the baking sheet and cook for about 10 minutes until semi-cooked and pliable, not crispy. Remove from oven and cut bacon into two halves. Keep the oven on.

Slice each jalapeño down the middle, scraping away some of the membrane and seeds depending on how spicy you like your peppers. Fill each jalapeño half with Jalapeño Cashew "Cheese" Spread. Wrap the bacon around each stuffed jalapeño half, securing with a wooden skewer. Place on a baking sheet and bake for 15 minutes. The bacon should be crispy and the jalapeño just starting to wilt. Serve immediately.

CHEF'S TIP:

The longer you bake the Jalapeño Cashew "Cheese" Spread, the more it tends to dry out. Though not as creamy or visually appealing as dairy cream cheese, it still packs addicting flavor. I bet you can't eat just one!

MAPLE BACON GLAZED BEETS

I like to tell people who don't like beets to please give this recipe a try. I've converted many beet haters into actually enjoying beets and asking for seconds from this recipe. —KW

SERVES 4

8 medium-sized beets, peeled and tops cut off

3 tbsp (45 ml) bacon fat, melted

1 tbsp (15 ml) pure maple syrup

Preheat oven to 400°F (200°C, or gas mark 6). Slice the beets into ¼-inch (6-mm) slices or you can dice them in ½-inch (1.3-cm) pieces. Place the sliced beets on a parchment-lined baking pan. Pour melted bacon grease over the beets and toss, making sure both sides are well coated. Drizzle the maple syrup over the top of the beets. Bake for 50 minutes to 1 hour or until beets are well roasted.

CHEF'S TIP:

Depending on how salty the bacon grease is, you probably won't need any extra salt. It's best not to salt them until you've tried them after they've baked. If they need more salt, sprinkle some on top.

BACON AVOCADO CUPS WITH BALSAMIC GLAZE

This is one of the most raved about recipes on my blog with over 200 positive reviews! Give them a try and you'll quickly learn why. —KW

SERVES 2–4

2 avocados

Fresh lemon slice

4 slices of bacon, cooked

3 tbsp (45 g) butter

1 tbsp (15 ml) balsamic vinegar

1 tsp (3 g) minced fresh garlic

Cut the avocados in half lengthwise and remove the pits. Rub the insides of the avocado with a few drops of lemon juice from a fresh lemon slice. If you are eating these right away, you can leave out the whole lemon part. The lemon just helps keep the avocado from turning brown. Crumble the bacon and stuff it into the avocado half where the pit was—use one piece of bacon per avocado half.

Over low heat, melt the butter, balsamic and garlic. Stir constantly for about a minute or two until the mixture is boiling. As soon as it boils, remove from heat and drizzle all over the avocado halves.

ROASTED ASPARAGUS AND BACON

Roasted asparagus makes a simple and elegant Paleo side dish. I like to add a bit of chopped bacon to make it even better. —KH

SERVES 4

1 bunch asparagus

1½ tbsp (23 ml) butter, ghee or coconut oil, melted

Sea salt, to taste

3 slices cooked bacon, chopped into tiny pieces

Preheat the oven to 425°F (220°C, or gas mark 7). Trim off tough ends of the asparagus and arrange in a single layer on baking pan. Drizzle with fat of choice and roll the spears to evenly coat. Roast for 10 to 15 minutes, depending on how thick your spears are, until tender but still crisp. Sprinkle with a bit of sea salt and bacon pieces. Serve and enjoy.

RED CABBAGE WITH BACON

I love cooking sautéed red cabbage with apple cider vinegar and bacon as a side for my Polish sausage. It's so simple to make, and the leftovers get better with time. —RM

SERVES 4

4 slices of bacon, cut in ½-inch (1.3-cm) pieces

½ white onion, diced

Salt and pepper to taste

½ head of red cabbage, medium-sized (sliced thinly)

1 tbsp (15 ml) apple cider vinegar

1½ tbsp (23 ml) maple syrup

½ cup (120 ml) chicken stock

1 tbsp (15 g) whole grain mustard

First, slowly fry the bacon bits over medium-low heat in a large deep skillet. Once the bacon is almost crispy, and you have rendered most of the bacon fat, raise the heat to medium and add the onions. Add salt and pepper and then sauté for about 4 minutes until translucent. Add the sliced cabbage and more salt and pepper to the pan.

Sauté, adding the apple cider vinegar and maple syrup as you toss. Once the cabbage has started to wilt, about 4 minutes, then add the chicken stock and grain mustard, mixing thoroughly. Seal the lid on the skillet and reduce heat to a low simmer for 30 minutes, stirring occasionally. The cabbage should be lighter in color and tender, but not mushy when done.

SAUSAGE AND BACON MUSTARD GREENS

One of my all-time favorite dishes, these greens are full of nutrients and will keep you satiated longer. Mustard greens have a unique taste and make for delicious leftovers. —RM

SERVES 4

6 slices bacon

½ pound (227 g) Andouille sausage (or your own preference)

1 tbsp (15 g) butter

1 pound (454 g) mustard greens, stemmed and chopped

½ cup (120 ml) chicken stock

1 tsp (3 g) red pepper flakes

Salt and pepper to taste

Fry the bacon in a deep sauté pan over medium heat. Once crispy, remove bacon to dry on a paper towel. In the same pan, fry the sausage over medium heat until fully cooked. Cut sausage into ¼-inch (6-mm) slices when done. Place on the side with the bacon.

Add 1 tablespoon (15 g) butter to the bacon and sausage grease in pan, then slowly add the greens tossing as you go so that they are fully coated in fat. Add the chicken stock and red pepper flakes to the greens. Add salt and pepper to taste.

Sauté over medium heat for 10 minutes until the greens are fully wilted and have a dark green color. Add the sausage chunks to the greens and then serve hot immediately. Sprinkle bacon pieces on top.

BACON CHICKEN LIVER PÂTÉ

Coarsely ground and rustic, this pâté features chicken liver, bacon, mushrooms and herbs. —RB

SERVES 14

½ pound (227 g) bacon

1 onion

4 cloves garlic

½ pound (227 g) mushrooms (I like a combination of oyster and chanterelle)

2 pounds (908 g) chicken livers

12 tbsp (355 g) butter

½ tsp salt

½ tsp black pepper

Leaves from ½ bunch parsley

Parsley and mushrooms for garnish

Carrot slices for serving

Roughly chop the bacon and fry in a large skillet over medium heat until lightly browned.

Coarsely chop the onion and garlic, then add to the bacon and cook until the onions are softened and lightly browned, about 10 minutes. Chop the mushrooms and add to the bacon mixture, then add the chicken livers. Cook, stirring occasionally, until the livers are cooked through but still slightly pink inside, 8 to 10 minutes.

As the livers cook, add the butter, a few tablespoons (30 to 45 g) at a time. Remove the skillet from the heat and season the livers with the salt and pepper. Allow the mixture to cool enough to handle.

Transfer the mixture to a food processor and pulse 3 to 4 times, just until a coarse paste is achieved. Stir in the parsley. Line a loaf pan with plastic wrap and scrape the chicken liver mixture into the pan. Cover with plastic wrap and refrigerate until the butter solidifies, at least several hours and preferably overnight.

Turn the pâté out onto a serving plate, distribute the parsley leaves and mushrooms over the top, and serve chilled.

PROSCIUTTO AND CASHEW "CHEESE" STUFFED MUSHROOMS

Cheesy mushroom caps are stuffed and baked with salty prosciutto. Double (or triple) this recipe for the perfect hors d'oeuvre party platter, or enjoy them as an easy gourmet dinner appetizer. —RM

SERVES 3

1 tbsp (15 ml) extra-virgin olive oil, plus more for greasing and drizzling

2 slices of prosciutto, chopped

½ tbsp (4 g) garlic, minced

1½ tbsp (6 g) chopped Italian parsley

⅓ cup (35 g) Jalapeño Cashew "Cheese" (page 508)

10 medium sized mushrooms

Pepper, to taste

Ground flaxseed, optional

Preheat the oven to 425°F (220°C, or gas mark 7). Heat the olive oil in a small skillet over medium-low heat. Lightly fry up the prosciutto for 4 minutes and then add the minced garlic. Sauté for 2 more minutes and then empty the contents of the skillet into a mixing bowl. Add the fresh parsley and cashew "cheese" to the bowl, mixing into a crumb-like consistency. Rinse any dirt from each mushroom and then break off the stems. Stuff each mushroom cavity with the cheese mixture. Lay the mushrooms stuffed-side up in a glass baking dish greased with olive oil. Lightly drizzle more olive oil on top of each mushroom. Top with freshly grated black pepper. Bake for 13 to 15 minutes or until mushrooms are soft. Serve hot.

Optional: Top each mushroom with ground flax seed before drizzling with oil as a grain-free bread crumb substitute.

GRILLED ENDIVE WITH PROSCIUTTO

Endive is always an impressive vegetable to make a dish with. Adding delicious prosciutto to this vegetable really highlights its flavors. Serve this as an appetizer or a side dish. —VM

SERVES 4

4 whole endive

2 tbsp (30 g) butter

8 slices of prosciutto di Parma

Sea salt and black pepper to taste

Preheat the oven to 350°F (180°C, or gas mark 4).

Rinse the endive and remove the outer leaves as well as the base. Place the endive into a steamer and steam for about 30 minutes, then let cool.

Once they're cool, cut the endives in half lengthwise and place a slice of butter on each half. Wrap each endive in prosciutto and place on a greased baking dish. Sprinkle with salt and black pepper. Bake the wraps for 15 to 20 minutes until the prosciutto is nice and crispy.

Serve as an appetizer or a tasty side to your favorite dish.

GRIDDLED WATERMELON AND PROSCIUTTO SPEARS

Here succulent watermelon is grilled with slices of salty prosciutto. Top the skewers off with fresh basil for a gourmet summer appetizer. —RM

SERVES 8

20 small wooden skewers

40 small seedless watermelon cubes

4 ounces (112 g) all-natural prosciutto

Handful of fresh basil, cut in strips

Thread each skewer with two pieces of watermelon and two small pieces of prosciutto, alternating between each. Use a griddle or flat skillet on the stove to sear each side of the watermelon skewers, about 1 minute on each side. If you need to use a drizzle of olive oil to keep them from sticking then do so, but I was able to sear them on a dry non-stick surface.

After removing from the heat, take a sliver of fresh basil and spear it on each skewer end while they are still hot. These babies taste good hot or at room temperature and are perfect for passing out at parties.

CHEF'S TIP:

Watermelon tends to release its juices when stored for a long time, so I prefer to make these fresh before consumption.

CASHEW, ROSEMARY PROSCIUTTO-WRAPPED DATES

Sweet and savory bites are always my favorite and this simple dish is a crowd pleaser for sure! Pop a few into the oven while preparing the rest of your meal for a tasty appetizer. —CP

SERVES 4

8 medjool dates

¼ cup (60 g) raw cashew butter

1 tsp (3 g) fresh rosemary, chopped

4 slices prosciutto

½ tsp smoked sea salt flakes

Preheat oven to 375°F (190°C, or gas mark 5).

Use a knife to make a thin slit in the dates, removing the pits and discarding.

Stuff a small amount of cashew butter into each date and sprinkle with a pinch of chopped rosemary.

Slice the prosciutto in half lengthwise into 1- to 2-inch (2.5 to 5-cm) strips, then tightly wrap a slice around each date.

Bake for 10 to 12 minutes or until prosciutto starts to turn crispy and golden brown. Remove from the oven and garnish with smoked sea salt flakes.

Serve warm and enjoy!

SWEET AND SPICY BACON CANDY

It's true that bacon makes everything taste good, but how about taking it to the next level by making sweet and spicy candied bacon? Sweet, savory and insanely delicious! Serve this at your next potluck and watch your guests go crazy over them. —JC

SERVES 8

¼ cup (50 g) coconut sugar

1 tsp (3 g) cayenne pepper

1 tsp (3 g) black pepper

8 pieces thick-cut bacon

Preheat oven to 375°F (190°C, or gas mark 5). Line a baking sheet with two pieces of parchment paper on top of each other. This is very important for easy cleanup since the coconut sugar hardens immediately as it cools.

In a small bowl, combine coconut sugar, cayenne pepper and black pepper. Lay down the bacon on a separate piece of parchment paper. Sprinkle ¼ teaspoon of the coconut sugar mixture on one side and spread it to coat the entire surface of the bacon. Flip to the other slide and spread another ¼ teaspoon of the coconut sugar mixture. Place coated bacon on the baking sheet and repeat for the remaining bacon strips. Bake it in the oven for 20 to 25 minutes. Remove from the oven and place the candied bacon on a parchment-lined plate. Let it cool for 10 to 15 minutes before serving.

SPICED SWEET POTATO APPLE FRUIT LEATHERS

These fall-flavored homemade fruit leathers are easy to make and can be taken with you on the go. —KH

SERVES 8–10

3 medium sweet potatoes

3 apples

½ tsp ground cinnamon

¼ tsp ground ginger

Pinch of ground cloves

A few scrapes of whole nutmeg

Preheat the oven to 400°F (200°C, or gas mark 6). Cut sweet potatoes in half. Peel and core apples and place both into a baking dish. Cover and bake for 30 minutes. Carefully remove apples and return sweet potatoes to oven, covered, and bake another 20 minutes, until completely soft. Allow to cool a bit.

Gently peel the skin from the sweet potatoes and place into food processor. Add the apples and spices. Purée until completely smooth. Cover mesh screens with parchment paper and pour mixture on top. Spread evenly until it is about ¼-inch (6-mm) thick. Dehydrate until no longer sticky and has a smooth surface, about 12 to 24 hours, depending on your dehydrator.

PIÑA COLADA GUMMY SNACKS

Gummy snacks are a great way to incorporate gut-healing gelatin into your diet. This recipe can be used with just about any fruit or berry combo to create endless variations. —KH

MAKES 64 (1-INCH [2.5-CM]) SQUARES

1 (13.5-ounce [378-g]) can full-fat coconut milk

1½ cups (240 g) chopped pineapple—fresh, frozen or canned; defrost first if using frozen

3-4 tbsp (45-60 ml) honey

4 tbsp (32 g) gelatin

In a blender, purée coconut milk and pineapple until smooth. Heat mixture in a medium pan to a very gentle boil. Continue to simmer for about a minute. Turn off heat. Whisk in honey and then the gelatin 1 tablespoon (15 ml) at a time. Continue to whisk until gelatin is completely dissolved. Pour into a 8 × 8-inch (20 × 20-cm) baking dish or any cute molds you may have. Place in fridge to set, at least 2 hours.

CHEF'S TIP:

Pineapple contains a naturally occurring enzyme called bromelain that inhibits gelatin from setting. Bromelain is broken down by the cooking process, so be sure to bring the mixture to a boil and cook for at least a minute. Your gummies will not set if you skip this step.

SUPERFOOD CITRUS AND PINEAPPLE GUMMIES

These Citrus and Pineapple Gummies offer a perfect combination of sweet and sour flavors. They taste like candy, but are packed with nutrients! —AV

SERVES 8

1 cup (235 ml) fresh-squeezed orange juice

¼ cup (60 ml) fresh-squeezed lemon juice

Juice of 1 lime

3-4 tbsp (24-32 g) gelatin

2 tsp (10 ml) honey

½ cup (83 g) pineapple, chopped into ½-inch (1.3-cm) cubes

Combine orange juice, lemon juice, lime juice, gelatin and honey in a saucepan. Whisk until there are no lumps. Heat over low until the mixture is warm, but not boiling. Stir constantly. This step takes about 5 minutes. Pour the mixture into a glass dish. Allow it to sit out on the counter to cool for about 5 to 10 minutes. Add the chopped pineapples. Place the dish in the freezer to firm up for about 15 minutes. Store in the fridge. Enjoy straight out of the container or cut into bite-size pieces!

CHEF'S TIP:

For more of a traditional Jell-O consistency use 3 tablespoons (24 g) of gelatin. If you want it to be a little harder, more like candy, then use 4 tablespoons (32 g).

RASPBERRY ROSE GUMMIES

What could be more delightful to eat than a rose-scented and colored sweet like this? —NK

SERVES 6

1 cup (125 g) fresh raspberries

1½ cups (355 ml) full-fat coconut milk

4 tbsp (60 ml) maple syrup

1 tsp (5 ml) rose water

4 tbsp (32 g) powdered gelatin

Place raspberries into a blender and blend until well mixed. Pour raspberry mixture through a fine mesh sieve, placed over a mixing bowl and use a wooden spoon to extract as much juice as possible. Set the bowl aside.

Heat a saucepan on medium-low heat and add the coconut milk. Heat until warm but not boiling. Add the raspberry juice and maple syrup, mix to combine. Remove from the heat and stir in the rose water. Place the mixture into a clean blender and add the gelatin. Quickly blend for 30 seconds, so that everything is well mixed. Pour mixture into an 8-inch (20-cm) square glass dish. Place in the fridge to set for 2 to 3 hours. Remove from the fridge and cut into squares before serving.

CHEF'S TIP:
Use the raspberry mixture left over in the sieve as a spread.

MACA AND CACAO NIB GUMMIES

Want to add more gelatin to your diet? Try making these gut-friendly Maca and Cacao Nib Gummies for a delicious way to do so. —NK

SERVES 8–10

6 tbsp (48 g) gelatin powder

½ cup (120 ml) cold water

13½ ounces (378 g) full-fat coconut milk

¼ cup (60 ml) raw honey

⅓ cup (40 g) maca powder

3 tbsp (24 g) cocoa nibs

Sprinkle the gelatin over the cold water in a measuring cup, let sit for 5 minutes. Heat coconut milk in a medium saucepan over medium-low heat. Add the raw honey and stir. Stir the coconut milk making sure it doesn't come to a boil. Add the gelatin mixture to the milk and stir until dissolved. Remove from the heat and pour into a blender. Add the maca powder and blend until well combined. Stir in the cocoa nibs then pour into a silicone mold with 30 squares. Place in the fridge and allow to set for 1 to 2 hours. Keep any leftovers in a sealed glass container for up to a week.

BLINIS

There are different variations of the dainty blini where it can be made smaller than a pancake or as thin as a crepe. It is versatile enough to be paired with an endless variety of toppings that can range from sweet to savory and simple to elegant. Make these for Sunday brunch and top them with anything that your heart desires. —JC

SERVES 2

2 tbsp (16 g) almond flour

1½ tbsp (12 g) coconut flour

⅛ tsp baking soda

⅛ tsp sea salt

1 large egg

½ cup (120 ml) Date-Sweetened Almond Milk (page 502)

3 tbsp (45 g) butter or ghee, softened, divided

TOPPINGS SUGGESTIONS

Smoked salmon with coconut cream and chives

Pesto sauce with sun-dried tomatoes

Mashed avocado and crushed bacon

Sift together almond flour, coconut flour, baking soda and salt in a bowl to remove any lumps.

In another bowl, add the egg, almond milk and 1 tablespoon (15 g) of butter. Whisk until frothy. Slowly add the dry ingredients to the egg mixture. Whisk gently until combined. Let it stand for 5 minutes to let the flours get absorbed into the liquid.

In a small skillet over medium-low heat, spoon 2 tablespoons (30 ml) of batter into the middle. Swirl it around the skillet to ensure a thin and even layer. Let it cook for 1 minute. Flip and cook the other side for another minute. Fold into thirds and set aside on a serving plate. Repeat the same steps to make the rest of the blinis.

Generously spread the remaining butter on each blini. Add your choice of toppings.

CRANBERRY APRICOT GRANOLA

The word granola automatically brings about images of oats, a handful of nuts and a few pieces of dried fruit covered in a sweet sugary substance (read: high fructose corn syrup) and marketed as a healthy breakfast staple. This nut and seed blend is the perfect alternative to store-bought granola and can also be enjoyed as a pre-workout snack. Make sure you look for dried fruit sweetened with fruit juice instead of sugar. —JC

SERVES 24

1 pound (454 g) raw walnuts, roughly chopped

1 pound (454 g) raw sliced almonds

1 cup (150 g) raw pecans, roughly chopped

1 cup (150 g) raw pumpkin seeds

1 cup (150 g) raw sunflower seeds

1 cup (235 ml) coconut oil, melted

½ cup (120 ml) grade B maple syrup

1 tbsp (15 ml) vanilla extract

1 tbsp (8 g) ground cinnamon

1 cup (85 g) unsweetened shredded coconut

1 cup (145 g) dried cranberries

1 cup (130 g) dried apricots, roughly chopped

Preheat oven to 275°F (140°C, or gas mark 1). Line two baking sheets with parchment paper.

In a large bowl, add walnuts, almonds, pecans, pumpkin seeds and sunflower seeds. In a smaller bowl, add coconut oil, maple syrup, vanilla extract and cinnamon. Whisk to combine. Pour the coconut oil and maple syrup mixture over the nuts and seeds. Mix until well combined.

Divide the granola between the two baking sheets and spread them into a single layer. Bake for 20 to 25 minutes and check every 10 minutes to stir the granola and even it back out on each baking sheet. This prevents the granola from burning on one side.

Remove from the oven and add the coconut flakes, cranberries and apricots on top. Stir and let the granola cool completely for 30 to 40 minutes. Store in a glass container.

NUT-FREE GRANOLA

Paleo granola is mostly made out of nuts and for those who have nut allergies or are just limiting their nut consumption, a nut-free option is desirable. Pumpkin and sunflower seeds are the perfect crunchy alternative! —JC

SERVES 8

1 cup (150 g) pumpkin seeds

1 cup (150 g) sunflower seeds

2 tbsp (30 ml) coconut oil, melted

2 tbsp (30 ml) honey

1 tsp (5 ml) vanilla extract

¼ cup (20 g) unsweetened shredded coconut

¼ cup (30 g) cacao nibs

¼ cup (36 g) dried cherries, chopped

Preheat oven to 275°F (140°C, or gas mark 1). Line a baking sheet with parchment paper.

In a large bowl, add pumpkin and sunflower seeds. In a smaller bowl, add coconut oil, honey and vanilla extract. Whisk to combine. Pour the mixture over the pumpkin and sunflower seeds. Mix until well combined.

Spread the granola into a single layer on the baking sheet. Bake for 20 minutes and stir the granola to even it back out. Bake for another 10 minutes.

Remove from the oven and add shredded coconut, cacao nibs and dried cherries. Stir and let the granola cool completely for 30 to 40 minutes. Store in a glass container.

ROASTED CHESTNUTS WITH THYME BUTTER

Roasted chestnuts are a delightful treat during the colder months. Pair them with some butter and fresh thyme and you have a great snack to nibble on. —NK

SERVES 6–7

1 pound (454 g) fresh chestnuts

1 tsp (5 ml) walnut oil

⅓ cup (80 ml) water

2 tbsp (30 g) butter

3 tsp (4 g) chopped fresh thyme

Sea salt, to taste

Using a paring knife, score an X in the flat side of each chestnut, making sure not to cut into the chestnut meat. Toss the chestnuts with the walnut oil. Heat a 10- to 12-inch (25- to 30.5-cm) skillet with a lid over medium-low heat. Once the skillet is hot add the chestnuts and cover the skillet with a lid. Cook for 15 to 20 minutes, making sure to stir the chestnuts on a frequent basis. Add the water to the skillet then cover again and cook for around 5 to 8 minutes, stirring frequently until the water has evaporated and the chestnuts have softened. Remove from the heat. While the chestnuts are still warm peel and set aside.

Wipe dry any excess water in the skillet. Add the butter and allow to melt until frothing. Add in the fresh thyme and sea salt and mix. Quickly stir in the roasted chestnuts and coat with the butter. Serve warm.

CHEF'S TIP:

You can also roast the chestnuts in the oven. Preheat oven to 400°F (200°C, or gas mark 6). Again score an X into each chestnut, making sure not to cut through the meat. Roast in a baking tray for around 20 to 30 minutes or until the shells are splitting apart. Remove from the oven and allow to cool slightly before peeling.

PAPRIKA BUTTER FRIED ALMONDS

Dress up your almonds! These fried crunchy nuts will have you munching away! I love to make these on game days as a spicy snack mix for everyone to enjoy. —CP

MAKES 2 CUPS (300 G)

2 tbsp (30 g) butter

2 cups (300 g) raw almonds

½ tsp sea salt

½ tsp paprika

½ tsp garlic granules

¼ tsp freshly cracked black pepper

⅛ tsp cayenne pepper

Melt the butter in a large skillet over medium heat. Add almonds and sprinkle in salt and spices. Gently sauté over low heat for 8 to 10 minutes.

Remove from heat. Cool on parchment paper and enjoy!

SPICED APPETIZER NUTS

Simple everyday spices you have in your spice cabinet can add some zing to regular nuts. Coconut sugar adds some sweetness and enhances the savory spices so you'll be able to enjoy all sorts of flavors with each handful of nuts. —JC

SERVES 4

1 cup (150 g) raw almonds

1 cup (150 g) raw pecans

1 tbsp (15 ml) coconut oil, melted

2 tsp (10 g) ghee

1 tbsp (12 g) coconut sugar

¼ tsp black pepper

¼ tsp paprika

½ tsp garlic powder

⅛ tsp cayenne pepper

Preheat oven to 275°F (140°C, or gas mark 1). Line a baking sheet with parchment paper.

In a large bowl, combine almonds and pecans. Add the coconut oil and mix until well combined. Spread the nuts in a single layer on the baking sheet. Bake for 15 minutes and stir the nuts to even them out on the baking sheet. Bake for another 15 minutes.

Remove from the oven and coat with ghee. In a small bowl, combine coconut sugar, black pepper, paprika, garlic powder and cayenne pepper. Sprinkle seasoning on top of the nuts and mix until well coated. Let cool slightly for 10 minutes and serve warm.

COCONUT ALMONDS

The combination of honey and slightly sweet coconut makes for a delicious snack or a topping for a Paleo friendly dessert, such as or stewed fruit. —AV

SERVES 8

½ cup (40 g) desiccated unsweetened coconut

2 cups (300 g) raw whole almonds

1 tbsp (15 ml) coconut oil, melted

¼ tsp ground cinnamon

Dash of sea salt

2 tbsp (30 ml) honey

Preheat the oven to 350°F (180°C, or gas mark 4). Place the coconut in a large frying pan over low heat. Stir continuously until coconut turns golden, about 2 minutes. Immediately remove from heat to a bowl. Note that the coconut burns quickly, so do not step away from the stove.

Place the almonds in a bowl. Add the coconut oil, cinnamon and sea salt. Use your hands to mix and make sure the almonds are well coated. Place the almonds on a cookie sheet lined with parchment paper. Bake until toasted, about 10 minutes. You can mix them up once during the cooking time.

Place the almonds back in the bowl, add the honey and stir to combine. Sprinkle with the toasted coconut. Allow them to cool to set, about 30 minutes. Enjoy immediately or store in an airtight container.

RAW ALMOND BUTTER COCONUT BALLS

Make these raw almond butter coconut balls for a fun and delicious snack. Especially great for the little ones. —NK

SERVES 8

1 cup (240 g) cooked butternut squash, mashed

½ cup (120 g) almond butter

3 tbsp (45 ml) coconut oil, melted

2 tbsp (30 ml) maple syrup

¼ tsp vanilla extract

1 tsp (3 g) ground cinnamon

¼ tsp sea salt

6 tbsp (48 g) coconut flour

1 cup (85 g) unsweetened shredded coconut

In a large mixing bowl combine the butternut squash, almond butter, melted coconut oil, maple syrup and vanilla extract. Mix in the cinnamon and pinch of salt. Sift in the coconut flour and mix. Cover and refrigerate for an hour. Remove from the fridge and use your hands to roll the mixture into even-sized balls. As you make the balls, roll them in the shredded coconut. Store in an airtight container in the fridge for a week or freeze in individual portions.

APRICOT & CARDAMOM BARS

Apricots and cardamom are a match made in heaven. This wonderfully fragrant combination creates a unique and refined treat out of simple ingredients. —VM

SERVES 16

Coconut oil for greasing

⅓ cup (80 g) unsalted butter

3 tbsp (45 ml) honey

½ cup (65 g) dried apricots, finely chopped

2 eggs

1 cup (120 g) almonds, ground

1 tsp (3 g) ground cardamom, plus ½ tsp for sprinkling

Preheat the oven to 350°F (180°C, or gas mark 4). Take a 7 × 10-inch (17.8 × 25-cm) baking pan and grease with coconut oil. Line the pan with parchment paper, allowing for enough to hang over the edges.

In a small saucepan, melt the butter and honey over low heat and let cool. While you're melting the honey and butter, soak the diced apricots in a bowl with hot water for about 2 minutes, then drain.

In a separate bowl, whisk the eggs until they are light and fluffy. Now fold the eggs, diced apricots, ground almonds and cardamom into the honey/butter mixture and mix well. Spread the mixture evenly into the pan and bake for 20 minutes.

Let the bars cool before cutting. Once they are cool, cut the bars into 16 servings and enjoy!

COCONUT CHOCOLATE BARS

Drum roll please! Ladies and gentleman, let me introduce one of the best low-carb snacks you will ever try. It's also probably one of the easiest! —VM

SERVES 5

1 cup (85 g) shredded coconut, unsweetened

⅓ cup (80 ml) coconut cream

1 tsp (5 ml) vanilla extract, divided

1 packet of stevia, divided

4 tbsp (60 ml) coconut oil or 2 ounces (56 g) cocoa butter

2 tbsp (16 g) unsweetened cocoa powder

In a large mixing bowl add the shredded coconut, coconut cream, half the vanilla extract and half the stevia packet together and mix well. Line a cookie sheet with parchment paper and add the shredded coconut mixture to the sheet. Shape the shredded coconut into a flat rectangles about 4 × 6-inches (10 × 15-cm), and about 1-inch (2.5-cm) thick.

Place the shredded coconut bars in the freezer for about 2 hours, or until frozen solid.

(continued)

While the coconut bars are freezing, melt the coconut oil, or cocoa butter in a small sauce pan over low heat. Add the cocoa powder and the remaining stevia and vanilla extract to the pan and mix well for about 2 minutes. Let the mixture cool to room temperature, but make sure that it remains in liquid form.

Take the bars from the freezer and dip them into the cocoa mixture. Place the bars on the lined cookie sheet and refrigerate them until the coating has hardened.

Keep the bars in the fridge to maintain their candy-like consistency and enjoy!

CHEF'S TIP:
Instead of using the coconut oil to coat the bars, you could use 2 ounces (56 g) cocoa butter, so they remain hard at room temperature.

COCONUT CHERRY BARS

Having healthy snacks around helps avoid reaching for unhealthy choices when we are in a hurry. These little bars are loaded with nutrient-dense almonds, naturally sweet dates, and healthy fats from coconuts to keep you fueled up for hours. Dried cherries are my favorite addition to homemade bars. —KH

SERVES 8–12

1 cup (150 g) raw almonds

½ cup (90 g) dates

½ cup (75 g) dried cherries, unsweetened

½ cup (120 ml) coconut butter, melted

⅛ tsp sea salt

2 tbsp (30 ml) water

1 tbsp (15 g) nut butter—almond, cashew or sunflower

¼ cup (20 g) shredded coconut, unsweetened

Line an 8 × 8-inch (20 × 20-cm) baking pan with parchment paper. Set aside.

Coarsely chop almonds in food processor and place in a bowl. Place dates, cherries, coconut butter, salt, water and nut butter in a food processor and process into a paste. You may need a bit more water but add slowly. Add chopped almonds and coconut shreds. Pulse until well combined. Mixture should be tacky but not sticky-wet.

Dump mixture into lined pan and press evenly down into bottom of pan. Place pan in the freezer for 30 minutes, remove and cut into eight to twelve bars. Store in sealed container in refrigerator. Separate each layer with parchment paper.

HAZELNUT SESAME BARS

Store-bought bars can be expensive and full of unwanted ingredients. Make your own for easy snacking on the go. —KH

SERVES 9–12

1 cup (180 g) dates, pitted

½ cup (120 ml) coconut butter, melted

2 tbsp (30 g) almond butter

¼ tsp sea salt

3 tbsp (45 ml) filtered water

1 cup (150 g) hazelnuts, raw

2 tbsp (16 g) sesame seeds

In food processor, process dates, coconut butter, almond butter, salt and water until they form a paste. Add hazelnuts and pulse until nuts are broken down into tiny bits. Add sesame seeds and pulse to combine. You may need to add a bit of water here. Mixture should be tacky but not sticky wet. Add water a tiny bit at a time. Press mixture firmly into a 9 × 11-inch (23 × 28-cm) baking pan that is lined with parchment paper. Use the back of a spatula or your fingers to even out the top. Place in freezer for about an hour then remove and cut into desired-sized bars. Store in fridge, separating layers with parchment paper.

RAW HEMP ALGAE BARS

This recipe is so simple because it consists mostly of tossing the ingredients into a food processor, then letting the bars set in the refrigerator. The sticky sweetness of the dates, paired with the coconut and the crunch of the nuts makes for a balanced, tasty snack —RB

SERVES 6

½ cup (75 g) pistachios

½ cup (75 g) pumpkin seeds

¾ cup (60 g) shredded unsweetened coconut

¾ cup (120 g) packed, pitted dates, chopped

¼ cup (60 ml) orange juice

¼ cup (60 ml) coconut oil, melted

¼ cup (30 g) hemp seeds

½ tsp spirulina

In a food processor, pulse the pistachios, pumpkin seeds, shredded coconut and dates until the mixture is crumbly and sticky.

Move to a medium mixing bowl and stir in the orange juice, coconut oil, hemp seeds and spirulina. Press into an 8-inch (20-cm) square cake pan or glass dish.

Chill in the refrigerator for at least 1 hour, then slice and serve.

CHEF'S TIP:
Increase the dates to a whole cup (160 g) if you like your raw energy bars more sticky than crumbly.

RAW SUPERFOOD BARS

These raw energy bars are packed with superfoods like chia, sea-buckthorn and bee pollen. —RB

SERVES 6

30 large dates, pitted

2 cups (160 g) shredded unsweetened coconut

½ cup (75 g) chia seeds

½ cup (60 g) sea-buckthorn powder

2 tbsp (16 g) bee pollen

2 pinches salt

4 tbsp (60 ml) red palm oil

Pulse the ingredients in a food processor until a thick dough forms. Press the mixture into a greased 8-inch (20-cm) square cake pan. Chill for 1 hour or until very firm. Carefully cut into bars and serve chilled or at room temperature.

CHEF'S TIP:
The red palm oil heightens the red hue, but can stain utensils and color your hands. Coconut oil can be subbed instead.

SPICED BUTTERNUT SQUASH FRIES

These butternut squash fries infused with the warming spices of cinnamon, nutmeg, cloves and ginger make a delicious side or snack to enjoy. —NK

SERVES 2

1 medium butternut squash, peeled, seeded and cut into fries

2 tsp (6 g) ground cinnamon

¼ tsp ground nutmeg

⅛ tsp ground cloves

⅛ tsp ground ginger

¼ tsp sea salt

1 tbsp (15 ml) coconut oil, melted

Hazelnut oil, for topping, optional

Preheat oven to 425°F (220°C, or gas mark 7). Line a large baking tray with parchment paper. Place butternut squash fries in a large mixing bowl and add in the cinnamon, nutmeg, cloves, ginger and sea salt. Mix well. Place the fries onto the lined baking tray and drizzle with the melted coconut oil. Bake for 15 to 20 minutes then remove from the oven, flip the fries over and bake for another 15 to 20 minutes. Serve warm with a drizzle of hazelnut oil on top.

CREAMY BACON-WRAPPED DATES

I usually prep these, stage them in the oven and turn the oven on as soon as the first dinner guests arrive. Greeting guests with warm, gooey cashew cream, crunchy bacon and sweet dates always impresses them. These are usually gone within minutes! —AV

SERVES 10 (2 PER PERSON)

1 cup (110 g) raw, whole cashews

Filtered water for soaking

⅓ cup (80 ml) water

1 heaping tbsp (20 g) nutritional yeast from non-GMO beets

2 tbsp (6 g) chives, chopped

6 large basil leaves, chopped

¼ cup (10 g) fresh parsley

1 clove garlic

1 tbsp (15 ml) fresh lemon juice

¼ tsp lemon zest

¼ tsp pepper

½ tsp sea salt

20 Medjool dates, slit, seeds removed

10 pieces bacon, cut in half

Place the cashews in a bowl and cover them with filtered water. Allow them to soak for 5 to 6 hours. Preheat oven to 400°F (204°C). Remove the cashews from the water, rinse them and place them in a food processor. Add ⅓ cup (80 ml) filtered water and pulse until cashews are creamy, about 2 minutes. Add the yeast, chives, basil, parsley, garlic, lemon juice, lemon zest and pepper and pulse until well combined, about 1 more minute. Adjust salt to taste. Fill dates with cashew filling. Securely wrap each date in a half-piece of bacon. Arrange dates on a wire rack and set on a baking sheet. Bake for 15 minutes or until bacon is cooked through. Serve warm.

PANCETTA-WRAPPED FIGS WITH WALNUTS

Figs are harvested twice a year in California, in early summer and late summer or early fall. I always grab a basket or two as soon as I see them at the market. In my opinion, not many other fruits can compete with the sweet flavor and the soft texture of a fresh, ripe fig. Crunchy walnuts and savory pancetta provide the perfect accompaniment to this honeyed fruit. —AV

SERVES 12 (2 PER PERSON)

24 walnut pieces

12 large black mission figs, sliced in half

24 strips pancetta, very thinly sliced

FOR THE VINAIGRETTE

2 tsp (10 ml) extra-virgin olive oil

2 tsp (10 ml) balsamic vinegar

1 tsp (5 ml) champagne vinegar

2 tsp (1 g) mint, chopped

1 tsp (1 g) chives, chopped

Sea salt and pepper to taste

Preheat oven to 350°F (177°C). Chop walnuts and press into the center of each fig. Wrap a piece of pancetta around the fig. Place figs on a baking sheet and cook for 30 minutes or until pancetta is browned. While they cook, stir the vinaigrette ingredients. Add salt and pepper to taste. Arrange figs on a platter and drizzle with vinaigrette.

PROSCIUTTO-WRAPPED MELON

Prosciutto e melone is a classic Italian appetizer, perfect for a summer party. I chill my cantaloupe before making this dish to make it extra refreshing. The fresh ground black pepper adds the perfect amount of heat and complexity to this simple appetizer. —AV

SERVES 8

4 cups (720 g) ripe cantaloupe, chilled and cut into 2-inch (5-cm)-long and 1-inch (2-cm)-wide pieces

10 mint leaves, julienned

½ tsp pepper

2 tbsp (30 ml) champagne vinegar

4 ounces (113 g) thinly sliced prosciutto, torn into 1 inch (2-cm) strips

In a medium-sized bowl, combine the cantaloupe, mint leaves, black pepper and champagne vinegar. Wrap one piece of prosciutto around each piece of melon.

SMOKED SALMON NORI WRAPS WITH WASABI MAYO

Iodine is a trace mineral that plays an essential role in optimal thyroid function. We should be conscious of iodine when following a Paleo diet. Many people may not be getting enough iodine when processed foods are eliminated and table salt is replaced by sea salt. Nori (dried seaweed pressed into thin sheets) is a great source of iodine. These rolls are a tasty way to include it in your diet. They are perfect as an appetizer, or in a larger portion for a light lunch. —AV

SERVES 6

4 sheets of nori

8 (4-ounce [113-g]) pieces smoked wild salmon

1 English cucumber, julienned

2 carrots, peeled and julienned

4 tbsp (55 g) of Homemade Wasabi Mayonnaise (page 227), divided

Place one sheet of nori on a flat surface. Place two pieces of salmon, some cucumber and carrot, and 1 tablespoon (14 g) of wasabi mayo, about 2 inches (5 cm) from the bottom edge.

Starting with the bottom edge, roll the nori around the fillings, pressing gently while you roll. The edges of the nori will stick together if slightly moistened; run warm water over your finger, then run your finger along the inside edge of the top flap. Press the moistened edge to the roll to seal. Repeat with the remaining rolls. Cut each roll into six pieces.

IKRA, OR POOR MAN'S CAVIAR (MIDDLE EASTERN EGGPLANT SPREAD)

When most of us think of a Middle Eastern eggplant appetizer, baba ghanoush comes to mind. Although it's a fantastic dip, my favorite Middle Eastern eggplant dish is the lesser-known ikra. The recipe for ikra varies from household to household, and even within a household! My dad grills the vegetables for this dish, while my mom broils them. I am a novice on the barbecue, so I usually prepare this my mom's way. I love the smoky flavors complemented by subtle sweetness from the tomatoes. Traditionally ikra is served with pita bread, but I often eat it by itself or with sliced cucumbers. —AV

SERVES 12

3 medium eggplants

1 green bell pepper

1-2 serrano peppers

6 tomatoes, deep red and flavorful

½ medium onion

5 cloves garlic

2 tbsp (30 ml) extra-virgin olive oil

2 tbsp (30 ml) fresh lemon juice

1 tsp (5 g) sea salt

½ tsp pepper

Preheat oven to 350°F (177°C). Pierce each eggplant in several places with a fork and place on a baking sheet. Roast in the oven until soft (about 1 hour), turning over once. Allow eggplant to cool. Once cooled cut it in half lengthwise. Scoop out the flesh and place it in a medium-sized bowl. Discard the peel. Change oven setting to broil. Place peppers, tomatoes and onion under the broiler for 20 minutes, turning once halfway through. Allow to cool. Peel the skin from the tomatoes and peppers. In a food processor mix eggplant, tomatoes, peppers, onion and garlic. Transfer to a medium-sized bowl. Add olive oil, lemon juice, salt and pepper. Adjust salt and pepper to taste. Refrigerate for 3 hours to allow spread to cool and flavors to meld.

SARDINE SPREAD

I rarely use canned products but fresh sardines are hard to come by. Sardines are loaded with nutrients, so it is worth the trade-off! They are a great source of omega-3 fats, vitamin D, vitamin B12 and selenium. If you do find fresh sardines, they taste delicious grilled! —AV

SERVES 6

1 tbsp (15 g) ghee

½ sweet onion, chopped

1 clove garlic, minced

8 ounces (227 g) canned sardines, drained and mashed

½ cup (115 g) avocado (about 1 medium)

3 tbsp (45 ml) fresh lemon juice

½ tsp lemon zest

¼ tsp cayenne pepper

Cucumber slices for dipping

Heat ghee in a saucepan over medium heat. Sauté onions until soft, about 7 minutes. Add garlic and sauté until fragrant, about 2 minutes. Place onions, garlic, sardines, avocado, lemon juice, lemon zest and cayenne pepper in a food processor and blend until smooth. Serve with cucumber slices for dipping.

GRILLED LAMB HEARTS AND LIVER WITH SPICY CHIMICHURRI

Liver is rich in iron and other minerals, choline and B vitamins, especially vitamins B6 and B12. In addition, it's a good source of the fat-soluble vitamins A, D and K. Heart is a rich source of Coenzyme Q10 and a helpful substance that supports many body processes.

In Armenian cuisine organ meats are often served simply, grilled and sprinkled with sea salt. Because of its milder flavor, lamb offal is preferred over beef.

Heart is a perfect introduction to organ meats. Once it's trimmed, you're left with tender muscle flesh, which resembles other muscle meats in flavor.

Liver and heart are quite lean. I add a sauce to the classic grilled version to add some fat to the dish. Let's face it; it will also help disguise the strong flavor of liver for those who are new to it!—AV

SERVES 6–8

1 pound (454 g) lamb heart, well-trimmed of exterior fat and interior veins and ventricles, cut into 1-inch (2-cm) cubes

1 pound (454 g) lamb liver, trimmed of tough membranes and veins, cut into 2 inch (5-cm) slices

Coarse sea salt

Serve with Cilantro Chimichurri (page 510)

Thread the heart and liver slices loosely on skewers and sprinkle with sea salt. Grill over hot coals, about 5 minutes per side, until the center is pink but firm. Do not overcook, as the heart and liver can get really tough. Drizzle with chimichurri and serve.

SALMON CEVICHE WITH MANGO AND CUCUMBER

Ceviche is a Latin American preparation using citrus acid to "cook" fish. Because this dish isn't cooked with heat, use the freshest fish possible. During salmon season, we often make ceviche with fish we buy directly from fishermen off their boats—a real treat! —AV

SERVES 4

1 pound (454 g) salmon fillet, skin removed, diced

1 serrano pepper, minced

3 tbsp (10 g) scallions, chopped

1 mango, peeled and diced

½ cup (90 g) cucumber, peeled and chopped

¼ cup (10 g) cilantro, finely chopped

1 tbsp (3 g) mint leaves, chopped

¼ cup (60 ml) each fresh lemon, lime and orange juice

¼ tsp sea salt

¼ tsp pepper

1 avocado, chopped

In a medium-sized bowl combine salmon, serrano pepper, scallions, mango, cucumber, cilantro and mint. Add lemon, lime and orange juices, salt and pepper and make sure all of the ingredients are well coated. Place in the refrigerator for 1 to 2 hours. Fold in avocado, taking care not to smash. Adjust salt and pepper to taste and serve.

COCONUT SHRIMP WITH MANGO SALSA

I worked as a server at a restaurant through graduate school. Coconut shrimp was one of my favorite appetizers. Of course, the version I consumed at the restaurant I worked at was loaded with vegetable oils and doused in white flour. What I love about the Paleo diet is that I can enjoy my old favorite foods without the guilty conscience. My old favorites are improved with their Paleo face-lifts! —AV

SERVES 4

½ cup (50 g) coconut flour

2 tbsp (15 g) arrowroot starch

½ tsp cayenne

½ tsp sea salt

2 eggs, lightly beaten

1 cup (75 g) dried shredded coconut

1 pound (455 g) fresh shrimp, shelled and deveined

½ cup (120 ml) coconut oil for frying

Mango Salsa (page 250), for serving

In a medium-sized bowl mix together coconut flour, arrowroot starch, cayenne and salt. Place the beaten eggs in a second bowl. Place the shredded coconut in a third bowl. Hold the tail of each shrimp and dip it in the egg mixture, making sure both sides are covered. Dip each shrimp in the coconut flour mixture, then back into the egg mixture. Once the shrimp is coated with egg a second time, dip it into the shredded coconut. Make sure it is well coated with coconut. Place a heavy-bottomed skillet on medium-low heat and add the coconut oil. Once the coconut oil has melted add the shrimp to the skillet. Cook shrimp for about 5 minutes on the first side, and an additional 2 to 3 minutes on the second side. (It works best to cook these a bit longer on a lower heat so the coconut does not burn.) Serve with mango salsa.

SHRIMP WITH PAPAYA COCKTAIL SAUCE

Although I love shrimp, I have never been a fan of restaurant shrimp with cocktail sauce. Too often the shrimp is served with prepackaged, too-sweet, ketchup-tasting sauce. This papaya version is a fruity and refreshing take on an old classic. —AV

SERVES 8

FOR THE COCKTAIL SAUCE

1 medium papaya, diced (about 2 cups [480 g])

2 tsp (10 g) freshly grated horseradish

1 tbsp (15 ml) champagne vinegar

2 tbsp (30 ml) fresh lime juice

1 tsp (5 ml) raw honey

1 serrano pepper, chopped

½ tsp sea salt

FOR THE SHRIMP

Zest of 1 lemon

¼ cup (60 ml) fresh lemon juice

1 tbsp (15 ml) sea salt

1 bay leaf

3 quarts (2.8 L) water

2 pounds (900 g) large shrimp, peeled and deveined

Prepare the cocktail sauce by placing the papaya, horseradish, vinegar, lime juice, honey, pepper and salt in a food processor. Pulse a few times until well combined. Do not grate the horseradish too far in advance, since within a few hours it can turn drab and bitter.

Prepare the shrimp by adding lemon zest, lemon juice, salt and the bay leaf to the water. Bring to a boil, then reduce to a simmer. Add the shrimp and poach until opaque, about 3 to 4 minutes. Serve shrimp along with papaya cocktail sauce.

CHEF'S TIP

Choose organic papayas; nonorganic papayas are sometimes genetically modified.

SWEET POTATO SALMON CAKES

Salmon is often revered for its high omega-3 fat content, and is also a great source of vitamin B12, tryptophan, selenium and vitamin D (which is not found in many foods).

I often use canned salmon in this recipe because the salmon flavor is not as prominent when combined with the rest of the ingredients. Buying canned salmon offers a great opportunity for a Paleo foodie to save money. Reserve the fresh salmon for a recipe where it's the star. —AV

SERVES 4 (3 PER PERSON)

¼ cup (10 g) parsley, chopped

¼ cup (10 g) scallions, chopped

¼ cup (45 g) red bell pepper, chopped

12 ounce (340 g) canned, boneless pink salmon or cooked fresh salmon

1 medium sweet potato, peeled, boiled and mashed

2 eggs, separated

¼ tsp cayenne pepper

½ tsp sea salt

¼ tsp pepper

2 tbsp (30 ml) coconut milk (see page 503 for Homemade Coconut Milk)

2 tbsp (15 g) coconut flour

2 tbsp (15 g) arrowroot starch

¼ cup (60 ml) coconut oil for frying

In the bowl of a food processor combine parsley, scallions and red bell pepper. Pulse a few times until well combined. In a medium bowl, combine the parsley, scallion and red bell pepper mixture, salmon, sweet potato, egg yolks, cayenne, sea salt, black pepper, coconut milk, coconut flour and arrowroot starch. Mix using your hands, until all the ingredients are well combined.

Make the mixture into patties, about the size of your palm and 1-inch (2.5-cm) thick. This mixture should make about twelve patties. Heat a heavy-bottomed skillet, such as cast iron, over medium heat. Add coconut oil. Using a pastry brush, coat both sides of each patty with egg whites. Once coconut oil is melted, add the salmon cakes to the pan and cook for 3 to 5 minutes per side. Cook in batches so as not to overcrowd the pan. Add more coconut oil as needed. Cook until well browned, crispy and heated through.

SPICY SAUSAGE- AND WALNUT-STUFFED MUSHROOMS

One-bite appetizers give parties a more intimate feel, making room for lively conversation. I recently shared these savory treats with my book club. (If you saw our spread, you might call it a wine and food club!) The fiery sausage pairs perfectly with the earthy mushrooms, making this appetizer an instant crowd-pleaser! —AV

SERVES 6

18–24 crimini mushrooms

1 tbsp (15 g) ghee

½ pound (225 g) spicy Italian sausages

¼ cup (60 g) shallots, finely minced

2 cloves garlic, minced

¼ tsp fennel seeds

2 tbsp (15 g) walnuts, chopped

¼ cup (10 g) fresh parsley, chopped

Sea salt and pepper to taste

1 tbsp (15 g) butter, melted

(continued)

Preheat oven to 375°F (190°C). Pull the stems off the mushrooms and chop the stems, keeping the mushroom caps whole. Heat the ghee in a medium skillet over medium heat. Remove the sausage meat from the casings and crumble into the skillet. Sauté gently until meat is cooked through. Use a slotted spoon to remove the sausage, leaving the fat behind. Using the remaining sausage fat, sauté the shallots and mushroom stems until tender, about 5 to 7 minutes. Then add garlic, fennel seeds and walnuts and sauté until fragrant, about 1 to 2 minutes. Add parsley and the sausage mixture back in. Make sure the meat and mushroom mixture is thoroughly mixed. Adjust salt and pepper to taste. Toss mushroom caps with melted butter. Generously fill with stuffing. Place on a baking sheet and cook for 20 minutes or until well browned.

HOMEMADE NUT BARS

These nut bars make a filling, sweet treat. If you will be hosting kids or toddlers as guests, these are always a hit! —AV

SERVES 8

½ cup (85 g) almonds

½ cup (60 g) walnuts

13 dates, pits removed and chopped (a little more than a cup)

¾ cup (55 g) shredded coconut

1 tbsp (15 ml) coconut oil

½ tsp cinnamon

¼ tsp nutmeg

Add the almonds and walnuts to a food processor and blend until you have a fine, flour texture. Next add the dates, shredded coconut, coconut oil, cinnamon and nutmeg. The coconut oil should be soft. If it is really hard, melt it before adding. Blend until the ingredients are well combined. The mixture should be slightly sticky. Put the mixture in a square or rectangular glass dish. Use the back of a spoon to push on it and pack it in tight. Place it in the refrigerator to set for at least an hour. Slice it into squares and serve or store in the refrigerator.

POTATOES IN "CHEESE" SAUCE

Adapting this traditional Peruvian dish to be both grain-free and dairy-free was a feat, since the sauce is normally made with both cheese and cream and thickened with cracker crumbs. My husband told me that my "cheese" sauce is frighteningly authentic, and I think you'll agree. Some like to really turn up the heat in this dish, but it's up to you how hot to make the sauce. —AT

SERVES 4–6

2–2½ pounds (905–1021 g) Yukon gold potatoes, peeled

FOR THE "CHEESE" SAUCE

1 cup (235 ml) Slow Cooker Chicken Broth (page 170)

4 tbsp (28 g) unflavored gelatin

1 cup (235 ml) canned full-fat coconut milk

2 tbsp (30 ml) extra-virgin olive oil

¼ cup (32 g) nutritional yeast

1½ tsp (7 ml) red palm oil, for color

½ tsp ground turmeric

1 tsp (6 g) fine Himalayan salt

½–3 tbsp (5–27 g) minced ají amarillo or another chile pepper (see note in recipe introduction)

1 tsp (2 g) granulated onion

1 tsp (3 g) granulated garlic

2 tbsp (30 ml) apple cider vinegar

2 tbsp (16 g) tapioca starch dissolved in 2 tbsp (30 ml) water

FOR SERVING

2–3 large hard-boiled eggs, peeled and sliced

4–6 leaves romaine lettuce

¼ cup (25 g) sliced black olives (Peruvian botija olives are ideal)

Sprig of curly-leaf parsley, for garnish

Begin by cooking the potatoes. Place the peeled potatoes in a 4-quart (3.8-l) or larger pot and cover with water. Bring to a boil over high heat, then lower the heat to a gentle boil and cover, cooking until the potatoes are tender, 25 to 30 minutes.

Meanwhile, prepare the "cheese" sauce. Pour the chicken broth into a medium pot. Slowly sprinkle the gelatin, about 1½ teaspoons (3.5 g) at a time, or top of the broth to "bloom" it. Do this slowly so that clumps do not form. Once all of the gelatin has been added, heat the pot over medium heat until the gelatin has dissolved.

Whisk in all the remaining sauce ingredients and cook for about 5 minutes. Remember to make a slurry by combining the tapioca starch with the water before adding it to the pot, otherwise it won't dissolve evenly.

Reduce the heat to low and cover, to keep it warm until the dish is ready to serve.

Meanwhile, prepare the serving ingredients. Hard-boil the eggs by placing them in a pot with a lid and covering with at least 1 inch (2.5 cm) of water. Heat, uncovered, over high heat until the water reaches a rolling boil, then cover with the lid and turn off the heat, but leave on the burner. Let sit for 10 to 12 minutes, then drain and run the eggs under cool water.

Drain the potatoes and place in a bowl or on a plate. Carefully, without burning your fingers, slice the potatoes crosswise into three or four slices each.

To assemble the dish, arrange the lettuce leaves on your serving dish. Layer the potato slices evenly on top of the leaves. Pour the warm cheese sauce on top. Garnish with sliced hard-boiled eggs, olives and a sprig of parsley. Serve immediately.

FRIED RIPE PLANTAINS

Maduros are made from very ripe plantains that are a blend of yellow and black (not yet mostly black) and are a staple side dish throughout Latin America. They are one of my favorite starchy sides to go with just about anything. I love the way the natural sugars caramelize during cooking to provide a lovely sweet contrast to any savory main dish. —AT

SERVES 2–3

2 ripe or very ripe plantains (yellow and black; should give when pressed but not be mushy)

2-4 tbsp (28-56 g) fat of choice (coconut oil recommended, but lard, ghee and avocado oil also work)

Coarse sea salt, for garnish

To peel ripe plantains, first slice off both tips with a knife, then cut a slit in the skin down the length of the plantain. Lift off the peel with your fingers.

You can cut the plantains one of two ways: into disks about ¾-inch (2-cm) thick or on the bias (diagonally) into oblong strips about ½-inch (1.3-cm) thick. The latter option results in a more visually interesting dish and is likely how you have been served maduros at a restaurant.

In a large skillet, heat your fat of choice over medium heat until shimmering, 3 to 5 minutes. Carefully add the slices to the heated fat (they should sizzle when dropped in), cooking on each side for 3 to 5 minutes, or until they have turned a nice golden brown and have partially caramelized. Be careful not to burn.

Serve immediately with any main dish, garnished with coarse sea salt.

MASHED GREEN PLANTAINS WITH ONIONS

Mangú is a ubiquitous side dish in the Dominican Republic and you will often find it served with eggs and salami for breakfast. However, it pairs well with just about any main dish in this cookbook. The "pickled" onion topping provides a wonderful contrast of flavor for this hearty, sticks-to-your-ribs side dish. You can even use the onions to garnish steak or pork chops, too! —AT

SERVES 4–6

FOR THE *MANGÚ*

4 green plantains, peeled and cut

1 tsp (6 g) plus 1 pinch of fine Himalayan salt, divided

¼ cup (60 ml) extra-virgin olive oil, butter (if tolerated), lard or ghee

½ cup (120 ml) cold water

FOR THE *CEBOLLA*

2 tbsp (30 ml) extra-virgin olive oil

1 large red onion, cut into thin slices

1 tsp (6 g) fine Himalayan salt

2 tbsp (30 ml) distilled white vinegar or coconut vinegar

Prepare the mangú. To peel green plantains, first slice off both tips with a knife, then cut one or two slits in the skin down the length of the plantain. If the peel does not lift off easily you can loosen it by soaking the plantains in a bowl of water with about 1 tablespoon (6 g) of salt for 10 to 15 minutes.

Cut the peeled plantains in half through the center and then cut each piece in half lengthwise. Place in a pot and cover with 1 inch (2.5 cm) of water plus the pinch of salt and heat over high heat until boiling. Boil for 20 to 25 minutes, or until the plantains are fork-tender.

Meanwhile, prepare the cebolla. In a large skillet, heat the olive oil over medium heat. Add the sliced onion and salt and sauté until the onion is tender, about 5 minutes. Reduce the heat to low and stir in the vinegar. Keep warm over low heat until ready to serve with the mangú.

Once the plantains are tender, drain them and place in a large mixing bowl. Add your fat of choice and 1 teaspoon (6 g) of salt. Use a potato masher or a sturdy fork to mash the plantains. After the fat has combined with the plantains, add the cold water and continue to mash for another minute or two, until it forms a nice creamy consistency. Using cold water supposedly improves the texture of the mashed plantains and helps them stay soft when reheating leftovers. If necessary, you can add extra water ¼ cup (60 ml) at a time, until the texture is very smooth.

Serve the mangú with a generous portion of cebolla on top.

Store leftovers in the fridge in an airtight container. You can reheat leftovers in a covered dish in the oven.

TWICE-FRIED GREEN PLANTAINS

Green plantains that are fried, smashed and fried again are called tostones in some parts of Latin America and patacones in others. To make preparing these crispy bits of starchy deliciousness much easier, I recommend spending a few dollars on what is called a tostone press, which you can order online or pick up at your local Latin American grocery store. You can also use a sturdy glass or jar or even a flat meat mallet, too. Tostones can go well with just about any main dish or can be eaten as an appetizer or snack—think of them as hearty chips. —AT

SERVES 2–3

2 green plantains

4–6 tbsp (56–84 g) fat of choice (coconut oil, lard or avocado oil)

Coarse sea salt

1–2 tbsp (1–2 g) chopped fresh cilantro, for garnish

Slice the tips off the plantains with a knife, then cut one or two slits in the skin down the length of the plantain. If the peel does not lift off easily you can loosen it by soaking the plantains in a bowl of water with about 1 tablespoon (6 g) of salt for 10 to 15 minutes.

Slice the peeled plantain crosswise into disks ¾- to 1-inch (2- to 2.5-cm) wide.

In a large skillet, heat your fat of choice over medium heat until shimmering, 3 to 5 minutes. Carefully add the disks to the heated fat, cooking on each side for 2 to 4 minutes, or until they have turned a darker, more golden color. Do not allow to brown.

Remove the disks from the oil and flatten, using a tostone press (recommended) or a sturdy glass/jar or flat meat mallet. If using a tostone press, place the disk in the recessed circle and then clamp down the lid on top.

Return the flattened plantain disks to the hot oil and fry for an additional 2 to 3 minutes on each side, or until crispy and browned. You will likely need to work in batches to fry the flattened disks.

Add extra cooking fat as needed, because these will absorb quite a bit of fat as they cook.

Top with a sprinkling of coarse sea salt and a garnish of cilantro and serve immediately; tostones do not reheat well. Serve with your favorite main dish. Use mojo de ajo, or your favorite sauce, for dipping.

YELLOW CAULIFLOWER "RICE"

This is a grain-free, low-carb option for Puerto Rican style yellow "rice" that has all the flavor of the original dish but without the grains. It is extremely easy to prepare with the help of a good food processor and can be a really tasty way to pack more vegetables into your diet. —AT

SERVES 6

1 head cauliflower

¼ cup (60 ml) extra-virgin olive oil

2 tbsp (30 g) sofrito

1½ tsp (3 g) ground turmeric

1 tsp (6 g) fine Himalayan salt

½ red bell pepper, diced, optional

¼ cup (25 g) sliced green olives, optional

Remove the stem and outer leaves from the cauliflower and cut it into several smaller chunks. In a food processor, using the blade attachment, pulse the cauliflower for about 10 seconds. Scrape down the sides and continue to pulse until all the cauliflower is riced, working in batches if necessary.

Heat the olive oil in a large (12-inch [30.5-cm]) skillet over medium heat. Add the sofrito and cook until it is fragrant, 2 to 4 minutes (longer if cooking with frozen sofrito).

Add the turmeric, salt and cauliflower and cook, stirring frequently, for about 3 minutes. Add the bell pepper and olives, if using, and cook for about 5 minutes more, until the cauliflower is cooked throughout and the bell pepper is tender.

CHEF'S TIP

You can also grate the cauliflower with a box grater to "rice" it. The pieces won't be as uniform as they would be in a food processor, but it will still work!

WHITE OR YELLOW MALANGA "RICE"

Cauliflower rice isn't everyone's cup of tea, and sometimes you really want (and need) something starchy to pair with your meals, so I developed this, which I dub the best Paleo rice replacement ever. It is made from the malanga root and is just as easy to make as cauli-rice and helps soak up the juices on your plate. You can serve this rice replacement without the seasoning if you want a plain white "rice" option with your meal and with dishes traditionally served with white rice. —AT

SERVES 4

FOR PLAIN WHITE "RICE"

2 malanga roots or 1 small taro root (about 1–1½ pounds [450–680 g])

FOR PUERTO RICAN YELLOW "RICE"

2 tbsp (30 ml) olive oil

1 tbsp (15 g) sofrito

½ tsp fine Himalayan salt

1 tsp (2 g) ground turmeric

½ tsp freshly ground black pepper

To prepare plain white "rice," peel the malanga roots and cut each into four or five large chunks.

Place a few chunks in a food processor and pulse for 8 to 10 seconds. Scrape down the sides with a spatula and remove any large pieces that did not begin to rice. Pulse for 8 to 10 more seconds, then empty the processor. Add any large chunks that were removed and repeat the process until the entire root is ground up. Be careful not to overprocess, otherwise it will turn the "rice" into more of a dough-like consistency.

Place a vegetable steamer basket in a pot with a lid and pour about 1 inch (2.5 cm) of water in the bottom of the pot. Heat it over high heat.

Place the riced malanga in the steamer basket, spreading it evenly over as much of the surface as you can. If it is a small basket, you may need to work in batches (you don't want the malanga layered too thick or the inside won't cook).

When the water boils, cover the pot with the lid and lower the heat to a low boil. Steam the malanga rice for about 10 minutes. About halfway through, carefully stir the malanga rice around to help with even cooking.

Carefully remove from the steamer basket and fluff the cooked malanga rice with two forks.

To make Puerto Rican–style yellow rice, while the malanga is steaming, heat the olive oil in a large skillet over medium heat for 1 to 2 minutes. Add the sofrito, salt, turmeric and black pepper and stir for 2 to 4 minutes (longer if cooking with frozen sofrito), until sizzling and fragrant. Add the cooked malanga rice to the pan and quickly stir to combine and coat it, letting the flavors combine for 30 to 60 seconds. Remove from the pan immediately and serve.

SWEET OR SAVORY MASHED BONIATO

This sweet root vegetable is a type of sweet potato commonly used in Latin America and goes by different names in different countries; when buying it in the United States, you will most often see it labeled as "boniato." It has a unique sweet flavor and a starchier, drier consistency than the yellow sweet potatoes we typically eat in the United States. It is quite versatile and can be made into a sweet or savory side dish, depending on your mood. —AT

SERVES 4–6

2 pounds (905 g) boniato (also called batata)

FOR A SWEET MASH

1 (13.5-ounce [399-ml]) can full-fat coconut milk

1 tsp (2 g) ground cinnamon

1 tsp (2 g) aniseeds

1–2 tbsp (15–30 g) sweetener (coconut sugar or honey work well), optional

FOR A SAVORY MASH

2 tbsp (30 ml) extra-virgin olive oil

1 small onion, diced

4 cloves garlic, minced

Juice of 2 limes

1 cup (235 ml) Slow Cooker Chicken Broth (page 170)

1 tsp (2 g) dried oregano

1 tsp (6 g) fine Himalayan salt

Peel the boniato roots and cut into cubes about 2 inches (5 cm) across. Place in a pot and cover with water by 1 inch (2.5 cm). Bring to a boil over high heat, then lower the heat to a simmer and cover. Cook until the chunks are fork-tender, about 20 minutes.

Drain the cooked boniato to a large bowl. Since boniato can be fibrous inside, I recommend using an immersion blender or a food processor to make a smooth purée for the sweet version. You can also simply use a potato masher or even a sturdy fork for a chunkier consistency, if you prefer—this works well for the savory version.

For a sweet mash, combine the coconut milk with the cooked boniato and mash, then combine with the remaining sweet ingredients and mix well. Serve immediately.

For a savory mash, while the boniato is boiling, heat the olive oil in a pan over medium heat for 1 to 2 minutes, then add the onion and cook until translucent, 8 to 10 minutes. Add the garlic and continue to cook for an additional 1 to 2 minutes, until the garlic is fragrant. Turn off the heat and add the lime juice to the pan, stirring to scrape up any browned bits from the pan, mash the drained boniato with the chicken broth, then add the onion mixture and sprinkle the oregano and salt on top. Stir to combine well and serve immediately.

GREEN BANANAS IN OIL AND VINEGAR

I never knew how versatile green bananas, called guineitos, could be before learning to cook Puerto Rican food. It turns out that you can make an incredible tamale-like dough from them and they also make a unique and delicious side dish. Escabeche refers to an ancient oil and vinegar method of preservation, but in the modern kitchen it serves as a flavorful marinade for the bananas. —AT

SERVES 4–6

5-6 green bananas

½ medium white onion, cut into rings

¼ cup (60 ml) coconut vinegar or distilled white vinegar

½ cup (120 ml) extra-virgin olive oil

½ tsp fine Himalayan salt

3 ajíes dulces or 1 small red bell pepper, diced

3 large cloves garlic, minced

6 whole black peppercorns

2 bay leaves

12–15 green Manzanilla olives (optional)

Cut the tips off the green bananas and cut two to three slits down the length of each peel. Place the bananas in a large pot and cover with water. Bring to a boil and cook for 15 to 20 minutes over medium-low heat, until the peels are easily removed and the bananas are tender. Take care not to overcook or the bananas will fall apart. Note that the cooking water may turn black, but this is normal.

In a bowl, cover the onion ring slices with the vinegar and set aside.

While the bananas are cooking, combine the oil, salt, ajíes dulces, garlic, peppercorns and bay leaves in a saucepan and cook over medium-low heat for about 20 minutes, to infuse the flavors into the oil. Do not allow the oil to get too hot. Just before draining the bananas, add the onion and vinegar (and olives, if using), increasing the heat to medium and cook for about 5 minutes, to lightly soften the onion.

Drain the bananas and allow to cool enough to handle. Remove the peel and slice into 1-inch (2.5-cm) disks. You may plunge them in an ice bath to quickly cool them, if desired.

Place the sliced bananas in a glass dish with a lid and pour the marinade on top. Cover and refrigerate several hours or overnight to allow the bananas to soak up the flavor. Serve chilled.

BOILED YUCA WITH TANGY GARLIC SAUCE

Yuca has a mild yet distinctive flavor that begs to be paired with a flavorful sauce. This humble root really comes alive when you let it simmer with tangy, garlicky mojo criollo sauce. You will find this dish on the menu at most Cuban restaurants and it will surely become a new family favorite. —AT

SERVES 4

1½–2 pounds (680–905 g) yuca (frozen works well)

Juice of 1 lime

½ tsp fine Himalayan salt

¾ cup (175 ml) Mojo Criollo (page 520)

1 small white or yellow onion, sliced into rings

If using fresh yuca, peel the root with a knife or sharp vegetable peeler, ensuring you remove all traces of the pink/purple layer just beneath the skin. Cut off both tips and cut the root crosswise into lengths of about 3 inches (7.5 cm). Inspect the flesh to ensure it is pure white with no soft spots, discolorations or black speckles. Discard any such areas.

Place the yuca, lime juice and salt in a pot and cover with about 2 inches (5 cm) of water. Bring to a boil over high heat. Lower the heat to a slow boil and cook, uncovered, for 25 to 30 minutes, or until the yuca is easily pierced with a fork.

When the yuca has about 5 minutes left to cook, pour the mojo criollo into a large skillet with the onion rings and heat to a gentle bubble to soften the onion.

Remove the cooked yuca from the water and pull out the fibrous stringy piece from each core.

Add the cooked yuca to the skillet and toss to combine with the sauce. Let the flavors mingle for 3 to 5 minutes, stirring a few times. The sauce will thicken during this time as some of the starch from the yuca cooks out. Serve as a starchy side to your favorite main dish. Leftovers will not reheat well; see the note as to how to use them.

CHEF'S TIP

A tip for cooking leftover yuca con mojo is to form it into patties to fry. Mash the yuca and onion together and form into small balls, then flatten and fry in your fat of choice in a large skillet until crispy, 3 to 5 minutes per side.

CILANTRO-SPICED YUCA FRIES

Yuca is an excellent replacement for white potatoes, especially as an alternative to French fries. French fries can take forever to cook if you are pan frying them, but these are ready much quicker. You can make yuca frita from either the fresh root or frozen chunks. I always prefer to work with frozen whenever possible, but in this case it is a bit easier to work with the fresh root. The trick to perfectly crispy on the outside yet tender on the inside yuca fries is to cut them to the right thickness and not boil them for too long before frying. —AT

SERVES 2–4

1–2 pounds (455–905 g) fresh or frozen yuca

About ¼ cup (56 g) fat for frying (avocado oil or lard recommended)

Fine Himalayan salt

Chopped fresh cilantro, for garnish (optional)

If you are using fresh yuca, remove the peel with a sharp knife or vegetable peeler. Ensure that you remove all of the pink/purple layer beneath the tough outer peel. Cut the root crosswise into lengths of about 3 inches (7.5 cm). Cut each in half lengthwise and cut out the woody stem in the center of the root. Cut each piece into sticks about ¾-inch (2-cm) thick. Inspect the flesh to ensure it is pure white with no soft spots, discolorations or black speckles. Discard any such areas.

If you are using frozen yuca, add the pieces to a pot and cover with water. Bring to a boil, then lower the heat to a simmer and cook for several minutes, until thawed enough to cut. Drain and cut as described for fresh yuca.

Place the yuca sticks in a pot and cover with water. Bring to a boil over high heat, then lower the heat to a low boil and cook them for 10 to 15 minutes. They should be tender when pierced with a fork, but not falling apart. Drain the water and either fry the yuca sticks immediately or store them, covered, in the fridge to fry later or the following day.

In a small to medium skillet, heat your fat of choice over medium heat for 3 to 4 minutes. Add the yuca sticks and fry them for 2 to 3 minutes per side, or until they are lightly golden brown and crisp on the outside. Use additional fat as needed.

Sprinkle with salt to taste and garnish with chopped cilantro. Enjoy alone or with your favorite dipping sauce.

BRAZILIAN GARLICKY COLLARD GREENS

There isn't a whole lot of greenery in traditional Latin American cuisine, so I had to be sure to include this delicious recipe for collard greens that is a common side dish in Brazil. You can substitute your favorite variety of kale, if you prefer. It is such a simple cooking method but really makes the greens taste wonderful! —AT

SERVES 2–4

1 bunch collard greens (7 or 8 leaves)

2 tbsp (30 ml) extra-virgin olive oil

4–6 cloves garlic

¼ tsp fine Himalayan salt

Prepare the collard leaves by cutting away the thick stem. Lay each leaf flat on your cutting board, slice out the stem with a V shape, then cut the leaf in half by slicing above the V-shaped cut.

Place about six leaf halves in a stack and roll them up tightly to do a chiffonade cut. Slice thin strips (½ inch [1.3 cm] or less) crosswise, then carefully do one lengthwise cut through the center so that you are left with short ribbons of collards. Repeat until all leaves are cut into ribbons.

In a large skillet, heat the olive oil over medium heat for about 1 minute. Add the garlic and salt and sauté until the garlic is nice and fragrant, 1 to 2 minutes. Stir in the collard ribbons and sauté them, stirring frequently, until they are softened and bright green in color, 4 to 8 minutes. If they begin to turn dark, they are overcooking and may be bitter. Serve fresh with your favorite main dish.

VEGETABLE BLACK "BEANS"

This is a lower-carb vegetable-based bean replacement that you can use in tons of different recipes or enjoy as a side. It is seasoned in the style of Venezuelan black beans, called caraotas negras. Using eggplant yields a firmer texture than zucchini, but both taste great. See page 291 for an alternative recipe that is starchy and has a more robust texture. —AT

SERVES 4–6

8 ounces (225 g) bacon

1½ pounds (680 g) zucchini, sliced, or eggplant, cubed

1 small onion, diced

1 small red bell pepper, diced

1 tbsp (7 g) cumin

1½ tsp (3 g) dried oregano

1 tbsp (15 ml) molasses

1 tbsp (15 ml) balsamic vinegar or freshly squeezed lime juice

2 tbsp (16 g) tapioca starch

2 tbsp (30 ml) water or Slow Cooker Chicken Broth (page 170)

Fine Himalayan salt, to taste

In a large skillet, cook the bacon over medium heat until it is crispy, 8 to 12 minutes depending on the thickness. Transfer to a paper towel–lined plate, leaving the bacon fat in the skillet.

Cook the zucchini or eggplant in the rendered bacon fat. You may need to add additional fat if using eggplant, because it really soaks it up. Cook until tender, 8 to 10 minutes for zucchini and 10 to 15 minutes for eggplant.

Add the onion, pepper, cumin, oregano, molasses and vinegar to the pan and cook for about 5 more minutes. In a small bowl, create a slurry of the tapioca starch and water (or broth), pour it into the pan and cook for 2 minutes more.

Transfer the contents of the pan and the crispy bacon to a food processor or blender and blend until smooth. Season with salt to taste.

YUCA BLACK "BEANS"

Of all the non-Paleo foods to create a Paleo-friendly replacement for, beans were the hardest to replicate. This dish has the authentic flavor of the Venezuelan black bean dish caraotas negras. I think that the base of yuca to replace the beans helps re-create some of the same texture as eating real beans, but o course it won't fool anyone into thinking they are eating actual beans. Caraotas negras are one of the four components of what is considered the national dish of Venezuela: Pabellón criollo. You may also use it as a filling for Pupusas con Chicharrón o "Queso" (page 145) If you prefer a lower-carb option, see page 290 for an alternative recipe. —AT

SERVES 4–6

6 ounces (170 g) bacon

11 ounces (310 g) peeled yuca

8 ounces (225 g) white or baby portobello mushrooms

1 small onion, diced

1 small red pepper, diced

2 cups (475 ml) Slow Cooker Chicken Broth (page 170)

1 tbsp (15 ml) molasses

1 tbsp (15 ml) balsamic vinegar or freshly squeezed lime juice

1 tbsp (7 g) ground cumin

Fine Himalayan salt, to taste

In a large skillet, cook the bacon over medium heat until it is crispy, 8 to 12 minutes depending on the thickness. Transfer to a paper towel–lined plate, leaving the bacon fat in the skillet.

Meanwhile, coarsely "rice" the peeled yuca using a food processor. Cut it into several smaller chunks, then pulse 10 to 20 times. Do not overprocess. Set aside in a bowl and wipe out the food processor bowl

Fry the mushrooms, onion and red pepper in the rendered bacon fat until softened, about 5 minutes, then remove with a slotted spoon. Coarsely process the mushroom mixture with the crispy bacon in the food processor. Do not overprocess; you want the mixture to be slightly chunky.

Add the yuca and broth to the skillet and cook, stirring frequently, for 15 minutes, or until very thick. Return the mushroom mixture to the pan along with the rest of the ingredients, including salt to taste, and mix well. Cook for about 5 minutes longer.

CHAPTER 5

SOUPS & SALADS

There's nothing quite as satisfying as a crisp, refreshing salad or a soothing and nourishing bowl of soup. Often soups and salads are the first place people turn when trying to eat a healthier diet. Both are so easy to put together and can create a simple and healthy meal with minimal effort. Either one can be reworked into a small side dish or a larger main course. A soup or a salad can take on many different interesting flavors and combinations to suit any preference or need.

The soups and salads in this section run the gamut from more traditional recipes like 1-Pot Chicken Soup (page 300) and Cream of Mushroom Soup (page 318), to new inspiring creations like Asian Crab Soup with Mustard Greens (page 320). Don't forget about the amazing salads, like the Fresh Fig & Roasted Butternut Squash Salad (page 294) or, one of my favorites, the Raw Marinated Beet Salad (page 327) with apple and mint.

With all the soup and salad recipes featured in *1,001 Paleo Recipes* you can make a quick and easy side to spice up your lunch or impress your dinner guests with a rare new favorite!

POMEGRANATE AND FENNEL SALAD

This pomegranate and fennel salad has crisp flavors and festive colors. It makes for a perfect starter for a holiday dinner. —AV

SERVES 4

2 oranges

1 large fennel bulb, thinly sliced

½ cup (50 g) pomegranate seeds

7–8 mint leaves, chopped

1 tbsp (15 ml) olive oil

1 tbsp (15 ml) red wine vinegar

Salt and pepper to taste

Fennel leaves for garnish

Segment the orange by using a sharp knife to cut off both ends of the orange to reveal the flesh. On a cutting board, stand the orange upright and slice off the peel and pith in strips, following the contour of the fruit. You should be left with just the orange flesh. Use a paring knife and hold the orange over a bowl to catch the citrus juices. Slip the knife between one of the segments and the connective membrane. Cut until you reach the middle of the orange, but don't cut through any of the membrane. Do the same to the other side that is still attached the membrane. It should become loose, leaving a perfect membrane. Do this to all of the remaining segments for both oranges.

Toss the fennel, orange, pomegranate seeds, mint leaves, olive oil and red wine vinegar to coat. Season with salt and pepper. Serve topped with fennel leaves.

WARM BEET, KOHLRABI AND WATERCRESS SALAD

This Warm Beet, Kohlrabi and Watercress Salad offers a delightful combination of slightly sweet flavors from the beets and kohlrabi contrasted with the bracing peppery bite of the watercress. —AV

SERVES 4

3 large kohlrabi, both ends trimmed and peeled

3 medium beets, both ends trimmed and peeled

4 tbsp (60 ml) melted ghee—or cooking fat of choice

Leaves from 1 bunch watercress

⅓ cup (50 g) walnuts, chopped

FOR THE VINAIGRETTE

1 tbsp (15 ml) champagne vinegar

1 tbsp (15 ml) fresh-squeezed orange juice

1 tbsp (15 ml) fresh-squeezed lime juice

¼ tsp Dijon mustard

¼ tsp dried tarragon

¼ tsp sea salt

¼ tsp black pepper

2 tbsp (30 ml) olive oil

Preheat oven to 375°F (190°C, or gas mark 5). Spiralize the kohlrabi and beets using a vegetable spiralizer. Lay them on two baking sheets. Drizzle each of the baking sheets with 2 tablespoons (30 ml) of ghee and use your hands to toss them so they are well coated. Cook for about 10 to 15 minutes or until the beets and kohlrabi have softened. Keep a close eye to keep them from burning.

While the vegetables are cooking, make the vinaigrette. Whisk together all of the ingredients, except the olive oil. Once everything is thoroughly mixed, slowly drizzle in the olive oil, while you continue to whisk. This will help the dressing emulsify.

(continued)

Immediately move the beets and kohlrabi to a large bowl and add the watercress. Mix them together, so the heat from the beets and kohlrabi will wilt the watercress.

Toss the salad with the vinaigrette, top it with walnuts and serve immediately. Alternatively, you can allow it to chill and serve it cold.

CHEF'S TIP:

If you include any dairy in your diet, crumbled goat cheese is a welcomed addition to this salad!

FRESH FIG & ROASTED BUTTERNUT SQUASH SALAD

This salad is a great option to toss together when entertaining, as it is colorful, showy and full of flavor. I love pairing sweet with salty, and the prosciutto spirals add a nice touch for a hearty fall salad. —CP

SERVES 4–6

2 pounds (908 g) butternut squash

1 tbsp (15 ml) olive oil

½ tsp sea salt

5 ounces (140 g) mixed greens

3 ounces (90 g) prosciutto

10 fresh figs, sliced

1 recipe Grainy Mustard Champagne Vinaigrette (page 513)

Preheat oven to 400°F (200°C, or gas mark 6).

Peel, seed and slice the squash. Cut the squash into 1-inch (2.5-cm) cubes. Place squash in a baking dish and toss together with oil and salt.

Roast for 40 minutes, stirring squash halfway through. Remove from the oven and set aside to cool.

In a large salad bowl, arrange mixed greens, figs, prosciutto and squash. Drizzle a few spoonfuls of dressing and toss together. Add more dressing as needed.

CURRIED CARROT AND SWEET POTATO SOUP

This creamy carrot and sweet potato soup is a delicious way to include some nourishing bone broth in your diet. The sweet potato makes for a naturally sweet and luxuriously creamy soup, while the curry powder and cayenne add some heat. This soup is elegant enough to serve at the start of a holiday dinner, but simple enough to whip up for a weeknight meal. —AV

SERVES 4

2 tbsp (30 ml) coconut oil

1 large leek (white and light green parts only), thinly sliced

1½ pounds (680 g) carrots, peeled and coined

3 cloves garlic, minced

1 tsp (3 g) sea salt

1 tbsp (9 g) madras curry powder

1 tbsp (8 g) fresh ginger, grated

Pinch of cayenne

1 Japanese sweet potato, peeled and chopped

2 cups (470 ml) coconut milk

2 cups (470 ml) Slow Cooker Chicken Broth (page 170)

Chopped chives for garnish

Red pepper flakes for garnish

In a large pot, melt the coconut oil. Add the leeks and carrots. Stirring often, cook until the leeks are soft and the carrots are fragrant, about 10 minutes. Add the garlic, salt, curry powder, ginger and cayenne; stir for 2 to 3 minutes. Add the sweet potato, coconut milk and chicken broth. Bring the soup to a simmer and cook for 45 minutes or until the carrots are tender and the sweet potato is cooked through. Allow the soup to cool slightly. Purée with an immersion blender until smooth. Garnish with chives and red pepper flakes.

ROASTED RED PEPPER TOMATO SOUP

Warm and comforting, this soup combines roasted red peppers and tomatoes for a delightful blend of vegetables. Use warm Grain-Free Fluffy White Dinner Rolls (page 522) to dip into the soup. —CP

SERVES 4–6

1 pound (454 g) fresh tomatoes

1 red bell pepper

1 red onion, medium

3 large cloves garlic, peeled

1 tbsp (15 ml) olive oil

1 tsp (3 g) salt

1 tsp (3 g) dried oregano

½ tsp fresh cracked black pepper

1 tbsp (15 g) butter

¾ cup (180 ml) Slow Cooker Chicken Broth (page 170)

15 ounces (420 g) tomato sauce

½ cup (30 g) chives, chopped for garnish

Whipped coconut cream or crème fraîche, to garnish

Preheat oven to 375°F (190°C, or gas mark 5).

Cube tomatoes, red pepper and onion. Place on baking sheet with garlic. Drizzle with olive oil and sprinkle with salt, oregano and pepper. Slice butter into small pieces on top of vegetables. Roast for 30 minutes, stirring after 15 minutes.

Allow roasted vegetables to cool for 10 minutes. Purée vegetables, broth and tomato sauce in blender until smooth, scraping down the sides several times while blending.

Heat tomato soup in a saucepan allowing the soup to slowly simmer for a few minutes to blend the flavors together. Serve warm topped chives and whipped coconut cream or crème fraîche.

Use Grain-Free Fluffy White Dinner Rolls to dip in soup

CLASSIC LAMB STEW

Chunks of tender lamb are bathed in a light, fragrant broth. Serve with a piece of crusty Paleo bread and curl up with your soup and a great book. —RM

SERVES 5

3 pounds (1.4 kg) lamb shoulder meat

7 cloves garlic, divided

1 tsp (3 g) oregano

1½ cups (355 ml) red wine, divided

2 tbsp (30 ml) extra-virgin olive oil

½ white onion, chopped

Salt and pepper, to taste

1 tbsp (8 g) sweet paprika

1 (12-ounce [340-g]) jar roasted red peppers, sliced

1 (10-ounce [280-g]) can plum tomatoes, cored, seeded and diced

1 tbsp (4 g) chopped Italian parsley

2½ cups (588 ml) chicken stock

4 carrots, chopped

1 bay leaf

2 pounds (908 g) fingerling potatoes, optional

Slice the lamb meat in to 2 × 2-inch (5 × 5-cm) pieces. Mince three cloves of garlic. Add garlic, oregano and ½ cup (120 ml) of the wine to a large bowl and whisk to create a marinade. Add the lamb to the marinade and let sit in the refrigerator at least 3 hours, or preferably overnight.

(continued)

Take the meat out, drain it in a colander and pat dry with paper towels. Heat olive oil in a large Dutch oven or stock pot on medium-high heat. Sear the lamb meat in batches on all sides. It should take about 8 minutes per batch. When finished searing, reserve the meat on the side and then add the chopped onion to the pan. Add salt and pepper. Sauté for about 5 minutes until onions are soft. Then mince the remaining four cloves of garlic and add them to the onions and cook another minute. Now add the meat back in to the pot as well as the paprika, red peppers, tomatoes, parsley, remaining red wine, chicken stock, carrots and bay leaf. Bring the pot to a boil and then reduce to medium low heat and simmer covered for 2 hours. At the 2-hour point, add the fingerling potatoes and simmer covered for an additional hour or until the potatoes are tender. Remove the bay leaf and serve hot in shallow bowls.

CHEF'S TIP:
Although lamb shoulder works best, any cut of lamb will do.

LEBERKNÖDEL: LIVER DUMPLINGS AND BONE BROTH

The ultimate nourishment! Paleo liver dumplings to warm and nourish the body in the cold winter months. They also help to keep colds and flu away in a wonderfully natural way! —VM

SERVES 4

¼ pound (112 g) beef liver

¼ pound (112 g) ground beef

1 egg

1 shallot, finely chopped

2 cloves garlic

2 tbsp (8 g) fresh parsley, chopped, plus more for garnish

1 lemon, zested

¼ cup (60 ml) melted butter

Sea salt and black pepper, to taste

1 quart (940 ml) beef stock

Clean the veins from the liver and cut it into small cubes. Place the liver into the food processor along with the ground beef and blend until smooth.

Add the egg, shallot, garlic, parsley, lemon zest, melted butter, salt and pepper to the meat mixture and blend well.

In a medium saucepan bring the beef stock to a boil over medium heat. Take the meat mixture and hand roll into as many golf ball–sized meatballs you can form. Once you are done rolling meatballs, lower them into the boiling beef stock, and then lower the heat to a simmer for 10 to 15 minutes.

Serve in a bowl with the broth and garnish with the fresh parsley and enjoy.

CREAMY BACON SOUP

Who doesn't love bacon? This soup is creamy and dreamy and topped with crunchy bacon. Perfect for a cold winter night! —HH

SERVES 4–6

7 slices bacon

2 tbsp (30 ml) bacon grease, or amount leftover from cooking bacon

1 small onion, diced

6 cloves garlic, diced

½ tsp oregano

½ tsp sage

½ tsp thyme

½ of a medium-large cauliflower head, chopped

2½ cups (590 ml) Slow Cooker Chicken or Beef Broth (page 170 or 171)

½ tsp salt

¼ tsp paprika

½ tsp pepper

¾ cup (180 ml) full-fat canned coconut milk

Place the bacon slices in a pan, then turn on the heat to medium. Cook, flipping every few minutes, until the bacon is browned and fully cooked. Place the bacon to cool and crisp up on a paper towel or brown paper bag. Pour the leftover bacon grease into a soup pot and turn the heat to medium-high. Once the grease is hot, sauté the onions and garlic for about a minute, then add the oregano, sage and thyme. Cook until the onions are slightly translucent, about 3 to 5 minutes. Add the chopped cauliflower and cook for about 2 minutes. Add the broth, salt, paprika and pepper and bring to a boil. Turn the boil down to a simmer and cook, covered, until the cauliflower is soft and fork tender.

Once the cauliflower mixture has cooked fully, turn off the heat. Using an immersion blender, purée the cauliflower fully. Add the coconut milk and purée again. If using a regular blender, allow the mixture to cool for at least 30 minutes before blending to avoid damaging your blender.

On a cutting board, chop the cooked bacon into small bits or strips. Add the chopped bacon to the soup pot and mix with a spoon. Serve and enjoy.

CHEF'S TIP:

You can use either chicken or beef broth for this recipe. If using beef broth, the flavor will be a little heartier, earthy and rich. If using chicken broth, it will be a little lighter.

SAUERKRAUT AND HAM SOUP

This is one of my favorite recipes to make with leftover Polish Easter food. It has a salty, tangy flavor and adds a bonus serving of healthy probiotics. —RM

SERVES 2–3

2 slices bacon

1 cup (150 g) leftover ham, chopped

2 cloves garlic, minced

4 cups (940 ml) ham stock

Pepper to taste

1½ cups (375 g) lacto-fermented sauerkraut

Since this recipe is all about simplicity, I like to do this right in my medium saucepan so I only dirty one dish. Fry the bacon over medium heat. When the bacon is done, remove and add in chopped ham and stir it until the ham gets browned a bit. This adds amazing flavor.

Lower the heat and add minced garlic and sauté for 30 seconds. Then add the ham stock and season with pepper, cooking over medium heat until it begins to lightly simmer. Turn off the stove and throw in the sauerkraut, stir and serve immediately with bacon crumbled on top.

CHEF'S TIP:

To preserve the live probiotics in the sauerkraut, stir them into the hot, but not boiling, soup immediately before serving.

BOILED PORK RIBS SOUP

Boiled ribs soup or *Nilaga* is a humble Filipino dish that can be made using either pork ribs or beef chunks. This version uses pork ribs that are simmered low and slow to extract all the flavor and nutrients from the bones. Load it up with vegetables for a complete meal. —JC

SERVES 4

2 pounds (908 g) pork ribs, separated into individual rib pieces

6 cups (1410 ml) water

2 medium onions, quartered

2 tsp (6 g) whole peppercorns

1 tbsp (15 ml) fish sauce

Sea salt

½ pound (227 g) baby potatoes

1 tbsp (15 g) toasted onions

1 head green cabbage, quartered, hard core removed

1 cup (130 g) baby carrots

In a large stockpot, add pork ribs, water, onions and peppercorns. Bring to a boil, about 10 to 15 minutes. Remove any scum that floats to the surface. Reduce heat to low. Cover and simmer for 2 hours. Check it periodically to skim any additional scum from the pork.

Add fish sauce and season with sea salt to taste. Add baby potatoes and toasted onions. Cover and cook for about 10 minutes. Increase heat to medium. Add cabbage and baby carrots. Cover and let the vegetables cook for 5 to 8 minutes until tender. Ladle into bowls and serve hot.

CHEF'S TIP:

Toasted onions adds a nice nutty flavor to the soup and can be bought at any grocery store or spice shop. If you can't find any, onion powder will do.

GARLIC SOUP WITH BROCCOLI RABE AND POACHED EGGS

Most garlic and egg soup recipes I have seen call for day-old bread. By swapping out the bread for broccoli rabe, we end up with a more flavorful and nutritious meal. The slightly bitter and spicy flavor of the broccoli rabe pairs perfectly with the rich flavor of the runny egg yolk. —AV

SERVES 4

2 tbsp (30 g) ghee

1 medium onion, sliced

6 cloves garlic, chopped

6 cups (1410 ml) Slow Cooker Chicken Broth (page 170)

1 tsp (3 g) sea salt

1 pound (454 g) broccoli rabe, chopped

4 eggs

Splash of white vinegar

Fresh parsley, garnish

In a stockpot, heat ghee over medium heat. Cook the onion until soft and translucent, about 7 minutes. Add the garlic and cook until fragrant, about 1 minute. Add the chicken broth and salt and bring to a simmer. Reduce the heat and simmer for 15 minutes. Add the broccoli rabe and simmer for another 10 minutes.

Crack the eggs into four small bowls. Make sure the soup stays at a simmer. Add a splash of white vinegar to the soup. Slide the eggs into the soup and simmer until the whites are firm and the yolks are runny, about 4 minutes. Ladle each poached egg and some soup into each bowl, top with a sprig of parsley and serve.

TURKEY EGG DROP SOUP

This recipe is a great use of leftovers from Thanksgiving. I always keep the turkey carcass to make turkey stock, then I use leftover meat to make this easy comforting soup. —RM

SERVES 2

4 cups (940 ml) turkey stock

1 cup (140 g) leftover turkey meat

1 clove garlic, minced

⅛ tsp minced ginger

¼ tsp salt

⅛ tsp black pepper

½ tbsp (4 g) arrowroot flour

2 eggs

1 avocado, sliced

Reserve ¾ cup (180 ml) of turkey stock in a small bowl and pour the rest into a saucepan. Add turkey meat to the saucepan and stir in garlic, ginger, salt and pepper. Bring to a gentle boil. Whisk the arrowroot flour with the reserved turkey stock until smooth.

In a separate bowl, whisk the two eggs. Once the turkey stock is boiling, slowly stir in the arrowroot mixture until soup thickens.

Using a fork, drizzle the egg into the boiling soup a little at a time until it is all in. Take off heat, pour in bowls and top with avocado slices.

EGG DROP MUSHROOM SOUP

Shiitake mushrooms are a very aromatic type of fungi that have an earthy yet subtle flavor. It takes something ordinary to a whole new level. This soup uses bone broth as a base to make it more nutritious, but any type of broth will do. —JC

SERVES 4

4 cups (940 ml) Slow Cooker Chicken Broth (page 170)

1 cup (70 g) shiitake mushrooms, sliced

2 pieces boneless, skinless chicken thighs, diced

1 tbsp (15 ml) coconut aminos

1 tsp (3 ml) fish sauce

Black pepper

1 egg, beaten

Combine broth, mushrooms and chicken in a pot over medium heat.

Bring to a boil and reduce heat to low. Let it simmer until the chicken is cooked, about 5 to 7 minutes. Add the coconut aminos and fish sauce. Season with black pepper to taste. Simmer for 1 minute. Gently stir the soup to create a swirling motion. Slowly drizzle the egg while stirring the soup constantly. This will prevent the egg from clumping and will help produce thin strands that thicken the soup. Ladle into bowls and serve hot.

1-POT CHICKEN SOUP

This 1-pot Paleo chicken soup recipe is a great healing recipe that's easy to digest and is good for the gut. I like to make a big pot of this soup to save in jars in the fridge for easy lunches or dinners. —HH

SERVES 4–6

1 yellow onion

6 cloves garlic

1 pound (454 g) carrots

2 tbsp (30 g) ghee or coconut oil

½ tsp parsley

½ tsp sage

½ tsp oregano

½ tsp thyme

2 boneless, skinless chicken breasts

6–8 cups (1410–1880 ml) Slow Cooker Chicken Broth (page 170)

1 tsp (3 g) sea salt

1 tsp (3 g) pepper

6 ounces (168 g) tomato paste

3 cups (90 g) fresh baby spinach

Finely chop the onions and garlic, slice the carrots and set aside. Place the ghee in a large soup pot over medium-high heat until it melts. Add the onions and stir with a wooden spoon for 1 minute. Then, add the garlic and stir for 1 minute. Next add the herbs. Cook until the onions are soft, about 3 to 5 minutes. Add the carrots and stir for a few minutes. Add the chicken to the pot then add the broth to cover the chicken. Add salt and pepper, then turn the heat to high and allow the liquid to come to a boil. Once it starts boiling, turn the heat to low, place a lid on top and cook for about 50 to 60 minutes.

After the soup is done cooking, turn off the heat and remove the chicken breasts with tongs and place on a plate. Allow to cool for at least 10 minutes or until they're cool to the touch. Shred the chicken into thick strands.

Place the shredded chicken back into the soup pot, turn the heat back on to medium and stir. To add the tomato paste place the paste in a bowl and add 1 cup (235 ml) of the soup broth into the bowl and mix the paste until it's a liquidy consistency. Then add that to the soup until it's fully incorporated. Next, add the spinach to the soup and stir until it's wilted. Turn off the heat and serve.

THE FLU SHOT

This is the best first defense against getting sick! It's one the best home remedies to PREVENT getting sick. Drink 4 to 5 cups (950 to 1190 ml) per day at the first onset of symptoms. The sooner you take it the better it will work! —VM

MAKES 2 QUARTS (1892 ML)

1 whole chicken, or 2–3 pounds (908–1362 g) of chicken parts on the bone

2 large onions, sliced into quarters

2 cloves garlic, peeled

1 large piece fresh ginger, peeled and cut into slices (about 4 inches [10 cm])

2 tbsp (36 g) Celtic sea salt

Apple cider vinegar

Pinch of cayenne

Put the chicken and vegetables into a large stock pot with 4 quarts (3.6 L) of water. Let the ingredients sit in the stock pot with the water for an hour and then cook over low heat for 4 hours.

Once the broth is ready, pour yourself a cup with 2 tablespoons (30 ml) of apple cider vinegar and a pinch of cayenne.

GINGER CHICKEN SOUP

Serve this one-pot ginger chicken soup to warm your family's bellies once the colder months arrive. A Filipino favorite more commonly known as tinola, it has flavorful clear broth that is infused with garlic, onion and fish sauce as it simmers with the chicken. —JC

SERVES 4

1 tbsp (15 ml) tallow or coconut oil

4 cloves garlic, minced

1 inch (2.5 cm) ginger, thinly sliced

1 small onion, thinly sliced

1 pound (454 g) chicken wings

1 pound (454 g) chicken drumstick

2 tsp (10 ml) fish sauce

4 cups (940 ml) water

1 small green papaya, sliced

1 bunch spinach

Sea salt

Heat tallow in a Dutch oven over medium-high heat. Add garlic, ginger and onion. Sauté until fragrant, about 1 to 2 minutes. Add chicken wings and drumstick. Season with fish sauce. Sauté and reduce heat to medium. Cover and let it cook for 5 to 8 minutes. Add water and simmer until chicken is cooked, about 10 minutes. Add papaya and simmer for 5 more minutes. Mix in spinach and season with sea salt to taste. Turn off heat once spinach is wilted. Ladle into bowls and serve hot.

COOKS TIP:

Green papaya can be found at most Asian stores. If you don't have access to any, just omit it and double the amount of spinach.

CHICKEN ASPARAGUS SOUP

Gently drizzling a beaten egg into hot soup forms delicate strands that act as a natural thickener without the need for any starches. The next time you are feeling under the weather, try this alternative to classic chicken noodle soup. —JC

SERVES 4

1 tbsp (15 g) ghee or tallow

2 cloves garlic, minced

2 medium shallots, chopped

¾ pound (340 g) asparagus spears, woody ends trimmed, cut into 2-inch (5-cm) pieces

½ pound (227 g) cooked chicken, shredded

32 ounces (945 ml) Slow Cooker Chicken Broth (page 170)

1 large egg, beaten

¼ cup (25 g) green onions, chopped

Add ghee to a Dutch oven over medium heat. Add garlic and shallots. Sauté until shallots become translucent, about 2 minutes. Add asparagus and shredded chicken. Sauté for 3 minutes. Add broth and bring to a boil. Reduce heat to low, cover and simmer for 30 minutes.

Gently stir the soup to create a swirling motion. Slowly drizzle the egg while stirring the soup constantly. This will prevent the egg from clumping and will help produce thin strands that thicken the soup. Simmer for a couple more minutes. Ladle into bowls and top with green onions. Serve immediately.

CHICKEN-FENNEL SOUP

Fennel is a surprising addition to an otherwise traditional soup. It brightens the flavor, allowing you to enjoy this recipe, even on a summer day! —AV

SERVES 4

2 tbsp (30 g) ghee

1 white onion, diced

1 fennel bulb, diced

2 carrots, chopped

3 ribs celery, chopped

3 cloves garlic, crushed

1 pound (454 g) boneless, skinless chicken thighs, or substitute chicken breast

1 tsp (3 g) salt

1 tsp (3 g) pepper

1 tsp (3 g) dried basil

1 tsp (3 g) dried parsley

4 cups (940 ml) Slow Cooker Chicken Broth, preferably (page 170)

Fresh parsley for garnish

Heat the ghee over medium heat in a large soup pot. Add the onions and sauté until translucent. Add fennel, carrots and celery and sauté until softened. Then add garlic and sauté for a minute until fragrant. Add the chicken to the pot and cook, until all sides are browned, about 7 minutes. Add salt, pepper, basil, parsley and broth. Bring to a light boil, then simmer for 25 minutes or until chicken is cooked through. Top with fresh parsley and serve!

CHICKEN SALAD BOATS

Belgian endives are a great Paleo and low-carb alternative to toast. Their crisp and slightly bitter flavor complements this creamy chicken salad nicely. —AV

SERVES 8–10

4 cups (560 g) cooked chicken, chopped

1 rib celery, diced

2 green onions, diced

¼ cup (40 g) red onions, diced

½ cup (60 g) red bell pepper, diced

1 tbsp (4 g) fresh sage, minced

1 tbsp (4 g) fresh parsley, minced

2 tsp (10 ml) fresh lemon juice

1 tsp (5 g) Dijon mustard

¾–1 cup (180–240 g) Homemade Mayonnaise (page 496)

Salt and pepper to taste

4–5 heads of Belgian endives

In a medium bowl combine the chicken, celery, green onions, red onions, bell pepper, sage, parsley, lemon juice and Dijon mustard. Fold in the mayonnaise starting with about ½ cup (120 g) and then add more until you reach the desired consistency. I like a creamier chicken salad that uses about 1 cup (240 g) of mayonnaise. Adjust salt and pepper to taste. Scoop the chicken salad onto the endive leaves and serve.

PERSIAN CHICKEN AND POTATO SALAD

This is a dish I grew up eating all the time. It reminds me of my childhood and my mum making this for us to take to school or packing it for a picnic lunch. I grew up calling this dish "Salad Olivieh" and I believe it takes its name from the Russian "Olivier Salad." It's a dish that comes together fairly quickly depending on how many of the ingredients you already have prepared but even if you're making it from scratch it's a fairly simple dish to put together. Best served cold this dish is excellent for on the go meals and great to serve at gatherings. —NK

SERVES 4–6

1 pound (454 g) russet potatoes

3 eggs

12 ounces (340 g) cooked shredded chicken

4 ounces (113 g) kalamata or green seedless olives, roughly chopped

9 ounces (255 g) frozen organic peas and carrots, thawed

8 ounces (280 g) dill pickles, diced

1½–2 cups (330–440 g) Homemade Mayonnaise (page 496)

¼ cup (60 ml) fresh lemon juice

¼ cup (60 ml) avocado oil

1 tsp (5 g) Dijon mustard

Sea salt and black pepper, to taste

Place the potatoes in a large pot with a lid. Add enough cold water to just cover the potatoes. Place on a high heat and bring to a boil. Once the water has come to a boil reduce the heat to medium, cover the pot with a lid and cook for 40 minutes until the potatoes are just softened but still holding their shape. Drain and rinse under cold water. Allow to cool before removing the skins. Place in the fridge to cool completely.

While the potatoes are cooling, wash, rinse and dry the same pot as you used to cook the potatoes. Add about an inch (2.5 cm) of water. Place over high heat until the water comes to a boil. Place a steamer basket carefully into the pot and carefully add the eggs. Cover with a lid and steam for 12 minutes. About 5 minutes before the eggs are done, fill a large mixing bowl with cold water and add some ice cubes. Once eggs are done, carefully move them to the ice water to completely cool down for 5 to 10 minutes. Once cooled, peel and refrigerate until potato has completely cooled down.

To assemble, place shredded chicken into a large mixing bowl, roughly chop and add the potatoes and eggs. Add the kalamata or green olives, organic peas and carrots and dill pickles. Mix through. Season with some sea salt and black pepper. In a separate smaller mixing bowl add the mayonnaise, lemon juice, avocado oil and Dijon mustard. Season with a bit more sea salt and black pepper and mix. Pour dressing over the ingredients in the large mixing bowl and mix together. Taste to check for seasoning. Place in a glass dish and cover. Place in the fridge for a couple of hours or preferably over night to let the flavors meld together. Serve cold.

CURRIED CHICKEN SALAD

This curried chicken salad is a treat for the taste buds. It bursts with sweet flavors from the fruit, savory from the curry and creamy from the avocado and mayonnaise. —AV

SERVES 12–14

Meat from 1 whole poached chicken (page 156) or 1 rotisserie chicken, diced

½ cup (75 g) dried apricots, finely diced

¼ cup (40 g) dried cranberries, finely diced

1 Gala apple, finely chopped

¼ cup (16 g) chives, minced

1 rib celery, finely chopped

2 tbsp (20 g) green onion, finely chopped, white part only

¼ cup (40 g) red onion, finely chopped

2 cups (500 g) Homemade Mayonnaise (page 496)

1 tsp (3 g) curry powder

Salt and pepper to taste

6–7 large avocados, halved

In a large bowl, combine the first eight ingredients. Fold in the mayonnaise and curry. Adjust salt and pepper to taste. Cut avocados in half, remove the pit and top with chicken salad. You can also slice the avocado into segments, making it easier to scoop out.

SPICY SHREDDED CHICKEN SALAD

Coconut milk and butternut squash purée make this chicken salad perfectly creamy without mayonnaise. —RB

SERVES 8

2 tbsp (30 ml) coconut oil

1 large leek, white part only

1 bunch celery, chopped

1 jalapeño pepper, cored and seeded

3 pounds (1.4 kg) shredded chicken

4 tsp (12 g) salt

½ tbsp (4 g) black pepper

⅔ cup (160 ml) coconut milk

2 cups (520 g) butternut squash purée

FOR THE GARNISH

Parsley

Jalapeño pepper

Chili flakes

Heat coconut oil over medium heat in a large skillet. Slice the leek into ribbons, then fry in the hot oil until soft but not browned.

Shred the celery and jalapeño in a food processor until finely diced. Add to the leeks, fry until soft (add more coconut oil if necessary to keep from sticking and burning), approximately 10 minutes.

In a large mixing bowl, combine the shredded chicken, vegetables, salt, pepper, coconut milk and squash purée until thoroughly mixed and creamy. Garnish with parsley, more jalapeño and chili flakes if desired.

CHEF'S TIP:

The heat in this recipe builds slowly bite after bite. More finely chopped jalapeño as a topping would take this from slow burn to white-hot.

SOUTHWEST CHICKEN SALAD

I love this Southwest spin on traditional chicken salad. Serve it in hollowed out tomatoes, avocado halves or lettuce wraps. —KW

SERVES 4–6

3 cups (420 g) cooked and shredded chicken, about 3 chicken breasts

1 lime, juiced

2 green onions, sliced, both green and white parts

¼ cup (15 g) fresh cilantro, chopped

½ tsp chili powder

¼ tsp ground cumin

¼ tsp garlic powder

Salt and pepper, to taste

4 tbsp (60 g) Homemade Mayonnaise (page 496)

Tomatoes, avocados or lettuce, for serving

Mix together all the ingredients in a bowl. Serve in a hollowed out tomato, a pitted avocado or wrap in lettuce. Keep any leftovers in the fridge for up to 4 days.

TARRAGON POTATO SALAD

The distinctive, slightly bittersweet flavor of tarragon adds a twist to this classic potato salad. —AV

SERVES 6

10 small potatoes, peeled and diced

½ cup (120 g) Homemade Mayonnaise (page 496)

3 scallions, chopped

3 tbsp (12 g) fresh tarragon, chopped

2 cloves garlic, minced

Bring 8 cups (1880 ml) of water to a boil in a large pot. Add diced potatoes to the water and boil until they can be pierced with a fork, about 10 minutes.

In a large bowl, combine the mayonnaise, scallions, tarragon and garlic. Remove the potatoes from the water and drain well. Allow them to cool, about 10 minutes. Add them to the dressing and toss gently to coat. Serve immediately or refrigerate for later.

CURRIED EGG SALAD

This spiced spin on the classic egg salad adds a new dimension of flavor. This is great to make ahead for school or work lunches or to bring on a picnic! —HH

SERVES 3–4

5 eggs

1 tbsp (15 ml) apple cider vinegar

1 tbsp (15 ml) olive oil

2 tsp (10 g) Dijon mustard

½ tsp lemon juice

1¼ tsp (4 g) curry powder

¼ tsp turmeric

¼ cup (40 g) diced onion

Place eggs in a pot with the vinegar and a sprinkle of salt. Cover with cold water and heat on high until boiling. Once it has reached a boil, turn down to a simmer for 5 minutes. Then, turn off heat and cover pot and let sit for about 15 minutes. Then, pour out hot water and rinse eggs with cold water until cooled. Peel eggs and put into a bowl. Use a knife and/or fork to mash eggs.

Add olive oil, Dijon mustard and lemon juice and mix well. Add curry, turmeric and onion and mix. If you like egg salad to be moister you can add more olive oil or Dijon mustard.

HUNGARIAN PEPPER STEW (LECSÓ)

My husband grew up eating this dish and after watching him make it so many times for us to enjoy I finally had to learn how to make it myself. This dish uses just a few simple ingredients but it has a real robust and delicious taste. —NK

SERVES 4

2 tbsp (30 g) ghee

1 medium yellow onion, diced

2 smoked sausages, diced

14 sweet Hungarian wax peppers or banana peppers cut in half length-wise, seeds and white parts removed and cut into even-sized slices

1 tbsp (8 g) sweet Hungarian paprika powder

Sea salt, to taste

1 (15-ounce [420-g]) can organic tomato sauce

Filtered water

Heat a large skillet on medium-low heat. Add ghee. Once the ghee is melted add the diced onion. Stir and cook for 5 minutes. Add the sausage to the skillet and mix, allow to cook for a few more minutes then add in the peppers. Add the paprika powder and stir to mix. Add a pinch of sea salt. Add the tomato sauce and stir, then add just enough filtered water to cover the contents in the skillet. Turn the heat up to high and let it come to a boil. Reduce the heat to low and allow to cook for another 30 to 40 minutes making sure to stir every now and then. Taste and adjust for seasoning before serving.

CHEF'S TIP:

Serve any leftovers with a fried egg on top for breakfast the next day. Hungarian wax peppers can be found in most grocery stores or farmers markets, just make sure to ask for the sweet kind.

HUNGARIAN CHICKEN STEW (CSIRKE PÖRKÖLT)

Csirke Pörkölt is a classic Hungarian dish. As with all the Hungarian dishes that my husband cooks at home, this one was passed on to him by his mum. Using just a few simple ingredients, this dish transforms itself to a tasty and comforting stew that you'll be sure to love. —NK

SERVES 4

2 tbsp (30 g) ghee

1 large yellow onion, diced

2 tsp (6 g) sweet Hungarian paprika powder

2 pounds (908 g) boneless, skinless chicken thighs, diced

Sea salt, to taste

15 ounces (420 g) organic tomato sauce

2 sweet Hungarian wax peppers, sliced down the middle with seeds and white parts removed

Heat a medium-large saucepan over medium heat. Add in the ghee. Once melted, add in the onion and cook, stirring frequently for about 10 minutes or until the onion has softened and is golden. Stir in the Hungarian paprika powder. Add in the chicken pieces and fry until browned on the outside, about 10 to 12 minutes. Season to taste with sea salt and add in the tomato sauce. Bring the sauce to a boil. Reduce the heat to medium-low and add in the sliced Hungarian wax peppers. Cook with the lid off the saucepan for 30 to 40 minutes or until the chicken has cooked through and the sauce has thickened. Taste and check for seasoning. Remove the Hungarian wax peppers before serving; alternatively, remove them and slice them to serve over the stew.

CHEF'S TIP:

If you can't find Hungarian wax peppers you can substitute banana peppers. When my husband cooks this dish he uses the peppers for flavor only and does not serve them with the dish. If you choose to serve them just remove from the saucepan and slice them into thin rings.

MOROCCAN HEART STEW

Beef stew meat and heart slowly cooked with spices, lemons and apricots! Imagine complex fragrant tones of cinnamon and cardamom, complemented by a clear note of lemon. The whole dish is brought to heavenly quality by the subtle sweetness of apricots that blend with the onions in the broth to create a smooth and creamy sauce. Are you hungry yet? I am! —VM

SERVES 4

2 pounds (908 g) beef heart, or lamb or turkey hearts, cut in 1-inch (2.5-cm) cubes

2 tbsp (30 ml) apple cider vinegar

2 tbsp (30 g) ghee, schmaltz or lard

3 cups (480 g) onion, sliced

2 tbsp (16 g) ginger, peeled and chopped

1 pound (454 g) beef stew meat

½ tsp ground cardamom

½ tsp ground cinnamon

½ tsp ground cayenne

½ tsp ground cloves

2 cups (470 ml) water or Slow Cooker Beef Broth (page 171)

1 lemon, sliced into rounds

Sea salt to taste

1½ cups (195 g) dried apricots, quartered

The night before you are to prepare this tasty stew, marinate the heart meat in the apple cider vinegar in the refrigerator overnight.

The following day, start by heating the fat—ghee, schmaltz or lard—in a Dutch oven, over medium heat. Add the onion and ginger to the pan and sauté until the onion is translucent, about 5 minutes.

Separate the meats into small batches, about 1 cup (225 g) of meat each. Quickly sear each batch of meat in a skillet over high heat, and set aside when done.

Add all of the spices to the Dutch oven with the onion and ginger, stirring well. Add all of the meat to the Dutch oven, mixing well into the spices.

Deglaze the skillet with a cup (237 ml) of water or broth, scraping all of the browned bits from the bottom. Add the deglazing liquid and remaining broth to the Dutch oven along with the lemon slices and a pinch of salt. Bring everything to a boil, then lower to a simmer and cook for 1½ hours, or until the beef heart is tender. When the heart is tender, add the apricots and simmer for an additional 10 minutes until the liquid has reduced and thickened.

MULLIGATAWNY SOUP

This soup is a rich, thick riff on a Mulligatawny recipe with meat rather than the traditional legumes. —RB

SERVES 4

FOR THE SOUP

1 sweet potato

4 tsp (20 ml) coconut oil, divided

1 tsp (3 g) salt, divided

1 pound (454 g) ground turkey

½ tsp black pepper

1 yellow onion, chopped

6 cloves garlic

3 tbsp (24 g) fresh ginger

1 jalapeño pepper, core and seeds removed

¼ cup (30 g) arrowroot flour

2 tbsp (16 g) coconut flour

1 tbsp (8 g) ground coriander

1 tsp (3 g) ground cumin

1½ tsp (4.5 g) ground turmeric

4 cups (940 ml) chicken stock or vegetable stock

(continued)

3 tbsp (45 ml) coconut oil

1 plum tomato, minced

2 tsp (4.5 g) Aleppo pepper

1 tsp (3 g) cumin seeds

1 tsp (3 g) coriander

1 tsp (3 g) black mustard seeds

2 dried chiles de arbol

½ tsp salt

FOR THE GARNISH

3 tbsp (12 g) minced cilantro

Coconut milk, to garnish

Preheat the oven to 450°F (230°C, or gas mark 8). Peel the sweet potato, cut into ½-inch (1.3-cm) cubes and toss with 2 teaspoons (10 ml) of coconut oil and ½ teaspoon of salt. Roast on a cookie sheet until soft and browned on the undersides, approximately 15 minutes.

In a thick-bottomed pan with high sides, warm 2 teaspoons (10 ml) of coconut oil over medium heat, then add the ground meat, ½ teaspoon salt and the black pepper. Cook, stirring frequently, just until the meat is no longer pink, approximately 10 minutes. Use a slotted spoon to remove the meat and set aside. Pour off all but 2 tablespoons (30 ml) of fat from the pan.

In a food processor, combine chopped onion, garlic cloves, ginger and jalapeño. Pulse to a fine shred, and then add to the hot fat remaining in the pan and cook until caramelized but not burnt, approximately 10 minutes.

Stir in the arrowroot flour, coconut flour, spices, stock, roasted sweet potato and cooked ground meat. Boil until thickened, approximately 20 minutes.

While the soup boils, prepare the sauce. Heat the coconut oil in a small skillet. Stir in the rest of the sauce ingredients, bring to a simmer, about 10 minutes, then remove from the heat.

Stir half of the sauce into the thickened soup, then stir in the cilantro and remove from the heat. Serve warm, garnished with more sauce and a dollop of coconut milk.

SPICY BEANLESS CHILI

As soon as the weather starts to get cold, I make a pot of this Spicy Beanless Chili and freeze it in batches for emergency meals. The chili gets its heat from Mexican chilies and jalapeños. A side of dinner rolls is the rightful companion for this hearty meal. —RM

SERVES 10

¼ cup (60 g) rendered bacon grease

3 pounds (1362 g) chuck roast, cubed

5 New Mexican green or red chilies, stemmed, seeded and chopped

5 cloves garlic, peeled and crushed

3 large jalapeño peppers, stemmed, seeded and chopped

1 large white onion, chopped

4 tbsp (32 g) chili powder

1 tbsp (8 g) ground cumin

2 tsp (6 g) oregano

3 tsp (8 g) salt

1 tsp (3 g) ground pepper

2 (15-ounce [420-g]) cans crushed tomatoes

3 chipotle chilies in adobo sauce, chopped

4–5 cups (940–1175 ml) beef stock

3–6 tbsp (24–48 g) masa harina, or coconut flour

Grain-Free Fluffy White Dinner Rolls (page 522), for serving

In a large stock pot over high heat, heat the bacon grease and sear the cubed meat until browned on all sides, about 1 minute per side. Lower the heat to medium-high. Add the chilies, garlic, jalapeños, onion and chili powder, stirring constantly for about 5 minutes until they get slightly soft. Add the cumin, oregano, salt and ground pepper, stirring for another 30 seconds.

Add the two cans of crushed tomatoes to deglaze the pan, stirring for about 1 minute. Then add the chipotles in adobo sauce and 4 cups (940 ml) of beef stock and bring to a boil. Reduce the heat to a simmer and cook partly covered for 3 to 4 hours until the meat is tender and the chili liquid reduces slightly. If it becomes too dry add more beef stock. Once the meat is tender, add 1 tablespoon (8 g) of masa harina or coconut flour at a time to thicken the chili. Stir and let the flour absorb before adding another tablespoon (8 g) until you get a nice consistency. Serve with the dinner rolls.

CHEF'S TIP:

Always wear protective gloves when handling hot peppers and wash every surface after contact to prevent skin/eye irritation.

FARMERS MARKET WINTER SOUP

Winter is a time when the farmers' market seems empty and depleted. Don't be discouraged, you can still get all the ingredients needed to make wonderful soups. This is the time of plentiful greens and sweet winter squashes, tender leeks and juicy carrots whose flavors blend beautifully into this easy, flavorful soup. I love to make this ahead of time and freeze some for later. —VM

SERVES 6

2 quarts (2 l) water, heat in a separate pot

3 tbsp (45 g) ghee, lard or coconut oil

1 large sweet onion or yellow onion, sliced

2 cloves garlic, peeled and smashed

3 ribs of celery, chopped into small pieces

3 carrots, chopped into small pieces

2 leeks, sliced

½ butternut squash, chopped into small cubes

1 tbsp (18 g) sea salt

1 pinch of red pepper flakes

1 bunch kale, remove stems and chop into small pieces

Black pepper to taste

Heat the water, and prepare all of the vegetables for cooking according to the ingredients list.

Melt fat of choice in an 8-quart (7.6-l) stock pot over low heat. Add the onions and garlic, and sauté them until they are fragrant and translucent. Raise the heat to medium and add the celery, carrots, leeks and butternut squash, cooking them until they all begin to soften, about 5 to 7 minutes.

Once the vegetables have softened, add as much or little water to the pot as you would like. Stir things well and then add the salt and red pepper flakes to the mix. Raise the heat until you reach a rolling boil. Once you have reached the rolling boil, lower the heat to a simmer and cook for 20 minutes, or until the vegetables are completely tender.

Add the kale to the pot and cook for 5 more minutes. When you have finished cooking the soup, you can serve it as is, or blend it with an immersion blender to the desired consistency. Sprinkle with black pepper to taste. Enjoy!

BUTTERNUT SQUASH SOUP

Healthy and easy comfort food. This simple soup will warm the bones and give you needed nourishment to feed the immune system! —VM

SERVES 4

1 butternut squash

2 quarts (2 l) Slow Cooker Chicken Broth (page 170)

1 pinch cayenne

1 pinch ground cumin

Sea salt and pepper to taste

Tahini or butter, for serving

Preheat the oven to 350°F (180°C, or gas mark 4). Prepare the butternut squash by cutting the squash in half and cleaning the seeds out of the belly. Lay the squash face-down on a cookie sheet and bake for about 40 minutes, or until soft.

Once the squash is done baking set it aside to cool. When the squash has cooled, scoop the flesh from the skin of the squash into a bowl. Now add a little squash and chicken broth to the blender, adding more and more until you have blended all of the squash.

Add the blended mixture to a pot over low heat. Add the remaining ingredients and bring the soup to a simmer and cook for about 5 minutes. Serve the soup with a generous scoop of tahini or butter and enjoy!

BUTTERNUT SQUASH AND BEEF CHILI STEW

Warm up in the cooler months with this delicious, veggie-filled stew with a spicy kick. —NK

SERVES 4

1 medium butternut squash, peeled, seeded and diced

Sea salt and black pepper, to taste

2 tbsp (30 g) ghee, divided

1 yellow onion, diced

2 cloves garlic, minced

6 medium carrots, peeled and diced

1 pound (454 g) beef stew meat, diced into even pieces

3 tbsp (24 g) chili seasoning, see below

6 ounces (168 g) mushrooms, diced

14 ounces (392 g) diced tomatoes, blended into sauce

2 cups (470 ml) Slow Cooker Chicken Broth (page 170)

6 ounces (168 g) baby spinach

2 tbsp (16 g) arrowroot flour, optional

CHILI SEASONING

¼ cup (32 g) chili powder

2 tbsp (16 g) garlic powder

1 tbsp (8 g) onion powder

2 tbsp (16 g) dried oregano

1 tbsp (8 g) paprika

2 tbsp (16 g) dried coriander

½ tbsp (4 g) dried marjoram

Preheat oven to 390°F (200°C, or gas mark 6). Line a large baking tray with parchment paper. Place diced butternut squash into a large mixing bowl and season with sea salt and black pepper. Mix well. Place the butternut squash onto the baking tray and drizzle with 1 tablespoon (15 g) ghee. Bake for 30 to 40 minutes or until tender.

Combine the chili seasoning ingredients and store any leftovers.

While the squash is baking add 1 tablespoon (15 g) ghee to a large heavy-bottomed pot with a lid. Heat over medium heat and add the diced onions. Sauté for around 5 minutes until softened then add the minced garlic. Cook for another 1 to 2 minutes. Add the carrots and cook for another 10 minutes or until the carrots start to soften. Add the diced beef and stir to brown, about 8 to 10 minutes. Season with some more sea salt and pepper. When the meat is just about cooked through add in the chili seasoning and mix. Add the mushrooms, tomatoes and chicken broth. Mix well.

Once ready stir in the butternut squash. Turn the heat down to low and cover the pot with a lid. Simmer for 20 to 30 minutes. Remove the lid and add the baby spinach. Cook until the spinach has wilted, around 2 to 3 minutes. Taste and adjust for seasoning accordingly. If you would like to thicken the stew, stir in 2 tablespoons (16 g) arrowroot powder after the stew is off the heat. Serve warm.

SWEET AND SPICY BUTTERNUT SQUASH SOUP

Sweetened with honey and spiced with cumin and cinnamon, this butternut squash soup makes a delicious and comforting meal. —NK

SERVES 4

1 (2-pound [908-g]) butternut squash, peeled, seeded and cut into even chunks

2 tbsp (30 g) ghee, divided

1 medium red onion, diced

1 tsp (3 g) ground cumin

1 tsp (3 g) ground cinnamon

½ tsp sea salt

¼ tsp black pepper

6 cups (1410 ml) Slow Cooker Chicken Broth (page 170)

2 tbsp (30 ml) raw honey

Preheat oven to 425°F (220°C, or gas mark 7). Line a large baking tray with parchment paper. Add butternut squash to the baking tray and drizzle with 1 tablespoon (15 g) ghee. Bake in the oven for 45 to 50 minutes or until tender.

Heat 1 tablespoon (15 g) ghee in a large heavy-bottomed pot over medium heat. Add the onions and fry for 10 minutes, then add the roasted butternut squash and cook, stirring for about 5 minutes. Add the cumin, cinnamon, sea salt and black pepper. Pour in the chicken broth and mix. Bring to a boil then reduce the heat and cook for another 10 minutes. Using an immersion blender, blend the mixture into a soup or blend the soup in batches in a blender. Once blended, mix in the raw honey. Check for seasoning and add more sea salt and black pepper if needed. Serve warm.

CREAMY CURRIED BUTTERNUT SQUASH SOUP

This golden soup combines roasted butternut squash with sautéed onions and rich spices. Deeply nourishing and deliciously creamy, this winter squash soup is the perfect meal for a chilly winter day. —KH

SERVES 4

1 large butternut squash

1 tsp (3 g) ground turmeric

½ tsp ground cumin

½ tsp ground coriander

¼ tsp ground cinnamon

¼ tsp ground cardamom

½ onion

2 tbsp (30 g) coconut oil or ghee

3–4 cloves garlic, minced

2–3 cups (470-705 ml) bone broth

1–1½-inch (2.5–3.8-cm) piece of fresh ginger, grated, depending on how gingery you like it

½ cup (120 ml) full-fat coconut milk

Sea salt, to taste

Cut butternut squash in half, seed, and cook until tender, about 45 minutes. Either bake in oven at 400°F (200°C, or gas mark 6) skin side down until soft or place into slow cooker with 1 inch (2.5 cm) of water on high for about 2 hours. Remove from heat and allow to cool.

Place all dry spices into small bowl and set aside.

Sauté onion in fat of choice for 5 to 7 minutes until onions begin to brown. Add garlic and cook another minute or two. Pour in spices and let them temper for a minute or two, stirring occasionally. They will get very fragrant. Do not let them smoke. Turn down heat if necessary.

Add 2 cups (470 ml) of bone broth, ginger and the coconut milk. Stir to combine. Scoop out all of the meat from the butternut squash and add to soup. Use an immersion blender or regular blender to completely purée the soup together. Add more broth if necessary. Rewarm, salt to taste and enjoy!

SWEET POTATO CHILI

This hearty, one-pot dinner recipe is the perfect comfort food on a chilly evening. Sweet potatoes, ground meat and savory spices combine perfectly for a heart and soul warming meal. Fresh cilantro and avocado are the perfect garnish. —KH

SERVES 6

2 bay leaves

2 tbsp (16 g) chili powder

1 tbsp (8 g) ground cumin

½ tsp dried oregano

½ tsp ground cinnamon

¼ tsp ground ginger

¼ tsp ground allspice

1½ tsp (4 g) sea salt

1 tbsp (15 g) ghee, butter or coconut oil

1 small onion, chopped fine

4 cloves fresh garlic, chopped fine

2 pounds (908 g) beef or bison

2 cups (500 g) red sauce or crushed tomatoes

2 cups (470 ml) Slow Cooker Chicken Broth, or Beef Broth (page 170 or 171)

4 cups (600 g) sweet potatoes, chopped into 1-inch (2.5-cm) pieces

¾ cup (90 g) celery, diced

FOR THE GARNISH

Avocado slices

Fresh cilantro

Combine all the spices and salt in a small bowl and set aside. Melt fat of choice in a large pot and cook onions until they begin to turn translucent, about 6 minutes and slightly brown. Add ground meat and garlic. Continue to cook until meat is completely browned, about 8 to 10 minutes.

Pour in red sauce or crushed tomatoes and broth. Add spice mixture. Give it a good mix, cover and let simmer for 5 minutes to meld the flavors. Add the sweet potatoes and celery, give another good mix, cover and let simmer very gently for 40 minutes, stirring a couple of times. Top with loads of avocado slices and fresh cilantro.

JALAPEÑO BACON SWEET POTATO SOUP

This soup is especially perfect for a cold fall day. The contrast of sweetness from the sweet potatoes and spiciness from the jalapeño peppers is a winning combination. —KW

SERVES 4

4 slices bacon

1 medium onion, chopped

4 jalapeño peppers, diced

3 cloves garlic, minced

4 cups (940 ml) Slow Cooker Chicken Broth (page 170)

5 medium sweet potatoes, diced

1 tsp (3 g) smoked paprika

½ tsp chili powder

½ tsp ground cumin

Salt and pepper, to taste

Fry bacon in a skillet over medium heat. Set aside. Use the bacon fat to cook the onion and jalapeño peppers for 5 minutes or until onion is translucent. Add garlic and cook for an additional minute. Add the chicken broth, sweet potatoes and spices and bring to a boil. Turn the heat down to low and simmer for 30 minutes. With an immersion blender, blender or food processor, process the soup until thoroughly blended and creamy. Top each serving with a piece of crumbled bacon.

CHEF'S TIP:

If you want less heat, remove most or all of the seeds from the jalapeños. For an extra tasty treat, top each serving with cilantro and chopped green onion. If you can tolerate dairy, a dollop of sour cream added to each serving is absolutely divine, too.

CARROT GINGER SOUP

I love having this soothing soup on cold winter nights. When I make it, I like to make a big batch and keep a jar in the freezer for easy access when I don't have time to cook. —HH

SERVES 6–8

1 small onion

6 cloves garlic

2 pounds (908 g) carrots

1 large knob of ginger (a roughly 3 × 5-inch [7.5 × 12.5-cm] piece), peeled and grated

2 tbsp (30 g) ghee, lard or oil

½ tsp oregano

½ tsp parsley

½ tsp sage

½ tsp thyme

1 tsp (3 g) salt

1 tsp (3 g) pepper

1 tsp (3 g) dried ginger, optional

4 cups (940 ml) Slow Cooker Chicken Broth (page 170)

Chop the onions, garlic and carrots and peel the ginger. Put the ghee in a large pot and heat on medium heat. Once the pan and oil is hot, add the onion to the pot and allow to cook for a couple minutes, then add the garlic. Cook the onions until they are soft and almost translucent. Add the carrots, oregano, parsley, sage, thyme, salt, pepper and dried ginger to the pot and stir. Then, grate the ginger into the pan and sauté for a couple minutes.

Add the bone broth until it covers the carrots. Put a top on the pot and allow the soup to come to a boil. Once it starts boiling, turn the heat down to low and let it gently simmer for 30 to 45 minutes or until the carrots are soft.

Once the carrots are soft, turn the heat off. If you have an immersion blender you can begin to purée the soup with that. If you have to use a blender to purée the soup, wait for the soup to cool for at least 30 minutes to an hour before transferring it to the blender. Once it's cool, pour part of the soup in the blender and purée, then transfer to a bowl. Continue until all the soup is puréed, then return the purée to the pot, reheat and serve.

APPLE KABOCHA SOUP

Have you ever had a soup that tastes just like apple and pumpkin pie in one delicious bite? That's exactly how this soup is. I wouldn't be surprised if this becomes one of your fall favorites. —VM

SERVES 4

1 cup (120 g) almond flour

¼ cup (60 g) ghee

2 apples, peeled, cored and sliced

1 whole kabocha squash, peeled, seeded and cubed

2 quarts (2 l) water OR 1 quart (1 l) water and 1 quart (1 l) Slow Cooker Chicken Broth (page 170)

1 pinch ground cardamom

1 pinch black pepper

Coconut cream, for serving

Heat a non-stick skillet over high heat and toast the almond flour for about 3 to 4 minutes. In a separate pot, melt the ghee over medium heat and then add the sliced apples. Let the apple sauté for about 5 minutes, and then add the kabocha squash. Raise the heat and sauté the mixture an additional 5 minutes.

Once the apples and kabocha have softened, add in the almond flour and 2 quarts (2 l) of water or water and chicken broth, the cardamom and the black pepper.

Lower the heat and let it cook for 30 minutes. After the 30 minutes, use an immersion blender to blend the soup until it's nice and smooth.

Serve with a nice dollop of coconut cream and the lightest dusting of cardamom.

BEET AND BASIL SOUP

My husband and I are not necessarily big fans of beets, but we both really enjoy this warm beet soup. The addition of our garden-fresh basil is especially tasty. —KW

SERVES 4

2 tbsp (30 ml) avocado oil or fat of choice

1 medium onion, diced

3 cloves garlic, minced

6 medium beets, peeled and diced

2 cups (470 ml) Slow Cooker Chicken or Beef Broth (page 170 or 171)

Sea salt and pepper to taste

¼ cup (15 g) fresh basil, chopped

Add fat of choice to a skillet over medium heat and sauté the onions and garlic until soft, about 5 minutes. Add in the beets and cook for an additional minute. Stir in the broth, sea salt and pepper. Turn the heat to medium-high and bring to a boil. Turn down the heat and simmer for 45 minutes or until the beets are tender. Using an immersion blender, process the soup until smooth and creamy. Top with 1 tablespoon (4 g) of chopped fresh basil per serving.

CHEF'S TIP:
If you tolerate dairy, adding a shaving or two of Pecorino Romano to each bowl is superb.

CREAM OF ZUCCHINI SOUP

An easy and tasty zucchini soup made with chicken broth, garlic and onion that is great for you!. —VM

SERVES 4

2 pounds (908 g) zucchini

2 cups (470 ml) Slow Cooker Chicken Broth (page 170)

½ white onion, thinly sliced

2 cloves garlic, thinly sliced

Sprig of fresh thyme

Sea salt

4 tbsp (60 ml) olive oil, plus extra to sauté and garnish

Cut the zucchini into large 2-inch (5-cm) pieces, reserving about a quarter of them on the side. Blanch the zucchini pieces in boiling, salted water for about 5 minutes. Once you take them out of the boiling water, submerge them in a bowl of ice water to cool them down and preserve their brilliant color.

After the zucchini have cooled, purée them in a blender along with the chicken broth until smooth.

In a large pan, sauté the onion, garlic and thyme with the oil over low heat. Take the remaining zucchini and cut them into 1-inch (2.5-cm) pieces. Add the zucchini to a pan over high heat, sautéing them until they are a little al dente, about 3 minutes.

Season the zucchini with sea salt to taste and then add to the zucchini purée. Serve the soup in shallow bowls, drizzling a little olive oil to finish. Enjoy!

SOUTHWESTERN ZUCCHINI SOUP

This soup is my favorite way to use up all of that extra summer zucchini. It's bursting with the flavors of cumin, fresh cilantro and lemon and perfectly creamy. You can add fresh jalapeños for a little extra kick. —KH

SERVES 4

1 small onion, chopped

2 tbsp (30 g) butter, ghee or coconut oil

3 cloves garlic

1 tsp (3 g) ground cumin

3 cups (360 g) zucchini, chopped into small pieces

1½ cups (180 g) yellow summer squash, chopped into small pieces

4 cups (940 ml) good quality homemade broth

2–3 tbsp (16–24 g) green chilies or jalapeños peppers, finely chopped, fresh or canned

1 cup (235 ml) full-fat coconut milk

Salt and pepper, to taste

¼ cup (15 g) cilantro, finely chopped

3 tbsp (45 ml) fresh lemon or lime juice

2 tbsp (16 g) nutritional yeast

Avocado slices, for garnish

Sauté onion in fat of choice until translucent and starting to brown, about 6 minutes. Add chopped garlic and ground cumin and sauté another minute or two. Add chopped zucchini and yellow squash and sauté for 3 to 4 minutes to soften. Add broth and green chilies/jalapeños. Cover and bring to a boil. Once it comes to a boil, turn off heat, leave lid on and allow flavors to meld for 10 minutes. Add coconut milk, salt and pepper to taste, cilantro, lemon/lime juice and nutritional yeast. Garnish with avocado slices. Serve immediately.

GREEN PEA SOUP

This bright green soup combines quality broth with rich ham and softened vegetables for a silky-sweet finish. —RB

SERVES 5

3 tbsp (45 ml) coconut oil

1 carrot

½ onion

2 cups (240 g) chopped ham

4 cups (940 ml) Slow Cooker Chicken Broth (page 170) or vegetable broth

2 (16-ounce [454-g]) bags frozen peas

5 mint leaves

FOR THE GARNISH

Mint leaves

Coconut yogurt

Cracked pepper

Heat the coconut oil in a large skillet over medium heat. Pulse the carrot and onion in a food processor until shredded, then add to the skillet.

Add the chopped ham and cook for 20 minutes, or until the vegetables are very soft. While they cook, combine the broth and frozen peas in a large pot and warm until thawed.

Purée the broth, peas and mint leaves in batches in a blender until as smooth as you prefer. Transfer back to the large pot, and add the softened carrots, onion and ham. Heat the mixture through.

Ladle into bowls and top with mint, coconut yogurt and freshly cracked pepper for garnish.

GREEN BEAN STEW WITH GARLIC CAULIFLOWER MASH

For this recipe I took one of my favorite dishes growing up called *Loobia Polo* or Green Bean Stew with Rice and turned it into a simple-to-make version that's still as flavorful as the original. —NK

SERVES 2–4

2 tbsp (30 g) ghee

1 yellow onion, finely chopped

¼ tsp turmeric

1 pound (454 g) beef stew meat, diced into even pieces

1 pound (454 g) green beans, cut into ½-inch (1.3-cm) pieces

1 tbsp (15 g) organic tomato paste

1 (16-ounce [454-g]) can organic tomatoes, blended

Juice of one small lemon

½ tsp ground cinnamon

Sea salt and black pepper, to taste

1 head cauliflower, washed, cored and diced into pieces

¼ tsp garlic powder

Heat a medium skillet on medium heat and add the ghee. Add the onion and cook for about 6 to 8 minutes or until translucent. Add the turmeric and mix together. Add the meat and brown. Add the green beans and cook for about 8 minutes before adding the tomato paste, canned tomatoes, lemon juice, cinnamon, sea salt and black pepper. Bring the sauce to a boil, then lower the heat to a simmer and cook, covered, for 15 to 20 minutes or until the meat is cooked through and the green beans are softened. Set aside.

To make the cauliflower mash, add cauliflower pieces to a large pot and cover with cold water. Bring water to a boil then lower the heat and cook for 20 to 30 minutes or until the cauliflower pieces are softened. Drain and add the cauliflower to a food processor or blender. Add the garlic powder and sea salt and black pepper, to taste. Mix until well combined and you reach a mash consistency.

Serve the stew over the cauliflower mash.

GREENS AND YAM SOUP

A hearty soup combining two of the healthiest vegetables: kale and sweet potatoes. A perfect combination of savory and sweet. —KH

SERVES 6

1 onion, chopped

2 large yams, peeled and roughly chopped

3 cups (705 ml) filtered water

1 bunch kale, washed and chopped, tough stems removed

1 bunch chard or spinach, washed and chopped, tough stems removed

5-6 cloves garlic, peeled

½ tbsp (2 g) fresh thyme, or ⅛ tsp dried

¼ tsp dried oregano

4 cups (940 ml) good quality homemade broth

Juice from one lemon

Salt and pepper, to taste

In small skillet, sauté onion until translucent and starting to brown, about 5 minutes. Set aside. Place yams into large pot with the water. Bring to boil, turn down heat and simmer, covered, for 10 minutes.

Add chopped greens, garlic and spices into pot with yams. Pour stock in and stir. Simmer, covered, for 20 minutes on low-medium heat. Let cool slightly, then add cooked onions and use immersion blender to purée smooth or purée in small batches with a blender. Add lemon juice. Salt and pepper, to taste.

EASY ROASTED VEGETABLE SOUP

Warming soup with homemade broth is the best way to take the chill off of a cold day. This simple soup combines roasted winter vegetables with fresh herbs to make a hearty, savory meal. Pairs well with Rosemary Garlic Flatbread (page 523). —KH

SERVES 6

2 carrots

2 small sweet potatoes, peeled

2 parsnips

2 potatoes, peeled

1 small onion

1 sprig fresh rosemary

3 tbsp (45 ml) coconut oil, ghee, beef tallow or duck fat, melted

3-4 cloves garlic, peeled

1 quart (940 ml) homemade broth, plus more to thin the soup if desired

1 tsp (3 g) unrefined salt

2 tbsp (8 g) fresh parsley, chopped, plus more for garnish

Salt and pepper, to taste

Preheat the oven to 400°F (200°C, or gas mark 6).

Roughly chop carrots, sweet potatoes, parsnips, potatoes and onion and place into a large bowl. Add the rosemary. Pour in fat of choice and toss until vegetables are coated. Roast veggies on a large baking pan for 30 to 40 minutes, throwing in garlic cloves halfway through and turning vegetables once—until soft and beginning to brown.

Remove from oven, remove sprig of rosemary and place veggies into a large soup pot. Add broth, salt and parsley. Purée with a hand immersion blender or in a regular blender, adding in more broth or water to thin to desired consistency. Salt and pepper, to taste. Garnish with fresh chopped parsley. Gently reheat and serve warm.

BROCCOLI SOUP

This broccoli soup is a tasty way to get a serving of vegetables. Adding the butter at the end creates a creamy texture and rich flavor that makes it almost like a cream-based broccoli soup. Make a big batch and save it for leftovers throughout the week! —HH

SERVES 4

1 small onion

5 cloves garlic

3 tbsp (45 g) ghee or oil

1 tsp (3 g) oregano

½ tsp parsley

1 tsp (3 g) sage

¼ tsp ginger

1–2 heads broccoli

5–6 cups (1175–1410 ml) Slow Cooker Chicken Broth (page 170)

4 tbsp (60 ml) melted butter or olive oil, optional for added texture

Salt and pepper, to taste

Dice the onion and garlic. Melt ghee over medium-high heat in a pot. Add onions and garlic and stir. Add spices and mix until the onions are almost translucent, about 3 to 5 minutes. Chop broccoli to same-sized bits. Chop the stalk a little finer so it cooks through. Add the broccoli to the pot and allow to cook for a few minutes. Add the broth to the pot and stir. Cover and allow it to come to a boil, then turn down to low and let simmer for about 20 to 30 minutes or until the broccoli is tender almost mushy.

The easiest way to blend the soup is to use an immersion blender. You can also put it into a blender or food processor, but let it cool down a bit before blending. Once it is blended, add the butter. This adds a creamy delicious texture and flavor. Add more butter, salt and pepper to your liking.

ICED BROCCOLI SOUP

This is a great soup to have during those hot summer days. Refreshing but cooling and creamy at the same time, it will hit the spot as a whole meal. —VM

SERVES 4

1 yellow onion, chopped

2 tbsp (30 ml) extra-virgin olive oil

2 cups (470 ml) Slow Cooker Chicken or Beef Broth (pages 170 and 171), chilled, fat removed

2 broccoli heads, cleaned and trimmed into florets

2 ounces (56 g) mushrooms, sliced

1 bunch chives, finely chopped

1 cup (235 ml) coconut milk

Sea salt and black pepper to taste

5–6 walnuts, for garnish

Pinch of nutmeg, for garnish

Cook the chopped onions with the olive oil in a saucepan for 5 minutes over low heat. Add the broth of choice and bring to a boil. Once it has reached a boil, add the broccoli and cook for another 5 minutes.

Add the mushrooms and chives, cooking for an additional 2 minutes. Take the soup off the heat and let it cool for a minute or two. Then put it in the food processor and blend until nice and smooth. Once the puréed soup has cooled completely refrigerate it for at least 2 hours. Add the coconut milk to the cold soup and blend one more time. Add sea salt and black pepper to taste.

Serve the soup garnished with walnuts and a sprinkle of nutmeg.

CREAM OF MUSHROOM SOUP

If you are dairy-free and miss those cream-based mushroom soups, this recipe is for you! I use puréed cauliflower and coconut milk to replicate that creaminess. —HH

SERVES 4–6

1 tbsp (15 g) ghee, butter or avocado oil

1 small onion, diced

6 cloves garlic, diced

½ tsp oregano

½ head of a medium cauliflower, chopped

1½ cups (105 g) chopped mushrooms, divided

2½ cups (590 ml) broth

½ tsp salt

½ tsp pepper

1 tbsp (15 g) butter, ghee or oil

¾ cup (180 ml) full-fat coconut milk, canned

In a large pot heat the ghee or oil and sauté the onions and garlic for a minute, then add the oregano. Cook until the onions are slightly translucent, about 3 to 5 minutes. Add the chopped cauliflower and the ½ cup (35 g) of chopped mushrooms and cook for about 2 minutes. Add the broth, salt and pepper and bring to a boil. Turn the boil down to a simmer and cook, covered, until the cauliflower is soft and fork tender.

While the cauliflower mixture is cooking, heat 1 tablespoon (15 ml) of butter or oil on medium-high heat in a separate pan and sauté the remaining chopped mushrooms. Sautée until soft and slightly browned, about 5 to 7 minutes, then turn off the heat and set aside.

Once the cauliflower mixture has cooked fully, turn off the heat. Using an immersion blender, mix the cauliflower until it is fully puréed. Add the coconut milk and purée again. If using a regular blender, allow the mixture to cool for at least 30 minutes before blending to avoid damaging your blender. Once the mixture is fully puréed, add the sautéed mushrooms to the soup pot and mix with a spoon.

CLAM CHOWDER

Chowder is usually full of flour and butter, but this grain-free version is lighter and gets its creaminess from softened potatoes and a good dose of coconut milk. Stir in the bacon immediately before serving for a crispy contrast to the creamy soup. —JC

SERVES 4

¾ pound (340 g) bacon, chopped into ½-inch (1.3-cm) pieces

4 large shallots, chopped

1 pound (454 g) potatoes, chopped into ¼-inch (6-mm) pieces

1 cup (235 ml) vegetable broth

8 ounces (227 g) clam juice

2 (10-ounce [280-g]) cans clams in juice

½ cup (120 ml) coconut cream

Sea salt

Black pepper

¼ cup (15 g) chives, chopped

In a Dutch oven pan over medium-high heat, pan fry bacon for 10 to 12 minutes until crispy. Remove and set aside.

Drain excess fat and leave 2 tablespoons (30 ml) in the pan. Add shallots and potatoes. Sauté for 5 minutes. Add broth, clam juice and liquid from canned clams. Scrape the bottom of the pan, stir and bring to a boil.

Reduce heat to low. Cover and simmer for 20 minutes until potatoes are soft. Lightly mash cooked potatoes with a wooden spoon until the sauce thickens slightly. Add coconut cream and clams. Season with sea salt and black pepper to taste. Stir and simmer uncovered for 5 minutes.

Turn off the heat and stir in the bacon pieces. Immediately spoon into bowls and top with chopped chives. Serve hot.

MARYLAND CRAB SOUP

Being a Baltimore native, I'm very serious about my crab cakes and crab soup. I use the leftover shells from family crab feasts to make a fragrant stock, then add traditional veggies and blue crab meat. —RM

SERVES 8

8 cups (1880 ml) crab stock (see Chef's Tip)

1 (14.5-ounce [406-g]) can diced tomatoes

½ pound (227 g) green beans, cut in thirds

3 carrots, chopped

1 potato, peeled and cubed

1 celery rib, chopped

1 yellow onion, chopped

1 cup (150 g) corn kernels, optional

2 bay leaves

1 teaspoon (3 g) fresh ground pepper

Old Bay seasoning, to taste

2 cups (240 g) blue crab meat

Salt to taste

Heat the stock in a large pot over medium heat. Add all the vegetables and spices and let simmer for about an hour, until tender. Add the crab meat and allow to simmer for an additional 30 minutes. Remove the bay leaves and serve immediately. Store leftovers in the refrigerator for up to a week.

CHEF'S TIP:

To make an easy crab stock, fill a stock pot with the leftover crab shells and legs then cover with water and simmer for 2 hours. Strain the stock using a colander lined with cheese cloth.

THAI COCONUT SOUP WITH SHRIMP OR CHICKEN

This is my Paleo and healthy version of a Thai classic. Now you don't have to feel deprived of your favorite exotic foods! —VM

SERVES 2

FOR THE BROTH

4 cups (940 ml) Slow Cooker Chicken Broth (page 170)

1½ cups (355 ml) full-fat coconut milk

3 kaffir lime leaves, or the zest of 1 lime

1 inch (2.5 cm) fresh lemongrass, cut into slices

1 cup (60 g) fresh cilantro

3 or 4 dried Thai chilies, or 1 jalapeño pepper sliced

1 inch (2.5 cm) fresh galangal root or ginger root

1 tsp (6 g) sea salt

FOR THE SOUP

3½ ounces (98 g) uncooked shrimp or chicken thigh meat

1 tbsp (15 ml) fish sauce (I use Red Boat)

1 ounce (28 g) red onion, sliced thinly

1 ounce (28 g) mushrooms, any kind, sliced

Juice of 1 lime

1 tbsp (4 g) cilantro, chopped to garnish

Simmer all of the broth ingredients in a sauce pan over low to medium heat for 20 minutes. Strain and return to the same pan.

Bring the broth back to a simmer and then add the protein of choice. Add the fish sauce, onions and mushrooms and let simmer for 10 minutes or until the protein is done. Add the lime juice, garnish with cilantro and serve!

KOREAN FUSION SOUP

This soup really helped me to kick a terrible cold. Ever since then it has been one of my go-tos every time I get sick. The fragrant aroma of the garlic and ginger along with the healing nourishment of the homemade chicken stock is everything one could need when they get sick. I hope it will nurse you back to health and delight the senses as well. —VM

SERVES 4

1 quart (1 l) Slow Cooker Chicken Broth (page 170)

1 bunch kale, stemmed and roughly chopped

2–3 cloves garlic

1-inch (2.5-cm) slice of ginger (more if you like)

¼ cup (32 g) Korean hot pepper flakes, or red chili pepper flakes

4 tbsp (60 ml) fish sauce (I use Red Boat)

2 eggs, optional (see Chef's Tip)

In a medium stock pot over high heat, bring the chicken stock to a nice boil. While the chicken stock is coming to a boil, add all the remaining ingredients to a food processor and blend well. Add the mixture to the chicken stock and simmer for 2 to 3 minutes. You can adjust the taste of the soup by adding more fish sauce or chili flakes to the desired taste.

Serve very hot, so it will open the sinuses and give you a good detoxing sweat!

CHEF'S TIP:

If you like you can add a couple of eggs and let them simmer with the soup until done. They will poach nicely in the soup. Serve them whole or stir them in for a different effect.

ASIAN CRAB SOUP WITH MUSTARD GREENS

Crab, mushrooms, and mustard greens swim in a light spicy broth. It's then topped with crunchy bacon to complete the complex flavor profile. —RM

SERVES 3–4

2 slices bacon

1 cup (70 g) shiitake mushrooms, sliced

1 tsp (3 g) red pepper flakes

1 tsp (3 g) salt

Pepper, to taste

4 cloves garlic, minced

1 tbsp (8 g) fresh ginger, minced

1 cup (140 g) shredded cooked chicken

3 cups (750 g) mustard greens

6 cups (1410 ml) chicken stock

1 cup (120 g) blue crab meat

1 tbsp (15 ml) fish sauce

1 tbsp (4 g) Thai basil

Cook the bacon in a sauté pan over medium heat until crispy, about 5 minutes. Reserve bacon and keep the fat in the pan. Add the mushrooms, red pepper flakes, salt and pepper and cook about 5 minutes until the mushrooms have softened. Add the minced garlic and ginger and stir in for about a minute. Add the chicken and mustard greens.

Stir everything together and keep cooking until the greens have wilted. Now add the chicken stock, crab meat, fish sauce and basil and simmer for about 10 minutes. Pour into serving bowls and crumble bacon on top, then serve.

ORIENTAL GOJI BERRY SOUP

Goji berries are used in Chinese medicine to promote healthy liver function, immunization, longevity and even eyesight. These sweetly sour berries are used in a lot of traditional cooking as well. —RM

SERVES 2

1 tbsp (15 g) chicken fat, other animal fat, or coconut oil

2 cups (140 g) sliced mushrooms

Salt and pepper, to taste

1 tbsp (8 g) minced ginger

2 tsp (6 g) red pepper flakes

4 cloves garlic, minced

2 cups (280 g) shredded chicken

4 cups (940 ml) Slow Cooker Chicken Broth (page 170)

1 tbsp (4 g) dried Thai basil

1 tbsp (15 ml) fish sauce

¼ cup (38 g) goji berries

1 green onion, sliced

Cilantro to garnish

Heat your choice of fat in a sauté pan over medium heat. Add sliced mushrooms. Salt and pepper the mushrooms and cook down for a few minutes, then add the minced ginger, pepper flakes, garlic and shredded chicken. Sauté together for another 2 minutes then add the chicken stock, Thai basil and fish sauce. Bring to a simmer and add goji berries and green onions. Allow to simmer for 5 minutes and then plate. Garnish with a few cilantro leaves.

CHEF'S TIP:

If you don't have any already cooked shredded chicken, use ½ chicken breast sliced in to extremely thin strips and add at the same time you sauté the mushrooms.

WAKAME SEAWEED SALAD

Although seaweed is not a vegetable that is very commonly eaten outside of Asian countries, it is a great food to include in your daily diet. It is very nutrient dense and is one of the few dietary sources of magnesium and iodine! The flavor of the seaweed is almost reminiscent of seafood, yet much milder. The citrus and vinegar help to tame the ocean flavors while the sesame seeds add a wonderful crunch. —HH

SERVES 2

2 ounces (56 g) dried wakame seaweed, about 1 large package

1½ tsp (7.5 ml) apple cider vinegar

1 tsp (5 ml) lemon juice

1 tsp (5 ml) sesame seed oil or avocado oil

1 tsp (5 ml) coconut aminos

2 green onion stalks

½ tsp sea salt

2 tsp (6 g) toasted sesame seeds

Place the dried wakame in a large bowl (it will expand a lot) and fill with lukewarm water. Let it soak and expand for about 10 minutes. While the seaweed is soaking, prepare the dressing by combining the apple cider vinegar, lemon juice, sesame oil and coconut aminos in a small bowl and set aside. Then, chop the green onions and set aside.

Once the seaweed has soaked for about 10 minutes, drain the water from the bowl. Place one piece at a time on a cutting board and cut into thin long slices, then place into a bowl. Once you have sliced all of the seaweed, place the dressing mixture over the seaweed and toss to cover evenly. Sprinkle with sea salt and sesame seeds and mix. Then, top with the chopped green onions.

THAI CRUNCH CHOP SALAD

This Thai chop salad will have you wanting an extra serving of your vegetables! It is made Paleo with the addition of a creamy almond butter dressing and slightly tangy with the addition of soy-free coconut amino and vinegar. Serve with slices of grilled chicken for a complete dinner for warm summer nights. —CP

SERVES 6

FOR THE DRESSING

½ cup (30 g) fresh cilantro

¼ cup (60 ml) macadamia nut oil

3 tbsp (45 g) almond butter

2 tbsp (30 ml) coconut aminos

1 tbsp (15 ml) rice vinegar

1 lime, juiced

½ tsp fish sauce

¼ tsp fresh cracked black pepper

2 cups (200 g) shredded green cabbage

2 cups (200 g) shredded red cabbage

2 carrots, shredded

4 green onions, chopped

1 mango, sliced

⅓ cup (40 g) slivered almonds, toasted

Blend all dressing ingredients together in a blender. Scrape down the sides of the blender and briefly blend again.

Add shredded cabbage, carrots and green onions together in a bowl. Toss salad together with the dressing.

Plate and garnish with sliced mango and a sprinkle of toasted almonds.

ASIAN NOODLE SALAD

A crunchy salad of vegetables and kelp noodles in a light, spicy dressing. —RB

SERVES 6

FOR THE SALAD

1 small Napa cabbage

½ small purple cabbage

½ bunch green onion

1 red pepper

1 yellow pepper

½ small bunch cilantro

3 large handfuls baby spinach

1 large handful bean sprouts

1 (12-ounce [340-g]) package kelp noodles

FOR THE DRESSING

2 tbsp (30 ml) olive oil

2 tbsp (30 ml) coconut aminos

1 tbsp (15 ml) honey

1 tbsp (15 ml) sesame oil

Juice of ¼ lime

1 clove garlic

1 (2-inch [5-cm]) piece raw ginger, peeled

½ serrano pepper, seeds removed

½ tsp salt

FOR THE GARNISH

Sesame seeds

Thinly chop the Napa cabbage, starting at the head and working toward the base. Place in a large mixing bowl. Thinly slice the purple cabbage into strips, then wash and dice the green onions. Add to the Napa cabbage.

Halve the bell peppers and remove the pith and seeds. Thinly slice and add to the mixing bowl.

Roughly chop the cilantro and spinach and add to the other vegetables. Top with the bean sprouts and noodles, then mix well.

To make the dressing, combine the ingredients in a blender. Purée until completely smooth and then drizzle over the vegetables and noodles. Toss to coat, then top with sesame seeds and serve.

CHEF'S TIP:

Feel free to play around with crunchy vegetables in different combinations. Use carrots instead of peppers, or add mushrooms and top with cashews.

ASIAN CUCUMBER SALAD WITH SESAME GINGER DRESSING

The Sesame Ginger Dressing transforms ordinary cucumber into something unique and flavorful. This dish goes especially well with the Sesame-Crusted Salmon (page 102). —KW

SERVES 4

1 clove garlic, minced

1 tsp (3 g) fresh ginger, grated

1 tbsp (15 ml) olive oil

1 tbsp (15 ml) toasted sesame oil

1 tbsp (15 ml) coconut aminos

1 tbsp (15 ml) apple cider vinegar

1 tsp (5 ml) honey, optional

2 cucumbers, spiralized into noodles

FOR THE TOPPINGS

Green onions, sliced

Toasted sesame seeds

Avocado slices

Combine the garlic, ginger, oils, coconut aminos, vinegar and honey in a small bowl and stir to combine. Toss the cucumber noodles with the dressing and refrigerate at least 10 minutes. When ready to serve, top each serving with green onion, toasted sesame seeds and sliced avocado.

SEARED ALBACORE SALAD WITH CHIPOTLE AIOLI

The delicate albacore is paired with crunchy cabbage and spicy chipotle aioli for a simple and delicious meal. —AV

SERVES 4

4 (6-ounce [168-g]) albacore tuna fillets

Salt and pepper

2 tbsp (30 ml) avocado oil

1 cup (120 g) green cabbage, shredded

1 cup (120 g) purple cabbage, shredded

½ cup (32 g) cilantro, chopped

¼ cup (50 g) green onion, chopped

2 tbsp (30 ml) olive oil

2 tbsp (30 ml) lime juice

CHIPOTLE AIOLI

1 cup (240 g) Homemade Mayonnaise (page 496)

2 tsp (10 ml) fresh lime juice

1 clove garlic, minced

2 tsp (10 g) Chipotle Peppers in Adobo Sauce (page 518), chopped

Generously season albacore fillets with salt and pepper. Heat a cast iron skillet or heavy-bottomed pan over medium-high heat and coat it with the avocado oil. Lay the seasoned tuna in the hot oil and sear for 1 minute on each side to form a light crust. Depending on the size of the skillet, this may need to be done in batches. Remove the tuna and allow it to cool for 3 to 5 minutes. Once cooled, slice each fillet of tuna with a very sharp knife into 4 or 5 slices.

In a bowl, mix together the cabbage, cilantro, green onion, olive oil and lime juice. Salt and pepper to taste. Set aside.

To make the chipotle aioli, whisk mayonnaise with lime juice, garlic and Chipotle Peppers in Adobo Sauce. Season with salt and pepper. Chill until ready to serve.

To serve, divide the cilantro salad equally onto four plates, top with albacore and 1 to 2 tablespoons (15 to 30 g) of chipotle aioli.

FRESH GRILLED SARDINES WITH PERSIAN SALAD

This Persian salad, known as Salad Shirazi, is a delicious salad that can be enjoyed alongside chicken or fish or just as a refreshing salad on its own. Eating fresh sardines may feel intimidating, but let me tell you they are full of flavor and paired with this salad, they make a great meal. —NK

SERVES 1–2

7 ounces (196 g) cucumber, peeled and diced

1 red bell pepper, diced

1 small red onion, diced

1 tbsp (8 g) dried mint

Sea salt and black pepper, to taste

¼ cup (60 ml) fresh lime juice

1 tbsp (15 g) ghee

3 fresh sardines, cleaned and butterflied

Place cucumber, bell pepper and onion into a mixing bowl. Add in the dried mint and season with sea salt and black pepper. Mix well, cover then place in the fridge for 20 minutes. Remove from the fridge and stir in the lime juice. Cover and place back in the fridge.

Place a medium square grill pan over medium-high heat. Add in the ghee. While the pan is heating season both sides of the sardines with sea salt and black pepper. Place sardines skin-side down into the grill pan. Cook for 2 minutes then flip over and cook for another minute or two on the other side. Serve alongside the Persian Salad.

CHEF'S TIP:

Traditionally this salad is made with tomatoes; I substitute red bell peppers in here as I don't do well with tomatoes, but feel free to make this with tomatoes instead.

WINTER CHOP SALAD WITH ROASTED BRUSSELS SPROUTS

Sweet, crunchy apples give this salad a bit of pop! This salad is great to make up in advance as it lasts a while in the fridge. You can always top with any leftover sliced meat for a complete, healthy meal. —CP

SERVES 4–6

1 pound (454 g) Brussels sprouts, quartered

1 tbsp (15 ml) olive oil

1 tbsp (15 g) Dijon mustard

¼ tsp sea salt

Fresh cracked pepper

1 tbsp (15 g) butter

3 cups (210 g) kale, deveined and finely chopped

1 cup (100 g) red cabbage, thinly sliced

1 golden delicious apple, cored and thinly sliced

FOR THE DRESSING

3 tbsp (45 ml) olive oil

2 tbsp (30 g) Dijon mustard

2 tbsp (30 ml) champagne vinegar

1 tbsp (15 ml) apple cider vinegar

2 tsp (10 ml) fresh lemon juice

2 large cloves garlic, crushed

½ tsp ground cumin

¼ tsp sea salt

½ tsp fresh cracked pepper

Preheat oven to 375°F (190°C, or gas mark 5). Slice Brussels sprouts in quarters or halves, depending on the size, and toss with oil, mustard and salt and pepper. Place on baking sheet and top with slices of butter. Roast for 25 minutes, stirring halfway through. Cool completely.

While sprouts are roasting, make the dressing by whisking together all ingredients.

Mix the kale, cabbage and apple with half of the dressing, tossing with your hands or spoon.

Place the leafy vegetables and apples in a large serving bowl, topping with roasted Brussels sprouts. Drizzle remaining dressing on top, toss together and serve.

CHEF'S TIP:
This salad can be stored in the refrigerator for up to 3 days and will still taste great and crunchy.

ROASTED VEGETABLE SALAD

Roasted yams and beets add a bit of warmth to this hearty cool-weather salad. Lightly dressed with a lemony dressing, this salad pairs well with savory meats or stews. —KH

SERVES 4

FOR THE DRESSING

3 tbsp (45 ml) fresh lemon juice

3 tbsp (45 ml) olive oil

1½ tbsp (23 ml) honey

Pinch of salt

3 medium yams, peeled and chopped into 1-inch (2.5-cm) cubes

2 golden beets, peeled and chopped into 1-inch (2.5-cm) cubes

3 tbsp (45 ml) coconut oil, ghee or butter, melted

¼ tsp salt

2 red beets, peeled and chopped into 1-inch (2.5-cm) cubes

12 ounces (340 g) salad mix

2 tbsp (16 g) pumpkin seeds or sunflower seeds, for garnish

Preheat the oven to 375°F (190°C, or gas mark 5).

Combine all ingredients for dressing and mix well. Set aside.

Place the chopped yams and golden beets into a large bowl. Pour melted fat of choice and salt in and mix well. Gently toss in the red beets. Spread evenly onto large baking pan and roast for 45 minutes to 1 hour, until soft and beginning to brown, turning every 20 minutes. Remove from heat and allow to cool.

Place salad greens into large bowl and toss with dressing. Divide dressed greens evenly onto four plates, scoop roasted vegetables on top and garnish with pumpkin or sunflower seeds. Serve immediately.

HUNGARIAN CUCUMBER SALAD (UBORKASALÁTA)

This simple cucumber salad is another Hungarian dish passed on to me by my husband. It's refreshing and simple to make. Perfect for those warm summer days. —NK

SERVES 4

2 large cucumbers

1 tsp (6 g) sea salt, divided

1 cup (235 ml) filtered water

2 tbsp (30 ml) white wine vinegar

2 tsp (10 ml) raw honey

1 tsp (3 g) sweet Hungarian paprika powder

Peel and thinly slice the cucumber, a mandolin works best for this. Place into a mixing bowl and sprinkle with ½ teaspoon of sea salt. Mix well. Cover and set aside for an hour. After that time pour into a strainer and rinse with cold water. Place into a clean mixing bowl. In a separate mixing bowl add the filtered water, white wine vinegar, raw honey, paprika powder and ½ teaspoon sea salt. Mix well. Pour the dressing over the cucumber and let sit in the fridge for at least an hour before serving.

OLIVE, POMEGRANATE AND WALNUT SALAD

Salty olives, paired with sweet bursts of pomegranate seeds and crunchy walnuts make this a delightfully tasty salad. —NK

SERVES 4–6

12 ounces (336 g) pitted green olives, some chopped in half, some left whole

5 ounces (140 g) pomegranate seeds

2 ounces (56 g) walnuts, roughly chopped

2 small cloves garlic, minced

2 tbsp (8 g) fresh mint, chopped, divided

3 tbsp (45 ml) extra-virgin olive oil

Sea salt and black pepper, to taste

Place olives, pomegranate seeds, walnuts, garlic and 1 tablespoon (4 g) fresh mint into a medium-sized mixing bowl. Mix well. Add the extra-virgin olive oil, sea salt and black pepper and stir. Cover and place in the fridge for at least an hour before serving. To serve, sprinkle 1 tablespoon (4 g) fresh mint on top.

ROASTED GOLDEN BEET SALAD

Golden beets provide this delicious gluten-free fall salad with a bit of sweetness and pops of color. This roasted beet salad is tossed together with a simple vinaigrette and generously topped with savory bacon and feta crumbles. —CP

SERVES 6

2 golden beets, medium size

1 tbsp (15 ml) olive oil

½ tsp sea salt

½ pound (227 g) bacon

5 ounces (140 g) mixed baby lettuces

4 ounces (112 g) soft goat feta, optional

⅓ cup (50 g) pine nuts, toasted

8–10 basil leaves, thinly sliced

FOR THE DRESSING

½ cup (120 ml) olive oil

¼ cup (60 ml) champagne vinegar

1 tbsp (15 ml) lemon juice

1 tbsp (15 g) Dijon mustard

½ tsp sea salt

Fresh cracked black pepper

Preheat oven to 400°F (200°C, or gas mark 6). Line a baking sheet with parchment paper. Thinly slice golden beets, place on baking sheet and lightly brush with olive oil and sprinkle with salt.

Roast for 25 to 30 minutes, depending on thickness of beet slices, or until edges begin to turn golden brown and crisp. Cool completely.

Cook bacon in a large skillet, set aside to cool and then crumble into small pieces.

In a large serving bowl, assemble salad by laying the lettuce at the bottom, then beets and garnishing with remaining ingredients.

Mix together all dressing ingredients.

Drizzle desired amount of dressing over the salad, lightly toss and serve. Store any remaining dressing in the refrigerator.

RAW MARINATED BEET SALAD

The marinade in this recipe masks the bitterness of the beets, while the apple and mint add a pop of flavor and sweetness. This is a great appetizer or first course salad to serve at a dinner party. —HH

SERVES 2–3

2 small/medium beets, peeled and diced

Garlic Dijon Vinaigrette (page 514)

1 small Fuji apple, diced

7-9 mint leaves

Salt to taste

Place the beets in a container with Garlic Dijon Vinaigrette covering them. Store in the fridge overnight. The beets will take on the flavor of the dressing.

Remove the beets from the container with a fork or slotted spoon and put into a bowl. Put the diced apple and chopped mint leaves in the bowl and mix. Then sprinkle with salt.

CHICKEN SALAD WITH CITRUS, AVOCADO AND BEETS

I had this salad in a restaurant one day and was so pleased with the combinations of flavors that I went right home to re-create it. The flavors are fresh and light. A perfect lunch salad. —KH

SERVES 2–3

3 small beets, red or golden

1 small red onion, cut into thin rounds

3 cups (705 ml) boiling water

2 tbsp (30 ml) apple cider vinegar

3 cups (60 g) sunflower sprouts or arugula

2 cups (280 g) cooked and chopped chicken

1 small grapefruit, peeled and separated into segments

1 avocado, chopped or sliced

FOR THE DRESSING

2 tbsp (30 ml) white wine vinegar

2 tbsp (30 ml) fresh lemon juice

3 tbsp (45 ml) olive oil

1 tsp (5 ml) raw honey

¼ tsp grated fresh ginger

2 pinches of sea salt

Fresh pepper

Preheat the oven to 400°F (200°C, or gas mark 6). Wash and trim beets. Place in a baking dish, cover and bake until tender, about 45 to 60 minutes. Remove from oven and allow to cool. Once cool, peel and slice into thin rounds.

Place red onion rings in a small colander in the sink. Pour the boiling water over onions and drain. Place into small bowl, add apple cider vinegar and give it a good mix. Set aside. Process all dressing ingredients in a blender until well combined. Set aside.

To assemble salad: place sunflower sprouts or arugula in center of plate. Top with chopped chicken. Arrange sliced beets, vinegar-soaked onions, grapefruit slices and avocado in any way that makes you happy. Drizzle with dressing and enjoy!

NASTURTIUM AND PEACH SALAD

This delectable edible flower has a spicy, peppery flavor. The entire plant is edible, too. The peppery flavor of the nasturtiums complements the sweetness of the peaches in this salad perfectly. And don't skip the coconut-toasted pecans, they make the recipe! —AV

SERVES 8

FOR THE TOASTED PECANS

1 tbsp (15 ml) coconut oil, melted

½ tsp ground cinnamon

¼ tsp ground nutmeg

½ cup (75 g) pecans

FOR THE VINAIGRETTE

1 tbsp (15 g) peach, smashed

1 or 2 nasturtiums, smashed

1 tbsp (15 ml) fresh lemon juice, preferably Meyer lemon

2 tbsp (30 ml) olive oil

½ tsp raw honey

½ tsp stone-ground mustard

Salt and pepper to taste

FOR THE SALAD

8 ounces (227 g) mixed salad greens

1 peach, pit removed and sliced

20 nasturtiums, flowers and leaves

Preheat oven to 300°F (150°C, or gas mark 2). Combine coconut oil, cinnamon and nutmeg. Pour coconut oil mixture over the pecans and toss to coat evenly. Arrange on a baking sheet, and bake for about 15–20 minutes or until nuts are lightly browned.

Smash the peach and nasturtium reserved for the vinaigrette. I did this with a cocktail muddler. Whisk together all of the ingredients. Adjust salt and pepper to taste.

Place the salad greens in a shallow dish. Arrange the peach slices, nasturtiums and toasted pecans on top. Drizzle with vinaigrette and serve!

PEAR AND PERSIMMON FALL SALAD

I always look forward to that time of year when I can bite into a sweet, juicy persimmon. Here I added them to a salad including pears, almonds and greens and dressed this fall-inspired salad with a honey mustard vinaigrette. —NK

SERVES 4–6

FOR THE SALAD

5 ounces (140 g) arugula

1 green pear, mostly firm, cut into sticks

1 red pear, mostly firm, cut into sticks

2 ripe Hachiya persimmons, peeled and cut into sticks

2 ounces (56 g) slivered almonds, divided

FOR THE DRESSING

⅓ cup (80 ml) raw apple cider vinegar

2 tbsp (30 ml) raw honey

1 tbsp (15 g) Dijon mustard

⅔ cup (160 ml) extra-virgin olive oil

½ tsp sea salt

¼ tsp black pepper

Place arugula, pears, persimmons and 1 ounce (28 g) slivered almonds into a large mixing bowl. Mix well and set aside. In a small mixing bowl add the raw apple cider vinegar and whisk in the honey and Dijon mustard. In a steady, slow stream add the extra-virgin olive oil while whisking constantly at the same time until blended. Season with sea salt and black pepper and whisk thoroughly. Cover salad and the dressing and place in the fridge before serving. Dress the salad just before serving and top with 1 ounce (28 g) slivered almonds.

CHEF'S TIP:

The recipe for the dressing makes a lot of dressing, so feel free to set some aside to use at a later time if desired.

APPLE, POMEGRANATE BUTTERLEAF SALAD

Fresh, crunchy pomegranate seeds add pops of color to this simple salad. Butter leaf is such a light variety of lettuce that this salad serves up as a refreshing side to a heavier meal. —CP

SERVES 4–6

1 pomegranate

2 small heads of butter leaf lettuce

2 small apples, sliced

½ cup (75 g) toasted pecans, chopped

1 recipe Grainy Mustard Champagne Vinaigrette (page 513)

Start by seeding the pomegranate. Slice pomegranate in half and use your fingers to gently remove the seeds. Set seeds aside in a bowl.

Assemble butter leaf lettuce leaves, sliced apples, pomegranates and toasted pecans in a large bowl. Drizzle with desired amount of dressing.

Toss together, plate and serve!

STRAWBERRY ASPARAGUS SPRING SALAD

This is a refreshing springtime salad bursting with fresh flavor. I think you'll especially love the special details like the easy candied walnuts. The balsamic dressing is equally fantastic with vibrant light lemon flavors. Be sure to use fresh, in-season produce for the best flavors —KW

SERVES 6+

FOR THE DRESSING

3 tbsp (45 ml) balsamic vinegar

2 tbsp (30 ml) olive oil

1 lemon, zested and juiced

Salt and pepper, to taste

1 tbsp (15 ml) honey, optional

2 tsp (10 g) butter or coconut oil

1 tbsp (15 ml) honey

½ cup (75 g) walnuts

Pinch of sea salt

1 bunch of fresh asparagus, cut into 1-inch (2.5-cm) pieces, about 2 cups (240 g)

1 pint (300 g) of strawberries, about 2 cups (300 g), sliced

Combine the vinegar, oil, lemon juice and zest, and salt and pepper and honey (if using). Stir until well mixed.

For the candied walnuts: in a skillet over medium heat, melt the butter and the honey. Add in the walnuts and stir until the walnuts are sticky and well coated. Add a dash of sea salt to them. Set aside to cool.

Snap the tough ends off the asparagus. I do this by gently bending the asparagus and they will naturally snap off where they are supposed to. After the tough ends are off, slice the asparagus on an angle into 1-inch (2.5-cm) pieces. Bring a pot of water to a boil and boil the asparagus for 3 minutes. Drain and rinse with cold water. Combine the asparagus with the sliced strawberries in a large bowl. Add the dressing to the bowl. Next stir in the candied walnuts. Add some fresh pepper and sea salt to the top. I like to add some additional fresh lemon zest/spirals to the top of the salad, too.

CUCUMBER, MINT AND POMEGRANATE SALAD

Bursting with the freshness of cucumber and mint and dressed with the tart flavor of pomegranate molasses, this tasty and refreshing salad can be enjoyed on its own or as a side salad with your desired meal. —NK

SERVES 4–6

2 long cucumbers, sliced into thin rounds

1 cup (120 g) pomegranate seeds

2 tbsp (8 g) fresh chopped mint, divided

2 tsp (10 ml) pomegranate molasses

3 tbsp (45 ml) extra-virgin olive oil

Sea salt and black pepper to taste

Place sliced cucumber into a medium-sized mixing bowl. Add the pomegranate seeds and 1 tablespoon (4 g) chopped mint, mix well. In a small mixing bowl add the pomegranate molasses, extra-virgin olive oil, sea salt and black pepper. Stir to mix. To serve, pour the dressing over the top of the cucumber mixture then add another 1 tablespoon (4 g) of fresh mint over the top.

CHEF'S TIP:

Pomegranate molasses can be purchased in Middle Eastern grocery stores or online. It has a tangy flavor.

CUCUMBER SALAD

This cool, crisp salad is elegant and well balanced. It's a perfect accompaniment to a variety of dishes, such as Sri-Lankan Grilled Chicken (page 72). —AV

SERVES 4

2 large cucumbers

1 tsp (3 g) salt

2 tbsp (30 ml) apple cider vinegar

1 tbsp (15 ml) sesame oil

Partly peel the cucumbers and thinly slice them. In medium-sized bowl mix the cucumbers with the salt. Let stand for about 45 minutes or until cucumbers look wilted. Rinse and drain. Squeeze the excess liquid out of the cucumbers. Place cucumbers in a bowl and add the apple cider vinegar and sesame oil. Place in the fridge to cool for about an hour. Serve cold.

CUCUMBER AND TOMATO SALAD

This side dish exudes vibrance thanks to the combination of crisp cucumber and plump tomatoes. The apple cider vinegar gives it some tang that is balanced by the freshness of the mint, making it a wonderful summery side. —JC

SERVES 2

1 cucumber, sliced

1 cup (150 g) grape tomatoes, halved

2 medium shallots, sliced

3 tbsp (12 g) fresh mint, chopped

VINAIGRETTE

¼ cup (60 ml) extra-virgin olive oil

3 tbsp (45 ml) apple cider vinegar

½ tsp dried parsley

½ tsp dried chives

Sea salt

Black pepper

Combine cucumber, grape tomatoes, shallots and fresh mint in a bowl.

Make the vinaigrette by whisking together extra-virgin olive oil, apple cider vinegar, parsley and chives. Season with sea salt and black pepper to taste. Pour the vinaigrette over the cucumber and tomato salad. Toss it lightly until combined. Refrigerate for half an hour before serving.

KIWI KALE SALAD WITH MACADAMIA NUTS

Kiwi is a sweetly acidic fruit that cuts through the usual bitterness of kale, perfectly complementing this salad. The macadamia nuts provide an earthy crunch as well as an added benefit of healthy omega-3s. —RM

SERVES 3–4

8 cups (560 g) kale, about 10 stalks

4 tbsp (60 ml) extra-virgin olive oil, plus more for drizzling

2½ tbsp (37 ml) apple cider vinegar

1½ tsp (7.5 ml) raw honey

2 kiwis

Black pepper, to taste

Crushed macadamia nuts for topping

Remove the ribs from the kale stalks and then wash them in a colander, shaking them dry. Rip them into bite-sized pieces and dump them into a large mixing bowl. Lightly drizzle some olive oil on top of the kale. Massage the kale for about 4 minutes with your hands. The point is to wilt the kale slightly by breaking down the cell structure. This gives it a velvety texture and makes it taste less bitter.

In a small bowl, mix together 4 tablespoons (60 ml) olive oil, the apple cider vinegar and honey. Skin the kiwis by cutting the ends off and then slicing the skin off in thin strips. You can slice the kiwi or chop into cubes. Drizzle the light dressing on top of the kale. Mix in the kiwi slices and top with chopped macadamia nuts and fresh black pepper.

MASSAGED KALE SALAD WITH ALMONDS AND CRANBERRIES

Massaging raw kale transforms it from a tough, slightly bitter leaf to a delectable salad, especially when balanced with sweet cranberries and crunchy almonds. And it only takes a few minutes! —AV

SERVES 4

¼ cup (40 g) shallots, thinly sliced and soaked

1 bunch kale, stalks removed and leaves chopped (I prefer curly kale)

Juice of 1 orange, divided

3 tbsp (45 ml) olive oil, divided

Sea salt and pepper

½ cup (75 g) dried cranberries, preferably sweetened with apple juice

¼ cup (40 g) almonds, chopped or slivered

1 tbsp (15 ml) balsamic vinegar (I prefer a thick syrupy variety)

Place the shallots in a bowl and cover with filtered water. Let them sit for at least 10 minutes. This will help take the bite out. Then drain the water and discard. In a large serving bowl, combine the kale, half of the orange juice, 1 tablespoon (15 ml) of olive oil and some sea salt. Massage with your hands until the kale starts to soften, about 2 to 3 minutes. Now add the cranberries, almonds and shallots to the kale. In a separate bowl, whisk together the remaining olive oil, orange juice, and balsamic vinegar. Pour over the salad and toss to combine. Adjust salt and pepper to taste.

CHEF'S TIP:

For a little extra crunch, use raw almonds and toss them with a little bit of coconut oil, about ½ teaspoon. Toast them in a toaster oven for just a few minutes, until they are crispy, then chop them up and use them in the salad.

KALE PINE NUT SALAD

This is a knock-off of my favorite salad at The Standard Spa, my favorite local hangout in Miami. The sweet golden raisins cut through the tart apple cider vinegar, making this salad perfect for lunch on the bay. —RM

SERVES 2–4

3–4 cups (210–280 g) kale, stemmed and ripped

2 tbsp (30 ml) extra-virgin olive oil

1 tbsp (15 ml) apple cider vinegar

¼ cup (30 g) matchstick carrots

¼ cup (38 g) golden raisins

¼ cup (38 g) pine nuts

Avocado, optional, sliced

Goat cheese, optional

Add the kale to a medium-sized mixing bowl. Drizzle the olive oil onto the kale and massage with your hands for a few minutes. This helps break down the cell structure of the kale and allows it to be digested more easily while tasting less bitter.

Pour the apple cider vinegar onto the kale and then toss. Add the carrots, raisins and pine nuts on top. Serve with sliced avocado or goat cheese for added flavor complexity.

ARUGULA AND SPINACH SALAD

This salad is inspired by one of my friends who shared with me her lemon tahini dressing. I must say I eat this every week with different vegetables added in and I've also had it for breakfast on a few occasions! Seriously, it's that good. The dressing keeps for at least 3 days in the fridge but it never lasts longer than a day at home. —JC

SERVES 4

FOR THE LEMON TAHINI DRESSING

Juice and zest of 1 lemon

1½ tbsp (23 g) tahini

¼ cup (60 ml) extra-virgin olive oil

¼ tsp sea salt

FOR THE SALAD

1 (6-ounce [168-g]) bag baby arugula

1 (6-ounce [168-g]) bag baby spinach

1 medium avocado, sliced

1 (13.5-ounce [378-g]) can whole artichoke hearts, drained and cut in half

¼ cup (40 g) roasted red peppers, sliced

4 strips bacon, cooked

Combine all the lemon tahini dressing ingredients in a glass jar. Cover it tightly and give it a good shake until everything is well combined.

Assemble arugula and spinach on individual salad plates. Top with sliced avocado, artichoke hearts, roasted red peppers and bacon. Serve drizzled with lemon tahini dressing or with the dressing on the side.

FAVORITE HEARTY SALAD

Enjoy a big bowl of this hearty salad that is chock full of different flavors and textures plus some healthy fats thanks to the avocado. Zesty roasted red pepper vinaigrette gives it a bright and sweet taste that packs a punch! —JC

SERVES 2

1 (6-ounce [168-g]) bag spring mix

8 ounces (227 g) cooked chicken, sliced

1 (8.5-ounce [240-g]) can artichoke hearts, drained and cut in half

3 ounces (84 g) white button mushrooms, sliced

1 green bell pepper, cut into strips

½ cup (75 g) grape tomatoes

2 small cooked beets, sliced

1 avocado, sliced

2 tbsp (16 g) red onions, thinly sliced

FOR THE ROASTED RED PEPPER VINAIGRETTE

2 tbsp (30 ml) apple cider vinegar

2 tbsp (30 ml) lemon juice

Zest of 1 lemon

½ cup (120 ml) extra-virgin olive oil

3 ounces (84 g) roasted red peppers

1½ tsp (7.5 ml) raw honey

½ tsp garlic powder

⅛ tsp cayenne pepper

¼ tsp sea salt

¼ tsp black pepper

2 tbsp (16 g) raw pumpkin seeds, plus more for garnish

Divide spring mix into two bowls. Add chicken, artichoke hearts, mushrooms, bell peppers, tomatoes, beets, avocado and red onions. Place in the fridge to chill for 15 minutes.

Prepare roasted red pepper vinaigrette by combining all vinaigrette ingredients in a deep bowl or cup. Using an immersion blender, pulse until the vinaigrette becomes smooth and creamy. Drizzle on top of chilled salad and top with pumpkin seeds before serving.

BBQ CHICKEN SALAD

Eating Paleo means the usual cheese, beans and tortilla strips found in regular BBQ chicken salads are off the table. Instead, pile on vegetables and chicken and pour a generous serving of smoky sweet dressing for a healthy, filling meal. This is so much healthier and more affordable than the ones offered at BBQ restaurants. —JC

SERVES 2

1 romaine lettuce heart, chopped

1 small cucumber, chopped

1 cup (150 g) grape tomatoes, halved

2 tbsp (16 g) red onions, thinly sliced

2 stalks green onions, chopped

8 ounces (227 g) boneless, skinless cooked chicken, cut into bite-sized pieces

2 tbsp (30 ml) Paleo-friendly BBQ Sauce

FOR THE DRESSING

1 tbsp (15 g) Homemade Mayonnaise (page 496)

1 tbsp (15 ml) Homemade Coconut Milk (page 503)

1 tsp (5 ml) apple cider vinegar

½ tsp raw honey

1 tsp (3 g) chives, chopped

¼ tsp onion powder

⅛ tsp sea salt

⅛ tsp black pepper

Combine lettuce, cucumber, tomatoes, red onions and green onions in a bowl. Divide between 2 serving plates. In a separate bowl, add chicken and BBQ sauce. Toss to combine. Place BBQ chicken on top of the salad.

Combine all the dressing ingredients in a small bowl. Drizzle it on top of the BBQ chicken salad. Serve immediately.

TACO SALAD

This is a simple taco salad that can be made any day of the week because it comes together in less than half an hour. The seasoned beef pairs well with Bacon Guacamole (page 252) and it's packed with vegetables to keep you full and satisfied. —JC

SERVES 4

1 tsp (3 g) tallow or ghee

1 small onion, chopped

1 pound (454 g) ground beef

½ tsp garlic powder

½ tsp onion powder

½ tsp black pepper

¼ tsp oregano

¼ tsp ground cumin

¼ tsp cayenne pepper

¼ tsp sea salt

2 romaine hearts, chopped

2 roma tomatoes, chopped

1 large avocado, sliced

1 cup (240 g) Bacon Guacamole (page 252)

½ cup (120 ml) salsa

¼ cup (15 g) cilantro, chopped

Add tallow to a wok or skillet over medium-high heat. Add onion and sauté until it begins to soften, about 2 to 3 minutes. Add ground beef and sauté for 3 to 5 minutes until browned. Season with garlic powder, onion powder, black pepper, oregano, cumin, cayenne pepper and sea salt. Sauté for a few more minutes and adjust the sea salt if necessary.

Turn off heat and let it cool for 8 to 10 minutes. Serve on lettuce topped with tomatoes, avocado, Bacon Guacamole, salsa and cilantro.

CARAMELIZED ONION AND BEET SOUP

The sweet and smoky caramelized onions paired with the earthy beets give this soup a rich and satisfying flavor that simultaneously evokes sophistication and comfort.—AV

SERVES 6

2 pounds (907 g) fresh beets, peeled and chopped

5 cups (1183 ml) Slow Cooker Chicken Broth (page 170), divided

½ tsp sea salt

¼ tsp pepper

2 tbsp (30 g) butter

1 large onion, thinly sliced

1 carrot, peeled and diced

Place the beets in a large stockpot. Add 4 cups (950 ml) chicken broth, salt and pepper. Cover and cook for 45 minutes or until beets are tender. Meanwhile, heat the butter in a large skillet over medium heat. Sauté the onion and carrot, constantly stirring until carrots are tender and onion is soft, and they give off a sweet aroma. Once onion and carrots are soft, add them to the beets and broth. Let the soup cool a little bit, then transfer to a blender, add the additional broth and blend until smooth. Place the soup back into a pot and adjust salt and pepper to taste. Bring back to a simmer and serve.

WATERCRESS SOUP

Watercress can be hard to come by, so I snatch it up whenever I see it to make this soup. The watercress adds the perfect amount of pepper and spice to an otherwise sweet soup. —AV

SERVES 4

3-4 tbsp (44-60 g) butter

1 cup (150 g) yellow onions, finely chopped

4 cups (950 ml) Slow Cooker Chicken Broth (page 170)

1 medium sweet potato, peeled and diced

3 sprigs thyme

½ tsp sea salt

¼ tsp pepper

3 cups (540 g) watercress

Melt the butter in a heavy pot. Add the onions and sauté until translucent. Add the chicken broth, sweet potato, thyme, salt and pepper. Bring to a boil, reduce heat and simmer, partially covered, until sweet potato is very tender, about 20 minutes. Remove the thyme sprigs from the soup and discard.

Meanwhile, remove the leaves from the watercress and rinse. Add the watercress to the pot, cover, remove from heat and allow to cool. Put soup in a food processor and process until smooth. Return the soup to the pot and add more broth if it seems too thick. Adjust salt and pepper to taste and simmer until heated through.

CHEF'S TIP

I prefer Japanese sweet potato for this soup, as it is sweeter than most sweet potatoes.

HOPAR'S CHUNKY GAZPACHO

When I was growing up, my *hopar* (Armenian for dad's brother) owned an Italian restaurant. I loved the gazpacho they served, so refreshing on hot Los Angeles summer nights. It truly hit the spot! I asked him for the recipe and he didn't remember the amounts, but he did remember all the ingredients. I experimented until I got it right!—AV

SERVES 8

½ cup (40 g) each red and green bell peppers, finely chopped

½ cup (120 g) shallot, finely chopped

3 cloves garlic, finely chopped

½ cup (90 g) cucumbers, peeled and finely chopped

2 tbsp (6 g) scallions, finely chopped

6 tomatoes, peeled, seeded and diced

3 cups (710 ml) tomato juice

¼ cup (60 ml) red wine vinegar

2 tbsp (30 ml) extra-virgin olive oil

2 tbsp (5 g) fresh dill, chopped

1½ tbsp (22 ml) high-quality balsamic vinegar

1 tsp (5 g) sea salt

In a large bowl, combine bell peppers, shallot, garlic, cucumbers, scallions, tomatoes, tomato juice, red wine vinegar, olive oil and dill. Cover and refrigerate, preferably overnight. Add balsamic vinegar and salt and serve.

THAI-INSPIRED CHICKEN SOUP

This Thai take on chicken soup is so refreshing that you can even enjoy it on a summer day! The homemade broth is a powerhouse full of easily digested nutrients, such as calcium and magnesium. It is also rich in collagen, gelatin and amino acids.—AV

SERVES 8

1 stalk lemongrass, trimmed, peeled and chopped

8 cups (1.9 L) Slow Cooker Chicken Broth (page 170)

1 large shallot, chopped

3 cloves garlic, chopped

1 tsp (5 g) sea salt

3 kaffir lime leaves

1 (2-inch [5-cm]) piece of fresh ginger, peeled and chopped

3 tbsp (45 ml) fish sauce, divided

1½ pounds (680 g) boneless, skinless chicken thighs, thinly sliced about 2 inches (5 cm) long and ½ inch (1 cm) wide

2 Thai peppers, chopped

1 red bell pepper, sliced

2 cups (360 g) zucchini (2 medium or 1 large), chopped in circles, then halved

1 cup (65 g) shitake mushroom, sliced, stems removed if tough

½ cup (15 g) fresh basil, julienned

2 tbsp (30 ml) fresh lime juice

Cut the top off the lemongrass, remove the tough outer layers and cut into four pieces. Heat chicken broth, lemongrass, shallot, garlic, salt, kaffir lime leaves, ginger and 2 tablespoons (30 ml) fish sauce in a heavy stockpot over medium-low heat. Bring to a light simmer, cover and cook for 30 minutes. Strain broth through a mesh sieve, discard solids and return broth back to the stockpot. Add the chicken, Thai peppers, bell pepper and zucchini. Simmer for 15 minutes. Add the shitake mushrooms and simmer for another 10 minutes. Turn off the heat. Add the basil, lime juice and additional tablespoon of fish sauce. Adjust seasoning to taste.

KALE, SHITAKE MUSHROOM AND BEEF SOUP

Soup is one of our favorite meals. We love the flexibility it offers, as our fridge is always filled with a variety of vegetables from local farms. Soup allows us to get creative in the kitchen and mix and match combinations. This soup is one of our favorites. With their earthy flavor, the mushrooms add the perfect richness and depth.—AV

SERVES 4

½ cup (120 g) shallots, chopped

2 tbsp (30 g) ghee, plus more if needed

1½ pounds (455 g) beef stew meat, cut into 1-inch (2-cm) chunks

1½ cups (115 g) shitake mushrooms, stems removed, chopped

1 carrot, peeled and diced

4 cloves garlic, minced

2 tomatoes, peeled and chopped

4 cups (950 ml) Slow Cooker Beef Broth (page 171)

1 tsp (5 g) sea salt

½ tsp pepper

½ tsp red pepper flakes

1 bunch curly kale, stems removed and leaves chopped

1 tbsp (15 ml) coconut aminos

Heat a heavy-bottomed pot or Dutch oven over medium-high heat. Add ghee and shallots, and lightly sauté shallots until translucent, 5 to 7 minutes. Add the meat, stir and brown it on all sides, about 5 minutes. Set aside.

Add more ghee if needed. Add the chopped shitake mushrooms and cook for 3 to 5 minutes or until mushrooms are browned. Add carrots and garlic and sauté until fragrant, 1 to 2 minutes. Add tomatoes, beef broth, browned beef, salt, pepper and red pepper flakes. Bring to a simmer, then lower heat and cook for 30 minutes or until meat and vegetables are tender. Add kale and coconut aminos and cook for an additional 10 minutes or until kale is tender. Adjust salt and pepper to taste and serve!

SLOW-COOKER HAWAIIAN OXTAIL SOUP

Oxtail is a tough but flavorful cut of meat that becomes very tender when cooked slowly. This Hawaiian version of oxtail soup is thin and light. The toppings are reminiscent of a Vietnamese pho. Traditionally this soup calls for peanuts but due to their creamy nature, cashews are a perfect Paleo substitute.

Oxtail bones have a lot of collagen, which makes for a gelatinous stock. Gelatin has many benefits, including improving digestion and soothing the GI tract. —AV

SERVES 6–8

3 pounds (1.4 kg) oxtail

1 strip orange peel (zest, not the pith)

4 cloves garlic

3 star anise

1 (2-inch [5-cm]) piece of fresh ginger, peeled

1 tbsp (15 g) sea salt

½ cup (85 g) cashews

Filtered water

1 tbsp (15 ml) apple cider vinegar

1 bunch mustard greens

¼ tsp chili pepper flakes

FOR GARNISH

Coconut aminos

Fresh cilantro

Scallions, chopped

Fresh ginger, grated

Place oxtail, orange peel, garlic cloves, star anise, ginger, salt and cashews in a slow cooker. Cover with filtered water. Add the apple cider vinegar. Cook on low for 10 to 12 hours. Allow the soup to cool. Move to a stockpot with a lid and chill in the refrigerator overnight.

By the next day, the fat will have solidified. Pull the fat off the oxtail and remove the star anise, orange peel and ginger. Bring the soup to a simmer. Add the mustard greens and the chili pepper flakes. Cook for 7 to 10 minutes or until mustard greens are tender. The meat can either be stripped from the bones before serving or the oxtails can be served bone in. Serve with coconut aminos, fresh cilantro, chopped green onions and freshly grated ginger for garnish.

CHEF'S TIP
For best results, trim oxtail of any excess fat. Better yet, ask your butcher to trim it for you!

SLOW COOKER BEEF BURGUNDY

Beef Burgundy, also known as Beef Bourguignon, is an iconic French recipe. It is a sumptuous and comforting slow-cooked stew. It is delicious over mashed potatoes or cauliflower mash. —AV

SERVES 6

6 pieces bacon, chopped

1 large onion, chopped

2 large carrots, peeled and chopped

4 cloves garlic, minced

2½ pounds (1.1 kg) beef stew meat or chuck roast, cut into 2-inch (5-cm) cubes

Salt and pepper

2 tbsp (30 ml) tomato paste, preferably in a glass jar

1½ cups (350 ml) Pinot Noir

2 cups (475 ml) Slow Cooker Beef Broth (page 171)

1 bay leaf

10 fresh thyme sprigs

1 cup (150 g) of onions, sliced

8 ounces (230 g) of mushrooms, stems discarded and sliced

2 tbsp (30 g) butter

¼ cup fresh parsley leaves, minced for garnish

Cook bacon until crisp, in a heavy-bottomed pot with a lid or a Dutch oven over medium-high heat. Remove the bacon from the pan with a slotted spoon and set aside. Pour bacon fat into a small bowl or a glass jar, leaving enough behind to sauté the vegetables, about 1 tablespoon. Add chopped onion and carrots to the skillet and sauté until soft, about 5 to 7 minutes, then add garlic cloves and sauté until fragrant, about 1 minute. Transfer the vegetables to a bowl and set aside. Generously add salt and pepper to the beef. Add another tablespoon of bacon fat if needed to the pot. Brown the beef, turning to make sure all sides are browned, about 7 minutes. Add the tomato paste, stirring frequently to make sure beef is well coated and cook until tomato paste goes from a bright red to a brick color, about 45 seconds. Add the wine, and use a wooden spoon to scrape up any brown bits from the bottom of your pot. Add the broth, bay leaf, and thyme. Cover the pot with a lid and turn the heat down to low. Cook for 1½ hours covered. Cook for an additional 30 minutes uncovered to allow the sauce to thicken. Discard thyme sprigs and bay leaf. Fifteen minutes before the beef is ready, prep the sliced onions and mushrooms for garnish. Add butter to a medium-sized saucepan and turn heat to medium. Add onions and sauté for 5 minutes, add mushrooms and sauté for an additional 10 minutes, or until onions and mushrooms are tender. Add cooked and chopped bacon back to the beef. Adjust salt and pepper of beef to taste. Garnish with chopped parsley and mushroom and onion sauté and serve.

CHAPTER 6

DESSERTS

You wouldn't find an ice cream maker or a cupcake pan in the Paleolithic era. Nor would you use them in most other "diets." That's because desserts tend to stray into the gray area of a Paleo lifestyle. For me, embarking on a real-food journey for the first time looked a lot less bleak with a few mounds of fresh whipped coconut cream along the way.

Today there are tons of dairy- and grain-free substitutions available, making it even easier to ditch the wheat and prepare baked goods and candies with all-natural, nutrient-dense ingredients. My philosophy is if you are going to splurge on birthday cake—check out the Chocolate Birthday Cake with Chocolate Frosting (page 353)—it might as well be made from the best whole ingredients possible and a healthy dose of self-love.

The desserts in this section range from traditional classics such as Egg-Free Pumpkin Pie (page 367), to quirky flavor combinations like Bacon Browned Butter Cupcakes (page 364). Of course, Paleo desserts should be limited to special occasions—they're a treat! And in limiting consumption, that will make each sweet morsel even more appreciated.

HONEY LEMON FIGS WITH GHEE

When figs are in season, enjoy them in abundance, especially if you're lucky enough to have your very own tree in your backyard. Frying fresh figs in ghee and then drizzling with some raw honey is the perfect treat to satisfy your sweet tooth craving. —JC

SERVES 4

¼ cup (60 g) ghee

1 pound (454 g) fresh black figs, cut in half

2 tbsp (30 ml) raw honey

Zest of 1 lemon

Melt ghee in a cast iron pan over medium heat. Add figs cut-side down and fry for 5 minutes. Flip to the other side and fry for 3 minutes. Turn off heat and add honey. Mix until well combined. Let it cool in the pan for 5 minutes. Transfer to a serving plate and top with lemon zest. Serve warm.

COCONUT CHOCOLATE-COVERED BANANAS

These chocolate-covered bananas are delicious and very simple to make. They make a perfect treat for kids! —AV

SERVES 6

5 ounces (140 g) dark chocolate chips

1 tsp (3 g) ground cinnamon

1 tbsp (15 ml) coconut oil

3 medium bananas, peeled and halved crosswise

½ cup (60 g) shredded coconut

In a heatproof bowl, combine chocolate chips, cinnamon and coconut oil and place it over a pot of simmering water. Stir until mixture is melted and smooth. It takes about 3 to 5 minutes. Keep a close eye on it to make sure that it doesn't burn. Set it aside and allow it to cool.

Meanwhile, line a baking sheet with parchment paper. Insert sticks into the bananas. When the chocolate is ready, dip the bananas into the bowl or spoon the chocolate over the bananas. Tilt the banana and allow the excess chocolate to drip off and back into the bowl. Use your hands or a spoon to sprinkle the shredded coconut over the banana. Repeat on all sides, until it is covered. Place the bananas on the parchment lined baking sheet and set in the freezer for 30 minutes or until the chocolate has hardened.

CASHEW BUTTER TRUFFLES

If you love the combination of nuts and chocolate, these simple truffles are for you! They are more of a bite-sized snack than a traditional chocolate truffle. The combination of creamy dates and nuts makes for the perfect treat. —CP

MAKES ABOUT 20 TRUFFLES

2 cups (300 g) raw cashew pieces

½ cup (75 g) raw almonds

½ cup (75 g) raw walnuts

1 cup (180 g) dates, pitted

½ tsp sea salt, for soaking

2 tbsp (30 ml) coconut oil

1½ tsp (4.5 g) ground cinnamon

FOR THE CHOCOLATE GLAZE

¼ cup (30 g) cacao powder

¼ cup (60 ml) coconut oil

2 tbsp (30 ml) maple syrup or raw honey

1 tbsp (5 g) finely shredded, unsweetened coconut, for garnish

Before you begin, line a baking sheet with parchment paper and place in the freezer.

Soak the nuts, dates and salt in water for 2 hours.

Drain and pat nuts and dates dry to remove any excess moisture. Add coconut oil and cinnamon. Using a food processor or immersion blender, purée until a smooth yet thick mixture forms.

Chill in refrigerator for 15 minutes.

Make the chocolate glaze by whisking together all ingredients.

Using a cookie scoop, scoop cashew butter mixture into small balls continuing to form with your hands.

Dip cashew centers in chocolate glaze and place on frozen cookie sheet to allow the chocolate to harden. Sprinkle with shredded coconut.

Place the truffles in the refrigerator for 30 minutes to harden before enjoying!

CHEWY DOUBLE CHOCOLATE COOKIES

Double dark chocolate cookies are studded with chocolate chips for a rich flavor with each bite. These chewy cookies have a denser cake-like texture and are great to whip up on a whim when craving some chocolate! —CP

MAKES 16

8 tbsp (120 g) butter, softened

2 cups (240 g) almond flour

¼ cup (30 g) cacao powder

¼ cup (50 g) coconut sugar

1 tsp (3 g) baking soda

Pinch of sea salt

2 tbsp (30 ml) raw honey

½ cup (85 g) dark chocolate chips

2 egg whites

Preheat the oven to 350°F (180°C, or gas mark 4). Line a baking sheet with parchment paper.

Slice butter into small pieces and set aside to soften. In a separate bowl, sift together all dry ingredients making sure that flour mixture is smooth.

Using a hand blender, briefly whip butter and honey until fluffy. Fold into flour mix making a clumpy cookie dough. Mix in chocolate chips.

In another bowl, whip egg whites until soft peaks begin to form. Gently fold in egg whites, mixing to form a fluffy ball of cookie dough. Use a cookie scoop to scoop onto baking sheet.

Bake for 11 to 14 minutes. Allow to cool briefly before transferring to a cooling rack. Best served fresh and warm.

ROSEMARY LAVENDER COOKIES

Sweet and savory biscuits for an afternoon treat! These cookies are not too sweet but pair nicely with a charcuterie platter or a cup of hot coffee. —CP

MAKES ABOUT 10 COOKIES

1 cup (120 g) almond flour

2 tbsp (16 g) coconut flour

½ tsp baking soda

1 tbsp (6 g) fresh rosemary, finely chopped

1 tbsp (6 g) dried lavender

5 tbsp (75 g) butter, softened

1 tbsp (15 ml) maple syrup

1 tsp (5 ml) vanilla extract

Raw honey for brushing tops of cookies, optional

Preheat the oven to 350°F (180°C, or gas mark 4). Line a baking sheet with parchment paper.

In a small mixing bowl toss together flours, baking soda and chopped rosemary.

Using the back of a wooden spoon or a mortar and pestle, gently crush the lavender to release the oils. Add this to the dry mixture.

Whip butter, maple syrup and vanilla extract. Fold in flour and mix until the dough comes together. Shape dough into a log and wrap in waxed paper. Refrigerate for 1 hour.

Unwrap dough and slice into ½-inch (1.3-cm) round cookies.

Bake for 10 minutes or until cookies begin to turn golden brown.

Cool on baking sheet for 10 minutes before transferring to a cooling rack as they will firm up as they cool.

While the cookies are still warm, brush with raw honey if desiring something slightly sweeter.

CARAMEL SHORTBREAD COOKIES

A grain- and refined sugar–free homemade Girl Scout Samoas cookie made healthy in the comforts of your kitchen. Butter shortbread drizzled with honey caramel and chocolate topped with toasted coconut. These cookies take a bit of love to make but are always worth it! —CP

MAKES 20 COOKIES

10 tbsp (150 g) butter

2 cups (240 g) almond flour

¼ cup (30 g) coconut flour

¼ cup (50 g) coconut sugar

¼ tsp baking soda

2 tsp (10 ml) vanilla extract

FOR THE HONEY CARAMEL

½ cup (120 ml) raw honey

2 tbsp (30 g) nut butter—almond, pecan or cashew butter

1 tsp (5 ml) vanilla extract

FOR THE CHOCOLATE DRIZZLE

½ cup (120 g) raw cacao butter, chopped

5 tbsp (40 g) cacao powder

1 tbsp (15 ml) raw honey

¼ cup (42 g) unsweetened, toasted coconut flakes for dusting

Slice butter and set aside to soften for 1 hour. Preheat oven to 350°F (180°C, or gas mark 4). Line a baking sheet with parchment paper.

Sift together all dry cookie ingredients. Add softened butter and vanilla. Use a pastry cutter or your hands to mix in butter. Wrap dough in parchment paper and chill in refrigerator for 1 hour.

Place chilled dough between two large sheets of parchment paper. Roll dough into a thin layer, between ¼- to ½-inch (6-mm to 1.3-cm) thick.

Use a 2½-inch (6.4-cm) cookie cutter to cut out round cookies. Roll extra dough scraps into a ball, roll out again and cut remaining cookies.

Place on a parchment-lined baking sheet. Bake for 12 minutes or until cookies are golden brown.

Transfer cookies to a cooling rack and cool completely before assembling.

While cookies are baking, make the caramel. In a small saucepan, on low-to-medium heat, add honey. Heat for 35 minutes, stirring occasionally. Small bubbles should rise from the pan but you do not want to boil or burn the honey.

Remove from heat and stir in nut butter and vanilla. The caramel will thicken as it cools.

Make the chocolate drizzle by melting together all ingredients over low heat. Set aside to cool.

To assemble cookies, spread a thin layer of warm caramel over the top of cookies. Place all cookies on parchment lined baking sheet and generously drizzle chocolate and toasted coconut over the tops and sprinkle with toasted coconut.

Store remaining cookies in refrigerator. Best served at room temperature or slightly chilled.

CHEF'S TIPS:

Caramel is easiest to work with when slightly warm; if necessary you can heat it slightly again to make it pliable. I think these cookies are best served chilled or the next day if you happen to have any leftovers as the flavors continue to blend together beautifully!

PUMPKIN CHOCOLATE CHIP COOKIES

If you love pumpkin and chocolate chip cookies, you are in for a treat. These cookies have all the flavors of fall and are sure to impress any guests. —KW

MAKES 24

⅓ cup (80 g) butter, ghee or coconut oil, melted (I use butter)

⅓ cup (80 g) pumpkin purée

⅓ cup (80 ml) maple syrup or liquid sweetener of choice

1 large egg

1 tsp (5 ml) pure vanilla extract

⅔ cup (80 g) tapioca flour or arrowroot

⅓ cup (40 g) coconut flour

1 tsp (3 g) Pumpkin Pie Spice (page 505)

½ tsp baking soda

Pinch of sea salt

⅓ cup (60 g) chocolate chips

Mix together the butter, pumpkin purée, maple syrup, egg and vanilla extract. Add the tapioca flour, coconut flour, pumpkin pie spice, baking soda and salt and stir until combined. Add the chocolate chips. Refrigerate batter for 30 minutes or longer—the batter will stiffen up in the fridge. Preheat oven to 375°F (190°C, or gas mark 5). Drop the batter by spoonfuls onto a parchment-lined cookie sheet. Flatten the cookies with your fingers or the back of a spoon. Bake for 12 to 15 minutes or until lightly golden brown.

CHEF'S TIP:

To make the cookies really pretty, press a few additional chocolate chips onto the tops of each cookie once they come out of the oven.

GINGERBREAD MEN COOKIES

One of my favorite holiday cookies is gingerbread men! These cookies have a wonderful, soft, almost cakey texture and spiced molasses flavor. These cookies perfectly accompany a cup of hot cider near the fire. —HH

SERVES 4

FOR THE COOKIES

3 tbsp (24 g) ground flax seeds

½ cup (60 g) almond flour

⅓ cup (40 g) coconut flour

2 tbsp (16 g) arrowroot

¼ tsp salt

½ tsp baking soda

⅓ cup (65 g) coconut sugar

1 tsp (3 g) ground cinnamon

1 tsp (3 g) ground ginger

½ tsp ground cloves

¼ cup (60 ml) coconut oil, melted

2 tbsp (30 ml) molasses

FOR THE FROSTING

1 (13.5-ounce [378-g]) can full-fat coconut milk refrigerated overnight

1 tsp (5 ml) raw honey or maple syrup

Preheat the oven to 350°F (180°C, or gas mark 4). Line a cookie sheet with parchment paper. In a small bowl mix ground flax seeds with 3 tablespoons (45 ml) warm water. Let it sit until the mixture thickens and jells. In a food processor or mixing bowl, mix together dry ingredients. Then add flax mixture, melted coconut oil and molasses.

Sprinkle a cutting board or countertop with almond flour—do not use coconut flour or arrowroot because it will dry out the cookies. Roll out the cookie dough with a rolling pin until it's flat and even. It should be about ¼-inch (6-mm) thick or less. Use gingerbread men cookie cutters to cut out as many gingerbread men as you have room to do. Place the gingerbread men cookies on the lined baking sheet. Roll the remaining dough into a ball and use the rolling pin to roll it flat again. Cut out more gingerbread men and repeat this process until the dough is gone. Bake for 10 to 15 minutes. Let cool.

To make the frosting, make sure you've refrigerated a can of full-fat coconut milk overnight. Open the can and scoop out the hardened coconut cream from the top and discard the clear thin liquid left at the bottom. Put the coconut cream in a bowl and add honey or maple syrup. Blend with a hand mixer or an immersion blender for a few minutes until it's softened up a bit. Use a piping bag to create designs with the frosting. Keep the frosted gingerbread men refrigerated.

CHEF'S TIP:

These cookies can easily be made into gingersnaps by omitting the frosting and forming the dough into flat rounds instead of rolling it out and cutting out gingerbread men.

PUMPKIN SNICKERDOODLES

A creative twist on the classic festive cookie adding spice and pumpkin. These snickerdoodles are not overly sweet making for a nutritious afternoon treat with a cup of hot coffee or tea during the chilly winter months. —CP

MAKES 10

4 tbsp (60 g) butter

1¼ cups (150 g) almond flour

2 tbsp (16 g) coconut flour

3 tbsp (36 g) coconut sugar

¼ tsp sea salt

½ tsp baking soda

1 tsp (3 g) ground cinnamon

¼ tsp ground nutmeg

1 tbsp (15 ml) raw honey

3 tbsp (45 g) pumpkin purée

FOR THE CINNAMON SUGAR SPRINKLES

2 tbsp (24 g) coconut sugar

1 tsp (3 g) ground cinnamon

Thinly slice butter and set aside to soften. Preheat oven to 350°F (180°C, or gas mark 4). Line a baking sheet with parchment paper.

In a small bowl, stir together cinnamon sugar sprinkles and set aside.

Sift together all dry ingredients.

Use a fork or pastry cutter to mix in honey, pumpkin and butter. Continue to stir with a spatula until a small ball of dough has formed. Chill dough in refrigerator for 1 hour.

Scoop dough into small balls, continuing to form small round shapes with your hands. Roll snickerdoodles in cinnamon sugar sprinkles.

Place balls onto baking sheet about 2 inches (5 cm) apart. Use the bottom of a drinking glass to gently flatten cookies. Bake for 14 to 16 minutes. Transfer to a cooling rack to cool completely; the cookies will firm up as they cool.

Share and enjoy. Use any leftover cinnamon sugar sprinkles to sweeten your morning cup of coffee.

EGG–FREE CHOCOLATE CHIP COOKIES

If you are sensitive to eggs, but still love a good chocolate chip cookie, these are for you! I use flaxseeds as a binder in place of eggs. —HH

SERVES 4

3 tbsp (24 g) ground golden flaxseeds

⅓ cup (40 g) coconut flour

½ cup (60 g) almond flour

2 tbsp (16 g) arrowroot powder

¼ tsp salt

½ tsp baking soda

¼ cup (50 g) coconut sugar

¼ cup (60 ml) coconut oil, melted

½ tsp vanilla extract

⅓ cup (60 g) chocolate chips

Preheat the oven to 350°F (180°C, or gas mark 4). In a small bowl mix ground flaxseeds with 4 tablespoons (60 ml) warm water. Let it sit until the mixture thickens and jells, about 1 to 2 minutes.

In a food processor or mixing bowl, mix together dry ingredients. Then add flax mixture, melted coconut oil and vanilla extract and mix well. Gently fold in the chocolate chips.

Take a large spoonful of the cookie dough, roll it into a ball and then flatten into a cookie shape. The cookies will not rise or expand much in the oven, so make them the size and shape that you want them to be. Place the flattened dough onto a cookie sheet lined with parchment paper. Bake at 350°F (180°C, or gas mark 4) for 10 to 15 minutes. Let cool before eating.

CHEF'S TIP:
To grind flaxseeds, grind in a small coffee or spice grinder.

EGG–FREE CHOCOLATE CHIP & ALMOND COOKIES

These cookies are the guilt-free answer to your chocolate chip cookie cravings. —RB

SERVES 10

2 cups (240 g) almond flour

1 cup (80 g) shredded unsweetened coconut

1 tsp (3 g) cream of tartar

½ tsp baking soda

¼ tsp salt

3 tbsp (45 ml) coconut oil

3 tbsp (45 ml) maple syrup

1 tbsp (15 ml) vanilla extract

½ cup (85 g) chocolate chips

½ cup (75 g) slivered almonds

Preheat the oven to 350°F (180°C, or gas mark 4). Line a cookie sheet with parchment paper, set aside.

Combine all ingredients except the chocolate chips and slivered almonds in a food processor and pulse until thoroughly combined. Add the chocolate chips and slivered almonds and pulse for a few moments more until broken down into the dough to your preference.

Shape approximately ¼ cup (60 g) of dough for each cookie into discs and set on the parchment paper-lined cookie sheet. Bake in the preheated oven for 20 minutes, or until the edges of the cookies are lightly browned.

PEPPERMINT CHOCOLATE COOKIE BALLS

I made these as a holiday treat for my family one year. They ate the whole batch in one sitting. I knew I had created a winner. The best part is that they do not require any baking. —KH

MAKES 20

1 cup (120 g) blanched almond flour

3 tbsp (24 g) raw cacao, or unsweetened cocoa powder

¼ tsp sea salt

3 tbsp (45 ml) coconut oil, melted

2 tbsp (30 ml) honey

½ tsp peppermint extract

2 tbsp (22 g) mini chocolate chips

FOR THE DRIZZLE

¼ cup (60 ml) coconut butter, melted

1 tbsp (15 ml) honey

¼ tsp peppermint extract

Hot water

In a large bowl, mix together almond flour, raw cacao, sea salt, coconut oil, honey and peppermint extract until well combined. Fold in chocolate chips. Form small spoonfuls of the dough into cute little balls and place onto baking sheet lined with parchment paper. Refrigerate for about 30 minutes to harden.

In a small bowl, combine melted coconut butter and honey into a creamy paste. Add peppermint extract and 1 teaspoon (5 ml) of hot water at a time to create a drizzle consistency. You may need to add a bit more water if it's too thick or a bit more melted coconut butter if it's too thin. Use a spoon, squeeze bottle or plastic bag with a tiny corner cut out to drizzle onto the cookie balls. Store in fridge.

FLOURLESS CHOCOLATE COOKIE

These delicious flourless cookies are chewy and soft, almost like a brownie but more like a cookie. We keep ours in the freezer for a tasty cold treat. —KH

SERVES 9

1½ cups (225 g) raw sunflower seeds, preferably soaked and dehydrated

1 cup (200 g) coconut sugar

½ cup (60 g) raw cacao powder or unsweetened cocoa powder

¼ tsp sea salt

¼ cup (45 g) mini chocolate chips

3 eggs whites

1 tsp (5 ml) vanilla extract

Preheat the oven to 350°F (180°C, or gas mark 4) and line a baking sheet with parchment paper or a silicone baking sheet.

Process sunflower seeds in a food processor for 1½ minutes, until they resemble coarse flour. Pour into large bowl.

Process coconut sugar in food processor for 1½ minutes to create a finer sugar. Pour into bowl with ground sunflower seeds.

Add cacao powder, sea salt and mini chocolate chips and mix to combine. Set aside.

In another large bowl, using a hand blender, whip egg whites until foamy but not stiff, about 30 seconds. Fold in vanilla extract. Add dry ingredients to egg whites and stir gently to combine.

Spoon batter onto prepared baking sheet in nine evenly spaced mounds, leaving about 2 inches (5 cm) in between. Bake for 14 minutes, until cookies are slightly puffed and glossy. Slide entire parchment paper or silicone mat onto wire rack to cool completely. Enjoy!

CHEF'S TIPS:

This recipe makes nine large cookies because that's how I roll when it comes to chocolate. You can also make eighteen smaller cookies if you like. Just lessen the bake time by a minute or two.

Soaking and dehydrating nuts and seeds makes them more digestible. I do my sunflower seeds in big batches and keep them in the fridge for easy use. Soak 4 cups (600 g) of seeds in water and ½ tablespoon (4 g) of salt overnight. Drain and rinse. Dehydrate at 110°F (43°C) for 24 hours, or until completely dry.

FLOURLESS ALMOND CHOCOLATE CHIP COOKIES

This spin on the traditional chocolate chip cookie is a great way to eat Paleo and still have your cake too. For a crispier cookie, make them small and thin. For a chewy cookie, make them bigger and thicker. —KH

MAKES ABOUT 20

1 cup (250 g) almond butter

¼ cup (60 ml) honey

1 egg

½ tsp sea salt

¼ cup (20 g) shredded coconut, unsweetened

½ tsp baking soda

½ cup (85 g) chocolate chips

½ cup (75 g) sliced almonds

Preheat the oven to 325°F (170°C, or gas mark 3). Mix almond butter and honey in a large bowl until smooth. Add egg, salt, shredded coconut and baking soda and mix again. Fold in chocolate chips and sliced almonds. Using a tablespoon, form the dough into round balls and place on baking pan lined with parchment paper or a silicone baking mat. Press balls down slightly, depending on how thick you want your cookies. Bake 8 to 11 minutes until cookies are golden brown. Let cool completely before removing from pan.

NUTTY RAISIN TODDLER COOKIES

Soft little cookies perfect for the little ones in your life. They are lightly sweetened and loaded with protein-rich almond flour and nuts. Big people love these cookies too. —KH

MAKES 20–28

1½ cups (180 g) almond flour

¼ tsp baking soda

½ tsp ground cinnamon

½ tsp sea salt

5 tbsp (75 ml) coconut oil, melted

2 tbsp (30 ml) honey

1 tsp (3 g) chia seeds

½ tsp vanilla extract

¼ cup (32 g) finely chopped nuts—almond, cashew, hazelnut or macadamia

¼ cup (32 g) raisins, soaked in water for 10 minutes and roughly chopped

Preheat the oven to 325°F (170°C, or gas mark 3) and line baking pan with parchment paper or silicon baking mat.

Combine almond flour, baking soda, cinnamon and salt in a large bowl.

Combine coconut oil, honey, chia seeds and vanilla in a smaller bowl. Pour the oil-honey combo into dry mix and stir until well combined. Fold in nuts and raisins.

Roll dough into tablespoon (15 g)-sized balls and place onto baking sheet. Flatten with your fingertips until about a half-inch (1.3-cm) thick. Keep them as round as possible as they do not change shape as you bake them. Bake 8 to 11 minutes, until the bottom of cookies is nice and golden. Let cool completely on baking sheet.

GRAIN–FREE THUMBPRINT COOKIES WITH CHIA BERRY JAM

The homemade chia berry jam in these soft and chewy cookies is ridiculously easy to make. These cookies make a perfect holiday gift. —KH

MAKES 24 COOKIES

FOR CHIA BERRY JAM

1½ cups (225 g) berries, fresh or frozen, defrost if frozen

2 tbsp (30 ml) honey or maple syrup

2 tsp (6 g) chia seeds

¼ tsp vanilla extract

FOR COOKIE DOUGH

1 egg

⅓ cup (80 ml) coconut oil, melted

¼ cup (60 ml) raw honey or real maple syrup

2 tsp (10 ml) vanilla extract

¼ tsp sea salt

2 cups (240 g) blanched almond meal

To make the chia berry jam, bring berries and sweetener of choice to a low simmer in a small pan. Once the berries release their liquid, about 2 to 3 minutes, add the chia seeds. Continue to simmer on low for 10 minutes, stirring occasionally. Remove from heat, add vanilla and let cool.

For the cookies, preheat the oven to 350°F (180°C, or gas mark 4). Combine egg, coconut oil, sweetener of choice, vanilla and salt in a large bowl. Add almond flour slowly and mix to thoroughly combine.

Roll dough into small balls and place on a baking sheet lined with parchment paper or a silicone baking mat. Using your thumb, create a little indentation in each cookie ball. Spoon a small amount of chia berry jam onto each cookie. Bake for 10 to 12 minutes. Allow to cool for 10 minutes then transfer to baking rack to cool completely.

GRAIN-FREE GINGER COOKIES

Ginger cookies are my favorite! I use real molasses and fresh ginger to give them just the right flavor. I use sunflower seeds as the base to make them nut-free. —KH

MAKES 24 COOKIES

½ cup (75 g) sunflower seeds, preferably soaked and dehydrated

2 tbsp (16 g) coconut flour

¼ cup (60 ml) maple syrup or honey

2 tbsp (30 ml) coconut oil, melted

1 tbsp (15 ml) blackstrap molasses

1 (2-inch [5-cm]) piece fresh ginger, peeled and grated

1 tsp (3 g) ginger powder

¼ tsp baking soda

¼ tsp sea salt

Coconut sugar for topping, optional

Process sunflower seeds in food processor for 1½ minutes until broken down into a coarse flour. Add the rest of the ingredients and pulse until you have a fully combined dough. It will begin to roll into a ball. Place dough in fridge for 30 minutes to chill.

Preheat the oven to 350°F (180°C, or gas mark 4), and line a baking sheet with parchment paper or a silicone baking mat. Roll tablespoon (15 g)-sized scoops of dough into uniform balls. Drop onto baking sheet. Using a wet fork, press each dough ball to flatten. Sprinkle with optional coconut sugar. Bake for 10 to 12 minutes, until bottom of cookie begins to brown, less time for chewier cookie, more for crispier cookie.

DOUBLE CHOCOLATE CARAMEL WHOOPIE BITES

The ultimate chocolate ooey-gooey dessert! Mini double chocolate whoopie pies stuffed with warm caramel sauce—the result is a bite of chocoholic heaven. —RM

SERVES 12

FOR THE WHOOPIE BITES

½ cup (60 g) blanched almond flour

½ cup (120 g) almond butter

¼ cup (60 ml) raw honey

1 egg

2 tbsp (16 g) raw cacao powder

1 tbsp (15 ml) coconut oil

½ tsp baking salt

½ tsp baking soda

½ cup (85 g) dark chocolate chips

FOR THE SALTED CARAMEL SAUCE

¼ cup (60 ml) unsalted butter

3 tbsp (45 ml) coconut milk

½ cup (100 g) coconut sugar

½ tsp sea salt

Preheat the oven to 350°F (180°C, or gas mark 4). Line two baking sheets with unbleached parchment paper. In a large mixing bowl, mix all of the whoopie pie ingredients except the chocolate chips together, making sure to add the baking soda last. Once smooth, mix in the chocolate chips. Scoop heaping tablespoons (15 g) of batter onto the baking sheet, in rows about 2 inches (5 cm) apart from each other. Bake for about 7 to 9 minutes until a tester comes out clean.

While the whoopie pies are cooling, make the caramel sauce. In a heavy-bottomed saucepan, add all of the salted caramel ingredients and gently boil for 2 minutes. It should thicken slightly. If you want a thicker sauce, boil for about 1 more minute. The caramel sauce will thicken as it cools. Set the caramel aside on the warm stove.

(continued)

After the caramel is prepared, match up same-sized whoopie halves to each other. Spoon about half of a tablespoon (7.5 ml) of caramel onto one side of a whoopie pie pair and sandwich the two together. Store in an airtight container if they are going to be eaten soon, if not then just store them in the fridge. Serve at room temperature.

FROZEN CHOCOLATE CRUNCH BITES

My go to sweet treat when craving some chocolate! These frozen crunch bites hit the spot every time and are full of quality proteins and fats to keep you satisfied longer. Maca is a Peruvian superfood that can help balance hormones and increase energy. —CP

MAKES 10–12 CANDY BITES

1 cup (240 g) almond butter

½ cup (120 ml) coconut oil

½ cup (60 g) cacao powder

¼ cup (30 g) maca powder

½ cup (42 g) finely shredded, unsweetened coconut

2 tbsp (16 g) ground flaxseed

3 tbsp (45 ml) raw honey

¼ tsp sea salt

Line a baking sheet with parchment paper and place in the freezer for 15 minutes.

Combine all ingredients in a bowl and use a hand blender to mix together. Chill chocolate batter in the refrigerator for 15 minutes.

Remove the sheet from the freezer and use a small cookie scoop to scoop drops of batter onto the sheet.

Immediately place in the freezer for 15 minutes to harden before serving.

Enjoy cold and store any remaining chocolate bites in the refrigerator.

PUMPKIN SPICE POPPERS

These gooey poppers are a fun and tasty treat. They are perfect for holiday potlucks! No one ever realizes that they are gluten-free. —AV

MAKES 24

Coconut oil for greasing muffin tins

½ cup (120 g) canned pumpkin purée (not pumpkin pie filling)

½ cup (120 ml) butter (or palm shortening), melted

5 eggs, beaten

1 tsp (5 ml) vanilla

⅓ cup (80 ml) honey

½ cup (60 g) coconut flour

¼ tsp sea salt

½ tsp ground cinnamon

½ tsp ground nutmeg

¼ tsp ground allspice

⅛ tsp ground cloves

½ tsp baking soda

FOR THE COATING

½ cup (120 ml) butter, melted

2 tbsp (30 ml) maple sugar or coconut sugar

1 tbsp (8 g) ground cinnamon

Preheat oven to 350°F (180°C, or gas mark 4) and use coconut oil to coat the mini muffin tin. In a bowl, combine the pumpkin, butter, eggs, vanilla and honey. Whisk until thoroughly mixed. Sift together coconut flour, salt and all the spices. Add the dry ingredients to the wet ingredients. Whisk to combine. Let sit for 5 minutes to allow the coconut flour to absorb the wet ingredients. Add baking soda, stir until baking soda is mixed through. Fill mini-muffin tins until almost full. Bake for 15 minutes or until a toothpick inserted in the center comes out clean. Allow muffins to cool for a few minutes by either removing them from the pan and setting them on a cooling rack or leaving them in the pan and tipping them on their sides.

Melt the butter on the stove top on low heat, watching it carefully to make sure that it doesn't burn. Place melted butter in a small bowl. Mix the maple, or coconut, sugar and cinnamon in a separate small bowl. After poppers have cooled for a few minutes, dip them in the butter and roll them in the sugar mixture. Enjoy!

APRICOT BITES

Dried apricots dipped in chocolate with some nuts and a coconut sugar icing may be too pretty to eat but they are a delight to serve at any holiday gathering. Change it up a little by using different types of nuts and other add-ins. —JC

SERVES 6

¼ cup (44 g) chocolate chip morsels

1 tsp (5 g) ghee or coconut oil

12 dried apricots

2 tbsp (16 g) raw almonds, chopped

3 tbsp (36 g) coconut sugar

1½ tsp (7.5 ml) water

Prepare a double boiler by placing a small saucepan on the stove. Fill it halfway with water. Set a glass or metal bowl that fits snugly on top of it and turn on the heat to medium-high. Bring water to a boil and reduce heat to medium-low until it is just simmering. Add the chocolate chips and ghee. Gently stir until the mixture melts completely, about 3 to 5 minutes. Turn off heat. Let it sit to cool slightly for 3 to 5 minutes.

Line a baking sheet with parchment paper.

Grab an apricot and dip it halfway in the melted chocolate. Sprinkle with almonds and give them a gentle pat so that they stick to the chocolate. Place it on the parchment-lined baking sheet. Repeat for the rest of the apricots.

Place the coconut sugar in a coffee or spice grinder and pulse until it is a powder-like consistency. Place the powdered coconut sugar in a small bowl and add water. Stir to dissolve it completely. Add a little bit more water one drop at a time if the consistency is too thick. Drizzle the coconut sugar icing on top of the apricots.

Place the baking sheet in the fridge for at least 30 minutes to cool and harden the chocolate and coconut sugar icing before serving.

PUMPKIN SPICE DATE BARS

These date bars aren't overly sweet because they have an equal ratio of dates to nuts so each serving is packed with a lot of crunch! Swap out the pumpkin spice for cinnamon or even cocoa powder for an entirely new spin on these date bars. —JC

SERVES 8

10 Medjool dates, pitted

1 tsp (5 ml) vanilla extract

3 tbsp (24 g) raw almonds, chopped

2 tbsp (16 g) raw walnuts, chopped

2 tbsp (16 g) raw pecans, chopped

1 tsp (3 g) Pumpkin Pie Spice (page 505)

In a food processor, add dates and vanilla extract. Pulse until everything sticks together and forms into a ball.

Knead together the date mixture, almonds, walnuts, pecans and pumpkin spice in a bowl, using your hands to combine. Flatten the mixture into a ½-inch (1.3-cm)-thick square sheet. Wrap it in parchment paper and refrigerate for at least an hour or until firm. Slice into ¾-inch (2-cm) pieces and enjoy. Leftovers will keep in the fridge for 3 to 4 days.

FLOURLESS PEPPERMINT FUDGE BROWNIE BARS

If you are a chocolate lover, you will absolutely love these rich and fudge-y brownie bars. They are perfectly decadent with just the right amount of sweetness. —KW

SERVES 16

4 eggs

¼ cup (60 ml) butter or coconut oil, melted

½ cup (120 ml) pure maple syrup or sweetener of choice

1 tsp (5 ml) pure vanilla extract

½ tsp pure peppermint extract

Pinch of sea salt

½ cup (60 g) cacao powder or unsweetened cocoa powder

½ cup (88 g) chocolate chips or dark chocolate pieces

FOR THE CHOCOLATE TOPPING

¼ cup (44 g) chocolate chips or dark chocolate pieces

1 tbsp (15 g) butter or coconut oil

Preheat oven to 350°F (180°C, or gas mark 4). Mix eggs, melted butter, maple syrup, vanilla, peppermint extract and sea salt together until well combined. Stir in cacao (or cocoa) powder until silky smooth. I use an immersion blender to get it nice and smooth. Pour the batter into a parchment-lined or well-greased, 8 × 8-inch (20 × 20-cm) baking pan—the batter will be very runny. Sprinkle ½ cup (88 g) of chocolate chips all over the top. Bake for 25 minutes and then let cool.

When the brownie bars are cool to the touch, make the chocolate topping by melting chocolate chips and butter over low heat and stir until smooth and melted. Spread chocolate topping all over the brownie bars.

Place in the refrigerator for at least 1 hour.

DATE-SWEETENED BROWNIES

This date-sweetened brownie recipe is delicious and just the right amount of sweetness despite having no processed sugar in it. The texture is perfect; moist, fudgy squares that melt in your mouth. —HH

SERVES 4

8 dates soaked in ¼ cup (60 ml) warm water

2 tbsp (16 g) ground flax seeds soaked in 2 tbsp (30 ml) water

3 ounces (84 g) unsweetened baking chocolate

½ cup (120 ml) coconut oil

4 tbsp (60 ml) whole milk, coconut milk or almond milk

1 tsp (5 ml) vanilla extract

½ cup (60 g) almond flour

¼ cup (30 g) coconut flour

1 tsp (3 g) baking soda

½ cup (75 g) walnuts (optional)

Preheat oven to 350°F (180°C, or gas mark 4). Remove the pits from the dates and soak in the warm water for a few minutes. Then, in another bowl combine ground flaxseeds and water and allow to congeal.

Using a double boiler, melt the baking chocolate and coconut oil together. Put the dates and water in a food processor and chop into a paste. Add flax mixture, milk and vanilla. Then, add dry ingredients and process. Last, add melted chocolate and coconut oil and mix until all ingredients are combined.

Pour batter into an 8-inch (20-cm) baking dish that is either oiled or lined with parchment paper. Place walnuts on top. Bake at 350°F (180°C, or gas mark 4) for 30 to 35 minutes. Let cool for at least 20 minutes before eating.

Blueberry Ice Cream, page 385

Fruity Coconut Breakfast Tart, page 471

Mixed Berry Crisp, page 372

Apple Pie Pancakes, page 451

Strawberry Shortcake, page 375

Maca and Cacao Nib Gummies, page 269

Zucchini Spaghetti with Creamy Alfredo Sauce, page 98

Kale Pine Nut Salad, page 332

Kale Guacamole, page 251

Honey Mustard Brussels Sprouts, page 225

Bacon Cabbage Chuck Roast Stew, page 158

Simple Coconut Flour Cake, page 355

utrient-Rich Berry Smoothie, page 479

Sugar-Free Trail Mix with Coconut Clusters, page 401

Mini Winter Squash Pies, page 368

Coconut Flour Donut Holes, page 406

Oven-Roasted Parsnip Fries with Ras el Hanout, page 216

Pumpkin Chocolate Chip Cookies, page 343

Chocolate Banana Breakfast Shake, page 483

Pear and Persimmon Fall Salad, page 328

Roasted Root Vegetable Frittata, page 86

Red Pepper "Hummus," page 243

Caramelized Onion & Sausage Breakfast Hash, page 431

Easy Slow Cooker Chicken Verde, page 153

Pesto Chicken with Zucchini Noodles, page 25

Chili Lime Chicken Wings, page 207

Chocolate Banana Ice Cream Sandwich, page 381

Gyro Meatballs, page 63

esh Fig & Roasted Butternut Squash Salad, page 294

Bok Choy Stir-Fry, page 187

armers Market Winter Soup, page 309

Eaked Chicken with Pistachio Tapenade, page 30

Slow Cooker Apple Crumble, page 168

Spicy Fish Sticks, page 105

Hungarian Chicken Stew, page 306

Savory Garlic Herb Biscuits, page 525

w Almond Butter Coconut Balls, page 273

Spaghetti Squash Cilantro Fritters, page 433

Ingredient Nut Butter Cookies, page 417

Curried Carrot and Sweet Potato Soup, page 294

Moroccan Heart Stew, page 307

Blueberry Lemon Donuts, page 470

Fluffy Banana Pancakes, page 194

Salmon Balls, page 104

sin "Cereal," page 194

Roasted Herbed Chicken, page 23

rsian-Spiced Beef and Roasted Butternut Squash, page 4

Mini Personal Frittata, page 430

Parsnip Chips, page 188

Sweet and Spicy Bacon Candy, page 267

Venison Ragout, page 53

Rosemary Garlic Flatbread, page 523

n & Crispy Pizza Crust, page 528

Truffled Cauliflower Mash, page 238

conut Chocolate Bars, page 273

Cinnamon Banana Pecan Crunch, page 401

Chocolate Salted Caramel Cupcakes, page 363

Italian Meatballs, page 59

Creamy Bacon Soup, page 296

Grain-Free Ginger Cookies, page 349

CHOCOLATE BIRTHDAY CAKE WITH CHOCOLATE FROSTING

This Paleo Chocolate Birthday Cake is moist and decadent. It is rich, so I recommend serving it with Coconut Whipped Cream (page 504) to balance out the flavors. —AV

SERVES 12–14

FOR THE CAKE

1 cup (175 g) chocolate chips

2 tbsp (30 ml) coconut oil, plus more for greasing the pans

8 eggs

2 cups (470 ml) coconut cream

2 tsp (10 ml) vanilla

½ cup (120 ml) honey

1 cup (120 g) coconut flour, sifted

½ cup (60 g) cocoa powder, sifted

½ tsp sea salt

1 tsp (3 g) baking soda

FOR THE FROSTING

1 cup (175 g) chocolate chips, melted in a double boiler

1 cup (235 ml) palm shortening

½ cup (120 ml) honey

1 tsp (5 ml) vanilla

2 tbsp (30 ml) of coconut cream

Pinch of sea salt

1 pint (340 g) strawberries, sliced

Preheat oven to 350°F (180°C, or gas mark 4). While the oven is preheating, melt the chocolate and the coconut oil in a double boiler. Prepare the cake pans by lining the bottom with parchment paper and greasing the sides with coconut oil. Set aside. In a food processor combine the eggs, coconut cream, vanilla, melted chocolate and honey. Then add the sifted coconut flour, cocoa powder and salt (I sift them all together) to the food processor. Once everything is all combined, add the baking soda and give it one last whirl.

Evenly distribute the batter between the two cake pans. Bake them for 30 minutes or until a toothpick inserted in the middle comes out clean. Allow the cakes to cool for 15 minutes.

While the cake is baking, whip up the chocolate frosting. Melt the chocolate in a double boiler. Add the melted chocolate, palm shortening, honey, vanilla, coconut cream and sea salt to a bowl. Use a hand mixer to blend until it is all well mixed, creamy and smooth. Using a spatula, spread a layer of frosting on top of one of the cakes. Line the middle of the cake with strawberries. Place the other cake on top of the strawberries. Now frost the sides of the cake and the top.

TRIPLE CHOCOLATE TRIFLE

Layers of chocolate cake chunks, fresh berries, Coconut Whipped Cream and chocolate pudding. All housed in cute mason jars for a rustic presentation. —RM

SERVE 2–4

FOR THE CHOCOLATE PUDDING

1 (14-ounce [392-g]) can full-fat coconut milk

¼ cup (60 ml) pure maple syrup

¼ cup (30 g) unsweetened Dutch process cocoa

Pinch of sea salt

FOR THE CHOCOLATE CAKE

¼ cup (30 g) coconut flour

¼ cup (30 g) unsweetened Dutch process cocoa

½ tsp baking soda

Pinch of salt

3 large eggs

⅓ cup (80 ml) pure maple syrup

2 tbsp (30 g) almond butter or sunbutter

1 tbsp (15 ml) coconut oil, melted, plus more for greasing the pan

1 tsp (5 ml) vanilla extract

(continued)

2 squares extra-dark chocolate

Raspberries, optional

Fresh whipped cream or Coconut Whipped Cream (page 504), optional

Make the chocolate pudding first so it has time to chill thoroughly. In a medium saucepan, mix all of the pudding ingredients together and bring to a boil. Turn the heat down to medium and simmer for 15 to 25 minutes, depending on your stove. Whisk the pudding every few minutes as you are preparing the cake batter. When ready, the pudding should coat the back of a wooden spoon. It will get thicker once chilled. Remove from the stove and cool to room temperature before chilling for an hour in the fridge.

Meanwhile, preheat the oven to 350°F (180°C, or gas mark 4). In a large mixing bowl, whisk together the dry ingredients for the cake. In a separate smaller bowl, whisk the eggs along with the other wet ingredients until combined. Mix the wet ingredients into the large bowl, making sure to smooth out any clumps of coconut flour.

Grease a standard 9-inch (23-cm) loaf pan with coconut oil. Pour the cake batter into the loaf pan and bake for 20 to 25 minutes. The cake should be about 1½ inches (3.8 cm) high. Cool the cake completely and cut into 1½-inch (3.8-cm) cubes.

Make dark chocolate shavings by using a potato peeler along the edge of a chocolate square—it helps to freeze the shavings before sprinkling them onto the trifle. Use small mason jars to layer the cake bits, pudding, chocolate shavings and raspberries. Serve chilled with Coconut Whipped Cream.

VANILLA CAKE WITH CHOCOLATE FROSTING

Cake is one of my favorite desserts, but making a grain-free version can sometimes be tough and can often result in a dense brick. This cake uses a combination of coconut and almond flour to create a great fluffy texture. Since both of these flours have some shortfalls when it comes to baking, blending them makes for a good texture and flavor. The dates are used to sweeten the cake, but also help to add a creamy richness. —HH

SERVES 6

FOR THE CAKE

2¼ cups (405 g) pitted dates in ½ cup (120 ml) water

8 eggs, whites and yolks separated

1 cup (120 g) coconut flour

½ cup (60 g) almond flour

1 tsp (5 ml) apple cider vinegar

½ tsp salt

1½ tsp (7.5 ml) vanilla extract

½ cup (120 g) butter or coconut oil

1¼ cups (295 ml) coconut milk or whole milk

1¼ tsp (4 g) baking soda

FOR THE CHOCOLATE FROSTING

2 (13.5-ounce [378-g]) cans coconut cream or refrigerated full-fat coconut milk

½ cup (60 g) cocoa powder

1 tsp (5 ml) vanilla

Dash of salt

⅓ cup (80 ml) raw honey

Shredded unsweetened coconut, optional, for garnish

Preheat the oven to 350°F (180°C, or gas mark 4). Grease two 8-inch (20-cm) round cake pans. Boil the water and pour over dates in a dish. Let soak for about 10 minutes. Put dates along with soaking water in a food processor and blend until it becomes a paste.

Put egg yolks in the food processor with the dates. Add flours, vinegar, salt, vanilla, butter, milk and baking soda and mix until well blended.

With a hand mixer, whisk the egg whites until they're fluffy and form stiff peaks. Gently fold the egg whites into the batter until fully incorporated. Pour the batter into the greased cake pans. Bake for 15 to 25 minutes or until firm and a toothpick inserted through the cake comes out clean. Set the cake aside to cool.

Using a whisk, lightly whisk the coconut cream for a few minutes until it's fluffy. Add the remaining frosting ingredients and whisk. If you want a firmer frosting to work with, refrigerate it for 30 minutes. If you want a more drizzly frosting leave it at room temperature. Frost the cake and sprinkle with unsweetened shredded coconut, optional.

CHEF'S TIP:

To make coconut cream, refrigerate a can of coconut milk overnight. Scoop the thick white coconut cream off the top. Discard the thin clear liquid left on the bottom.

SIMPLE COCONUT FLOUR CAKE

Every grain-free baker has a basic yellow cake recipe. This is mine. It's simple, perfectly moist, and can be used with almost any frosting or topping. —KH

MAKES 1

Ghee or coconut oil for oiling pan

½ cup (60 g) coconut flour

½ tsp baking soda

¼ tsp sea salt

3 eggs

½ cup (120 ml) ghee or coconut oil, melted

¼ cup (60 ml) full-fat coconut milk

⅓ cup (80 ml) maple syrup or honey

2 tsp (10 ml) vanilla extract

2 egg whites

Preheat the oven to 350°F (180°C, or gas mark 4). Oil a 9-inch (23-cm) round cake pan and line bottom of pan with parchment paper cut into a circle to fit the bottom.

In a large bowl, sift together coconut flour, baking soda and salt. Set aside.

In another bowl, whisk together the three eggs, fat of choice, coconut milk, maple syrup or honey and vanilla until foamy. Add wet to dry and mix well to combine.

In another large bowl, beat the two egg whites with a hand mixer until thick soft peaks form. Fold very gently into cake batter. Bake for 28 to 30 minutes, until toothpick inserted into center comes out clean and cake is golden.

CHEF'S TIP:

There is a fine art to whipping and folding egg whites. It is helpful if you use a VERY clean bowl, make sure that no egg yolk gets into the whites and use room-temperature eggs.

CHOCOLATE FROSTING

Chocolate makes everything better, right? This rich and decadent chocolate frosting is my go-to frosting for cupcakes and birthday cakes. Make it once and I think you'll see why! —KW

FROSTS 1 (8-INCH [20-CM]) CAKE

½ cup (120 g) butter, at room temperature

½ cup (60 g) cacao or cocoa powder

½ cup (120 ml) maple syrup

¼ cup (30 g) tapioca starch

Pinch of sea salt

Whip the butter on high speed until light and fluffy. Add in the remaining ingredients and continue whipping until everything is combined.

CHEF'S TIP:

If you cannot tolerate dairy, substitute palm shortening for the butter.

MATCHA TEA WHOOPIE PIES

These whoopie pies are perfectly moist and spongy, with the right amount of fluff in between. Packed with the earthiness of matcha tea, these green-tinted cakes are both a treat and an afternoon pick-me-up. —RM

MAKES 6

FOR THE CAKES

2 cups (240 g) almond flour

2 eggs

½ cup (120 ml) full-fat coconut milk

⅓ cup (65 g) coconut palm sugar (or ¼ cup [60 ml] raw honey)

1 tbsp (15 ml) bourbon vanilla extract

3 tsp (8 g) matcha tea

1½ tsp (4 g) baking soda

½ tsp baking powder

FOR THE FILLING

3 egg whites

½ cup (120 ml) raw honey (or raw turbinado sugar)

¼ tsp cream of tartar

Pinch salt

2 tsp (6 g) matcha

1 tsp (5 ml) lime juice

1 tsp (3 g) lime zest, plus more for garnish

½ tsp bourbon vanilla extract

Preheat the oven to 350°F (180°C, or gas mark 4). Line two baking sheets with parchment paper. In a large mixing bowl, add all of the cake ingredients except the baking soda and baking powder. Mix with a whisk and then whisk in both the baking powder and soda. Using a cookie scoop for uniformity, divide the batter between the cookie sheets. I like doing six cakes per tray (makes six big whoopie pies) but you can separate it to twelve mini cakes per tray. Bake for 13 to 15 minutes, until slightly firm to the touch. If you are making mini whoopie pies, bake for about 10 minutes. The cakes should be soft and moist, like an airy muffin top.

While the cakes are cooling, make your matcha meringue. Simmer a couple inches (5 cm) of water in a small saucepan on the stove. Combine the egg whites, honey, cream of tartar and salt in a medium metal mixing bowl. Set the mixing bowl over the simmering water, making sure the bottom of the metal bowl doesn't touch the hot water. Whisk the egg white mixture for a couple minutes or until the honey is melted. Caution: if the mixture gets too hot then the egg whites will scramble.

Remove the bowl and start whipping the meringue mixture with a handheld mixer. This process should take about 4 to 5 minutes until you reach stiff peaks. Add the matcha, whipping with the mixer until fully incorporated (about 30 seconds). Then gently fold in the lime juice, zest and vanilla. Match up like-sized cakes. Using a spatula or pastry bag, divide the meringue evenly between each whoopie pie. Sprinkle with extra lime zest and enjoy.

GOOEY CHOCOLATE BANANA SWIRL CAKE

This cake starts with the banana batter, then gets chocolate swirled through it to make a fun and pretty banana chocolate swirl cake. The flavor is rich and sweet and the texture is ooey and gooey with a crisped top crust. Perfect for kids! —HH

SERVES 4

FOR THE CAKE

2 ripe bananas

¼ cup (30 g) ground flax seeds mixed with ¼ cup (60 ml) warm water

1¼ cups (180 g) almond flour

½ cup (60 g) coconut flour

½ tsp salt

2 tsp (6 g) baking soda

⅓ cup (80 ml) coconut oil

⅓ cup (80 ml) full-fat coconut milk, canned

1 tsp (5 ml) apple cider vinegar

FOR THE CHOCOLATE SWIRL

¼ cup (60 ml) coconut oil

½ cup (60 g) cacao or cocoa powder

¼ cup (50 g) coconut sugar, honey or maple syrup

Preheat the oven to 350°F (180°C, or gas mark 4). Mash up the bananas or process in a food processor until smooth. In a separate bowl mix the ground flax seeds and warm water and let sit for a few minutes until it jells. Add the remaining cake ingredients, including the jelled flax and water to the food processor and mix together.

To make the chocolate swirl, in a double boiler, melt the coconut oil and add the cacao and sweetener until well blended. Turn off the heat. Pour the banana mixture into a 5 × 9–inch (12.5 × 23–cm) loaf pan. Use a silicone spatula to smooth it out evenly. Carefully drizzle the chocolate mixture in a zig-zag motion over the batter. Then use a butter knife or skewer to drag up and down to create a design in the cake.

Put the cake in the oven and bake for 25 to 35 minutes. Remember this is a gooey moist cake; since there are no eggs, the center will be a bit gooey while the top will be crispier.

LEMON PUDDING CAKE

If you've never had a pudding cake, you are in for a treat. The top is a cake, while the bottom has a very thin layer of pudding. The fresh lemon flavor makes this pudding cake divine. —KW

SERVES 4

4 eggs, whites and yolks separated

¾ cup (180 ml) full-fat coconut milk

¼ cup (60 ml) honey or sweetener of choice

1 tsp (5 ml) vanilla extract

Zest and juice of 1 lemon

Pinch sea salt

3 tbsp (24 g) coconut flour

Coconut oil for greasing

Preheat oven to 350°F (180°C, or gas mark 4). Whisk egg whites with a hand or stand mixer until stiff peaks form. In a separate bowl, mix together egg yolks, coconut milk, honey, vanilla, lemon juice and zest and sea salt. Stir in coconut flour. Briefly mix together the eggs whites and the lemon/yolk mixture. It will turn runny. Pour mixture into a well-greased 1-quart (1-l) ramekin or round baking dish. Bake for 45 minutes or until the center feels spongy when you gently poke it. Let cool and enjoy either warm or cold.

CHEF'S TIPS:

You can also use small, individual ramekins and bake for 25 to 30 minutes or until center feels spongy when poked.

LEMON BERRY SKILLET CAKE

Skillet cakes are not only easy to make, they are fun to share as well. This cake combines zesty lemon with fresh berries to create a moist grain-free cake that will please even the pickiest of eaters. —KH

SERVES 6–8

Coconut oil or ghee for oiling skillet

½ cup (60 g) coconut flour

¼ tsp sea salt

½ tsp baking soda

6 eggs

6 tbsp (90 ml) maple syrup or honey

½ cup (120 ml) coconut oil or ghee, melted

6 tbsp (90 ml) full-fat coconut milk

1 tsp (5 ml) vanilla extract

1 tbsp (15 ml) fresh lemon juice

Zest from 1 lemon

1 cup (150 g) mixed berries (strawberries, blueberries and raspberries)

Preheat the oven to 350°F (180°C, or gas mark 4) and liberally oil skillet with fat of choice.

Sift together coconut flour, sea salt and baking soda. Set aside.

Whisk eggs until nice and foamy. Then add sweetener of choice, coconut oil or ghee, coconut milk, vanilla, lemon juice and zest. Mix again to thoroughly combine. Slowly add dry to wet. Mix until combined. Allow to sit for 2 to 3 minutes to allow coconut flour to absorb.

Pour into greased skillet. Gently spread evenly across bottom of skillet. Pour berries on top. Bake for 28 to 30 minutes, or until cake is firm in center and lightly golden.

MINI POUND CAKES WITH PEACHES, BLACKBERRIES AND CREAM

Hints of orange and honey provide these dense cakes with extra sweetness and moisture. Baking with coconut flour results in a denser cake, but once you garnish with whipped cream or coconut cream and fresh fruit, the presentation is beautiful and the taste is delicious. A classic summer favorite in our house! —CP

MAKES 12

6 eggs

6 tbsp (90 ml) butter, melted

½ cup (120 ml) plain yogurt or coconut milk

¼ cup (60 ml) raw honey

1½ tsp (7.5 ml) vanilla extract

¾ cup (90 g) coconut flour, sifted

¾ tsp baking soda

1 heaping tsp (2 g) fresh orange zest

8 ounces (227 g) fresh blackberries

2 peaches, peeled and sliced

8 ounces (227 g) heavy whipping cream or whipped coconut cream

Preheat oven to 350°F (180°C, or gas mark 4). Generously grease muffin tins with butter or line tins with baking cups.

In a bowl, use a hand blender to mix together wet ingredients. Sift in dry ingredients and continue to blend until a smooth batter forms. Fold in orange zest.

Spoon batter into baking tins about two-thirds full.

Bake for 17 to 20 minutes or until a tester comes out clean. Let the cakes cool for about 10 minutes before inverting onto a cooling rack to cool completely.

As the cakes are cooling, prepare the whipping cream by using a hand blender to whip for 2 to 3 minutes or until cream is thick and fluffy. Prepare peaches and blackberries.

Assemble by cutting the mini cakes in half and garnishing with a large spoonful of cream and fruit.

STRAWBERRY LIME CAKE

I've served this strawberry lime cake at many summer BBQs and parties and it's always a big hit. No one can believe it's grain-, dairy- and refined-sugar-free! —KW

SERVES 9 +

FOR THE CAKE

4 eggs

2 limes, zested and juiced

¼ cup (60 ml) coconut oil or butter

⅓ cup (80 ml) pure raw honey

½ cup (118 ml) milk of choice (coconut or almond milk)

1 tsp (5 ml) pure vanilla extract

½ cup (60 g) coconut flour

1 tsp (3 g) baking soda

¼ tsp sea salt

FOR THE WHIPPED CREAMY ICING

1 (14-ounce [392-g]) can full-fat coconut milk

1 lime, zested

2 tbsp (30 ml) pure raw honey

1 tsp (5 ml) pure vanilla extract

Pinch sea salt

FOR THE TOPPINGS

1½ cups (225 g) diced strawberries

Preheat oven to 350°F (180°C, or gas mark 4). In a bowl, combine the eggs, lime juice and zest, coconut oil, honey, milk and vanilla. Mix well. Add the coconut flour, baking soda and salt. Mix until well combined. Pour the batter into a greased 8 × 8-inch (20 × 20-cm) baking dish. Bake for 20 to 25 minutes or until done in the center. Check the top at the 15- and 20-minute mark and make sure it's not over-browning. If it is, place some foil over the top until it's finished cooking. Let cool.

Refrigerate the can of coconut milk overnight for best whipped results. Use just the coconut cream that has risen to the top from the can of coconut milk—You can use the leftover coconut water for smoothies or save it for another use. Place just the coconut cream in bowl or stand mixer. Whip until peaks form. Once it's whipped, add the lime zest, honey, vanilla and a pinch of sea salt. Whip once more until it's thoroughly incorporated.

Once cooled, frost with the whipped icing. Place in the refrigerator for at least one hour. Top with diced strawberries. Slice and serve. Keep any leftovers in the fridge.

CINNAMON CARDAMOM PEAR CAKE

Having guests over for some afternoon tea? Why not serve this delicious cake that highlights the beauty of pears? —NK

SERVES 8

Coconut oil, for greasing the cake pan and cooking the pears

2 medium pears, slightly soft, peeled and sliced into even rounds

1½ cups (180 g) almond flour

2 tsp (6 g) ground cinnamon

1 tsp (3 g) ground cardamom

¼ tsp baking soda

¼ tsp sea salt

2 large eggs, whites and yolks separated, at room temperature

⅓ cup (80 ml) raw honey, melted

¼ cup (60 ml) melted coconut oil

1 tsp (5 ml) vanilla extract

⅛ tsp cream of tartar

(continued)

Preheat oven to 350°F (180°C, or gas mark 4). Line a 9 × 1½-inch (23 × 3.8-cm) round cake pan with parchment paper and grease using a little coconut oil. Set aside. Heat 1 tablespoon (15 ml) coconut oil in a medium-large skillet over medium heat. Add the sliced pears to the pan and cook on either side for 1 to 2 minutes. Remove the pear slices to a paper towel-lined plate and set aside.

In a large mixing bowl sift in the almond flour, then add the cinnamon, cardamom, baking soda and sea salt. Mix well and set aside.

In another large mixing bowl, mix together the egg yolks, raw honey, melted coconut oil and vanilla extract using an electric mixer. Set aside. Using another large clean mixing bowl, add the egg whites and the cream of tartar. Using a whip attachment on an electric beater or stand mixer whip the egg whites until they form soft peaks.

Add the egg yolk mixture to the bowl with the almond flour mixture and mix well. Take a spatula and add one third of the egg white mixture and fold through. Do this two more times until all the egg white mixture is folded through, making sure to fold gently.

Now layer pear slices on the bottom of the cake pan. Pour the cake batter over the top of the pears and use a spatula to flatten and spread the batter evenly over the top. Place in the oven and bake for 25 to 30 minutes or until a toothpick or fork inserted in the middle comes out clean. Remove from the oven and allow to cool before flipping over and serving.

RAW CHEESECAKE

This cheesecake is so decadent and delicious! I use a mixture of cashews and coconut cream for the cream cheese texture. Make this for a birthday or bring to a potluck and it will be a hit! —HH

SERVES 6–8

FOR THE CHEESECAKE

2 cups (300 g) cashews, soaked overnight in warm water to cover

1 (13.5-ounce [378-g]) can coconut cream

⅓ cup (80 ml) coconut oil

Juice of ½ lemon

½ tsp vanilla

½ cup (60 g) powdered coconut sugar

FOR THE CRUST

1½ cups (270 g) dates

1¼ cups (150 g) almond flour

2 cups (300 g) chopped walnuts

2 tbsp (16 g) coconut flour

½ cup (60 g) cacao powder or cocoa powder

1 tbsp (15 ml) coconut oil, for greasing

¾ cup (60 g) shredded coconut

FOR THE CHOCOLATE DRIZZLE

½ cup (85 g) chocolate chips, Enjoy Life brand is gluten- and dairy-free

Cover the dry cashews with warm water in a bowl, and let soak overnight or for at least 8 hours. Also place a can of coconut milk in the fridge overnight to make coconut cream.

Cover the dates with hot water and let soak for at least 10 minutes. After the dates have soaked, drain the water from the bowl and place the dates in a food processor. Blend the dates until a paste forms. Then, place almond flour, chopped walnuts, coconut flour and cacao powder in the food processor and blend with the dates. The resulting mixture should be a thick doughy consistency. If it is too dry you can add a small amount of water, but you don't want it to be very wet. It needs to stick together firmly in a ball. Press this crust mixture into the bottom of a spring-form pan that has been greased with coconut oil. Sprinkle the shredded coconut over the crust evenly and place into the refrigerator.

For the cheesecake filling, drain the water from the cashews and blend the cashews in a clean food processor until it resembles a paste. Open the can of refrigerated coconut cream and scoop the cream off of the top and discard the clear liquid at the bottom. Put the cream into the food processor. Add the coconut oil, lemon juice and vanilla and process until all of the liquids are smooth and there are no lumps. Add the powdered coconut sugar to the food processor and blend. Once the mixture is blended well and there are no lumps, pour the cheesecake mixture into the chilled crust. Refrigerate for 3 to 5 hours or until the cheesecake has hardened.

When you are almost ready to serve the cheesecake you can apply the chocolate drizzle. In a double boiler, melt the chocolate chips on medium heat. Remove the cheesecake from the spring-form pan. Take large spoonfuls of the melted chocolate and drizzle it over the cheesecake.

CHEF'S TIP:

Coconut cream can be made by putting 1 (13.5-ounce [378-g]) can of full-fat coconut milk in the fridge overnight. In the morning, the cream will separate and you can scoop it off the top of the can of coconut milk.

To powder coconut sugar, simply blend in a coffee or spice grinder.

CHERRY CHOCOLATE CUPCAKES

I've served these cupcakes at both kid and adult birthday parties and they always go over well. They are an especially delicious treat for chocolate lovers. —KW

MAKES 12

4 eggs

¾ cup (180 ml) coconut milk

¼ cup (60 ml) coconut oil, melted

⅓ cup (80 ml) honey

1 tbsp (15 ml) vanilla extract

½ cup (60 g) coconut flour

¼ cup (30 g) cocoa powder

½ teaspoon baking soda

Pinch of sea salt

½ cup (75 g) pitted cherries, chopped

12 additional cherries for decorating

Preheat oven to 350°F (180°C, or gas mark 4). In a large bowl, whisk together the eggs, coconut milk, coconut oil, honey and vanilla extract until well blended. Stir in the coconut flour, cocoa powder, baking soda and sea salt until combined. Fold in the pitted chopped cherries. Pour the batter into a cupcake lined muffin pan, filling each liner three quarters of the way full, and bake for 20 to 25 minutes or until an inserted toothpick comes out clean. Frost with Chocolate Frosting (page 356). After frosting, top each cupcake with a whole cherry.

COCONUT CUPCAKES WITH CHOCOLATE FROSTING

These coconut flour cupcakes are a fun sweet treat for birthdays, special occasions or those days when you just need a cupcake! The texture is very moist, light and pretty close to a regular cupcake despite using coconut flour, which can be tricky to work with since it soaks up so much moisture. The frosting is very rich and creamy, so if you're a frosting fan like me, you'll want to lick that off first! —HH

SERVES 6

FOR THE CAKE

¼ cup (60 ml) coconut oil, melted

½ cup (60 g) coconut flour

1½ tsp (4.5 g) baking soda

Dash of salt

¼ cup (50 g) coconut sugar

1 tsp (5 ml) vanilla extract

½ cup (120 ml) coconut milk

4 eggs

1 tsp (5 ml) apple cider vinegar

FOR THE FROSTING

½ cup (120 ml) coconut oil, at room temperature

¼ cup (60 ml) coconut butter

¼ tsp vanilla

4–6 tbsp (30–50 g) powdered coconut sugar

4 tbsp (30 g) cacao or cocoa powder

¼ cup (19 g) shredded coconut, for decorating

Preheat the oven to 350°F (180°C, or gas mark 4). Melt the coconut oil and combine with remaining cupcake ingredients in a food processor or bowl, mix well.

Place batter in a muffin tin lined with cupcake liners. The cupcakes will rise a small amount, so you can fill the muffin liner about three quarters full. Bake for about 20 to 30 minutes or until a toothpick inserted comes out clean and the tops are slightly browned.

For the frosting, beat the coconut oil in a bowl with an electric mixture or hand blender. The coconut oil will soften up a bit. Add the coconut butter, vanilla and powdered coconut sugar and blend until mixed. Then add the cacao or cocoa powder and mix again.

Keep in the fridge until the cupcakes are cooled and ready to frost. The frosting will harden if it's in the fridge for longer than 30 minutes. To soften, leave at room temperature for 30 minutes then blend again with a hand mixer until it breaks up and softens.

Top the cupcakes with the frosting and sprinkle with shredded coconut. Store the cupcakes in the fridge and let sit at room temperature 30 to 60 minutes before eating to allow the frosting to soften.

CHEF'S TIP:
To make powdered coconut sugar, place the desired amount of coconut sugar into a coffee grinder and grind into a fine powder.

DOUBLE CHOCOLATE CUPCAKES

These double chocolate grain-free cupcakes will give any store-bought cupcake a run for its money! On top of the rich chocolatey goodness and moist cakey texture, it's also a whole lot better for you than any store-bought cupcake. —HH

SERVES 6

FOR THE CUPCAKES

¼ cup (60 ml) coconut oil

½ cup (60 g) coconut flour

1½ tsp (4.5 g) baking soda

Dash of salt

¼ cup (50 g) coconut sugar

2 tbsp (16 g) cacao powder or cocoa powder

1 tsp (5 ml) vanilla extract

⅔ cup (160 ml) full-fat coconut milk, canned

4 eggs

1 tsp (5 ml) apple cider vinegar

FOR THE FROSTING

½ cup (120 ml) coconut oil, room temperature

¼ cup (60 ml) coconut butter

¼ tsp vanilla

Dash of salt

4–6 tbsp (30–50 g) powdered coconut sugar

4 tbsp (30 g) cacao or cocoa powder

Unsweetened shredded coconut, optional

Preheat the oven to 350°F (180°C, or gas mark 4). Melt the coconut oil and combine with remaining cupcake ingredients in a food processor or bowl, mix well. Place batter in a muffin tin lined with cupcake liners. The cupcakes will rise a small amount, so only fill the muffin liner about three quarters full. Bake for about 20 to 30 minutes or until a toothpick inserted comes out clean and the tops are slightly browned.

For the frosting, place the coconut oil in a bowl and beat with a hand mixer. The coconut oil will soften up a bit. Add the coconut butter, vanilla, salt and powdered coconut sugar and blend with the hand mixer until mixed. Then add the cacao or cocoa powder and mix again.

Keep in the fridge until the cupcakes are cooled and ready to frost. The frosting will harden if it's in the fridge for longer than 30 minutes. To soften, leave at room temperature for 15 to 30 minutes then blend again with a hand mixer until it breaks up and softens. Top the cupcakes with the frosting and sprinkle with shredded coconut. Store the cupcakes in the fridge and let sit at room temperature 30 to 60 minutes before eating to allow the frosting to soften.

CHEF'S TIP:

To make powdered coconut sugar, place the desired amount of coconut sugar into a coffee grinder and grind into a fine powder.

CHOCOLATE SALTED CARAMEL CUPCAKES

The easy salted caramel sauce in this recipe is so versatile, I love to drizzle it on everything. It is the perfect complement to dark chocolate and oozes from the center of these decadent cupcakes. —RM

SERVES 12

FOR THE CUPCAKES

1 cup (120 g) almond flour

½ cup (60 g) tapioca starch

⅓ cup (40 g) unsweetened cocoa powder

½ tsp ground cinnamon

1 tsp (3 g) baking soda

½ tsp sea salt

⅓–½ cup (80–120 ml) raw honey

¼ cup (60 ml) coconut oil, melted

4 eggs

½ tbsp (7.5 ml) vanilla extract

FOR THE CHOCOLATE BUTTERCREAM FROSTING

2 sticks (225 g) butter

⅔ cup (115 g) chocolate chips (I prefer Enjoy Life brand)

Pinch of salt

FOR THE SALTED CARAMEL SAUCE

¼ cup (60 g) unsalted butter

3 tbsp (45 ml) coconut milk

½ cup (100 g) coconut sugar

½ tsp sea salt

(continued)

For the cupcakes: Preheat the oven to 350°F (180°C, or gas mark 4) and line a cupcake tray with paper or silicon liners. Combine all dry ingredients together in a large mixing bowl. Mix together all the liquid ingredients in a small bowl, and then combine with the dry ingredients. Divide the batter evenly in the cupcake liners and bake for 15 to 18 minutes until a toothpick comes out clean when inserted in the middle.

For the chocolate buttercream frosting, melt all of the ingredients in a small saucepan on the stove until fully incorporated. Pour into a freezer-safe bowl and freeze until solid. Remove from the freezer and bring to room temperature. Whip the stiff chocolate butter with a handheld mixer for about 5 minutes, until the buttercream becomes light brown and fluffy. Set aside.

Add all of the salted caramel ingredients to a heavy-bottomed saucepan and gently boil for 2 minutes. If you want a thicker sauce, boil for about 1 more minute. The caramel sauce will thicken more as it cools. Set the caramel aside.

Prepare the cooled cupcakes by punching a hole from the center top of each one. You can use the back side of a pastry bag's metal tip or a paring knife. Fill each cupcake with 1 teaspoon (5 ml) caramel sauce. Use a pastry bag to frost each cupcake with buttercream. Drizzle more caramel sauce on top. Store cupcakes in an airtight container in the fridge and bring to room temperature before eating.

CHEF'S TIP:

If the caramel sauce is too warm, then it might melt the frosting, but too cooled and it's hard to drizzle. I find it's easiest to fill a plastic sandwich baggie with the caramel sauce, gently warm it between my hands, and then cut a ¼-inch (6-mm) slit in the corner. Then drizzle on top of frosting.

BACON BROWNED BUTTER CUPCAKES

Browned butter has a nutty taste with gorgeous flecks of gold. When whipped into buttercream, it's so light and delicate. In this recipe, bacon becomes the metaphorical cherry on top. —RM

SERVES 12

4 slices thick bacon

1 cup (120 g) almond flour

½ cup (60 g) tapioca flour

⅓ cup (40 g) unsweetened cocoa powder

1 tsp (3 g) baking soda

½ tsp ground cinnamon

½ tsp sea salt

½–¾ cup (120–180 ml) Grade B maple syrup

¼ cup (60 ml) bacon fat

4 eggs

½ tbsp vanilla extract

¼ cup (45 g) chocolate chips (I prefer Enjoy Life brand)

FOR THE BROWNED BUTTERCREAM FROSTING

2 sticks (225 g) unsalted butter

⅓ cup (80 ml) raw honey

In a heavy-bottomed saucepan, fry the bacon on the stove, saving the bacon grease for the oil used in the cupcakes. Reserve the crispy cooked bacon off to the side. Preheat the oven to 350°F (180°C, or gas mark 4).

For the cupcakes: Combine all dry ingredients together in a large mixing bowl. Mix together all the liquid ingredients in a small bowl and then combine with the dry ingredients. Mix well and then stir in the chocolate chips. Line a cupcake tray with 12 cupcake liners. Divide the batter evenly between each liner. Bake for 15 to 17 minutes, the middle should be slightly soft to the touch when finished.

For the frosting: lightly wipe out the heavy-bottomed sauce pan with a clean paper towel. Melt the butter in the sauce pan over medium heat. Continue cooking, stirring constantly and keeping an eye on it, until the butter just starts to turn a golden color, about 4 to 6 minutes. It will be frothy and bubbly. Remove from heat and stir in the raw honey until fully melted. Pour the browned butter mixture into a freezer-safe bowl, cover and pop in the freezer until fully hardened. Remove the cold butter from the freezer and let it come to room temperature. Whip the butter for about 5 minutes with a hand mixer until it turns into a light, fluffy frosting. Frost each cooled cupcake with the browned buttercream and sprinkle bits of crumbled bacon on top. Leftover cupcakes should be stored in an airtight container in the fridge for up to 8 days. Bring them to room temperature before enjoying.

GINGERBREAD CUPCAKES

A classic spicy gingerbread flavor topped with mounds of fluffy meringue frosting! This holiday recipe can be served as cupcakes or muffins. —RM

SERVES 12

FOR THE CUPCAKES

1 cup (120 g) blanched almond meal

½ cup (60 g) tapioca starch

¼ cup (30 g) coconut flour

3 tsp (8 g) ground ginger

2 tsp (6 g) ground cinnamon

1 tsp (3 g) baking soda

½ tsp sea salt

¼ tsp ground cloves

¼ tsp ground allspice

4 eggs

⅓ cup (80 ml) molasses

⅓ cup (80 ml) maple syrup

¼ cup (60 ml) coconut oil

1 tsp (5 ml) vanilla extract

FOR THE FROSTING

¼ cup (60 ml) maple syrup

2 egg whites, at room temp

½ tsp lemon juice

¼ tsp vanilla extract

Dash ground cinnamon

Crystalized ginger, for garnish

Preheat the oven to 350°F (180°C, or gas mark 4). In a large mixing bowl, mix together all of the dry cupcake ingredients. In a medium mixing bowl, mix together all of the wet ingredients. Whisk together the dry and wet ingredients and combine until fully incorporated. Line a cupcake tray with paper liners and distribute the batter evenly. Bake for 15 to 20 minutes until a toothpick comes out clean when inserted in the middle. Cool completely.

It's best to have each frosting ingredient prepped before starting this process. In a small saucepan over medium heat, boil the maple syrup for about 1 minute, or until a candy thermometer reads 220°F (104°C). At the same time, use a hand mixer or a stand mixer to whip the egg whites, lemon juice and vanilla extract to stiff peaks. Once you have stiff peaks, slowly drizzle the boiling maple syrup into the egg whites. If you pour it in too fast then you will scramble the eggs. The pouring process should take about 1 minute. Sprinkle a dash of cinnamon into the frosting. Continue mixing until the frosting looks glossy. Frost the gingerbread cupcakes with the meringue frosting and sprinkle with crystallized ginger. Cupcakes can be stored in an airtight container for 5 days in the fridge.

CHEF'S TIP:
These cupcakes can easily be made into muffins by omitting the frosting and sprinkling with crystalized ginger prior to baking. They are the perfect holiday treat!

CINNAMON BUN IN A MUG

This easy solo recipe is more of a cinnamon cake than a bun, but it still has that signature "cream cheese" icing, made here from a few simple ingredients. It is a Paleo staple that eases the transition from conventional diets. —RM

SERVES 1

2 tbsp (16 g) coconut flour

1 tsp (3 g) ground cinnamon

Dash salt

Dash ground nutmeg

1 egg

2 tbsp (30 ml) almond milk, unsweetened

1½ tbsp (23 ml) raw honey

½ tsp vanilla extract

½ tsp baking powder

FOR THE ICING

1 tbsp (15 g) coconut butter

1 tbsp (15 ml) almond milk, unsweetened

1 tsp (5 ml) raw honey

½ tsp lemon juice

Mix all of the cinnamon cake ingredients in a large coffee mug, mixing in the baking powder last. Microwave for 2 minutes. Mix all of the icing ingredients in a small bowl, drizzling over the hot mug cake. Enjoy immediately.

CHEF'S TIP:

This mug cake can also be baked in the oven, using an oven-safe mug, at 350°F (180°C, or gas mark 4) for 15 minutes.

EGG-FREE CHOCOLATE PIE

This rich, creamy and decadent chocolate pie is a great dish to bring to a dinner party. It looks impressive, yet the filling is very easy to make and the nutty crust is one of the BEST parts of the whole dish! —HH

SERVES 4

2 (13.5-ounce [378-g]) cans coconut cream

¼ cup (60 ml) raw honey—or substitute coconut nectar for a vegan alternative

⅔ cup (80 g) cacao powder or cocoa powder

¼ tsp sea salt

½ tsp vanilla

1 Egg-Free, Grain-Free Pie Crust (page 528), cooled

Shaved dark chocolate, for garnish

Scoop the coconut cream out of the cans and put in a large mixing bowl—you can reserve a small portion, about 2 tablespoon (30 ml) of the coconut cream, to top the pie like whipped cream if you want. Whisk the coconut cream until the lumps are broken up and it is a fluffy whipped cream consistency. Once the coconut cream is smooth and fluffy like whipped cream, add the honey, cacao powder, sea salt and vanilla and gently mix it with the whisk until it is fully blended and there are no lumps.

Place the chocolate coconut cream filling in the thoroughly cooled pie crust. Spread it evenly and place in the refrigerator for an hour or more to allow it to set. To serve, you can place a small amount of whipped coconut cream on top for garnish and add shaved dark chocolate.

EGG-FREE PUMPKIN PIE

This Paleo and vegan pumpkin pie is such a delicious winter treat. It would make a perfect addition to the holiday table, no matter whom you're sharing with. —HH

SERVES 4

Egg-Free, Grain-Free Pie Crust (page 528)

2 tbsp (16 g) ground flax seeds soaked in 2 tbsp (30 ml) warm water

2 cups (520 g) pumpkin purée

⅓ cup (65 g) coconut sugar

¼ cup (60 ml) full-fat coconut milk, canned

2 tbsp (16 g) arrowroot

1 tsp (5 ml) vanilla

2 tsp (6 g) Pumpkin Pie Spice (page 505)

2 tbsp (30 ml) honey

Prepare the pie crust with the recipe provided on page 528.

Set the oven to 325°F (170°C, or gas mark 3). Combine the ground flaxseeds and water in a dish and set aside to jell. Once the flax mixture has jelled, use a food processor or blender to mix all the ingredients together until it is smooth. Pour the filling into the pie shell and bake at 325°F (170°C, or gas mark 3) for 30 to 40 minutes. Once it is done baking, allow it to cool and set for at least an hour.

CHEF'S TIP:
Grind flaxseeds in a coffee grinder.

SWEET POTATO PIE

No holiday meal is complete without a real sweet potato pie. The hazelnut crust gives it a special touch. This pie is so healthy and nutrient-dense that I don't mind if my kids eat it for breakfast. —KH

SERVES 6–8

FOR CRUST

¾ cup (112 g) hazelnuts, preferably soaked and dehydrated

1 cup (120 g) almond meal

¼ tsp sea salt

4 tbsp (60 ml) coconut oil, butter or ghee, melted

2 tbsp (30 ml) honey

2 cups (500 g) cooked sweet potato purée

3 eggs

⅔ cup (160 g) sweetened condensed coconut milk

2 tbsp (30 g) coconut oil, butter or ghee, softened

½ tsp ground cinnamon

½ tsp ground allspice

½ tsp ground ginger

2 pinches ground cloves

½ tsp sea salt

Prepare crust by preheating oven to 350°F (180°C, or gas mark 4). Process hazelnuts in food processor until they resemble a coarse flour. Add the rest of crust ingredients and pulse until well combined. Press mixture into a glass pie dish and bake for 12 minutes to firm up a bit. You will not see much of a color change in the crust. Allow to cool completely.

To make pie filling: Preheat the oven to 400°F (200°C, or gas mark 6). With a hand blender, combine sweet potato purée and eggs until smooth and creamy. Add the remaining ingredients and mix again until well incorporated. Be mindful not to overprocess as the sweet potatoes can get pasty and sticky.

Pour into cool, prepared pie crust and bake for 10 minutes. Then turn oven down to 325°F (170°C, or gas mark 3) and bake until set, about 40-45 minutes. Allow to cool completely. Serve as is or garnish with coconut cream. Enjoy!

MINI WINTER SQUASH PIES

Mini desserts are my favorite. These cute little mini pies are baked in their own shells and are reminiscent of a traditional pumpkin pie. —KH

SERVES 6

3 small winter squash

5 eggs

1 cup (235 ml) full-fat coconut milk

4 tbsp (60 ml) honey or maple syrup

1 tsp (3 g) ground cinnamon

½ tsp ground cardamom

¼ tsp ground ginger

⅛ tsp ground cloves

⅛ tsp ground nutmeg

¼ tsp sea salt

2 tsp (10 ml) vanilla extract

Ghee, butter or coconut oil to grease baking pan and squash skins

Preheat the oven to 400°F (200°C, or gas mark 6). Lightly grease a large baking pan or cookie sheet. Cut winter squash in half horizontally, scoop out the seeds and stringy parts and rub outer skins liberally with fat of choice. Bake squash, cut-side down, for 30 to 40 minutes until insides are soft. Remove from oven and allow to cool enough to handle.

Reduce oven heat to 350°F (180°C, or gas mark 4). Carefully scoop out inner meat of squash, leaving a thin layer inside to provide support for the shell. Place all ingredients into blender and purée until creamy and smooth. Taste and adjust for flavor and sweetness.

Arrange the six squash shells skin-side down on the baking sheet. Pour the creamy mixture into each shell. Bake for 35 to 40 minutes, until the filling is set. Allow to cool slightly. Serve either warm or at room temperature.

MINI BLUEBERRY TARTS

These sweet Mini Blueberry Tarts make for a beautiful dessert. I like to add a tiny mint leaf to each one. —KW

SERVES 12

FOR THE TART

3 eggs

⅓ cup (80 ml) melted butter or ghee

3 tbsp (45 ml) pure honey or pure maple syrup

1 tsp (5 ml) pure vanilla extract

¾ cup (90 g) coconut flour

2 tbsp (16 g) arrowroot powder

Pinch of sea salt

Zest of half lemon, optional

FOR THE BLUEBERRY FILLING

2 tbsp (16 g) gelatin

Juice of 1 lemon

1 tbsp (13 g) coconut oil

3 cups (450 g) blueberries, divided

2 tbsp (30 ml) pure raw honey or pure maple syrup

Pinch of sea salt

12 mint leaves, for garnish

Preheat oven to 325°F (170°C, or gas mark 3). Mix the wet tart ingredients in a mixing bowl. Add the dry tart ingredients and mix until dough forms. Form the dough into a ball. Refrigerate for 1 hour. After it's been refrigerated, form the dough into twelve equal, golf-ball-sized balls. Press each ball until it's flat into a regular-sized muffin-lined tray. Bake for 15 minutes.

As the tarts are baking, mix the gelatin and lemon juice together. Set aside. It will form a big clump—that's ok. Place the coconut oil and 1 cup (150 g) of blueberries in a small pot over medium heat. Cook and stir for about 4 to 5 minutes until the blueberries burst and it's mostly liquid. Turn the heat to low and dump in the lemon-gelatin. Stir until gelatin is completely dissolved—about a minute. Take the pot off the heat and stir in the honey, sea salt and remaining blueberries. Once the tarts are finished cooking, spoon the blueberry filling over each tart. Refrigerate for at least 30 minutes or until the gelatin has set.

RAW FRUIT TART

This raw fruit tart is so delicious! The whipped coconut cream is so light and rich and really adds a nice texture to the tart. The date sweetened crust brings a nutty flavor that pairs beautifully with the sweet fruit and cream. —HH

SERVES 4

FOR THE CRUST

1 cup (180 g) pitted dates

1½ cups (180 g) almond flour or almond meal

1½ tbsp (23 ml) water

FOR THE FILLING

1 (13.5-ounce [378-g]) can coconut cream

1½ tbsp (12 g) powdered palm sugar

TOPPING

1 apple

1 kiwi

4 strawberries

¼ cup (38 g) blueberries

Finely chop the dates in a food processor, then add almond flour and water. The water is added to keep the dates and almond flour together a little better, you can add more as you see fit. Press this crust into a standard-sized tart pan and put in the fridge.

Whisk the coconut cream by hand in a bowl for a few minutes until it become a little lighter. Add the powdered palm sugar and whisk. Put the coconut cream over the crust and put in the fridge and let solidify for about 30 minutes. Cut the fruit into thin flat slices and place on top of the coconut cream in a decorative design. I used apples, kiwi, strawberries and blueberries, but you can use any fruit that you have on hand.

CHEF'S TIP:

To powder the palm sugar, blend in a coffee grinder. It will make a finer powdered sugar version of the coarse palm sugar. If you use apples on your tart, squirt a little lemon juice on them to keep them from getting brown. Lemon juice is a natural preservative!

BAKED PEARS WITH CRANBERRIES AND ORANGE COCONUT CREAM

I serve these baked pears during the holidays and my guests just adore them. Not only do they make a beautiful presentation, but they are absolutely delicious. —KW

SERVES 4

2 pears, cut in half

4 tsp (20 g) butter or coconut oil

Pinch of ground cinnamon and ground nutmeg

1 cup (145 g) cranberries

½ of an orange, zested and juiced, zest divided in half

1 tbsp (15 ml) pure honey, optional

FOR THE WHIPPED ORANGE COCONUT CREAM

½ cup (120 ml) coconut cream

⅛ tsp pure vanilla extract

½ tbsp (7.5 ml) pure honey

Pinch ground cinnamon

Preheat oven to 350°F (180°C, or gas mark 4). Place pears cut side up in a baking dish. Place 1 teaspoon (5 ml) of butter on top of each pear. Add a pinch of cinnamon and nutmeg to each pear half. Add the cranberries on and around the pears. Sprinkle half the zest from the orange half on top of the pears and cranberries. Squeeze the juice from the orange half over the fruit. If you are using honey, drizzle honey over the pears. Bake for 25 to 30 minutes or until pears are softened.

With a stand or electric mixer, whip coconut cream until peaks form. Add the other half of the zest from the half orange, vanilla, honey and pinch of cinnamon. Continue whipping until well incorporated, about 15 to 30 seconds longer. Top with whipped orange coconut cream.

MINI BLUEBERRY COBBLERS

Everything mini is better! This recipe for warm personal Blueberry Cobblers can be doubled and then frozen before baking for easy portion control. —RM

SERVES 2

FOR THE FILLING

1½ cups (225 g) blueberries

1 tbsp (15 ml) lemon juice

1 tbsp (8 g) arrowroot starch

1 tbsp (15 ml) raw honey

FOR THE TOPPING

1 egg

2 tbsp (16 g) coconut flour

1 tbsp (8 g) blanched almond flour

1 tbsp (15 ml) raw honey

1 tbsp (15 ml) unsweetened almond milk

1 tbsp (15 ml) virgin coconut oil

1 tbsp (8 g) sliced almonds

Dash salt

Vanilla coconut ice cream, for serving

Coconut Whipped Cream (page 504), for garnish

Preheat the oven to 375°F (190°C, or gas mark 5). In a small mixing bowl, gently mix together the filling ingredients. The honey may be clumpy; that's ok. Fill two greased medium-sized ramekins. Place both ramekins on a baking sheet and bake for 13 minutes.

Mix together the topping ingredients. The batter should be pretty wet, not clumpy or crumbly. Remove the ramekins from the oven and scoop the batter on top. You can spread it flat or leave it looking rustic in small rounds. Bake in the oven for another 17 to 20 minutes. The topping should be fully baked. Serve immediately with vanilla coconut ice cream or Coconut Whipped Cream.

BERRY COBBLER

This Berry Cobbler is surprisingly simple to whip together and uses healthy ingredients like fiber-rich coconut flour. To make this recipe extra special, top each serving with a dollop of whipped coconut cream. —KW

SERVES 9

1 tbsp (15 ml) coconut oil

4 cups (600 g) of frozen or fresh mixed berries or any fruit

1 lemon, juiced and half of it zested

4 eggs

¼ cup (60 g) coconut oil, butter or ghee

¼ cup (60 ml) pure raw honey or pure maple syrup

½ cup (120 ml) coconut milk or any other type of milk

2 tsp (10 ml) pure vanilla extract

½ cup (60 g) coconut flour

¼ tsp ground cinnamon

1 tsp (3 g) baking soda

¼ tsp salt

Preheat oven to 350°F (180°C, or gas mark 4). In an 8 × 8-inch (20.3 × 20.3-cm) baking dish, mix 1 tablespoon (15 ml) coconut oil, fruit, fresh lemon juice and lemon zest. In a bowl, mix together eggs, ¼ cup (60 ml) coconut oil, honey, coconut milk and vanilla. Mix in the coconut flour, cinnamon, baking soda and salt until it forms a batter. Drop the batter by spoonfuls all over the top of the fruit. You can leave it as spoonfuls or smooth it out. Bake for 35 minutes or until fruit is bubbly and top is done and golden brown.

BAKED STREUSEL-TOPPED PEARS

This is an elegant dessert that doesn't require a lot of prep time. Cinnamon streusel pears are baked in warm juices, resulting in an explosion of flavor. —RM

SERVES 4

¼ cup (38 g) chopped pecans

2 tbsp (24 g) coconut sugar

1 tbsp (15 g) butter or coconut oil, melted

1 tbsp (8 g) ground flaxseed

1 tsp (3 g) tapioca flour

½ tsp ground cinnamon

Pinch salt

2 green Bosc pears, peeled, halved, cored

¼ cup (60 ml) apple juice

Preheat the oven to 375°F (190°C, or gas mark 5). In a small mixing bowl, mix together all of the streusel ingredients except the pears and apple juice. Lay the four pear halves in a small baking dish, cut-side up. Spoon the streusel topping evenly on the pear halves. Pour the apple juice in the bottom of the baking dish. Cover loosely with aluminum foil and bake for 45 minutes. Remove the foil and bake for another 10 minutes, until the streusel is lightly browned. Serve warm with a drizzle of the leftover juice from the baking dish.

APPLE CRUMBLE

Love apples? Turn them into a delicious spiced crumble, perfect for those cold days or when you want to enjoy something warm and sweet. —NK

SERVES 4–6

1 tbsp (15 ml) fresh lemon juice

4 apples

2 cups (240 g) almond flour

1 tsp (3 g) ground cinnamon, plus more for topping

½ tsp ground nutmeg

¼ tsp ground cloves

¼ tsp ground ginger

¼ tsp sea salt

½ cup (120 ml) coconut oil, melted

¼ cup (60 ml) raw honey

½ tsp vanilla extract

¼ cup (38 g) sliced almonds

Preheat oven to 350°F (180°C, or gas mark 4). Line a 10½ × 7-inch (26.7 × 17.8-cm) baking dish with parchment paper. Fill a mixing bowl with water and add the lemon juice. Core, peel and cut the apples into ¼- to ½-inch (6-mm to 1.3-cm) slices. Add the apples to the lemon juice water as you slice them. Set aside.

In a medium-sized mixing bowl sift in the almond flour. Add the cinnamon, nutmeg, cloves, ginger and sea salt. Mix well. In another mixing bowl add the coconut oil, raw honey and vanilla extract and mix. Mix the coconut oil mixture into the almond flour mixture.

Drain the apples, rinse and pat dry. Place sliced apples on the bottom of the baking dish. Using your hands sprinkle the crumble over the top of the apples. Add the sliced almonds on top. Cover the top of the baking dish with foil, then place in the middle rack of the oven to bake for 50 minutes. Remove the foil and bake for another 10 to 12 minutes until the top browns and crisps. Remove from the oven and sprinkle with some more cinnamon. Serve warm.

PEACH BERRY CRISP

This peach berry crisp comes together in just a few minutes. If you own individual tart baking dishes or small ramekins, consider using those instead of the pie dish. It will make a nice presentation and you can serve directly from the dish. —KW

SERVES 4–6

3 cups (450 g) mixed nuts, chopped

2 tbsp (30 ml) coconut oil, melted plus more for greasing

½ cup (60 g) almond meal

3 peaches, diced

1½ cups (225 g) raspberries, fresh or frozen, diced

1½ cups (225 g) blueberries, fresh or frozen

¼ cup (60 ml) honey

Preheat oven to 350°F (180°C, or gas mark 4). In a bowl combine nuts, coconut oil and almond meal. In a second bowl combine fruit and honey. Grease an 8-inch (20-cm) pie dish with coconut oil. Take about half the nut-almond meal mixture and pack it down with a spoon to create a bottom layer. Add fruit mixture to the dish.

Add remaining nut-almond meal mixture to the top. Bake for 30 minutes. Serve warm alone or with ice cream on top.

CHEF'S TIP:
You can use fresh or frozen berries.

MIXED BERRY CRISP

This is a rustic dual-recipe that can be made as a dessert, and then served again for breakfast the next morning. Everyone will love it. —RM

SERVES 10

FOR THE BERRIES

6 cups (900 g) mixed berries (or 2 cups [300 g] blueberries, 2 cups [300 g] strawberries, 1 cup [150 g] blackberries, 1 cup [150 g] raspberries)

¼ cup (50 g) coconut sugar

2 tbsp (16 g) tapioca flour

1 tsp (3 g) ground cinnamon

1 tsp (5 ml) lemon juice

Dash of salt

FOR THE CRISP TOPPING

¾ cup (112 g) sliced almonds

½ cup (75 g) chopped pecans

¼ cup (20 g) unsweetened coconut flakes

¼ cup (30 g) nut flour, like cashew

1 tbsp (8 g) tapioca flour

½ tsp ground cinnamon

4 tbsp (60 g) cold butter, cubed

Coconut Whipped Cream (page 504), for serving

Preheat the oven to 375°F (190°C, or gas mark 5). Gently mix all of the berry ingredients together in a large mixing bowl. Spoon them into a greased 9 × 11-inch (23 × 28-cm) baking dish. Mix together all of the topping ingredients in a separate bowl. Use your hands to incorporate the cold butter cubes into the nut mixture, making a crumbly crisp topping. Sprinkle it evenly on top of the berries. Bake for about 45 minutes until the crisp just starts to turn golden and the berry juices are bubbly. Serve with Coconut Whipped Cream.

CHEF'S TIP:
This crisp can be made all year round by using bags of frozen organic berries that were picked and frozen at season's peak.

PEAR BERRY HAZELNUT CRISP

Warm fruit crisp topped with fluffy whipped cream has always been one of my absolute favorite desserts. A crisp is the simpler friend to pie but still so comforting and tasty! This pear berry hazelnut crisp is simply made grain free and Paleo by creating a crumb topping of nuts, coconut and maple sugar. I chose to use maple for a rich fall flavor. This crisp is simple to make and perfect for holiday entertaining, as even those who don't eat grain free will enjoy! Make sure to serve garnished with a scoop of your favorite vanilla ice cream or a spoonful of fluffy whipped cream. —CP

SERVES 8

Coconut oil for greasing pan

4 pears, not fully ripe or mushy

½ cup (75 g) blueberries

1 tbsp (15 ml) lemon juice

2 tsp (10 ml) vanilla extract, divided

2 tsp (6 g) ground cinnamon, divided

6 tbsp (90 g) butter, room temperature

¾ cup (90 g) hazelnut flour

⅓ cup (37 g) cashews

⅓ cup (25 g) finely shredded coconut

⅓ cup (63 g) plus 1 tbsp (12 g) maple sugar

½ tsp ground cardamom

½ tsp ground nutmeg

¼ tsp salt

Whipped cream or vanilla ice cream, optional for serving

Preheat oven to 350°F (180°C, or gas mark 4). Generously grease a 9-inch (23-cm) pie pan with coconut oil.

Peel the pears and cut into bite-sized cubes. Toss together pears, blueberries, lemon juice, half vanilla extract and half cinnamon. Set aside.

In a food processor, add butter, hazelnut flour, cashews, shredded coconut, maple sugar and spices. Pulse several times until a crumbly mixture forms. Scrape down the sides of the bowl and pulse again.

Pour fruit mixture into pie pan. Crumble hazelnut dough over the top of the pears. Sprinkle the remaining tablespoon (12 g) of maple sugar over the top.

Bake for 30 to 35 minutes or until crisp is golden brown. Serve warm with whipped cream or a scoop of vanilla ice cream.

CHEF'S TIP:

I have found that a firmer, not completely ripe pear works best as they will not release as much juice when baked.

POACHED SUMMER FRUIT CROSTATA

Delicious, sweet peaches and plums make this wonderful grain-free crostata a tasty dessert to enjoy. —NK

SERVES 6–8

FOR THE DOUGH

3 pounds (1.4 kg) yuca

⅓ cup (80 ml) avocado oil

1 tsp (5 ml) vanilla extract

1 tsp (3 g) ground cinnamon

3 tbsp (45 g) maple sugar

¼ tsp sea salt

3 tbsp (24 g) coconut flour, optional

FOR THE POACHED FRUIT

1 cup (235 ml) water

5 plums, sliced into wedges

5 peaches, sliced into wedges

1 vanilla pod, split down the middle

2 cinnamon sticks, broken in half

3 tbsp (45 ml) raw honey, slightly melted to be runny

(continued)

Place a large pot of water to boil on the stove. Slice the tops and ends off the yuca and remove the thick outer layer from the yuca, making sure to also remove any brown spots or blemishes. Slice the yuca into even medium-sized pieces. When the water has come to a boil add the yuca pieces, turn the heat to medium low and cover with a lid. Cook yuca for 20 to 25 minutes or until fork tender. Strain the yuca and let rest for 5 minutes.

To make the poached fruit, place water, plums, peaches, vanilla pod, cinnamon sticks and raw honey into a large heavy-bottomed pot. Stir to mix. Place on medium heat with the lid on and let cook 15 to 20 minutes or until the fruit has softened but still mostly holding their shape. Remove from the heat and strain through a fine mesh sieve, placed over a bowl to catch the liquid from the poached fruit. Discard the vanilla pod and cinnamon sticks. Set the fruit aside to cool while you make the dough.

Place the rested, strained yuca into a high-powered blender or food processor. Add the avocado oil, vanilla extract, ground cinnamon, maple sugar and sea salt. Blend until a dough forms.

Remove from the blender or food processor and transfer to a piece of parchment paper on top of a cutting board. Allow to cool. While the yuca is cooling, preheat oven to 400°F (200°C, or gas mark 6) and line a large baking sheet with parchment paper. As the yuca cools remove any fibrous pieces from the dough. Allow to cool for 10 to 15 minutes then check the dough for stickiness; if the yuca is still a little sticky, sprinkle 1 tablespoon (8 g) coconut flour at a time into the yuca and press into the dough to help absorb any stickiness.

Once ready use your hands to form the dough into a circle, around ½-inch (1.3-cm) thick. Strain any leftover liquid as best as you can from the poached fruit then spoon the poached fruit mixture into the center of the yuca dough. Use your hands to fold over the outside edges of the dough all around to meet with the fruit, making sure to overlap the edges slightly as you go around. Carefully place onto the lined baking sheet and bake for 30 to 35 minutes. Remove from the oven and allow to cool before serving.

CHEF'S TIP:
You can use the leftover liquid from the poached fruit to make a simple syrup. Just boil down the liquid in a small saucepan until it reduces and thickens. You can use this to drizzle on top of pancakes the next morning.

APPLE GALETTE

Galette is a traditional French pastry filled with sweet or savory ingredients. Its rustic and free-form design allows for simple baking without all the fuss of a traditional pie. This apple galette is perfect for the holidays served with a spoonful of whipped cream or even a breakfast treat with a hot cup of coffee! —CP

SERVES 8

FOR THE CRUST

6 tbsp (90 g) butter

1½ cups (180 g) almond flour

3 tbsp (24 g) coconut flour

1 tbsp (12 g) coconut sugar

½ tsp arrowroot starch

½ tsp baking soda

¼ tsp salt

1 tsp (3 g) ground cinnamon

¼ tsp ground nutmeg

1 egg, whisked

FOR THE APPLE FILLING

2 tbsp (30 g) butter

2 large apples

1 tbsp (15 ml) lemon juice

1 tsp (5 ml) hazelnut extract

1 tbsp (12 g) coconut sugar

1 tsp (3 g) ground cinnamon

¼ tsp ground nutmeg

Pinch of ground cloves

¼ tsp sea salt

FOR THE GLAZE

2 tbsp (30 ml) butter, melted

2 tbsp (30 ml) raw honey

Slice the butter into thin slices and set aside to soften. Preheat oven to 350°F (180°C, or gas mark 4). Line a baking sheet with parchment paper.

Sift together dry ingredients. Use a pastry cutter or clean hand to mix in butter. Fold egg into flour mixture and continue to shape until crumbly mixture turns into a ball of dough. Chill in refrigerator for 1 hour.

Warm a skillet on low, melting butter in the pan. Peel, core and cut apples into thin slices. In a mixing bowl, stir together all apple filling ingredients and spices. Sauté apples for about 5 to 8 minutes to soften slightly.

Assemble the gallette by placing chilled dough onto a parchment-lined baking sheet. Place another layer of parchment paper on top. Using a rolling pin, roll out dough into a thin circle. Remove top layer of parchment paper.

Scoop apples into center of crust leaving a 1-inch (2.5-cm) border. Use a soft-edged knife to fold up edges of the crust.

Bake for 25 minutes, brush with butter and honey glaze, then continue to bake for 5 minutes.

Allow the galette to briefly cool before slicing. It is best when served fresh and warm, topped with whipped cream.

STRAWBERRY SHORTCAKE

Grain-free strawberry shortcakes are surprisingly easy to make! If you need a recipe to impress, you should give this one a try. —KW

SERVES 4

4 eggs

1 lemon, juiced

¼ cup (60 ml) butter or coconut oil, melted

2 heaping tbsp (30 ml) pure honey or other sweetener of choice

2 tsp (10 ml) pure vanilla extract

½ cup (60 g) coconut flour

½ tsp ground cinnamon

½ tsp baking soda

¼ tsp sea salt

2 cups (300 g) strawberries, diced

WHIPPED COCONUT CREAM

1 (13.5-ounce [378-g]) can full-fat coconut milk (must be full-fat) or 1 (13.5-ounce [378-g]) can coconut cream, chilled in the fridge for a few hours

1 tbsp (15 ml) pure honey (or other sweetener of choice), more or less to taste

1 tsp (5 ml) pure vanilla extract

In a mixing bowl, mix together eggs, lemon, butter, honey and vanilla. Add the coconut flour, cinnamon, baking soda and salt. Put the shortcake mixture in the fridge for 15 minutes—if you skip this step, the shortcakes will be thin and flat like a pancake. Still yummy, but definitely not as pretty!

Preheat the oven to 350°F (180°C, or gas mark 4). Drop eight heaping spoonfuls of dough onto a parchment-lined or greased cookie sheet in equal-sized portions. Bake for 15 minutes or until lightly golden. Scoop just the thick, hardened cream out of the refrigerated can of coconut milk—save the coconut liquid for smoothies!—and whip with a hand or stand mixer until nice and fluffy. Add in honey and vanilla extract and continue whipping for 30 seconds. Store the whipped coconut cream in the fridge until you are ready to use it.

Top four of the shortcakes with a dollop of whipped coconut cream. Add ½ cup (75 g) of strawberries on top of each whipped cream–topped shortcake. Add another shortcake on top of each one. Add another dollop of whipped coconut cream and enjoy.

CHEF'S TIP:

If you can tolerate dairy, fresh whipped cream using heavy whipping cream—instead of coconut cream—is delicious, too.

BITE-SIZED STRAWBERRY SHORTCAKES

These little bite-sized strawberry shortcakes make a perfect dessert for a party. They are really easy to make and only require a minimal number of dishes. All things key in my book! —AV

MAKES 26 TO 28

4 eggs

2 tbsp (30 ml) raw honey

1 cup (235 ml) coconut cream

2 tsp (10 ml) vanilla extract

½ cup (60 g) coconut flour, sifted

Coconut oil for greasing baking dish

½ tsp baking soda

⅛ tsp sea salt

1 pint (340 g) strawberries, sliced

Coconut Whipped Cream (page 504)

Preheat the oven to 350°F (180°C, or gas mark 4). Grease a mini muffin pan with coconut oil.

Whisk eggs, raw honey, coconut cream and vanilla together. Add coconut flour and allow the batter to sit for about 5 minutes, so the coconut flour can absorb the wet ingredients. Add the baking soda and sea salt and make sure that it is thoroughly mixed. Place a heaping tablespoon (15 g) of batter into each cup of the mini muffin pan. Fill the cups until they are almost full, but have a little room left at the top. Cook for about 18 minutes or until a toothpick inserted comes out clean. After they have cooked, remove them from the pan and set on a wire cooling rack. Allow to cool for 10 minutes.

While the shortcakes are cooling, make the Coconut Whipped Cream. Use a serrated knife to cut the shortcakes in half horizontally. Place a dollop of whipped cream on one half of a shortcake, add a couple of slices of strawberries and then top with the other half. Serve immediately or store in the refrigerator.

CHEF'S TIP:

You can substitute whole coconut milk for coconut cream in the batter, but I think the results are better with the cream.

LEMON COCONUT PETIT FOURS

Petit fours are a delicate and elegant mini cake traditionally served with British high tea. These grain-free petit fours would be a wonderful addition to a real food tea party, a child's birthday party or a sophisticated luncheon. They can be made ahead and keep well in the fridge or freezer. —HH

SERVES 4

FOR THE CAKE

¾ cup (135 g) dates

½ cup (60 g) coconut flour

½ cup (120 ml) whole milk or coconut milk

3 eggs, whites and yolks separated

½ tsp vanilla

½ tsp baking soda

¼ tsp salt

1 tsp (3 g) lemon rind, plus more for decorating

FOR THE FROSTING

⅔ cup (160 ml) coconut cream

2 tbsp (30 ml) raw honey

1 tbsp (15 ml) lemon juice

Preheat the oven to 350°F (180°C, or gas mark 4). Grease a standard-sized loaf pan. Pour 3 tablespoons (45 ml) boiling water over the dates in a heat-safe bowl and let soak for about 15 minutes. Once the dates have soaked, put them in a food processor along with soaking water and mix until you have a paste-like consistency. Add coconut flour, milk, egg yolks, vanilla, baking soda, salt and lemon rind and mix. Whip the egg whites with a stand mixer with the whisk attachment or a hand mixer until foamy and stiff peaks form. Gently fold egg whites into the batter. Pour the batter into the greased pan and even out the top with a spatula or spoon. Bake for 20 to 30 minutes or until an inserted toothpick comes out clean.

For the frosting, whisk the coconut cream in a bowl by hand for a few minutes to make it lighter and creamier. Add raw honey and lemon juice and whisk until fully incorporated.

Allow the cake to cool completely before frosting. Once the cake has cooled, cut the top off with a knife to make it flat and even. Cut small 2- to 3-inch (5- to 7.5-cm) squares or circles out of the cake. Cut the shapes in half widthwise and frost the middle. You can use the prepared frosting, but it will be very thin. For a thicker middle frosting, just use plain coconut cream sprinkled with lemon zest. Then place the other half of the cake on top of it. Drizzle the prepared frosting over the small cake shapes and use a spatula or knife to frost the sides evenly. Once you've frosted each petit four, refrigerate to allow the frosting to harden. Top with a bit of lemon rind.

CHEF'S TIP:

Coconut cream can be purchased in cans or you can skim the cream off the top of refrigerated cans of coconut milk. Refrigerate a can of full-fat coconut milk overnight to solidify the cream.

CREAMY CHOCOLATE ICE CREAM

Making ice cream is a fun activity to do in the kitchen together—get everyone involved, gathering around to talk and laugh as the ice cream churns away. You can top with whatever desired toppings or flavorings you prefer. This chocolate ice cream is pure creamy goodness and will have you scooping a second serving! —CP

SERVES 4–6

2½ cups (588 ml) coconut milk, full-fat and unsweetened

½ cup (60 g) cacao powder

⅓ cup (80 ml) maple syrup

3 egg yolks

1 tsp (5 ml) vanilla extract

FOR THE TOPPING

Toasted coconut

Chocolate chips

Fresh berries

Real whipped cream

Chopped nuts

Place all ingredients in a blender. Blend, scrape down the sides and blend again.

Heat a saucepan to low. Add the ice cream mixture and slowly heat for about 15 minutes, stirring occasionally so the cream does not burn. Steam will begin to rise when the mixture is hot enough, but you do not want the mixture to bubble or boil.

Transfer ice cream batter to a clean bowl and chill in the refrigerator for 4 hours.

Pour into the ice cream maker and churn according to manufacturer's instructions. Transfer ice cream to a bowl and freeze for 15 minutes before serving.

Top with toasted coconut, chocolate chips, berries, a scoop of whipped cream, chopped nuts or any of your favorite toppings.

CHEF'S TIPS:

You can make the ice cream batter the morning or even night before you want to serve. Simply pour into your ice cream maker when you are ready to churn.

COFFEE ICE CREAM

For this coffee ice cream recipe, I use actual coffee grounds. I've found that works best because you still get that nice ice cream consistency along with the strong coffee flavor. I used decaf so we wouldn't get a coffee buzz, but if you do want that buzz feel free to use regular! —HH

SERVES 2

2 tbsp (16 g) decaf coffee grounds

1 (13.5-ounce [378-g]) can full-fat coconut milk

2½ tbsp (37.5 ml) raw honey

½ tsp vanilla

¼ tsp salt

Grind coffee is very finely. If you're using a large or commercial grinder, make sure it's set to espresso.

In a bowl combine all ingredients and whisk well. Let cool in the fridge for a while—some ice cream makers suggest that you do this before you start churning. Follow the directions for your ice cream maker to churn into ice cream.

MAPLE COCONUT ICE CREAM

This ice cream is one of my favorites. With a good ice cream maker, the texture comes out just like real ice cream! —HH

SERVES 2

1½ cups (355 ml) coconut milk

3–5 tbsp (45–75 ml) maple syrup, depending on how sweet you want it

¼ tsp salt

Combine coconut milk, maple syrup and salt and mix well using a whisk or spoon. Put in your ice cream maker and process according to the manufacturer's directions.

MAPLE PECAN ICE CREAM BITES

These ice cream bites are little pieces of creamy maple goodness that melt in your mouth. The chopped pecans and shredded coconut add a nice crunch. I like to keep these ice cream bites in the freezer for when I want a wholesome sweet snack! —HH

SERVES 4

½ cup (120 ml) coconut cream

2½ tsp (12 ml) maple syrup, add more if you want it to be sweeter

Dash salt

¼ tsp vanilla

¼ cup (38 g) chopped pecans

2 tbsp (10 g) shredded coconut

Whip the coconut cream, maple syrup, salt and vanilla in a bowl with a hand mixer or whisk. You can taste this coconut cream to determine if it's sweet enough or if it needs more maple syrup. Put the mixture in a loaf pan lined with wax paper. Sprinkle chopped pecans and shredded coconut over it and put in the freezer. Allow it to harden, then cut into smaller pieces to serve.

CHEF'S TIP:

Coconut cream can be purchased in cans or you can skim the cream off the top of refrigerated cans of coconut milk. Refrigerate a can of full-fat coconut milk overnight to solidify the cream.

MAPLE AND CHOCOLATEY BACON CRUNCH ICE CREAM

Chocolate-covered bacon bits are mixed into luscious folds of maple coconut ice cream. This is a summertime treat like no other. —RM

MAKES 2 PINTS (940 G)

1 cup (235 ml) maple syrup

4 cups (940 ml) full-fat coconut milk

1 pack gelatin

Pinch salt

6 egg yolks

3 tbsp (45 g) unsalted butter

4 pieces of thick cut bacon

3-4 ounces (84-112 g) dark chocolate (72%)

In a small saucepan, reduce the maple syrup by about half over medium heat. Set aside. Pour coconut milk in a medium saucepan and sprinkle gelatin on top without stirring. Let sit for 1 minute and then whisk in. Turn the stove on medium and then whisk in the reduced maple syrup and pinch of salt. Lightly simmer the mixture until just before boiling. Then in a mixing bowl, beat the egg yolks until light in color. Slowly temper the eggs with the hot maple cream mixture. Add the butter and then turn off the stove. Mix it for 5 minutes using an immersion blender or regular blender. Bring to room temperature before chilling for at least 6 hours or overnight. You want it to be plenty cold before churning in the ice cream maker.

Prior to churning, fry the bacon until crisp but not burnt. Trim off any excess rubbery fat from the bacon. Layer a baking sheet with parchment paper. Melt chocolate using a double boiler and then dip bacon strips in it. Lay on baking sheet. Chill for 15 minutes and then cut into small bite-sized pieces.

Follow the directions of your ice cream maker and churn the maple ice cream. Throw in the chocolate bacon pieces toward the end of churning when it's the consistency of soft serve. Pack into pints or an airtight container and freeze before serving.

CHEF'S TIP:

Using a microwave to cook the bacon produces a dryer, jerky-like bacon which works better for this recipe. Bacon grease doesn't pair well with ice cream.

PUMPKIN SOFT SERVE

Many of us make soft serve from bananas as an easy Paleo treat. Add some pumpkin and spices for a fun seasonal treat. —KH

SERVES 4

1 cup (250 g) pumpkin purée, frozen in ice cube tray

2 ripe bananas, sliced into pieces and frozen

¼ cup (60 ml) non-dairy milk of choice

½ tsp vanilla extract

2 tbsp (30 ml) maple syrup or honey

½ tsp ground cinnamon

¼ tsp ground ginger

¼ tsp ground cardamom

Pinch of ground cloves

Remove frozen pumpkin cubes and banana slices from freezer and allow to soften for 5 minutes. Place all ingredients into a high-powered blender or food processor and blend until creamy smooth, scraping down sides as necessary. Serve immediately.

CHEF'S TIP:

One teaspoon (3 g) of pumpkin spice powder can be used in place of the individual spices in this recipe.

CREAMY PEPPERMINT ICE CREAM WITH DARK CHOCOLATE FUDGE DRIZZLE

Most holiday desserts are baked and warm, but this creamy ice cream is festive, fun and refreshing with a hint of peppermint. Creamy coconut milk makes up the base for this Paleo-friendly ice cream, so if you are looking for a lighter dessert for the holidays, this treat will have everyone scooping for seconds! —CP

SERVES 6

2½ cups (588 ml) coconut milk, full-fat and unsweetened

¼ cup (60 ml) raw honey

3 egg yolks

1 tsp (5 ml) peppermint extract

FOR THE DARK CHOCOLATE FUDGE DRIZZLE

3½ ounces (100 g) dark chocolate

2 tbsp (30 ml) coconut milk

2 tbsp (30 ml) water

½ tsp peppermint extract

In a small saucepan, combine all ice cream ingredients. Heat the sauce pan to low and slowly heat the mixture for about 15 minutes. Stir occasionally so the mixture doesn't burn. Steam will begin to rise when it is hot enough but you do not want it to bubble or boil. Transfer to a clean bowl and chill in the refrigerator for 4 hours.

Churn in an ice cream maker and freeze according to your ice cream maker's instructions.

Over low heat, melt the fudge ingredients together, stirring so that the chocolate does not burn.

Scoop ice cream and drizzle with warm fudge sauce!

CHEF'S TIPS:

Generally, ice cream needs to be chilled in the freezer for 20 to 30 minutes after churning and before serving. If your fudge sauce is too thick, add 1 to 2 more tablespoons (15 to 30 ml) of water to desired consistency.

CHOCOLATE AND ROASTED HAZELNUT GELATO

Chocolate and Roasted Hazelnut Gelato, or Gelato al Bacio, is a classic Italian ice cream. Inspired by the famous chocolates Baci Perugina, it has quickly become a summer favorite. This is the Paleo version, which gets remarkably close to the original. —VM

SERVES 4

3 bananas, peeled then frozen, then cut into coins

1 cup (150 g) toasted hazelnuts

¼ cup (30 g) dark cacao powder

1 tbsp (15 ml) vanilla extract

Take the bananas out of the freezer and let them sit out for about 10 minutes to soften.

While the bananas are sitting out, add the hazelnuts to the food processor and blend until they reduce to a nice flour. Add the remaining ingredients, including the bananas and blend until everything has mixed smoothly.

The gelato should be a perfect consistency to serve now, or you can store it in the freezer for later. If you choose to freeze and serve later, make sure to let the gelato sit out for about 30 minutes once you take it out of the freezer.

CHUNKY MONKEY ICE CREAM

So long wasting money and ingredient quality on pints of Ben & Jerry's. This is a dairy-free knock-off recipe with gobs of chocolate-covered walnuts swirled into banana ice cream. —RM

SERVES 4

4 egg yolks

4 cups (940 ml) full-fat coconut milk

1 cup (120 g) frozen ripe bananas, thawed

¾ cup (180 ml) maple syrup

1 vanilla bean, scraped (or 1 tsp [5 ml] vanilla extract)

Half a package of gelatin

3 ounces (84 g) dark chocolate (72% cocoa)

1 cup (150 g) chopped walnuts

Whisk egg yolks in mixing bowl until frothy. Take about 1 cup (235 ml) of the coconut milk and set aside in a small bowl. Blend bananas and remainder of the coconut milk together in a blender. Heat resultant coconut banana mixture on medium-low heat until just below boiling. Add maple syrup and vanilla bean/extract to the coconut milk and stir well. Take the reserved coconut milk and sprinkle gelatin on top. Allow to set for 1 minute, then pour into the hot coconut milk and stir for several more minutes.

Using a ladle, slowly add the hot mixture to your egg yolks, tempering them while whisking continuously so they don't scramble. Once one third of it is incorporated, you can start adding the rest more quickly, but all the while continuing to whisk. Then pour the mixture back in to the saucepan and heat on medium-low, continuing to stir until the mixture is thick enough to coat the back of a spoon. Once it reaches this point, it is ready to be transferred to a container and then cooled to room temperature.

Chill the mixture for at least 6 hours or overnight. Before churning the chilled mixture, melt the dark chocolate using a double boiler and layer a baking sheet with parchment paper. Coat the chopped walnuts in chocolate and then lay on parchment paper. Pop them in the fridge before you start churning. Follow the instructions for your ice cream maker. Add the chocolate walnuts when the ice cream has been churned to soft-serve consistency. Freeze the ice cream in an air-tight container. Let it sit out of the freezer to warm for 5 minutes before serving.

CHOCOLATE BANANA ICE CREAM SANDWICH

This chocolate banana ice cream sandwich recipe is the perfect summer treat. Despite the "ice cream" being only bananas, the texture is very reminiscent of real dairy-based ice cream. The soft, nutty chocolate cookies pair perfectly with the creamy banana "ice cream." —HH

SERVES 4

4 ripe bananas

1 cup (120 g) almond flour

½ cup (60 g) cocoa powder

2 tbsp (16 g) coconut flour

⅓ cup (60 g) coconut sugar

¼ cup (30 g) ground flax seeds

½ tsp baking soda

¼ tsp salt

½ tsp vanilla extract

½ cup (120 ml) coconut oil, melted

1 egg

Before you start the recipe make sure that you peel and slice the bananas and freeze them for 1½ to 2 hours.

Preheat the oven to 350°F (180°C, or gas mark 4). Combine all the ingredients except the bananas in a bowl, mixer or food processor. Shape dough hunks into balls and flatten and form into large circles on a cookie sheet lined with parchment paper. Bake for about 6 to 9 minutes. Cookies will be firm. Set aside to cool.

Once the cookies have cooled, start the banana ice cream. Put frozen bananas in a food processor. Run the processor until the bananas are fully blended into a creamy, ice cream-like texture. You may have to stop the processor a few times and scrape the sides to incorporate all the bananas.

To form the ice cream sandwiches, take one cookie and top the flat side with desired amount of banana ice cream, then top it with another cookie. If the banana ice cream is too creamy to hold up on its own, put it in the freezer for about 20 to 45 minutes until it's hard enough to hold, but soft enough to work with. Store ice cream sandwiches in the freezer.

SALTED CARAMEL BROWNIE ICE CREAM BARS

Coconut milk ice cream gets sandwiched between salted caramel sauce and brownies. You can either make your own dairy-free ice cream or buy a pint of it from your local natural food store. These are a fun summertime treat that the family can make together. —RM

SERVES 12

FOR THE BROWNIES

1 cup (120 g) almond flour

¾ cup (90 g) cocoa powder, unsweetened

½ cup (60 g) arrowroot flour

¼ cup (30 g) coconut flour

4 eggs

½ cup (120 ml) raw honey

¼ cup (60 ml) coconut milk

1 tbsp (15 ml) vanilla extract

1 cup (235 ml) melted oil—butter or coconut oil, plus more for greasing

¼ cup (45 g) chocolate chips, optional

FOR THE SALTED CARAMEL SAUCE

½ cup (100 g) coconut sugar

¼ cup (60 g) butter or ghee

3 tbsp (45 ml) coconut milk

½ tsp sea salt

¼ tsp vanilla extract

Pint of homemade coconut milk ice cream or So Delicious brand's vanilla

Preheat the oven to 350°F (180°C, or gas mark 4). In a medium mixing bowl, mix together all of the dry brownie ingredients. In a separate mixing bowl, mix together all of the wet ingredients. Then blend together until smooth. Line a 9 × 13-inch (23 × 33-cm) cake pan with parchment paper, leaving a few inches (7.5 cm) of parchment paper hanging over both sides for easy brownie removal. Grease with coconut oil or butter. Pour the brownie batter into the pan and bake for 20 minutes or until an inserted toothpick comes out clean.

Meanwhile, use a small saucepan on the stove to make the salted caramel sauce. Place all of the caramel sauce ingredients in the saucepan and gently simmer for 3 minutes. The sauce will also thicken once it cools. Set aside.

Cool the baked brownies to room temperature before drizzling two-thirds of the caramel sauce on top, reserving the last of the caramel sauce at room temperature. Pop the whole pan in the freezer to harden, about 10 minutes.

During this time, start thawing out the ice cream to a soft-serve consistency for about 15 minutes, making sure it doesn't get too runny. Once the caramel brownies are really cold, gently use the extra parchment paper sides to remove them from the cake pan. Cut the brownie sheet in half with a very sharp knife. Spread the ice cream evenly on one half and then use the other half to sandwich it. Place it back in the parchment-lined cake pan and then freeze it for at least 2 hours or until solid.

Cut the brownie sandwiches into bars while frozen, then let them sit at room temperature for a few minutes to soften a bit. Drizzle with reserved caramel sauce and eat immediately.

HONEY SWEETENED LEMON CURD

This Paleo lemon curd is entirely sweetened with honey and is on the tarter side, but absolutely fabulous spread on your favorite baked goods or even eaten by the spoonful! I like to top a spoonful of curd with toasted coconut flakes or churn into Honey Sweetened Lemon Curd Ice Cream (page 383). —CP

MAKES ABOUT 1½ CUPS (355 ML)

8 tbsp (120 g) butter

¼ cup (60 ml) raw honey

5 egg yolks

½ cup (120 ml) lemon juice

Dash of sea salt

Melt butter in a double boiler over low heat.

Whisk honey, egg yolks, lemon juice and salt in a bowl. Add to the melted butter. Continue stirring for about 10 to 15 minutes or until curd begins to thicken.

Transfer lemon curd to a clean container and place in the refrigerator. Allow curd to cool for a minimum of 4 hours.

CHEF'S TIP:
Be patient with the process of heating, stirring and thickening as it results in the best texture in the end!

HONEY SWEETENED LEMON CURD ICE CREAM

Tart and tangy lemon curd ice cream sweetened entirely with raw honey for a sweet, creamy treat. —CP

SERVES 4–6

½ cup (120 g) Honey Sweetened Lemon Curd (page 383)

1½ cups (355 ml) unsweetened, full-fat coconut milk

1 cup (235 ml) coconut cream or heavy cream

2 egg yolks

⅓ cup (115 g) raw honey

Make the lemon curd and refrigerate for 4 hours.

To make the ice cream, whisk together milk, cream, yolks and honey. Pour into a saucepan and heat until milk mixture starts to steam. Remove from heat and whisk in lemon curd. Chill ice cream batter for 4 hours in the refrigerator or make an ice bath to quicken the process.

Freeze and churn in an ice cream maker according to maker's instructions. Scoop and serve!

CHEF'S TIP:
You will have extra lemon curd but it stores fabulously in the refrigerator and is a delicious topping to your favorite scone or biscuit recipe. The curd can be prepared a few days in advance and then simply added to the ice cream when needed.

SAFFRON ROSE WATER AND PISTACHIO ICE CREAM

Ice cream that is dairy-free can be easy to make at home. Here I show you how to take a classic Persian ice cream recipe and turn it into a dairy-free treat, and the best part is you don't even need an ice cream maker to make it! —NK

SERVES 4–6

1 (13.5-ounce [378-g]) can full-fat coconut milk

2 tsp (10 ml) vanilla extract

4 egg yolks

3 tbsp (45 ml) raw honey

½ tsp crushed saffron, dissolved in ¼ cup (60 ml) of boiled water

1 tbsp (15 ml) rose water

4 ounces (112 g) chopped pistachios, for garnish

Create a double boiler by adding water to a medium saucepan and bringing to a boil. Lower the heat to a simmer then place a mixing bowl big enough to fit over the top of the saucepan on top, making sure that the bottom and sides of the mixing bowl do not come into contact with the water underneath. Add the coconut milk and vanilla extract. Stir to mix and warm up, making sure the mixture does not boil.

While the coconut milk is heating up, add the egg yolks to another mixing bowl. Take ¼ to ½ cup (60 to 120 ml) of the warm coconut milk mixture and add it to the egg yolks slowly, while whisking at the same time. Take another ¼ to ½ cup (60 to 120 ml) of the coconut milk mixture and again slowly add to the egg yolks while whisking. Pour the egg yolk mixture back into the remaining coconut milk in the double boiler. Using a wooden spoon, continue to mix for about 5 minutes or until a thick custard forms. If you think the coconut milk mixture is getting too hot, lift the bowl off the simmering water, mix and return. When the custard has thickened, remove the bowl from the heat and set aside to cool.

Once cool enough to be able to comfortably touch add the honey, saffron and rose water. Whisk to combine. Place in a freezer-safe container and place in the fridge to cool completely. After the ice cream mixture has cooled, place it in the freezer. Remove from the freezer and mix every 30 minutes for 2 to 3 hours until set. Remove the ice cream from the freezer and allow to sit out for 10 minutes. Once softened, stir in the chopped pistachios. Place back in the freezer until ready to serve.

LAVENDER ICE CREAM

This ice cream will make you want to jet off to Paris in a heartbeat! The aromatic flavor of bergamot in the Earl Grey with the floral notes of the lavender produces a light and refreshing dessert. —JC

SERVES 6

2 cups (470 ml) Homemade Coconut Milk (page 503)

1 cup (235 ml) Date-Sweetened Almond Milk (page 502)

½ cup (120 ml) raw honey

¼ cup (16 g) loose-leaf Earl Grey tea

1 tbsp (4 g) dried lavender

5 large egg yolks, room temperature

1 tsp (5 ml) vanilla extract

In a saucepan over low heat, add coconut milk, almond milk and honey. Stir for 2 to 3 minutes until it starts to simmer, but make sure it does not boil. Once milk is hot and honey has been dissolved, remove from heat.

Place the tea and lavender in a large cotton or paper tea bag. Drop it into the heated milk and gently stir. Cover the saucepan and infuse the milk with tea for 30 minutes or longer for a much stronger flavor. Remove tea bag and turn on heat to low. Warm the milk for 2 to 3 minutes. Remove from heat.

In a small bowl, beat the egg yolks with vanilla extract. Whisk the egg mixture 1 tablespoon (15 ml) at a time into the warm milk. Once all the eggs are incorporated into the milk, return the saucepan to the stove and turn on heat to low. Stir it constantly until it has thickened enough to coat the back of a wooden spoon. Remove from heat and pour into a bowl. Let the custard chill in the fridge for at least 5 hours.

Freeze the cooled mixture using an ice cream maker following the manufacturer's instructions. Place ice cream in a container and freeze for another hour before serving.

CHEF'S TIP:

Not all types of dried lavender are edible. Make sure you get culinary grade ones that are used for cooking or baking. Use 4 tea bags as a substitute for loose-leaf tea.

BLUEBERRY ICE CREAM

This recipe makes the most beautiful ice cream I have ever had. Enjoy the creaminess of coconut with the fresh flavor of blueberry in this dairy-free Paleo ice cream alternative. —KH

SERVES 6–8

2½ cups (375 g) fresh blueberries

½ cup (120 ml) maple syrup

⅛ tsp sea salt

2 (13.5-ounce [372-g]) cans full-fat coconut milk

½ tsp vanilla extract

Bring blueberries, maple syrup and salt to a boil in a medium pot. Turn down heat a bit and simmer softly for 3 to 4 minutes, until berries begin to pop open. Remove from heat and allow to cool slightly.

Add blueberry mixture, coconut milk and vanilla extract to blender. Process until creamy smooth. Place into fridge until very cold, overnight is best.

Pour into an ice cream maker and process according to manufacturer's instructions. Serve immediately as soft serve or place into freezer-safe container and freeze until firm enough to scoop.

INSTANT COCONUT MANGO FROZEN YOGURT

Frozen yogurt is my favorite treat on a hot day and this recipe provides instant satisfaction! This is a great afternoon snack to serve to your kids and I like to top mine with toasted coconut and chopped nuts or even dark chocolate shavings. —CP

SERVES 2

1½ cups (270 g) frozen mango chunks

1 cup (240 g) plain coconut yogurt

1 tbsp (15 ml) raw honey, optional, for something sweeter

Toasted coconut and slivered almonds, for garnish

Place mango, yogurt and honey in the blender and blend till smooth.

Divide into two cups and top with toasted coconut or almonds if desired.

Serve immediately.

CHEF'S TIP:

When mangos are in season, I usually peel and cut a few up, then freeze them to keep on hand.

WATERMELON LIME SORBET

Enjoy this treat on a warm summer's day when watermelons are plentiful and at their best. It is refreshing and tasty. —KW

SERVES 6

4 cups (480 g) watermelon, cubed

2 limes, juiced

3 tbsp (45 ml) honey

¼ tsp sea salt

Place the watermelon chunks in the freezer until frozen, about 2 hours. Once frozen, place the watermelon in a blender with the remaining ingredients. Blend until smooth.

CREAMY MATCHA STRAWBERRY FROZEN POPS

When the warmer weather hits try this delightfully creamy dairy-free ice cream to stay cool and refreshed. —NK

SERVES 6

8 ounces (227 g) fresh strawberries, stems removed

1½ tsp (4.5 g) matcha powder

1 tbsp (15 ml) just-boiled water

2 cups (470 ml) full-fat coconut milk

3 tbsp (45 ml) pure maple syrup

Roughly chop strawberries and place in a blender. Blend until puréed. Pour the mixture evenly into six popsicle molds. Place in the freezer and allow to set for 1 to 2 hours. Wash and dry the blender. Sift the matcha powder into a large measuring cup and sprinkle the boiled water over it. Stir to mix.

Mix the coconut milk , matcha powder mixture and maple syrup. Pour into the blender and blend for 20 seconds. Remove the molds from freezer and remove the tops. Pour the matcha mixture evenly into each mold, place the tops back on the place back in the fridge for another 3 hours or until set.

CHEF'S TIP:

To easily remove the tops of the molds just run under hot water until they easily release.

AVOCADO FROZEN TREATS

Avocado pairs so well with all different flavors. One of my absolute favorite ways to eat it is in desserts. These delicious Creamsicles will have you reevaluating everything you thought you knew about the use of avocados. —RM

SERVES 4–6

2 ripe Hass avocados

1 (13.5-ounce [378-g]) can full-fat coconut milk

⅓ cup (80 ml) raw honey

2½ tsp (12 ml) fresh lemon juice

Seeds from ½ vanilla bean, scraped

In a food processor or blender, fully combine all ingredients on high for 2 minutes until creamy. Spoon the mixture into BPA-free popsicle molds. Freeze for at least 2 hours until solid. To release the popsicles, run each mold under warm water for 5 seconds.

CANTALOUPE MINT PALETAS

This recipe uses very little honey to sweeten, as the cantaloupe is already really sweet These are so refreshing and would make a perfect healthy dessert for a summer gathering. —AV

SERVES 8

2 cups (320 g) cantaloupe, peeled, seeded and cut into chunks

¼ cup (60 ml) freshly squeezed lime juice

2 tsp (10 ml) honey (optional)

Pinch of sea salt

1 tbsp (6 g) fresh mint leaves, chopped

Place the cantaloupe, lime juice, honey and sea salt in a blender or food processor. Blend until smooth. Add mint and pulse for a few more seconds, until it is combined into the cantaloupe mixture. Pour cantaloupe mixture into popsicle molds and freeze for 6 hours to overnight.

COCONUT FUDGE FROZEN POPS

These coconut fudge pops are a fun summer indulgence. I use whipped coconut cream to create a creamy fudgy texture. —HH

SERVES 4

2 (13.5-ounce [378-g]) cans coconut cream

4 ounces (112 g) unsweetened baking chocolate

½ cup (120 ml) honey

½ tsp vanilla extract

Refrigerate the coconut cream overnight before you make this recipe.

Melt the baking chocolate in a double boiler and set aside to cool. Using a hand mixer, whisk the coconut cream for a few minutes until it's fluffy.

Add the honey and vanilla to the cream and mix. Add the chocolate and mix. Put the mixture into popsicle molds and freeze until completely hardened, about 3 to 5 hours.

CHEF'S TIP:

Coconut cream can be purchased in cans or you can skim the cream off the top of refrigerated cans of coconut milk. Refrigerate a can of full-fat coconut milk overnight to solidify the cream.

TANGY COCONUT LIME MACAROONS

A bite-sized taste of the tropics—a tangy, yet sweet coconut macaroon. Serve with vanilla ice cream for an extra special treat! —CP

MAKES 18

2¼ cups (190 g) finely shredded coconut flakes

½ cup (60 g) almond flour

Zest of 1 lime

Dash of sea salt

¾ cup (180 ml) unsweetened, full-fat coconut milk

2 tbsp (30 ml) raw honey

2 tbsp (30 ml) fresh lime juice, about 1 lime juiced

Preheat oven to 250°F (120°C, or gas mark 1⁄2). Line a baking sheet with parchment paper.

In a medium bowl, combine coconut, almond flour, lime zest and sea salt.

Pour in the coconut milk, honey, and lime juice and mix together.

Using a 1½ tablespoon (23 g) cookie scoop, drop small macaroon balls onto parchment-lined baking sheet. It is best to scoop, dragging the scoop up the side of the bowl to densely pack in the macaroon batter.

Bake for 40 to 45 minutes. Allow macaroons to cool briefly and then transfer to refrigerator to cool for 1 hour before serving. Macaroons keep in refrigerator for about 5 days.

CHEF'S TIP:

Use finely shredded coconut flakes as the fineness of the coconut will ensure the macaroons stay together—I recommend Let's Do Organic brand. Macaroons are best served slightly chilled as they will firm up. These can be prepared ahead of time for a quick snack after swimming or as a simple dessert for those hot nights.

DOUBLE CHOCOLATE COCONUT MACAROONS

A bite-sized cookie dipped in rich chocolate glaze. I love to make a batch of these and keep on hand when needing just a small bit of chocolate. These double chocolate macaroons are not overly sweet and make for a healthy afternoon snack as well. —CP

MAKES 18

2 cups (170 g) finely shredded coconut, unsweetened

½ cup (60 g) cacao powder

¼ cup (30 g) almond flour

¾ cup (180 ml) coconut milk, full-fat and unsweetened

3 tbsp (45 ml) maple syrup

Pinch of Celtic sea salt

FOR THE GLAZE

3 tbsp (45 g) raw cacao butter, chopped

2 tbsp (16 g) cacao powder

1 tbsp (15 ml) coconut oil

1 tbsp (15 ml) raw honey

Preheat oven to 250°F (120°C, or gas mark ½). Line two baking sheets with parchment paper, placing one in the freezer.

In a mixing bowl, sift together all macaroon ingredients, until a thick, crumbly batter forms.

Firmly pack macaroon batter into a medium, 1½ tablespoons (23 g) cookie scoop, by scooping and dragging along the sides of bowl. Drop onto baking sheet. Bake for 40 minutes.

While the macaroons are baking, melt together all glaze ingredients in a small saucepan over low heat.

Transfer macaroons to a cooling rack and cool completely, allowing the macaroons to harden.

Once the macaroons are cooled, dip macaroons in chocolate and place on frozen cookie sheet, allowing the glaze to set. Chill macaroons in refrigerator for 30 minutes before serving.

POMEGRANATE PANNA COTTA

Panna cotta makes for the perfect Paleo-friendly dessert. It is luscious and creamy, looks elegant, but is simple to make—although your guests would never guess! Don't skimp on the mint garnish here, it not only adds the perfect hint of green, but it also adds a pleasant layer of complexity to the dessert. —AV

SERVES 8

1 tbsp (8 g) gelatin

1 cup (235 ml) coconut milk

3 cups (705 ml) coconut cream

⅓ cup (80 ml) honey

½ tsp vanilla

2 tbsp (30 ml) fresh lime juice

1 tsp (3 g) lime zest

FOR THE POMEGRANATE LAYER

1½ cups (150 ml) pomegranate seeds (1½–2 pomegranates)

2 cups (470 ml) filtered water

1 tsp (5 ml) honey

3 tsp (8 g) gelatin

Small fresh mint leaves for garnish

24 whole pomegranate seeds for garnish

Add the gelatin to the coconut milk in a small bowl. Stir to combine and let it sit for 5 minutes. Heat a medium-sized heavy saucepan over medium heat; add the coconut cream, honey and vanilla. Whisk until the honey is dissolved and the mixture is well combined, about 2 to 3 minutes. Add the milk and gelatin mixture to the saucepan and vigorously whisk until well combined and the gelatin has dissolved, about 2 to 3 minutes. Make sure the mixture does not come to a boil. Remove the mixture from the heat and stir in the lime juice and the lime zest.

Pour the mixture evenly into individual serving glasses. Allow it to sit on the counter top to cool slightly. Refrigerate until set, 6 to 8 hours.

Place the pomegranate seeds in a medium-sized saucepan and cover with the water. Bring the heat to medium and cook the pomegranate seeds uncovered for about 20 minutes. Keep a close eye on them; if the water is getting close to boiling, bring the temperature down. Strain the seeds through a mesh strainer. Use a wooden spoon and press down on the seeds to get more of the juice out. Once it seems like there is no more juice left in the seeds, discard the seeds and put the juice back into the sauce pan. Bring the heat to medium, add the honey and whisk until completely dissolved. Once the honey is dissolved, add the gelatin and whisk vigorously until the gelatin is dissolved, about 2 to 3 minutes. Make sure the mixture does not come to a boil. Pour the mixture into another container and leave it out on the countertop and allow it to cool for about 10 minutes. If you pour it into the cups with the coconut cream when it is too warm, it might become murky, as it will mix with the cream layer. Once the pomegranate mixture is cool, pour it over the cream mixture until it forms a thin layer of red. Once all of the servings are covered with the pomegranate layer, allow them to set in the fridge for about 4 hours. Once they are set, garnish them with mint and pomegranate and serve.

MATCHA POMEGRANATE PANNA COTTA

Traditionally panna cotta is made with cream or cream and milk. This Paleo-friendly version uses coconut milk for that creamy taste and is infused with the vibrant flavors of matcha and pomegranate. —NK

SERVES 4

2 cups (470 ml) full-fat coconut milk

2¼ tsp (7 g) gelatin power

3 tbsp (45 ml) cold water

4 tbsp (60 ml) raw honey

2 tsp (6 g) matcha powder

2 tbsp (16 g) pomegranate seeds

Heat a saucepan on medium heat. Add the coconut milk and allow to warm gently, making sure it doesn't boil. Sprinkle the gelatin over the cold water in a measuring cup. Allow the gelatin to sit for 5 minutes. When the coconut milk is warm to the touch add the raw honey and mix. Remove the coconut milk mixture from the heat and sift in the matcha powder. Whisk the matcha into the coconut milk mixture.

Take ¼ cup (60 ml) of the mixture and pour it over the gelatin and mix. Pour the rest of the coconut milk mixture into a measuring cup and then pour everything into a blender. Blend for 30 seconds and then pour the contents back into the measuring cup for easier pouring. Pour the mixture into your desired serving containers and place in the fridge to set for a couple of hours. When ready to serve remove from the fridge and add ½ tablespoon (4 g) of pomegranate seeds on top of each panna cotta.

CHEF'S TIP:

If you don't have a blender you can use an immersion blender instead.

TURKISH DELIGHT PANNA COTTA

This decadent rose-colored panna cotta was inspired by the flavors of Turkish delight. Infused with the scent of rose water this dessert is sure to win over anyone who tastes it. —NK

SERVES 4

2 cups (470 ml) full-fat coconut milk

3 tbsp (45 ml) raw honey

2¼ tsp (7 g) gelatin powder

3 tbsp (45 ml) cold water

2 tsp (10 ml) organic beet juice

1 tbsp (15 ml) rose water

Roughly chopped pistachios, to serve

Heat the coconut milk in a medium saucepan over medium heat and add the raw honey. Stir to mix. Allow the mixture to warm up but make sure it doesn't come to a boil. In a medium-sized mixing bowl, sprinkle the gelatin powder over the cold water and let sit for 5 minutes.

While the gelatin is resting, check the mixture in the saucepan by dipping the tip of your finger in, it should feel warm but not hot. Remove the saucepan from the heat and mix in the beet juice and rose water. Pour the mixture over the gelatin in the bowl and use a whisk to mix well. Add the mixture into a glass measuring cup with a spout for easier transfer. Pour into your desired serving containers and place in the fridge to set for 2 to 3 hours. The panna cotta should still have a little jiggle to it when set. To serve, add some roughly chopped pistachios on top.

LEMON PANNA COTTA

Creamy, delicious panna cotta always makes me happy. Add a bit of zesty lemon, and you have a stellar dessert that is sure to please. Healthy coconut and gut-healing gelatin make it a perfect Paleo alternative. —KH

SERVES 3

1 (13.5-ounce [378-g]) can full-fat coconut milk, divided

Zest from 2 lemons

1½ tsp (4 g) gelatin

5 tbsp (75 ml) honey or maple syrup

1 tsp (5 ml) vanilla extract

Lemon zest, optional, for garnish

Whisk together 1 cup (235 ml) of the canned coconut milk and lemon zest in a medium pan. Bring to just below a boil, turn off heat, cover and allow to infuse. Pour the rest of the coconut milk into a shallow bowl and sprinkle the gelatin evenly over the surface and allow to bloom for 10 minutes.

Once gelatin has bloomed, gently reheat the coconut milk/lemon mixture to just below a boil and whisk in the coconut milk/gelatin until completely dissolved. Turn off heat. Whisk in the sweetener of choice and vanilla. Strain with a sieve and pour into three small dishes and allow to chill until set, at least 4 hours.

Run a sharp knife around the edge of each cup and unmold onto a serving plate, and garnish as desired or you can place the chilled cups into a hot water bath for a minute or two to make removal a bit easier.

VANILLA CHAI LATTE PANNA COTTA

Panna cotta is one of my favorite desserts. Although it sounds and looks sophisticated, it is easy to make. It's also a perfect recipe for those following an Autoimmune Paleo Protocol and for those that are allergic to eggs. This recipe is grain-, egg- and dairy-free! —AV

SERVES 6

1 cup (235 ml) coconut milk

1 tbsp (8 g) gelatin

3 tbsp (45 ml) chai tea (or 4 to 6 chai tea bags)

3 cups (705 ml) coconut cream

¼ cup (60 ml) raw honey

1 tsp (5 ml) vanilla

6 dried figs, chopped for garnish, optional

Place the coconut milk in a small bowl and add the gelatin to it. Stir to combine and set aside. If using loose tea, place the tea in a large mesh tea ball and set it aside. Heat a medium-sized heavy saucepan over medium heat, add the coconut cream, honey and vanilla. Whisk until the honey is dissolved. Add the tea and simmer at a low heat for 10 minutes. Make sure the mixture does not come to a boil. Remove the tea ball or the tea bags and discard. Add the milk and gelatin mixture to the saucepan and vigorously whisk until well combined and the gelatin has dissolved. Again, take care to not bring the mixture to a boil. Remove the mixture from the heat and pour it evenly into individual serving glasses. Allow it to sit on the countertop to cool slightly. Refrigerate until set, 6 to 8 hours. Top with dried figs and serve!

PUMPKIN PANNA COTTA

Panna cotta is such a perfect dessert. It is simple to make, uses the nourishing food gelatin and you can easily change the flavors based on what is in season. This combination with pumpkin and spices makes for a delicious fall treat. —AV

SERVES 6–8

1 cup (235 ml) coconut milk

1 tbsp (8 g) gelatin

2 cups (470 ml) coconut cream

1½ cups (375 g) pumpkin purée

⅓ cup (80 ml) honey or maple syrup

½ tsp vanilla

½ tsp ground cinnamon

¼ tsp ground nutmeg

¼ tsp ground cardamom

Coconut Whipped Cream (page 504) and chopped almonds, optional

Place the milk in a small bowl and add the gelatin to it. Stir to combine and let it sit for 5 minutes. Heat a medium-sized heavy saucepan over medium heat, add the coconut cream, pumpkin purée, honey or maple syrup, vanilla, cinnamon, nutmeg and cardamom. Whisk until well combined, about 2 to 3 minutes. Add the milk and gelatin mixture to the saucepan and vigorously whisk until well combined and the gelatin has dissolved, about 2 to 3 minutes. Make sure the mixture does not come to a boil. Remove the mixture from the heat and pour it into individual serving glasses. Allow it to sit on the countertop to cool slightly. Refrigerate until set, 6 to 8 hours.

COCONUT FLAN

With its vanilla flavored cream and caramelized sauce, this is the perfect Paleo version of a Latin favorite. —KH

SERVES 6

2 (13.5-ounce [378-g]) cans full-fat coconut milk

1 cup (200 g) coconut sugar, divided

⅛ tsp sea salt

1 tsp (5 ml) vanilla extract

1 tbsp (8 g) lemon zest

2 tbsp (30 ml) water

6 eggs

In a small saucepan, heat coconut milk until beginning to bubble at the sides. Add ½ cup (100 g) of coconut sugar and whisk until completely dissolved. Allow to simmer gently for 20 minutes to reduce. It will reduce by a third to one half of original volume. Remove from heat and add salt, vanilla and lemon zest. Mix to combine. Allow to cool for at least 10 minutes.

Preheat the oven to 325°F (170°C, or gas mark 3). Fill a large baking dish one third full of water and place in oven to heat up.

In a small saucepan or skillet, heat ½ cup (100 g) of coconut sugar and the water over medium heat until completely dissolved and beginning to bubble. Stir constantly with a wooden spoon to prevent burning. Once it is syrupy, carefully pour equal amounts into six ramekins.

Whisk the eggs together in a medium bowl. Slowly, pour a gentle stream of the reduced coconut milk mixture into eggs, whisking constantly to prevent eggs from cooking.

Pour mixture into caramel-lined ramekins. Place ramekins into the hot water bath in oven and bake for 45 to 50 minutes until custard is set. Center may still be a bit wiggly. Remove the baking dish from oven and remove ramekins from baking dish. I use tongs here. Allow to cool slightly then place into fridge for several hours. To serve, run a knife along the sides of the ramekins and carefully invert onto plate, allowing caramel to flow over custard.

BAKED PUMPKIN CUSTARD

This custard is delicious enough to be a dessert but healthy enough to be a side dish to any meal. Bursting with the flavors of warming spices, it's a wonderful addition to any holiday dinner. Try making it in individual ramekins for a fun twist. —KH

SERVES 6

8 egg yolks

2 cups (500 g) pumpkin purée

5 tbsp (75 ml) honey

½ tsp vanilla extract

1 (13.5-ounce [378-g]) can full-fat coconut milk

½ tsp ground cinnamon

¼ tsp ground ginger

¼ tsp ground cardamom

Pinch of ground cloves

Pinch of freshly grated nutmeg

¼ tsp sea salt

Preheat the oven to 350°F (180°C, or gas mark 4). Fill a large baking dish one-third full with water and place into oven to warm up.

Combine egg yolks, pumpkin purée, honey and vanilla extract in a medium bowl.

In a saucepan, gently heat coconut milk, all spices and sea salt until edges barely start to bubble. DO NOT BOIL. Slowly whisk half of coconut milk mixture into egg mixture to temper the eggs. Return the mixture to saucepan and stir with a wooden spoon over low heat until it thickens, about 5 minutes.

Pour into an 8 × 8-inch (20 × 20–cm) baking dish. Place the baking dish into prepared larger baking dish to make a water bath for even cooking. Then bake for 45 to 50 minutes, until set and toothpick inserted in the center comes out clean. Serve and enjoy. Store leftovers in fridge.

CHEF'S TIP:

I like to bake custards in a hot water bath for more even cooking. This step is not absolutely necessary but does make for a better end result. And if you don't have all the spices listed above, you can substitute 1 teaspoon (3 g) of pumpkin pie spice.

BLACKBERRY BRÛLÉE

Whether it is custard, flan or brûlée, creamy, rich desserts have always been popular. This Paleo version combines creamy coconut with fresh blackberries to make the perfect end to any dinner party. —KH

SERVES 6

Coconut oil, butter or ghee for oiling ramekins

2 cups (300 g) fresh blackberries

5 egg yolks

4 tbsp (60 ml) honey

2¼ cups (530 ml) full-fat coconut milk

1 vanilla bean, cut lengthwise and seeds scraped

Pinch of sea salt

¼ tsp ground cinnamon

6 tbsp (72 g) coconut sugar, optional, for hard topping

Preheat the oven to 325°F (170°C, or gas mark 3). Place large baking dish filled one-third full with water in oven to heat up. Lightly oil six ramekins. Divide blackberries evenly in the bottom of ramekins.

Whisk egg yolks and honey together in a medium bowl. In a saucepan, slowly heat coconut milk, split vanilla bean pod and scraped seeds, sea salt and cinnamon until edges barely begin to bubble. DO NOT BOIL. Remove vanilla bean pod.

Slowly whisk half of the coconut milk mixture into egg mixture to temper the eggs. Return the mixture to saucepan and stir with a wooden spoon over low heat until it thickens, about 5 minutes.

Strain the custard into the six ramekins right over the berries. Place ramekins in the water-filled baking dish and bake 35 to 40 minutes, until custard is set. Carefully remove baking dish from oven and remove ramekins. Tongs are useful here. Refrigerate for at least 4 hours.

To add hard caramel topping: Sprinkle 1 tablespoon (12 g) of coconut sugar evenly across top of each dessert. Broil 1 to 2 minutes until sugar melts. Watch it carefully as it burns quickly.

CRÈME BRÛLÉE (FOR TWO!)

I've always had a love affair with crème brûlée, and the sound of breaking through the torched sugar with a spoon. These cute little personal crème brûlées are dairy-free and taste just like the classic recipe. —RM

SERVES 2

⅓ vanilla bean

1 cup (235 ml) full-fat coconut milk

2 eggs yolks

2 tbsp (30 ml) raw honey

2 tbsp (30 g) raw sugar or palm sugar, for garnish

2 strawberries, for garnish

Preheat oven to 325°F (170°C, or gas mark 3). Slit the vanilla bean down the center with a paring knife, scraping the inside of the bean. Deposit the scrapings and the bean inside a small saucepan over medium heat. Add the coconut milk and simmer gently, not boiling it, for about 5 minutes or until slightly thicker.

In a medium mixing bowl, beat the egg yolks and honey until light in color. Remove the vanilla coconut milk from the stove and slowly temper the eggs in the mixing bowl. Strain the mixture through a fine mesh sieve into two medium ramekins, saving the vanilla bean pod for later use.

Lay the ramekins in an 8 × 8-inch (20 × 20-cm) glass baking dish, and pour in hot water until halfway up the sides of the ramekins. Bake for 40 to 45 minutes, or 30 minutes for shallow wide ramekins, until the tops are lightly browned but the insides still seem liquidy. When you give them a shake you should see that it isn't firm. Remove and cool for 5 minutes. Cover the ramekins with plastic wrap and chill for at least 2 hours.

Remove from the fridge right before serving and dab away any moisture on top of the crème. Sprinkle 1 tablespoon (15 g) raw sugar on top of each, shaking it to cover the surface evenly. If the sugar is too thick then the underside won't get torched. Torch the sugar about 2 inches (5 cm) away from the surface, holding the flame perpendicular and making small circles. The sugar will bubble up and brown beautifully. Garnish with fresh strawberries.

(continued)

FLOURLESS CHOCOLATE RASPBERRY SOUFFLÉS (FOR TWO!)

Chocolate soufflés are an elegant treat for your special someone and you don't have to spend all night in the kitchen with this easy recipe. Great for Valentine's Day. —RM

SERVES 2

2 ounces (56 g) bittersweet chocolate

2 tbsp (30 ml) heavy cream or full-fat coconut milk

1 tsp (5 g) butter or coconut oil, plus extra for ramekins

1½ tbsp (23 ml) raw honey

1 egg yolk

2 egg whites

Pinch of salt and cream of tartar

RASPBERRY SAUCE

¾ cup (112 g) fresh/frozen raspberries

½ tsp raw honey

½ tsp lemon juice

Grease two 5- or 6-ounce (148- or 177-ml) ramekins with your fat of choice and set aside on a small baking sheet. Preheat the oven to 375°F (190°C, or gas mark 5). On the stovetop, fill one third of a small saucepan with water and bring it to a boil. Place chocolate, cream, butter and honey in a medium metal bowl. Set the metal bowl in the boiling water and stir until the mixture melts, and then take it off the heat. Whisk in the egg yolk. In a different clean bowl, beat the egg whites with a hand mixer until frothy. Add the salt and cream of tartar until you have stiff peaks. Fold the egg whites into the chocolate mixture gently. Divide the mixture between the two ramekins and bake on a baking sheet for 15 to 18 minutes. The top should be set but insides soft.

While the soufflés are baking, reduce the raspberries, honey and lemon juice in a covered small saucepan over medium-low heat for about 7 minutes. It should have the consistency of thick sauce. If you want to take it a step further, strain out some of the seeds with a fine mesh strainer. Serve the soufflé immediately with a generous drizzle of raspberry sauce.

KABOCHA SQUASH SOUFFLÉ

If you are like, "kabocha what?" no worries, you can easily substitute sugar-pie pumpkin or even canned pumpkin in this recipe. But, if you do notice some kabocha squash at the market, I encourage you to pick some up and try this recipe or even eat it simply roasted. Kabocha squash has a sweet flavor and a moist, fluffy texture. It's really delicious! —AV

MAKES 6 INDIVIDUAL SOUFFLÉS

2 cups (500 g) kabocha squash purée (substitute canned pumpkin)

¾ cup (180 ml) coconut milk

3 tbsp (45 ml) pure maple syrup

½ tsp ground cinnamon, plus more for sprinkling

½ tsp ground nutmeg

3 eggs, lightly whisked

1 tbsp (8 g) arrowroot starch/powder

½ tsp cream of tartar

Coconut oil for ramekins

Preheat oven to 350°F (180°C, or gas mark 4). In a large bowl, mix together the kabocha squash purée, coconut milk, maple syrup, cinnamon and nutmeg. Add the whisked eggs, arrowroot powder and cream of tartar. Make sure it is all well mixed. Grease the ramekins with the coconut oil. Fill them up with the squash mixture until almost full. Cook for 45 to 50 minutes or until a toothpick inserted comes out clean. Try not to open the oven door often, use the oven light instead to check on them. Sprinkle with some cinnamon and serve. Enjoy!

PUMPKIN SOUFFLÉ

Soufflés make such an impressive dessert. Make sure to serve them right away since they deflate quickly. —KW

SERVES 4

4 eggs, whites and yolks separated

1 cup (240 g) roasted pumpkin or canned pumpkin

¼ cup (60 ml) pure maple syrup, pure honey or sweetener of choice (I use maple syrup)

1 tsp (5 ml) pure vanilla extract

1 tbsp (8 g) pumpkin pie spice

2 tsp (10 ml) coconut oil or butter for greasing

Preheat oven to 350°F (180°C, or gas mark 4). Whip egg whites only until peaks form. Mix together the yolks, pumpkin, maple syrup, vanilla and pumpkin pie spice until well mixed. Gently incorporate the pumpkin-yolk mixture into the beaten egg whites. It's very important not to over mix at this point. Fold the combined egg mixture into a well-greased soufflé dish, pie dish or small individual ramekins. Bake until mixture is cooked throughout and top is puffed and golden brown, about 30 minutes.

SWEET POTATO MOUSSE

This dessert highlights the natural sweetness of sweet potatoes. No added sweetener is necessary to enjoy a delightful treat. —NK

SERVES 2

Coconut cream, from the top of 1 (13.5-ounce [378-g]) can of full-fat coconut milk left in the fridge overnight

1 vanilla pod, cut in half, seeds scraped out and saved

1 cup (120 g) mashed sweet potato, left to cool in the fridge

1 tbsp (8 g) ground cinnamon

¼ tsp ground cardamom

¼ tsp ground nutmeg

⅛ tsp sea salt

Place a mixing bowl to chill in the fridge for a couple of hours. Add chilled coconut cream to the chilled bowl and add the vanilla seeds. Using an electric mixer whip the cream to soft peaks. Add the mashed sweet potato, cinnamon, cardamom, nutmeg and sea salt. Gently fold the ingredients together until combined. Divide between two small glasses or ramekins. Place in the fridge for at least an hour to set.

CHIA CHOCOLATE MOUSSE

This rich and satisfying chocolate mousse is an easy yet healthy dessert recipe that will wow any dinner guests. Chia seeds are an integral part of this recipe since they help to thicken the mousse and give it that signature mousse texture. —HH

SERVES 2

⅓ cup (40 g) unsweetened cocoa powder

2 tbsp (16 g) powdered coconut sugar

¾ cup (180 ml) coconut milk

2 tbsp (16 g) ground chia seeds

Mix all ingredients together using a food processor or an immersion blender. Place in a bowl or in individual ramekins and put in the fridge to solidify for about 30 minutes to 1 hour.

CHEF'S TIP:

To powder the coconut sugar and grind the chia seeds, simply grind each in a small coffee grinder. The ground chia seeds will make a powder that will thicken the mixture and create a jelly-like pudding texture.

CHOCOLATE ESPRESSO MOUSSE

This recipe is so easy to make and just requires a little patience to wait for the mousse to set in the fridge. The espresso adds a coffee kick to the rich chocolate mousse. It would be a great dessert to throw together for dinner guests . . . just make sure you set it up in the morning! —HH

SERVES 3–4

16 ounces (474 ml) full-fat canned coconut milk

2 tbsp (30 ml) raw honey

½ tsp vanilla

¼ tsp sea salt

3 tbsp (24 g) finely ground espresso beans

3 tbsp (24 g) cacao powder or cocoa powder

Combine ingredients in a wide-mouth mason jar or a large bowl. Mix all ingredients with an immersion blender, hand mixer or blender/food processor. This step is important because you need something powerful to really mix everything together—just a regular whisk or a mixing spoon will not work.

Once everything is thoroughly mixed, place the mixture in a jar and keep it in the fridge overnight. In the morning the mixture will be solid and ready to eat!

CHEF'S TIP:

Make sure you use full-fat canned coconut milk or the recipe may not work. If you use light coconut milk or watered down coconut milk that comes in soy milk-style boxes, it won't solidify properly.

CRANBERRY ORANGE LOAF

The combination of cranberries and oranges is a delightful match. You will especially love the glaze that goes over this loaf. —KW

MAKES 1

FOR THE LOAF

6 eggs

1 orange, zested and juiced, about ¼ cup (30 g) zest and ¼ cup (60 ml) juice

½ (13.5-ounce [378-g]) can coconut milk, or ¾ cup (180 ml)

⅓ cup (80 ml) pure honey or sweetener of choice

2 tbsp (30 ml) coconut oil, plus more for greasing

1 tsp (5 ml) pure vanilla extract

⅔ cup (80 g) coconut flour

1 tsp (3 g) baking soda

¼ tsp sea salt

1½ cups (225 g) fresh cranberries

FOR THE GLAZE

2 tbsp (30 ml) melted butter or coconut oil

2 tbsp (30 ml) honey or sweetener of choice

1 tbsp (15 ml) coconut milk

1 orange, juiced and half of it zested, about 2 tbsp (30 ml)

½ tsp pure vanilla extract

Pinch sea salt

Preheat oven to 350°F (180°C, or gas mark 4). Combine the wet loaf ingredients together. Add the dry ingredients. Fold in the cranberries. Pour into a greased, regular-size loaf pan. Bake for 45 minutes to 1 hour, or until center is cooked through. While the loaf is cooking, combine glaze ingredients until well mixed. Refrigerate glaze ingredients until loaf is done cooking and has cooled. Once loaf is done cooking and has cooled, pour glaze over the loaf.

PUMPKIN BREAD WITH CARAMEL GLAZE

This is one of my favorite fall treats. The bread is decadent and perfectly sweet. Don't leave out the caramel glaze—it's the best part! —KW

MAKES 1

FOR THE PUMPKIN BREAD

4 eggs

1 cup (225 g) roasted pumpkin or canned pumpkin

⅓ cup (80 ml) pure maple syrup or pure honey

¼ cup (60 ml) coconut oil

1 tsp (5 ml) pure vanilla extract

½ cup (60 g) coconut flour

1 heaping tbsp (8 g) Pumpkin Pie Spice (page 505)

½ tsp baking soda

¼ tsp sea salt

Butter or coconut oil, for greasing

3 tbsp (24 g) roasted pumpkin seeds

FOR THE CARAMEL GLAZE

2 tbsp (30 ml) butter or coconut oil

2 tbsp (30 ml) coconut milk or any other milk of choice

½ tsp arrowroot powder

½ tsp pure vanilla extract

½ tsp ground cinnamon

Pinch of sea salt

2 tbsp (30 ml) pure honey or pure maple syrup

Preheat oven to 350°F (180°C, or gas mark 4). In a mixing bowl, combine all liquid pumpkin bread ingredients.

Stir in the dry ingredients, except the pumpkin seeds. Spread into a lightly greased standard-size bread loaf pan greased with butter or coconut oil. Top the pumpkin batter with the pumpkin seeds. Bake for 35 to 40 minutes or until center is cooked through.

In a small saucepan, melt the butter over medium-low heat. Stir together the coconut milk and arrowroot powder and pour that in with the butter. Add vanilla, cinnamon and sea salt. Stir until it starts to simmer and gets a little bit thicker. Remove from heat and stir in the honey until well mixed (by removing the pot from the heat, it preserves the enzymes of the raw honey). Let the glaze cool for 10 to 15 minutes before pouring over the pumpkin bread.

BLUEBERRY COCOA BREAD

This is a sweet Paleo bread that can be enjoyed at breakfast with a cup of tea, or as dessert with a cold glass of almond milk. —RM

SERVES 10

¼ cup (30 g) Dutch process cocoa powder

2 tbsp (16 g) coconut flour

1 tsp (3 g) ground cinnamon

½ tsp baking soda

½ tsp baking powder

Pinch of salt

2 eggs, whisked

¾ cup (180 g) sunbutter (or other nut butter)

¼ cup (60 ml) raw honey

1 tsp (5 ml) vanilla extract

1 cup (150 g) blueberries

½ tsp coconut oil for greasing the pan

Preheat the oven to 375°F (190°C, or gas mark 5). Sift powdered ingredients into one bowl and stir wet ingredients into another bowl, keeping the blueberries separate from both. Add the wet ingredients to the dry ingredient bowl, mix thoroughly, then lightly fold the blueberries into the mix. The mix will be very thick so try to be gentle with the blueberries. Grease a standard loaf pan with the coconut oil, making sure to grease the sides. Pour in the bread batter, smoothing the top and sides evenly. Bake in the oven for 25 to 35 minutes, making sure the middle isn't wet. Best served at room temperature.

CINNAMON BANANA BREAD

An easy-to-make banana bread that uses bananas, eggs and coconut flour as its base, flavored with the warming spices of cinnamon, nutmeg and cloves. Try this delicious recipe for a tasty Paleo-friendly banana bread. —NK

SERVES 4–6

FOR THE TOPPING

3 tbsp (45 ml) melted ghee or coconut oil

2 tbsp (30 ml) raw honey, melted

FOR THE BANANA BREAD

2 ripe bananas

3 eggs

½ cup (60 g) coconut flour

½ cup (120 ml) melted ghee or coconut oil

¼ cup (60 ml) raw honey

1 tbsp (15 ml) vanilla extract

1 tsp (3 g) ground cinnamon

¼ tsp ground nutmeg

¼ tsp ground cloves

½ tsp baking soda

¼ tsp sea salt

Preheat oven to 350°F (180°C, or gas mark 4). Line a 9 × 5-inch (23 × 12.7-cm) loaf pan with parchment paper. In a small bowl mix together the ingredients for the topping and set aside. Add the bananas, eggs, coconut flour, ghee or coconut oil, raw honey, vanilla extract, cinnamon, nutmeg, cloves, baking soda and sea salt into a food processor. Process until well blended. Pour into the lined loaf pan then pour the topping on top. Bake for 20 to 25 minutes or until a toothpick or fork placed in the middle comes out clean.

PUMPKIN CHOCOLATE CHIP BREAD PUDDING

Your house will smell incredible as this Pumpkin Bread Pudding bakes. This is really more of a hybrid between a pumpkin bread and bread pudding. It is comforting and delicious! Plus, it is easier to make than traditional bread pudding. —AV

SERVES 8

Coconut oil for greasing pan

1 cup (235 ml) coconut milk

6 eggs

3 tbsp (45 ml) maple syrup

1½ cups (375 g) pumpkin purée

1 tsp (5 ml) vanilla

1 cup (120 g) coconut flour

Pinch of salt

1 tsp (3 g) ground cinnamon

½ tsp ground nutmeg

¼ tsp ground cloves

¼ tsp ground ginger

¼ tsp ground cardamom

½ tsp baking soda

½ cup (75 g) chocolate chips

Coconut Whipped Cream (page 504), for topping

Preheat oven to 350°F (180°C, or gas mark 4). Grease a loaf pan with coconut oil and set aside. In a large bowl, whisk together coconut milk, eggs, maple syrup, pumpkin purée and vanilla. In a separate bowl, sift together coconut flour, salt, cinnamon, nutmeg, cloves, ginger and cardamom. Add the coconut flour mixture to the bowl with the wet ingredients. Stir until well combined. Allow the mixture to sit for about 10 minutes, so the coconut flour can effectively absorb the wet mixture. Add the baking soda and chocolate chips. Stir to combine. Pour the batter into the loaf pan.

Bake for 50 minutes or until a toothpick inserted comes out clean. Serve warm topped with Coconut Whipped Cream.

BLUEBERRY BREAD PUDDING

Bread pudding is the ultimate comfort food and you can still enjoy this traditional favorite on the Paleo diet. Serve hot or cold. It is delicious on its own but amazing with maple syrup or dairy free ice cream on top. —KH

SERVES 6

Coconut oil or ghee for greasing pan

1 Simple Coconut Flour Cake (page 355)

¾ cup (112 g) blueberries

1 (13.5-ounce [378-g]) can full-fat coconut milk

3 eggs

¼ cup (60 ml) maple syrup or honey

2 tbsp (30 ml) coconut oil or ghee, melted

1 tsp (5 ml) vanilla extract

¼ tsp unrefined salt

2 tsp (6 g) ground cinnamon

Pinch of ground nutmeg

Preheat the oven to 350°F (180°C, or gas mark 4). Grease an 8 × 8-inch (20 × 20-cm) baking dish.

Chop simple coconut flour cake into 1-inch (2.5-cm) cubes, and place into greased pan with the blueberries.

In a large bowl, whisk together coconut milk, eggs and sweetener of choice and melted coconut oil/ghee. Add vanilla, salt, cinnamon and nutmeg. Whisk again until fully incorporated.

Pour wet mixture over bread cubes and blueberries. Give the pan a little shake to cover most of the bread cubes. Bake at 350°F (180°C, or gas mark 4) for 35 to 40 minutes, or until toothpick comes out clean in the center. Serve hot or room temperature.

HEAVENLY SWEET POTATO PUDDING

Everybody loves individual desserts. This recipe takes hearty sweet potatoes and makes a lightly spiced and heavenly creamy baked pudding that you will want to enjoy again and again. —KH

SERVES 6

Coconut oil, butter or ghee for oiling ramekins

1½ cups (375 g) cooked, mashed yam

¼ cup (60 ml) honey

½ tsp sea salt

¼ tsp ground cinnamon

¼ tsp ground allspice

¼ tsp ground ginger

Pinch of ground cloves

5 eggs, beaten

1¼ cups (295 ml) coconut milk

2 tsp (10 ml) vanilla extract

FOR THE OPTIONAL GARNISH

3 tbsp (15 g) shredded coconut, unsweetened

1½ tbsp (18 g) coconut sugar

¼ tsp ground cinnamon

Fill a large baking pan halfway with water and place into oven on the center rack. Preheat the oven to 350°F (180°C, or gas mark 4). Lightly oil six ramekins.

Combine mashed yams and honey in a large bowl. Add sea salt and spices. Mix well to combine. Stir in the beaten eggs and mix again until well combined. Pour in coconut milk and vanilla. Stir again.

If using optional garnish, combine shredded coconut, coconut sugar and cinnamon in a small bowl. Set aside.

(continued)

Spoon the yam mixture into oiled ramekins, dividing it equally among the six cups. Sprinkle with optional garnish if desired. Carefully place ramekins into the baking pan with the hot water in the oven. Bake for 35 to 40 minutes, until pudding is solid and a toothpick comes out clean. It's OK if the center is a bit soft, as it will continue to cook after coming out of oven. Carefully remove baking pan from oven. Then remove individual ramekins from the pan. Allow to cool completely before serving. This pudding tastes the best at room temperature or cold out of the fridge. Store leftovers in fridge, tightly covered.

GRANOLA CRUNCH DARK CHOCOLATE PUDDING CUPS

Thick, rich chocolate pudding meets crunchy roasted granola for a simple sweet treat. These bite-sized granola pudding cups are delightful for an afternoon snack and a fun way to include your friends or children in the cooking process. —CP

SERVES 12

2 tsp (10 ml) coconut oil for brushing muffin tins

1 recipe Crunchy Roasted Granola (page 474), uncooked, about 3½ cups (525 g)

3½ ounces (100 g) dark chocolate, 70% cacao

¾ cup (180 ml) coconut milk, room temperature

2 tsp (6 g) gelatin

FOR SERVING

8 ounces (227 g) whipped cream or coconut cream

Fresh berries

Dark chocolate shavings

Preheat the oven to 300°F (150°C, or gas mark 2). Lightly brush muffin tins with coconut oil and set aside.

Make the granola. Drop a spoonful of granola mixture into each muffin tin. Press the mixture into the bottom and up the sides, forming to the shape of the muffin tins. Bake for 25 to 28 minutes or until golden brown. Allow the granola cups to cool for 15 minutes.

While the cups are cooling, melt the chocolate over low heat in a small saucepan. Pour in the coconut milk, stirring continuously. Sprinkle the gelatin on top, remove from heat and continue to stir for 3 minutes or until the gelatin is completely dissolved.

Pour the chocolate pudding into the granola cups and refrigerate for 2 hours.

When ready to serve, use a knife to gently pry cups out of the tins. Serve garnished with whipped cream, fresh berries and/or dark chocolate shavings if desired.

CHEF'S TIPS:

When you are mixing the granola ingredients in the food processor, pulse slightly more than you would to normally make granola, but be careful not to turn the granola into nut butter.

Make sure your coconut milk is room temperature before adding to the chocolate otherwise the melted chocolate will clump.

CHOCOLATE PEPPERMINT CUPS

These fun little treats are the perfect combination of chocolate and peppermint. Made in individual muffin liners, they make perfect gifts for Paleo friends. —KH

SERVES 10

1 cup (150 g) nuts (almond, cashew, hazelnut, macadamia or pecan)

1 cup (235 ml) coconut oil

½ cup plus 2 tbsp (150 g) almond butter

4 tbsp (60 ml) honey

½ cup (60 g) raw cacao, or unsweetened cocoa powder

½ tsp sea salt

1¼ tsp (7 ml) peppermint extract

¾ cup (60 g) unsweetened shredded coconut

Line a muffin tin with ten muffin liners. Set aside. Pulse nuts in food processor several times until broken into tiny pieces. Set aside.

In a double boiler, melt the coconut oil. Add the almond butter, honey, raw cacao, sea salt and extract. Stir until completely melted and smooth. Remove from heat and fold in shredded coconut and chopped nuts. Mix to thoroughly combine.

Pour into lined muffin tins. Place into freezer to harden for at least 2 hours. Store leftovers in the freezer.

CINNAMON BANANA PECAN CRUNCH

When you want a slightly sweet dessert that hits the spot, fried bananas with a coconut butter sauce is so good it will make you feel guilty for indulging! Have no fear, this dessert has no added sugar and gets its sweetness from almost ripe bananas and the luscious coconut butter. —JC

SERVES 2

2 tbsp (30 g) ghee

2 green tipped bananas, sliced in to 1-inch (2.5-cm)-thick rounds

1 tbsp (15 ml) coconut butter, melted

1 tsp (5 ml) coconut oil, melted

½ tsp ground cinnamon

2 tbsp (16 g) raw pecans, chopped

Melt ghee in a cast iron pan over medium heat. Add bananas and fry for 3 to 5 minutes. Flip to the other side and cook for another 3 to 5 minutes until golden brown. Remove and set aside on a serving plate.

Mix together coconut butter, coconut oil and cinnamon in a small bowl. Drizzle it on the fried bananas and top with pecans. Serve warm.

SUGAR-FREE TRAIL MIX WITH COCONUT CLUSTERS

Trail mix with coconut butter clusters are a handy snack on the go or a quick pre-workout fuel. The tiny bits of espresso beans will give you a little boost but since there's no sugar here, you won't come crashing down once the caffeine wears off! —JC

SERVES 8

1 cup (150 g) raw cashews

1 cup (150 g) raw pecans

1 cup (150 g) raw macadamia nuts

¼ cup (38 g) raw sunflower seeds

1 tbsp (15 ml) ghee, melted

⅛ tsp ground allspice

⅛ tsp ground cardamom

⅛ tsp ground nutmeg

¼ tsp ground ginger

½ tsp ground cinnamon

2 tbsp (30 ml) coconut butter, melted

3 tbsp (16 g) unsweetened shredded coconut

2 tbsp (16 g) espresso beans, coarsely ground

Add cashews, pecans, macadamia nuts and sunflower seeds to a large bowl. Add ghee and mix until the nuts are coated.

Heat a skillet over low heat. Add nuts and toast them for 15 to 20 minutes. Stir constantly to prevent the bottom from burning. Turn off heat.

In a small bowl, combine allspice, cardamom, nutmeg, ginger, cinnamon and coconut butter. Pour it on top of the toasted nuts. Add shredded coconut and espresso beans. Mix well to combine. Spread the mixture on a parchment-lined baking sheet. Freeze for at least 45 minutes to an hour until the trail mix clusters are hardened and set. Place trail mix in glass jars and cover tightly. Refrigerate for up to a week.

CHEF'S TIP:

Not a coffee fan? Substitute cacao nibs for the espresso beans, or omit it entirely.

MAPLE VANILLA ROASTED ALMONDS

Since these sweet, crunchy, maple-coated almonds taste like candy, you're bound to eat more than just a handful. Serve these to kids instead of sugary candy and they won't even know they're eating something that's good for them. —JC

SERVES 8

2 tbsp (30 ml) coconut oil, melted

2 tbsp (30 ml) maple syrup

¼ tsp vanilla extract

Pinch of sea salt

2 cups (300 g) raw almonds

Preheat oven to 350°F (180°C, or gas mark 4). Line a baking sheet with parchment paper.

In a small bowl, combine coconut oil, maple syrup, vanilla extract and sea salt.

Add almonds to another bowl. Pour coconut oil and maple syrup mixture on top and mix well until the almonds are evenly coated with the mixture. Arrange the almonds evenly on the baking sheet. Bake for 10 to 15 minutes. Stir halfway through the baking time then even the mixture out. Make sure to watch it closely during the last 5 minutes so it doesn't burn. Let it cool completely before transferring into glass jars.

SALTED CHOCOLATE ENERGY CLUSTERS

These energy clusters can be made with any dried superfoods. Sometimes I like to add golden berries along with spirulina and hemp seeds. Macadamia nuts, which are high in omega-3's, can also be subbed for the almonds. —RM

MAKES 14

½ cup (75 g) raw almonds

¼ cup (38 g) raw cashews

¼ cup (38 g) raw pumpkin seeds

¼ cup (20 g) coconut flakes

⅛ cup (16 g) goji berries

⅛ cup (16 g) raw cacao nibs

⅛ cup (16 g) dried cranberries

⅛ cup (16 g) bee pollen

4 ounces (112 g) soy-free, dark chocolate (70% or higher)

Course sea salt, for garnish

Line a baking tray with unbleached parchment. Mix all of the ingredients except the chocolate together in a small mixing bowl. Using a double boiler, melt the chocolate fully. Mix the melted chocolate into the berry and nut mixture until everything is covered completely.

Spoon about 2 tablespoons (30 g) worth of mixture into separate clusters on the parchment paper. Piling them high instead of flat and wide will help them stick together after they cool. Sprinkle with course sea salt before popping the tray in the freezer for 30 minutes. You can eat them straight out of the fridge or freezer or let them come to room temperature first.

LOADED FRUIT AND NUT MORSELS

These single-serve discs of chocolate are loaded with dried fruit and nuts and are both beautiful to look at and delicious to eat. The addition of salt balances the sweetness, making it all the more enjoyable. —JC

SERVES 8

1 cup (175 g) chocolate chip morsels

1 tbsp (15 ml) ghee or coconut oil

¼ cup (38 g) dried cranberries, chopped

¼ cup (38 g) golden raisins, chopped

2 tbsp (16 g) pecans, chopped

2 tbsp (16 g) pistachios, chopped

1 tsp (5 g) coarse sea salt (I like Himalayan)

Prepare a double boiler by placing a small saucepan on the stove. Fill it halfway with water. Set a glass or metal bowl that fits snugly on top of it and turn on the heat to medium-high. Bring water to a boil and reduce heat to medium-low until it is just simmering. Add the chocolate chips and ghee. Gently stir until it melts completely, about 3 to 5 minutes. Turn off heat. Let it sit to cool slightly for 3 to 5 minutes.

Line a baking sheet with parchment paper. Scoop a teaspoon (5 ml) of melted chocolate onto the baking sheet and form it into a circle that is 2 inches (5 cm) in diameter. Top it with cranberries, raisins, pecans, pistachios and sea salt. Repeat until all the chocolate is used up.

Place the baking sheet in the fridge for at least 30 minutes to cool and harden the chocolate before serving.

ROSE WATER SPICED STEWED FRUIT

Stewed fruit is a simple and delicious way to enjoy something sweet. Adding rose water to the mix adds a subtle floral note. —NK

SERVES 4

1 tbsp (15 ml) fresh lemon juice

4 medium apples

4 medium plums

1 cup (235 ml) water

1 vanilla pod, split down the middle

3 cinnamon sticks, broken in half

1 tsp (5 ml) rose water

Coconut cream, optional

Crushed pistachios, optional

Fill a large mixing bowl with water. Add in the lemon juice and mix. Peel, core and slice the apples into even slices about ½- to 1-inch (1.3- to 2.5-cm) thick. Place apples into the lemon water as you slice them to prevent them from going brown. Slice the plums in half and remove the stones. Slice into quarters.

Place a heavy-bottomed pot with a lid over medium heat. Drain the apples from the lemon water and add to the pot along with the plums and 1 cup (235 ml) of water. Add the vanilla pod along with the cinnamon sticks to the pot. Place a lid on the pot and let cook for 20 minutes. Remove the lid and add in the rose water. Stir and continue to cook until the juices have reduced and the fruit is softened.

To serve, discard the vanilla pod and cinnamon sticks. Place the fruit in a serving bowl and top with some coconut cream and pistachios if desired.

STEWED APPLES

Cooking with real food means that you can let the beauty of the food shine through. These stewed apples are a perfect example. Using fresh apples and some spices you can create a delicious dessert. Great on its own or served with a dollop of Coconut Whipped Cream (page 504) or even with some homemade dairy-free vanilla ice cream. You will love eating these spicy warm apples. —NK

SERVES 6

2 tbsp (30 ml) butter

2 pounds (908 g) Honeycrisp apples, peeled, cored and cut into ½-inch (1.3-cm) slices

¼ tsp sea salt

3 tbsp (45 ml) raw honey

1 tsp (3 g) ground cinnamon

¼ tsp ground cloves

¼ tsp ground nutmeg

¼ tsp ground ginger

¼ cup (38 g) crushed hazelnuts

Coconut Whipped Cream (page 504), for serving, optional

Heat a 10- to 12-inch (25- to 30.5-cm) skillet—a cast iron skillet preferably—with a lid over medium heat. Add the butter. When the butter has melted add the apple slices and mix. Add in the sea salt and continue cooking for 5 minutes. Add in the raw honey, cinnamon, cloves, nutmeg and ginger. Mix to combine. Reduce the heat, cover and cook for 10 to 15 minutes until the apple slices have softened but are still mostly holding their shape. Remove from the heat and add the crushed hazelnuts and coconut cream on top. Serve warm.

SIMPLE SAUTÉED APPLES

This simple dish is multi-functional. It can be served as dessert, a side dish without the added toppings or reheated for breakfast. —RM

SERVES 8

4 large apples, tart

1 tbsp (15 ml) lemon juice

¼ cup (60 g) butter

2 tsp (6 g) arrowroot flour

½ cup (120 ml) cold water

½ cup (120 ml) or less of Grade B maple syrup

1 tbsp (8 g) ground cinnamon

Dried unsweetened coconut flakes, optional

Chopped walnuts, optional

Peel, core and cut apples into ¼-inch (6-mm)-thick pieces. Toss the apples with the lemon juice to keep them from browning during the coring process. In a large skillet over medium heat, melt the butter then add the apples. Stir constantly for 6 minutes until slightly tender.

Mix the arrowroot flour and cold water, then add to skillet. Stir in maple syrup and cinnamon, bringing to a boil for 2 minutes, stirring constantly. Remove from heat and garnish with a heaping spoonful of coconut flakes and nuts. Serve warm.

STRAWBERRY PILLOWS

This decadent dessert is a version of my favorite pastry item at my local market. It's a tower of cake, whipped coconut cream, chocolate sauce and strawberries. Absolute Heaven. —RM

SERVES 5

FOR THE CAKE

¼ cup (30 g) coconut flour

½ tsp baking soda

Pinch salt

3 large eggs

¼–⅓ cup (60–80 ml) maple syrup

2 tbsp (30 g) almond butter

1 tsp (5 ml) vanilla extract

Butter or coconut oil, for greasing

FOR THE CHOCOLATE SAUCE

½ cup (89 g) chocolate chips (I prefer Enjoy Life brand)

½ cup (120 ml) unsweetened almond milk

½ tsp vanilla

FOR THE WHIPPED COCONUT CREAM

1 (13.5-ounce [378-g]) can coconut milk, chilled overnight

1 tsp (5 ml) vanilla extract

2 tsp (10 ml) maple syrup

1 pint (300 g) strawberries, trimmed and quartered, for garnish

Preheat the oven to 350°F (180°C, or gas mark 4). In a small mixing bowl, combine all dry ingredients for the cake. In a larger mixing bowl, combine all wet ingredients for the cake. Whisk the dry ingredients into the wet ingredients, letting the batter rest for 5 minutes while you grease a 9-inch (23-cm) loaf pan with butter or coconut oil. Give the batter a final stir, then pour it into the loaf pan. Bake for 20 minutes until a toothpick inserted in the center of the cake comes out clean. Cool completely.

Using a double boiler, melt the chocolate chips and almond milk, stirring constantly so the chocolate doesn't burn, about 5 minutes. Reduce the sauce until it is slightly thinner than hot fudge consistency. Stir in the vanilla extract. Cool to room temperature.

Gently remove the coconut milk can from the fridge and scrape off the collected cream from the top. In a mixing bowl, whip all of the coconut cream ingredients together with an electric mixer for about 4 minutes until the cream can hold its version of a "stiff peak."

Now just assemble everything together. I like to cut the thin loaf cake into five slices. Then I slice the tops off and smear each piece with chocolate sauce, then sandwich them with coconut cream and strawberries in between. Layer more whipped cream and strawberries on top so they become light fluffy stacks of chocolate, cream and strawberries. Serve immediately.

CHEF'S TIP:

Every element can be made the day prior, so that assembling this dessert is a piece of cake.

COCONUT BERRY JELLY CUPS

These Coconut Berry Jelly Cups are a fun way to enjoy delicious bright berries and also a great way to get in some gut-healing gelatin. Sweetened naturally by berries and coconut water this is a great dessert that can be enjoyed by all. —NK

SERVES 2

1¼ cups (295 ml) coconut water, divided

1 tbsp (8 g) gelatin powder

¼ cup (38 g) mixed frozen berries

Add ¼ cup (60 ml) coconut water to a small saucepan. Sprinkle the gelatin powder over the coconut water, and allow it to sit for 3 minutes. Add in another ¼ cup (60 ml) coconut water and place the saucepan over low heat. Stir until the gelatin has dissolved, about 1 to 2 minutes. Remove from the heat. Place in a large measuring cup, mix the remaining coconut water with the gelatin mixture from the saucepan.

Divide the frozen berries evenly between two 8-ounce (240-ml) cups. Pour the coconut mixture over the top and place in the fridge to set for 1 to 2 hours. Once set serve in the cups or carefully remove the jelly cups from their containers by running warm water under and around the cups until the they slide out of their containers, and serve on individual plates.

HORCHATA GELATIN

Horchata is a classic Mexican drink made from rice, vanilla and cinnamon. I took the concept of horchata and turned it into a creamy Jell-O using almond milk. —NK

SERVES 2–4

2 cups (470 ml) unsweetened almond milk

3 tbsp (45 ml) raw honey

1 tsp (5 ml) vanilla extract

½ tbsp (4 g) ground cinnamon, plus more for dusting on top

1 tbsp (8 g) gelatin powder

Place almond milk into a medium saucepan over medium-low heat. Allow the almond milk to warm up but not boil. Once it's warm, stir in the raw honey until dissolved, around 1 to 2 minutes. Mix in the vanilla extract and ground cinnamon. Transfer to a blender and add the gelatin powder. Blend for 30 seconds until well mixed. Pour into your desired containers and place in the fridge to set for a couple of hours.

PUMPKIN CUPS

A no-fuss version of pumpkin pie that is low-carb and grain-free. Use crushed pecans for an added crunch to these custard cups. —RM

SERVES 4–5

1 (15-ounce [420-g]) can of 100% pumpkin purée

½ cup (120 ml) full-fat coconut milk

⅓ cup (80 ml) Grade B maple syrup

3 eggs and 1 egg yolk

1 tsp (5 ml) bourbon vanilla extract

1 tsp (3 g) ground cinnamon

1 tsp (3 g) ground ginger

½ tsp ground nutmeg

¼ tsp ground allspice

½ tsp lemon zest

Pinch of sea salt

Virgin coconut oil or butter, for greasing

Coconut Whipped Cream (page 504), for garnish

Crushed pecans, for garnish

Preheat oven to 350°F (180°C, or gas mark 4). Boil a medium pot of water on the stove. Mix all ingredients in a large mixing bowl with a whisk. Oil four or five individual ramekins with virgin coconut oil or butter. Fill ramekins three quarters full with pumpkin mixture. Place a dish towel at the bottom of a deep baking dish to prevent the ramekins from sliding during the baking process. Nestle each ramekin on top of the dish towel and fill the baking dish with boiling water, about halfway up the ramekin sides. Bake in the oven for 25 to 35 minutes. If you use extra-large ramekins, you may have to bake about 45 minutes total. The pumpkin center should jiggle slightly but be semi firm on top. Cool first then chill for 3 hours. Serve with Coconut Whipped Cream and crushed pecans.

COCONUT FLOUR DONUT HOLES

These coconut flour donut holes are such a fun recipe for kids. The texture is a little different from your regular wheat-flour donut since it's a little denser, but the flavor is sweet and delicious! —HH

SERVES 6

FOR THE DONUTS

⅓ cup (40 g) coconut flour

¼ tsp baking soda

¼ cup (50 g) coconut sugar

1 tsp (3 g) ground cinnamon

¼ tsp salt

2 eggs

¼ cup (60 ml) coconut oil

FOR THE TOPPING

2 tbsp (30 ml) coconut oil

¼ cup (50 g) coconut sugar

1 tbsp (8 g) ground cinnamon

Preheat the oven to 350°F (180°C, or gas mark 4). Combine the donut ingredients in a mixing bowl or food processor and mix well. Set up a mini muffin tin with muffin liners. Roll small amounts of the dough into little balls and place in the muffin liners. Bake for about 10 minutes. Remove from the oven and let cool.

Melt coconut oil and set aside. Combine coconut sugar and cinnamon on a plate. Brush each donut hole with a little bit of coconut oil. Roll the donut hole in the cinnamon sugar. Repeat with all the donut holes.

CARROT CAKE DONUTS

A Paleo version of a donut that is reminiscent of the best carrot cake you have ever tasted. The lemon glaze makes them extra delicious. —KH

SERVES 6

¾ cup (90 g) blanched almond flour

2 tbsp (16 g) coconut flour

½ tsp baking soda

¼ tsp unrefined sea salt

½ tsp ground cinnamon

¼ tsp ground ginger

Pinch of ground cloves

¼ cup (20 g) unsweetened shredded coconut

2 eggs

6 tbsp (90 ml) coconut oil, melted

4 tbsp (60 ml) maple syrup or honey

½ cup (70 g) grated carrot, packed

½ cup (75 g) raisins, soaked in water for 10 minutes, drained and roughly chopped

1 tbsp (8 g) grated fresh ginger

FOR THE LEMON GLAZE

¼ cup (60 ml) coconut butter, softened

¼ cup (60 ml) full-fat coconut milk

1 tsp (5 ml) lemon juice

1½ tsp (7.5 ml) raw honey

Water to thin, if necessary

Preheat the oven to 350°F (180°C, or gas mark 4) and grease a donut pan with coconut oil.

Combine almond flour, coconut flour, baking soda, salt, cinnamon, ginger, cloves and shredded coconut in a large bowl.

In a separate bowl, whisk together eggs, coconut oil and sweetener of choice. Fold in grated carrots, raisins and fresh ginger. Add wet to dry and mix until well incorporated. Allow to sit for a couple of minutes to let the coconut flour absorb.

Place the batter in a piping bag or a large resealable bag with the end cut off so there is about a half-inch (1.3-cm) opening. Fill each cavity in the donut pan three quarters full. Give the pan a little shake or two to let the batter settle. Bake for 18 minutes, or until toothpick inserted comes out clean and edges are just beginning to brown. Remove from oven. Let cool for 5 minutes then tip over onto a cooling rack. Allow to cool completely before adding glaze.

To make the glaze, place all glaze ingredients into high-speed blender. Process until smooth and creamy. Add water a tiny bit at a time if it's too thick to pour. Pour into shallow bowl. Dip each donut into glaze with a twisting motion to let extra run back into bowl or just drizzle over the donuts in any fashion that you desire. Place back onto cooling rack.

MAPLE GLAZE DONUTS

These were the first Paleo donuts I ever made. The texture is perfect. The maple glaze is divine. If you are going to eat a donut, might as well make it one of these. —KH

SERVES 6

Ghee or coconut oil, for greasing

1¼ cups (150 g) blanched almond flour

2 tbsp (16 g) coconut flour

½ tsp sea salt

½ tsp baking soda

2 eggs

4 tbsp (60 ml) full-fat coconut milk

4 tbsp (60 ml) maple syrup or honey

4 tbsp (60 ml) coconut oil, melted

½ tsp vanilla extract

FOR THE MAPLE GLAZE

½ cup (75 g) raw cashews

¼ cup (60 ml) maple syrup

4 tbsp (60 ml) coconut butter, melted

2 tbsp (30 ml) coconut oil, melted

2 tbsp (30 ml) filtered water, plus more if necessary

Preheat the oven to 350°F (180°C, or gas mark 4). Lightly grease the donut pan with ghee or coconut oil.

Combine almond flour, coconut flour, salt and baking soda in a medium bowl. Set aside.

In another large bowl, whisk together eggs, coconut milk, maple syrup, coconut oil and vanilla until thoroughly combined. Add dry ingredients to wet and stir to combine. Place the batter in a piping bag or large resealable bag with the end cut off so there's about a half-inch (1.3-cm) opening.

Fill each cavity in the donut pan three-quarters full. Give the pan a little shake or two to let the batter settle. Bake for 18 to 20 minutes, or until toothpick inserted comes out clean and edges are just beginning to brown. Remove from oven. Let cool for 5 minutes then tip over onto a cooling rack. Allow to cool completely before adding glaze.

To make the glaze, place all glaze ingredients into a high speed blender. Process until smooth and creamy. Add more water a tiny bit at a time if it's too thick to pour. Pour into shallow bowl. Dip each donut into glaze with a twisting motion to let extra run back into bowl. Place back onto cooling rack.

TOASTED COCONUT HAYSTACKS

Chocolate haystacks can be made with anything and everything. From pretzels to chow mein noodles, the possibilities are endless. Of course these little gluten bombs are far from healthy, so here's a Paleo-friendly version made with toasted coconut, chocolate and crunchy bits of cacao nibs. A decadent yet healthy treat that you can definitely indulge in. —JC

SERVES 6

¼ cup (44 g) chocolate chip morsels

2 tsp (10 ml) ghee or coconut oil

½ tsp vanilla extract

1 cup (85 g) unsweetened shredded coconut, toasted

1 tbsp (8 g) cacao nibs

Prepare a double boiler by placing a small saucepan on the stove. Fill it halfway with water. Set a glass or metal bowl that fits snugly on top of it and turn on the heat to medium-high. Bring water to a boil and reduce heat to medium-low until it is just simmering. Add the chocolate chips and ghee. Gently stir until it melts completely, about 3 to 5 minutes. Turn off heat. Add vanilla extract and mix well.

Combine shredded coconut and cacao nibs in a bowl. Pour in the melted chocolate mixture and mix until well combined. Using a tablespoon, scoop the chocolate haystacks and place them on a parchment-lined baking sheet. Pat down to slightly flatten and compress the haystack to help the coconut and chocolate stick together. Place the baking sheet in the freezer for 20 to 25 minutes to harden the chocolate. Serve and enjoy.

CANDIED BACON

Candied bacon is the perfect combination of sweet and savory. I typically add a few slices to my breakfast burgers with a fried egg on top. This bacon also makes a devilish midnight snack! —RM

SERVES 4

Coconut oil, for greasing

⅓ cup (80 ml) maple sugar or coconut sugar

Dash cayenne

1 pound (454 g) sliced bacon

Preheat the oven to 350°F (180°C, or gas mark 4). Line a baking sheet with foil for easy clean up and then place a wire rack on top. Grease the rack with coconut oil. Pour the maple sugar on a plate and mix in the dash/pinch of cayenne. Lightly dip both sides of the bacon into the sugar. Lay out the slices flat on the wire rack. Bake for 30 to 35 minutes, until almost crispy and syrupy. The bacon should be at a jerky-like consistency and not burnt. Serve warm.

CHOCOLATE HAZELNUT BACON

At the county fair during summer time, there is always a stall that sells concoctions such as chocolate dipped bacon. At $5 to $6 apiece, it is ridiculously expensive! Make it at home and you'll get eight pieces for the same price you'll pay for one at the fair. —JC

SERVES 8

1 pound (454 g) bacon strips, cut in half

½ cup (85 g) chocolate chip morsels

½ tbsp (7.5 g) ghee or coconut oil

¼ cup (38 g) hazelnuts, chopped

Preheat oven to 375°F (190°C, or gas mark 5). Line a baking sheet with parchment paper.

Lay down the bacon strips side by side on the baking sheet. Bake for 15 minutes on one side, flip and bake for another 15 minutes. Remove from the oven and set cooked bacon on a wire rack to cool.

Place a small saucepan on the stove to create a double boiler to melt the chocolate. Fill it halfway with water. Set a glass or metal bowl that fits snugly on top of it and turn on the heat to medium-high. Bring water to a boil and reduce heat to medium-low until it is just simmering. Add the chocolate chips and ghee. Gently stir until it melts completely, about 3 to 5 minutes. Turn off heat.

Line another baking sheet with parchment paper.

Dip a slice of bacon halfway in the melted chocolate. Sprinkle with hazelnuts and place bacon on the parchment-lined baking sheet. Repeat for the rest of the bacon slices. Place baking sheet it in the fridge for at least 30 minutes to cool and harden the chocolate before serving.

FIG AND WALNUT CHOCOLATE BARK

Making your own chocolate at home is easy and the best part is that you know exactly what ingredients go into it. Add some dried figs and walnuts for some sweetness and crunch. —NK

SERVES 4–6

½ cup (120 ml) coconut oil

5 tbsp (75 g) salted butter

2 tbsp (16 g) cacao powder

1 tbsp (15 ml) raw honey

3 ounces (84 g) dried figs, roughly chopped

1 ounce (28 g) walnuts, roughly chopped

Line a small baking sheet with parchment paper. Add the coconut oil to a small saucepan over medium-low heat and melt. Once melted add the butter and whisk. Once the butter has melted add the cacao powder and raw honey. Whisk to combine. Once everything is well mixed, remove from the heat and stir in the chopped figs and walnuts. Pour the mixture onto the lined baking sheet, and spread around as evenly as possible, making sure to spread the figs and walnuts out evenly. Place in the freezer to set completely for a couple of hours. Once set, remove from the freezer and break into shards. Keep in the freezer and enjoy as desired.

CHEF'S TIP:

If using unsalted butter, add ¼ teaspoon sea salt to the mixture in the saucepan before stirring in the figs and walnuts. Also don't worry if the mixture doesn't spread into a perfect shape on the baking sheet as this is more of a free-form homemade chocolate bark.

COCONUT MILK CUSTARD

Flan is a custard with a caramel sauce that is popular throughout Latin America. Flan de coco is made with coconut milk, but is usually mixed with whole milk or condensed milk. Luckily, it tastes just as rich and wonderful when made with all coconut milk—including condensed coconut milk, which you can make at home or purchase in cans. —AT

MAKES 2 (5-INCH [12.5-CM]) MINI FLANS TO SERVE 4–6

½ cup (115 g) coconut sugar or grated panela

4 large eggs

1 (13.5-ounce [399-ml]) can full-fat coconut milk

1 cup (235 ml) condensed coconut milk (purchased or make your own; see Chef's Tip on page 411)

1 tbsp (15 ml) vanilla extract

Preheat the oven to 350°F (180°C).

Make the caramel sauce by combining the sugar with 2 tablespoons (30 ml) of water in a saucepan and heating over medium heat. Cook until slightly thickened, swirling occasionally to dissolve the sugar, 6 to 8 minutes.

Meanwhile, thoroughly blend the eggs, coconut milks and vanilla, either using a whisk or electric mixer or blender.

Pour the caramel sauce into the bottom of two 5-inch (12.5-cm) pie dishes, carefully tilting to swirl it along the sides. Allow to rest for about 5 minutes.

Divide the egg mixture evenly among the dishes.

Prepare a hot water bath by boiling water. Place your dishes in the bottom of an 9 × 13-inch (23 × 33–cm) ovenproof glass dish (or equivalent pan) and pour in enough hot water so that it comes about 1 inch (2.5 cm) up the sides of the dish. Take care not to get water in the flan itself and not to splash hot water while transferring the dish to the oven.

Bake for about 1 hour, or until a knife comes out clean when inserted into the center of a flan and the middle no longer wiggles if you shake the pan (remove from the water bath before testing for wiggles!). Wear sturdy ovenproof mitts to lift them from the water bath, or slip a cooking spatula (the kind you would flip pancakes with) underneath to lift. Be very careful not to burn yourself!

Allow the flan to cool for at least 20 minutes before refrigerating. Cover with plastic wrap and let chill for several hours before serving.

Release the flans onto a serving plate (make sure it has a lip to catch the sauce) by using a butter knife to gently loosen the edges. Place the plate on top of the dish and quickly flip it over to release or to the plate. The caramel sauce will drizzle out on top.

Serve each slice with a generous spoonful of caramel.

CHEF'S TIP:
You will need a large baking dish or roasting pan to make the hot water bath. Ensure that your mini pie dishes are small enough to fit inside the vessel you will use for your water bath. Two 5-inch (12.5-cm) mini pie pans fit perfectly inside of a 9 × 13-inch (23 × 33-cm) glass baking dish.

CAKE SOAKED IN 3 "MILKS"

Tres leches means "three milks" and in the traditional version this would be a blend of heavy cream, evaporated milk and sweetened condensed milk. Luckily, this dessert can be made dairy-free thanks to our friend the coconut. This cake is delicious any time you get a hankering for it, but since it is served chilled, it is especially refreshing in the summer months. —AT

SERVES 9–12

FOR THE CAKE

1 cup (112 g) sifted coconut flour

2 tbsp (16 g) tapioca starch, plus more for dusting the pan

1 tbsp (14 g) unflavored gelatin

2 tsp (8 g) baking soda

¼ tsp fine Himalayan salt

½ cup (120 ml) melted coconut oil, plus more for greasing the pan

⅔ cup (120 g) coconut sugar or grated panela

2 large eggs, or ½ cup (125 g) applesauce

½ tsp vanilla extract

1 tsp (5 ml) apple cider vinegar

⅔ cup (157 ml) water

FOR THE THREE MILKS

½ cup (120 ml) coconut cream

½ cup (120 ml) coconut milk

½ cup (120 ml) sweetened condensed coconut milk (purchased or make your own; see Chef's Tip)

Preheat the oven to 350°F (180°C).

To prepare the cake, in a mixing bowl, combine the coconut flour, tapioca starch, gelatin, baking soda and salt and stir well.

In a separate mixing bowl, combine the coconut oil, sugar, egg, vanilla and vinegar and whisk vigorously or beat with an electric mixer. Stir in the water.

Gradually add the dry ingredients to the wet, stirring often, until all ingredients are combined. The resulting batter will be extremely thick.

Grease an 8-inch (20.5-cm) square baking dish with coconut oil and dust lightly with tapioca starch. Use a spatula to scrape the batter into the dish, spreading it evenly so that there are no air bubbles in the batter and smoothing the top. Bake for 30 to 40 minutes, or until the edges have begun to pull away from the sides and the top is lightly crisped and has darkened. Due to the combination of coconut flour and coconut sugar, the cake does not turn a golden color. Be careful not to burn the cake. Allow it to remain in the dish while you prepare the milks.

Prepare the three milks: In a bowl, thoroughly combine the coconut cream, coconut milk and sweetened condensed coconut milk.

Transfer the cake to a serving platter by placing it on top of the pan and quickly inverting it. Or, if your baking dish has a lid, you may leave it there if you prefer. Use a fork or toothpick to prick holes all over the top of the cake. Pour the three-milk mixture on top in an even layer. Cover and chill in the refrigerator for at least 1 hour before serving.

CHEF'S TIP:
To make condensed coconut milk, place 1 cup (235 ml) of coconut milk in a saucepan and bring to a boil, stirring constantly to prevent bubbling over. Immediately lower the heat to low and stir in 2 to 4 tablespoons (30 to 45 g) of your sweetener of choice. Allow to simmer, stirring occasionally, until reduced by half (you should have ½ cup [120 ml]), 30 to 40 minutes.

COCONUT MILK PUDDING

The word tembleque means "wiggly" or "wobbly" and it is the perfect name for this creamy pudding. This dish is naturally dairy-free, thanks to the coconut milk base, although it is traditionally made with cornstarch as the thickener. For a lower-carb, Paleo-friendly option, gelatin works wonderfully to set this pudding. —AT

SERVES 6–8

2 tbsp (28 g) unflavored gelatin

2 (13.5-ounce [399-ml]) cans coconut milk

5–6 tbsp (100–120 g) honey, coconut sugar or grated panela

Pinch of fine Himalayan salt

Ground cinnamon, for garnish

Bloom the gelatin by pouring ½ cup (120 ml) of water into the bottom of a small saucepan and then sprinkling the gelatin slowly on top of the water. Do not add the gelatin too quickly or clumps can form. Whisk the mixture to encourage wetting, if needed.

Add the remaining ingredients, except the cinnamon, to the saucepan and heat over medium heat, whisking frequently, until all the gelatin and your choice of sweetener have dissolved.

Pour into a 9-inch (23-cm)-diameter × 1¼-inch (3-cm)-deep pie mold and allow to set for several hours in the refrigerator until firm. Serve in slices, almost like a crustless cheesecake for a traditional presentation. You can also pour the mixture into six to eight small bowls, ramekins or other vessels. Sprinkle a generous amount of cinnamon on top before serving chilled.

"RICE" PUDDING

Arroz con dulce is a very typical dessert served throughout Latin America. This version is done in the style of Puerto Rico. It turns out that in this case, yuca makes the absolute perfect grain-free rice replacement. As it simmers in the coconut milk, it naturally thickens to a pudding-like consistency, thanks to the starch cooking out of the yuca. This stuff tastes like the real deal! —AT

SERVES 4

About 5 ounces (140 g) yuca

2 cups (475 ml) coconut milk

1 tsp (2 g) ground cinnamon, plus more for garnish

½ tsp ground ginger

¼ tsp ground cloves

5–6 tbsp (75–90 g) coconut sugar or grated panela

¼ cup (35 g) raisins

If using fresh yuca, peel the root with a knife or sharp vegetable peeler, ensuring you remove all traces of the pink/purple layer just beneath the skin. Cut off both tips and cut the root crosswise into sections about 3 inches (7.5 cm) long. Cut each in half lengthwise and cut out the woody stem in the center of the root. Inspect the flesh to ensure it is pure white with no soft spots, discolorations or black speckles. Discard any such areas.

If using frozen yuca, remove any remnants of the woody core.

Place the yuca in a food processor and pulse, using the blade attachment, to "rice" the yuca. Do not overprocess.

Place all the ingredients, except the raisins, in a pot and bring to a simmer over medium heat. Simmer for about 15 minutes, stirring constantly, until it is very thick and the yuca pieces are tender. Fold in the raisins and transfer to a serving dish. Place in the refrigerator to chill before serving. Garnish with cinnamon before serving.

PUERTO RICAN SPICE CAKE

Hojaldre is a delightful Puerto Rican spice cake. These flavors just scream "holidays" and I'm sure you'll love to make it. This base cake recipe is one of my specialties and borrows a note from traditional baking in my home state of Georgia by adding gelatin to the dry ingredients. This ensures an incredibly moist cake, whereas Paleo cakes generally tend to be on the dry side. Also, if you opt to use applesauce instead of the egg, the cake will be even moister! Traditional recipes call for a sweet wine, but you can also use plain grape juice. —AT

SERVES ABOUT 16

FOR THE CAKE

2 cups (224 g) sifted coconut flour

4 tbsp (32 g) tapioca starch, plus more for dusting the pan

2 tbsp (28 g) unflavored gelatin

4 tsp (16 g) baking soda

½ tsp fine Himalayan salt

2 tsp (3 g) ground cinnamon

2 tsp (4 g) ground nutmeg or mace

1 tsp (2 g) ground cloves

1 cup (235 ml) melted coconut oil or palm shortening, plus more for pan

1½–1¾ cups (338–294 g) coconut sugar or grated panela

4 large eggs, or 1 cup (245 g) applesauce

1 tsp (5 ml) vanilla extract

2 tsp raw (10 ml) apple cider vinegar

⅔ cup (160 ml) sweet wine (Moscato works well)

⅔ cup (157 ml) water

FOR THE POWDERED SUGAR

¼ cup (60 g) coconut sugar or panela (or other unrefined granulated sweetener)

1½ tsp (12 g) tapioca starch

To prepare the cake, preheat the oven to 350°F (180°C).

In a mixing bowl, combine the coconut flour, tapioca starch, gelatin, baking soda, salt and spices and stir well. In a separate mixing bowl, combine the coconut oil, sugar, eggs, vanilla and vinegar and whisk vigorously or beat with an electric mixer. Stir in the wine and water. Gradually add the dry ingredients to the wet, stirring often, until all the ingredients are combined. The resulting batter will be extremely thick and almost doughlike, but the resulting cake will be very moist, so don't be alarmed.

Grease a 9-inch (23-cm)-diameter × 3-inch (4.5-cm)-deep fluted Bundt pan and dust lightly with tapioca starch. Use a spatula to scrape the batter into the pan, pressing it down and spreading it evenly so that there are no air bubbles in the batter.

Bake for 50 to 60 minutes, or until the top is lightly crisped and has darkened. A toothpick inserted into the center will come out mostly clean—however, due to the moist nature of this cake, some crumbs may still stick even when the cake is cooked through. Also, due to the combination of coconut flour and coconut sugar, the cake does not turn a golden color, and instead darkens slightly. Be careful not to burn the cake. Allow to cool in the pan for at least 30 minutes, then transfer very carefully to a serving plate to finish cooling. The texture of this cake is too delicate for a wire rack.

Prepare the powdered sugar: In a coffee grinder or high-powered blender, pulverize the coconut sugar and tapioca starch together. If purchasing powdered sugar, be sure to read the ingredients to make sure it contains tapioca starch and not cornstarch. Dust the top of the cake with the powdered sugar and serve.

PUMPKIN BONIATO CRUSTLESS PIE

The word cazuela means "cooking pot" and in most parts of Latin America it is used to describe stewed meats with vegetables. However, in Puerto Rico cazuela is a crustless pumpkin and boniato pie that is traditionally dairy-free, thanks to the use of coconut milk. It is typically thickened with eggs, but since eggs and I don't get along very well, I developed this egg-free version that is just as delicious. If you wish to be very traditional, make this using boniato and calabaza squash, or for a shortcut, use canned pumpkin and substitute white sweet potatoes for the boniato. —AT

SERVES 9–12

1¾ cups (394 g) mashed boniato or white or yellow sweet potatoes (from about 1 pound [455 g] peeled and cubed root)

1¾ cups (394 g) mashed calabaza squash (from about 1 pound [455 g] peeled and seeded squash), or 1 (15-ounce [425-g] can pumpkin purée)

1½ cups (355 ml) coconut milk

4 tbsp (60 g) unflavored gelatin

½–⅔ cup (115–150 g) coconut sugar

1 tsp (2 g) ground cinnamon

½ tsp ground ginger

½ tsp aniseeds

½ tsp ground cloves

¼ tsp fine Himalayan salt

Place the peeled and cubed boniato and calabaza in a pot and cover with water. Bring to a boil over high heat and cook until all the pieces are fork-tender, about 20 minutes. Drain, place in a mixing bowl and mash to a smooth consistency. If the boniato is particularly stringy, purée the mixture in a food processor or with an immersion blender until very smooth.

Pour the coconut milk in a small pot and gradually sprinkle the gelatin on top, whisking frequently to combine it. Do not allow clumps to form. Once all of the gelatin has been wetted, heat the pan over medium heat, whisking often, until all the gelatin dissolves smoothly.

Combine all the remaining ingredients with the boniato mixture and pour in the coconut milk mixture. You can add the sugar gradually and taste the batter until it is as sweet as you like. Pour the batter into an 8-inch (20.5-cm) square glass dish, cover and refrigerate for several hours until set. Serve chilled.

GUAVA-STUFFED CAKE

Guayaba (a.k.a. guava) is a tropical fruit that is a favorite in desserts throughout Latin America. You can readily find guava paste in stores or order it online. This cake is soft and fluffy with a warm, gooey filling and oh so delicious! —AT

SERVES 9–12

1 cup (112 g) sifted coconut flour

2 tbsp (16 g) tapioca starch, plus more for dusting the pan

1 tbsp (14 g) gelatin

2 tsp (8 g) baking soda

¼ tsp fine Himalayan salt

½ cup (120 ml) coconut oil, plus more for greasing the pan

⅔ cup (120 g) coconut sugar or grated panela

2 eggs, or ½ cup (125 g) applesauce

½ tsp vanilla extract

1 tsp (5 ml) apple cider vinegar

⅔ cup (157 ml) water

⅔ cup (157 ml) coconut milk

10–12 ounces (283–340 g) guava paste, cut into about 16 slices

Preheat the oven to 350°F (180°C).

In a mixing bowl, combine the coconut flour, tapioca starch, gelatin, baking soda and salt and stir well.

In a separate mixing bowl, combine the coconut oil, sugar, eggs, vanilla and vinegar and whisk vigorously or beat with an electric mixer. Stir in the water and coconut milk. Gradually add the dry ingredients to the wet, stirring often, until all the ingredients are combined. The resulting batter will be extremely thick.

Grease an 8-inch (20.5-cm) square baking dish with coconut oil and dust lightly with tapioca starch. Use a spatula to scrape half of the batter into the dish, spreading it evenly so that there are no air bubbles in the batter. Add a layer of guava paste slices to cover, then add the remaining batter on top of the guava paste, smoothing it out with the spatula.

Bake for 30 to 40 minutes, or until the top is lightly crisped and has darkened. Due to the combination of coconut flour and coconut sugar, the cake does not turn a golden color. Be careful not to burn the cake. Can be served hot while the filling is gooey (how I prefer it) or at room temperature.

STEWED SPICED RIPE PLANTAINS

Plantains are so extremely versatile and can be appropriate for breakfast, lunch, dinner and dessert! This recipe utilizes very ripe plantains that are mostly black and soft to the touch. They are naturally very sweet on their own and pair wonderfully with the warm spices. In the fall when everyone is going crazy for "pumpkin spice" everything, make a batch of these! —AT

SERVES 2–4

1 cup (235 ml) water

¼ cup (60 g) coconut sugar or grated panela sugar

1 tsp (2 g) ground cinnamon

½ tsp aniseeds

¼ tsp ground cloves

1 tbsp (15 ml) coconut oil

2 large, very ripe (mostly black) plantains, peeled and cut into 4 pieces

In a small pot, combine all the ingredients, except the plantains, and stir well. Add the plantains and bring to a boil, then lower the heat to medium, cover and cook for 15 to 20 minutes, or until the sauce thickens and the plantains are cooked throughout and tender.

Serve with a generous portion of sauce and enjoy!

ALMOND CAKE

This grain-free almond cake recipe is moist, slightly-sweet and rich. It's a great easy and simple recipe to make for friends or family. —HH

SERVES 6

1½ cups (180 g) + 2 tbsp (16 g) almond meal

½ tsp baking soda

½ tsp apple cider vinegar

1 tbsp (15 g) ghee or coconut oil

¼ tsp sea salt

3 eggs

½ cup (120 ml) honey

Preheat the oven to 325°F (170°C, or gas mark 3). Make sure that the ghee or coconut oil is softened, but not melted. In a food processor or mixing bowl, place all the dry ingredients and mix. Then, add in the remaining ingredients and process until everything is combined. Grease a 9 × 5-inch (23 × 12.5-cm) loaf pan with ghee or coconut oil. Place the batter into the loaf pan. Place the pan in the oven and bake for 45 to 55 minutes or until a toothpick inserted through the middle comes out clean.

CHOCOLATE CAKE

This grain-free chocolate cake is a tasty, fluffy and chocolatey delight! It goes great with the Maple Coconut Ice Cream (page 378). —HH

SERVES 4

½ cup (60 g) almond flour

½ cup (60 g) cocoa powder

2 tbsp (16 g) coconut flour

½ cup (100 g) + 2 tbsp (24 g) coconut sugar

¼ tsp salt

1 tsp (3 g) baking powder

½ tsp vanilla

¼ cup (60 ml) milk or coconut milk

3 eggs, whites and yolks separated

¼ tsp apple cider vinegar

1 tbsp (15 g) butter or coconut oil, to grease the pan

Preheat the oven to 350°F (180°C, or gas mark 4). Combine all ingredients except for the egg whites and mix in a food processor or with a mixer. With an electric mixer, beat egg whites until stiff peaks form. Gently fold egg whites into the batter.

Use butter or coconut oil to grease a standard-sized loaf pan then add the batter to the pan. Bake for 15 to 20 minutes or until a toothpick inserted in the middle comes out clean.

BIG CHOCOLATE COOKIES

These chocolate cocoa cookies are like those big tasty cookies that you see at coffee shops that are just begging to be dipped into a cup of tea or coffee! But these are grain-free and naturally sweetened, so you can rest easy knowing that they're a healthy indulgence. —HH

SERVES 8

1 cup (120 g) almond flour

½ cup (60 g) cocoa powder

2 tbsp (16 g) coconut flour

⅓ cup (65 g) coconut sugar

¼ cup (30 g) ground flax seeds

½ tsp baking soda

¼ tsp salt

½ tsp vanilla extract

½ cup (120 ml) coconut oil, melted

1 egg

Preheat oven to 350°F (180°C, or gas mark 4). Line a cookie sheet with parchment paper. Combine ingredients in a bowl, mixer or food processor. Make sure that the coconut oil is melted (76°F [24°C]). Shape dough hunks into balls and flatten and form into large circles on the cookie sheet. Bake for about 6 to 9 minutes. Cookies will be firm.

CHOCOLATE CHIP COOKIES

I have to say that these grain-free chocolate chip cookies are the best I've had! When baking grain-free, I like to combine almond flour and coconut flour. What one flour lacks, the other makes up for. Coconut flour alone can be a bit crumbly and almond flour can be a bit dense and heavy, but together they make a darn good cookie! —HH

SERVES 12–16

1 cup (120 g) almond flour

⅓ cup (40 g) coconut flour

¾ cup (150 g) coconut sugar

½ cup (120 ml) coconut oil, softened

¼ tsp salt

1 tsp (3 g) baking soda

1 tsp (5 ml) vanilla

2 eggs

¾ cup (130 g) chocolate chips

Preheat the oven to 350°F (180°C, or gas mark 4). Combine all ingredients except the chocolate chips in a food processor and mix well. Make sure you soften or melt the coconut oil so it's easier to combine. Gently fold in the chocolate chips manually with a spoon—do not mix it with the food processor or it will chop up all the chocolate chips. Take small bits of the dough and shape into a round cookie and place on a cookie sheet lined with parchment paper. Bake for 10 to 15 minutes or until slightly browned on top. If you feel the cookies right out of the oven they may feel a bit soft, but allow them to cool and they will harden.

4-INGREDIENT NUT BUTTER COOKIES

These cookies will be the easiest cookies that you have ever made. —KH

MAKES 12

1 cup (250 g) unsalted nut butter

¼–⅓ cup (60–80 ml) maple syrup or honey, or ½–¾ cup (100–150 g) coconut sugar

½ tsp sea salt

1 egg, beaten

Preheat the oven to 350°F (180°C, or gas mark 4) and line baking sheet with parchment paper.

In a large bowl, combine nut butter, sweetener of choice and salt until creamy smooth. Add in egg and mix until completely incorporated. Scoop out tablespoon (15 g)-sized portions of dough and drop onto prepared baking sheet. Gently flatten with fingers to desired cookie thickness. These cookies do not flatten on their own. If you are using coconut sugar, dough will be thick enough to roll into tablespoon (15 g)-sized balls and then flatten to desired thickness.

Using a wet fork, make a crisscross pattern on top of each cookie. Bake at 350°F (180°C, or gas mark 4) for 10 to 12 minutes, or until golden brown. Cool and serve.

CHEF'S TIP:

For a softer cookie, use wet sweetener like maple syrup or honey. For a crisper cookie, use a dry sweetener like coconut sugar.

EGG-FREE, NO-BAKE COOKIE BALLS

These no-bake cookie balls taste almost like sweet and nutty cookie dough. I love serving these easy Paleo cookie balls with a cup of tea. —HH

SERVES 4

3 tbsp (24 g) ground flax seeds, soaked in 3 tbsp (45 ml) warm water

⅓ cup (40 g) coconut flour

½ cup (60 g) almond flour

2 tbsp (16 g) arrowroot

¼ tsp sea salt

¼ cup (50 g) coconut sugar

¼ cup (60 ml) softened coconut oil

½ tsp vanilla extract

1 tsp (5 ml) honey or sub coconut nectar for a vegan alternative

In a small bowl, mix the ground flax seeds and warm water. Allow to sit until it jells. Mix dry ingredients together in a food processor or mixing bowl. Add wet ingredients, including flax mixture, and mix well. The result will be a thick crumbly dough-like consistency. If the dough is too crumbly to form into balls add another tablespoon (15 ml) of honey. Roll portions of the dough into balls and they're ready to eat! Store extras in the refrigerator.

CHEF'S TIP:

To grind flaxseeds, put them in a clean coffee grinder.

CHOCOLATE CHIP, COCONUT SNACK BALLS

This is one of my favorite easy treat recipes. It's packed with great nutrients and is a healthy treat you can feel good about eating. —KW

MAKES 25

1½ cups (120 g) unsweetened coconut flakes

½ cup (120 g) nut butter of choice

½ cup (120 ml) coconut oil, melted or softened

1 tsp (5 ml) pure vanilla extract

⅔ cup (116 g) mini chocolate chips

Combine all the ingredients except mini chocolate chips in a bowl and stir until well incorporated. Stir in mini chocolate chips. Roll out into bite-size balls.

Refrigerate or freeze until hardened.

CHEF'S TIP:

Keep any leftovers in the refrigerator or freezer. To make this even more simple if you don't feel like rolling into balls, just spread the mixture into an 8 × 8-inch (20 × 20-cm), parchment-lined baking pan. Refrigerate until hardened and cut into squares.

COOKIE DOUGH BALLS

This is one of my favorite sweet treats! The dry richness of the coconut butter and the creamy nutty almond butter combine to make an excellent base for the pop of sweetness from the chocolate chips. Not only are these Paleo cookie dough balls delectable, but they are also really easy to make. You can whip up a batch in probably 5 to 10 minutes. —HH

MAKES 10

½ cup (120 g) coconut butter

2 tbsp (30 g) almond butter

1 tsp (5 ml) raw honey or maple syrup

¼ cup (38 g) chocolate chips

Combine coconut butter, almond butter and honey in a bowl and mash together with a fork until all the ingredients are combined and you have a dough-like consistency. Add the chocolate chips and mix well. Form small spoonfuls of the dough into balls. Refrigerate for about 30 minutes to harden. Enjoy them as they are, or add to dairy-free ice cream to make cookie dough ice cream . . . my favorite!

5-MINUTE RAW FUDGE BALLS

These simple fudge balls are almost like a rich, textured and nutty truffle, but the thing that I love about this recipe is that it is much quicker and easier than most traditional truffle recipes and has all-natural ingredients! —HH

SERVES 2

¼ cup (30 g) raw cacao powder or cocoa powder, plus more for rolling

¼ cup (20 g) shredded coconut

2 tbsp (30 ml) raw honey

1 tbsp (15 ml) coconut milk or almond milk

2 tbsp (30 g) raw almond butter

Place all ingredients in a bowl and mix with a fork until thoroughly combined. If the mixture is too wet to form into balls, add a little bit of cacao powder, 1 teaspoon (3 g) at a time until it reaches the desired consistency. If it's too dry, add more milk 1 teaspoon (5 ml) at a time until it reaches the desired consistency. Roll small portions of the batter into balls and roll in the cacao powder. They're ready to eat immediately! Store any extras in the fridge.

PUMPKIN FUDGE BALLS

If you like fudge and pumpkin, you are in for a treat. These pumpkin fudge balls are easy to assemble and always get rave reviews. —KW

SERVES 8

1 (15-ounce [420-g]) can pumpkin purée or 2 cups (500 g) cooked fresh pumpkin purée

1¾ cups (400 g) coconut butter, warmed

¼ cup (60 ml) coconut oil, melted

½ cup (120 ml) honey

1 tsp (5 ml) vanilla extract

1 tbsp (8 g) Pumpkin Pie Spice (page 505)

Using a food processor or blender, process all the ingredients until smooth and creamy. Pour the mixture into an 8 × 8-inch (20 × 20-cm) square pan. Refrigerate for 4 hours or until fully set. Cut into 16 squares. Using your hands, form each square into balls. Keep refrigerated.

CHEF'S TIP:

Rolling them into balls makes for a prettier presentation, but if you are running short on time, omit rolling them and just serve the pumpkin fudge as squares.

AUTUMN CHOCOLATE BITES

These chocolate bites have all the beautiful colors of fall—thanks to the cranberries, apricots and pumpkin seeds—yet they are so simple to make. If you are a chocolate lover, I think you will especially enjoy these. —KW

MAKES ABOUT 12

½ cup (60 g) cacao powder

¼ cup (60 ml) coconut oil, melted

2 tbsp (30 ml) honey or sweetener of choice

½ tsp pure vanilla extract

Pinch sea salt

TOPPINGS

12 whole pecans

Dried cranberries

Dried apricots, cut into small pieces

Pumpkin seeds

Few pinches of Pumpkin Pie Spice (page 505)

In a bowl, combine all chocolate ingredients until well mixed and smooth. Cover a cookie sheet with parchment paper. Spoon out 12 circles, about a teaspoon or two (5 to 10 g) each, of chocolate over the parchment paper. Press 1 pecan in the middle of each chocolate. Gently press the remaining toppings in the chocolate. Sprinkle pumpkin spice over the chocolates. Freeze until firm.

Store in the freezer.

CHOCOLATE COCONUT FUDGE BALLS

These are the perfect bite-sized treat when you are looking for something a little sweet, yet still want to stay healthy. The dates provide just the right amount of natural sweetness—no added sugars necessary! —KW

MAKES 32

1½ cups (225 g) walnuts, soaked overnight and drained

½ pound (227 g) dates, pitted

½ cup (60 g) cocoa powder

1 tsp (5 ml) vanilla extract

Pinch of sea salt

1 cup (80 g) unsweetened shredded coconut

Process walnuts, dates, cocoa powder, vanilla extract and sea salt in a food processor until a thick paste forms. Roll into bite-sized balls. Roll each ball in the shredded coconut. Refrigerate any leftovers.

EASY HEALTHY FUDGE RECIPE

You can make this easy fudge recipe in less than five minutes! If you are looking for an easy and healthy treat recipe, I think you'll love this one. —KW

SERVES 8

1 cup (230 g) coconut butter, softened

½ cup (120 g) nut or seed butter

1 tsp (5 ml) vanilla extract

3 tbsp (45 ml) honey or sweetener of choice

⅓ cup (80 g) chocolate chips

Mix softened coconut butter, nut butter, vanilla and honey together in a bowl until well combined. Pour and spread into a parchment-lined 8 × 8-inch (20 × 20-cm) baking pan. Pour the chocolate chips all over the top of the fudge. I gently press the chocolate chips down into the fudge with my hands.

Refrigerate or freeze until hardened. Cut into squares to serve.

CHEF'S TIP:

Keep any leftovers in the refrigerator or freezer.

EASY, HEALTHY HOMEMADE DARK CHOCOLATE

High-quality, organic chocolate bars from the store can be very expensive. I bet you didn't know that making your own high-quality chocolate is so simple and so inexpensive, did you? —KW

SERVES 4

½ cup (60 g) cacao powder

¼ cup (60 ml) coconut oil, melted

2 tbsp (30 ml) pure raw honey or pure maple syrup, or more or less to taste

½ tsp pure vanilla extract

Pinch of sea salt

Combine all the ingredients in a small bowl and stir until well mixed and smooth. You can pour the chocolate into candy molds to make chocolate candy, you can put the chocolate into a cake decorator—or plastic bag with the edge cut off—and pipe out chocolate chips or you can pour the chocolate onto wax or parchment paper and make bars. Freeze until hardened—about 30 minutes. Store the chocolate in the fridge.

CHEF'S TIP:

I came up with this based on my personal taste tests:
1 tablespoon (15 ml) honey = about 85% dark chocolate
1½ tablespoons (23 ml) honey = about 73% dark chocolate
2 tablespoons (30 ml) honey = about 60% dark chocolate

CHOCOLATE PEPPERMINT CANDIES

These candies contain rich dark chocolate with a boost of peppermint to make for a decadent yet cooling and fresh treat that will melt in your mouth. I love making these candies for the holidays and bringing them to parties and family dinners. —HH

MAKES 20

4 ounces (112 g) baking chocolate

3 tbsp (45 ml) honey

2 tbsp (30 ml) coconut oil

¼ tsp peppermint extract

Place the baking chocolate, honey and coconut oil in a double boiler on medium heat. Allow the ingredients to melt while occasionally stirring. Do not allow to get too hot, just hot enough to melt it and mix it together. Once the chocolate and coconut oil has melted and all ingredients are mixed, turn off the heat, add the peppermint extract and allow the mixture to cool for about 5 minutes. Place the melted chocolate mixture into silicone candy molds and place in the freezer for 2 to 3 hours to harden. Store leftover candies in the fridge or freezer.

CHEF'S TIP:

Make sure you keep these candies in the refrigerator or a cool place since they melt easily.

CHOCOLATE BARK

I almost always have these homemade chocolate bars in my freezer. They're great to have around if I want a little square of dark chocolate, but don't want a store-bought one loaded with processed sugar and preservatives! This chocolate bar can also make a great gift. You can wrap it in wax paper and give it away to friends, just try to keep it cool because if it's too hot it can melt! —HH

SERVES 4

¼ cup (60 ml) coconut oil

4 ounces (112 g) unsweetened baking chocolate

¼ cup (60 ml) honey

OPTIONAL TOPPINGS

Nuts

Coarse sea salt

Shredded coconut

Dried fruit

Melt the unsweetened chocolate and coconut oil in a double boiler on medium-high heat. Line an 8 × 8–inch (20 × 20–cm) Pyrex dish with parchment paper or grease with extra coconut oil. When all of the chocolate and coconut oil is melted, mix gently with a spoon. Add the honey and mix thoroughly to combine. Pour the mixture into the Pyrex dish and freeze for about 10 to 15 minutes.

Remove the chocolate from the freezer to add toppings. The chocolate should be slightly harder, but still melted enough to hold the toppings. Sprinkle whichever toppings you want. One of my favorite combos is walnuts, shredded coconut and coarse sea salt.

Put the chocolate back in the freezer and allow to freeze for about 1 to 2 hours until it is hard. After it has hardened you can break it apart into smaller pieces. Store in the refrigerator or freezer. It does not need to be thawed before serving since it will melt in your mouth!

DARK CHOCOLATE– COVERED STRAWBERRIES

Heighten any romantic evening with this simple recipe. Making chocolate-covered strawberries at home is a much more economical way than buying them from a chocolatier—and without any questionable ingredients! —RM

SERVES 5

¼ cup (38 g) crushed almonds

¼ cup (20 g) shredded unsweetened coconut flakes

1 pound (454 g) fresh strawberries, washed and dried

6 ounces (168 g) dark chocolate, chopped

Line two baking sheets with parchment paper or wax paper. Separate the almonds and shredded coconut on two small plates off to the side. On the stove, boil water in a small saucepan. Add the chopped chocolate to a separate medium metal bowl and place on top of the small saucepan of boiling water, creating a double boiler. Immediately turn off the stove and stir the chocolate until fully melted.

Dip each strawberry by holding the green leaves and coating the berries evenly with chocolate. Let any excess chocolate drip off and then coat each strawberry in crushed almonds and/or coconut flakes. Lay them on the parchment trays and repeat the process. Pop the trays on the bottom shelf of the fridge for 15 minutes, or until the chocolate is set. Indulge immediately.

EASY LEMON FRUIT DIP

This fresh flavored dip is rich and creamy—you'd never guess it was made without dairy. Fresh strawberries and this dip are a winning combination. —KW

SERVES 6

1 (13½-ounce [378-g]) can full-fat coconut milk, refrigerated overnight

1 lemon, zested and juiced

2 tbsp (30 ml) pure raw honey, or sweetener of choice

1 tsp (5 ml) pure vanilla extract

Scoop just the cream that has risen to the top of the refrigerated coconut milk can and place in a bowl or stand mixer. You can use the remaining liquid for a smoothie or discard it, but we won't need it for this recipe. Whip the coconut cream with a hand or stand mixer until peaks form (just like regular whipped cream). After peaks form, add the remaining ingredients and mix until well incorporated. Keep refrigerated until ready to serve.

CHEF'S TIP:
I like to double my recipe when serving for parties. Using coconut milk out of a carton or using light coconut milk will not work for this recipe.

3-INGREDIENT BANANA ICE CREAM

This banana ice cream is quick and easy with just three ingredients! The texture is rich and creamy, just like real ice cream. When I serve this recipe to people and tell them it's only bananas and chocolate, they don't believe me! —HH

SERVES 2

2 bananas

½ cup (85 g) chocolate chips, optional

3 tbsp (24 g) cocoa powder, optional

Peel and slice both bananas and place on a plate lined with parchment paper. Place in the freezer for 1½ to 2 hours. After bananas have been frozen, start melting the chocolate chips in a double boiler on the stove for the optional chocolate drizzle. Put frozen bananas in a food processor and blend—this will also work with a Vitamix, but do not attempt with any other blender. After about 30 seconds it may still be chunky. Stop blending and scrape the sides down with a spoon, continue blending until it is smooth. Once it's smooth, scoop the banana ice cream out of the food processor and drizzle the melted chocolate over the ice cream.

If you want chocolate ice cream, simply add 3 tablespoons (18 g) cocoa powder to the food processor and blend. Once it's all mixed it's ready to go!

2-INGREDIENT PEACH SOFT SERVE

All you need for this recipe is peaches and coconut milk. Super simple. It's the perfect soft serve on a hot summer day. —KH

SERVES 2

2 cups (300 g) frozen peach slices

¼ cup (60 ml) full-fat coconut milk, you may need more

Process peaches in food processor until you get a creamy texture. Scrape down the sides, add coconut milk and process again until creamy smooth. Eat. Enjoy. Be happy.

PINEAPPLE MINT SORBET

This pineapple mint sorbet recipe is so easy to make. If you want a healthy and sweet treat, you can whip this up in 5 minutes! The mint adds freshness and the mango adds a nice tangy element to the super sweet pineapple, but just use more pineapple if you prefer a sweeter sorbet. —HH

SERVES 2

½ cup (85 g) frozen pineapple

⅓ cup (50 g) frozen mango

6-8 mint leaves, chopped

Combine ingredients in a food processor or strong blender (I recommend a Vitamix or possibly a Ninja blender). Blend until it reaches the consistency of sorbet. Scoop out of the food processor or blender and serve!

CREAMY ORANGE FROZEN TREATS

These make a fun, natural and juicy treat on those hot summer days! —HH

SERVES 4–6

1½ cups (355 ml) orange juice

½ tsp orange zest

½ cup (120 ml) full-fat coconut milk, canned

In a blender, combine all ingredients and blend. Pour the mixture into Popsicle molds and freeze for about 2 to 3 hours to harden.

CHAPTER 7

BREAKFASTS, SMOOTHIES & DRINKS

Breakfast is not only my absolute favorite meal of the day, but it's also the most important! Starting your day off right with a hearty breakfast will leave you energized and productive all day long.

If your mornings are rushed, take a moment the night before to prepare an egg frittata, like the Broccoli Spinach Frittata with Caramelized Onions (page 428), to have on hand all week long—or whip up a batch of Autumn-Spiced Allergy-Free Breakfast Cookies (page 469).

If you like to start the day off with a smoothie, you're in luck. We've got heaps for you to pick from, like the Nutrient-Rich Berry Smoothie (page 479), Rise and Shine Green Smoothie (page 484) and Berry Avocado Smoothie (page 483). Want a morning pick-me-up with a little buzz? Check out the Peppermint Mocha Latte (page 489).

Lazy weekend mornings can be a great chance to chat over a cup of coffee, gather around the table and make a meal together with friends or family. Treat yourself to something special on the weekends by making Blueberry Cobbler Pancakes (page 455), Asparagus & Smoked Salmon Creamy Eggs Benedict (page 425) or even Pumpkin Spice Donuts with Vanilla Glaze (page 470)!

ASPARAGUS & SMOKED SALMON CREAMY EGGS BENEDICT

This creative twist on eggs Benedict uses fresh asparagus spears as the base of this delightful egg dish. Eggs Benedict is my absolute favorite weekend breakfast treat, but sometimes I am too lazy to go through all the steps of baking homemade bread and poaching eggs so I came up with this simplified version to serve on a cozy morning or even when you have guests over! The addition of smoked salmon slices makes this a power breakfast to keep you satisfied all morning. —CP

SERVES 4

1 recipe Lemon Hollandaise Sauce (page 500)

3 tablespoons (45 g) butter, divided

1 bunch asparagus, ends trimmed

1 clove garlic, crushed

8 eggs

⅓ cup (80 g) coconut milk

½ tsp sea salt

¼ tsp white pepper

4 ounces (112 g) smoked salmon

¼ cup (20 g) micro greens

Prepare the Lemon Hollandaise Sauce and set aside.

Melt half the butter in the skillet over medium high heat. Sauté the asparagus stalks and garlic for 5 o 10 minutes or until soft; timing depends on thickness of asparagus. Remove the asparagus from the pan and se aside.

While the asparagus is cooking, whisk together eggs, milk, salt and pepper.

Melt remaining butter in hot skillet and pour in eggs. Scramble briefly, then turn down the heat to low. Slowly cook the eggs, using a spatula to stir and fold as this process will result in fluffy, soft cooked eggs

Plate the asparagus, layering salmon and eggs on top. Garnish with a drizzle of hollandaise and pinch of microgreens.

SUN–DRIED TOMATO PESTO BREAKFAST SANDWICHES

Breakfast sandwiches have always been my favorite. I usually try to keep a few extra Grain-Free Fluffy White Dinner Rolls (page 522) on hand for a quick, comfort food breakfast! —CP

SERVES 4

1 tbsp (15 g) butter

4 eggs

4 Grain-Free Fluffy White Dinner Rolls (page 522)

½ cup (120 g) Fresh Basil Pesto (page 509)

¼ cup (40 g) sun-dried tomatoes, chopped

1 avocado, sliced

Warm a skillet to medium heat. Melt the butter and fry eggs.

Slice the rolls in half, and lightly toast in the toaster oven.

Spread a layer of pesto on each side of toasted roll, then top with a fried egg, sprinkle of sun-dried tomatoes and avocado slices. Enjoy immediately.

FRUITY BREAKFAST PIZZA WITH GRANOLA CRUST

With a granola crust, soaked coconut and fruit, this pizza is a simple, sweet and endlessly customizable breakfast treat. —RB

SERVES 4

½ cup (40 g) shredded unsweetened coconut

¼ cup (60 ml) coconut milk or ½ cup (120 g) coconut yogurt

1 cup (180 g) granola plus 2 tbsp (20 g) for garnish

1 cup (145 g) dried fruit (dates, cherries, prunes or raisins work well)

2 tbsp (30 ml) coconut oil

⅓ cup (50 g) chopped grapes

⅓ cup (50 g) chopped pichuberries

2 tbsp (16 g) pomegranate seeds

Combine the shredded coconut and coconut milk or yogurt, set aside to soften.

Combine the granola, dried fruit and coconut oil in a food processor, pulse until a rough dough forms. Shape into a disc on your serving plate, and refrigerate while you prepare the fruit.

Wash and chop the grapes and pichuberries, then spread the shredded coconut on top of the chilled granola crust. Pile the pichuberries, grapes and pomegranate seeds on top, then finish with 2 tablespoons (20 g) of granola as garnish. Serve chilled.

CHEF'S TIP:
Pichuberries are also called ground cherries.

KALE AND ARTICHOKE CREAMY BAKED EGG CUPS

Combining sautéed power greens with creamy coconut milk provides these savory baked eggs with the perfect amount of richness and nutrition for your morning. I like to garnish with a sprinkle of cashew meal for a slightly crispy, buttery yet dairy-free topping. —CP

SERVES 4

2 tbsp (30 ml) olive oil, divided

2 cups (140 g) kale, deveined and finely chopped

½ cup (120 g) canned artichoke hearts, drained and chopped

3 green onions, chopped

1 clove garlic, crushed

4 eggs

¼ cup (60 ml) coconut milk

2 tbsp (16 g) cashew meal

½ tsp sea salt

¼ tsp fresh cracked black pepper

¼ cup (15 g) fresh basil, finely chopped

Preheat the oven to 350°F (180°C, or gas mark 4) and a skillet to medium heat.

Drizzle half the olive oil in the skillet and grease each ramekin with the rest of the oil.

Sauté the kale, artichoke hearts, onions and garlic for 2 minutes or until soft.

Add a scoop of vegetables to each ramekin and crack an egg on top. Drizzle a spoonful of the coconut milk over each egg, and sprinkle with cashew meal, salt and pepper.

Bake for 13 to 16 minutes or until the whites are set and the yolks are soft. Garnish with basil and serve warm.

TOMATO POACHED EGGS WITH BASIL

Shakshuka is a traditional Tunisian dish made by poaching eggs in a thick, simmering tomato sauce. This is a hearty meal that can be enjoyed for breakfast or dinner. It requires minimal preparation, but still tastes gourmet! Typically served with pita bread, I like to dip a thick slice of my Grain-Free Fluffy White Dinner Rolls (page 522) in the warm tomato sauce for a grain-free alternative. —CP

SERVES 4

1 tbsp (15 ml) olive oil

½ red onion, finely chopped

4 cloves garlic, crushed

½ tsp paprika

½ tsp Italian herbs

½ tsp dried oregano

½ tsp sea salt

¼ tsp fresh cracked black pepper

2 cups (140 g) fresh spinach, chopped

2 cups (480 g) tomato purée

½ cup (120 ml) Slow Cooker Chicken Broth (page 170)

8 eggs

½ cup (30 g) fresh basil, thinly sliced

In a large skillet over medium heat, sauté the onions with olive oil, garlic and spices for 10 minutes or until onions are softened. Mix in the chopped spinach.

Pour tomato purée and chicken broth into the pan and heat until the sauce starts to simmer. Crack the eggs over the tomato sauce, place a lid on top of the pan and cook for 7 to 9 minutes or until egg whites are set and yolks are soft.

Serve garnished with fresh basil.

SCALLION FRITTATA

Stovetop frittatas cook in just 10 minutes or less and you'll want a basic recipe such as this to keep in your rotation. The coconut cream makes the frittata nice and fluffy, but coconut milk will also yield the same result. Adding coarse salt at the end gives a nice burst of flavor bite after bite. —JC

SERVES 2

4 large eggs

2 tbsp (30 ml) coconut cream or Homemade Coconut Milk (page 503)

1 cup (100 g) scallions, chopped

¼ tsp black pepper

2 tbsp (30 g) of butter or ghee

¼ tsp coarse salt (I prefer Himalayan)

Crack eggs in a bowl and whisk until light and frothy. Add coconut cream, scallions and black pepper. Mix well to combine.

Add butter to a cast iron pan over medium heat. Pour in the egg mixture and give it a quick stir to lightly mix the butter with the eggs. Reduce heat to low. Cover and let it cook for 8 to 10 minutes until the top of the eggs is set. Sprinkle with coarse salt before slicing and serving.

PERSIAN HERB FRITTATA (KOOKOO SABZI)

A great way to enjoy fresh herbs is by adding them to a frittata. This recipe for Persian Herb Frittata uses herbs like parsley, dill and cilantro to create an earthy and flavorful dish. —NK

SERVES 6–8

2 tbsp (16 g) dried barberries

1 cup (60 g) packed fresh parsley

1 cup (60 g) packed fresh dill

1 cup (60 g) packed fresh chives

1 cup (60 g) packed fresh cilantro

8 eggs

1 tsp (3 g) baking powder

Sea salt and black pepper, to taste

¼ cup (38 g) walnuts, toasted and roughly chopped

2 tbsp (30 g) ghee

Preheat oven to 400°F (200°C or gas mark 6). Soak barberries in cold water for 10 minutes, drain and set aside. Take the fresh herbs and chop as finely as possible, then place into a large mixing bowl. Whisk eggs in a separate mixing bowl. Add the baking powder, sea salt and black pepper and mix well. Pour the egg mixture into the chopped herbs, add the toasted walnuts and barberries. Mix until well combined. Place a medium-large ovenproof skillet over medium heat and add the ghee. Once heated pour the frittata mixture in, making sure to spread it around the skillet. Fry over medium-low heat for 7 to 9 minutes. Carefully transfer the skillet to the oven and bake for 15 to 20 minutes, or until set. Carefully remove from oven and allow to cool for 5 to 10 minutes before serving.

CHEF'S TIP:

Barberries are small dried berries that are used extensively in Persian cooking. They are vibrant red in color and have a sharp flavor You can buy barberries online or at a Persian grocery store where they will often be called zereshk.

BROCCOLI SPINACH FRITTATA WITH CARAMELIZED ONIONS

A simple egg dish that can be served as breakfast, lunch or dinner. Pairs well with a big green salad for a satisfying meal. —KH

SERVES 4–6

4 cups (280 g) broccoli florets, chopped into bite-sized pieces

2 tbsp (30 g) ghee, butter or coconut oil

1 small onion, chopped into thin half rings

4 cloves garlic, minced

4 cups (280 g) packed baby spinach, washed and roughly cut

½ tsp sea salt

¼ tsp oregano, dried

7 eggs, beaten

Avocado, for serving

Salsa, for serving

Fermented veggies, for serving

Preheat the oven to 350°F (180°C, or gas mark 4). Lightly steam broccoli until it starts to turn bright green, about 5 minutes, then remove from heat, rinse with cool water and set aside.

Melt fat of choice in a large skillet. Sauté onions for 20 to 25 minutes until translucent and brown, stirring occasionally to prevent sticking. Add garlic and sauté another minute or two. Add spinach and a pinch of sea salt and stir. Let cook until spinach is wilted, about 3 to 4 minutes. Add rinsed and drained broccoli, oregano and rest of sea salt. Stir until well combined and remove from heat.

Pour eggs on top of veggies and shake pan slightly to get egg mixture to settle into the vegetables. Bake for 20 to 25 minutes until baked all the way through. Serve with avocado, salsa and fermented veggies of choice.

SUMMER VEGETABLE FRITTATA

One of the best things about summer (aside from the nice weather) is all the yummy produce that's in season. This recipe uses some of summer's best veggies like zucchini and tomatoes. —HH

SERVES 4

1 small onion

6 cloves garlic

1 zucchini

1 tbsp (15 g) ghee

6 eggs

1½ tbsp (23 ml) full-fat coconut milk

½ tsp salt

½ tsp pepper

2 tbsp (16 g) sun-dried tomatoes

½ tsp thyme

½ tsp oregano

1 tomato

2 tbsp (8 g) fresh chopped basil

Preheat the oven to 350°F (180°C, or gas mark 4). Finely chop the onions and garlic. Wash the zucchini and slice in half lengthwise then chop into small slices widthwise. Heat the ghee in a 6½-inch (16.5-cm) cast iron pan over medium heat. When hot, put the onions in the pan and stir for a minute. Then, add the garlic and stir. Crack the eggs into a separate bowl then add the coconut milk, salt and pepper and whisk until well beaten. Add the sun-dried tomatoes to the egg mixture and set aside. Add the thyme and oregano to the onion and garlic and continue to cook until the onions are slightly translucent, about 3 to 5 minutes. Add the zucchini and mix, cooking until the zucchini has softened, about 4 to 6 minutes. Slice the tomato into slices like you would put on a sandwich and set aside. Once the zucchini has softened, turn off the heat and add the egg mixture to the pan and gently mix so all of the ingredients are evenly distributed. Place the tomato slices on the top and use an oven mitt to transfer the pan to the oven. Allow the frittata to bake at for 20 to 25 minutes. Once you remove it from the oven allow it to cool for a few minutes then sprinkle with the fresh basil and serve.

SAUSAGE FRITTATA WITH ZUCCHINI & CARROT

Frittatas are a great way to start your morning. They also make a tasty, convenient on-the-go meal. —NK

SERVES 4–6

1 medium zucchini

2 medium carrots, peeled

1 tbsp (15 g) ghee

7 eggs, whisked

1 tsp (3 g) sweet Hungarian paprika

½ tsp garlic powder

Sea salt and black pepper, to taste

2 gluten-free sausages of your choice, cooked

Preheat oven to 350°F (180°C, or gas mark 4). Using a spiralizer or julienne peeler, spiralize or peel the zucchini and carrots into noodle strands or thin strips. Place in a mixing bowl and set aside.

Heat a medium oven-proof skillet over medium heat and add the ghee. Once the skillet is hot, add the zucchini and carrots. Cook for 10 minutes or until softened. While the vegetables are cooking mix the eggs, paprika, garlic powder, sea salt and black pepper in a separate bowl. Add the sliced sausage to the skillet and pour in the egg mixture. Cook over medium heat until the bottom of the frittata is set, about 7 to 9 minutes. Place in the oven to bake for 15 to 20 minutes or until the whole frittata is set.

ITALIAN PORK FRITTATA WITH BALSAMIC GLAZE

Try this delicious frittata filled with tasty pork, sweet balsamic glaze and woodsy herbs for a delicious meal that's perfect at any time of the day. —NK

SERVES 8

½ cup (120 ml) balsamic vinegar

2 tbsp (30 g) ghee

2 pounds (908 g) ground pork

2 tsp (6 g) dried parsley

2 tsp (6 g) dried oregano

1 tsp (3 g) dried basil

1 tsp (3 g) red pepper flakes

¼ tsp garlic powder

2 tsp (12 g) sea salt

½ tsp black pepper

1 zucchini, spiralized

12 eggs, whisked

Preheat oven to 350°F (180°C, or gas mark 4). Line a 12 × 9-inch (30.5 × 23-cm) baking dish with parchment paper. Cook the balsamic vinegar in a small saucepan over medium heat, stirring frequently until reduced by half and thickened, about 2 to 4 minutes, but keep an eye on it.

Heat a skillet over medium heat and add the ghee. Once heated add the ground pork and break up the meat as it cooks. Once almost cooked through add the parsley, oregano, basil, red pepper flakes, garlic, sea salt and black pepper. Cook the meat until browned. Remove from the heat and allow to cool for 5 minutes. Once cooled pour the meat mixture into the baking dish. Spread the spiralized noodles over the top of the meat mixture. Pour the whisked eggs over the top, making sure to cover the entire mixture. Bake for 25 to 30 minutes or until the eggs have set. Allow to cool before slicing.

To serve, drizzle balsamic reduction on top.

MINI PERSONAL FRITTATA

Who says you can't cook healthy meals for one? This recipe is perfect for single people who don't have time to make a huge gourmet breakfast, or Paleo individuals who live in a household where everyone else is stuck on a conventional diet. —RM

SERVES 1

Handful of spinach

1 tsp (3 g) sliced leeks

Olive oil

2 eggs

1 slice nitrate-free deli ham, diced

⅛ tsp sea salt

⅛ tsp black pepper

⅛ tsp garlic powder

Preheat the oven to 400°F (200°C, or gas mark 6). Sauté the spinach and leeks in a drizzle of olive oil until wilted, about 3 to 4 minutes. Remove and place in a small mixing bowl, along with the rest of the frittata ingredients. Pour the mixture into a greased 5-ounce (148-ml) ramekin. Place on a baking sheet in the oven and bake for 15 to 18 minutes. Serve hot.

YAM, CELERIAC ROOT & BACON HASH

This breakfast hash is a really tasty egg-free breakfast, but it is also amazing with a fried egg on top! If you have a busy schedule that doesn't leave you much time to prepare breakfast, you can make a big batch of this and enjoy it all week! —AV

SERVES 6

1 large yam, peeled and cut into ½-inch (1.3-cm) cubes

6 pieces bacon, diced

½ large onion, diced

1 celeriac root, peeled and cut into ½-inch (1.3-cm) cubes

1-2 tbsp (15-30 g) ghee

4 cloves garlic, minced

Sea salt and pepper

1 tsp (3 g) smoked paprika

1-2 tbsp (6-12) fresh parsley, minced

Bring water to a boil in pot that is large enough to hold the yam without crowding. Add a dash of salt and add the chopped yams. Cover and cook for 12 to 15 minutes, or until the yams are tender. They don't have to be all the way cooked through, as they will cook more when you sauté them. Once they are cooked, drain them in a colander. Try to drain as much liquid as possible.

In a large sauté pan, cook the bacon pieces until crispy. Use a slotted spoon and remove the cooked bacon and set aside. Sauté the onions in the remaining bacon grease for about 5 minutes, until translucent, then add the celeriac. Cook celeriac until soft, about 10 minutes. Celeriac is a thirsty vegetable and will absorb the bacon grease. If it absorbs too much of the bacon fat, then add some ghee to the pan, so the hash doesn't burn.

Once the celeriac is soft, add yams and garlic and cook until yams brown slightly. Generously season the hash with salt and pepper and gently mix in the smoked paprika and bacon. Top with chopped parsley and serve!

CARAMELIZED ONION & SAUSAGE BREAKFAST HASH

Browning sausage creates the most pleasing kitchen aroma and this savory breakfast hash will make your mornings delightful. I like to use a spicy pork breakfast sausage, but you really can use whatever type of meat or flavor you desire. —CP

SERVES 6

1 tbsp (15 g) butter

1 small red onion

5 mushrooms

2 cups (140 g) spinach

¼ tsp sea salt

¼ tsp fresh cracked black pepper

1 pound (454 g) breakfast sausage

4-8 eggs

½ cup (35 g) micro greens

Hot sauce, optional

Heat a large skillet to medium heat and melt butter in skillet.

Thinly slice onions and mushrooms. Sauté with salt and pepper in the pan for 10 minutes or until they begin to soften. Transfer onions and mushrooms from the pan to a bowl and set aside.

Brown and crumble sausage in the pan until completely cooked, about 10 minutes. Add onions, mushrooms and spinach and sauté until mixed.

Crack eggs on top of hash, place the lid over the skillet and cook for 6 to 8 minutes or until eggs are cooked to your liking.

Serve garnished with micro greens or even a dash of your favorite hot sauce!

CHEF'S TIP:

This sausage breakfast hash is great to make ahead of time without the eggs to keep for a quick breakfast option. Simply cook the sausage and vegetables and store in the refrigerator until ready to eat then warm and top with a fried egg as desired.

ROSEMARY SWEET POTATO HASH

Hash for breakfast is the best thing ever. Pair it with any type of protein and you've got yourself a meal! Caramelized onions and rosemary give sweet potatoes a sweet and aromatic flavor plus the addition of pumpkin seeds adds a bit of a crunch. —JC

SERVES 2

2 medium sweet potatoes, cubed

1 small onion, thinly sliced

1½ tbsp (6 g) fresh rosemary, roughly chopped

1 tbsp (15 ml) ghee or tallow, melted

Sea salt

Black pepper

2 tbsp (16 g) raw pumpkin seeds

¼ tsp red pepper flakes

Preheat oven to 375°F (190°C, or gas mark 5). Line a baking sheet with parchment paper.

In a bowl, combine sweet potatoes, onion and rosemary. Drizzle with ghee and toss to combine. Season with sea salt and black pepper. Spread the sweet potatoes and onions evenly on the baking sheet. Bake for 15 minutes. Stir and bake for 10 more minutes.

Mix in the pumpkin seeds and season with red pepper flakes. Bake for an additional 3 to 5 minutes. This will be enough to lightly toast the pumpkin seeds without burning them. Let cool for a few minutes before serving.

BACON & BEET BREAKFAST ROOT HASH

Root hash is my kind of comfort food for breakfast. I like to fry it with bacon and ruby red beets, then serve it straight from the skillet for a beautiful rustic meal to start the day. —RM

SERVES 4

1 rutabaga or turnip

1 cup (140 g) frozen yuca root (cut into 1-inch [2.5-cm] pieces)

1 medium-sized beet

1 carrot

1 parsnip

5 slices bacon, diced

½ white onion, sliced thin

Garlic salt and pepper, to taste

Dash cayenne pepper

2–3 eggs

Peel and chop all vegetables in uniform pieces, about 1-inch (2.5-cm) cubes. Boil all veggies except onions for 15 minutes.

In a large skillet, fry the diced bacon pieces. Reserve the cooked bacon on the side.

Fry the onions in the hot bacon grease until soft, then add the boiled and drained veggies. Add garlic salt, pepper and cayenne pepper to taste. Brown the veggies on each side for about 5 minutes. Some areas should be slightly crispy.

Add the bacon bits and stir. Crack 2 or 3 eggs inside the skillet and cook sunny side up. Serve immediately.

SPAGHETTI SQUASH CILANTRO FRITTERS

This straightforward breakfast dish uses only a few ingredients for easy prep, but doesn't skimp on flavor with spices and fresh herbs. —RB

SERVES 4

2 spaghetti squash

½ tsp cayenne

¼ tsp salt

4 tsp (12 g) coconut flour

¼ cup (15 g) diced cilantro

2 tbsp (30 ml) coconut oil

Pierce the spaghetti squash several times on each side with a sharp knife and place on a plate. Microwave on high for 8 minutes, then rotate top-side down and microwave for another 8 minutes. It may be necessary to cook the spaghetti squash one at a time.

Slice open the two spaghetti squashes, being careful of the hot escaping steam, and set aside to cool. Once cool enough to handle, squeeze the excess water out of the spaghetti squash strands using your hands or by rolling tightly in paper towels. The spaghetti squash are drained enough when the strands have been reduced to 1 cup (255 g) total.

Load the drained squash, cayenne, salt and coconut flour into a food processor and pulse for 20 seconds until thoroughly mixed. Stir in the diced cilantro and heat the coconut oil in a small skillet over medium heat.

Scoop small dollops, approximately 3 tablespoons (45 g) each, of the spaghetti squash batter into the skillet, and cook for 5 minutes or until browned but not burnt. Flip the fritters and cook for 5 minutes more.

Remove the fritters to a paper towel-lined plate to drain, and repeat the cooking method with the remaining batter. Serve warm.

SWEET POTATO LATKES

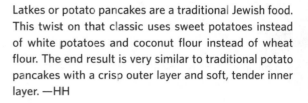

Latkes or potato pancakes are a traditional Jewish food. This twist on that classic uses sweet potatoes instead of white potatoes and coconut flour instead of wheat flour. The end result is very similar to traditional potato pancakes with a crisp outer layer and soft, tender inner layer. —HH

MAKES 12

1 large sweet potato

Half small or medium onion

2 eggs

½ tbsp (4 g) coconut flour

½ tsp salt and pepper

2 tbsp (30 ml) coconut oil or avocado oil for the pan

Shred sweet potato and onion and place in a clean kitchen towel and squeeze out the moisture. Set aside, still on the towel. In a large bowl whisk eggs, coconut flour, salt and pepper together. After the shredded potato and onion has sat for a few minutes, try to squeeze out a little more moisture. Add the sweet potato and onion to the egg mixture and mix well.

Heat coconut oil or avocado oil in a cast iron skillet. If you use a larger skillet you may need to add more oil because the pancakes have to fry in a good layer of oil. Once oil is hot add small spoonfuls of the mixture to the skillet and flatten into a circle with a spatula. Cook for a few minutes on one side until golden brown, then flip and cook the other side. Place on a paper towel after frying to catch excess oil.

BAKED EGGS WITH SWEET POTATOES

These baked eggs topped with porky goodness are ideal for a leisurely Sunday brunch. Prepare the sweet potato and onion mixture the night before so all you need to do the next day is assemble everything and pop the ramekins in the oven. You'll have just enough time to brew a fresh pot of coffee before these baked eggs are ready to be devoured. —JC

SERVES 2

1 tsp (3 g) ghee

3 strips bacon, chopped

1 medium sweet potato, chopped into small pieces

1 small onion, chopped into small pieces

1 sprig fresh rosemary, chopped

¼ tsp black pepper

4 large eggs

Preheat oven to 375°F (190°C, or gas mark 5). Lightly grease four individual serving–sized ramekins with the ghee.

Add bacon to a cast iron pan over medium-high heat. Fry it until crispy and golden brown, about 10 to 12 minutes. Set aside. Add sweet potato, onion, rosemary and black pepper into the same cast iron pan with bacon fat. Sauté and let it cook for 8 to 10 minutes until the sweet potatoes have softened.

Equally divide the sweet potato and onion mixture among the four ramekins. Crack an egg on top of each one. Place ramekins on a baking sheet and bake in the oven for 6 to 8 minutes depending on how you want the eggs cooked.

Let them cool for 5 minutes and top with fried bacon before serving.

BAKED EGGS

These baked eggs can make a fun appetizer or brunch item for guests! The tomato sauce adds a nice acidic and slightly sweet flavor while the greens add texture. —HH

SERVES 4

Ghee, butter or oil, for greasing

4 tbsp (60 g) tomato sauce

4 tsp (12 g) finely chopped garlic

4 tsp (12 g) finely chopped greens—beet greens, chard or kale

4 egg

Dash of almond flour, sage, salt and pepper for each

Preheat the oven to 375°F (190°C, or gas mark 5). Rub four 6-ounce (168-g) ramekins with ghee, butter or oil to prevent sticking. In each ramekin, put 1 tablespoon (15 g) tomato sauce. Mix in 1 teaspoon (3 g) each of garlic and greens in each. Crack one egg into each ramekin, then sprinkle each one with almond flour, sage, salt and pepper. Cook in the oven for 10 to 15 minutes.

GINGER APPLE BREAKFAST SAUSAGE

I like to make these flavorful sausages in big batches and save them in the fridge or freezer for easy breakfasts. The spiced kick of the ginger and the hint of sweetness from the apple, take simple ground pork to new flavorful heights. —HH

MAKES ABOUT 12

1 small onion

4 cloves garlic

1 small green apple

1 pound (454 g) ground pork

2 tsp (6 g) grated fresh ginger, peeled

1 tsp (3 g) garlic powder

¾ tsp ginger powder

½ tsp thyme

1 tsp (3 g) oregano

1 tsp (3 g) salt

1 tsp (3 g) pepper

2 tbsp (30 ml) coconut oil, lard or ghee

Finely dice the onion, garlic and green apple and place in a mixing bowl. Place the ground pork into the mixing bowl along with the grated ginger and the remaining ingredients—garlic powder, ginger powder, thyme, oregano, salt and pepper—except for the oil. Use a large wooden spoon or your hands to mix the ingredients together. You can also use a food processor or stand mixer.

Once all the ingredients are mixed together, form palm-sized patties of the pork mixture. You can either pan-fry the sausages or bake them. To pan fry, heat up the coconut oil, lard or ghee in a pan on medium-high heat. Place the patties in the pan and cook for about 5 minutes on each side until cooked all the way through or until a meat thermometer placed through the middle of the patty reads 140°F (60°C).

To bake, place the patties on a baking sheet lined with parchment paper. Bake at 350°F (180°C, or gas mark 4) for 25 to 30 minutes, flipping halfway through.

HOMEMADE MAPLE APPLE BREAKFAST SAUSAGE

This will quickly become your favorite sausage recipe. The rich flavors of sage and fresh herbs combine well with the sweetness of apples and maple. Finger-licking good! —KH

SERVES 4–6

¼ medium onion

1 clove fresh garlic

1 medium apple, peeled, cored and quartered

1 tbsp (15 ml) coconut oil, butter or ghee

1½ tbsp (23 ml) maple syrup

1 pound (454 g) ground pork

2 tbsp (8 g) fresh herbs, finely chopped—basil, cilantro, oregano or parsley

1 tsp (3 g) sea salt

½ tsp ground sage, dried

In a small food processor, purée onion and garlic. Add apple pieces and pulse until apple is broken up into tiny pieces but not puréed.

Sauté the onion-garlic-apple mixture in the fat of choice over medium heat for 5 to 7 minutes, until it softens and begins to brown a bit. Allow to cool slightly.

In a large bowl, add maple syrup to ground pork and mix thoroughly. Add the rest of the ingredients, including onion-garlic mixture and mix well. I use my hands. Shape into desired sized patties and either fry up now on medium-high heat for about 3 minutes each side or freeze for later. If freezing, separate layers with unbleached parchment paper.

PEAR, GINGER AND TURKEY PATTIES

The pear gives these patties a slight hint of sweetness, while the ginger adds some zest. These patties are easy enough to make for a weekday breakfast, but elegant enough for a weekend brunch! —AV

MAKES 10

1 ripe pear, peeled and chopped

1 pound (454 g) ground turkey

2 cloves garlic, minced

1 tsp (3 g) fresh ginger, grated

1 tsp (3 g) fresh sage, minced

1 tsp (3 g) fresh rosemary, minced

1 tsp (3 g) sea salt

½ tsp black pepper

1–2 tbsp (15–30 ml) coconut oil

Pulse the pear in a food processor until it is smooth. In a medium bowl, combine turkey, pear, garlic, ginger, sage, rosemary, salt and pepper. Shape mixture into small patties by rolling them into a ball in the palm of your hand and then flattening them. The mixture should make about 10 patties.

Heat 1 tablespoon (15 ml) of coconut oil in a heavy-bottomed pan, like cast iron. Add only enough patties so they are not crowded in the pan. You will have to cook these in two batches. Cook them for 4 to 5 minutes on the first side, until lightly browned and the patty lifts from the pan easily. Flip and cook them on the second side for 2 to 3 minutes, or until they are browned on both sides and no longer pink inside. Move cooked patties to a plate and set aside. Add more coconut oil if needed and cook the second batch of patties. Enjoy!

ROASTED TOMATO SHAKSHUKA

This is a traditional Israeli egg dish that can be made with many variations; this one is my roasted tomato version . . . I love roasted tomatoes and their caramelized flavor. —VM

SERVES 2

1½ pounds (680 g) cherry tomatoes, or any sweet, small heirloom tomatoes

Sea salt

½ tbsp (4 g) cumin seeds

¼ cup (60 ml) olive oil

1 yellow onion, chopped

1 red bell pepper, sliced into long strips

Leaves from two sprigs of thyme, chopped

1 tbsp (4 g) parsley, chopped

1 pinch cayenne

4 eggs

Preheat the oven to 350°F (180°C, or gas mark 4). After you have washed the tomatoes, cut them in half and lay them on a lightly oiled cookie sheet. Season the tomatoes with sea salt, and then place them in the oven for about 30 minutes, or until they are fully roasted and caramelized.

While the tomatoes are roasting in the oven, heat a large pan over medium heat, toasting the cumin seeds. Add the olive oil and chopped onions, sautéing them until they are nice and soft. Add the sliced peppers, finely chopped herbs and the roasted tomatoes that just came out of the oven. Then add the cayenne and season with sea salt. Mix everything together and bring the mixture to a simmer. Make sure to add water as needed, you want the dish to maintain a sauce-like consistency.

Break the eggs into the pan, spacing them evenly. Cook the eggs over the tomato mixture for 10 minutes, until the egg whites set and the yolks remain soft and runny. Serve immediately.

KALE & EGGS BENEDICT

This Kale & Eggs Benedict with a nourishing hollandaise sauce is a different take on the classic breakfast dish, as the eggs are fried instead of poached. The delicious flavor of butter permeates this dish while the egg yolk provides a boost of nutrition for the start of the day! —VM

SERVES 1

4 tbsp (60 g) butter

1 clove garlic, peeled

2 ounces (56 g) raw baby kale, washed and trimmed from stems

2 eggs, whites and yolks separated

1 tbsp (15 ml) coconut cream

Sea salt and black pepper to taste

Heat a small skillet over medium heat, melting 1 tablespoon (15 g) of butter. Smash and peel the clove of garlic, sautéing for 1 minute. After rinsing the kale, add it to the skillet, cover and cook for 5 minutes; stirring occasionally. Remove the kale and keep warm.

Take one egg and separate the yolk from white, setting aside the yolk. Add the second egg to the egg whites and fry to the desired consistency.

In a small saucepan melt the remaining butter, then add the coconut cream to it, mixing well until hot but not boiling. In a food processor, add the egg yolk, a pinch of salt and ground black pepper. Pulse slowly while adding the coconut cream mixture gradually. Mix the coconut cream mixture until you create a smooth cream.

Plate the warm kale, adding the fried egg on top. Dress the eggs and kale with the coconut hollandaise, and enjoy!

CRISPY HAM EGGS BENEDICT

Whenever I go to a breakfast restaurant, my eyes always wander to eggs Benedict and often I have mine served over sautéed spinach, but it just isn't the same without the bread! I re-created this classic favorite using Paleo-friendly ingredients and you will want to eat this every day for breakfast! —CP

SERVES 4

1 tsp (3 g) salt

2 tsp (10 ml) white vinegar

1 tsp (5 ml) olive oil

8 slices Canadian bacon

8 eggs

Grain-Free Fluffy White Dinner Rolls (page 522), sliced in half

2 cups (140 g) spinach

1 recipe Lemon Hollandaise Sauce (page 500)

¼ cup (20 g) microgreens

Warm a skillet to medium heat. Begin to simmer a pot of water to poach the eggs. Add salt and vinegar to the pot of simmering water.

Drizzle the oil into the skillet and place the Canadian bacon throughout the pan. Cook for about 2 minutes per side or until slightly crispy, rotate and continue to cook on the other side for an additional minute or until slightly crispy.

Crack each egg into a small bowl or ramekin then carefully drop them into the simmering water. Cook the eggs for 1 to 2 minutes until the whites are cooked and the yolks are soft, then carefully remove with a slotted spoon.

Slice the rolls in half and toast until warm and slightly crispy. Layer with a few leaves of spinach and slice of crispy Canadian bacon. Top with a poached eggs and a generous drizzle of Lemon Hollandaise Sauce. Garnish with micro greens.

CHEF'S TIP:

You may have leftover hollandaise sauce, depending on how much you like to use for eggs Benedict, but the sauce lasts in the refrigerator for a few days.

PERFECT SOFT-BOILED EGGS

I recommend that you try this method starting with 5 minutes, then adjust accordingly based on how your eggs turned out. The perfect soft-boiled egg should have firm whites that are cooked through, and a runny yolk. Some people find that 4 minutes works best for them, while others find that 6 minutes works best. I encourage you to try the below method a few times and find the timing that works best on your stove! —AV

SERVES 1

Water

2 eggs

Fill a pot with enough water to cover the eggs. Bring the water to a boil. Once the water is boiling, use a spoon to gently lower the eggs into the water. Cook uncovered for 5 minutes. I recommend using a timer. Use a slotted spoon to carefully remove the eggs from the water and run them under cold water. Peel and enjoy!

PAN-SEARED SMOKY STEAK AND EGGS

Filet mignon is my absolute favorite cut of meat and I created this dish to have the buttery flavor with each bite. The addition of smoked sea salt makes this pan-seared steak come alive and will have you eating steak and eggs for breakfast! —CP

SERVES 2

2 filet mignon steaks

½ tsp sea salt

½ tsp smoked sea salt flakes, plus additional for garnish

¼ tsp fresh cracked black pepper

2 tbsp (30 g) butter

1 shallot, thinly sliced

2 eggs, poached

Remove steak from the refrigerator and season with both salts and pepper. Set the steak aside to come to room temperature for 1 hour.

When you are ready to cook, warm a cast iron skillet to medium-high heat for several minutes so that the pan is evenly heated. Melt butter in the skillet.

Sear the steaks for 4 to 4½ minutes, flip then continue cooking for an additional 4 to 4½ minutes, for medium-rare steak, depending on the thickness of your steaks.

Remove steak from the pan and set aside to rest for 5 minutes.

Sauté the shallots in the leftover butter and steak juices of the pan until they turn slightly crispy. Plate steak with a poached egg, crispy shallots and a few pinches of smoked salt flakes.

CHEF'S TIP:

Searing time depends on the thickness of your filets and the desired degree of cooking. For medium to medium well, sear for an additional minute or two. Keep in mind that filets are meant to be served medium rare and slightly pink. They will also continue to cook as they rest.

EGGS WITH SMOKED SALMON

Smoked salmon and fluffy scrambled eggs are one of my favorite breakfast dishes. Red onions and capers are wonderful accompaniments and I usually double them up because I like the bold and tangy flavors they add to the eggs. —JC

SERVES 2

6 large eggs, room temperature

2 tbsp (30 ml) ghee or tallow, melted

½ tsp sea salt

½ tsp dried chives

½ tsp dried shallots

3 ounces (84 g) smoked salmon

1 tbsp (15 g) red onions, thinly sliced

1 tbsp (15 g) capers, drained

Preheat a skillet over low heat. Crack eggs in a bowl and add melted ghee. Whisk until light and frothy. Add sea salt, chives and shallots. Give it a stir to combine. Pour mixture into the skillet and gently stir once every minute. Let it cook for 5 to 8 minutes until it begins to set and it's not runny anymore.

Transfer eggs to a serving plate and top with smoked salmon, red onions and capers.

AVOCADO & SALMON LOW CARB BREAKFAST (2 WAYS)

A simple, but delicious breakfast combining two of my favorite ingredients—avocado and salmon. The avocado is used as its own serving cup and stuffed with a tasty salmon cream, to create fun avocado boats. —VM

SERVES 1

1 ripe avocado

2 ounces (56 g) wild smoked salmon

2 tbsp (30 ml) extra-virgin olive oil

Juice of 1 lemon

Sea salt and black pepper to taste

Cut the avocado in half and remove the pit. In a food processor, add the wild smoked salmon, olive oil, lemon juice, sea salt and black pepper. Pulse the ingredients until they are coarsely chopped. Scoop a generous serving of the salmon mixture into each avocado, season with sea salt and ground black pepper, and serve.

ALTERNATE VERSION

Cut avocado and wild smoked salmon into small cubes. In the food processor, blend the avocado, wild smoked salmon, olive oil and lemon juice. Season with sea salt and ground black pepper and serve.

TRUFFLED SPRING GREEN ASPARAGUS OMELET

This savory breakfast omelet is filled with seasonal spring greens and fragrant truffle oil. I love making this rolled omelet as it is so rich and gourmet in flavor but so simple to prepare. —CP

SERVES 1

1 tbsp (15 g) butter

5 asparagus stalks

3 eggs

2 tbsp (30 ml) coconut milk

⅛ tsp sea salt

⅛ tsp white pepper

½ cup (35 g) fresh baby arugula

1 green onion, chopped

Handful of Pecorino Romano shavings, optional

1 tsp (5 ml) truffle oil

Heat a skillet to medium heat. Melt butter in pan.

Chop off tough ends of the asparagus stalks. Sauté in butter for 5 to 10 minutes, depending on the thickness of your asparagus. Asparagus turns a brighter green as it begins to soften.

While asparagus is cooking, whisk together eggs, milk, salt and pepper. Remove asparagus from skillet and set aside.

Pour egg batter into the pan, allow the edges to sizzle slightly then turn the heat down to low. Cook until the middle is no longer runny. Add asparagus, arugula, green onions and handful of Parmesan shavings, if using, into center of omelet.

Use a spatula to carefully fold in half and slide onto a plate creating a rolled omelet.

Serve topped with a drizzle of truffle oil.

CHEF'S TIP:

Truffle oil isn't a cooking oil as the high heat will decrease its flavor, but it is a fragrant, finishing oil.

DATE & WALNUT OMELET

Enjoy this delicious omelet filled with the sweetness of dates and the crunch of walnuts for a sweet take on your morning eggs. —NK

SERVES 6

2 ounces (56 g) Medjool dates, pitted

3 ounces (84 g) walnuts

1 tbsp (15 g) ghee or coconut oil

6 eggs

½ tsp ground cinnamon

¼ tsp sea salt

Place dates and walnuts into a food processor and process until well combined. Add ghee or coconut oil to a 10-inch (25-cm) skillet and heat over medium heat. Whisk the eggs then stir in the date and walnut mixture, cinnamon and sea salt. Pour into the skillet and cook until the bottom of the omelet is cooked through, carefully flip over and cook the other side before serving.

PERSIAN SPINACH AND EGG OMELET

This Persian Spinach and Egg Omelet is a classic dish called *Nargesi Esfenaj*. The eggs in this dish represent narges, or narcissus, the golden flower that blooms in the spring. —NK

SERVES 2

2 tbsp (30 g) ghee

1 yellow onion, sliced into half moons

½ tsp turmeric

2 cloves garlic, minced

14 ounces (392 g) baby spinach

½ tsp sea salt

¼ tsp black pepper

4 eggs

1 tbsp (8 g) crushed walnuts, optional

Heat a 10- to 12-inch (25- to 30.5-cm) skillet over medium heat. Add the ghee. Once heated, add the onions and cook until golden, about 10 to 15 minutes. Add the turmeric and stir. Add the minced garlic and fry for 1 minute. Add the spinach in batches and cook until wilted. Add the sea salt and black pepper and mix well. Break one egg at a time into the skillet, making sure not to break the yolk. Cook for 5 to 7 minutes or until the eggs are just set sunny-side-up. Top with crushed walnuts if desired.

BEET GREEN AND CARROT ROLLED OMELET

These rolled omelets are a fun way to serve up breakfast to your family. —NK

SERVES 6–7

1 tbsp (15 g) ghee

1 cup (120 g) grated carrot

2 cups (140 g) sliced beet greens

¼ tsp garlic powder

½ tsp sea salt, divided

¼ tsp black pepper

10 eggs

Preheat oven to 350°F (180°C, or gas mark 4). Line a 10 × 15-inch (25 × 38-cm) rimmed baking tray with parchment paper, making sure that the parchment paper slightly hangs over the shorter ends of the baking tray. Heat a medium-large skillet over medium-low heat. Add the ghee. Once heated add the carrots, cook for around 5 minutes before adding the beet greens. Add the garlic powder, ¼ teaspoon sea salt and black pepper. Stir to cook for another 3 to 4 minutes. Remove from the heat and set aside.

In a large mixing bowl whisk together the eggs and another ¼ teaspoon sea salt. Pour the egg mixture into the lined baking tray, making sure the mixture covers the surface. Add the beet green and carrot mixture from the skillet and spread evenly over the top of the eggs. Place in the oven and bake for 15 to 20 minutes. Remove from the oven and allow to cool slightly. Then, starting at one of the shorter ends, lift the parchment paper and roll up the omelet as tightly as possible. Peel back the parchment paper as you go. Once rolled, place seam side down onto a chopping board. Cut into ½- to 1-inch (1.3- to 2.5-cm) slices.

CHORIZO OMELET

Chorizo and omelets were just meant to be. Pair it with fresh salsa and Super Easy Guacamole (page 190) and you have the perfect breakfast! —VM

SERVES 4

8 eggs

1 cup (60 g) cilantro, chopped, reserving some for garnish

1 jalapeño pepper, seeded and chopped finely

Sea salt to taste

1 tbsp (15 g) lard or butter

2 chorizo sausage links

2 medium sweet potatoes, peeled, boiled lightly, and sliced

Salsa, optional, for serving

Super Easy Guacamole (page 190), optional, for serving

Add the eggs, cilantro, jalapeños and salt to a bowl and whisk together. Melt the fat over medium heat in a large omelet pan.

Crumble the chorizo into the omelet pan, cooking for 2 to 3 minutes. Add the sliced sweet potatoes to the chorizo along with a little more fat if needed.

Cook the mixture for about 5 minutes before adding the egg mixture by pouring it evenly over the chorizo and sweet potatoes. Do not stir the eggs so they start to immediately form the omelet.

Cover the pan and lower the heat for about 5 minutes, or until the omelet has set. Flip the omelet once it has set and cook for another 3 minutes. Garnish with cilantro and some salsa and/or Super Easy Guacamole and enjoy!

GREEN EGGS QUICHE

Eggs take on spinach and herbs to make a fun green colored quiche that would be a delight on the breakfast table! This is a filling meal that will get you through the rest of the morning until lunchtime rolls in. —JC

SERVES 2

2 tbsp (30 g) ghee or tallow

1 large shallot, chopped

1 bunch spinach

6 large eggs

¼ cup (15 g) fresh parsley, chopped

¼ cup (15 g) fresh chives, chopped

2 tbsp (30 ml) Homemade Coconut Milk (page 503)

¼ tsp black pepper

¼ tsp sea salt

Add ghee to a cast iron pan over medium heat. Add shallot and sauté until caramelized, about 10 minutes. Add spinach and sauté until wilted, about 2 to 3 minutes.

Crack eggs in a bowl and whisk until frothy. Stir in parsley, chives, coconut milk, black pepper and sea salt. Pour mixture into the pan. Mix it with the caramelized shallots and spinach so the egg is distributed evenly. Reduce heat to low, cover and cook for 15 minutes.

Turn on broiler to low. Uncover and move the pan to the oven and broil for 5 minutes. Let cool for a few minutes before cutting and serving.

ZUCCHINI & TURNIP CRUSTLESS QUICHE

Zucchini has a wonderful flavor that complements the turnip. This quiche makes for an excellent main dish, a great brunch on a Sunday morning or to have throughout the week before work. —VM

SERVES 4

1 large zucchini

Ghee or coconut oil for sautéing

2 cloves garlic, thinly sliced

8 eggs

½ cup (120 ml) coconut cream

1 bunch fresh herbs (thyme, rosemary, tarragon, chives, etc.)

A pinch sea salt

A pinch ground black pepper

Salad turnips, chopped into ½-inch (1.3-cm) cubes

Preheat the oven to 325°F (170°C, or gas mark 3). Grease an 8 × 8-inch (20 × 20-cm) baking dish and set aside. Blanch the zucchini and then let it cool. Once it has cooled, cut it into 1-inch (2.5-cm) pieces and set to the side.

Heat the ghee in a skillet over medium heat and sauté the garlic until it is very fragrant. Add the zucchini to the garlic and sauté until they have cooked through, about 5 minutes. In a separate bowl, whisk the eggs and coconut cream together with the herbs and a pinch of salt and pepper. Line the baking dish with the zucchini and turnips and then cover with the egg mixture.

Bake for 45 minutes or until it has browned on top.

CHEF'S TIP:

This dish can be served warm or cold. It makes a great breakfast or appetizer if cut in little squares and served as a finger food.

PORK SAUSAGE & CHARD CRUSTLESS QUICHE

If you love to have eggs and sausage, then this is the dish, but better! Pork sausage and chard bring back the flavors of the south that are sure to satisfy anyone's appetite. —VM

SERVES 4

Ghee or coconut oil for greasing

1 pound (454 g) ground beef

1 pound (454 g) pork sausage

1 bunch Swiss chard, chopped and stemmed

8 eggs

½ cup (120 ml) coconut cream

½ tsp sea salt

½ tsp ground black pepper

Preheat the oven to 325°F (170°C, or gas mark 3). Grease an 8 × 8-inch (20 × 20-cm) baking dish with ghee and set to the side. In a large skillet over medium heat, brown the beef and sausage and then drain the excess fat if needed. Set the meat aside and let that cool. Add the chard to the skillet and sauté until the leaves begin to wilt, about 3 minutes. Let the chard cool and set aside.

In a separate bowl, whisk the eggs together with the coconut cream and a pinch of salt and black pepper. Add the chard to the egg mixture and mix well. Line the baking dish with the meat mixture. Then pour the egg mixture over the meat and bake for 45 minutes, or until the top has nicely browned.

BACON TURMERIC FRITTATA

The combination of bacon, eggs, turmeric and parsley makes for a quick, easy and savory meal. —RB

SERVES 6

4–6 pieces of bacon

1 onion

6 eggs

1 (3-inch [7.5-cm]) piece of fresh turmeric root

½ tsp salt

½ tsp black pepper

Parsley, for garnish

Preheat oven to 400°F (200°C, or gas mark 6). In a dry skillet over medium heat, fry the bacon, turning once, until cooked. Remove to a paper towel-lined plate, pour off all but 1 teaspoon (5 ml) of the bacon grease, reserve the rest.

Dice the onion, or pulse in a food processor until finely shredded. Sauté the onion until tender, approximately 10 minutes. Remove from heat and let cool while you prepare the eggs.

By hand or with a mixer, whip the eggs until frothy. Peel the turmeric, then grate into the eggs. Stir in the softened onion, salt and pepper.

Use the reserved bacon fat to grease a 9-inch (23-cm) pie plate. Pour in the turmeric egg mixture, and bury the bacon pieces halfway. Cook the quiche in the preheated oven for 20 minutes. Remove and let cool slightly, then sprinkle with fresh parsley. Serve warm.

CHEESY CAULIFLOWER SWIRL FRITTATA

Cheesy cauliflower frittata gets a visual upgrade with a chopped red bell pepper swirl. Grass-fed cheddar from humanely-raised animals, eaten in moderation, is a fantastic addition to add melty texture and savory flavor for those who tolerate dairy. —RB

SERVES 4

1 tbsp (15 ml) coconut oil, plus more for greasing pan

1 small cauliflower

½ cup (60 g) finely grated cheddar

½ tsp salt

2 eggs

1 red bell pepper

Preheat the oven to 350°F (180°C, or gas mark 4). Using coconut oil, grease a non-stick 8-inch (20-cm) fluted tart or pie pan with a removable bottom and set aside.

Roughly chop the cauliflower, then pulse in a food processor until very finely chopped, approximately the consistency of couscous. Melt 1 tablespoon (15 ml) of coconut oil in a large skillet over medium heat. Cook the chopped cauliflower, stirring frequently, until softened, about 15 minutes. Transfer the cauliflower to a bowl and stir in the grated cheese, making sure it's incorporated fully into the mixture as it melts. Add the salt.

Allow the cheesy cauliflower mixture to cool until it is just warm to the touch, then stir in the eggs. Beat until mixed, then spoon into the greased pan and level with the back of a spoon.

Dice the bell pepper, or finely shred in a food processor. Using your fingers, sprinkle the pepper in a rough spiral on top of the cauliflower mixture. Clean up the edges, using the tip of a knife, until you have a tidy geometric design.

Bake in the preheated oven for 1 hour or until browned on the top. Remove from the oven and allow to cool to room temperature. Remove from pan and serve.

MUSHROOM ONION FRITTATA BITES

These are tiny, protein-packed bites of breakfast goodness. —RB

SERVES 8

2 tbsp (30 ml) coconut oil, plus more for greasing muffin tin

2 onions

½ pound (227 g) mushrooms

1 cup (140 g) cooked chicken, chopped or shredded

⅓ cup (80 ml) coconut milk

¼ tsp salt

¼ tsp black pepper

5 eggs

Preheat oven to 350°F (180°C, or gas mark 4). Grease a 24-cup mini muffin tin with coconut oil, set aside.

Melt the 2 tablespoons (30 ml) of coconut oil in a medium skillet over medium-low heat. Thinly slice the onions and cook in the skillet until very soft and brown, approximately 20 minutes. Be sure to stir occasionally to avoid scorching. Remove the onions to a medium mixing bowl to cool.

Pulse the mushrooms in a food processor or dice very fine. Cook in the skillet until soft and all of the liquid has evaporated, approximately 15 minutes. Add to the onions in the mixing bowl.

Once the mushrooms and onions have cooled, add the chicken, coconut milk, salt and pepper. Whisk in the eggs, then spoon into the muffin tin. Cook in the preheated oven for 15 minutes until just set. Remove and let sit for 10 minutes; serve warm.

SUN-DRIED TOMATO FRITTATA

This full-flavored frittata can be prepared ahead: make the tomato, zucchini and pancetta mixture the night before, then crack the eggs and pop it in the oven in the morning. —RB

SERVES 4

2 tsp (10 ml) coconut oil, divided

1 onion

1 zucchini

4 ounces (112 g) oil-packed sun-dried tomatoes

¼ pound (112 g) pancetta, sliced

5 eggs

¼ tsp salt

¼ tsp pepper

Preheat oven to 350°F (180°C, or gas mark 4). Grease an 8-inch (20-cm) cast iron skillet with 1 teaspoon (5 ml) of coconut oil and set aside.

Melt 1 teaspoon (5 ml) coconut oil in a medium skillet over medium heat. Pulse the onion and zucchini in a food processor until finely shredded, then cook in the skillet until soft and translucent, about 10 minutes.

While the zucchini and onions soften, drain the oil from the sun-dried tomatoes, roughly chop and add to a medium mixing bowl. Dice the pancetta, then add to the tomatoes.

When the onions and zucchini are soft, add to the pancetta and tomatoes. Mix thoroughly and let cool to room temperature. Whisk in eggs, salt and pepper and pour into the cast iron skillet. Cook in the preheated oven for 1 hour and 15 minutes or until firm. Serve warm.

SWEET PEPPER FRITTATA

This simple frittata recipe comes together in 15 minutes and is made of only three ingredients: sweet peppers, ham and eggs. —RB

SERVES 8

Coconut oil, for greasing pan

1 cup (120 g) sweet peppers, chopped

2 cups (280 g) ham, chopped

4 eggs

3–4 little sweet peppers, for garnish

Preheat oven to 350°F (180°C, or gas mark 4). Grease a 9-inch (23-cm) pie plate, and set aside.

Place the chopped peppers and ham into a food processor and pulse until grated very fine. Transfer to a medium mixing bowl and crack four eggs over the mixture, and then combine thoroughly with a fork.

Spoon mixture into the greased pie plate, level with the back of a fork. Slice the little sweet peppers into strips and lightly press them into the egg mixture. Bake in the preheated oven for 1 hour or until firm. Serve warm.

CHEF'S TIP:
I used baby sweet peppers for this, but full-sized bell peppers would work just as well. If you like it spicy, shred half of a jalapeño into the mixture before spooning it into the pie plate.

TOMATO AND HAM EGG MUFFINS

These portable, savory muffins are filled with mini tomatoes that burst with sweetness on that first bite! The Homemade Coconut Milk (page 503) makes them extra fluffy. They can be eaten hot or cold for breakfast, lunch or dinner. —JC

SERVES 6

1 tsp coconut oil

1 pint (300 g) mini heirloom tomatoes, cut in half

6 slices cooked ham, chopped

8 large eggs, room temperature

½ cup (120 ml) Homemade Coconut Milk (page 503)

2 tbsp (30 ml) ghee, melted

3 tbsp (18 g) green onions, chopped

½ tsp garlic powder

½ tsp onion powder

½ tsp sea salt

¼ tsp black pepper

Preheat oven to 375°F (190°C, or gas mark 5). Lightly coat a muffin pan with coconut oil. Evenly distribute tomatoes and ham among the muffin cups.

In a bowl, add eggs, coconut milk, ghee, green onions, garlic powder, onion powder, sea salt and black pepper. Whisk until frothy. Pour mixture into the muffin pan until each cup is two-thirds full. Bake for 30 to 35 minutes until eggs are set. Let cool for 5 minutes before removing the egg muffins from the pan.

THREE MUSHROOM EGG MUFFINS

Using three different kinds of mushrooms makes these egg muffins extra special. Select a variety of bold, medium and mild flavors that won't overpower each other. Crimini, shiitake and chanterelle are a good mix to start off with. —JC

SERVES 4

1 tbsp (15 ml) coconut oil, divided

¾ cup (53 g) crimini mushrooms, chopped

¾ cup (53 g) shiitake mushrooms, chopped

¾ cup (53 g) chanterelle mushrooms, chopped

1 leek, green and white parts, chopped

8 large eggs

¼ cup (60 ml) Homemade Coconut Milk (page 503)

½ tsp garlic powder

½ tsp onion powder

½ tsp sea salt

½ tsp black pepper

Preheat the oven to 375°F (190°C, or gas mark 5).

Add 2 teaspoons (10 ml) coconut oil to a pan over medium heat. Add the mushrooms and leeks and sauté until softened, about 8 to 10 minutes. Set aside to cool.

Crack the eggs into a bowl. Add the coconut milk, garlic powder, onion powder, sea salt and black pepper. Whisk until frothy.

Combine the egg mixture with the cooled mushrooms and leeks. Mix well. Grease a 12-cup muffin pan with the remaining 1 teaspoon of coconut oil. Pour the egg mixture in the muffin pan and bake for 10 to 15 minutes until eggs are set.

CHEF'S TIP:
Any combination of mushrooms can be used in lieu of crimini, shiitake and chanterelle.

MEAT MUFFINS

Muffins don't always have to be sweet. Make these meat muffins with ground beef, eggs and veggies, and enjoy them throughout the week or as an on-the-go snack. —NK

SERVES 8–10

1 tbsp (15 g) ghee or coconut oil

1 small red onion, diced

1 clove garlic, minced

1 pound (454 g) ground beef

½ tsp sea salt

¼ tsp black pepper

6 ounces (168 g) grated carrots

13 ounces (364 g) grated zucchini

½ tbsp (4 g) red pepper flakes

¼ cup (15 g) fresh flat leaf parsley, chopped

12 large eggs

Heat a 10- to 12-inch (25- to 30.5-cm) skillet over medium heat. Add the ghee or coconut oil. Add the onion and cook for 5 minutes then add the garlic and cook for another minute. Add the meat and use a wooden spoon to break up the meat as it cooks. Once the meat is almost cooked through, season with sea salt and black pepper. Add the grated carrot and cook for 5 minutes. Add the zucchini and cook for another 5 minutes. Stir in the pepper flakes and parsley. Remove from the heat and allow to cool for 10 minutes.

While the mixture is cooling preheat oven to 350°F (180°C, or gas mark 4) and line two regular 12-cup muffin pans with muffin/cupcake liners. Whisk the eggs in a large mixing bowl then add the meat mixture into the eggs and mix. Pour the egg-meat mixture into lined muffin trays. Bake for 15 to 20 minutes or until set.

CHEF'S TIP:

If you only have one muffin pan you can cover the remaining mixture and refrigerate to bake the following day. These muffins make a great portable meal or snack and can even be frozen.

JIANBING (CHINESE BREAKFAST CREPE)

Jianbing is a Chinese crepe with egg and filling sold from street stalls as breakfast or a late-night snack. Toppings vary, but mine includes meat, fresh herbs and fiery chili sauce. —RB

SERVES 1

FOR THE CREPE

1 tbsp (15 ml) coconut oil

1 egg

⅓ cup (40 g) arrowroot flour

Pinch salt

FOR THE FILLING

1 egg

Scant 1 cup (140 g) cooked meat (ground, shredded or diced)

⅛ cup (8 g) chopped cilantro

⅛ cup (10 g) chopped green onion

1 tbsp (15 ml) Paleo-friendly chili sauce

½ tsp black sesame seeds

Heat the coconut oil in a small non-stick or cast iron skillet over medium-high heat.

Whisk the egg, arrowroot flour and salt together until batter is completely free of lumps. Pour batter into the hot oiled skillet. Cook for 1 minute. Crack an egg over the crepe, then smear the white and yolk together all over its surface.

Pile on the meat, cilantro, green onion, chili sauce and sesame seeds. Cook just enough for the egg to set, then fold the crepe in half or roll over the filling using a spatula. Transfer to a plate and serve warm.

CURRIED CARROT WAFFLE STACK

This curried carrot waffle stack borrows the flavors of India in delicious layers. —RB

SERVES 3

FOR THE TOMATOES

1 pint (300 g) cherry tomatoes

1 tbsp (15 ml) olive oil

¼ tsp salt

FOR THE LAMB

½ pound (227 g) ground lamb

¼ tsp salt

¼ tsp black pepper

FOR THE WAFFLES

1 pound (454 g) carrots

8 eggs

½ cup (60 g) coconut flour

½ tsp salt

2 tbsp (16 g) curry powder

2 tbsp (30 ml) olive oil

FOR THE GARNISH

Cashew butter

Cilantro

Chili flakes

Preheat the oven to 350°F (180°C, or gas mark 4). Toss the cherry tomatoes with olive oil and salt, then spread on a cookie sheet. Bake in the preheated oven for 40 minutes (stirring occasionally to prevent burning) until very soft and thoroughly roasted. Remove from the oven and let cool.

While the tomatoes are roasting, prepare the ground lamb. In a dry skillet, cook the ground lamb over medium heat until no longer pink, breaking up chunks with a spoon or spatula. Add the salt and pepper. Raise the heat to medium-high under the lamb when cooked for 5 minutes to brown the meat, stirring frequently to prevent burning. Remove from the heat and let cool.

While the lamb is cooking, prepare the waffles. Roughly chop the carrots after peeling and removing the ends. In a food processor, combine the chopped carrots, eggs, coconut flour, salt, curry powder and olive oil. Pulse until the carrots are roughly shredded.

Heat a waffle iron until hot and spoon the waffle batter onto its griddle. Cook for approximately 10 minutes or until browned on top and cooked through—time may vary depending on the waffle iron.

Divide the waffles into fourths and arrange two per plate. Top with the ground lamb and roasted tomatoes, then drizzle cashew butter over the stacks and add cilantro leaves and a sprinkle of chili flakes.

JALAPEÑO WAFFLES

This easy version of grain-free waffles is the perfect thing to whip up either on a lazy weekend morning or in the Monday–Friday rush. The jalapeños add a pop of spicy unexpected flavor. Serve with melted ghee for a savory rendition or with whipped coconut cream and maple syrup for a sweet version. —RB

SERVES 2

8 eggs

8 tbsp (120 ml) coconut oil

½ cup (60 g) coconut flour

⅛ tsp salt

1 jalapeño pepper, seeded and diced

Preheat a waffle-maker according to the product directions.

In a large mixing bowl, whip the eggs until frothy using a hand mixer or whisk. Slowly add the coconut oil, while whipping the mixture continuously, until well-combined.

Stir in the coconut flour, salt and diced jalapeño until a stiff batter forms. Spoon into the preheated waffle-maker, and cook according to waffle-maker instructions until browned on both sides and a tester inserted comes out clean.

EGGY ONION BREAKFAST BREAD

This breakfast bread has crumbled bacon worked into the grain-free, nut-free dough and is topped with caramelized onions. —RB

SERVES 6

4 tbsp (60 ml) coconut oil, divided

½ onion

½ cup (60 g) coconut flour

½ tsp salt

½ tsp baking soda

1 tsp (3 g) cream of tartar

4 eggs

4 pieces of bacon, cooked and finely chopped

½ cup (120 ml) coconut milk or water

1 green onion, thinly sliced

Preheat oven to 350°F (180°C, or gas mark 4). Line an 8-inch (20-cm) square cake pan with parchment paper, set aside.

Warm 2 tablespoons (30 ml) of coconut oil in a medium skillet over medium heat. Slice the onion into thin rounds and cook in the skillet for approximately 10 minutes or until browned, flipping once to cook evenly. Transfer to a paper towel-lined plate, let cool.

Combine the coconut flour, salt, baking soda and cream of tartar in a medium mixing bowl.

In a small mixing bowl, whisk the eggs with the crumbled bacon, remaining coconut oil and coconut milk or water. Stir the wet ingredients into the coconut flour mixture, then spoon into the parchment paper-lined pan.

Press the cooked onions into the top of the batter and cook at 350°F (180°C, or gas mark 4) for approximately 1 hour or until browned around the edges and cooked through. Top with sliced green onion and serve warm.

COCONUT FLOUR BLUEBERRY PANCAKES

My family loves pancakes! But regular pancakes are too boring for us. Adding fresh blueberries, vanilla and cinnamon are just what pancakes need. Each delicious bite is anything but boring. —KW

MAKES 16–20

4 eggs

1 cup (235 ml) milk

3 tbsp (45 ml) pure raw honey or maple syrup

1 tbsp (15 ml) pure vanilla extract

½ cup (60 g) coconut flour

1 tsp (3 g) baking soda

Pinch ground cinnamon

Pinch sea salt

1 cup (150 g) blueberries

Coconut oil or butter for frying

Pure maple syrup, for serving

Whisk the eggs with the milk, honey and vanilla. Add the coconut flour, baking soda, cinnamon and salt to the liquid mixture. Stir until well combined. Gently fold in the blueberries. Let the pancake mixture sit for 2 to 3 minutes or until it reaches a normal pancake batter consistency. Pour the batter into 3-inch (7.5-cm) circles on a griddle, greased with coconut oil or butter, over medium-low heat. Once the pancakes have tiny bubbles all over, about 5 minutes, it's time to flip. Continue cooking for about a minute longer until both sides are golden brown. Serve with pure maple syrup.

SKILLET CHOCOLATE CHIP BANANA PANCAKE

This giant pancake is a cinch to whip together and a delicious treat when the mood strikes for something a little sweet. I like to serve it as a special breakfast treat with a drizzle of pure maple syrup. —KW

SERVES 4

2 ripe bananas, mashed

2 eggs

½ tsp vanilla

½ tsp ground cinnamon

½ cup (60 g) tapioca flour

2 tbsp (16 g) coconut flour

½ tsp baking soda

¼ tsp sea salt

2 tbsp (22 g) chocolate chips

3 tbsp (45 g) ghee or coconut oil, melted

Preheat oven to 375°F (190°C, or gas mark 5). Combine the bananas, eggs and vanilla. Add the cinnamon, tapioca flour, coconut flour, baking soda and sea salt and stir until thoroughly mixed. Fold in the chocolate chips. Add the melted ghee to a 10-inch (25-cm) skillet. Pour the batter over the melted ghee and bake for 25 minutes or until golden brown and inserted toothpick comes out clean.

SPICED CHESTNUT FLOUR PANCAKES

Chestnut flour has a hint of spice to it naturally and a very fine grind, making for a very light pancake batter. These pancakes store fabulously, and we usually eat them so quickly that I like to double the batch and save the rest for breakfast throughout the week. —CP

SERVES 3–4

1 cup (120 g) almond flour

½ cup (60 g) chestnut flour

½ tsp baking soda

1 tsp (3 g) ground cinnamon

¼ tsp ground nutmeg

¼ tsp ground ginger

¼ tsp ground cardamom

4 eggs

½ cup (120 ml) coconut milk

3 tbsp (45 ml) butter, melted

1½ tsp (7.5 ml) vanilla

½ tsp lemon juice

2 tbsp (30 g) butter, for greasing griddle

Heat a griddle to medium-low heat.

Use a hand mixer to blend together all pancake ingredients. Scrape down the sides of the bowl and blend again.

Add a pat of butter to the griddle. Drop a spoonful of pancake batter onto the hot griddle, cooking pancakes for a minute then flip to the other side and cook for an additional minute.

Repeat process until all batter is used.

Serve pancakes with a spoonful of warm apple cinnamon maple syrup. Garnish with butter, whipped cream or additional maple syrup as desired.

APPLE PIE PANCAKES

Don't let the long ingredient list intimidate you. These are easy to make and have all the flavors of a warm apple pie. —KW

MAKES 18–20

1 tbsp (15 g) coconut oil, butter or ghee

2 cups (300 g) diced apples, about 2 medium apples

2 tsp (6 g) ground cinnamon

4 eggs

1 cup (235 ml) milk of choice

2 tbsp (30 ml) pure raw honey or sweetener of choice

1 tsp (5 ml) pure vanilla extract

½ cup (60 g) coconut flour

½ tsp baking soda

1 tsp (3 g) ground cinnamon

Pinch of ground nutmeg

Pinch of sea salt

3 tbsp (45 ml) additional milk of choice

3 tbsp (45 g) butter, ghee or coconut oil

2 tbsp (30 ml) pure maple syrup

Additional coconut oil, butter or ghee for cooking pancakes

Melt 1 tablespoon (15 ml) of coconut oil over medium heat in a skillet. Add the diced apples and cinnamon. Cook until apples are soft, about 5 to 8 minutes.

While apples are cooking, mix the pancake ingredients by combining eggs, milk, honey and vanilla and then adding coconut flour, baking soda, cinnamon, nutmeg and salt. When the apples are done cooking, fold half of the apple mixture into the pancake batter and stir. Add to the apples left in the skillet, the milk, butter and maple syrup and stir until butter is melted. Set aside this apple pie topping until the pancakes are finished cooking.

Pour the pancake batter onto a well-greased skillet over medium-low in your desired pancake size. Smaller pancakes, about 3-inches (7-cm) wide, are easiest to flip. Once bubbles appear over the top of the pancakes, it's time to flip. Flip and continue cooking for about 1 minute or until both sides are golden brown. Serve with the apple pie topping.

BANANA SPICE PANCAKES

These fluffy banana spice pancakes are a wonderful Saturday morning gluten-free and grain-free breakfast idea that requires minimal effort. I love them because the flavor of banana and cinnamon sort of reminds me of banana bread, which is a comfort food for me. —HH

SERVES 2–3

2 ripe bananas

3 eggs

½ cup (60 g) almond flour

¼ tsp baking soda

½ tsp vanilla extract

½ tsp ground cinnamon

¼ tsp ground cloves

¼ tsp ground nutmeg

2 tbsp (30 g) butter or coconut oil for frying

Maple syrup, for serving

Purée the bananas with an immersion blender, fork or stand blender. Add remaining ingredients—except for the butter, reserve that for the pan—and mix well with an immersion blender or whisk. Heat up the butter or coconut oil in a cast iron skillet or pan. Put a little less than ¼ cup (60 ml) of batter for each pancake. Let cook for a few minutes on one side, then flip and let cook through on the other side. Serve with maple syrup.

CHEF'S TIP:

An immersion blender makes very quick work of puréeing the bananas, not to mention it's a nice thing to have around the kitchen for soups, sauces, etc.!

SOUFFLÉ SPICE PANCAKES

Crispy edges and a sweet spice flavor make for a delicious, healthy pancake made entirely of nut butter, mashed squash and whipped eggs. I like to make a batch of these each week to keep on hand for a simple breakfast or snack full of nutrients! —CP

MAKES 16

1 cup (240 g) cooked kabocha squash

1 tsp (5 ml) coconut oil, for roasting squash

5 eggs, whites and yolks separated

¾ cup (190 g) creamy almond butter

⅓ cup (80 ml) coconut milk

1 tsp (5 ml) vanilla extract

1 tsp (3 g) ground cinnamon

½ tsp ground nutmeg

¼ tsp ground cloves

⅛ tsp ground ginger

¼ tsp Celtic sea salt

2 tbsp (30 g) butter, for greasing griddle

Preheat oven to 375°F (190°C, or gas mark 5). Line a baking sheet with parchment paper.

Using a sharp knife, carefully cut squash in half and quarters. Grease orange side of squash with a thin layer of coconut oil. Roast for 40 minutes. Allow to cool before removing squash from their skins and mashing.

Heat a griddle to medium heat.

Separate the eggs, putting the whites in one bowl and the yolks in another. Use a hand blender to whip the egg whites until soft peaks begin to form.

Add squash, almond butter, milk, vanilla and spices to bowl with egg yolks. Use a hand blender to blend to a smooth batter. Fold egg whites into the yolk mixture and lightly mix to a form a fluffy batter.

Melt a small amount of butter on griddle and spoon batter onto hot griddle.

Cook for about 2 to 3 minutes, flip, then continue to cook on the other side. Pancakes will be soufflé like yet should still be cooked thoroughly. Repeat process with remaining batter.

Serve with butter, maple syrup, whipped cream and a side of bacon.

CHEF'S TIP:

These pancakes take a while to cook so be patient before flipping. If your griddle is the right heat, the batter should slightly sizzle when dropped onto the buttered griddle. Pancakes store well in refrigerator and freezer, wrapped between layers of parchment paper. I usually save the rest of the squash in the freezer to make another batch of pancakes later.

PUMPKIN SPICE PANCAKES

The addition of the pumpkin purée really makes for a heartier, fluffier pancake when compared to plain coconut flour pancakes. These are a great breakfast to serve for a lazy autumn Saturday morning! —HH

SERVES 2–3

¼ cup (30 g) coconut flour

⅓ cup (85 g) pumpkin purée

1 tsp (3 g) pumpkin pie spice

¼ tsp sea salt

¼ tsp vanilla

3 eggs

½ tsp baking soda

¼ tsp apple cider vinegar

2 tbsp (30 ml) full-fat coconut milk

1 tbsp (12 g) coconut sugar

2 tbsp (30 g) coconut oil or ghee, for greasing

Mix together all ingredients except the oil and blend with an immersion blender or food processor. Make sure that there are no lumps of the pumpkin in the batter. Heat the coconut oil or ghee in a skillet over medium heat (I like to use a cast iron griddle). Wait a moment for the pan to heat up. Place about ⅓ cup (80 ml) or less of batter in the skillet and slightly flatten and round with a spoon. Let cook for a few minutes or until the pancake has firmed a little, then flip with a spatula. Repeat for the remaining batter. Enjoy just plain or with maple syrup!

PEACH COBBLER PANCAKES

These pancakes are topped with warm peaches and a crunchy cobbler. It's a combination of my favorite breakfast item and a traditional peach cobbler dessert. —RM

SERVES 2

FOR THE PEACH TOPPING

3–4 peaches, peeled and sliced

¼ cup (60 ml) water

1 tbsp (15 ml) maple syrup

½ tsp lemon juice

¼ tsp ground cinnamon

1 tsp (3 g) coconut flour

FOR THE PANCAKES

½ cup (120 g) almond butter

2 tbsp (16 g) coconut flour

1 tbsp (8 g) ground flax seed

¼ tsp baking soda

½ tsp ground cinnamon

¾ cup (180 ml) egg whites (from about large 4 eggs)

2 tbsp (30 ml) maple syrup

½ tsp vanilla extract

FOR THE COBBLER TOPPING

2 Caramel Shortbread Cookies (page 342), crumbled

Butter or ghee for pancakes

In a small saucepan over medium heat, combine peach topping ingredients except the coconut flour. Simmer for 10 to 15 minutes until the water reduces by half, then stir in the coconut flour and reduce heat to warm.

Heat a large skillet over medium-low heat. Stir together the dry pancake ingredients in a mixing bowl. Then whisk in the wet pancake ingredients until smooth. Test a small dollop of pancake mix on the skillet. It should lightly sizzle and then small air bubbles will appear on the surface, about 2 to 3 minutes per side. Adjust your heat if you have to: it shouldn't burn too quickly nor take too long to cook.

Make the pancakes about 4 inches (10 cm) in diameter. Flip once bubbles form on one side. Cook for another minute before removing from heat. Slather some butter or ghee on each pancake before stacking. Top pancake stacks with the warm peaches and then crumble cookies on top. Serve immediately.

CHEF'S TIP:

I like to store my pancakes on an oven-safe plate inside a warm oven. It keeps them nice and toasty until all the pancakes are finished cooking. Lightly buttering each pancake also keeps them moist.

MAPLE BACON PANCAKES

Dipping bacon in pancake syrup is a must, so naturally combining these two sweet and savory flavors into one dish just makes sense. —RM

SERVES 2

5 pieces of bacon

½ cup (120 g) almond butter

¾ cup (180 ml) egg whites (from about 4 eggs)

2 tbsp (30 ml) maple syrup, plus ¼ cup (60 ml) for topping

2 tbsp (16 g) coconut flour

1 tbsp (8 g) ground flax seed

¼ tsp baking soda

Butter, for topping

Fry the bacon until crispy. Reserve on the side on paper napkins and pour off the leftover bacon grease for future use. Turn the skillet down to medium-low.

Mix all the wet ingredients together in a medium-sized mixing bowl. Add the dry ingredients and whisk to combine. Cut up the fried bacon into small pieces, dumping half into the wet pancake batter and mixing thoroughly. The second half will be mixed into ¼ cup (60 ml) of maple syrup in a small bowl for topping.

Test a tiny bit of pancake batter on the skillet to check temperature. Use about 2 tablespoons (30 g) of batter to make small pancakes. Cook for 2 to 3 minutes on one side until you see bubbles and then flip, cooking for another 1 to 2 minutes. Times may vary depending on your stove. Serve hot with grass-fed butter and the mixed bacon maple syrup on top.

CHEF'S TIP:

It's easier to pour the batter first, then spread it out with a spoon making them 4 inches (10 cm) in diameter. The ending result is a thinner, rounder pancake.

BEST GINGERBREAD PANCAKES

These are the best Paleo pancakes to serve during the holiday season. They are light and fluffy and bursting with traditional gingerbread flavor. —RM

SERVES 2

½ cup (60 g) almond flour

2 tbsp (16 g) coconut flour

1 tbsp (8 g) ground flax seed

Pinch of salt

¼ tsp baking soda

½ tsp ground cloves

½ tbsp (4 g) ground ginger, plus more for garnish

½ tbsp (4 g) ground cinnamon, plus more for garnish

½ tbsp (4 g) ground nutmeg

¾ cup (180 ml) egg whites

2 tbsp (30 ml) raw honey

½ tsp bourbon vanilla extract

Coconut oil, for cooking

¼ cup (60 ml) Grade B maple syrup, for garnish

Mixed roasted holiday nuts (pecans, cashews, chestnuts)

Heat a griddle over medium-low heat. Mix all dry ingredients in one bowl and all wet ingredients in a separate bowl. Whisk to combine.

Drizzle some coconut oil on the griddle before ladling out ¼ cup (60 g) of batter per pancake. You will have to spread the batter thinly and evenly on the griddle, making it circular, in order to have thin pancakes. Flip after 2 to 3 minutes on one side, and then cook for another minute on the other. These pancakes can burn easily if you are not careful.

Add a dash each of ginger and cinnamon to the maple syrup. Garnish with mixed holiday nuts and Ginger Cinnamon Maple Syrup. Serve immediately.

BLUEBERRY COBBLER PANCAKES

These light and airy medallions aren't your ordinary blueberry pancakes. They are topped with a warm blueberry compote with a crumb cobbler topping. It's traditional taste with a modern twist. —RM

SERVES 2

FOR THE BLUEBERRY SPREAD

1½ cups (225 g) blueberries

2 tbsp (24 g) coconut sugar

1 tsp (5 ml) lemon juice

1 tsp (3 g) tapioca starch

FOR THE PANCAKES

½ cup (60 g) almond flour

¼ cup (30 g) tapioca starch

2 tbsp (16 g) coconut flour

2 tbsp (24 g) coconut sugar

1 tbsp (8 g) ground flax seed

1 tsp (3 g) ground cinnamon

¼ tsp baking soda

Pinch of salt

¾ cup (180 ml) egg whites (from about 4 large egg)

1 tbsp (15 ml) coconut oil, plus extra for skillet

½ tsp vanilla extract

FOR THE COBBLER TOPPING

1½ tbsp (12 g) ground flax

1 tbsp (8 g) sliced almonds

1 tbsp (8 g) chopped pecans

½ tbsp (7.5 ml) honey

Dash ground cinnamon

In a small saucepan, combine all of the blueberry spread ingredients and cook for 5 minutes over medium heat, until the blueberries have broken down and the spread has thickened. Keep warm on the side.

Heat a large flat skillet to medium-low heat. Whisk all of the pancake ingredients together in a large mixing bowl. Grease the pan with coconut oil. Test a small dollop of pancake batter on the skillet, and adjust the heat if necessary. Pour 2 tablespoons (30 g) worth of batter at a time and use a spatula to spread the pancakes into thin circles. Cook for 2 minutes, until air bubbles come to the surface. Flip the pancake and cook for another minute. Fry the pancakes in small batches, and keep the cooked pancakes on a pan in a warm oven.

After finishing the batter, quickly combine all of the cobbler topping ingredients in a small bowl and then cook for 4 minutes in the same greased skillet, stirring constantly. Pour a heaping serving of blueberry spread on top of the pancakes, and then crumble the cobbler topping. Serve immediately.

ROSE WATER CHAI PANCAKES

Adding chai tea and rose water to these pancakes turns them into a deliciously exotic treat! Enjoy them warm with some homemade Rose Water Mixed Berry Chia Jam (page 195) on top. —NK

SERVES 4

3 eggs

2 cups (240 g) almond flour

½ cup (120 ml) almond milk

¾ cup (180 ml) cooled chai tea (made from 3 chai tea bags)

1 tsp (3 g) baking powder

1 tsp (3 g) ground cinnamon

1 tsp (5 ml) vanilla extract

1 tsp (5 ml) rose water

3 tbsp (45 ml) raw honey or maple syrup

2 tbsp (30 g) ghee

(continued)

Add eggs to a large mixing bowl and whisk. Sift in the almond flour, then add the almond milk, cooled chai tea, baking powder, cinnamon, vanilla extract, rose water, honey or maple syrup. Mix well and let the batter rest for 10 minutes. Heat up a medium skillet over medium-high heat and add 1 tablespoon (15 g) ghee. Once the skillet is heated, take ¼ cup (60 ml) measure of the batter and pour into the skillet. When the batter starts to bubble on top, about 2 to 3 minutes, carefully flip the pancakes over and cook for another 2 minutes or so on the other side. Continue until the batter is finished.

COCONUT BERRY PANCAKE

Pancake for one? This simple to make pancake can be made in no time at all and enjoyed as a special treat just by you. —NK

SERVES 1

1 ripe banana

2 eggs

2 tbsp (30 ml) coconut cream

1 tsp (3 g) ground cinnamon

¼ tsp ground nutmeg

¼ tsp ground cardamom

¼ tsp sea salt

1 tbsp (15 ml) coconut oil

¼ cup (38 g) mixed fresh berries, to top

Raw honey or maple syrup, to top

Place banana, eggs, coconut cream, cinnamon, nutmeg, cardamom and sea salt into a blender or food processor and mix well. Heat a medium skillet over medium-low heat and add the coconut oil. Once heated pour in the pancake batter and allow to cook on one side for 3 to 4 minutes or until done. Flip over the pancake and continue to cook the other side until done. Transfer to a plate and top with berries and a drizzle of raw honey or maple syrup.

PUMPKIN SPICE DUTCH BABY

I grew up eating Dutch Babies in Northern Europe. I was excited to create a Paleo version that is just as light and fluffy. The trick to a perfect Dutch Baby is a scorching hot skillet. —KH

SERVES 4–6

5 eggs

¾ cup (180 ml) dairy-free milk of choice

¾ cup (188 g) cooked, puréed pumpkin

¾ cup (90 g) almond flour

½ tsp sea salt

½ tsp ground cinnamon

¼ tsp ground ginger

⅛ tsp ground cloves

½ tsp vanilla extract

3 tbsp (45 g) butter or ghee

A big handful of chocolate chips, for garnish

Preheat the oven to 450°F (230°C, or gas mark 8) and place skillet into oven. Combine eggs and milk in a large bowl and whisk vigorously. Add pumpkin purée, almond flour, salt, spices and vanilla extract. Mix well to thoroughly combine.

Remove skillet from oven. Drop in ghee or butter and return to oven for 2 to 3 minutes, until completely melted. Remove skillet from oven and pour pumpkin spiced batter into skillet. Do not stir. The butter/ghee will pool on top of the batter. Place back in oven. Bake for 16 to 20 minutes, until turning golden brown and slightly crispy at edges. Throw a handful of chocolate chips on top and serve warm.

ORANGE BLOSSOM AND WALNUT DUTCH BABY PANCAKE

This delightful fluffy pancake made in a searing hot cast iron skillet, infused with orange blossom and topped with crunch walnuts and citrusy orange zest will make a treat you won't soon forget. —NK

SERVES 6–8

6 eggs

1 cup (235 ml) light coconut milk

1 tsp (5 ml) orange blossom water

3 tbsp (45 ml) raw honey

¼ cup (30 g) coconut flour

¼ cup (30 g) tapioca flour

½ tsp baking soda

¼ tsp sea salt

1 tsp (3 g) orange zest

1 tbsp (15 g) ghee

Crushed walnuts, to garnish

Preheat oven to 500°F (250°C, or gas mark 10). Once the oven has preheated place a 12-inch (30.5-cm) cast iron skillet in the middle rack of the oven to heat up for 10 minutes. Place eggs, coconut milk, orange blossom water and honey into a blender. Blend until well mixed. Add in coconut flour, tapioca flour, baking soda and sea salt. Blend again until ingredients are well mixed. Stir in the orange zest.

After 10 minutes carefully remove the cast iron skillet and close the oven door. Quickly add in the ghee to the hot skillet. When melted, pour in the pancake batter. Carefully place back in the oven and bake for 10 minutes or until the pancake has puffed up and has a golden color to it. Carefully remove from the oven and allow to cool for a few minutes. To serve, add some crushed walnuts on top and serve warm.

CHERRY CLAFOUTIS

Clafoutis is a traditional French baked pastry studded with sweet cherries and covered in a buttery, custard-like batter. This sweet breakfast or dessert is simple to make but has a rich and gourmet flavor, making it a great option to serve when guests are over. Top with a drizzle of maple syrup or a spoonful of fluffy whipped cream. —CP

SERVES 4

1 pound (454 g) fresh cherries

6 eggs

1 cup (235 ml) coconut milk

¼ cup (30 g) coconut flour, sifted

2 tbsp (30 ml) maple syrup

1 tsp (5 ml) vanilla extract

2 tbsp (30 g) butter

1 tbsp (12 g) maple sugar, for dusting

⅓ cup (40 g) slivered almonds, toasted

Whipped cream, to garnish (optional)

Preheat oven to 350°F (180°C, or gas mark 4).

Pit cherries and slice in half. Set aside. In a large mixing bowl, use a hand blender to mix together eggs, milk, flour, syrup and vanilla to a smooth batter.

On the stove, warm a large oven-proof skillet to low heat. Melt butter in skillet, spreading the butter around the bottom and up the sides of pan.

Pour the batter into the skillet and turn stove heat off. Arrange cherries evenly throughout the pan.

Bake 13 to 17 minutes or until the middle is cooked through. As it comes out of the oven, sprinkle with maple sugar and slivered almonds. Slice and serve garnished with whipped cream, fresh cherries and an extra drizzle of maple syrup if desired.

CARROT PANCAKES WITH ALMOND BUTTER

Eating Paleo doesn't mean not being able to enjoy old favorites like pancakes on occasion. These carrot pancakes are simple to make, have classic flavors like cinnamon, nutmeg and clove, and can be made sweetener-free. —NK

SERVES 4

½ cup (120 g) puréed carrots

4 eggs

1 tsp (5 ml) vanilla extract

2 tsp (6 g) ground cinnamon

¼ tsp ground nutmeg

¼ tsp ground cloves

¼ tsp sea salt

2 tbsp (16 g) coconut flour

¼ tsp baking soda

Coconut oil or ghee for greasing the pan

Almond Butter (page 506), to serve

Raw honey or maple syrup, to sweeten, optional

Add the carrot, eggs, vanilla, cinnamon, nutmeg, cloves, sea salt, coconut flour and baking soda to a food processor. Process until the ingredients are well mixed. Transfer the mixture to a mixing bowl.

Heat a large skillet over medium heat and add some coconut oil or ghee. Once heated, add ¼-cup (60-ml) scoops of the pancake mix in batches to the pan. Cook on one side for 3 to 4 minutes before flipping over to cook the other side for another few minutes. To serve add some almond butter on top and sweetener of your choice, if desired.

PUMPKIN PIE SPICE SQUASH CREPES

I remember the first time I tried a crepe. I was instantly hooked on the light and airy taste and I quickly replaced my love of pancakes with them. Of course back then I was eating crepes filled with gluten and topped with all sorts of sugary concoctions, so I'm happy that I now have a Paleo friendly version like these Pumpkin Pie Spice Squash Crepes, flavored with warming spices like cinnamon, nutmeg and cloves, which I can enjoy on special occasions. —NK

SERVES 3

¾ cup (90 g) arrowroot flour

3 tbsp (24 g) squash flour

1 tsp (3 g) ground cinnamon

¼ tsp ground nutmeg

⅛ tsp ground cloves

⅛ tsp ground allspice

⅛ tsp ground ginger

¼ tsp sea salt

2 eggs, whisked

1 cup (235 ml) canned full-fat coconut milk

1 tsp (5 ml) vanilla extract

2 tbsp (30 ml) raw honey

Ghee or coconut oil, for frying

In a medium-sized mixing bowl, sift the arrowroot flour and squash flour. Add the cinnamon, nutmeg, cloves, allspice, ginger and sea salt and mix. In another medium-sized mixing bowl, add the eggs, coconut milk, vanilla extract and raw honey and mix. Add the egg mixture into the dry ingredients and use a whisk to mix everything together until well incorporated.

Heat an 8-inch (20-cm) skillet over medium-low heat, add some ghee or coconut oil. Swirl the skillet so the cooking fat spreads evenly around the skillet. Once the skillet is heated, pour in ⅓ cup (80 ml) of the batter. Immediately swirl the skillet around so that the batter completely covers the bottom of the skillet. Cook on one side for around 2 minutes or until you see the edges of the crepe browning. Carefully flip over and cook on the other side for 1 to 2 minutes before transferring to a paper towel-lined plate. Continue this process until the batter is finished. You may have to add a little more cooking oil as you cook the crepes. Serve warm topped with some apples and a dusting of cinnamon or with a topping of your choice.

CHEF'S TIP:

Squash flour can be purchased online or you can use coconut flour in place of the squash flour.

CREAMY HERBED CREPES

Most crepes have a sweet element to them. I don't have much of a sweet tooth so I thought I would try to make a crepe that played up the savory, herbal notes you'd find in a great garden. This crepe delivers just that. Enjoy! —VM

SERVES 4

FOR THE CREPES

8 eggs

1 cup (235 ml) unsweetened coconut milk

3 tbsp (24 g) coconut flour

1 tsp (6 g) sea salt

Coconut oil for frying

FOR THE FILLING

1 ounce (28 g) butter

1 clove garlic, finely chopped

2 tbsp coconut flour

1 cup (235 ml) coconut cream

½ tsp sea salt

Freshly ground white pepper

1 sprig of fresh rosemary, finely chopped

1 small bunch of fresh parsley, finely chopped

1 small bunch of fresh basil, finely chopped

Preheat the oven to 350°F (180°C, or gas mark 4). Mix all of the ingredients for the crepes in a bowl until a smooth batter has formed.

Heat the coconut oil in a non-stick skillet over medium heat. Pour 3 to 4 tablespoons (45 to 60 ml) of batter onto the skillet, swirling the batter around to cover the surface evenly. Cook the crepe for 1 to 2 minutes, or until golden brown.

Flip the crepe and cook 1 minute on the other side. Repeat this process until you have made as many crepes as you can.

In a separate saucepan, melt the butter with the garlic. Add the coconut flour and let it brown for a few minutes with the butter. Add the coconut cream and mix well. Cook the sauce until it begins to simmer, stirring frequently, about 5 minutes. As the sauce begins to reach a boil, remove the sauce from the heat and season with salt and pepper. Add the herbs and mix well.

Place a crepe in a greased baking dish, fill it with 2 tablespoons (30 ml) of filling and fold closed. Repeat the process until you have filled all of the crepes.

Place the dish in the oven for about 5 minutes to warm, and then serve immediately!

STUFFED BANANA FRENCH TOAST

Slices of banana are sandwiched snuggly between layers of sunflower butter and French toast. The most decadent of all brunch items, this dish is sure to wow any houseguest in the morning. —RM

SERVES 6

1 loaf Easy and Amazing Banana Bread (page 526)

Crunchy sunflower butter

1 banana, thinly sliced

Coconut oil for skillet

4 eggs

¼ cup (60 ml) almond milk or any milk alternative

½ tbsp (4 g) ground cinnamon

1 tsp (5 ml) vanilla extract

Maple syrup, for topping

Butter, for topping

Slice bread loaf evenly into twelve slices to make six stuffed sandwiches.

Take two pieces of bread, spreading about 1 tablespoon (15 g) of sunflower butter on one and covering the other one with thin slices of banana. Assemble. Repeat until you have six sandwiches.

Heat a skillet over medium heat with a tablespoon (15 g) of coconut oil. In a wide shallow bowl, whisk eggs, almond milk, cinnamon, and vanilla together. Making one at a time, submerge the sandwich into the egg mixture coating thoroughly. Immediately set it on the skillet, cooking on both sides for about 4 minutes.

Repeat until all stuffed French toasts are cooked. Add a pad of butter and drizzle with pure maple syrup.

CHEF'S TIP:

Sub out the banana slices for 1½ tablespoons (23 g) grape preserves per sandwich for stuffed sunflower butter & jelly French toast treat.

PUMPKIN FRENCH TOAST

Pumpkin and fall spices meet grain- and nut-free sandwich bread for the perfect autumn flavored French toast. A Paleo-friendly, healthy comfort food breakfast, whipped cream not optional! —CP

SERVES 6

3 eggs

¾ cup (180 ml) coconut milk

⅔ cup (165 g) pumpkin purée

3 tbsp (45 ml) maple syrup

1 tbsp (15 ml) vanilla extract

1 tbsp (8 g) ground cinnamon

½ tsp ground nutmeg

¼ tsp ground cardamom

¼ tsp ground cloves

Grain- and nut-free sandwich bread

2 tbsp (30 g) butter, for melting on griddle

FOR THE TOPPING

Whipped cream or coconut whipped cream butter

Maple syrup

Chopped pecans

Bacon slices

Heat a large griddle or skillet to medium heat.

Make the milk batter by blending together all ingredients, except the bread and butter. Slice bread into thin slices about ½-inch (1.3-cm) thick.

Place the bread in a large rectangular dish—a 9 × 13–inch (23 × 33–cm) baking dish works well. Pour milk batter on top, covering all toast slices. Allow the toast to soak for 1 to 2 minutes per side, for about 3 to 4 minutes total.

Melt a pat of butter on griddle. If the griddle is hot enough, butter should sizzle slightly. Place toast slices on the hot griddle, cooking for about a minute or until golden brown then rotating to the other side to continue cooking. Repeat process to cook the remaining toast.

Serve warm garnished with toppings of your choosing.

CHEF'S TIP:

If your sandwich bread is a few days old, let it soak in the milk batter for a few extra minutes.

PUMPKIN SPICE WAFFLES

A healthy twist on the classic autumn favorite, these pumpkin waffles are made nut-free with coconut flour and sweetened entirely with applesauce. Serve with butter, whipped maple nut butter or even whipped coconut cream for a fall-flavored breakfast treat. —CP

MAKES 6

½ cup (60 g) coconut flour, sifted

½ tsp baking soda

1½ tsp (4.5 g) ground cinnamon

½ tsp ground nutmeg

¼ tsp ground ginger

Pinch of ground cloves

¼ tsp sea salt

6 eggs, whites and yolks separated

1 cup (250 g) pumpkin purée

⅔ cup (160 ml) coconut milk

⅔ cup (165 g) applesauce

6 tbsp (90 ml) butter, melted

1 tsp (5 ml) vanilla extract

Coconut oil, for greasing waffle maker

Turn on the waffle maker and warm to medium-low heat.

In a large mixing bowl, sift together all dry ingredients. Using a hand blender, whip egg whites until stiff peaks begin to form.

Combine the wet ingredients with the egg yolks and blend. Add the wet to the dry and blend until a smooth batter forms. Slowly fold together the egg whites and waffle batter, being careful to not completely flatten the fluffy egg whites.

Lightly brush the heated waffle maker with coconut oil and scoop batter into center of mold. Fill the waffle iron about half full as the batter will spread as it cooks. Cook the waffles until ready, about 1 to 2 minutes, then repeat with remaining batter.

Serve hot with butter, maple syrup and a dollop of whipped cream.

CHEF'S TIP:
These are best cooked slowly on low heat—I use heat settings between 2 and 3. I use a thin circular waffle maker, so if using a thicker, Belgian-style waffle maker, the cooking time may vary.

MINI BLUEBERRY BREAD

Everything is cuter in mini form! For this Mini Blueberry Bread, I use tiny bread pans to create a perfect rounded top. Each loaf can be frozen and then defrosted at a later time for a more personalized treat. —RM

SERVES 8

1½ cups (180 g) almond flour

¾ cup (90 g) arrowroot powder

¼ cup (30 g) golden flaxseed meal

½ tsp baking soda

⅛ tsp sea salt

4 eggs

1 tbsp (15 ml) lemon juice

1 tsp (5 ml) bourbon vanilla extract

3 tbsp (45 ml) raw honey

1 tsp (5 ml) apple cider vinegar

1 cup (150 g) blueberries

Preheat the oven to 350°F (180°C, or gas mark 4). In a medium mixing bowl, mix together all of the dry ingredients. In a separate mixing bowl, beat the eggs, lemon, vanilla extract, honey and vinegar for about 2 minutes with a whisk.

Mix the dry ingredients into the wet ingredients. Once smooth, fold the blueberries in gently. Divide the batter into three greased mini loaves—mine are about 3 × 5½-inches (7 × 14-cm). Set the three mini pans on a single baking sheet and bake for 25 to 30 minutes until the tops are golden and a toothpick comes out clean when inserted into the center.

Serve warm with honey butter or coconut butter.

CHEF'S TIP:
You can bake this recipe in a standard loaf pan for 35 minutes, although it will be shorter in height.

RASPBERRY CACAO NIB BREAKFAST BUNDT CAKES

Breakfast Bundt cakes made with coconut flour and studded with sweet red raspberries will have you eating cake for breakfast. Crunchy cacao nibs give these little cakes a rich flavor finished with a drizzle of sweet honey glaze. —CP

MAKES 8

Coconut oil or butter, for greasing

6 eggs

½ cup (120 g) whole milk, plain yogurt or coconut yogurt

6 tbsp (90 g) butter, melted

¼ cup (60 ml) + 1 tbsp (15 ml) raw honey

1 tsp (5 ml) vanilla extract

¾ cup (90 g) coconut flour, sifted

¾ tsp baking soda

⅓ cup cacao nibs

8 ounces (227 g) fresh raspberries

HONEY BUTTER GLAZE

2 tbsp (30 ml) raw honey

2 tbsp (30 g) butter

Preheat oven to 350°F (180°C, or gas mark 4). Generously grease mini Bundt pans with coconut oil or butter.

In a mixing bowl, blend together eggs, yogurt, butter, honey and vanilla. Sift in coconut flour and baking soda. Scrape down the sides of the bowl and blend until smooth. Fold in cacao nibs and raspberries, stirring just until raspberries are crushed and release their color and juice.

Spoon batter into mini Bundt cake pans, filling two-thirds full. Bake for 23 to 27 minutes or until a tester comes out clean. Cool for 10 minutes before inverting onto a cooling rack.

While the cakes are cooling, make the glaze by melting together honey and butter. Remove from heat and allow to cool and thicken for a few minutes. Drizzle over warm cakes, serve and enjoy!

ORANGE POPPY SEED BUNDT CAKES

Grain- and gluten-free orange poppy seed Bundt cakes make for a sweet breakfast bread. Sweetened with fresh juice and raw honey, these mini grain-free Bundt cakes are moist and delicious with each bite. —CP

MAKES 8

Coconut oil or butter, for greasing

6 eggs

½ cup (120 g) whole milk, plain yogurt or coconut yogurt

½ cup (120 ml) fresh orange juice

4 tbsp (60 ml) butter, melted

4 tbsp (60 ml) raw honey

¾ cup (90 g) coconut flour, sifted

¾ tsp baking soda

1 tsp (3 g) orange zest

1 tbsp (8 g) poppy seeds

FOR THE ORANGE HONEY GLAZE

4 tbsp (60 g) butter

2 tbsp (30 ml) fresh orange juice

2 tbsp (30 ml) raw honey

Preheat oven to 350°F (180°C, or gas mark 4). Generously grease mini Bundt pans with coconut oil or butter.

In a large mixing bowl, blend together eggs, yogurt, juice, butter and honey. Sift in coconut flour and baking soda. Blend until a smooth batter forms, scraping down the sides of bowl with a spatula. Fold in zest and poppy seeds.

Spoon batter into mini Bundt cake pans, filling two-thirds full. Bake for 22 to 25 minutes or until a tester comes out clean. Cool for 5 to 10 minutes before inverting on a cooling rack.

While the cakes are cooling, melt together glaze ingredients in a small saucepan. Bring the glaze to a simmer and simmer for 5 minutes. Set aside to cool as it will thicken as it cools.

Slowly pour glaze over cakes in small amounts, allowing the glaze to soak into the cakes. Best served slightly warm.

Bundt cakes can be made ahead of time and stored in an airtight container. Simply heat in the oven and pour warm glaze over when ready to serve.

Coconut flour can be very dense but allowing the glaze to slowly soak into the cakes makes for a sweet, luscious taste with every bite.

STRAWBERRY BREAKFAST CAKE WITH A CINNAMON CRUNCH TOPPING

This breakfast cake pairs well with your morning tea or coffee for an early morning treat. You can use fresh or frozen strawberries. —KW

SERVES 6

6 eggs

¼ cup (60 ml) coconut oil or butter, melted

¼ cup (60 ml) pure raw honey or pure maple syrup

½ cup (120 ml) coconut milk or milk of choice

1 tbsp (15 ml) pure vanilla extract

½ cup (60 g) coconut flour

1 tsp (3 g) baking soda

¼ tsp sea salt

1½ cups (225 g) strawberries, diced (reserve ½ cup [75 g] for topping)

FOR THE CINNAMON CRUNCH TOPPING

1 cup (150 g) nuts/seeds of choice

½ cup (40 g) shredded unsweetened coconut flakes

2 tbsp (30 ml) honey

2 tbsp (30 g) butter or coconut oil

1 tbsp (8 g) ground cinnamon

Pinch of sea salt

Preheat oven to 350°F (180°C, or gas mark 4). In a large bowl, mix together the eggs, oil or butter, honey, milk and vanilla. Add the coconut flour, baking soda and salt and stir until combined. Fold in 1 cup (150 g) of the strawberries. Pour into a lightly greased 8 × 8-inch (20 × 20-cm) baking pan.

To make the cinnamon crunch topping, combine all the ingredients in a bowl and mix well. Place spoonfuls of the topping all over the top. Finally, add ½ cup (75 g) of the diced strawberries over the top. Bake for 45 minutes or until center is cooked through.

CHEF'S TIP:
If you need to bake it longer than 45 minutes, you may need to add foil to the top so the topping doesn't burn.

ORANGE POPPY SEED FLAX MUFFINS

These grain-free orange poppy seed flax muffins are light and sweet from a combination of orange juice and honey. —RB

MAKES 8

2 tbsp (30 ml) coconut oil, plus more for greasing pan

½ cup (75 g) golden flax meal

¼ cup (30 g) coconut flour

¼ cup (30 g) arrowroot starch

1 tsp (3 g) baking soda

2 tsp (4.5 g) cream of tartar

2 tbsp (16 g) poppy seeds

¼ tsp salt

¼ cup (60 ml) honey

½ cup (120 ml) orange juice

4 eggs, room temperature

(continued)

Preheat oven to 375°F (190°C, or gas mark 5). Grease a muffin tin with coconut oil or prep with muffin liners.

In a medium mixing bowl, combine flax meal, coconut flour, arrowroot starch, baking soda, cream of tartar, poppy seeds and salt.

In a small mixing bowl, combine 2 tablespoons (30 ml) of coconut oil, honey and orange juice.

Crack the eggs and separate the egg whites into a medium mixing bowl, add the egg yolks to the honey mixture. Whip the egg whites using a hand mixer until soft peaks form.

Work the honey mixture into the dry mixture, and mix that into the whipped whites. Spoon the batter into the prepared muffin tin, then bake for 40 minutes, until the muffins are browned on the top and a tester inserted comes out clean.

CINNAMON VANILLA MUFFINS

These Cinnamon Vanilla Muffins are a great low-sugar addition to any breakfast. Despite using only coconut flour, which can sometimes be too dense, these muffins have a nice fluffy and moist texture. —HH

SERVES 6

¼ cup (60 ml) coconut oil

½ cup (60 g) coconut flour

½ tsp baking soda

¼ tsp sea salt

1½ tsp (4.5 g) ground ginger, optional

1½ tsp (7.5 ml) vanilla extract

2 tbsp (30 ml) raw honey

½ cup (120 ml) + 2 tbsp (30 ml) coconut milk

4 eggs

½ tsp apple cider vinegar

1½ tsp (4.5 g) ground cinnamon + extra for dusting

Preheat the oven to 350°F (180°C, or gas mark 4). Melt the coconut oil and combine with all the remaining muffin ingredients. Blend in a food processor or bowl, mixing until smooth. Place batter in a muffin tin lined with muffin liners. The muffins will rise a very small amount, so you can fill the muffin liner about three-quarters full, almost to the top.

Before you place the muffins into the oven, sprinkle each muffin top with a bit of cinnamon. Bake for about 20 to 30 minutes or until a toothpick inserted comes out clean and the tops are slightly browned and hardened. Make sure you let the muffin cool before eating. If you try to eat it without letting it cool, it may crumble.

CHEF'S TIP:

This recipe is very low-sugar and is not very sweet. If you prefer a sweeter muffin add 2 more tablespoons (30 ml) of honey or maple syrup. When working with coconut flour, the batter will be much thicker than traditional muffin batter— this is normal. Do not add more moisture as it will ruin the muffin consistency.

CRANBERRY MUFFINS

These Cranberry Muffins are a delicious sweet snack without much sugar . . . just a touch of honey! The addition of the tart cranberries adds a nice sour pop that contrasts nicely with the sweet muffin. —HH

SERVES 4

¼ cup (60 ml) coconut oil

½ cup (60 g) coconut flour

½ tsp baking soda

Scant ¼ tsp sea salt

1½ tsp (4.5 g) ground ginger, optional

1 tsp (5 ml) vanilla extract

2 tbsp (30 ml) raw honey

½ cup (120 ml) + 2 tbsp (30 ml) coconut milk

4 eggs

½ tsp apple cider vinegar

½ cup (55 g) fresh cranberries—you can also use whole, frozen cranberries but do not use dried cranberries

Preheat the oven to 350°F (180°C, or gas mark 4). Melt the coconut oil and combine with all the remaining muffin ingredients except the fresh cranberries. Blend in a food processor or bowl until smooth. With a spoon or spatula, gently fold the cranberries into the batter. I use whole frozen cranberries and do not defrost them, and it turns out great. Place batter in a muffin tin lined with muffin liners. The muffins will rise a very small amount, so you can fill the muffin liner about three-quarters full. Bake for about 20 to 30 minutes or until a toothpick inserted comes out clean and the tops are slightly browned and hardened.

BLUEBERRY GINGER MUFFINS

Ginger adds the perfect amount of spice to complement the sweet flavor of these muffins. These are perfect to make in the summer when blueberries are plentiful and ripe. —KH

MAKES 10 REGULAR OR 24 MINI MUFFINS

5 tbsp (40 g) coconut flour

¼ tsp unrefined sea salt

¼ tsp baking soda

¼ cup (20 g) unsweetened shredded coconut

3 eggs

¼ cup (60 ml) maple syrup or honey

2 tbsp (30 ml) full-fat coconut milk

¼ cup (60 ml) coconut oil or ghee, melted

1 tsp (5 ml) vanilla extract

1 tbsp (8 g) grated fresh ginger

¾ cup (112 g) fresh blueberries

Preheat the oven to 350°F (180°C, or gas mark 4). Line muffin tins with 24 mini muffin liners or regular unbleached muffin liners.

Sift together coconut flour, salt and baking soda. Add shredded coconut. Set aside. Whisk eggs in a medium bowl. Add sweetener of choice, coconut milk, melted fat of choice, vanilla extract and grated ginger. Mix to combine. Then add the dry ingredients to the wet ingredients, and mix until thoroughly combined. Fold in the blueberries.

Bake mini muffins for 16 to 18 minutes and regular muffins for 22 to 24 minutes, until muffins are firm in the center and lightly golden.

PEACH MUFFINS

These summertime muffins are a perfect, portable breakfast or snack when on the go. You can make them with either coconut flour or almond flour (see Chef's Tip). Both variations are delicious. —KH

SERVES 9

½ cup (60 g) coconut flour, sifted

¼ tsp baking soda

½ tsp sea salt

4 eggs

½ cup (120 ml) ghee or coconut oil, melted

½ cup (120 ml) maple syrup or honey

½ tsp vanilla extract

1¼ cups (180 g) peeled, pitted and diced peaches, divided

Preheat the oven to 350°F (180°C, or gas mark 4) and line muffin tin with muffin liners.

Combine coconut flour, baking soda and salt in a small bowl. Set aside. In a large bowl, whisk together eggs, ghee/coconut oil, maple syrup and vanilla. Add dry to wet and mix again until thoroughly combined. Fold in 1 cup (150 g) of diced peaches.

Divide mixture evenly among nine muffin liners. Sprinkle remaining diced peaches on top of each muffin to make them pretty. Bake 25 to 27 minutes, or until toothpick comes out clean and muffins are golden.

CHEF'S TIP:

Almond flour variation: Substitute 2 cups (240 g) of blanched almond flour for coconut flour. Increase baking soda to 1 teaspoon (3 g). Add ½ cup (40 g) of unsweetened shredded coconut. Reduce to 3 eggs. Reduce bake time to 22 to 25 minutes. Makes 12 regular muffins.

CHOCOLATE WALNUT BUTTER MINI MUFFINS

These mini muffins are a decadent treat. Using the walnut butter adds moisture and a rich unique nutty flavor to the chocolate. —HH

MAKES 7–10

2 cups (300 g) walnuts

⅓ cup (40 g) cocoa powder

¼ cup (60 ml) raw honey

2 tbsp (30 ml) coconut oil

½ tsp baking soda

1 egg

Dash of salt

To start, make walnut butter paste in the food processor. Put the walnuts in the food processor and blend. At first it will become crumbly and look sort of like ground walnuts, but continue to blend, stopping along the way to scrape the sides, until it is a thick, nut butter paste-like consistency. It will be a little thicker than store-bought almond butter. Once you have the walnut paste, add all of the remaining ingredients to the food processor and blend.

Line a mini muffin tin with liners. I like to use silicone mini muffin liners, which makes it easier to remove the muffin from the liner once it's done. Make a ball the size of the mini muffin cup and put it in the liner. Bake at 350°F (180°C, or gas mark 4) for about 10 to 15 minutes or until firm.

CHOCOLATE MUFFINS

This coconut flour chocolate muffin recipe is a great healthy snack for when you have a chocolate craving or want something a little sweet! Sometimes, baking with coconut flour can result in a dense, dry baked good, but these muffins have a lighter, fluffier texture than most heavier coconut flour treats. —HH

SERVES 6

¼ cup (60 ml) coconut oil

½ cup (60 g) coconut flour

½ tsp baking soda

Dash salt

¼ cup (50 g) coconut sugar, use 2–4 tbsp (25–50 g) more if you like your muffins sweeter

2 tbsp (16 g) cacao powder or cocoa powder

1 tsp (5 ml) vanilla extract

⅔ cup (160 ml) coconut milk

4 eggs

1 tsp (5 ml) apple cider vinegar

Preheat the oven to 350°F (180°C, or gas mark 4). Melt the coconut oil and combine with remaining muffin ingredients in a food processor or bowl, mix well. Place batter in a lined muffin tin. The muffins will rise a small amount, so you can fill the muffin liner about three-quarters full. Bake for about 20 to 30 minutes or until a toothpick inserted comes out clean and the tops are slightly browned.

CARROT GINGER MUFFINS

This is hands down the best muffin recipe I have created. Perfectly moist without being dense and lightly sweet with just the right amount of spice. Go ahead. You will love them. —KH

MAKES 36 MINI OR 12 REGULAR

2 cups (240 g) blanched almond flour

½ tsp sea salt

1 tsp (3 g) baking soda

½ tsp allspice

½ tsp powdered ginger

Pinch of clove

½ cup (40 g) shredded coconut, unsweetened

3 eggs

½ cup (120 ml) coconut oil, melted

½ cup (120 ml) maple syrup or honey

1-2 tbsp (8-16 g) grated fresh ginger

1 cup (120 g) grated carrot

¾ cup (112 g) raisins, soaked in water for 10 minutes and drained

Preheat the oven to 350°F (180°C, or gas mark 4). In a large bowl, combine almond flour, salt, baking soda, spices and coconut shreds. In a smaller bowl, whisk together eggs, oil and syrup. Add fresh ginger, grated carrot and raisins. Stir wet ingredients into dry. Spoon batter into paper-lined muffin tins. Bake for 18 to 20 minutes for mini muffins and 24 to 26 minutes for regular muffins. Cool and serve.

BUTTERNUT SQUASH APPLE HAZELNUT MUFFINS

Spice muffins have always been one of my favorite muffins and these are made with squash and apples, the perfect way to get a serving of fruits and vegetables in a sweet form. Serve warm with a slice of butter and add a side of eggs and bacon for the perfect fall breakfast! —CP

MAKES 10

1 cup (250 g) butternut squash

1 cup (120 g) almond flour

½ cup (60 g) hazelnut flour

3 tbsp (36 g) + 1 tbsp (12 g) maple sugar, divided

1 tsp (3 g) baking soda

2 tsp (6 g) ground cinnamon

½ tsp ground nutmeg

¼ tsp ground cardamom

3 eggs

4 tbsp (60 ml) butter, melted

2 tsp (10 ml) vanilla extract

2 tsp (10 ml) lemon juice

1 apple, grated

Preheat oven to 350°F (180°C, or gas mark 4). Bring a small amount of water to a boil in a steamer pot. Generously grease muffin pan with butter or line with muffin liners.

Peel, seed and slice butternut squash. Place squash in the steamer basket and steam for 15 to 20 minutes or until tender to touch with a fork. Remove from steamer to allow any water to drain out so that the squash is not watery.

While the squash is cooking and cooling, sift together all dry ingredients: flours, 3 tablespoons (36 g) maple sugar, baking soda and spices.

In a separate bowl, combine all wet ingredients—eggs, butter, vanilla and lemon—blending with a hand blender.

Once squash is cool enough to touch, mash on a plate until smooth. Measure out a cup of squash and add to the bowl with wet ingredients and blend. Add the dry ingredients and blend until smooth, scraping down the sides of the bowl. Fold in grated apples.

Scoop batter into muffin pan, filling three-quarters full. Sprinkle remaining maple sugar on top. Bake for 30 to 35 minutes or until a tester comes out clean. Serve the muffins warm with butter.

PUMPKIN MUFFINS

These pumpkin muffins burst with fall flavors. They are loaded with healthy fats, fiber and protein that will leave you feeling satisfied and energized. Grab them for a light breakfast or an afternoon snack, or top them with Coconut Whipped Cream (page 504) for dessert. —AV

MAKES 12

½ cup (120 g) canned pumpkin purée (not pumpkin pie filling)

½ cup (120 ml) butter or palm shortening, melted

5 eggs, beaten

1 tsp (5 ml) vanilla

⅓ cup (80 ml) honey

½ cup (60 g) coconut flour

½ tsp ground cinnamon

½ tsp ground nutmeg

¼ tsp ground allspice

⅛ tsp ground cloves

¼ tsp sea salt

½ tsp baking soda

FOR THE TOPPING

½ tsp coconut sugar

½ tsp ground cinnamon

Preheat oven to 350°F (180°C, or gas mark 4). Place liners in the muffin pan and set aside. In a bowl, combine pumpkin, butter or palm shortening, eggs, vanilla and honey. Whisk until thoroughly mixed. In a small bowl, sift together coconut flour, spices and salt. Add the dry ingredients to the wet ingredients. Whisk to combine.

Let sit for 5 minutes to allow the coconut flour to absorb the wet ingredients. Add baking soda, stirring until baking soda is mixed through. Fill baking cups three-quarters full with the batter. Mix the coconut sugar and cinnamon together and sprinkle it on top of the muffins. Bake for 15 minutes or until a toothpick inserted in the center comes out clean. Allow muffins to cool for a few minutes by either removing them from the pan and setting them on a cooling rack or leaving them in the pan and tipping them on their sides.

PUMPKIN BANANA MINI FLOURLESS MUFFINS

These little flourless muffins are so great and are perfect for those who are sensitive to nuts or to coconut since they don't contain either flour. The texture is a little different than flour-based baked goods so these will be a little more gooey and rich. —HH

MAKES 12

3 tbsp (24 g) ground flax, soaked in 3 tbsp (45 ml) warm water

1 medium banana

¾ cup (195 g) cooked pumpkin or sweet potato, roasted and peeled

½ tsp baking soda

3 tbsp (24 g) arrowroot

½ tsp apple cider vinegar

1 tsp (3 g) pumpkin pie spice

1 tbsp (12 g) coconut sugar

Preheat oven to 325°F (170°C, or gas mark 3). In a small bowl mix the ground flax and warm water together and allow to jell. Mash the banana and pumpkin together in a separate bowl. Add remaining ingredients to the banana pumpkin mixture including the flax mixture. Make sure there are no lumps. I use an immersion blender to make mixing easier.

Place mini muffin liners in the mini muffin tin and scoop the batter into the muffin liners. You can fill it until the muffin liner is almost full with batter. It will rise a little bit, but not enough to overflow. Bake for about 30 minutes. Make sure you let the muffins cool to set before eating.

PUMPKIN CHOCOLATE CHIP MINI MUFFINS

These pumpkin chocolate chip mini muffins are a great treat or snack for the fall season. They are moist little bites with yummy pops of chocolatey sweetness! —HH

SERVES 12

¼ cup (30 g) coconut flour

⅓ cup (85 g) pumpkin purée

1 tsp (3 g) pumpkin pie spice

¼ tsp sea salt

¼ tsp vanilla

3 eggs

½ tsp baking soda

¼ tsp apple cider vinegar

2 tbsp (30 ml) full-fat coconut milk

1 tbsp (12 g) coconut sugar

⅓–½ cup (60–85 g) chocolate chips

Preheat the oven to 350°F (180°C, or gas mark 4). Mix together all the ingredients except for the chocolate chips and blend with an immersion blender or food processor. Make sure that there are no lumps of the pumpkin in the batter. Gently stir in the chocolate chips (you can put more or less depending on your preference). In a mini muffin tin lined with mini muffin liners scoop the batter into each muffin cup almost to the top. Bake for 10 to 20 minutes or until a toothpick inserted comes out clean.

CHEF'S TIP:

When working with coconut flour, the moisture level will be very different from regular muffin batter, so do not add or take anything away from the stated ingredients if it looks too dry—this is normal. This recipe only works with mini muffins, not regular sized muffin tins.

AUTUMN-SPICED, ALLERGY-FREE BREAKFAST COOKIES

I love eggs for breakfast, but on quick mornings these macaroon-like cookies are my favorite grab and go breakfast. These spiced breakfast cookies are free of allergens and make a great breakfast or lunchbox snack for the kids! A mixture of coconut and sunflower seeds packs these cookies with quality fats and proteins keeping you energized throughout the morning. —CP

MAKES 16

¾ cup (110 g) raw sunflower seed kernels, shells removed

2 tbsp (30 ml) coconut oil, melted

1 tbsp (15 ml) honey

¼ cup (60 g) applesauce

3 tbsp (45 ml) coconut milk

1 tbsp (15 ml) vanilla extract

1½ tsp (4.5 g) ground cinnamon

½ tsp ground nutmeg

½ tsp ground cardamom

¼ tsp salt

1½ cups (120 g) finely shredded coconut

½ cup (75 g) golden raisins

Preheat oven to 275°F (140°C, or gas mark 1). Line a baking sheet with parchment paper.

Add seeds, oil, honey, applesauce, coconut milk, vanilla and all spices to a food processor. Pulse several times, then scrape down the sides of the bowl to incorporate all ingredients. Blend again for about a minute until mixture begins to turn into a smooth paste, but not to the point of a nut butter consistency.

(continued)

Next, add shredded coconut and pulse again. Remove blade from food processor and fold in golden raisins. Alternatively, you can transfer batter to a clean bowl and fold in raisins.

Use a medium cookie scoop, about 1½ tablespoons (12 g) size, to scoop the batter, dragging along the side of the bowl to densely pack in the cookie batter. Drop onto parchment lined baking sheet. Bake for 32 to 36 minutes.

Serve fresh from the oven—or slightly chilled, my preferred way—with a hot cup of coffee or a glass of almond milk.

CHEF'S TIP:
These are breakfast cookies, so please note that they are not sweet like a dessert. They are very dense cookies and will not rise or expand. Cookies last in the fridge for about a week.

BLUEBERRY LEMON DONUTS

The flavor combination of blueberry and lemon was made for baked goods. These donuts are no exception. Going Paleo doesn't mean you have to miss out on enjoying a delicious donut! —RM

SERVES 6

FOR THE DONUTS

8 Medjool dates

3 eggs

¼ cup (60 ml) coconut oil, plus more for greasing

¼ cup (30 g) arrowroot flour

3 tbsp (24 g) coconut flour

1 tbsp (15 ml) honey

1 tbsp (15 ml) lemon juice

1 tsp (5 ml) vanilla

¼ tsp baking powder

Pinch salt

½ cup (75 g) blueberries

FOR THE ICING

¼ cup (60 g) palm shortening

3 tbsp (45 ml) raw honey

2 tbsp (30 ml) lemon juice

Zest from half a lemon

Preheat the oven to 350°F (180°C, or gas mark 4). Using a food processer, blend all of the donut ingredients, except the blueberries, for about 4 minutes. Scrape down the sides of the processor and blend until smooth. Gently mix the blueberries into the batter with a spatula.

Grease a donut pan with coconut oil. Fill each donut mold to the top. Bake for 20 minutes.

In a small mixing bowl, mix together all of the icing ingredients. Remove the baked donuts from the oven and let sit for 5 minutes. Pop out each donut from the pan and drizzle with the lemon icing.

PUMPKIN SPICE DONUTS WITH VANILLA GLAZE

A light pumpkin spice flavored donut dipped in sweet vanilla glaze for a classic fall favorite. Serve with a side of eggs, bacon and hot coffee for a delicious breakfast treat or top with a scoop of warm vanilla ice cream for dessert. —CP

MAKES 8

Coconut oil, for greasing donut pan

1 cup (120 g) almond flour

2 tbsp (24 g) coconut sugar

2 tsp (6 g) arrowroot powder

1 tsp (3 g) ground cinnamon

¼ tsp ground nutmeg

¼ tsp baking soda

2 eggs

4 tbsp (60 g) pumpkin purée

4 tbsp (60 g) butter, melted

1 tsp (5 ml) vanilla extract

4 tbsp (60 ml) butter, melted

1 tbsp (15 ml) coconut milk

½ vanilla bean, split open and scraped

1 tsp (3 g) gelatin

2 tbsp (24 g) coconut sugar

Preheat the oven to 350°F (180°C, or gas mark 4). Generously grease the donut pan with coconut oil.

In a mixing bowl, sift together all dry ingredients. In a separate bowl, blend wet ingredients.

Add the dry to the wet and continue to blend until a smooth batter has formed.

Scoop the batter into a plastic bag, snip the end and pipe batter into the donut pan, filling about two-thirds of the way to the top. Use a small spatula to smooth out the tops.

Bake for 10 minutes or until a tester comes out clean. Transfer donuts to a cooling rack.

Over low heat, melt butter in a small saucepan. Stir in coconut milk and vanilla bean. Sprinkle gelatin over the top and continue stirring until dissolved. Add coconut sugar and continue stirring until glaze is smooth.

Remove from heat and allow to cool for 3 to 5 minutes to thicken. Dip the donuts in warm glaze, swirling them to allow the glaze to soak in. Place the donut on the cooling rack. Repeat with the remaining donuts.

Enjoy warm with a cup of coffee or hot apple cider!

FRUITY COCONUT BREAKFAST TART

This breakfast tart features fresh fruit piled over an almond butter drizzle on a coconut flour crust. —RB

SERVES 2

FOR THE CRUST

½ cup (60 g) coconut flour

½ cup (120 ml) coconut milk

¼ cup (60 ml) coconut oil

¼ cup (50 g) coconut sugar

FOR THE TOPPING

2 tbsp (30 g) almond butter

1 banana

1 handful blackberries

1 handful champagne grapes

Freeze-dried strawberries

Preheat oven to 350°F (180°C, or gas mark 4). Line a cookie sheet with parchment paper, set aside.

In a medium mixing bowl, combine the crust ingredients. Transfer the dough to the parchment-lined cookie sheet and roll the dough out to ¼-inch (6-mm) thickness, then shape into a disc. Bake in the preheated oven for approximately 15 minutes or until the edges are lightly brown.

Drizzle the almond butter over the coconut crust using a circular motion. Slice the banana and arrange over the almond butter, then scatter on the blackberries, grapes and strawberries.

PEACH PIE BREAKFAST BAKE

If you want to make a healthy, delicious breakfast that will serve a crowd, try this recipe. It's a protein-rich, sweet breakfast casserole that has all the flavors of peach pie. —KW

SERVES 6

2 tbsp (30 ml) coconut oil

4 peaches, peeled and sliced

8 eggs, whites and yolks separated

6 tbsp (90 ml) pure maple syrup or sweetener of choice

1 tbsp (8 g) ground cinnamon

1 tbsp (15 ml) pure vanilla extract

FOR THE TOPPING

1 cup (150 g) walnuts

¼ cup (38 g) sunflower seeds

¼ cup (25 g) shredded unsweetened coconut

2 tbsp (16 g) coconut flour

2 tbsp (30 ml) pure maple syrup or sweetener of choice

5 tbsp (75 ml) butter, melted

½ tsp ground cinnamon

Pinch sea salt

Preheat oven to 350°F (180°C, or gas mark 4). Place the coconut oil and peaches in a 9 × 13-inch (23 × 33-cm) baking dish. Whip the egg whites until peaks form. Set aside. Mix together the yolks, maple syrup, cinnamon and vanilla. Fold the yolk mixture into the peaked egg whites. Place the egg mixture all over the peaches. Bake for 15 minutes.

While it's baking, make the topping by mixing all the topping ingredients together. After 15 minutes is up, gently place the topping all over the eggs. Bake for an additional 10 to 15 minutes or until thoroughly cooked through.

BAKED GRAPEFRUIT CRISP

Baking a grapefruit brings out all the natural sweetness of the usually very tart fruit. If you've never baked a grapefruit before, you are in for a real treat! —KW

SERVES 2

1 grapefruit

2 tbsp (16 g) sliced almonds

2 tbsp (16 g) chopped walnuts

3 tbsp (15 g) unsweetened coconut flakes

2 tbsp (30 ml) honey

Pinch of ground cinnamon

Pinch of salt

Preheat oven to 350°F (180°C, or gas mark 4). Cut the grapefruit in half. You may need to cut a slight bit off the bottoms of both halves so they sit nice and upright. With a knife, remove the white membrane in the centers of the grapefruit and remove any seeds that you see. Run your knife around the outer edge of the grapefruit so the segments easily come out when it's ready to eat.

Mix up the rest of your ingredients in small bowl. Put equal amounts of the crisp on top of the grapefruit. Place the grapefruit on a cookie sheet and bake for 10 minutes. After the 10 minutes is up, turn on the broiler and broil for about 2 to 3 minutes until top is golden brown and crisp. Watch carefully while it's under the broiler so it doesn't burn. You may also need to rotate the cookie sheet a few times when it's under the broiler.

BREAKFAST-IN-BED BERRY COBBLER (FOR TWO!)

This is the perfect romantic breakfast to make on any special occasion, or just because. The warm bubbling berries are topped with a crisp golden crumble, and portioned perfectly for two. —RM

SERVES 2

FOR THE FILLING

2½ cups (375 g) berries (blackberries, blueberries, raspberries)

½ tbsp (7.5 ml) maple syrup

½ tsp arrowroot starch

FOR THE CRUMBLE

⅓ cup (40 g) almond flour

2 tbsp (16 g) sliced almonds

2 tbsp (16 g) arrowroot starch

½ tsp ground cinnamon

¼ tsp baking powder

1½ tbsp (23 ml) maple syrup

½ tsp coconut oil

Whipped coconut cream, for serving

Preheat the oven to 425°F (220°C, or gas mark 7). In a small saucepan over medium-low heat, simmer the berries and maple syrup for 10 minutes, stirring occasionally. Add the arrowroot starch and simmer until reduced, about 5 minutes. You don't want it to have too much liquid or be too dry.

Mix the almond flour, sliced almonds, arrowroot, cinnamon and baking powder together. Then mix in the maple syrup and coconut oil. The mixture should be crumbly.

Grease a large oven-safe mug the size of a bowl, or two ramekins, with your choice of oil. Fill the mug with the berries and then spoon the crumbles evenly on top.

Place on the center rack in the oven and bake for 10 minutes. The top should be semi-crispy and golden. Serve in bed with whipped coconut cream, two spoons and a good morning kiss!

CHEF'S TIP:

In the winter months use organic frozen berries from a natural foods store. They are plump and flavorful!

COCONUT BERRY PARFAIT

When it comes to breakfast I like to keep things simple and nothing could be simpler than mixing some fresh berries with some coconut milk. Adding a little rose water adds a hint of floral note to this delicious creamy dessert. —NK

SERVES 2

1 cup (235 ml) chilled full-fat coconut milk

1 tsp (5 ml) rose water

1 tbsp (15 ml) raw honey

1 tsp (3 g) ground cinnamon

½ cup (65 g) fresh berries

Coconut flakes for topping, optional

Pour coconut milk, rose water, honey and cinnamon into a mixing bowl. Mix well. Place ¼ cup (32 g) of berries on the bottom of two small glasses. Pour over the coconut milk mixture. Add another ¼ cup (32 g) of berries over the top. To serve, sprinkle some coconut flakes on top.

TROPICAL AÇAÍ BERRY BOWLS

Living in Hawaii, I absolutely love a refreshing açaí bowl heaped generously with my favorite toppings of nuts, toasted coconut and cacao nibs. It's the perfect chilly amount of sweet and crunch on a hot day. Açaí, coconut and macadamia nuts are also foods high in healthy fats, which can naturally protect your skin from sunburns! —CP

SERVES 2

1 (3½ ounce [98 g]) packet açaí berry, unsweetened and frozen

½ banana, frozen

½ cup (75 g) frozen blueberries

4 ounces (120 ml) full-fat coconut milk

FOR THE TOPPINGS

8 ounces (227 g) plain whole fat yogurt

2 tbsp (8 g) toasted coconut flakes

2 tbsp (20 g) macadamia nuts, chopped

2 tbsp (20 g) cacao nibs

1 mango, peeled and cubed

Remove açaí packet from freezer and set out for 5 minutes to slightly thaw.

Blend frozen açaí, banana, blueberries and coconut milk until smooth.

Scoop yogurt into bowls, top with açaí blend, toppings and mango cubes.

CRUNCHY ROASTED GRANOLA

Crunchy granola has always been one of my favorite treats so I re-created it using a combination of nuts and coconut for a Paleo-friendly cereal. This roasted granola is simply delightful with the perfect amount of crunch. Great with yogurt for breakfast or even Creamy Chocolate Ice Cream (page 377) for a sweet bite! I love making a batch for friends as this granola makes for a great gift and way to introduce others to healthy eating. —CP

MAKES ABOUT 4 CUPS (600 G)

2 cups (300 g) raw almonds

1 cup (150 g) raw macadamia nuts

½ cup (75 g) cacao nibs

½ cup (40 g) finely shredded coconut, unsweetened

¼ cup (35 g) ground golden flaxseed

¼ cup (60 ml) coconut oil

2 tbsp (30 ml) maple syrup or raw honey

1 tbsp (15 ml) vanilla extract

Preheat oven to 300°F (150°C, or gas mark 2). Line a baking sheet with parchment paper.

Place all ingredients in the bowl of a food processor and pulse several times. Scrape down the sides of the bowl and pulse again.

Scoop granola onto a baking sheet, spreading into an even layer. Bake for 30 minutes or until granola begins to turn golden brown. Remove from the oven and cool completely before enjoying.

Serve with yogurt a scoop of Creamy Chocolate Ice Cream or my favorite way, by the spoonful!

Store remaining granola in an airtight container in a cool location.

PUMPKIN SPICE GRANOLA

Pumpkin and autumn spices make for fall cheer in a cup. Nuts and seeds are great brain food, rich in vitamins, minerals and essential fatty acids which will energize your morning, giving you strength all day long! —CP

MAKES ABOUT 3 CUPS (500 G)

1 cup (150 g) raw almonds

1 cup (150 g) raw walnuts or pecans

1 cup (150 g) raw pumpkin seeds

¼ cup (35 g) finely ground flaxseed

2 tsp (6 g) ground cinnamon

½ tsp ground nutmeg

¼ tsp ground ginger

5 tbsp (80 g) pumpkin purée

¼ cup (60 ml) coconut oil

2 tbsp (30 ml) maple syrup

1 tsp (5 ml) maple extract

Preheat oven to 300°F (150°C, or gas mark 2). Line a baking sheet with parchment paper.

Using a food processor, pulse the nuts several times. Add the remaining ingredients and pulse until a crumbly mixture forms.

Scoop granola onto a baking sheet, filling the entire sheet and spreading into an even layer. Bake for 15 minutes, stir and bake for an additional 15 to 20 minutes or until granola turns fragrant and golden brown.

Cool completely before enjoying. Serve with yogurt, milk or even by the spoonful.

FIG PISTACHIO GRANOLA

The addition of purple figs and green pistachios gives this breakfast granola a pop of color for a cheerful morning. —CP

MAKES ABOUT 2 CUPS (400 G)

1 cup (150 g) raw almonds

1 cup (150 g) raw pistachios

2 tbsp (30 ml) coconut oil

2 tbsp (30 ml) maple syrup or raw honey

2 tbsp (30 g) applesauce

1½ tsp (7.5 ml) vanilla extract

½ tsp ground nutmeg

½ tsp ground cinnamon

½ cup (75 g) dried figs, about 12

Preheat oven to 300°F (150°C, or gas mark 2). Line a baking sheet with parchment paper.

Add all ingredients except figs to a food processor. Pulse nuts into small pieces about the size of oats. Chop figs into small chunks. Fold pieces into nut mixture.

Spoon nut granola onto parchment-lined baking sheet, spreading evenly. Use the back of a spatula to flatten nuts into a thin, even layer. Nut mixture should be packed closely together.

Bake for 25 minutes. Allow to cool completely before breaking into clusters. Store remaining granola in an airtight container in the refrigerator.

Serve with plain yogurt or simply by the spoonful.

CHEF'S TIP:
For a less sweet version, I replace 1 tablespoon (15 ml) maple syrup/raw honey with 1 tablespoon (15 ml) coconut oil.

MAPLE PECAN GRANOLA

This delicious and easy-to-make granola recipe is an excellent protein-filled snack to have around the house. Drizzling the nuts and seeds with coconut oil and maple syrup then toasting them makes for delightful flavor-filled crunchy clusters. I like to have it for breakfast sometimes with coconut milk, like cereal! —HH

SERVES 4

1 cup (150 g) pecans or walnuts

¾ cup (112 g) slivered almonds

¼ cup (20 g) shredded coconut

¼ cup (38 g) pumpkin seeds

3 tbsp (24 g) ground chia seeds

1 tsp (3 g) ground cinnamon

¼ tsp sea salt

2 tbsp (30 ml) maple syrup

1 tbsp (15 ml) coconut oil, melted

¼ cup (38 g) raisins

Preheat the oven to 300°F (150°C, or gas mark 2). Combine all ingredients except for the raisins in a bowl and mix well to incorporate the maple syrup and chia seeds with the other ingredients. Spread the mixture on a baking sheet lined with parchment paper. Bake for about 10 to 15 minutes, mixing halfway through, or until the granola is crispy and golden brown. Be careful not to burn. Remove granola from the oven and let cool, then add the raisins. Save in a jar for breakfast or a snack.

CHEF'S TIP:

Raisins tend to get too hard and lose their juiciness if you bake them in the oven, so mix them in with the granola afterward. To grind the chia seeds, put them in a coffee grinder.

"OATMEAL"

This Paleo "oatmeal" is packed with protein so it will keep you satiated for the whole morning. Since there are no grains and very little sugar, you won't get a blood sugar spike or sugar crash later in the day like many usually do when eating grains and sugar in the morning. The almond meal is at the heart of this recipe since it helps bring a nutty flavor, heartiness and rough texture that is reminiscent of oatmeal. —HH

SERVES 1

FOR THE BASE

1 banana

2 eggs—or omit eggs and include additional 2 tbsp (16 g) ground flax or chia for a vegan alternative

¼ cup (60 ml) coconut milk or almond milk

¼ cup (30 g) almond meal

1 tbsp (8 g) ground flax seeds

1 tbsp (8 g) gelatin (for protein, omit for vegan)

FOR OPTIONAL ADD-INS

Blueberries

Strawberries

Cinnamon

Milk

Nuts

Seeds

Put the banana, eggs and milk in a unheated saucepan and blend with an immersion blender until the banana is puréed. Add the dry ingredients and mix once more with the blender or whisk until combined. Turn the heat to medium and continuously stir until the mixture starts to thicken and bubble slightly, about 2 to 5 minutes. Turn off heat and put the oatmeal in a bowl. Top with your favorite toppings—I use blueberries and a little cinnamon—and enjoy!

CHEF'S TIP:

Be sure to use almond meal, not almond flour. Almond meal is ground almonds with the skins on and is a bit rougher in texture than almond flour, which is made from blanched almonds and typically much finer than almond meal. The almond meal gives this recipe better texture.

COCONUTTY BERRY CEREAL

Missing your morning cereal? Try this grain-free version made with shredded coconut, cashew butter, dates and fruit for those times when you want to enjoy the occasional bowl of cereal. —NK

SERVES 1–2

1 cup (235 ml) coconut milk

½ cup (40 g) unsweetened shredded coconut

2 tbsp (30 g) cashew butter

1 tbsp (8 g) ground cinnamon

1 tsp (5 ml) vanilla extract

3 Medjool dates, pitted

¼ tsp sea salt

¼ cup (35 g) fresh blueberries

¼ cup (35 g) fresh sliced strawberries

Chopped hazelnuts, for garnish

Place coconut milk, shredded coconut, cashew butter, cinnamon, vanilla extract, Medjool dates and sea salt in a blender. Blend until well incorporated then pour into a bowl. Add blueberries and strawberries on top. Serve with some chopped hazelnuts on top.

BERRY CHIA PUDDING

Chia pudding is the perfect alternative to oatmeal or porridge due to its similar consistency once mixed in with any type of liquid. I like to eat this as a snack or post-breakfast meal. Once the pudding is ready, just add your favorite fruits and dig in. —JC

SERVES 2

½ cup (70 g) chia seeds

2 dates, pitted and finely chopped

2 cups (470 ml) Homemade Coconut Milk (page 503)

1 small banana, sliced

4 fresh strawberries, sliced

½ cup (75 g) fresh blueberries

2 tbsp (16 g) pumpkin seeds

Add chia seeds and dates to a bowl. Slowly pour in coconut milk and stir constantly to prevent clumping. Stir until it starts to thicken. Let it sit for 5 to 10 minutes until it turns into a jelly-like consistency. Stir every couple of minutes to redistribute the coconut milk.

Divide chia pudding into two serving bowls. Top with banana and strawberry slices, blueberries and pumpkin seeds. Serve immediately or chill in the fridge for 25 to 30 minutes.

BLUEBERRY, COCONUT AND CHIA SEED PUDDING WITH DRIED APRICOTS

This must be one of the world's easiest breakfasts, I mean desserts . . . hmm, I think I will call it a bressert. Either way the best part about it is that it's sugar-, dairy- and grain-free! —VM

SERVES 2

2 dried apricots, chopped

1 cup (150 g) blueberries, plus more for garnish

1 tbsp (15 ml) coconut oil, melted

¼ cup (60 ml) coconut cream

½ cup (60 g) chia seeds

Few drops of vanilla extract

Soak the dried apricots in warm water for about 20 minutes. When the apricots are done soaking, add all of the ingredients to the blender and blend until nice and smooth.

Pour the mixture into a bowl and refrigerate it for about 10 to 15 minutes. Garnish with some fresh blueberries and enjoy!

BANANA NUT CHIA PUDDING

Chia pudding is an easy way to take nutrient-dense goodness with you when you go. Less than 5 minutes of prep in the evening sets you up to wake up and go in the morning. —KH

SERVES 2

2 cups (470 ml) dairy-free milk of choice

4 dates, pitted, or 2 tbsp (30 ml) honey or pure maple syrup

2 bananas

Pinch of ground cinnamon

1 tsp (5 ml) vanilla extract

4–6 tbsp (32–48 g) chia seeds

FOR THE TOPPINGS

¼ cup (32 g) raisins

2 tbsp (16 g) raw cashews, roughly chopped

2 tbsp (16 g) raw almonds, roughly chopped

Place milk, dates, bananas, cinnamon and vanilla into high-powered blender. Process until smooth and dates are all broken up and incorporated. Pour into glass jar. Add chia seeds and cover with tight fitting lid. Shake until well incorporated. Place in fridge overnight or at least 4 hours. Cover the toppings with water to soak overnight. In the morning, drain toppings and rinse well. Pour over chia pudding. Enjoy.

CHEF'S TIP:

The amount of chia seeds used will determine the consistency. Less means a thinner pudding. More means a thicker pudding. Experiment to see what you like.

PUMPKIN PIE CHIA PUDDING

I love anything pumpkin. Add some spices and you have a fun, seasonal chia pudding to add to your breakfast rotation. —KH

SERVES 2–3

2 cups (470 ml) non-dairy milk of any kind

1 cup (250 g) cooked pumpkin purée

3–4 tbsp (45–60 ml) maple syrup or honey

1 tsp (5 ml) vanilla extract

½ tsp ground cinnamon

¼ tsp ground ginger

¼ tsp ground allspice

4–6 tbsp (32–48 g) chia seeds

FOR THE OPTIONAL TOPPINGS

Chocolate chips

Fresh fruit

Shredded coconut

The night before, place all ingredients, except for chia seeds, into a blender and purée until smooth. Pour chia seeds into a glass jar; pour pumpkin pie flavored liquid over seeds. Place cap on jar and give it a good shake. Place in fridge over night. Your amazing pumpkin pie pudding will be ready to devour in the morning! For a decadent treat, try adding a few chocolate chips.

APPLE CHIA KIWI PUDDING

Looking to change things up for your morning meal? Try this tasty Apple Chia Kiwi Pudding for a nice way to start your day! —NK

SERVES 2

1 cup (235 ml) full-fat coconut milk

½ medium apple, diced

2 tbsp (30 ml) raw honey or maple syrup

½ tsp vanilla extract

¼ tsp sea salt

¼ cup (32 g) chia seeds

2 kiwi fruit, sliced for serving

Place coconut milk into a blender. Add the diced apple, honey or maple syrup, vanilla extract and sea salt. Blend until the ingredients are well mixed. Transfer the mixture to a large mixing bowl then stir in the chia seeds. Pour the mixture into two 10-ounce (280-g) ramekins. Place in the fridge overnight or for 3 to 4 hours until the chia seeds absorb the milk, resembling tapioca pudding. To serve, place the sliced kiwi fruit on top.

NUTRIENT-RICH BERRY SMOOTHIE

This tasty smoothie is packed with healthy fats and protein so it will keep your blood sugar levels stable and it will keep you full! —AV

SERVES 1

1 tbsp (15 ml) coconut oil

½ avocado

2 tbsp (16 g) gelatin

1 cup (235 ml) coconut water (or liquid of your choice)

1 tsp (5 ml) raw honey (optional)

1 cup (150 g) frozen mixed berries

Blend the coconut oil, avocado, gelatin, coconut water and honey (if using). Once this is well blended, add the berries and blend until smooth. It's important to not add all the ingredients at once because the cold berries will freeze the coconut oil so you will end up with lots of little hard beads of coconut oil in your smoothie. Enjoy!

CREAMY GREEN SMOOTHIE WITH SPINACH & PAPAYA

Fresh, tropical and creamy, this coconut-based green smoothie is great to whip up for a quick breakfast or lunch on the go. I often add gelatin for extra protein. —CP

SERVES 2

1 heaping cup (150 g) frozen papaya

1 cup (150 g) ice, about 2 handfuls

1 cup (70 g) fresh spinach leaves

½ cup (120 ml) coconut milk

½ cup (120 g) plain, full-fat yogurt

1 tbsp (15 ml) raw honey, optional

Blend all ingredients together. Serve and enjoy immediately.

CHEF'S TIP:

I usually cube fresh papaya when it's in season to freeze and use in smoothies. Simply cube, spread out on a baking sheet, freeze until frozen then transfer fruit to a resealable plastic bag.

DARK CHOCOLATE, RASPBERRY MILKSHAKE

Living in Hawaii, sometimes it's just too hot to cook eggs for breakfast, so I frequently enjoy this creamy, nutritious milkshake! The cacao adds a rich flavor contrast to the tartness of raspberries. Because this is designed for breakfast, it is not on the sweet side, although you can add a spoonful of honey if desired. —CP

SERVES 2

1 cup (250 g) frozen raspberries

½ cup (120 ml) coconut milk

½ cup (120 g) whole-fat, plain yogurt

2 tbsp (16 g) raw cacao powder

1 tbsp (8 g) gelatin

2 tbsp (30 ml) raw honey, optional

Crunchy Roasted Granola (page 474), optional, for garnish

Add all ingredients to a blender and blend on high for about 20 seconds or until smooth.

Divide between two cups and serve. Great garnished with Crunchy Roasted Granola.

CHEF'S TIP:

Gelatin provides a rich, healthy source of protein to your morning and also promotes healthy bones, teeth and joints as well as good digestion and immunity.

TRIPLE BERRY SMOOTHIE

For all the berry lovers out there, this fantastic smoothie will brighten up your day in an instant! The Date-Sweetened Almond Milk adds a touch of creaminess that blends wonderfully with the frozen berries. —JC

SERVES 1

½ cup (75 g) frozen strawberries

½ cup (75 g) frozen blueberries

½ cup (75 g) frozen blackberries

1 cup (235 ml) Date-Sweetened Almond Milk (page 502)

Combine all ingredients in a blender. Blend for 40 seconds or until the smoothie is completely puréed. Pour into a glass and serve immediately.

ULTIMATE GREEN SMOOTHIE

At home we love to juice all kinds of vegetables for the ultimate green drink. It usually takes quite a bit of effort to clean the juicer afterwards so when we want vegetable juice in a jiffy, I just throw all our juice ingredients in a blender and give it a quick whirl. The result is a vibrant green smoothie in less than half the time it takes to clean the juicer! —JC

SERVES 2

1 cup (70 g) baby spinach

1 rib celery, chopped

1 small apple (I like Pink Lady or Fuji)

1 handful fresh parsley

½ cup (120 ml) coconut water

Juice of 1 lemon

¼ tsp turmeric powder

Combine spinach, celery, apple, parsley and coconut water in a blender. Blend for 40 seconds or until the smoothie is completely puréed. Add lemon juice and turmeric. Pulse for a few more seconds to combine. Pour into two glasses and serve immediately.

AVOCADO BANANA SMOOTHIE

This reminds me of the ice-blended avocado shake that I used to enjoy during the summer months when I was a child. I added spinach to this one to make it more nutritious while the bananas and the Date-Sweetened Almond Milk help create a texture that is reminiscent of soft serve ice cream. —JC

SERVES 1

1 small avocado, pitted and sliced

1 small frozen banana

2 cups (140 g) baby spinach

¾ cup (180 ml) Date-Sweetened Almond Milk (page 502)

Combine all ingredients in a blender. Blend for 40 seconds or until the smoothie is completely puréed. Pour into a glass and serve immediately.

CHEF'S TIP:
Other types of nut milk can be substituted for the almond milk.

BANANA PEACH SMOOTHIE

Bananas and peaches produce a fresh flavor that makes me think of sandy beaches and warm summer nights. Give this super simple smoothie a try and it will instantly transport you and your taste buds to the tropics. —JC

SERVES 1

1 small frozen banana

1 fresh peach, pitted and sliced

¾ cup (180 ml) coconut water

Combine all ingredients in a blender. Blend for 40 seconds or until the smoothie is completely puréed. Pour into a glass and serve immediately.

CHEF'S TIP:
Substitute coconut milk for the coconut water for a creamier texture.

MOCHA FREEZE

This smoothie is so much healthier than the ones you can get at your local coffee joint because there's no high fructose corn syrup or caramel coloring added. Who would want that anyway? Coffee, chocolate, a little bit of almond milk, some honey and you're good to go. —JC

SERVES 1

1 cup (235 ml) brewed coffee, frozen into cubes

½ cup (120 ml) Date-Sweetened Almond Milk (page 502)

1 tbsp (8 g) cacao powder

1 tsp (5 ml) raw honey

½ tsp vanilla extract

Combine all ingredients in a blender. Blend for 40 seconds or until the smoothie is completely puréed. Pour into a glass and serve immediately.

CHEF'S TIP:
Other types of nut milk can be substituted for the almond milk.

PIÑA COLADA

There's no rum in this piña colada but you won't even notice it! I like to toss in some mangos to tone down the tanginess of the pineapple and add just the right amount of sweetness. Sprinkle a little bit of shredded coconut on top for added flair! —JC

SERVES 1

1 cup (165 g) fresh pineapple, cut into chunks

1 cup (165 g) fresh mango, cut into chunks

½ cup (120 ml) Homemade Coconut Milk (page 503)

1 tbsp (5 g) shredded coconut

Combine pineapple, mango and coconut milk in a blender. Blend for 10 to 15 seconds or until the smoothie is completely puréed. Pour into a glass and top with shredded coconut. Serve immediately.

CHEF'S TIP:
Substitute coconut water for the coconut milk for a lighter drink.

CHOCO MINT DREAM

Remember those peppermint patties and thin mints? Well, you can enjoy the same flavors without overloading your body with a ton of sugar. The avocado may seem weird but it makes this drink so smooth you won't even taste it! —JC

SERVES 1

1½ tbsp (12 g) cacao powder

1 small avocado, sliced

6–8 fresh mint leaves

1 cup (235 ml) Date-Sweetened Almond Milk (page 502)

2 tsp (10 ml) raw honey

Combine all ingredients in a blender. Blend for 40 seconds or until the smoothie is completely puréed. Pour into a glass and serve immediately.

CHEF'S TIP:
Other types of nut milk can be substituted for the almond milk.

CARROT CAKE SMOOTHIE

Try this deliciously creamy smoothie, reminiscent of carrot cake, for a tasty way to start your morning. —NK

SERVES 1–2

1½ cups (355 ml) full-fat coconut milk

1 medium carrot, peeled and grated

½ frozen banana

1 tbsp (15 g) almond butter

1 tsp (3 g) ground cinnamon

¼ tsp nutmeg

1 tsp (5 ml) vanilla extract

¼ tsp coconut oil

Raw honey or maple syrup, to sweeten

Toasted coconut flakes, to garnish, optional

Put all of the ingredients into a blender. Blend until well mixed. Sprinkle toasted coconut flakes on top if desired.

ALMOND BANANA SMOOTHIE

Looking for a tasty, nutritious and quick-to-make-on-the-go breakfast? Try this Almond Banana Smoothie packed with goodness. —NK

SERVES 1–2

1½ cups (355 ml) almond milk

1 cup (150 g) frozen sliced bananas

1 cup (70 g) fresh spinach

5 pitted medjool dates, chopped

1 tsp (3 g) ground cinnamon

1 tsp (5 ml) vanilla extract

1 tbsp (8 g) chia seeds

Place almond milk into a blender. Then place the rest of the ingredients in and blend until well mixed.

WATERMELON SMOOTHIE

This refreshing drink is perfect for a hot summer day. It's especially hydrating and loaded with digestive health benefits. —KW

SERVES 4

4 cups (480 g) watermelon chunks, frozen

1 cup (235 ml) coconut water

3 limes, juiced

10 mint leaves

Pinch of sea salt

Put all of the ingredients in a high-powered blender. Blend until smooth and creamy. Enjoy!

CHEF'S TIP:
I keep a whole bag of watermelon chunks in my freezer for this recipe. You should freeze the watermelon chunks for at least 2 hours or until completely frozen.

HEALTHY PEPPERMINT SHAKE

Minty, creamy deliciousness awaits you. This shake is packed with healthy fats that will keep you full for hours. —KW

SERVES 4

1 (13.5-ounce [378-g]) can coconut milk

1 avocado, peeled and seed removed

3 tbsp (45 ml) honey

1 cup (150 g) ice

1 tbsp (15 ml) pure vanilla extract

1 tsp (5 ml) pure peppermint extract

Put everything in the blender and blend.

CHOCOLATE BANANA BREAKFAST SHAKE

This breakfast shake is packed full of protein and healthy fats and will keep you full for hours. Both kids and adults love this shake. —KW

SERVES 1

1 banana (frozen bananas are especially nice to use)

¾ cup (180 ml) full-fat coconut milk

1 handful of fresh leafy greens

2 tbsp (30 g) nut butter

2 tbsp (16 g) collagen

1 tbsp (8 g) cacao powder

½ tsp pure vanilla extract

¼ tsp ground cinnamon

1 or 2 dates, optional, for extra sweetness

Place all ingredients in a blender or food processor and blend until smooth and creamy.

MATCHA SMOOTHIE

This refreshing matcha smoothie is not only delicious, but it comes loaded with health benefits. Matcha is finely milled, whole leaf, green tea powder and some even say it's the superfood of superfoods. Since incorporating this matcha smoothie into my daily regimen, I've noticed some wonderful benefits. One such benefit is a sustained and focused energy that lasts me throughout the day. —KW

SERVES 2

½ cup (120 ml) coconut or almond milk

2 cups (300 g) ice

2 tsp (6 g) matcha

2 tsp (10 ml) maple syrup

¼ tsp vanilla extract

Put all ingredients into a blender and blend until smooth.

BERRY AVOCADO SMOOTHIE

This recipe includes grass-fed collagen hydrolysate gelatin for protein. This is a form of water-soluble gelatin that is a great supplement with beneficial amino acids and protein that can support joint, hair and skin health. —HH

SERVES 1

¾ cup (112 g) frozen berries

3 tbsp (24 g) collagen hydrolysate gelatin

¾ cup (180 ml) full-fat canned coconut milk or Date-Sweetened Almond Milk (page 502)

¼ of an avocado

1 tbsp (15 ml) coconut oil

Place all ingredients into a blender and blend on high until smooth. Add water or ice cubes to reach desired consistency.

CHEF'S TIP:
I like to use grass-fed gelatin from either Great Lakes or Vital Proteins.

RISE AND SHINE GREEN SMOOTHIE

Say good morning to the day with this fresh, invigorating green smoothie. Ginger adds a warming quality and is wonderful for digestion. A squeeze of lemon adds a refreshing twist to any green smoothie. —KH

SERVES 1

1 banana, fresh or frozen

½ apple, cored and chopped

1 cup (70 g) chopped spinach

1 cup (235 ml) Homemade Coconut Milk (page 503)

½-inch (1.3-cm) piece of fresh ginger

Small squeeze of fresh lemon juice, to taste

2–3 ice cubes, optional if you like a cold smoothie

Place all ingredients into blender. Process until smooth. Enjoy immediately.

CREAMY TROPICAL TURMERIC SMOOTHIE

Get a dose of anti-inflammatory goodness in this creamy smoothie that combines tropical fruits with healing spices. You can use either fresh or dried turmeric. —KH

SERVES 1

1 banana

¾ cup (120 g) pineapple chunks, fresh or frozen

1 cup (235 ml) Homemade Coconut Milk (page 503), or ¾ cup (180 ml) full-fat canned coconut milk plus ¼ cup (60 ml) water

Fresh turmeric, peeled, about the size of a small grape—or ¼–½ tsp ground turmeric

Fresh ginger, peeled, about the size of a small grape

1 tbsp (15 g) coconut butter or coconut oil

¼ tsp ground cinnamon

2 tbsp (16 g) hemp seeds

1 tbsp (8 g) gelatin hydrolysate

3–4 ice cubes, optional if you like a colder smoothie

Place all ingredients into a high-speed blender and process until creamy and smooth, about 45 seconds. Drink and enjoy! Your body will thank you!

CHEF'S TIP:

If you are new to turmeric, it's best to start out small. Add just a bit to your smoothie and see how you like it. You can always add more. Too much can be a bit bitter. My experience is that the body quickly develops a taste for this healing spice.

CHOCOLATE PROTEIN SMOOTHIE

Some days just call for a little chocolate. Here's an easy smoothie recipe that combines chocolate with nutrient-dense goodness. It's a delicious treat that you can feel good about having. —KH

SERVES 1

1 cup (235 ml) Homemade Coconut Milk (page 503)

1½ bananas

1 tbsp (8 g) gelatin hydrolysate

3 tbsp (24 g) hemp seeds, shelled

2 dates, pitted

2–3 tsp (6-8 g) raw cacao powder

1 tbsp (15 g) coconut butter

3–4 cubes of ice

Raw cacao nibs, optional, for garnish

Place all ingredients into a high-speed blender and process until creamy smooth—about 45 seconds. Drink and enjoy!

PUMPKIN SPICE SMOOTHIE

This smoothie is rich and slightly spiced, it's like a meal on its own. —KH

SERVES 2

2 cups (470 ml) Homemade Coconut Milk (page 503) or 1 cup (235 ml) full-fat canned, diluted with 1 cup (235 ml) water

1 banana, frozen or throw in a few ice cubes if not frozen

1 cup (250 g) pumpkin purée

1 tbsp (15 ml) maple syrup

½ tsp vanilla extract

½ tsp ground cinnamon

¼ tsp ground cardamom

¼ tsp ground ginger

⅛ tsp ground clove

⅛ tsp ground nutmeg

2 tbsp (16 g) gelatin hydrolysate

Combine everything in a blender. Purée until smooth. Drink and enjoy!

CHEF'S TIP:

You can substitute 1½ teaspoons (4 g) of Pumpkin Pie Spice (page 505) for the individual spices used.

THAI ZINGER SMOOTHIE

This smoothie was created while I daydreamed of traveling. The zesty ginger really complements the sweet, creamy flavors and evokes a feeling of being in exotic places. —KH

SERVES 1

1 banana, fresh or frozen

1 medium carrot

1 cup (150 g) mango or pineapple chunks, frozen

1 cup (235 ml) Homemade Coconut Milk (page 503)

1 tbsp (15 g) coconut oil

1–1½-inch (2.5–3.8-cm) piece of fresh ginger, peeled

4 ice cubes

Place everything into high-powered blender and process until smooth. Enjoy and dream about warmer places.

AVOCADO DATE SMOOTHIE

Adding avocado to a smoothie will make the creamiest smoothie you have ever had. I love this smoothie because it is thick enough to eat with a spoon. —KH

SERVES 1

1 banana, fresh or frozen

1 cup (235 ml) Homemade Coconut Milk (page 503), or any milk of choice

2 dates, pitted

½ large avocado

1 tsp (5 ml) vanilla extract

3–4 ice cubes, optional if you like a colder smoothie

Place all ingredients in blender. Process until creamy smooth. Enjoy!

BLUEBERRY GREEN SMOOTHIE

Green smoothies are packed with nutrients and taste delicious! I like using baby spinach because it tastes less bitter than other greens. This smoothie is lightly sweetened by banana and blueberries and has healthy fats and protein from the avocado and almond butter. —RM

SERVES 1

1 cup (70 g) baby spinach, packed

¾ cup (180 ml) unsweetened almond milk

¾ cup (112 g) frozen blueberries

1 kiwi

1 frozen banana

½ Hass avocado

1 tbsp (15 g) nut butter

Hemp seeds and cacao nibs, optional, for garnish

Put all of the ingredients into a blender. If using a Vita-mix, be sure to put liquid ingredients in first, then soft ingredients, then frozen ingredients on top. Blend on high for 3 to 4 minutes until smooth. Garnish with hemp seeds and raw cacao nibs, if desired.

BLENDED GREEN JUICE

No juicer? No problem. Making healthy green juice using a high-speed blender is easy and helps save money by avoiding the line at your local juice bar. —RM

SERVES 1

3 kale stalks, leaves only

Small handful parsley

2 celery ribs

½ cucumber

Juice from ½ lemon

½ cup (120 ml) cold water

1 apple

3 carrots

Wash each ingredient as the skin will be used as well. Cut up each of your veggies and fruits into 1-inch (2.5-cm)-thick pieces. In the order listed above, layer your ingredients into your Vitamix. Soft stuff on bottom, harder to blend stuff on top. Starting off at the lowest speed, blend the ingredients for 4 minutes while gradually increasing speed. Use a tamper or wooden spoon handle to get things moving along if it seems stuck. Then use a cheese cloth square to wring out the juice from the pulp into a glass. It may seem like a tedious process, but it's worth it.

CHEF'S TIP:

Use the leftover pulp to make veggie nut bread, or you can add a quarter of it back into your juice for added fiber.

SPARKLING REFRESHER

Ever since I've discovered the joys of drinking sparkling water, I've concocted different ways to make it more fun and appealing to drink. Any fruits that are in season can be used to flavor sparkling water and this citrus berry infusion is by far my favorite because it's super refreshing! —JC

SERVES 2

1 (750 ml) bottle of sparkling water

1 orange, halved and sliced

1 lemon, halved and sliced

1 cup (125 g) raspberries

1 bunch mint

Combine all the ingredients in a large pitcher. Cover and place it in the fridge for 30 minutes to allow the citrus and berries to infuse the water. Enjoy!

LEMON ROSE WATER ICED DRINK

This refreshing lemonade drink is perfect to enjoy on a hot summer's day. —NK

SERVES 2–4

3 cups (705 ml) water

⅓–1 cup (80–235 ml) raw honey

1 cup (235 ml) fresh lemon juice

1 tsp (5 ml) rose water

Ice

Place water and honey into a small saucepan. Place on medium-high heat and bring to a gentle boil making sure not to over heat. Stir frequently until the honey has dissolved. Remove from the heat and stir in the lemon juice and rose water. Pour into a glass pitcher. Taste to check the lemonade. If the mixture is not sweet enough add some more honey, up to 1 cup (235 ml), or if it is too sweet add in some more lemon juice. Place in the fridge for a few hours to chill. Serve over ice.

MINT LIME SPARKLERS

A refreshing, colorful drink of fresh herbs and lime juice topped with sparkling water. With a few garnishes, this simple drink looks extra fancy and is perfect for any backyard summer party. —CP

SERVES 1

3–4 fresh mint leaves

1 ounce (30 ml) fresh lime juice

Large handful of ice

Sparkling water

Slice of lime and sprig of mint to garnish

In a glass, muddle mint leaves with lime juice to extract flavor.

Add a handful of ice and fill with sparkling water.

Garnish with a slice of lime and sprig of mint.

BLACKBERRY FAUX-JITO

I typically make myself fancy "mocktails" as an afternoon pick-me-up. This is a virgin mojito sweetened with raw honey and blackberries, then topped with refreshing sparkling mineral water. —RM

SERVES 1

5 blackberries, plus more for garnish

5 mint leaves, plus more for garnish

3 lime slices, plus more for garnish

½–1 tbsp (7.5–15 ml) raw honey

Ice

6 ounces (180 ml) sparkling mineral water, chilled

In a pint glass, muddle blackberries, mint, limes and honey until fully mashed and dark in color. Fill the glass with ice. Pour in the sparkling water. Gently mix with a long spoon until fully incorporated. Garnish with a mint sprig, lime wheel and single blackberry. Drink up!

CHEF'S TIP:

If you don't have a bar muddler, then just use the handle of a wooden spoon and immediately rinse when done so the wood doesn't stain.

STRAWBERRY CUCUMBER KOMBUCHA

This is a virgin probiotic cocktail made with refreshing muddled strawberries and cucumber, then topped with ginger kombucha. Fizzy and fruity on a hot summer day. —RM

SERVES 1

3 slices cucumber, plus 1 for garnish

1 large strawberry, or 2 small

5 ice cubes

¾ cup (180 ml) ginger or original kombucha

In a tall bar glass, muddle the cucumber slices and strawberry together. If you don't have a muddler, just use the long handle of a wooden spoon. Fill the glass with ice cubes. Pour in the kombucha tea and mix together with a long spoon. Serve immediately with a cucumber slice.

CHEF'S TIP:

Entertaining guests at a luncheon or pool party? Multiply this recipe by 5 and serve in a large pitcher with pretty wine glasses. The kids will love it too.

SUGAR DETOX SPARKLY MINT LEMONADE

Giving up sugary sodas can be really tough when going Paleo or sugar detoxing. This fizzy tart lemonade is the perfect thirst quencher that is exciting to drink and healthy! —RM

SERVES 1

½ lemon

5 mint leaves

Ice cubes

Sparkling mineral water (I prefer Perrier)

Slice half a lemon into wedges. In a sturdy cup, about 12-ounce (355-ml) sized, muddle mint leaves and lemon for about a minute, or until you have plenty of minty lemon juice. If you don't have a muddler, use the skinny handle of a wooden spoon. Place about 5 ice cubes in the glass. Fill to the top with sparkling water. Mix with a spoon and drink immediately.

CHEF'S TIP:

For an afternoon energy lift, fill halfway with fresh green tea and half with sparkling water.

GINGER LIME CHIA FRESCA

A chia fresca is a delicious hydrating drink perfect to enjoy on hot summer days. This one uses fresh ginger and lime for a refreshing zing. —NK

SERVES 1

1 tbsp (8 g) chia seeds

1½ cups (355 ml) filtered water

Juice of ½ a small lime

4 thinly sliced pieces fresh ginger

Raw honey, to sweeten

Place chia seeds in the water and stir to mix. Let sit for 10 to 15 minutes so the chia seeds absorb the water and start to swell up. Add the lime juice and ginger and stir with a spoon. Sweeten as desired.

ICED COFFEE

Give your day a kick start by making this creamy iced coffee flavored with honey, cinnamon and vanilla. —NK

SERVES 1–2

½ cup (120 ml) cold brew coffee

2 cups (470 ml) coconut milk

2 tbsp (30 ml) raw honey

1 tbsp (15 g) coconut butter

1 tsp (3 g) ground cinnamon, plus more for dusting

1 tsp (5 ml) vanilla extract

Ice cubes

Place all ingredients into a high-powered blender. If using a non high-powered blender, crush the ice first before adding it in. Blend until well incorporated and enjoy cold.

ICED MATCHA LATTE

Want a little pick-me-up in the morning? Try this creamy iced latte filled with the uplifting goodness of matcha. —NK

SERVES 1

1 tsp (3 g) matcha powder

¼ tsp ground cinnamon

½ tsp pure vanilla extract

1 tbsp (8 g) collagen hydrolysate

3 tbsp (45 ml) just boiled water

1 cup (235 ml) full-fat coconut milk

1 tbsp (15 ml) pure maple syrup

1 cup (150 g) ice

Sift matcha powder into a large measuring cup. Add the cinnamon, vanilla and collagen hydrolysate. Pour over the boiled water and mix to dissolve. Add the coconut milk and maple syrup and mix. Pour into a high-powered blender and add the ice. Blend until well mixed and enjoy cold.

PEPPERMINT MOCHA LATTE

This peppermint mocha contains all-natural ingredients, unlike those chemical-laden ones from coffee shops. This sweet coffee drink has an espresso kick and makes a fun and soothing holiday treat! —HH

SERVES 1

1 shot espresso, 1 ounce (30 ml)

1 tbsp (8 g) cacao or cocoa powder

Scant ¼ tsp peppermint extract

½–1 tbsp (6–12 g) coconut sugar

½ cup (120 ml) almond milk or full-fat canned coconut milk

Ground cinnamon, for garnish

Brew espresso in a stovetop espresso maker. Pour the espresso into a mug and add the cocoa powder, peppermint extract and coconut sugar. Stir well.

To prepare the coconut milk (or almond milk), place in a saucepan or pot over medium heat. Turn off the heat. Once the milk is warm, begin to froth it with a milk frother. After a few minutes it will create fluffy latte foam. If you don't have a milk frother, slightly warm the milk, then blend it on high in a blender for a minute.

Pour the coconut milk into the mug containing the espresso, but leave a little bit of room so you can spoon some foam onto the top. Sprinkle with a little bit of cinnamon and enjoy!

CHEF'S TIP:
If you don't often make espresso or don't have an espresso maker you can always substitute the espresso for some very strong coffee.

S'MORES HOT COCOA

This decadent spin on hot cocoa will wow any house guest as you sit by the fire. Silky hot cocoa is topped with whipped meringue, crushed "graham," and a drizzle of fudge. It's like camping in the winter! —RM

SERVES 4

FOR THE HOT COCOA

2 (13.5-ounce [378-g]) cans coconut milk

¼ cup (30 g) raw cacao powder

¼ cup (50 g) coconut sugar

½ tsp ground cinnamon

½ tsp bourbon vanilla

FOR THE GRAHAM TOPPING

1 tbsp (8 g) finely chopped nuts (I use almonds)

½ tbsp (4 g) coconut flour

1 tsp (4 g) coconut sugar

½ tsp ground cinnamon

FOR THE MARSHMALLOW FLUFF TOPPING

¼ cup (60 ml) raw honey

2 egg whites, at room temperature

¼ tsp vanilla extract

FOR THE CHOCOLATE DRIZZLE

¼ cup (45 g) chocolate chips (I use Enjoy Life chocolate chips)

2 tbsp (30 ml) liquid from hot cocoa

In a medium saucepan combine all of the hot cocoa ingredients. Heat over medium-low until fully hot. Make sure the liquid doesn't boil. Meanwhile, combine all of the graham topping ingredients on a small plate and set aside.

For the marshmallow topping, heat the raw honey in a separate small saucepan over medium-low heat. You want the temperature to reach 240°F (116°C) with a candy thermometer before adding it to the egg whites, about 2 to 3 minutes. Start beating your egg whites and vanilla extract while the honey is reaching 240°F (116°C) with an electric hand-held mixer. Beat them until soft peaks form and then SLOWLY drizzle in the bubbling honey while continuing to beat the eggs. Beat them until stiff glossy peaks form. Set aside the marshmallow fluff while you melt the chocolate chips and 2 tablespoons (30 ml) of hot cocoa liquid in the microwave.

To assemble, turn the cocoa mugs upside down and rim the glasses with the melted chocolate. Immediately dip the rims into the graham topping. Pour the hot cocoa evenly into each mug. Top with a generous serving of marshmallow fluff and drizzle with more chocolate/graham topping.

Best when indulged in immediately, though each element can be saved in the fridge separately. The marshmallow fluff does tend to collect sugary liquid at the bottom of the bowl when not consumed immediately. Just scoop the fluff from the top, don't try to incorporate the liquid.

CHEF'S TIP:

The marshmallow fluff can be made without using a candy thermometer, but it can be tricky. Just boil the honey over medium heat for almost 1 minute before adding it to the egg whites.

SUPERCHARGED HOT CACAO

A twist on the popular Bulletproof Coffee, this warm drink is full of antioxidants and mild caffeine, along with healthy fats to keep you satiated throughout the day. —RM

SERVES 1

½ cup (120 ml) filtered water

½ cup (120 ml) full-fat coconut milk

2 tbsp (30 g) unsalted butter

2 tbsp (16 g) raw cacao powder (or regular cocoa powder)

¼ tsp vanilla extract

Dash ground cinnamon

3 tsp (15 ml) raw honey, optional

Bring the water and coconut milk to a boil in a small saucepan. Mix all other ingredients into the simmering liquid. Blend with an immersion blender or hand mixer until frothy. Transfer hot cacao to your favorite mug and drink up!

COFFEE JELLY AND ALMOND MILK TEA

This is popular in Asian bubble tea stores as an alternative or complement to boba (tapioca pearls) in milk teas or shakes. Making this homemade version is easy and so much better because it's dairy-free and only contains a teaspoon (4 g) of coconut sugar. —JC

SERVES 2

1¾ cups (410 ml) room temperature black coffee, decaf or cold brew

1½ tbsp (12 g) gelatin dissolved in ¼ cup (60 ml) cold water

1 tsp (4 g) coconut sugar

1½ cups (355 ml) Date-Sweetened Almond Milk (page 502)

½ cup (120 ml) water

2 tbsp (16 g) black assam tea leaves

Make the coffee jelly by mixing together the coffee, dissolved gelatin and sugar in a small bowl. Mix until the sugar is dissolved. Pour the mixture into a gelatin mold or regular glass pan and let it set in the fridge uncovered for 4 to 6 hours.

In a small saucepan over low heat, prepare the milk tea by combining almond milk and water. Let it simmer for 1 to 2 minutes. Turn off heat and add the tea leaves. Stir and let the leaves steep for 3 to 4 minutes. Strain out the tea leaves and pour the milk tea in a glass jar. Place it in the fridge for 45 minutes to 1 hour to cool.

Once the gelatin is set, cut it into bite-sized cubes. Fill a glass one-quarter full with the coffee jelly. Add cold milk tea and serve

CHEF'S TIP:
For stronger coffee, substitute the cold coffee with two shots of espresso plus 1 cup (235 ml) of water.

ICED MACA

Can't drink coffee? Try maca powder instead. It's a great alternative to coffee with its caramel notes and its ability to energize without the jitters and crashing of caffeine. —NK

SERVES 1

1 cup (235 ml) full-fat coconut milk

½ tbsp (4 g) maca powder

½ tsp vanilla extract

½ tsp cinnamon

2 tbsp (30 ml) raw honey

1 cup (150 g) ice

Add coconut milk to a high-powered blender. Sift in the maca powder then add the vanilla extract, cinnamon, raw honey and ice. Blend until well incorporated. If using a regular blender, crush the ice first before blending. Serve cold.

CHAI ICED TEA LATTE

Chai is a traditional Indian spiced tea. The aromatic spices add a wonderful kick to regular black tea, and when mixed with a cream or milk, it becomes a delicious treat! This version is chilled and uses non-dairy almond milk in place of regular milk and honey in place of processed sugar, so it's a perfect healthy Paleo beverage for summer. —HH

SERVES 4

4 cups (940 ml) water

4 black chai tea bags

¼ cup (60 ml) honey

¼ tsp ground cinnamon

¼ tsp ground cloves

¼ tsp ground coriander

¼ tsp ground ginger

2 cups (470 ml) unsweetened almond milk

Boil the water, then turn off the heat and place the tea bags in the hot water. Allow to steep for at least 5 minutes, or 10 minutes if you want the tea to be stronger and richer. After steeping, remove the tea bags and add the honey, cinnamon, clove, coriander and ginger and stir until it has completely dissolved. Allow the tea to cool. It will take a few hours.

If you are in a rush, add ice cubes to the water until it is room temperature, then transfer to the fridge. Be careful not to add too many ice cubes as it will water down the tea. Once the tea has completely cooled, add the almond milk to the tea and mix. Add ice cubes to cool further and enjoy!

PUMPKIN CHAI LATTE

Chai lattes are a delicious coffee alternative with less caffeine. Flavored with pumpkin and spices, this latte is festive for a cold autumn morning. —RM

SERVES 1

1 chai tea bag

1 cup (235 ml) hot water

1 tbsp (8 g) powdered coconut milk

1 tbsp (15 g) pumpkin purée

2 tsp (10 ml) grade B maple syrup

Dash ground cinnamon

Dash ground nutmeg

Dash ground ginger

Steep tea bag in very hot water for 1 minute, then remove. Whisk all other ingredients into the hot tea until slightly frothy. Relish the joy of one-upping the expensive coffee shop.

WASSAIL

Wassail is a traditional, usually spiked, apple cider that originated in medieval southwest England. This recipe has the addition of whipped eggs at the end to make the cider frothy and extra special. A pot of this simmering on the stove will perfume your whole house with the smell of spiced apples. —RM

SERVES 10–12

2 quarts (1880 ml) apple cider

Reusable tea bags

2 cinnamon sticks

6 cloves

3 allspice berries

Half an orange, sliced

½ tsp grated nutmeg

½ tsp powdered ginger

½ tbsp (7.5 ml) lemon juice

3 large eggs, whites and yolks separated

⅓ cup (80 ml) brandy, optional

In a medium pot, gently heat apple cider slowly over medium-low heat without boiling. Fill the tea bags with cinnamon sticks, cloves and allspice berries. You can also use organic cheesecloth and butcher's twine if you don't have tea bags. Add the spice bag and slices of orange to the pot, along with the nutmeg, ginger and lemon juice.

Once the cider is thoroughly heated and the spices incorporated, about 1 hour, you can stop here OR go on to the next step: In a small mixing bowl, beat the egg yolks with a hand mixer until light in color, about 1 minute. In a separate large mixing bowl, beat the egg whites until stiff peaks form, about 3 minutes. Fold the yolks into the whites, then use ½ cup (120 ml) hot wassail to temper the eggs by pouring them into the wassail slowly so they don't scramble. Then add the tempered eggs to the pot of wassail. Stir in the brandy, if using. Serve immediately.

LONDON FOG TEA LATTE

Inspired by the traditional London Fog Tea Latte, my version makes this a dairy-free and refined-sugar-free version for those following a Paleo template. —NK

SERVES 1

½ cup (120 ml) full-fat coconut milk

1 tsp (5 ml) vanilla extract

1 cup (235 ml) strongly brewed Earl Grey tea

Raw honey or maple syrup, to sweeten

Place coconut milk into a small saucepan and heat over medium-low heat. Stir the milk frequently. Once the milk is steaming, add the vanilla extract and mix through. Remove from the heat and pour into the brewed tea. Add raw honey or maple syrup. Use a milk frother to whisk until frothy. Serve warm.

CHEF'S TIP:

Use a blender to blend the tea for a frothy mixture if you don't have a milk frother.

ROOIBOS TEA LATTE

Need to give up the caffeine but still want to enjoy a cup of something warm in the mornings? Try some rooibos tea instead. Caffeine-free and full of robust flavor, this tea is a perfect replacement for coffee. —NK

SERVES 1

1 cup (235 ml) full-fat coconut milk

½ tsp pumpkin pie spice or ground cinnamon

2 tsp (10 ml) raw honey or maple syrup, to sweeten

1 tsp (5 ml) vanilla extract

1 cup (235 ml) brewed rooibos tea

Ground cinnamon, for garnish

Place coconut milk into a small saucepan and heat until warm but not boiling. Add the pumpkin pie spice or cinnamon and raw honey or maple syrup. Mix to combine. Remove from the heat and stir in the vanilla extract. Place brewed tea and coconut milk mixture into a blender. Blend the mixture for 30 to 60 seconds. Pour into your chosen cup and dust with some ground cinnamon.

TURMERIC TEA

A powerful liver-cleansing tonic, this tea is one of my favorite ways to include turmeric and ginger in my diet. Both spices provide anti-inflammatory health benefits, and the tea is delicious, warming and comforting. —KW

SERVES 1

Boiling water

2 tsp (6 g) fresh turmeric, finely grated

1 tsp (3 g) fresh ginger, finely grated

½ tsp ground cinnamon

Pinch black pepper

½ tsp pure vanilla extract

1 tsp (5 ml) pure raw honey or sweetener of choice

¼ cup (60 ml) coconut milk or milk of choice

Fill mug halfway full with boiling water. Add turmeric and ginger. Cover and let steep for 10 to 15 minutes. Strain out the turmeric and ginger. Stir in cinnamon, black pepper, vanilla and honey. Fill the rest of the mug with coconut milk and stir.

CHAPTER 8

PALEO ESSENTIALS

Paleo essentials make life more flavorful! They're both the building blocks on which recipes are built and the final touch that takes a finished dish to the next level. Often when folks take control of their nutrition and prioritize their health, condiments, sauces and the like are some of the first things cleaned out of the fridge after a glance at the ingredients. But there's hope! Paleo essentials are here to the rescue.

Another fantastic thing to keep in mind about Paleo essentials is that they can be batch-prepared and stored for later use. There's nothing like having a container of Homemade Mayonnaise (page 496) ready to pull together a rich chicken salad or crisp slaw or your favorite homemade dressing— check out the Grainy Mustard Champagne Vinaigrette (page 513) to take your salad to the next level. Master these Paleo Essentials and weave them into your routine for meals that don't compromise on flavor and don't skimp on the flavor building blocks that make a recipe memorable.

Plus, by making your own staples like Homemade Coconut Flour (page 505), Almond Flour (page 505) and even Homemade Hazelnut Spread (page 504), you can save money and know exactly where your Paleo basics are coming from.

HOMEMADE MAYONNAISE

Homemade mayo is one of those recipes that seems intimidating, but is actually quick and easy to make! It is delicious and healthy, unlike the junk-ridden store-bought varieties. Homemade mayo is great with lettuce wraps, egg salad, chicken salad and even as a base for many sauces. —AV

MAKES 1 CUP (235 ML)

1 large egg yolk or 2 small, at room temperature

1 tsp (3 g) stone ground mustard

1 tbsp (15 ml) fresh lemon juice

¼ tsp sea salt

¼ tsp freshly ground black pepper

1 cup (235 ml) high quality avocado oil or mild-tasting olive oil

In the bowl of a food processor fitted with the blade, place the egg yolk, mustard, lemon juice, salt and pepper. While it's running, add the avocado or olive oil to the insert. The insert should have a tiny little hole in it that will slowly drip the oil into the food processor. Leave the food processor running until all of the oil has completely dripped through. This emulsification process is key when making mayo. Trust me, the first time I ever made homemade mayo, I just poured the cup of oil right in with the ingredients and it just made a liquid-y mess and not a mayo. Adjust salt and pepper to taste.

CHEF'S TIP:

If your mayo didn't work out and needs fixing: Remove the mayo mixture from your food processor. Add another egg yolk to the bowl of your food processor, while it is running, slowly add the curdled/liquid-y mayo mess until it is all blended and creamy.

GREEN HERB MAYONNAISE

Mayonnaise is a delicious condiment that pairs well with many different foods like Spicy Fish Sticks (page 105). Brighten up this Paleo-friendly mayonnaise by stirring in some fresh herbs for a nutritious twist. —NK

SERVES 4–6

2 cups (500 g) Homemade Mayonnaise (page 496)

2 tbsp (8 g) fresh dill, finely chopped

2 tbsp (8 g) fresh flat-leaf parsley, finely chopped

2 tbsp (8 g) fresh chives, finely chopped

1 tbsp (15 ml) fresh lemon juice

¼ tsp garlic powder, optional

Place mayonnaise into a medium-sized mixing bowl. Stir in the fresh herbs. Add the lemon juice and garlic powder if desired. Place in a glass container with a secure lid in the fridge.

EASY 30–SECOND HOMEMADE MAYONNAISE

I never realized how it easy it is to make homemade mayonnaise. Once you make it homemade, you'll get spoiled and never want to go back. It's rich and creamy and so much better than store bought. And the great news is that you can make it in less than 30 seconds with an immersion blender! —KW

MAKES 1 CUP (360 G)

2 egg yolks at room temperature

Salt and white pepper, to taste

1½ tbsp (23 ml) apple cider vinegar or fresh lemon juice

1 tsp (3 g) dried ground mustard or Dijon mustard

⅓ cup (80 ml) refined coconut oil, melted

1 cup (240 ml) avocado oil

Put all of the ingredients in a tall, narrow cup in the order listed. The order of ingredients is important so make sure to start with the eggs and end with the oil. The reason this method works is because of the narrow cup so make sure to use a narrow cup and not a bowl.

With an immersion blender—sometimes called a stick blender—start at the bottom of the cup and work your way up until it's nice and smooth and creamy. You want to use the regular blending attachment not the whisk.

The mayo is ready to use right away. It must be stored in the fridge and keeps for about 2 weeks.

SWEET & SAVORY WHIPPED BUTTERS

Whipped butters are a great way to dress up a simple meal with gourmet flavor. I love to add a scoop to Easy and Amazing Banana Bread (page 526) or grilled carrots or any of your favorite roasted vegetables. —CP

MAKES 1 CUP (360 G) EACH FLAVOR

FOR WHIPPED MAPLE NUT BUTTER

8 tbsp (120 g) butter

½ cup (75 g) walnuts, finely chopped

¼ cup (60 ml) maple syrup

½ tsp ground cinnamon

FOR WHIPPED GARLIC HERB BUTTER

16 tbsp (240 g) butter

3 large cloves garlic, crushed

1 tbsp (15 ml) olive oil

½ tsp Celtic sea salt

2 tbsp (8 g) fresh basil, finely chopped

Slice butter into small cubes and bring to room temperature for about 20 minutes

Place the butter and remaining ingredients of your desired flavor in a mixing bowl. Use a hand blender to whip the butter until light and fluffy.

Add a scoop of flavored butter as a delicious topping to your desired food.

ROASTED GARLIC MARROW BUTTER

This rich and decadent topping is packed with flavor that will catapult your taste buds into overdrive. Serve it on top of the humble burger patty or some grilled steak for the ultimate indulgence. —JC

SERVES 12

1½ pounds (680 g) beef marrow bones

1 head of roasted garlic

½ cup (120 ml) ghee, melted

Sea salt

Black pepper

Preheat oven to 400°F (200°C, or gas mark 6).

Place marrow bones in a casserole dish and roast in the oven for 20 minutes. Scoop out the cooked marrow and place it in a food processor or blender. Add roasted garlic and ghee. Purée until smooth. Season with sea salt and black pepper to taste. Place marrow butter in the freezer for 8 to 10 minutes until it begins to solidify. Transfer it to a sheet of parchment paper and roll into a log. Freeze for at least 45 minutes to 1 hour until hard. Slice and use as needed.

CHEF'S TIP:

Roasted garlic can be bought at grocery stores. You can make your own by slicing off the top of a garlic bulb and adding 1 tablespoon (15 g) of ghee or coconut oil. Wrap the garlic in foil and bake in the oven at 375°F (190°C, or gas mark 5) for 40 to 45 minutes until soft.

CONFIT GARLIC

The concept of cooking something confit style is to cook it slowly in fat. Here I take that concept and translate it to these Confit Garlic by using Paleo-friendly fats like coconut oil or macadamia oil to confit the garlic. These make a great addition to any meal or as a condiment that can be enjoyed with some homemade burgers. —NK

SERVES 10–15

1¼ cups (295 ml) refined coconut oil or macadamia oil

30 large cloves garlic, peeled

Place coconut oil or macadamia oil into a medium saucepan over low heat. Once the oil is completely melted, add the garlic cloves. Cook over very low heat, making sure the mixture doesn't boil, for an hour or until the garlic has softened. Store in the fridge in a glass container for up to 2 weeks. To serve, remove desired amount of garlic cloves from the cooking fat and keep the rest refrigerated.

CHEF'S TIP:

Due to coconut oil's nature to turn solid when cold, when you want to enjoy some confit garlic, heat some water in a saucepan and place the jar in the water to melt the coconut oil.

GARLIC BUTTER BALSAMIC SAUCE

This garlic sauce is finger-licking good. If you want to spruce up a boring burger or meatloaf, drizzle this sauce over it and watch it transform from blah to amazing. —KW

MAKES ¼ CUP (60 G)

3 tbsp (45 g) butter

1 tbsp (15 ml) balsamic vinegar

1 tsp (3 g) fresh garlic, minced

Over low heat, stir the butter, balsamic and garlic in a small pot. Stir constantly for a minute or two until the mixture is boiling. As soon as it boils, remove from heat. Serve warm.

CHEF'S TIP:

I like to quadruple the garlic butter balsamic sauce recipe and keep some stored in a mason jar in the fridge so I can have it at all times. Once it's in the refrigerator, it will solidify and become spreadable like butter. You can either warm it back up so you can drizzle it or keep it cool so you can spread it.

HOMEMADE GHEE

Ghee or clarified butter is a traditional cooking oil from India that I use often. Ghee is essentially butter with the milk solids taken out so it burns cleaner and has a higher smoke point. It is also a good alternative for those who are sensitive to dairy but want that buttery flavor. Since the lactose and casein are mostly removed, many with dairy sensitivities can tolerate ghee. I use ghee almost exclusively when cooking in a skillet. I use it for scrambling eggs, sautéing vegetables, making stir-frys and more. —HH

MAKES ABOUT 16 OUNCES (454 G)

2 pounds (908 g) butter

Put butter in a pot on medium heat. Allow the butter to melt completely, then turn down to low. The butter will begin to sputter. Continue to let the butter gently simmer and sputter.

You will notice a whitish film accumulate on the surface, these are the milk solids. Use a wooden spoon to gently remove the surface milk solids in order to see to the bottom of the pan. There will also be solid bits at the bottom of the pan.

Once the butter is a clear golden hue and the solid bits at the bottom of the pan have begun to brown and toast, the ghee is done. This usually takes about 15 to 25 minutes. At this point turn the heat off and let cool for a few minutes.

Set up a strainer over a bowl to catch the ghee, and line the strainer with cheesecloth or a clean, thin, flour sack-style dishtowel. Pour the ghee through the strainer. The cloth will catch the milk solids and leave you with the remaining clarified butter.

Once the ghee has cooled, transfer it to a clean jar. Ghee does not need to be refrigerated and once it has fully cooled it will become solid, but still very pliable. I sometimes put my ghee into the fridge after it has cooled a bit so it solidifies faster, but it's up to you.

INDIAN SPICED GHEE

This spiced ghee can be used for flavoring soups, vegetables and savory meats. Simply use for sautéing or add to your foods after cooking. A great way to add a bit of variety to your meals. —KH

MAKES ABOUT 1½ CUPS (355 ML)

1½ cups (355 g) ghee

2 tsp (6 g) mustard seed

2 tsp (6 g) cumin seed

4 tsp (12 g) turmeric

2 tsp (6 g) ground coriander

½ tsp ground cumin

1 tsp (3 g) ground ginger

½ tsp ground cinnamon

3 tsp (8 g) fennel seeds

5 whole cardamom pods, crushed

Gently heat ¼ cup (60 g) ghee in a heavy-bottomed pan on low-medium. Once melted, add mustard and cumin seeds and turn down heat to low. Allow to cook for 3 to 4 minutes, stirring once in a while.

Add remaining spices to pot and continue to cook on low for 2 to 3 minutes, stirring occasionally. The spices will become fragrant.

Pour in the rest of the ghee and allow to warm on low for 20 minutes, uncovered. Be sure that it is very low. The ghee should not bubble in any way. The low heat is just to help the spices infuse. Remove from heat and allow to cool for 30 minutes. Strain with a fine mesh strainer into a glass jar. Enjoy!

WHIPPED JALAPEÑO HONEY BUTTER

This whipped butter is so unique but versatile. It can be spread on Paleo biscuits, slathered on lobster tails or used in sweet baking for a jalapeño kick. —RM

MAKES 2 CUPS (480 G)

8 ounces (227 g) unsalted butter

2 tbsp (16 g) jalapeño peppers

2½ tbsp (37 ml) raw honey

¼ tsp fine sea salt

Allow the butter to come to room temperature. Slice each jalapeño in half, place outer side up on a baking sheet and broil for 5 minutes, until skin looks lightly blackened. Cool the jalapeños and then remove the seeds and outer blackened layer of skin, then mince them.

In a medium-sized mixing bowl, whip the butter, honey and salt until light and fluffy, about 5 minutes. Beat in the minced jalapeños until smooth.

Serve immediately on Paleo biscuits or gluten-free non-GMO cornbread. Seal in an airtight container for about a month. Bring to room temp before serving.

LEMON HOLLANDAISE SAUCE

I could truly eat this hollandaise sauce by the spoonful! It is rich and buttery and slightly on the tangy side. Serve with Crispy Ham Eggs Benedict (page 437) or Asparagus & Smoked Salmon Creamy Eggs Benedict (page 425). —CP

MAKES ABOUT ¾ CUP (180 ML)

8 tbsp (120 ml) butter, melted

2 egg yolks, room temperature

2 tbsp (30 ml) lemon juice

¼ tsp salt

¼ tsp paprika

⅛ tsp cayenne pepper

Pour a small amount of hot water into a blender, cover with the lid and set aside for a few minutes. Melt the butter in a small saucepan. Pour the water out of the blender.

Next, blend together yolks, lemon juice, salt and spices. Scrape down the sides of the blender and continue to blend.

With the blender running on low, slowly drizzle in the melted butter and blend until it is completely incorporated. The sauce will thicken as it cools.

Serve a generous spoonful with eggs Benedict. Store remaining sauce in the refrigerator for up to 4 days.

CHEF'S TIP:
I love serving this sauce using Grain-Free Fluffy White Dinner Rolls (page 522) as the base for eggs Benedict. Save your extra 2 yolks from the roll recipe for the hollandaise sauce.

SWEET ONION MARMALADE

Caramelized onions and balsamic vinegar merge together to make a sweet spread. This marmalade can be a great gift idea. Just can it in mini jars and include a homemade bag of Paleo bread mix with baking instructions on the bag. —RM

MAKES ½ CUP (120 G)

1 tbsp (15 g) bacon fat

4 cups (640 g) onion, sliced

¼ cup (60 ml) water

1½ tbsp (23 ml) balsamic vinegar

1 tbsp (15 ml) pure maple syrup

Dash of salt and pepper

In a large skillet, heat the bacon fat until hot. Add the onion slices and stir, making sure the fat evenly coats the onions. Lay a heavy medium-sized skillet lid (smaller than the large skillet) directly on top of the onions for 15 minutes, stirring occasionally. This helps speed up the cooking process of the onions.

Stir the water into the onions and then cook covered, with a lid that fits now for 40 to 45 minutes depending on your stove temp. I like to stir the onions every 8 to 10 minutes to get beautiful browning. The last 15 minutes you really have to keep an eye on them as caramelizing onions can be tricky.

Mix in the balsamic vinegar, maple syrup and salt and pepper, and continue cooking for another 10 minutes. The mixture should become thick and gooey, with very little moisture. Store contents in an airtight container in the fridge for up to 2 weeks. This recipe can be easily doubled.

NO-FUSS BLUEBERRY SPREAD

This is an easy recipe to keep up your sleeve. I love topping pancakes or muffins with it, and once I even used a spoonful on top of vanilla coconut milk. It's so versatile. —RM

MAKES 1½ CUPS (360 G)

2 cups (300 g) fresh blueberries

2 tbsp (30 ml) raw honey

2 tsp (10 ml) fresh lemon juice

2 tsp (6 g) gelatin

2 tbsp (30 ml) cold water

Heat the blueberries, honey and lemon juice over medium heat in a small saucepan.

Cover with a lid for 4 minutes. Meanwhile, soak the gelatin in the cold water for 2 minutes. Then stir it in with the blueberries. Reduce the stove temp to low heat and cook for 6 more minutes while the blueberries break down.

The spread should be syrupy thick and not dry. Adjust the cooking time as needed for desired consistency. Serve warm over grain-free pancakes or coconut ice cream, or chill and use it as jelly on grain-free toast.

BLUEBERRY JAM

Summer berry season is my absolute favorite and this thick blueberry jam will have you enjoying this sweetness all year long. Blueberries are not only low glycemic but also full of antioxidants. Add a spoonful to a slice of toasted grain- and nut-free sandwich bread. —CP

MAKES 2 (8-OZ) JARS

1 pound (454 g) blueberries

2 tbsp (30 ml) raw honey

1 tbsp (15 ml) fresh lemon juice

2 tsp (6 g) gelatin

Toss together blueberries and honey in a saucepan over medium-low heat. Heat the berries for 15 minutes, stirring occasionally so they don't burn.

Next, crush the berries with the back of a large spoon or masher until the blueberries release their juices and the mixture starts to resemble jam. Stir in lemon and gelatin and continue heating for another 10 minutes, stirring occasionally.

Remove pan from heat and let it cool for 20 minutes before transferring to the refrigerator to finish cooling. The jam will thicken as it cools.

ORANGE & DATE CHUTNEY

If you love a good chutney, then you have to make this one. Sweet dates blend wonderfully with the delicate flavor of oranges, and subtle notes of ginger and apple. A great pairing for roasted meats, especially pork, or with fresh cheeses in a sandwich. —VM

MAKES 3 SMALL JARS (8 OUNCES [227 G])

12 ounces (336 g) apples, peeled and quartered

5 ounces (140 g) oranges, peeled and cut into small pieces

8 ounces (227 g) dates, pitted

2 tsp (6 g) fresh ginger root, grated

8 ounces (227 g) coconut sugar

½ tsp sea salt

1 cup (235 ml) apple cider vinegar

In a large pan over low heat, bring all of the ingredients to a slow boil.

Cook over low heat for 2½ hours, mixing often so the chutney will not stick and burn to the bottom of the pan. Once the chutney is cooked, pour the mixture into sterilized jars and seal.

Store the jars upside down until ready to use. For the best results, wait 2 weeks before serving and store in the refrigerator once you have opened the jar. Stores for about 3 weeks.

DATE-SWEETENED ALMOND MILK

A dairy-free milk alternative, slightly sweetened with dates and hints of vanilla. This almond milk makes a great coffee creamer or grain-free granola accompaniment. —CP

MAKES 4 CUPS (945 ML)

1½ cups (225 g) almonds

½ cup (90 g) dates, pitted

3½ cups (822 ml) warm water, for blending

1 tsp (5 ml) vanilla extract

¼ tsp ground cinnamon

Pinch of Celtic sea salt

In a glass or stainless steel bowl, soak almonds covered in 3 inches (7.5 cm) of water. Soak overnight or up to 24 hours. During the last hour of soaking, add dates to soften. Strain and rinse almonds and dates.

Add almonds and dates to a blender with the warm water, vanilla, cinnamon and salt.

Blend on high for about 2 minutes, depending on the power of your blender. The mixture will be thick and foamy but should be completely fluid.

Over a wide mouth container, pitcher or bowl, place cheesecloth, securing with a rubber band to hold the cloth in place.

Working in small batches, slowly pour some of milk through the cloth to strain out the almond meal. You may need to clean or change cloths several times.

Gather the cloth in your hands to press out any remaining milk. Discard the almond meal.

Store in glass containers in refrigerator for up to 5 days.

CHEF'S TIP:

I recommend storing the milk in glass containers as plastic easily absorbs flavors and could alter the taste of your milk.

HOMEMADE CASHEW MILK

Making your own nut milk at home couldn't be easier. Try this cashew milk recipe and you'll never want to buy nut milk from the store again. —NK

MAKES 1–2 SERVINGS

8 ounces (227 g) organic cashews

Filtered water

⅛ tsp sea salt

1 tsp (5 ml) vanilla extract, optional

2 tsp (10 ml) raw honey, optional

Soak cashews in 2 cups (470 ml) of filtered water overnight. Drain the cashews and add to a blender. Pour in 2 to 4 cups (470 to 940 ml) of filtered water. Add the sea salt, vanilla extract and honey, if using. Blend until combined. Pour through a nut milk bag or a cheesecloth-lined glass jar to remove the nut pieces. Store the cashew milk in the fridge for up to a week.

CHEF'S TIP:

The less water you add to the blender the thicker and creamier the resulting milk will be.

HOMEMADE COCONUT MILK

It's surprisingly easy and more nutritious to make your own coconut milk. You can make coconut milk using various methods, including making it from desiccated coconuts or from fresh coconuts. The latter takes a fair amount of work. This method relies on a store-bought package of shredded coconut. —AV

MAKES 4 CUPS (940 ML)

1 (8-ounce [227-g]) package unsweetened finely shredded coconut

4 cups (940 ml) very hot water, not quite boiling

Place the coconut and hot water in a blender and blend for about 45 seconds. Line a strainer with 2 layers of cheesecloth—or use a nut milk bag in place of the cheesecloth and strainer. Pour the contents of the blender through the cheesecloth-lined strainer or through the nut milk bag and into a large bowl. Pull the edges of the cheesecloth together or nut milk bag and squeeze the remainder of the coconut milk out. Refrigerate the coconut milk and use within 1 or 2 days.

SWEETENED CONDENSED COCONUT MILK

This dairy-free alternative can be used in any recipe that calls for sweetened condensed milk. It also makes a great non-dairy coffee creamer. —KH

MAKES ABOUT 10 OUNCES (280 G)

1 (13.5-ounce [372-g]) can of full-fat coconut milk

¼ cup (60 ml) honey or maple syrup

In a small saucepan, bring coconut milk to a gentle boil. Whisk in honey or maple syrup. Allow to actively simmer on medium heat for 25 to 30 minutes, stirring often. Mixture will thicken slightly, reduce by about a third, and darken just a bit. Allow to cool completely then store in glass container for up to 5 to 7 days.

COCONUT WHIPPED CREAM IN 30 SECONDS

Coconut whipped cream is a Paleo and dairy-free favorite. With this method it can be whipped up in less than a minute! —AV

SERVES 6–8

2 cups (470 ml) coconut cream, 2 cups (470 ml) Homemade Coconut Milk (page 503) or 1 (14.5-ounce [406-g]) can full-fat coconut milk

Up to 1 tbsp (15 ml) of raw honey

1 tsp (5 ml) vanilla

Place the coconut cream, Homemade Coconut Milk or the can of coconut milk in the refrigerator overnight. If using coconut cream or homemade coconut milk, I like to put it in a wide mouth mason jar. An hour before making the whipped cream, place the mixing bowl in the freezer to chill it.

If using coconut milk (not cream), remove the milk from the refrigerator and carefully scoop out the cream from the top of the container and into the mixing bowl. For coconut cream, you can just put the entire contents into the mixing bowl. You can save the remaining liquid from the coconut milk and add it to smoothies. Add vanilla and honey to taste to the mixing bowl and stir to combine. I use 1 tablespoon (15 ml) of honey, per 2 cups (470 ml) of coconut cream. If you are using coconut milk, you will have much less cream. I recommend starting with 1 teaspoon (5 ml) of honey and adjusting to taste from there. The honey should not be hard—you can put it in a small glass container and put it in a warm water bath to gently liquefy it.

Use an immersion blender and blend for 30 seconds, moving the blender up and down until peaks form. Serve immediately or store it in the fridge and blend it again right before serving.

HOMEMADE HAZELNUT SPREAD

A healthy alternative to the famous chocolate spread. This one tastes just as good . . . and does not contain a bunch of harmful ingredients! —VM

MAKES 1 PINT JAR

1 cup (150 g) hazelnuts

4 tbsp (60 g) butter, softened

¼ cup (30 g) raw cacao powder

1–4 drops liquid stevia

1 tsp (5 ml) vanilla extract

½ cup (120 ml) coconut water

Toast the hazelnuts in a dry skillet over low heat for about 10 minutes. Set them aside and let them cool. Once they have cooled, roll the hazelnuts between your hands to remove the skins. After you have removed the skins, place the hazelnuts in the blender or coffee grinder and reduce to a fine paste.

Place the hazelnut paste in the food processor along with the softened butter, raw cacao powder, liquid stevia and vanilla extract. Mix thoroughly, until smooth. Add the coconut water a little at a time and blend until you reach the desired consistency. Store in the refrigerator for up to 3 weeks. Let come to room temperature before serving.

HOMEMADE COCONUT BUTTER

With just a few ingredients it's easy to make your own creamy coconut butter at home. —NK

MAKES 10 OUNCES (20 TBSP [296 G])

10 ounces (280 g) unsweetened shredded coconut

1 tbsp (15 ml) coconut oil, melted

⅛ tsp sea salt

Add the shredded coconut, coconut oil and sea salt into a high-powered blender. Blend on high for 1 to 2 minutes. Transfer the mixture to a glass jar or container and store in dry cool place.

CHEF'S TIP:

Don't have a high-powered blender? You can also make this coconut butter in your food processor. Place ingredients as above into a food processor and process for around 8 to 10 minutes, making sure to stop the food processor frequently to scrape down the sides.

HOMEMADE COCONUT FLOUR

Coconut flour should only be made from the leftover coconut fiber from making Homemade Coconut Milk (page 503) because most of the moisture has been wrung out of it. Coconut flour must be very dry, so it can't be made by simply processing shredded coconut. —HH

MAKES ABOUT 1–2 CUPS (120–240 G)

Leftover coconut fiber from making Homemade Coconut Milk (page 503)

Spread out the leftover coconut fiber on a cookie sheet. Try to spread it out as much as possible and break up any clumps. You can either dry it in your oven on the lowest temperature setting until it is totally dry, about 2 to 4 hours, or use a dehydrator and dry it at about 130°F (54°C) until it is dry, a few hours. Once it is completely dry, process it in a food processor to break up all the clumps.

ALMOND FLOUR

Making your own almond flour is a cinch! I never buy it because I can make it so quickly. I usually just make the amount that I need right before I make a recipe with almond flour. For best results use blanched almonds. —HH

MAKES ABOUT 1 CUP (120 G)

1 cup (150 g) blanched almonds

Use blanched almonds (almonds that have had the skin removed), because these work the best for baking recipes. Put the almonds in a food processor. If you need 1 cup (120 g) of almond flour, put in 1 cup (150 g) of almonds. Pulse until you get a flour-like texture. Be careful not to pulse for too long because it can release the oils and create almond butter. You want it to be dry. That's it!

CHEF'S TIP:

You can buy blanched almonds at most health food stores. Blanched almonds have had the skins removed, so they will be off-white in appearance. They can be whole blanched almonds or slivered blanched almonds—both will work.

PUMPKIN PIE SPICE

Instead of spending extra money on store bought pumpkin pie spice, try making your own. It's so easy to make with ingredients you probably already have in your cabinets. —KW

MAKES 1 TABLESPOON (8 G) OF SPICE

2 tsp (6 g) ground cinnamon

¼ tsp ground ginger

¼ tsp ground cloves

¼ tsp ground nutmeg

¼ tsp ground allspice

Combine all ingredients in a small bowl and mix together.

CHEF'S TIP:

I usually triple or quadruple my recipe and store it in a little mason jar that I keep in my spice cabinet. This would make a fun little gift, too.

ALMOND BUTTER

It is so easy to make your own creamy almond butter. After you try this recipe you will wonder why people ever buy it! —HH

SERVES 4

2 cups (300 g) almonds, raw or roasted

Put the almonds into a food processor and blend. At first the almonds will turn into a dust-like texture. Continue to mix. Stop and scrape down the sides of the food processor if necessary. Continue to blend until the oils release and you get a creamy almond-butter texture. This may take up to 5 to 6 minutes of blending and stopping to scrape the sides.

CHEF'S TIP:

You can use either raw almonds or roasted almonds. The only difference it will make in the almond butter is the flavor—It just depends on your preference. The roasted almonds will create a smokier flavor, while the raw almonds will have a cleaner, lighter taste. If you are buying already roasted almonds, make sure you check the ingredients and watch out for any unwanted added oils or flavorings.

PUMPKIN-SPICED ALMOND BUTTER

Different flavored nut butters are expensive to buy, but you can make your own very easily! This pumpkin spiced version is a favorite at my house. We especially enjoy dipping apples in it. —KW

MAKES ABOUT 1 CUP (240 G)

1 cup (240 g) almond butter

3 tbsp (45 ml) pure maple syrup

2 tbsp (24 g) roasted pumpkin or canned pumpkin—add more, 1 tbsp (12 g) at a time, to the food processor if you want a creamier consistency

1 tbsp (8 g) Pumpkin Pie Spice (page 505)

1 tsp (5 ml) pure vanilla extract

Sea salt, to taste

Add ingredients to a food processor and process until desired consistency is reached.

CHOCOLATE ALMOND BUTTER

A simple homemade chocolate nut butter to be enjoyed by the spoonful or spread on a slice of warm grain- and nut-free sandwich bread. I love whipping up a batch of this sweet treat to give as an edible gift! —CP

MAKES ABOUT 2½ CUPS (450 G)

2 cups (480 g) creamy almond butter, preferably raw

6 tbsp (48 g) cacao powder

2 tbsp (30 ml) maple syrup

2 tbsp (30 ml) coconut oil, melted

1 tsp (5 ml) vanilla extract

1½ tsp (4.5 g) ground cinnamon

½ tsp Celtic sea salt

If your almond butter is hard or chilled, place the jar in a heat-proof bowl with hot water for 5 minutes.

Place all ingredients in a mixing bowl. Blend with a hand blender until thoroughly mixed.

Enjoy by the spoonful or spread on a slice of grain- and nut-free sandwich bread.

CHUNKY PISTACHIO MACADAMIA NUT BUTTER

Try a different spin on nut butters and make this sweet and savory pistachio macadamia nut combo. A little bit of honey gives it some sweetness and creamy ghee makes it oh-so-decadent; you won't be able to resist eating it by the spoonful! Look for shelled pistachios to save time and get this ready in a pinch. —JC

SERVES 48

3 cups (450 g) raw shelled pistachios

1 cup (150 g) raw macadamia nuts

4 tbsp (60 ml) raw honey

2 tbsp (30 ml) ghee, melted

¼ tsp sea salt

In a large skillet over low heat, add pistachios in a single layer. Toast for 10 minutes, stirring every couple of minutes to prevent one side from burning. Remove and set aside on a piece of parchment paper to cool. Add macadamia nuts to the same pan and toast for 5 to 8 minutes. Stir every couple of minutes. Remove and set aside to cool next to the pistachios.

Add 2½ cups (375 g) of cooled pistachios and ¾ cup (112 g) macadamia nuts to a food processor. Purée for 8 to 10 minutes until it turns into a creamy consistency. Make sure to scrape down the sides every couple of minutes.

Place the nut butter mixture into a bowl. Add the remaining ½ cup (75 g) of pistachios and ¼ cup (38 g) of macadamia nuts to the food processor. Pulse for 5 to 8 seconds to create chunky pieces. Add to the nut butter. Add honey, ghee and sea salt. Mix until well combined.

Transfer to glass containers and store at room temperature.

CHEF'S TIP:

A blender can also be used instead of a food processor. If you don't want chunky nut butter, place all the pistachios and macadamia nuts together to purée all at once.

CASHEW CREAM CHEESE

This Cashew Cream Cheese is a rich and creamy alternative to dairy-based cream cheese. It pairs well with both savory and sweet items like crackers or dates! —HH

MAKES 8–12 OUNCES (227–340 G)

1 cup (150 g) raw cashews

Enough water to cover the cashews

Sprinkle of sea salt

½ tsp garlic powder

½ tsp salt

Soak cashews in water and sea salt for 8 to 24 hours. Drain the water and put the soaked cashews in a food processor or blender along with garlic powder and salt. Blend until creamy. If you want it to be a little thinner you can add a little more water. Store in a jar in the fridge.

CHEF'S TIP:

This recipe can be made savory or sweet depending on how you want to use it. For sweet applications, you can omit the garlic powder and add a sweetener like honey or coconut sugar and other flavor-enhancers like cinnamon or vanilla extract.

EASY HERBED CASHEW CHEESE

If you miss cheese, this recipe is for you. Get the texture and flavor of a tangy soft cheese without the dairy. —KH

MAKES ABOUT 1½ CUPS (375 G)

1½ cups (375 g) raw cashews, soaked in water for 4–6 hours

6 tbsp (90 ml) full-fat coconut milk

1 tbsp (8 g) nutritional yeast

1 tbsp (15 ml) fresh lemon juice

½–1 clove garlic, crushed

Several grinds of fresh pepper

Sea salt, to taste

¼ cup (15 g) finely chopped fresh herbs (basil, chives, parsley, cilantro, dill)

Soak cashews in water for at least 4 to 6 hours. Drain and rinse well.

Process drained cashews and coconut milk in food processor until creamy smooth, about 5 to 7 minutes, scraping sides a time or two. Be patient here. This cheese is amazing when you get it nice and smooth.

Add the remaining ingredients, except the fresh herbs, and process another minute to fully incorporate. Feel free to add a teaspoon or two (5 to 10 ml) of liquid here if you prefer. I like mine pretty thick. Adjust the salt and pepper. Fold in fresh herbs. Place in fridge to cool completely. Serve and enjoy!

JALAPEÑO CASHEW "CHEESE" SPREAD

This recipe is a creative dairy-free alternative to cheese spread. It can be used as a veggie dip, spread on grain-free crackers or stuffed inside peppers. It's so addicting, I've been known to eat it straight from the fridge! —RM

SERVES 4

1½ cups (225 g) raw cashews, soaked

¼ cup (60 ml) water

3 tbsp (45 ml) white wine

3 tbsp (24 g) nutritional yeast

4 cloves garlic

2 tsp (10 ml) fresh lemon juice

1 tsp (3 g) Celtic sea salt

Ground black pepper

2 tbsp (16 g) raw jalapeño pepper seeds

Soak the cashews, fully submerged, for at least 2 hours. This will get them soft and helps to make a creamier cheese. Drain and blend the soaked cashews in a food processor, scraping the sides occasionally, until chunky.

Add in the other ingredients EXCEPT the jalapeño seeds and process, scraping the sides occasionally, until you have a smooth texture, at least 5 minutes. Taste the cheese mixture and fine-tune it before mixing in the jalapeño seeds with a spoon. Put in an airtight container and keep in the fridge for up to 5 days.

CHEF'S TIP:
Use the discarded jalapeño skins by stuffing this cheese spread inside and then baking them.

AVOCADO CREAM

Thanks to the avocado and coconut cream, this is a super quick and easy recipe loaded with healthy fat. The wonderful part about this cream is that you can pair it with just about everything that tastes great with an avocado. Go ahead; add a new twist to the dishes with this delicious cream! —VM

SERVES 1

1 avocado, peeled, seed removed

1 tbsp (15 ml) coconut cream

Juice of ½ lemon

Celtic sea salt

Mix all ingredient together until smooth and pair with your favorite cracker or use as a side dish.

DAIRY-FREE PARMESAN CHEESE

Certain dishes just call for a bit of Parmesan cheese. This cashew-based dairy-free version can be used in place of traditional Parmesan cheese in your Paleo meals. —KH

MAKES ABOUT 1 CUP (120 G)

¼ cup (30 g) nutritional yeast

1 cup (150 g) raw, unsalted cashews

1 tsp (3 g) salt

Process all ingredients in a food processor until the texture is crumbly like coarse flour. Store in airtight container in fridge for up to 3 to 4 weeks.

FRESH BASIL PESTO

Toasted pine nuts and macadamia nuts give this dairy-free pesto a rich buttery taste. Serve with scrambled eggs for a delightful meal full of flavor. You may also want to eat it by the spoonful as I sometimes do! —CP

MAKES 1 CUP (136 G)

¼ cup (38 g) raw pine nuts

¼ cup (38 g) raw macadamia nuts

4 ounces (112 g) fresh basil, about 4 cups

½ cup (120 ml) olive oil

3 cloves garlic

1 tsp (5 ml) lemon juice

1 tsp (3 g) sea salt

½ tsp fresh cracked black pepper

Preheat oven to 300°F (150°C, or gas mark 2). Spread nuts out on a baking sheet. Toast the nuts for 5 to 6 minutes or until fragrant and golden brown, watching carefully so they don't burn.

Allow the nuts to cool for a few minutes.

Combine all ingredients in a food processor. Blend for 30 seconds, scraping down the sides and blending for an additional 30 seconds.

Store pesto in the refrigerator for up to 5 days.

MACADAMIA NUT PESTO

Macadamia nuts add a delectable creamy flavor to a traditional pesto. They are also a great option when nuts are called for because they have a very low omega-6 content compared to their other nut friends. They are also a healthy source of magnesium, manganese, thiamine, copper and iron. —AV

MAKES 2 CUPS (470 ML)

1 cup (60 g) flat-leaf parsley

2 cups (120 g) fresh basil

3–4 cloves garlic

½ cup (120 ml) olive oil

¼ cup (40 g) macadamia nuts

2 tbsp (30 ml) fresh lemon juice, I used Meyer lemons

2 tsp (6 g) fresh oregano

¼ tsp sea salt

¼ tsp pepper

Combine all pesto ingredients in a food processor and blend until smooth.

VITAL GREEN PESTO

Pesto is not just for basil. I like to use other green herbs to make this fresh, green condiment to complement any dish. A great way to add a bit of living foods to every meal. —KH

MAKES ABOUT 1½ CUPS (375 G)

1 bunch cilantro, washed and dried

1 bunch parsley or basil, washed and dried

1 cup (235 ml) olive oil

1 cup (150 g) pumpkin seeds, raw

Sea salt, to taste

Place greens into food processor and pulse until coarsely chopped. Add olive oil and pumpkin seeds. Process until it forms a smooth paste. Feel free to leave pesto as chunky or smooth as you like it. Salt to taste. Transfer into clean glass jar. Store in fridge for up to 2 to 3 weeks.

SPINACH BASIL PESTO

This pesto is an easy and delicious way to use up the abundance of spinach and basil from a summer garden. Adding just a dollop or two of pesto can really jazz up any savory dish. —KW

MAKES ABOUT 1 CUP (240 G)

2 cups (140 g) fresh spinach leaves

1 cup (60 g) fresh basil leaves

3 cloves garlic, peeled

½ lemon, zested and juiced

½ cup (120 ml) extra-virgin olive oil

Sea salt and pepper, to taste

Pinch of red pepper flakes, optional

Using a food processor or blender, process all the ingredients until smooth.

CHEF'S TIP:

Freeze any leftovers in individual portion sizes. Also, if you can tolerate dairy, adding ½ cup (50 g) Parmesan or Romano cheese to the pesto is delicious.

CILANTRO CHIMICHURRI

Chimichurri is an easy way to add a blast of flavor to any savory dish. I especially enjoy this recipe over beef and chicken. —KW

MAKES ABOUT 1½ CUPS (360 G)

2 limes, juiced

½ cup (120 ml) olive oil

½ onion, roughly cut into chunks

4 cloves garlic

½ jalapeño pepper

1 bunch fresh cilantro, about 1 packed cup (60 g), stems are ok (see Chef's Tip)

1 bunch fresh parsley, about 1 packed cup (60 g), stems are ok

½ tsp ground cumin

Sea salt, to taste

Put all ingredients in a high-powered blender or food processor, starting with the lime juice and olive oil. Blend or pulse until everything is finely chopped.

CHEF'S TIP:

Don't worry about removing all the stems from the cilantro and parsley—there is a ton of flavor in those stems! I just grab the entire fresh bunch with my hand and twist the tops off in one move. The rougher bottom stems will be snapped off in your twist leaving you with the green leaves and softer stems. Put all those leaves and softer stems in the blender.

AVOCADO TZATZIKI SAUCE

Tzatziki sauce gets a makeover! I love serving this sauce with the Gyro Meatballs (page 63). —KW

SERVES 4

1 avocado

1 small/medium cucumber, or ½ large cucumber, cut in half and seeded

2 cloves garlic

1 tbsp (10 g) red onion, diced

Juice of 1 lemon

1 tbsp (4 g) fresh dill

¼ cup (30 g) sour cream, optional

Sea salt and pepper, to taste

Combine all ingredients together in a food processor or blender.

Blend until smooth and creamy. Add salt and pepper to taste.

EASY FERMENTED CUCUMBERS (PICKLES)

Tangy, crisp and easy to make, these counter pickles are a great way to get more fermented foods into your diet. —KH

MAKES ½ GALLON (1.9 L)

3 large cucumbers

½ onion, sliced into thin rounds

2½ tbsp (18 g) sea salt

2 tbsp (8 g) fresh dill, finely chopped or ½ tsp dried dill

Filtered water

2-3 tbsp (30-45 ml) juice from previously fermented vegetables, optional, to boost fermentation

Cut cucumbers into thin slices. Place cucumbers, onion, salt and dill into a large, clean glass jar. Pour in filtered water to cover—add extra juice from fermented veggies, if using. Give a little shake to dissolve salt. Let sit loosely covered on kitchen counter for 2 to 3 days then refrigerate.

QUICK AND EASY PICKLED RED ONIONS

Condiments make everything better. These zesty pickled onions are a great addition to burgers, salads or savory meats. And they are an amazingly beautiful purple color. —KH

SERVES 6

3 cups (705 ml) water

1 large red onion, sliced into thin rings/rounds

¼ cup (60 ml) raw, unfiltered, unpasteurized apple cider vinegar

Boil the water in a tea kettle or small pot. Place onion rounds into a sieve in the sink and pour boiling water over them. Drain and place into a shallow bowl. Pour in apple cider vinegar, stir and allow to sit on the counter to cool for about 30 minutes, stirring once or twice. Store, covered, in fridge for up to 2 weeks.

GOMASIO (SESAME SALT)

Gomasio is an Asian sesame seed condiment full of calcium, protein and fiber. It can be used to flavor vegetables, soup, salads and meats. —KH

MAKES ABOUT 1 CUP (165 G)

1 cup (150 g) sesame seeds

1 tbsp (15 g) sea salt

Dry-roast sesame seeds in a cast iron skillet over medium heat, tossing or stirring constantly, until light golden-brown, about 7 to 10 minutes. Be careful not to burn them. Allow to cool.

Put the sesame seeds and salt in a clean spice grinder, food processor or mortar and pestle and grind into a coarse meal—you should still see a few whole seeds in the mixture. Store in refrigerator; keeps for 6 to 8 weeks.

RANCH DRESSING (DAIRY-FREE, VEGAN)

This recipe is not quite as thick as some of the more mayo-textured ranch dressings that you sometimes see, but I like this thinner ranch to pour more easily over salad. —HH

MAKES 16 OUNCES (474 ML)

1 cup (235 ml) full-fat canned coconut milk

¼ cup (60 ml) + 1 tbsp (15 ml) apple cider vinegar

¼ cup (60 ml) + 1 tbsp (15 ml) olive oil

½ tsp parsley, fresh and chopped or dried

½ tsp dill, fresh and chopped or dried

½ tsp chives, fresh and chopped or dried

½ tsp sea salt

½ tsp pepper

½ tsp garlic powder

½ tsp onion powder

Shake the can of coconut milk before opening so it's not separated. In a bowl, combine the coconut milk, apple cider vinegar and olive oil. Use an immersion blender or blender to emulsify the liquids and the oil. Add the herbs, salt, pepper, garlic and onion powder to the liquids and blend. Keep the dressing in a jar in the fridge. It will last for at least a week.

CHEF'S TIP:
Fresh chopped herbs will lend a better flavor.

RANCH SEASONING

This seasoning blend is fantastic on chicken and vegetables. You can even make your own ranch dressing by adding these ingredients to Homemade Mayonnaise (page 496). —KW

MAKES ABOUT 3 TABLESPOONS (24 G)

2 tsp (6 g) dried parsley

1 tsp (3 g) onion powder

1 tsp (3 g) garlic powder

1 tsp (3 g) dried dill

1 tsp (3 g) dried chives

1 tsp (3 g) salt

1 tsp (3 g) pepper

Combine all ingredients together.

CHEF'S TIP:
Double, triple or even quadruple this recipe so you have extra seasoning to keep on hand. You can keep the spice rub in a sealed container in your pantry for up to a year.

THOUSAND ISLAND DRESSING

I was inspired to make this Thousand Island Dressing by the sauce that usually goes on "cheesy" kale chips. The tangy bell pepper adds a nice bite and a hint of sweetness to the creamy nutty cashew purée. This is a great dressing for salads or a rich dip for sliced veggies. —HH

SERVES 4

1 cup (150 g) soaked raw cashews

1 tbsp (8 g) sea salt

1 red bell pepper

Juice of 1 lemon

2 tbsp (30 ml) olive oil

2 tbsp (30 ml) water

½ tsp salt and pepper

¼ tsp turmeric

¼ tsp garlic powder

To soak cashews, put them in a bowl and cover completely with water and mix in the sea salt. Let soak for at least 2 hours. Drain water from the cashews. In a food processor, combine cashews with remaining ingredients and blend. Add more water for a thinner consistency.

CAESAR SALAD DRESSING

Caesar salad dressing used to be one of my favorite dressings. It's impossible to find a healthy, Paleo-friendly version, but luckily making your own is simple! —AV

MAKES ABOUT 1 CUP (235 ML)

2 tbsp (30 ml) fresh lemon juice

2 small cloves garlic

1 tsp (5 g) Dijon mustard

6–8 anchovy fillets packed in olive oil

2 large egg yolks

¼ tsp salt

¼ tsp pepper

½ cup (120 ml) avocado oil

2 tbsp (30 ml) olive oil

In the bowl of a food processor, combine lemon juice, garlic, mustard, anchovy fillets, egg yolks, salt and pepper. Blend together and mix thoroughly. With the processor running, add avocado oil and olive oil in a slow stream through hole in the lid. Adding the oil slowly is key to making the dressing. This will help it emulsify and become creamy. Most food processors have an insert with a little hole. You can just add your oil there and keep the food processor on until all the oil has mixed in.

GRAINY MUSTARD CHAMPAGNE VINAIGRETTE

This light champagne vinaigrette adds a pop of flavor to any salad but pairs particularly well with salads filled with fresh fruits. I like to make a batch to have on hand throughout the week. —CP

MAKES ABOUT ¾ CUP (180 ML)

½ cup (120 ml) olive oil

¼ cup (60 ml) champagne vinegar

1 tbsp (15 g) stone ground mustard

½ tsp sea salt

¼ tsp fresh cracked black pepper

Whisk together all ingredients.

Toss with your favorite salad.

Store any extra dressing in the refrigerator.

RASPBERRY BALSAMIC DRESSING

I have acres of wild raspberry bushes at my house and this is one dressing I make every year when the raspberries are in season. We also enjoy this dressing poured on top of grilled chicken and fish during the hot months of summer. —KW

SERVES 15

2 cups (300 g) fresh raspberries

½ cup (120 ml) balsamic vinegar

½ cup (120 ml) extra-virgin olive oil

2 tbsp (30 ml) honey

2 tsp (10 g) Dijon mustard

½ tsp dried oregano

½ tsp onion powder

Sea salt and pepper, to taste

Add all of the ingredients to a food processor or blender and blend until smooth and creamy.

CHEF'S TIP:
This dressing tastes the best after chilling in the refrigerator for a few hours.

ORANGE VINAIGRETTE

The fresh orange flavor is a welcome surprise in this easy vinaigrette. I usually make a big salad, add whatever vegetables I can find in my refrigerator and then top with grilled chicken or steak, almonds and orange segments. —KW

SERVES 6+

1 orange, zested and juiced

1 tsp (5 g) Dijon mustard

½ cup (120 ml) olive oil

¼ cup (60 ml) apple cider vinegar

¼ tsp ground cumin

Sea salt and pepper, to taste

Blend all ingredients in a blender or food processor until creamy.

CHEF'S TIP:
This also makes a fantastic marinade for all types of meat and fish.

GARLIC DIJON VINAIGRETTE

I use this Garlic Dijon Vinaigrette dressing for plain salads and also as a dip. Emulsifying the vinegar and oil together creates a thick, rich texture that complements the tart and slightly spicy dressing. You will want to put this vinaigrette on everything! —HH

SERVES 6–8

2–4 cloves garlic

1½ tsp (7.5 g) Dijon mustard

½ cup (120 ml) olive oil

½ cup (120 ml) balsamic vinegar

Salt and pepper to taste

Finely chop the garlic. Combine all ingredients in a jar or drinking glass. Use an immersion blender or regular blender to blend all ingredients together. The oil and vinegar will emulsify to create a thick, rich and creamy salad dressing.

WARM BACON DRESSING

Don't throw out that bacon fat! This warm bacon dressing makes eating a big pile of raw greens extra delicious. —KW

MAKES ¾ CUP (180 G)

⅓ cup (80 ml) bacon fat, warmed

⅓ cup (80 ml) apple cider vinegar

1 tbsp (15 g) Dijon mustard

1 clove garlic, minced

⅛ tsp pepper

Whisk all ingredients together and serve. Enjoy over salad greens, eggs, vegetables or even different kinds of meat.

CHEF'S TIP:
Keep it in the refrigerator but warm before using.

BACON DATE DRESSING

This savory and sweet salad dressing will add a unique flavor to any salad that you serve. Who doesn't love bacon? —KH

MAKES ½ CUP (120 ML)

5 tbsp (75 ml) olive oil

2 tbsp (30 ml) bacon fat (reserved from cooking bacon)

2 tbsp (30 ml) apple cider vinegar

1 piece of cooked bacon

4 dates, dried and pitted

¼ tsp sea salt

Combine all dressing ingredients in a blender or small food processor and process until smooth and the dates are all incorporated. Enjoy over your favorite salad.

BETTER THAN PEANUT SAUCE: ALMOND SATAY SAUCE

This sauce is the perfect way to spice up simple meals. Make a batch and enjoy it all week with Chicken Stir-Fry (page 76) or simple lettuce cups! —AV

MAKES 1 CUP (180 G)

½ cup (120 g) almond butter

Juice of 1 tangerine

Juice of 1 lime

1 small spicy pepper, chopped (I use jalapeños)

½ cup (120 ml) coconut aminos

½ tsp Paleo-friendly fish sauce

1 tsp (3 g) fresh grated ginger

¼ cup (60 ml) hot filtered water

Place almond butter, tangerine juice, lime juice, pepper, coconut aminos, fish sauce and ginger in a food processor. Blend until smooth. Add water and mix some more. If it is too thick for your liking, you can thin it out with more water. I find this thickness to work great as a dipping sauce and for a stir-fry sauce. You can eat it immediately, but I have found that if you let it sit for a few hours to overnight, the flavors improve. Store in the refrigerator in an air-tight container. Enjoy!

THAI SALAD DRESSING

Eating salads is more fun when you have delicious dressings to pour over them. This creamy dressing is perfect with any salad and tastes amazing with fresh cilantro and crunchy vegetables. —KH

MAKES ABOUT ¾ CUPS (162 G)

¼ cup (38 g) almond butter or sunflower seed butter

2 tbsp (30 ml) raw apple cider vinegar

2 tbsp (30 ml) fresh lemon juice

2 tbsp (30 ml) extra-virgin olive oil

1 tbsp (15 ml) coconut aminos

3 tbsp (45 ml) maple syrup or honey

2 cloves garlic, minced

1-inch (2.5-cm) knob of fresh ginger, peeled and chopped

½ tsp salt

⅛ tsp cayenne powder

2 tbsp (8 g) fresh cilantro

Water for thinning

Combine all ingredients in a high-powered blender and process until creamy and smooth. Add water 1 tablespoon (15 ml) at a time for a thinner consistency, if desired.

COOL RANCH AVOCADO DIP

I wanted a different variation of traditional guacamole so I created this Cool Ranch Avocado Dip. I especially enjoy using plantain chips or red pepper slices for dipping. —KW

MAKES 1½ CUPS (360 G)

1 ripe avocado

1 medium cucumber, cut in half lengthwise and seeded

1 lemon, juiced

2 cloves garlic

1 heaping tbsp (10 g) red onion, diced or 1 tsp (3 g) dried onion powder

1 tbsp (4 g) fresh dill or 1 tsp (3 g) dried dill

1 tbsp (4 g) fresh chives or 1 tsp (3 g) dried chives

1 tbsp (4 g) fresh parsley or 1 tsp (3 g) dried parsley

Sea salt, to taste

¼ cup (60 g) sour cream or Greek yogurt, leave out for dairy free

Plantain chips or red pepper slices for dipping

Put all ingredients in a high-powered blender. Blend until smooth and creamy. Serve with plantain chips or red pepper slices for dipping.

CHEF'S TIPS:

The longer this sits in the fridge, the better it is. I like to make it the night before I'm going to serve it.

BUFFALO RANCH DIPPING SAUCE

I especially love pairing this sauce with the Chicken Dippers (page 207). If you like extra spice, be sure to add more hot sauce and perhaps even a pinch or two of cayenne pepper. —KW

SERVES 4

¾ cup (180 g) Homemade Mayonnaise (page 496)

1 tsp (3 g) dried parsley

½ tsp garlic powder

½ tsp onion powder

½ tsp dried dill

½ tsp dried chives

Sea salt and pepper to taste

1–2 tbsp (15–30 ml) buffalo hot sauce, or more if you want more spice

Mix all ingredients together in a bowl. Refrigerate any leftovers for up to 1 week.

BLOOMING ONION SAUCE

This tasty sauce is great for sliced raw vegetables or drizzling over grilled chicken, but you'll definitely want to try it with the Baked Zucchini Fries (page 217), too. —KW

MAKES ¾ CUP (180 G)

½ onion, sliced

½ tsp sea salt

1 tbsp (15 ml) coconut oil or other fat of choice

1 tbsp (15 ml) apple cider vinegar

1 tbsp (15 ml) honey, optional

1 tsp (5 g) Dijon mustard

½ cup (120 g) Homemade Mayonnaise (page 496)

Place the onion, salt and oil into a skillet over medium-low heat. Cook for 20 to 25 minutes stirring occasionally until the onions turn golden brown and caramelize. Blend the caramelized onions, vinegar, honey and Dijon with a hand blender or food processor until fairly smooth. Stir in the mayonnaise. Keep any leftovers in the refrigerator for up to 1 week.

LEMON DILL DIPPING SAUCE

Lemon and dill are a classic combination, and this dipping sauce pairs well with all types of seafood. I especially like to serve this dipping sauce with Fish Sticks (page 104). —KW

SERVES 4

½ cup (120 g) Homemade Mayonnaise (page 496)

¼ cup (30 g) dill pickles, chopped

1 tsp (3 g) dried dill or 1 tbsp (4 g) fresh dill

1 tsp (3 g) garlic powder

½ tsp onion powder

Juice of ½ lemon, cut the other half in wedges for serving

Combine all the ingredients in a bowl and stir until well mixed. Place in the fridge for at least 10 minutes for the flavors to combine.

HONEY MUSTARD DIPPING SAUCE

The pungent flavor of mustard with the sweet taste of honey might be one of the most perfect food marriages. When combined with creamy homemade mayonnaise, it really becomes finger-lickin' good! This is the perfect accompaniment to Chicken Tenders (page 29) —AV

MAKES ½ CUP (120 ML)

½ cup (120 g) Homemade Mayonnaise (page 496)

2 tbsp (30 g) Dijon mustard

1 tsp (5 g) yellow mustard

2 tbsp (30 ml) raw honey

Stir together mayonnaise, mustards and honey. Store in an airtight container in the refrigerator for up to 5 days.

ANCHO CHILI SPICE RUB

This is one of our favorite spice rubs for pork and chicken. If you like extra heat, be sure to add a pinch or two of cayenne pepper, too. —KW

MAKES RUB FOR UP TO 5 POUNDS (2.3 KG) OF MEAT

2 tbsp (16 g) ancho chili powder

1 tbsp (8 g) smoked paprika

1 tbsp (8 g) garlic powder

1 tbsp (8 g) onion powder

1 tbsp (8 g) ground cumin

1 tsp (3 g) dry mustard

1 tsp (3 g) dried oregano

1 tsp (3 g) sea salt

1 tsp (3 g) pepper

Combine all the ingredients together. Rub on meat of choice and let marinate for 2 to 4 hours before cooking.

MANGO HABANERO HOT SAUCE

This mango habanero hot sauce goes well with many different dishes from savory to sweet. We especially love it over pulled pork. It's equally fantastic drizzled over vanilla ice cream, too. —KW

MAKES 2+ CUPS (470 ML)

3 mangos, pitted and skinned

4 habaneros, seeds removed

½ medium onion

4 cloves garlic

1 lime, juiced

1 tsp (3 g) sea salt

½ cup (120 ml) apple cider vinegar

½ cup (120 ml) water

1 tbsp (15 ml) honey

(continued)

Combine all the ingredients in a blender or food processor until smooth. Once smooth, place the mixture in a pot over medium heat. Bring to a simmer and let simmer for 20 minutes, stirring occasionally. Remove from heat, let cool and then store in the refrigerator.

CHEF'S TIP:

If you find the hot sauce is too spicy, stir in a bit more honey until it's to your liking. And if you like it extra spicy, consider leaving some or all of the seeds in the habanero peppers.

PARSLEY GARLIC AIOLI

Aioli is a delicious garlic mayonnaise that can accompany plantain chips, sweet potato fries or even be slathered on grilled meat. —RM

MAKES ¾ CUP (180 G)

1 egg yolk

2 garlic cloves, chopped

1 tbsp (4 g) fresh chopped parsley

1½ tbsp (23 ml) fresh lemon juice

½ tsp salt

Freshly ground pepper

¼ cup (60 ml) extra-virgin olive oil

¼ cup (60 ml) macadamia nut oil

Combine the egg yolk, garlic, parsley, lemon juice and salt and pepper in a food processer. While the motor is still running, pour a thin stream of extra-virgin olive oil slowly to create a thick emulsion. Do not rush this step or else it will separate! Do the same with the macadamia nut oil. Scrape the sides of the processor in order to blend all the chopped ingredients. You should have a thick creamy aioli when you're done. This recipe can be kept in the fridge for up to 6 days.

CHIPOTLE PEPPERS IN ADOBO SAUCE

Chipotle peppers in adobo sauce are one of my favorite ingredients. They add smoky heat and depth to otherwise simple dishes. I stopped using them when I started following a Paleo diet, as many of the canned varieties are loaded with questionable ingredients. I finally made my own recipe that tastes identical to the store-bought version. These add a delicious smoky heat when added to a pot-roast in the oven or the slow cooker.—AV

MAKES ABOUT 2 CUPS (470 ML)

7–10 chipotle peppers, stems removed and split lengthwise

1 cup (240 g) strained tomatoes in a jar

1 cup (235 ml) beef broth (substitute filtered water)

¼ cup (60 ml) apple cider vinegar

¼ cup (40 g) onion, minced

2 cloves garlic, crushed

2 tbsp (30 ml) honey

½ tsp sea salt

½ tsp ground cumin

¼ tsp ground cinnamon

⅛ tsp ground allspice

Pinch of ground cloves

Combine all of the ingredients in a pan and simmer, covered, on low for 30 minutes. Remove the lid and simmer on low for an additional 30 minutes to allow the sauce to thicken. Once the sauce has thickened, allow the peppers to cool and then store for later use. The sauce should keep in the fridge for about a week or you can freeze it for later use.

HOW TO PEEL & SEED TOMATOES

I rarely use canned tomato products because highly acidic foods, such as tomato sauce and stewed tomatoes, are more likely to leach chemicals like BPA from the lining of the can.

When a recipe calls for canned tomatoes, you can substitute fresh ones by blanching fresh tomatoes, then peeling, seeding and chopping them. This method is healthier and less wasteful, as you minimize your use of packaging.

As a rule of thumb, when a recipe calls for a 14.5-ounce (406-g) can of tomatoes, I use 5 to 6 whole tomatoes. —AV

Bring about 4 quarts (3.6 l) of water to a boil. Set up a cold bath of water in a large bowl with some ice cubes. Cut an X in the bottom of each tomato, drop the tomatoes in the boiling water carefully and cook for 1 minute or until skin starts to break. Remove a few tomatoes at a time and dunk in the cold bath. The skin should now easily peel off by hand. Peel the skin, cut the tomatoes in half and scoop or squeeze the seeds out. Chop and use as needed.

GARDEN FRESH TOMATO SAUCE

I come from an Italian family, and to us, there aren't many things better than a garden-fresh homemade tomato sauce. Butter and balsamic kick this sauce up a notch. I like to serve this with the Italian Meatballs (page 59). —KW

MAKES ABOUT 1½ QUARTS (1.5 L)

4 pounds (1818 g) tomatoes, skin removed

¼ cup (60 ml) olive oil

2 medium onions, diced

4 cloves garlic, minced

¼ cup (60 ml) balsamic vinegar

¼ cup (15 g) fresh basil, chopped

1 tbsp (4 g) fresh oregano, chopped

1 tbsp (4 g) fresh parsley, chopped

Pinch or two dried red pepper flakes

Salt and pepper, to taste

2 tbsp (30 g) butter

To get the tomato skins off easily, cut a shallow X into the stem end of the tomatoes. Place them in a pot of boiling water for 20 seconds each. Using a slotted spoon, take them out of the boiling water and immediately dip them in ice cold water for 10 seconds. The skins will peel right off!

After the skins are removed, roughly chop the tomatoes. You can get as many seeds out as you like or leave them in. Set cut tomatoes aside.

In a large pot, add the olive oil over medium heat. Add the onions and garlic and salt and cook for about 2 to 3 minutes or until onions are translucent. Pour in the balsamic vinegar and let simmer for about a minute. Add the chopped tomatoes, basil, oregano and parsley and red pepper flakes. Add some more salt and pepper, to taste. Bring to a boil and let simmer for 25 minutes, stirring occasionally. Right before you take it off the heat, stir in the butter.

You can leave the sauce chunky or you can blend it with an immersion blender until it reaches your desired consistency.

CHEF'S TIPS:
Resist letting this simmer for longer than 25 minutes. When you are using fresh herbs, it's important not to overcook them because they will lose their freshness and flavor.

CRAN-APPLE CRANBERRY SAUCE

Gone are the days of eating cranberry sauce out of a can. This recipe is simple to make and made with real ingredients. This recipe is a Thanksgiving favorite of mine. —KW

SERVES 8

¼ cup (60 ml) water

12 ounces (340 g) fresh cranberries

1 orange, peeled and cut into small pieces

1 apple, diced

¼ cup (60 ml) pure maple syrup

⅛ tsp ground cloves

In a skillet over medium heat, mix water, cranberries, orange and apple pieces. Cook, stirring often, until cranberries start to split open. Pour in maple syrup and ground cloves. Simmer for 10 minutes, stirring often. If you prefer a smoother cranberry sauce, blend all the ingredients until smooth. Chill and serve.

CRANBERRY SAUCE

Cranberry sauce is one of my favorite things about fall and Thanksgiving. Instead of using the usual processed white sugar, this cranberry sauce uses honey to sweeten the sour cranberries, which lends a richer depth of flavor. I love how the acidity of this sauce pairs with a savory meat like turkey or pork chops. —HH

SERVES 4-5

2 cups (220 g) cranberries

¼ cup (60 ml) honey

⅓ cup (80 ml) orange juice or juice of 1 orange

1 tsp (3 g) orange zest

½ tsp grated fresh ginger

Place all ingredients in a pot and turn heat to medium. Allow to simmer for about 8 to 10 minutes or until the mixture begins to bubble and foam and most cranberries are popped and mushed. Turn off the heat and allow to cool. There should still be a few whole cranberries left for texture, but most should be mushed.

MOJO CRIOLLO

Sour oranges are a wonderful seasoning agent in Cuban and Puerto Rican cuisine. The flavor is actually more bitter than sour and works well to impart a tangy flavor to everything from roasts to veggies to starchy sides. You can make a large portion and freeze it for later use, too. If sour oranges are unavailable in your area, I've given you two substitutions using more commonly available citrus fruits that you can try out. —AT

MAKES ABOUT 1½ CUPS (355 ML)

1 cup (240 ml) freshly squeezed sour orange juice

8-10 cloves garlic, peeled

1 tsp (2 g) dried oregano

1 tsp (6 g) fine Himalayan salt

¼ tsp freshly ground black pepper

2-4 tbsp (30-60 ml) extra-virgin olive oil, depending on recipe

In a blender or food processor, pulse the sour orange juice, garlic, oregano, salt, pepper and olive oil until the garlic is pulverized and you have a sauce with a creamy consistency.

Use immediately as a marinade. Store in fridge for a few days only. Freeze unused portions for use later.

Used as a traditional marinade for meats (especially pork), for yuca, served as a condiment for cooked meats or to season roasted or sautéed veggies. It is a very versatile marinade/dressing.

CHEF'S TIPS:

Sour oranges are also called bitter, Seville, marmalade or bigarade oranges and may be labeled naranja agria at Latin American markets. If sour oranges are unavailable, substitute ½ cup (120 ml) of freshly squeezed lime juice and ½ cup (120 ml) of freshly squeezed regular (sweet) orange juice. Or use ½ cup (120 ml) of freshly squeezed regular orange juice, ¼ cup (60 ml) of grapefruit juice and 1 tablespoon (15 ml) of lime juice.

CHAPTER 9

BREADS & CRACKERS

When we talk about the Paleo diet, breads and crackers are not the first thing to come to mind. There is room, however. for the occasional bread or cracker indulgence. Sometimes we just want some bread or a few crackers to complement our meal, and having some grain-free alternatives can make transitioning to a Paleo diet a bit easier.

What we have included in this section are a variety of bread and cracker recipes using high-quality, real-food ingredients. The focus here is to maintain eating nutrient-dense foods. There is definitely a learning curve when it comes to grain-free baking, but once you get to know your ingredients, it can be fun and exciting. So get to know your grain-free flour ingredients: coconut flour, almond flour, tapioca flour, nuts and seeds. And remember to use high-quality fats like coconut, ghee or butter. Other fats like tallow, lard and duck fat can be used as well.

Some of my favorites in this section include Savory Garlic Herb Biscuits (page 525) and Thin & Crispy Pizza Crust (page 528).

GRAIN-FREE FLUFFY WHITE DINNER ROLLS

A fluffy, white Paleo dinner roll so you can once again say pass the bread and butter at the table. Raw, creamy cashew butter makes these rolls light and fluffy. If you want to use these as a sweeter roll with butter and Blueberry Jam (page 502), simply omit the chopped rosemary. —CP

MAKES 8

2 egg whites

¾ cup (180 g) raw cashew butter

1 whole egg

2 tbsp (30 ml) butter, melted

Pinch of sea salt

¼ tsp baking soda

½ tsp lemon juice

½ tsp fresh rosemary, chopped

Handful of Parmesan cheese, optional

Preheat oven to 350°F (180°C, or gas mark 4). Line a baking sheet with parchment paper.

In a mixing bowl, use a hand blender to whip egg whites until soft, foamy peaks being to form.

In another bowl, use a hand blender to mix cashew butter, egg, butter, salt, baking soda, lemon juice and rosemary. This will be very thick.

Fold in egg whites and mix until smooth. You want this to be well blended but still keep the whites fluffy.

Use a spoon to drop batter onto baking sheet. Sprinkle a small handful of Parmesan over each roll, if desired.

Bake for 10 to 12 minutes then serve and enjoy immediately with butter.

CHEF'S TIPS:

Be sure to preheat your oven as you want to place these in the oven immediately after mixing. The sprinkle of Parmesan is optional but just helps give them a slightly crispy outside texture.

CRUMBLY BUTTER BISCUITS

Buttery biscuits complete every festive dinner. These classic biscuits are simple but can be garnished with butter, pesto, herbs or honey. Quick to make, butter biscuits provide a cozy addition to any weekend brunch or rainy day. Crumble biscuits as a topping for soup or even to make Thanksgiving stuffing. Sprinkle with cinnamon and drizzle with honey for a sweet treat! —CP

MAKES 8

2½ cups (300 g) almond flour

¼ cup (30 g) arrowroot powder

2 tbsp (16 g) coconut flour, sifted

½ tsp baking soda

½ tsp baking powder

½ tsp sea salt

6 tbsp (90 g) butter, softened

2 eggs, whites and yolks separated

Preheat oven to 375°F (190°C, or gas mark 5). Line a baking sheet with parchment paper.

In a mixing bowl, sift together all dry ingredients. Slice softened butter into flour and use a fork or pastry cutter to form a crumbly mixture. Mix in the egg yolks.

In a separate bowl whip egg whites until soft peaks begin to form. Gently fold egg whites into flour. The mixture will still be very crumbly.

Use a spoon to scoop dough into your hands and gently form flat round biscuits. Place on baking sheet.

Bake for 12 to 15 minutes or until edges are golden brown. Drizzle tops with honey or melted butter.

GRAIN-FREE FOCACCIA BREAD

Not all Paleo breads are created equal. This flavorful focaccia bread can be eaten as is or sliced thin for a savory sandwich bread. My favorite sandwich to make with this bread is salami, avocado and pesto. —KH

SERVES 4-6

1 cup (120 g) tapioca flour

¼ cup (30 g) coconut flour, sifted

1 tbsp (8 g) nutritional yeast

1 tsp (3 g) sea salt

½ tsp baking soda

3 eggs

¼ cup (60 ml) full-fat coconut milk

¼ cup (60 ml) ghee, melted

2 tbsp (8 g) finely chopped fresh herbs (rosemary, thyme, oregano, basil)

1 tbsp (15 g) ghee for skillet

Olive oil and salt, for garnish

Place a 10-inch (25-cm) cast iron skillet into the oven and preheat to 400°F (200°C, or gas mark 6).

Combine tapioca flour, coconut flour, nutritional yeast, salt and baking soda in a large bowl. Set aside.

In another bowl, whisk together eggs, coconut milk and melted ghee. Add chopped herbs and mix again. Pour wet into dry and mix until well incorporated.

Carefully remove skillet from oven and drop 1 tablespoon (15 g) of ghee into hot bottom of pan and swirl to cover. Pour bread mixture into pan and give pan a little shake to level it out.

Bake 11 to 13 minutes, until top of bread is golden and bread is pulling away from sides of skillet. Drizzle liberally with olive oil and sea salt before serving.

ROSEMARY GARLIC FLATBREAD

Sometimes you just want a little bread. This simple flatbread recipe is popular even with the non-Paleo crowd. The secret is in using a thick, hot pan to create a perfectly crispy flatbread. —KH

SERVES 4

½ cup (120 ml) full-fat coconut milk

¼ cup (60 g) ghee or coconut oil

1 cup (120 g) tapioca flour

¼ cup (30 g) coconut flour, sifted

½ tsp sea salt

1 egg, beaten

1 tsp (3 g) finely chopped fresh rosemary

1-2 tsp (3-6 g) finely chopped garlic

Olive oil and extra sea salt, for garnish

Preheat the oven to 450°F (230°C, or gas mark 8) and place a pizza stone, cast iron skillet or very thick pizza pan into oven to heat up.

Gently heat up coconut milk and ghee in a small saucepan until very warm but not boiling.

Combine tapioca flour, sifted coconut flour and salt in a large bowl. Pour coconut-ghee mixture on top. Mix until thoroughly combined. Allow to sit for a couple of minutes to cool and for coconut flour to absorb.

Add beaten egg and mix again until fully combined.

Place a large piece of parchment paper onto a cutting board and pour mixture into center. Using a spatula, evenly spread mixture until it is about ¼-inch (6-mm) thick. Sprinkle on rosemary and garlic. Carefully remove hot stone/pan from the oven and slide parchment paper onto it. Bake for 9 to 12 minutes, depending on how crispy you like it. Garnish with olive oil and sea salt.

BAGELS

Paleo bagels? Yes, it's true. They may not be your typical New York-style bagel, but it sure is fun to eat bagels again. —KH

SERVES 6

¼ cup (32 g) pumpkin seeds, preferably soaked and dehydrated

¼ cup (32 g) sunflower seeds, preferably soaked and dehydrated

2 tbsp (16 g) coconut flour

1 tbsp (8 g) arrowroot powder

2 tsp (6 g) poppy seeds

1 tbsp (8 g) hemp or sesame seeds

½ tsp unrefined sea salt

¼ tsp baking soda

½ tsp cream of tartar

4 eggs

3 tbsp (45 ml) ghee, melted (I highly recommend using ghee)

Preheat the oven to 350°F (180°C, or gas mark 4) and liberally grease a donut pan with ghee or coconut oil.

Process pumpkin and sunflower seeds in food processor for 10 seconds to break them up into coarse pieces. Add the coconut flour, arrowroot, poppy seeds, hemp seeds, salt, baking soda and cream of tartar. Pulse a couple of time to combine.

In a large bowl, beat the 4 eggs until well combined. Whisk in melted ghee or coconut oil. Add dry ingredients to wet and mix until well incorporated. Allow to sit for a couple of minutes to let the coconut flour absorb.

Fill each cavity in donut pan three-quarters full. Give the pan a little shake or two to let the batter settle. Bake for 12 to 14 minutes, or until toothpick inserted comes out clean and edges are just beginning to brown. Remove from oven. Allow to cool completely before removing from donut pan. Slice in half and pan toast in a bit of ghee or use a toaster oven.

CHEF'S TIPS:

I use soaked and dehydrated seeds whenever I can to make them more digestible. I usually do several pounds at a time and keep them in the fridge for baking and eating.

I use a combination of baking soda and cream of tartar to replace baking powder. Baking powder often has GMO cornstarch in it, which I like to avoid. If you do not have cream of tartar, you can just use 1 teaspoon (3 g) of baking powder in this recipe in place of the baking soda and cream of tartar.

SAVORY GARLIC HERB BISCUITS

These biscuits have a hearty texture that goes nicely with the savory garlic and herbs. They're a perfect accompaniment to scrambled eggs or gravy-drenched turkey and potatoes. —HH

MAKES 6

¼ cup (60 ml) coconut oil

½ cup (60 g) coconut flour

½ tsp baking soda

½–1 tsp (1.5–3 g) sea salt

½ cup (120 ml) + 2 tbsp (30 ml) coconut milk

4 eggs

1 tsp (5 ml) apple cider vinegar

1 tsp (3 g) garlic powder

½ tsp each of rosemary, thyme, sage

Preheat the oven to 350°F (180°C, or gas mark 4). Melt the coconut oil and combine with remaining biscuit ingredients in a food processor or bowl, mix well. Place batter in a muffin tin lined with muffin liners. The biscuits will rise a small amount, so you can fill the muffin liner about three-quarters full. Bake for about 20 to 30 minutes or until a toothpick inserted comes out clean and the tops are slightly browned.

SAVORY PUMPKIN BISCUITS

Paleo baking is an art form. And making fluffy, buttery biscuits is not easy. Here's a savory biscuit recipe that comes close to the biscuits of your pre-Paleo days. —KH

SERVES 8–10

2¼ cups (270 g) almond flour, plus more for dusting dough

¼ cup (30 g) arrowroot powder

1 tsp (3 g) sea salt

1 tsp (3 g) baking soda

¼ tsp ground cumin

2 eggs

¼ cup (60 ml) ghee, butter or coconut oil, melted

½ cup (125 g) cooked pumpkin purée

Preheat the oven to 350°F (180°C, or gas mark 4).

Combine almond flour, arrowroot, salt, baking soda and cumin in a medium bowl. In a large bowl, blend together eggs, melted fat of choice and pumpkin purée until well incorporated. Pour dry into wet and mix until dough forms.

Shape dough into a nice ball and dust with a bit of almond flour so it's not too sticky but not too dry. Be patient. Keep dusting until it feels like you can roll it out.

Roll dough out between two sheets of unbleached parchment paper until about 1½-inches (3.8-cm) thick. Using a biscuit cutter or a glass with a 2½- to 3-inch (6.4- to 7.5-cm) mouth, cut out biscuits and place them on a baking sheet lined with parchment paper or a silicone mat. Repeat process until you have used up all of the dough.

Bake for 15 to 18 minutes, until bottoms are beginning to brown.

EASY AND AMAZING BANANA BREAD

This is easily one of the most popular recipes on my blog. Many of my readers made this a weekly staple. I've even been told that it's the best banana bread recipe, Paleo or not. —KW

MAKES 1

4 very ripe bananas, mashed

¼ cup (60 ml) coconut oil, butter or ghee, melted

4 eggs

1 tsp (5 ml) pure vanilla extract

1½ tsp (4 g) ground cinnamon

½ cup (60 g) coconut flour

1 tsp (3 g) baking soda

¼ tsp sea salt

OPTIONAL ADD-INS

⅓ cup (60 g) dark chocolate chips

Walnuts

Pecans

Slivered almonds

Raisins

Preheat the oven to 350°F (180°C, or gas mark 4). Mix everything together in a medium bowl until well combined. Grease a standard-sized bread pan with coconut oil or butter, and pour in the batter. Bake for about 45 to 60 minutes or until center is set and top is golden.

CHEF'S TIP:

The bananas should be extremely brown, almost to the point when you would throw them away or freeze them. If they are not overly ripe, the bread will not be as sweet and probably not taste as good. If you are using non-ripe bananas, you should add about ⅓ cup (80 ml) of maple syrup to the batter.

NUT-FREE BANANA BREAD

Bananas are so sweet by themselves that this banana bread recipe is entirely fruit sweetened, but still completely delightful. Made with eggs and coconut flour, this nut-free bread is full of protein for a quick breakfast treat. Best served warm with a generous spoonful of Whipped Maple Nut Butter (page 497). —CP

MAKES 1

2 large bananas, firm and not fully ripe

¾ cup (90 g) coconut flour, sifted

6 eggs

6 tbsp (90 ml) butter, melted

⅓ cup (80 ml) coconut milk

¼ tsp ground nutmeg

1 tsp (3 g) ground cinnamon

1 tsp (3 g) baking soda

1 tsp (5 ml) vanilla extract

Dash of sea salt

Preheat the oven to 350°F (180°C, or gas mark 4). Line an 8.5 × 4.5-inch (21.6 × 11.4-cm) loaf pan with parchment paper cut to fit lengthwise. Lightly grease the uncovered sides.

Mash bananas with a fork until smooth. Combine all ingredients in a large mixing bowl and blend until a smooth batter forms. Scrape down the sides of the bowl and briefly blend again.

Pour batter into the greased loaf pan and bake for 45 to 50 minutes or until a tester comes out clean.

Allow bread to set and cool slightly before removing from pan by lifting up on the parchment paper.

Slice and enjoy warm, topped with a spoonful of Whipped Maple Nut Butter.

CHEF'S TIP:

I have found that when working with coconut flour, bananas will bake best when slightly on the firmer side and not produce a mushy baked good.

ORANGE CARDAMOM LOAF

Sweet citrus meets smoky cardamom for a delightful blend of flavors. This bread loaf is my favorite winter-time treat and makes for a delightful breakfast on chilly mornings. Bake, slice, toast, butter and enjoy! —CP

MAKES 1

Coconut oil, for greasing

2½ cups (300 g) almond flour

2 tbsp (16 g) coconut flour

2 tbsp (25 g) coconut sugar

1 tsp (3 g) baking soda

1 tsp (3 g) ground cardamom

¼ tsp ground cinnamon

¼ tsp ground nutmeg

Pinch of ground cloves

2 eggs

¾ cup (180 ml) coconut milk

4 tbsp (60 ml) butter, melted

4 tbsp (60 ml) fresh orange juice

2 tbsp (30 ml) orange zest

Preheat oven to 350°F (180°C, or gas mark 4). Lightly grease a loaf pan with coconut oil then line with parchment paper, allowing paper to hang over the edges of the loaf pan.

In a mixing bowl, sift together all dry ingredients.

In a separate bowl, use a hand mixer to blend eggs, coconut milk, butter and orange juice. Add dry ingredients to wet and blend until a smooth batter has formed. Fold in the orange zest.

Pour batter into the loaf pan. Bake for 45 to 50 minutes or until a tester comes out clean.

Allow to cool before removing from the pan. Slice, toast and enjoy!

CHEF'S TIP:

Almond flour is very moist and crumbly, especially when warm. Allow the loaf to completely cool before removing from the pan by gently pulling up on the parchment paper.

COCONUT FLOUR POP-OVERS

Meant to be eaten hot and steamy out of the oven, these little, fluffy, golden goodies are the perfect Paleo bread substitute. Enjoy them with butter and jam or serve them with a savory soup or stew. —KH

SERVES 8

5 eggs

½ cup (120 ml) non-dairy milk of choice

3 tbsp (24 g) coconut flour, sifted

¼ tsp sea salt

4 tsp (20 g) ghee or coconut oil

Preheat the oven to 425°F (220°C, or gas mark 7). Whisk eggs, milk, coconut flour and salt in a large bowl until fully incorporated and foamy.

Place ½ teaspoon ghee or coconut oil into each of eight cups of a muffin pan and place into the oven until the fat is sizzling hot, about 4 minutes. Carefully remove the muffin pan and pour batter into the eight cups over hot ghee or oil, filling about half-way up.

Bake for 20 minutes, until golden and fluffy, keeping the oven door closed so as not to deflate your pop-overs.

CHEF'S TIP:

These pop-overs will deflate soon after being taken out of the oven and are best served fresh and hot. Feel free to use muffin liners and omit the fat in the cups for easier clean up. They do, however, taste amazing with the ghee/coconut oil.

EGG-FREE, GRAIN-FREE PIE CRUST

It's nice to have a healthy go-to Paleo pie crust recipe, especially during the holidays or summer when peaches and berries are in season. This pie crust is egg-free and relatively easy to make considering that you don't have to roll it out with a rolling pin—you just press it into the pie dish! —HH

MAKES 1

6 tbsp (48 g) ground flaxseeds

⅔ cup (80 g) coconut flour

1 cup (120 g) almond flour

¼ cup (30 g) arrowroot

½ tsp sea salt

1 tsp (3 g) baking soda

½ cup (100 g) coconut sugar

½ cup (120 g) softened coconut oil, plus more for greasing

1 tsp (5 ml) vanilla extract

1 tbsp (15 ml) honey

Preheat the oven to 350°F (180°C, or gas mark 4). In a small separate bowl, mix the ground flaxseeds and 6 tablespoons (90 ml) warm water. Allow to sit until it jells. Mix dry ingredients together in a food processor or mixing bowl. Add wet ingredients, including flax mixture and mix well. The result will be a thick crumbly dough-like consistency.

Use extra coconut oil or butter to grease an 8- or 9-inch (20- or 23-cm) pie dish. Crumble the dough evenly over the pie dish. You will not roll out the dough with a rolling pin like traditional crusts. You simply have to press the dough into the crust so it forms the pie dish shape. Take a fork and puncture the crust a few times to avoid bubbling and lightly pre-cook the crust for about 5 minutes. Now you are ready to use your crust for pumpkin pie, pecan pie or any other treat you want to make!

CHEF'S TIP:
To grind the flaxseeds, blend them in a coffee grinder.

THIN & CRISPY PIZZA CRUST

When my husband and I gave up grains about six years ago, one food we really missed was pizza. This recipe exceeded all my expectations. Whenever I serve it to guests they can't believe it's grain-free. Numerous people have told me that it's the best pizza crust they've ever tasted, Paleo or not! —KW

MAKES 1

1 cup (120 g) tapioca flour or arrowroot powder

½ tsp sea salt

3 tbsp (15 g) Romano or Parmesan cheese, optional

⅓ cup (80 ml) avocado oil, olive oil or other fat of choice

⅓ cup (80 ml) water

1 tbsp (15 ml) apple cider vinegar

1 clove garlic, finely minced

1 egg

⅓ cup (40 g) coconut flour

1 tsp (3 g) Italian seasoning, optional

Preheat oven to 450°F (230°C, or gas mark 8). In a medium bowl, mix together the tapioca flour and sea salt—and cheese, if using. Set aside.

In a small pot over medium heat, bring the oil, water, apple cider vinegar and minced garlic clove to a boil. Remove it from the heat and add it to the tapioca flour bowl. Stir until combined. Set aside for about 2 minutes to cool.

Once it's not hot to the touch, add the egg. Stir until combined. Add the coconut flour and Italian seasoning, if using, and stir until the coconut flour is absorbed and it becomes dough. Form the dough into a ball and press or roll out on a parchment-lined or lightly greased pizza stone or baking pan. You will have enough dough to do a 12- to 14-inch (30.5- to 35.6-cm) circle.

Bake 14 to 15 minutes or just until the crust starts to become a very light golden brown. Remove from oven, add your toppings and bake for 3 to 5 more minutes.

CHEF'S TIPS:

I prefer my crust plain, without the optional cheese and seasoning. My husband likes his with the optional added cheese (Romano) and Italian seasoning. Try it both ways and see which one you like better!

TORTILLAS

When I first starting eating grain-free, I really missed eating tacos with a tortilla. When I created this recipe, my family couldn't get enough of them. We use these for tacos, wraps, crepes and more. —KW

MAKES 6

2 large eggs

1 tbsp (15 ml) melted butter, ghee or other fat of choice

½ cup (125 g) canned pumpkin or cooked, mashed sweet potato

1¼ cups (150 g) arrowroot powder or tapioca starch

¼ cup (30 g) ground flax or chia/flax blend

½ tsp sea salt

1 cup (235 ml) water

OPTIONAL

½ tsp chili powder for Tex-Mex tortillas

½ tsp vanilla and ¼ tsp cinnamon for dessert tortillas

Mix together eggs, melted butter, pumpkin or sweet potato until smooth. Stir in arrowroot or tapioca starch, flax blend and sea salt. (If you are using the chili powder or the vanilla/cinnamon, add it now). Add water and whisk until well combined. Batter will be runny.

Heat an 8-inch (20-cm) skillet on medium heat. Remove the pan from heat and using a ½ cup (120 g) measuring cup, add ½ cup (120 g) batter to the pan. Swirl the pan so the batter completely covers the bottom of the skillet. Put the pan back on the burner for about 30 seconds to 1 minute. You'll know it's time to flip when the tortilla moves around easily when you shake the pan. So flip and now cook the other side for 30 seconds to 1 minute.

Repeat for remaining batter. Make sure to give the batter a little stir each time. You will have enough for six tortillas if you use an 8-inch (20-cm) skillet and ½ cup (120 g) batter per tortilla.

AVOCADO & GOLDEN FLAX CRACKERS

This raw dehydrated cracker will go well with any dip. —VM

SERVES 4

1 bunch kale, washed and trimmed

1 cup (165 g) flaxseeds, soaked overnight in 2 cups (470 ml) of water

1 avocado

½ small red onion, peeled and soaked in cold water for 30 minutes

Juice of 1 lime

Pinch of Celtic sea salt

Pinch of chili powder, optional

To make this recipe, you will need a dehydrator.

Chop the kale into small pieces. Blend the kale and the remaining ingredients in the blender.

Spread the mixture thinly over dehydrator sheets and dry for about 4 hours at 175°F (80°C). Flip the spread and dry for another 4 hours, or until the crackers are dry and crispy.

Serve with your favorite spread and enjoy!

CHEF'S TIP:
You can also add a pinch of chili powder to the mix if you would like to spice up the crackers.

ROSEMARY & OLIVE OIL CRACKERS

These crackers are rich with the flavors of olive oil and rosemary with the satisfying crunch we all long for. This cracker is easy to make and easy on the carbs. It doesn't get much better than that. —VM

SERVES 30 CRACKERS

3½ ounces (98 g) whole flaxseeds

1½ ounces (42 g) chia seeds

1½ ounces (42 g) raw hemp hearts

2 tbsp (30 ml) coconut oil

2 tbsp (30 ml) olive oil

1 tbsp (18 g) sea salt

1 egg

1 egg white

2 sprigs fresh rosemary

½ cup (120 ml) water

Flaxseeds have the tendency to go rancid very fast. Because of this, I highly recommend making your own flour, so that it will be always fresh. Place the flax seeds into a coffee grinder and grind for about 10 seconds. Repeat the same grinding process with the chia seeds .

Preheat the oven to 300°F (150°C, or gas mark 2). Place the flax and chia meal into a large bowl with the hemp hearts, coconut oil, olive oil and sea salt. Mix the ingredients thoroughly. In a blender, add the egg, egg white, rosemary leaves and water and blend quickly for 10 seconds. Add the wet ingredients to the dry mixture and mix well.

Let the dough rest for about an hour. When it has finished resting the dough should be a little dry and ball up in the bowl. If the dough seems too dry, add a little water and mix thoroughly.

On a large working surface, lay out two large pieces of parchment paper. Place the dough on the paper and roughly flatten it to the same shape as the paper. Place the second paper on top of the dough and roll out to ¼-inch (6-mm) thick. Gently peel the top paper off the dough and then score it lightly with a serrated knife into nice little squares. Place the parchment paper with the cracker dough onto a cookie sheet and bake for 30 minutes.

Take the crackers from the oven and let cool, then gently peel the paper off. Break the cracker into bite-sized squares and enjoy!

"CHEESY" PALEO CRACKERS

If you miss crunchy foods on the Paleo diet, these crispy crackers will bring back fond memories of wheat crackers without the digestive upset. They are wonderful with Spicy Parsnip Hummus (page 240) or Roasted Garlic Pumpkin Hummus (page 241) —KH

MAKES 30–40

1 cup (150 g) raw sunflower seeds, preferably soaked and dehydrated

½ cup (75 g) raw pumpkin seeds, preferably soaked and dehydrated

½ cup (75 g) raw sesame seeds

¼ cup (30 g) nutritional yeast

3 tbsp (45 ml) coconut oil, melted

5 tbsp (75 ml) filtered water

½ tsp sea salt

Preheat the oven to 325°F (170°C, or gas mark 3).

Process sunflower and pumpkin seeds in food processor until you get a coarse flour-like consistency, about a minute or so. Add the rest of the ingredients and pulse until well combined. Mixture will stick together and begin to form a ball. If it doesn't form a ball, add a bit more nutritional yeast.

Roll out dough between 2 sheets of parchment paper. The dough should be no more than ¼-inch (6-mm) thick. Score the crackers into desired sizes with a pizza cutter.

Bake for 25 to 30 minutes, until crisp and beginning to brown. Allow to cool and enjoy. Store in an airtight container.

ABOUT THE AUTHORS

ARSY VARTANIAN is the founder and chef of the Paleo recipe and lifestyle blog, Rubies and Radishes and she is also the author of the cookbooks *The Paleo Foodie Cookbook* and *The Paleo Slow Cooker*. Arsy deeply enjoys spending time in her kitchen creating healthy, grain-free recipes for her family and her blog readers. She resides in a quaint beach town in California with her husband and daughter.

AMANDA TORRES, founder of the food and health website The Curious Coconut, has achieved life-changing results from adopting a Paleo diet. She has been featured in *Redbook*, The Huffington Post, *First for Women*, Mark's Daily Apple and others. She lives in Memphis, Tennessee.

CAROLINE POTTER is a Nutritional Therapy Practitioner and author of the blog Colorful Eats and her first print book, *All-American Paleo Table*. As much as she loves traveling, swimming in the ocean in the afternoon and exploring the beautiful world around, she also loves curling up on the couch with her husband for movie night. Caroline was diagnosed with Type 1 diabetes in college, which led to her developing a passion for nutrition, recipe creation and food photography. Caroline currently lives in Pearl Harbor, Hawaii, where her husband, Stephen, serves in the United States Navy. They love to cook together on the weekends and take their golden retriever, Libby, to the beach.

HANNAH HEALY is the creator of the real food and natural living blog Healy Eats Real. She loves creating delicious, nutrient-dense recipes and sharing everything she learns about nutrition and holistic health. Hannah's biggest passion is making delectable Paleo desserts with wholesome ingredients that you can enjoy on those special days when you need just a little something sweet!

JENNY CASTANEDA a foodie at heart, has great appreciation for different types of cuisine and is willing to try anything at least once, as chronicled on her blog, Paleo Foodie Kitchen. Her recipes and cooking style are mainly influenced by Asian and American flavors while also showcasing simple Filipino recipes that can be adapted to Paleo. Her first book, *One-Pot Paleo*, is a bestseller, and she has written numerous guest posts for top Paleo blogs, sharing simple recipes that cater to every palate. Aside from cooking, Jenny enjoys traveling, photography and obstacle course racing.

KATJA HEINO is the author and chef at the food and wellness blog, Savory Lotus. Combining her experiences as a registered nurse, home chef, yoga teacher, mama to two beautiful daughters and as a real-food lifestyle researcher, Katja hopes to inspire people to live healthier and more vibrant lives. Her passion lies in empowering people to take charge of their health by discovering the beauty of real food and natural remedies.

KELLY WINTERS is the creator of the popular Paleo and holistic living blog Primally Inspired. Her blog was created out of a deep love and desire to help her sister's family heal from a variety of health issues. Kelly loves creating easy, non-intimidating Paleo recipes for the overwhelmed and overworked who want to get healthy without going crazy in the process. She lives in Pennsylvania with her husband and her 100-pound, spoiled rotten, mutt.

NAZANIN KOVÁCS is the founder of the blog Cinnamoneats.com, soon to be NazKovacs.com. Since stumbling upon the Paleo lifestyle in 2011, she enjoys creating her own delicious and healthy real food recipes at home, often with a nod to her and her husband's Persian and Hungarian heritage, respectively. Nazanin's mission is to show everyone that cooking real food recipes can be easy, exciting and above all else delicious. Nazanin currently resides in Michigan with her loving and supportive husband.

RACHEL BALL is the creator of the healthy lifestyle blog Grok Grub, providing recipe and tips for wellness by cooking and eating real food made with whole ingredients. Raised by health-conscious parents, Rachel grew up with a Paleo nutritional approach and now shares her culinary creations as a way of giving back to the community and promoting a healthy lifestyle via home cooking. To "grok" means to understand, and that is Rachel's mission: to help her readers and the public understand and take ownership of their food, its preparation and its effect on personal health.

RACHEL MCCLELLAND is the 25-year-old food blogger behind South Beach Primal. After years of failed treatments for her chronic rosacea acne and IBS, she discovered that going grain- and dairy-free was the key to flawless skin and a healthy gut. That was four years ago, after moving to Miami Beach. When she isn't biking to her local CrossFit box or strengthening her yoga practice, she bartends on vibrant South Beach.

VIVICA MENEGAZ was born in Italy and, at 19, lived in Germany for 5 years. She lived in Spain before moving to California in the early nineties, becoming a food photographer and working for national and local magazines. This experience gave her the chance to visit (and try) many amazing restaurants, eating and photographing her way around Los Angeles. In 2009, Vivica moved to Northern California with her husband, cats and dog, and realized her passion for food and the desire to help others could come together in the ultimate calling: Nutrition. Vivica is certified as a Technician in Whole Food Nutrition and is studying for her clinician certification.